BRITISH WATERCOLOUR ARTISTS

up to 1920

ALEXANDER, Edwin John (1870-1926)
Daisy and Harebells. *Signed with initials, watercolour, 12in. x 6½in.*

The Dictionary of
BRITISH WATERCOLOUR ARTISTS
up to 1920

Volume I

H.L. Mallalieu

ANTIQUE COLLECTORS' CLUB

Printed in England
by the Antique Collectors' Club Ltd., Woodbridge, Suffolk

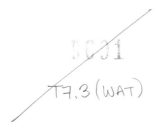

Contents

Acknowledgements

To list all the collectors, dealers and directors and staffs of museums to whom I owe a debt of gratitude for assistance and information would require another volume. It is invidious to do so, but I should especially like to thank the following: the Marchioness of Aberdeen and Temair and the late Marquess of Aberdeen and Temair; Lord and Lady Clitheroe; A.M. Cotman, Esq.; D.A. Fothergill, Esq.; Mr. and Mrs. D. Francis; Thomas Girton, Esq.; Sidney Gold, Esq.; Mr. and Mrs. Rainsford Hannay; Peter Hadley, Esq.; A.E. Haswell Miller, Esq.; Sir Oliver Millar; Dr. John Nesfield; the Earl of Oxford and Asquith; Matthew Pryor, Esq.; Mr. and Mrs. D. Scott, R.G. Searight, Esq.; Denis Thomas, Esq.; H. Cornish Torbock, Esq.; Ian Fleming Williams, Esq.; Mrs. E.M. Woodward; the Misses Yglesias; John Baskett; the Hon. C.A. Lennox-Boyd; Charles Chrestien; Michael Danny; William Drummond; Andrew Edmunds; Martyn Gregory; Richard Ivor; Beryl Kendal; Anthony Reed; John Robertson; Stanhope Shelton; Bill Thomson; Prue Heathcote-Williams; Andrew Wyld; Noel Annesley and Anthony Browne (Christie's); David Dallas and Mark Fisher (Phillips); John Newton (Sotheby's); Andrew Wilton and Reginald Williams (B.M.); John de Witt (Ashmolean); Francis Greenacre (Bristol); Denis Perriam (Carlisle); David Fraser (Derby); James Holloway (Edinburgh); Caroline Bruce (F.B.A.); Duncan Robinson (Fitzwilliam); Edward Archibald (Greenwich); A.G. Davies (Hertford); Eric J. Stanford (Reading); Dr. John Harris (R.I.B.A.); Malcolm Fry (R.W.S.); Martin Anglesea (Ulster); the Director and staff of the Mellon Centre and the Librarian and staff of the London Library.

Especially thanks are due to Jane Johnson for her researches and Sarah Danny for her typing. Also to Clive Butler for putting up with the mess with so few complaints.

A book of this sort can never hope to be fully comprehensive. That this one is as complete as it is is largely due to Caroline Smyth, who has worked with me at all stages of its preparation. It is her book as well as mine.

H.L.M., 1976

Note to the Second Edition

Once again it is impossible to thank everybody who has generously given information or time in aiding my revision of the Dictionary. The names which have been added to my personal roll of honour include: J.C. Bigg; Michael Bryan; Maurice Callow; Marcus Chambers; John C. Collins; Ian Cook; Esmé Gordon; Jeremy Lemmon; Brian and Rachel Moss; Jean Nielsen; Charles Nugent; Karen Turner; Henry Wemyss; and Donald Whitton. I am also indebted to the researches of Marshall Hall as embodied in his books on the painters of Northumbria and Cumbria.

My wife Fenella has not only provided very necessary encouragement. but through her alter ego, Fenella Rowse, the fruits of research which would otherwise certainly have escaped me.

H.L.M., 1986

Introduction to the Third Edition

The late David Jones, himself no mean painter as well as a poet, wrote that 'when the workman is dead, the work shall be remembered'. David Carritt, who had the best eye among the London picture dealers of the 1970s, was not encouraging when I told him that I was compiling a dictionary of British watercolourists. 'Oh dear,' he said. '*What* a dead end.' Thirty years later one would be unlikely to receive such a response even from the most fastidious, or supercilious, connoisseur of old masters. Rarity has added more than monetary value. Then there were still enough reasonably priced English watercolours by the leading members of the school available on the market to satisfy the comparatively small band of collectors and specialist dealers. In 1970 Agnew's 97th annual watercolour show could have been purchased in its entirety – 232 items, but admittedly no Turner or Sandby – for £54,938 (at a rough guess £440,000 today). As late as 1973 no auction of watercolours had yet produced a total of £100,000.

The collectors included a number of survivors from that happy period, the 1930s to the 1960s, when great bundles of drawings could be had inside and outside the many print and junk shops along the Charing Cross Road and in Bloomsbury for what now seems like nothing at all. Grander galleries were hardly more expensive. Those collectors revelled in their opportunities. Around 1970 I remember being shown into an upper room at Professor Jack Isaacs' house in Eltham. It had fitted cupboards all round, which I was assured were packed with drawings. However it was not possible to check because of the brown paper parcels and folders which stood like a sandbag barricade in front of them. It was accumulations of this kind that allowed scholarly collectors such as Iolo Williams, Martin Hardie, Dudley Snelgrove, Edward Croft-Murray, Leonard Duke, Cornish Torbock, Sir John Witt and their fellow pioneers to map the byways of the English School, as well as the peaks, rivers and prominent features.

My own interest I owe to my father, Sir Lance Mallalieu, who was an accomplished amateur, a talent inherited from his mother and shared with a younger brother, Dick. Not only did he encourage me to try to paint, but he first introduced me to some of the greatest watercolourists of the past. One Sunday morning, as the price for taking me out to lunch, he demanded that I show him the fine collection owned by my school. I had never bothered to look at them properly before, but there were Turners, Coxes, de Wints and Cotmans, and once I did look I was hooked. I fell instantly in love with a very green and splashy Brabazon impression of a Venetian Turner. That particular infatuation did not last, but the general passion remained.

Over the years the whole landscape of watercolour collecting has changed. It is not possible to accumulate in the old style any more, and nowadays few specialists would have the enthusiasm, knowledge and length of pocket needed to build up a collection of, say, Rowlandsons like Major Dent in the '50s, or even de Wints in the manner of Matthew Pryor in the '70s. Today's prices would horrify them. As in other fields, less and less of real quality is available for new collectors, even if the revival of enthusiasm for Victorian art greatly widened the scope. Fewer and fewer great discoveries remain to be made, although respectable amateur talents occasionally do still emerge from the privacy of their descendants' collections. Rather more than eight hundred completely new entries have been added to this edition, and many fall into that familial category.

Seven 'artists' have actually been ejected from the *Dictionary*. There is no evidence (or possibility) that Commander Edgar Montgomery Brunden, Alan Butler Clive, Daniel Hanlon, Edward Peter, John Stuart, il Cavaliere Milanese, Sir Piers Welfare or Kirsten Witherby ever actually painted or, indeed, existed. However, they did have a dual purpose in the first two editions. They served to protect the copyright, as suggested by the late publisher John Steel, and also to amuse the author. I did once subsequently and consequently see a photograph of a 'Brunden' owned by a London gallery. It was illustrating a magazine article by an auction house specialist.

As well as attempting to eliminate the grosser errors which had found their way into the first two editions, I have tried to pin down many of the unknown names and dates of prolific but obscure artists in the field. This has led to many hours among the registers then still at St Catherine's House which explains why some places of birth or death appear as the registry offices rather than the exact locations. Inevitably in this I have duplicated some of the work undertaken over the same period by Messrs. Stewart and Cutten for their admirably thorough *Dictionary of Portrait Painters in Britain, 1997.*

The late Sir Ellis Waterhouse, in his *Dictionary of British 18th Century Painters,* appears to have been the only previous lexicographer to pick up Sidney Hutchison's work on the admissions to the R.A. Schools (Walpole Society, XXXVIII, 1962), but Hutchison went no further than 1830. Since these records contain information of names and birth dates which came from the artists themselves, I have trawled the various volumes to 1900. On a significant number of occasions they contradict long accepted facts. This is also sometimes true of censuses and post office directories.

Further additions to my roll of honour, some of whom should have appeared earlier include: John Abbott and Philip Athill; Patrick Conner; Harriet Drummond; T.P.O'Connor-Fenton; the Knight of Glin; Penelope Gregory; Lowell Libson; the late Jeremy Maas and Rupert Maas; Delia, Lady Millar; the late Bill Minns; John Munday; Felicity Owen; Andrew Clayton-Payne; Peyton Skipwith.

My thanks are also due to Jodi Lawson, Alison Adnitt, Simon Fenwick, Aidan Flood, Rosalinda Hardiman, Sarah Hobrough, David Japes, Emma Lauze, Peggy Obrecht, Henrietta Pattinson, Mr and Mr Nicholas Williams and above all to Brian Cotton and Primrose Elliott at the Antique Collectors' Club. I trust that this third edition will continue to boil a pot for my family, especially since my children, Ilaira and Joshua, show some promise as amateurs, if not yet 'distinguished' ones, in Williams' phrase. My wife Fenella's distinction lies in a different field of art, ceramics.

As ever, I welcome further information on artists who are included, or who should be.

H.L.M. October 2002

The Colour Plates
A-L

ALLINGHAM, Helen (1848-1826)
Young Motherhood. *Signed, watercolour.*

ATKINSON, John Augustus (1775-c.1833)
Fishermen Launching their Boat in Choppy Sea.

AYLESFORD, Heneage Finch, 4th Earl of (1751-1812)
Ships in Harbour. *Pen and brown ink, grey wash and water-colour, 8½in. x 10½in.*

BARTHOLOMEW, Valentine (1799-1879)
Still Life with Roses. *Pencil and watercolour with touches of white heightening
and gum arabic, 18¼in. x 13in.*

**BARTLETT, William Henry
(1809-1854)**
Arabs on a Hilltop. *Watercolour,
6¼in. x 8⅜in.*

**BEAUCLERK, Lady Diana
(1734-1808)**
The artist's daughters, Elizabeth and
Mary. *Signed on backing,
watercolour, 8in. x 8in.*

BEARNE, Edward Henry (1844-)
Woman drawing water from a river – West Country. *Signed and dated 1879, watercolour, 21in. x 14½in.*

BENTLEY, Charles (1806-1854)
Ships off a Town in a Mountainous Landscape. *Signed and dated 1838,*
watercolour, 17¼in. x 23½in.

BONINGTON, Richard Parkes (1802-1828
Shipping off the Coast of France. *Signed with initials, watercolour
heightened with scratching-out, 5¼in. x 7¼in.*

BONINGTON, Richard Parkes (1802-1828)
Grandpapa. *Signed with initials, water and bodycolour. 7½in. x 5½in.*

BOYCE, George Price (1826-1897)
Godstow Nunnery and Lock, near Oxford. *Signed and dated September
1862, watercolour, 8in. x 21in.*

BOYS, Thomas Shotter (1803-1874)
View of Church of Saint Charles Borromeo, Antwerp. *Signed and dated*
1832, pencil and watercolour heightened with white and gum arabic,
10½in. x 7¾in.

BRABAZON, Hercules Brabazon (1821-1906)
Palazzo Dario, Venice. *Signed with initials, pencil, water and bodycolour, 6¾in. x 5¾in.*

BRANDOIN, Michel Vincent Charles (1733-1807)
The Castle of Grignan. *Extensively inscribed on reverse of original mount, pen and grey ink and watercolour with touches of white, 10¾in. x 17¼in.*

BUCK, Samuel and Nathaniel (1696-1779 and fl.1726-1753)
Pembroke Castle. *Pen and brown and grey ink, grey wash.*

BUTLER, Mildred Anne (1858-1941)
The Flowers of August (1900). *Signed and dated Oct. 1900,*
pencil and watercolour heightened with white.

CALLOW, William (1812-1908)
Dresden from the River Elbe. *Pencil and watercolour, 9in. x 13in.*

BURNEY, Edward Francis (1760-1848)
The Ardent Suitor (for *The Tatler*). *Pen and grey ink and watercolour, 3⅜in. x 2⅞in.*

CHAMBERLAYNE, General William John (1821-1910)
Jungle Cats. *Watercolour, 10½in. x 14½in.*

CHINNERY, George (1774-1852)
A Junk ar Sunset.

CONSTABLE, John (1776-1837)
Borrowdale by Moonlight. *Pencil and watercolour, 4¼in. x 9½in.*

CORBOULD, Edward Henry (1815-1905)
The Canterbury Pilgrims. *Signed and dated April 1873, water and bodycolour, 8¾in. x 38¾in.*

CONSTABLE, John (1776-1837)
Scene in Salisbury. *Signed and dated 1826, pen and grey ink and watercolour, 7¼in. x 10½in.*

COTMAN, John Sell (1782-1842)
An Aqueduct. *Pencil and watercolour, 9¼in. x 14¼in.*

COTMAN, John Sell (1782-1842)
Cow Tower, Norwich. *Pencil and watercolour, 13⅞in. x 10⅝in.*

COZENS, John Robert (1752-1797)
A View of London and the Thames from Greenwich. *Signed and dated 1792 on the artist's original wash-line mount, 14½in. x 20¾in.*

COZENS, John Robert (1752-1797)
Pays de Valais, Switzerland. *Signed on original mount and inscribed on the reverse, pencil and watercolour, 19¼in. x 26¾in.*

CRISTALL, Joshua (1768-1847)
A Bridge near Harrow. *Pencil and watercolour, 4¼in. x 7½in.*

DADD, Frank (1851-1929)
Hand Rearing. *Signed and dated 1888, watercolour, 19in. x 15in.*

DANBY, Francis (1793-1861)
The Approach of a Storm on Liensfjord, Norway. *Signed 'F. DANBY',*
watercolour with bodycolour, 7⅛in. x 11¾in.

DANIELL, Samuel (1755-1811)
A Girl by a South African River. *Watercolour, size unknown.*

DANIELL, William (1769-1837)
The Leven Estuary near Ulveston. *Signed with monogram, watercolour,*
6¼in. x 9½in.

DE WINT, Peter (1784-1849)
A Lock Gate near Nottingham, the Castle beyond. *Inscribed verso
'Original drawing of de Wint done before Mr. H. Sykes', pencil and
watercolour, 8½in. x 11½in.*

DUFFIELD, Mary Elizabeth (1819-1914)
A Still Life of Blossom, Tulip and a Bird's Nest on a Ledge.
Signed, pencil and watercolour heightened with white, 8⅜in. x 12⅛in.

DEVOTO, John
Study for the portrait
of the dwarf artist
Matthew Buckinger.
*Signed, pencil, pen and
grey and brown ink
and watercolour,
10in. x 6⅝in.*

DUNDAS, Adela 'Ada' (1840-1887)
From an album containing views in Italy, France and Switzerland.
Pencil, some with grey wash, the majority with watercolour,
13¾in. x 18¾in. and smaller.

EDWARDS, George (1694-1773)
Humming Bird, Waxwing, Bull and Gold Finches, Great Tit, Robin and
other birds. *Signed and dated 1732, bodycolour, 12in. x 20¼in.*

34

FIELDING, Anthony Vandyke Copley (1787-1855)
Shakespeare's Cliff, nr. Dover. *Inscribed on the reverse, 17⅛in. x 22in.*

FIELDING, Thales Angelo Vernet (1793-1837)
Landscape in France. *Signed, watercolour over traces of pencil, 5⅞in. x 11in.*

FRANCIA, François Louis Thomas (1772-1839)
'The Nelson, on the Stocks, building at Woolwich in the Year 1814'.
Pencil, pen and ink and watercolour, 5½in. x 7⅞in.

FRENCH, William Percy (1854-1920)
Sunlight and Bog. *Signed, watercolour, 10¼in. x 13½in.*

GAINSBOROUGH, Thomas (1727-1788)
Wooded Landscape with a Cottage and Cattle. *Black chalk and
watercolour heightened with white chalk and white and grey oil paint,
varnished, 8½in. x 11½in.*

GARDNER, William Biscombe (1847-1919)
Spring Tide on the Rother, before Rye, Sussex. *Signed, and inscribed on artist's board, watercolour, 5in. x 8in.*

GERE, Charles March (1869-1957)
Alison. *Inscribed in gold, water and bodycolour, 6¾in. x 5in.*

GIRTIN, Thomas (1775-1802)
Helmsley Castle, Yorkshire. *Signed, and inscribed on original mount, pencil and watercolour, 6½in. x 8½in.*

GOODALL, Edward Angelo (1819-1908)
Market Place, Segovia, Spain. *Signed, watercolour, c.1865, 12in. x 19in.*

GOSSELIN, Joshua (1739-1813)
View from Berges Hall. *Signed, inscribed and dated 1812, watercolour,*
8in. x 12¾in.

GRIMM, Samuel Hieronymus (1733-1794)
A View from Jenny's Whim, Pimlico, looking north towards the Pump
Houses of Chelsea Waterworks and London beyond. *Signed and dated S*
H. Grimm fecit 1774, inscribed 'From Jenny's Whim' under the mount,
pencil and grey ink and watercolour over traces of pencil on laid paper,
7⅛in. x 9¼in.

HOLLAND, James (1800-1870)
An Interior of a Fine Panelled Hall and Staircase decorated with
Classical Busts. *Signed with initials and dated '39, watercolour,*
heightened with bodycolour and scratching out, 19½in. x 15⅛in.

HUNT, William Henry (1790-1864)
Almost certainly 'Head of a Smuggler', exhibited at the O.W.S. 1832.
Signed, dated 1832, watercolour.

IBBETSON, Julius Caesar (1759-1817))
The Recalcitrant Donkey. *Pen and ink and watercolour, 18½in. x 11in.*

43

JACKSON, Samuel (1794-1869)
The Lodge, Broomwell House, Brislington. *Watercolour, 8⅞in. x 12⅞in.*

JOHNSON, Edward Killingworth (1825-1896)
Expectations. *Signed and dated 1878, watercolour heightened with white.*
26in. x 16½in.

LEAR, Edward (1812-1888)
Temple of Jupiter, Olympus, Athens, the Acropolis Beyond. *Extensively
inscribed and dated 14 June 1848, pencil, pen and brown ink and
watercolour, with touches of bodycolour, 10¾in. x 19¾in.*

LEWIS, John Frederick (1805-1876)
Study of an Arab Sheikh. *Signed with initials 'JFL./ARA', pencil and watercolour heightened with bodycolour, 8½in. x 7in.*

LEAR, Edward (1812-1888)
Abou Seer; the Second Cataract on the Nile. *Inscribed, numbered and dated 1867, watercolour, 11½in. x 21¼in.*

LINNELL, John (1792-1882)
Cloud Study. *Signed and dated 1815, pencil and watercolour,*
6¾in. x 9⁷⁄₁₆in.

A

ABBEY, Edwin Austin, R.A., A.R.W.S.
1852 (Philadelphia) - 1911 (London)
The son of a merchant, he took his first drawing
lessons from a local landscape painter and at a
writing school. He worked for a firm of wood
engravers and studied at the Pennsylvania
Academy before moving to New York to work
for *Harper's* in 1871. In 1878, he was sent to
England to illustrate an edition of Herrick and,
after a brief visit to New York three years later,
settled in London and the Cotswolds. He was a
member of the R.I. from 1883 to 1893,
transferring to the R.W.S. in 1895. He was
elected A.R.A. and R.A. in 1901 and 1902.

He was best known as a black and white
illustrator and his full watercolours are rare.
They are mostly of figure and genre subjects.
Illustrated: *The Comedies of Shakespeare*, 1904.
Examples: Ashmolean.
Bibliography: E.V. Lucas: *E.A.A.*, 1921. *A.J.*, 1911.
Yale University: *The E.A.A. Collection*, 1939. *Studio*,
Winter No. 1900-1; XXXI, 1901. *Apollo*, Sept., 1976.

ABBOT, Henry
1768 (London) - 1840 (London)
An artist who, in 1820, published twenty-four engravings of Roman antiquities after his own
drawings, which he had made on the spot in 1818.

ABBOTT, Arthur
1804 - 1843
An amateur landscape and figure painter who
visited Italy in 1838 and 1842. He had Exeter
connections, and also copied both Old Master
and contemporary artists.

ABBOTT, John White
1763 (Exeter) - 1851 (Exeter)
A friend and pupil of F. Towne (q.v.), he was
educated and spent nearly all his life in Exeter,
where he practised as a surgeon. In 1791 he made
his only extended journey outside the West
Country, a sketching tour of Scotland, the Lake
District, Lancashire, Derbyshire and Warwickshire. From 1793 to 1805 he exhibited oil
paintings at the R.A. as an honorary exhibitor. He
toured Monmouthshire in 1797 and again in 1827
when he also visited Gloucestershire and
Wiltshire. He exhibited again at the R.A. in 1810
and 1822. In 1825 he inherited the estate of
Fordlands, near Exeter, and in 1835 he was
appointed a Deputy Lieutenant for the County.

His drawing style is always very close to that
of his master, with neat pen outlines and light,
clear colour washes or grey wash. He rarely
approaches Towne's grandeur and is often at his
best dealing with the details of foliage, bank and
water. His drawings are generally mono-
grammed and often inscribed on the reverse.
See also: White, James, his uncle.

Examples: B.M.; V.A.M.; Ashmolean; Cecil Higgins
A.G., Bedford; Coventry A.G.; Exeter Mus.;
Fitzwilliam; Leeds City A.G.; Leicestershire A.G.;
N.G.; Scotland; Newport A.G.; Ulster Mus.; York A.G.
Bibliography: Walpole Soc., XIII, 1925. *Apollo*,
March 1933.

**ABERCROMBY, Juliet Janet Georgiana,
Lady 1840 (Naples) - 1915**
The daughter of the 2nd Earl of Camperdown,
she married the 4th Lord Abercromby in 1858.
She was a Lady-in-Waiting to the Queen from
1874 to 1885, when she resigned, according to
the Queen, in a huff. Victoria (q.v.) had
encouraged her drawing and painting, and she
had produced literary subjects and watercolour
copies of oil paintings. The Abercromby seats
were Fern Tower, Crieff, Perthshire, and
Tullibody Castle, Clackmannanshire.

ABNEY, Hepzibah
A landscape painter, who was working
between 1790 and 1822.

ABRAHAM, Francis Xavier, 'Frank'
1861 - 1932 (Hartshill)
A pottery designer, who studied at the Stoke-
on-Trent Art School and at South Kensington.
He then worked for a number of Staffordshire
firms and occasionally painted watercolours.
He exhibited at the R.A. in 1887.

ABRAHAM, Frederick Henry
1790 - 1845
A painter of churches who lived in Doncaster
and exhibited at the R.A. in 1833 and 1834.

ABRAHAM, Lilian
A London painter of flowers and genre
subjects. She exhibited at the R.I. and the
R.B.A. from 1880 to 1886.

ABSOLON, John, R.I.
1815 (Lambeth) - 1895 (Highgate)
A landscape and figure painter in oil and
watercolour and a book illustrator, he began his
career as a portraitist and scene painter at Drury
Lane and Covent Garden. He maintained this
theatrical connection, and in the 1880s he
collaborated with W.J. Callcott (q.v.) at the
Haymarket. He first exhibited at Suffolk Street in
1832, then in 1835 went to Paris for three years.
On his return he was elected to the N.W.S., from
which he resigned in 1858 to concentrate on oil
painting. However, he rejoined in 1861 and was
Treasurer for many years. He returned to Paris
for a time from 1839, working as a miniaturist,
and visited Italy and Switzerland in about 1858.
He also made drawings of the fields of Crécy and
Agincourt which were published by Graves in
1860. His pupil the Earl of Caernarvon secured
him a civil list pension.

His work is very varied in quality, and his

ABBOTT, John White (1763-1851)
Rebecca and Eleazar. *Signed with monogram and dated 1807, pen and grey ink and brown wash,
13¼in. x 19¾in.*

ABSOLON, John (1815-1895)
The Harvesters' Rest. *Pencil and watercolour heightened with white, 11½in. x 23¼in.*

drawing is sometimes rather sloppy, but he had a good eye for colour. His beach scenes can occasionally approach Constable at his most impressionistic.
Examples: B.M.; V.A.M.; Ashmolean; Grundy A.G., Blackpool; Leeds City A.G.; Sydney A.G.; Ulster Mus.; N.G., Tasmania; McClelland A.G., Victoria.
Bibliography: *A.J.*, 1862; 1895.

**ABSOLON, John de Mansfield
1840 (London) -**
The elder son of J. Absolon (q.v.), one of whose London addresses he used. He painted still lifes of dead birds as well as figure subjects in watercolour. He exhibited at Suffolk Street in 1862 and 1864.

**ABSOLON, Louis de Mansfield
1845 (London) -**
The younger son of J. Absolon (q.v.). He exhibited genre, figure and picturesquely architectural subjects at Suffolk Street, the N.W.S. and elsewhere between 1872 and 1889, and he lived in London.

ACLAND, Sir Henry Wentworth, Bt., F.R.S.   1815 (Killerton) - 1900 (Oxford)
Fourth son of Sir T.D. Acland (q.v.), he was educated at Harrow and Christ Church and from 1838 he spent nearly two years cruising in the Mediterranean. In 1840 he was elected a Fellow of All Souls and began to study medicine. From 1843 to 1845, he lived in Edinburgh and he later became Regius Professor at Oxford and

President of the B.M.A. In 1860 he visited America with the Prince of Wales and in 1890 he was created a baronet. He made illustrations for a number of his publications. He was a friend and touring companion of Ruskin.

His eldest son **Admiral Sir William Alison Dyke ACLAND Bt. (1847-1924)** drew towns and landscapes.
Published: *The Plains of Troy*, 1839. *The Oxford Museum*, 1859. &c.
Bibliography: J.B. Atlay: *Sir. H.W.A., Bt.,* 1903.

**ACLAND, Sir Thomas Dyke, 10th Bt.
1787 (London) - 1871 (Killerton)**
A son of the 9th Bt. and H.A. Fortescue (q.v.), he was well known as a politician, philanthropist and amateur artist. He was educated at Christ Church and was in and out of Parliament, where he was regarded as the head of 'the religious party', from 1812 to 1857. A number of his sketches of English and Continental scenery were worked up by F. Nicholson (q.v.).

Other members of the family who were amateur artists include his brother **Hugh Dyke ACLAND (1791-1834)** who painted a brown wash view in the Tyrol which passed through Sotheby's in June 1975. A **Caroline ACLAND** made rather weak brown wash drawings of Rome in about 1820. Sir Thomas's son, the 11th Bt., married a daughter of Sir C. and Lady Mordaunt (qq.v).

**ACOCK, Walter William
1850   - 1933 (Croydon)**
A painter of still lifes and landscapes who exhibited in 1870 and 1871, and taught drawing in Croydon. For the last thirty years of his life he was blind.

ACRAMAN, William Henry
A painter of landscapes and birds who was working in Hastings in 1851. He exhibited in London from 1856 to 1868. He was also a 'Professor and seller of Music', and compositions of his were published in 1886 and 1893.

**ADAM, James
1732 (Edinburgh) - 1794 (London)**
Architect and landscape draughtsman, he was the third son of William Adam and the younger brother of R. Adam (q.v.). He toured Italy from 1760 to 1763 with Clerisseau and Zucchi, returning to work in partnership with Robert in London, Edinburgh, Glasgow and elsewhere.
Examples: Soane Mus.; Register Ho., Edinburgh.
Bibliography: J. Swarbrick: *Robert Adam and his Brothers,* 1915. A.T. Bolton: *The Architecture of Robert and J.A.,* 1922. J.Fleming: *Robert Adam and his Circle,* 1962. D. Yarwood: *Robert Adam,* 1970. See *Writings in Honour of Harold Acton* (ed. Chaney & Ritchie), 1984. *Gentleman's Mag.,* 1794, ii.

**ADAM, Joseph Denovan, R.S.A., R.S.W.
1842 (Glasgow) - 1896 (Glasgow)**
The son and pupil of **Joseph ADAM**, a landscape

ACLAND, Sir Henry Wentworth (1815-1900)
The Cathedral at Aghadoe. *Pencil, pen and black ink and wash. heightened with white, size unknown.*

painter in oil and watercolour, who brought him to London at an early age. He studied at South Kensington and made several visits to Scotland, returning to live there in 1871. He exhibited at the R.A. from 1858 to 1880, and was elected A.R.S.A. and R.S.A. in 1884 and 1890. From 1887 he ran an art school near Stirling, and he had a considerable influence on the Glasgow School. He was particularly noted for his mountain landscapes with sheep and cattle in both oil and watercolour.

His son **Joseph Denovan ADAM, Yr. (c.1870-c.1935)** was an animal painter and sometimes collaborated with him. His watercolours are looser and wetter.

Examples: Glasgow A.G.

ADAM, Robert, F.R.S., F.S.A.
1728 (Kirkaldy) - 1792 (London)
The architect, he was the second son of William Adam, the Scottish Palladian. He was educated in Edinburgh, and was a competent artist by the age of fourteen. In 1754 he set off on the Grand Tour, travelling as far as Rome with the Hon. Charles Hope. In Rome he worked with Clerisseau, and in 1757 he moved to Venice and Diocletian's Palace on the Dalmatian coast. He returned to England the following January by way of the Rhine. He was the head of the family architectural partnership, setting up the London office, and for thirty years he imposed his style on British decoration. At the time of his death he was working on eight public and twenty-five private commissions. From 1765 he was Surveyor of Chelsea Hospital and from 1769 M.P. for Kinross.

His original drawings, as distinct from his plans and elevations, are romantic and picturesque in feeling. They are generally in ink and grey wash, and show castles and river gorges. He was much influenced by Piranesi in Rome and by his own studies at Diocletian's Palace.

Published: *Ruins of the Palace of the Emperor Diocletian at Spalatro,* 1764. *Works in Architecture of R. and J. Adam,* 1773-1822.

Examples: B.M.; V.A.M.; Exeter Mus.; Fitzwilliam; Leeds City A.G.; N.G., Scotland; Soane Mus.

Bibliography: P. Fitzgerald: *R.A.,* 1904. J. Swarbrick: *R.A. and his Brothers,* 1915. J. Fleming: *R.A. and his Circle,* 1962. D. Yarwood: *R.A.,* 1970. D. King: *The complete Works of R. and James A.,* 1991. A.A.Tait: *R.A., Drawings and Imagination,* 1993. *Gentleman's Mag.,* 1792, i. *Burlington,* LXXX, 1942; CXI, 1969; CXX, 1978. Kenwood: Exhibition Cat., 1953. *Connoisseur,* CXXXVII, 1956; CXLVI, 1960; July 1978.

ADAMS, Albert George
A landscape and coastal painter in oil and watercolour, he specialised in views on the South and South Welsh coasts and visited the Channel Islands in about 1877. He exhibited in London from 1854 to 1887.

ADAM, Robert (1728-1792)
Romantic landscape composition. *Pen and ink and watercolour, 8in. x 12½in.*

ADAMS, Caroline, Charlotte and Lucy
Three sisters who lived in Billericay, where their father was probably a doctor, and in London. Caroline exhibited from 1834 to 1837 and was teaching in London as early as 1828, and Lucy from 1815 to 1843. Both Lucy and Charlotte were candidates for the N.W.S. in 1839, Lucy trying again the following year, and one of them in 1848. In the B.M. there is a very impressive beach scene by Charlotte, rather in the earlier manner of Cox or Prout (qq.v.). While Caroline and Charlotte confined themselves to landscapes, Lucy also painted portraits and literary subjects. She may have been the author of *Ben Saunders, A Tale for Mothers,* 1852, and Charlotte may have produced improving literature from 1838 to 1866. They are unlikely to be the 'three Misses Adams' met by Farington in 1796.

ADAMS, Charles James
1859 (Gravesend) - 1931
A landscape painter who was a pupil of W. Pilsbury (q.v.). He lived and worked in London,

ADAMS, Charles James (1859-1931)
Changing Pastures. *Watercolour, signed, 14¾in. x 21¼in.*

Leicester and Surrey, and also studied at the Leicester School of Art. He made a number of lithographs early in his career and painted some watercolours, but the bulk of his work is in oil. He also painted animals, history and genre subjects.
Examples: Brighton A.G.; Leicestershire A.G.

ADAMS, James
1785 (Plymouth) - 1850
An architect and draughtsman who was a pupil of John Soane from 1806 to 1809. He entered the R.A. Schools in 1808 and exhibited designs at the R.A. in 1818 and 1819. At that time he was living in Plymouth and he designed the Freemasons' Hall there in 1827, also he made additions to Mount Edgcumbe House. A.F. Livesay of Portsmouth was an architectural pupil.
Published: *The Elements of the Ellipse* &c., 1818.

ADAMS, James L
A figurative and landscape painter in oil and watercolour. He exhibited at least from 1874 to 1880 and lived in Leeds.

ADAMS, John Clayton
1840   - 1906 (nr. Guildford)
A landscape painter who lived at Edmonton and near Guildford and exhibited at the R.A., the N.W.S. and elsewhere from 1863. The majority of his subjects were Surrey views.
Examples: V.A.M.

ADAMS, Robert
**   - 1595 (? Greenwich)**
The Surveyor of the Queen's Buildings, he drew platts and views of Middleburgh, the Thames and the Armada in 1588, largely for defensive purposes. The last were engraved by Abraham Ryther for Ubaldini's account in 1590.

ADAMS, William Dacres
1864   - 1951
A painter of landscapes and buildings, portraits and figure subjects who was educated at Radley and Exeter College, Oxford, and who studied under Herkomer (q.v.) at Bushey, and in Munich. He lived in London and later at Lewes.

ADAMSON, Miss A
A painter of fruit, flowers and birds' nests who changed her London address so often that one suspects that she may have been a governess. She exhibited from 1845 to 1869 and was an unsuccessful candidate for the N.W.S. in 1848, and the O.W.S. in 1868.

ADAMSON, Charles Murray
1820 (Newcastle) - 1894 (Newcastle)
A solicitor who was the son of a solicitor and scholar. He became a clerk to the Commissioners of Taxes, but devoted much of his energy to ornithology. He illustrated the second and third of his publications.
Published: *Sundry Natural History Scraps,* 1879; *More Scraps about Birds,* 1881; *Some More Illustrations of Wild Birds,* 1887.

ADAMSON, William
1818 (Newcastle) - 1892 (Cullercoats)
The elder brother of C.M. Adamson (q.v.), he took over his father's practice. He was a keen antiquary and the historian of the local militia. He produced rather crude architectural subjects and, around 1840, views of Cullercoats to which he later retired.

ADDEY, Joseph Poole
c. 1854   - 1922 (Watford)
A landscape, figure and portrait painter who exhibited at the R.H.A. from 1877. He taught at the Derry School of Art until 1888, when he moved to Dublin, later settling at Kingston-upon-Thames. He was active until at least 1914.

ADDISON, William Grylls
1851   - 1904 (Cranford)
A painter and etcher who lived in London and Kent and occasionally exhibited watercolours at the R.I. from 1876.
Examples: V.A.M.

ADYE, General Sir John Miller
1819 (Sevenoaks) - 1900 (Rothbury)
Soldier and sketcher, he was a member of a military family and entered Woolwich Academy in 1834. He was commissioned in the Artillery in 1836 and posted to Malta in 1840 and Dublin in 1843. He was at the Tower of London in 1848 during the Chartist troubles and also in Gibraltar. Thereafter he served in the Crimea from 1854 to 1856, in Ireland in 1857, and in India during the suppression of the Mutiny and for nine years thereafter. He returned to the Crimea in 1872 to report on the state of the war graves and in 1875 he was appointed Governor of Woolwich Academy. He was Chief of Staff to the expedition to Alexandria against Arabi Pasha in 1882 and was appointed Governor of Gibraltar at the end of that year. He was promoted general in 1884 and retired two years later to the house of his daughter, Lady Armstrong, where he continued to paint.
Published: *Recollections of a Military Life,* 1895. &c.

AFFLECK, William
1869 (Rochdale) - 1943 (Clapham)
A genre painter who also exhibited flowers, spring and autumn landscapes in London from 1890. He trained at South Kensington, Lambeth and Heatherley's, and was a member of the London Sketching Club. The Lambourne Valley in Berkshire was a favourite sketching ground, and his wife, Hilda Carruthers Billson, a favourite model. He worked for J. Salmon the postcard firm using the name 'William Carruthers'.

AGAR, John Samuel
1775   - 1858 (Hertford)
A painter of excellent military portraits in watercolour, much in the spirit of H. Edridge (q.v.) and the manner of D. Dighton (q.v.) or J.A. Atkinson (q.v.). He was descended from Charles and Jacques d'Agar, Huguenot portrait painters. In 1792 he entered the R.A. Schools as an engraver, winning a silver medal in 1798.

AGLIO, Agostino Maria
1777 (Cremona) - 1857 (London)
An Italian who settled in England in 1803, and worked as a scene painter, decorator, lithographer and landscape painter. Before his arrival in England he had visited Greece and Egypt with William Wilkins, R.A., and he worked with Wilkins in Cambridge in 1803 and 1804. In London he worked at the Opera House in 1804, Drury Lane Theatre in 1806 and the Pantheon in 1811. He also worked at the Olympic Theatre and Buckingham Palace. He visited France, Germany and Italy in 1825.

His watercolours, especially coastal views, are often very close to those of Constable, and indeed have often been attributed to the greater artist. They are usually rather free and blobby in technique, with slightly clumsy figures and a predominance of greys and blue-greens.

His son, **Agostino AGLIO, Yr. (1816-1885),** also known as Augustine, was a drawing master and sculptor, and he married a daughter of J. Absolon (q.v.). In 1831 he won a Silver Isis medal from the Society of Arts for a bust.
Published: *Twelve Pictures of Killarney. A Collection of Capitals and Friezes drawn from the Antique,* 1820. *Sketches and Decorations in Woolley Hall, Yorkshire,* 1821. *Studies of various Trees and Forest Scenery,* 1831. *Antiquities of Mexico,* 1830-48.
Examples: B.M.; V.A.M.; N.G., Scotland; Brighton A.G.
Bibliography: F. Sacchi: *Cenni sulla vita e le opere di A.A.,* 1868. *Apollo,* Nov. 1940; Nov. 1943.

AIKIN, Edmund
1780 (Warrington) - 1820 (Stoke Newington)
The youngest son of Dr. John Aikin, physician and author, he became an architect and draughtsman. He was articled to James Carr, architect of St. James's, Clerkenwell, and entered the R.A. Schools in 1801. He practised in London until 1814, then moving to Liverpool, but he also worked on dockyards at Sheerness, Portsmouth and elsewhere. His architecture is usually Greek in inspiration, but occasionally Islamic, or, under protest, Gothic.
Published: *Designs for Villas and other Rural Buildings,* 1808.
Bibliography: L. Aikin: *Memoir of John Aikin, M.D.,* 1823.

AIKMAN, George, A.R.S.A., R.S.W.
1831 (Edinburgh) - 1905 (Edinburgh)
The son of an engraver, with whom he trained before becoming an Edinburgh landscape painter and etcher. He was educated at the Edinburgh Royal High School and studied under Scott Lauder at the Trustees' School of Design. He exhibited at the R.S.A. and

AFFLECK, William (1869-1943)
'Will he come?' Watercolour, signed, 16½in. x 11¾in.

elsewhere from 1850 to 1905. His water-colours, of coasts, woods and brown moors, often have an admixture of bodycolour.
Illustrated: J. Smart: *A Round of the Links*, 1893. T. Chapman and J. Strathesk: *The Midlothian Esks*, 1895.
Examples: City of Edinburgh Coll.

AINSLEY, Colonel Henry Francis
c.1805 - 1879
He joined the Army in 1824 and was posted to India in 1849, serving in Sind from 1850 to 1853.
Examples: V.A.M.; India Office Lib.

AINSLEY, Samuel James
1806 - 1874
A landscape and figure painter and printmaker, who entered the R.A. Schools in 1829. He was in Italy in 1842 and 1843 working with G. Dennis on his *Cities and Cemeteries of Etruria*. He produced both wash and full colour drawings using a wet technique reminiscent of that of de Wint.
Examples: B.M.

AITKEN, James
(Newburgh, Fife) - 1935
A painter of rivers and landscapes in oil and watercolour who exhibited in London and Liverpool from 1880. He painted in France, Italy and Switzerland and lived on the Isle of Man, as did his son **John Ernest AITKEN (1880-1957),** a marine painter.

AITKEN, James Alfred, A.R.H.A., R.S.W.
1846 (Edinburgh) - 1897 (Glasgow)
A landscape painter in oil and watercolour who trained under H. McCulloch (q.v.) and then went with his family to Dublin where he entered the R.D.S. Schools. He exhibited at the R.H.A. from 1865 and was elected an Associate in 1871. The following year he married and moved to Glasgow, exhibiting at the R.S.A., the R.S.W. and the Glasgow Institute. He was a founder member of the R.S.W. as well as of the Pen and Pencil Club, and he travelled extensively in America and on the Continent.
Examples: Glasgow A.G.

ALABASTER, Mary Anne –
see CRIDDLE, Mary Anne, Mrs.

ALABASTER, Patricia Emma, Mrs. Henry, née Fahey
The daughter of J. Fahey (q.v.), she exhibited views of Cumberland and Spain at the N.W.S., Suffolk Street and elsewhere from 1864 to 1888. Her husband was also a painter, and they lived in London.

ALBERT see MARKES, Albert Ernest

ALBERT Charles Augustus Emmanuel, H.R.H. Prince **1819 (Rosenau) - 1861 (Windsor)**
An occasional etcher and draughtsman who took hints from many professional artists, including Sir E. Landseer (q.v.).
Examples: B.M.

ALBIN, Eleazar
1690 - 1759
A naturalist and painter of birds and flowers who changed his name from Weiss on coming to England from Germany. He worked in this country from 1713 to 1759.
    The Duchess of Beaufort was an early patron, and **Elizabeth ALBIN,** one of his numerous children, helped him colour his plates. Salmon gives his date of death as 1742.
Published: *Natural History of English Insects,* 1720. *Natural History of the Birds,* 1731-38. *A Natural History of Spiders,* 1736. *A Natural History of English Song-Birds,* 1737.
Bibliography: M.A. Salmon: *The Avrelian Legacy,* 2000. *Country Life,* 1963.

ALDAY, Paul
The proprietor of a Dublin music shop, he was an amateur violinist and watercolour painter. He exhibited with the Dublin Society of Artists in 1809 and at the R.H.A. in 1826 and 1827. For the most part he painted landscapes.

ALDIN, Cecil Charles Windsor
1870 (Slough) - 1935 (Mallorca)
A sporting and humorous artist and prolific illustrator. He studied at South Kensington under Calderon. He was a keen countryman

ALDIN, Cecil Charles Windsor (1870-1935)
'At the Horse Fair.' *Watercolour, 10in. x 14in.*

and was Master of the South Devonshire from 1914 to 1918. His style is made up of simple washes and outlines like that of Caldecott. There is sometimes the feel of a Japanese woodcut about his work.
Bibliography: C.A.: *Time I Was Dead*, 1934.

ALDRICH, Admiral Robert Dawes
    1809   - 1891 (Croydon)
The son of a naval officer from Stowmarket, he joined the Navy in 1824. He served on slavewatch on the African coast, on the 1850-51 Arctic expedition in search of Franklin and later in the Coast Guard. He was promoted to captain in 1860, rear-admiral in 1876 and admiral in 1887.
Examples: Greenwich.

ALDRIDGE, Frederick James
    1850   - 1933
A marine painter somewhat in the manner of T.B. Hardy, he lived at Worthing and painted the Channel coasts. He was a regular visitor to Cowes Week, and held exhibitions at Brighton in 1909 and Dorchester the following year. He exhibited in London from 1880 to 1901. His work is generally rather loose in drawing and the predominant colours are a yellow-green and brown.
Examples: Preston Manor, Brighton; Dudley A.G.

ALEFOUNDER, John
    1757   - 1794 (Calcutta)
The son of his namesake, an architect and surveyor in Colchester and London, he studied architecture at the R.A. Schools, winning the silver medal in 1782 and 1784. In the latter year he went to India, where he painted miniatures, and oil and watercolour portraits. He exhibited at the R.A. from 1777 to 1793, but at the end of the next year he killed himself.
Bibliography: *Gentleman's Mag.*, 1795, ii.

ALEXANDER, Edwin John, R.S.A., R.W.S., R.S.W.
    1870 (Edinburgh) - 1926 (Musselburgh)
His boyhood interest in botany and animal life, combined with the influence of Joseph Crawhall (q.v.), a friend of his father R.L. Alexander, R.S.A. (q.v.), formed his whole artistic outlook. In 1887 the two Alexanders and Crawhall made a long visit to Tangier, and in 1891 he studied under Fremiet in Paris. With E.E. Nicol, Yr. (q.v.), he lived in Egypt from 1892 to 1896. In 1904 he married and settled in Inveresk where he kept a large private zoo to supply himself with models. He

ALDRIDGE, Frederick James (1850-1933)
Making Port. *Signed with initials and dated 83, watercolour,*
                       14in. x 10in.

was elected A.R.S.A. and R.S.A. in 1902 and 1913, R.W.S. in 1910 and R.S.W. in 1911.

He is best remembered for his bird and animal drawings, in which, although accurate in detail, he avoids overloading the composition, and the effect is always rather simplified. Both in these and in his landscapes he often works on textured papers, fabrics, silks or linen. He knows exactly how best to work the defects and blemishes of his surfaces into the composition. His landscapes, informed by the current interest in Japanese art, show the same ability to select significant detail.

Illustrated: J.H. Crawford: *The Wild Flowers,* 1909. C.W.G. St. John: *Wild Sports and Natural History of the Highlands,* 1919.

Examples: B.M.; Aberdeen A.G.; Cartwright Hall, Bradford; Dundee City A.G.; Glasgow A.G.; Kirkaldy A.G.; N.G., Scotland.

Bibliography: O.W.S. Club, IV, 1926.

See Colour Plate

ALEXANDER, George
1832 - 1913

A self-taught landscape painter in oil and watercolour. He lived in Leeds and painted locally, in the Lake District and North Wales.

ALEXANDER, Herbert, R.W.S.
1874 (London) - 1946

A traditional romantic landscape and figure painter in the line of Palmer, Foster and J.W. North. He was educated in Cranbrook, Kent, and studied under Herkomer at the Slade. During the First World War he served in India and Mesopotamia. He was elected A.R.W.S. and R.W.S. in 1905 and 1927. He lived in Cranbrook for much of his life, and his subjects are often Kentish and show an eye for picturesque detail.

Examples: Ulster Mus.

Bibliography: *Studio,* XXXI, 1904.

ALEXANDER, John
1686 (? Aberdeen) - c.1766

A Scottish painter and engraver who was working in Rome in 1718. He was back in Scotland in 1720, where he painted portraits and mythological subjects. The B.M. has a drawing of Rome in pen and brown ink, blue and brown wash. It is rather untidy. He was a maternal grandson of George Jamesone, the portrait painter, and the father of Cosmo **ALEXANDER (1724-1772).**

ALEXANDER, Robert Graham Dryden
1875 (London) - 1945 (London)

An amateur landscape painter, who was the son of strict Presbyterian parents. Rather grudgingly, they allowed him a year or two to study art before placing him safely in the family business in the City. He studied at the B.M., the Hornsea School of Art where, through his future wife, he came under the influence of H.B. Brabazon (q.v.) and later at the Slade. The majority of his views are of

ALEXANDER, William (1766-1816)
Chinese conversation piece. *Pencil and watercolour, 3½in. x 4in.*

Essex subjects, since he lived in Brentwood and often stayed at Walton-on-the-Naze. He was a very rapid worker, which was lucky as he was only able to paint early in the morning, on Saturday afternoons (never on a Sunday) and during his two-week annual holiday.

He was most influenced by Turner, Constable, Brabazon and Wilson Steer and was a close friend of Sir George Clausen and of Mark Fisher. He was a regular exhibitor at the N.E.A.C. and in 1922 shared an exhibition at the Grosvenor Galleries with Sir Charles Holmes and others.

Examples: B.M.; V.A.M.; Ashmolean; Fitzwilliam.

ALEXANDER, Robert Love, R.S.A.
1840 (Kilwinning, Ayrshire) - 1923 (Edinburgh)

The painter of animals and occasional humans and landscapes, he was the father of E.J. Alexander (q.v.). He was apprenticed to a house painter and from 1875 paid many visits to the Continent, where he sketched in watercolour. He also visited Tangier in 1887 with Edwin, Pollock Nisbet and Joseph Crawhall, III (qq.v.). He was elected A.R.S.A. and R.S.A. in 1878 and 1888, and was briefly a member of the R.S.W. in 1900-1. Caw noted that while he mostly worked in oil, 'the watercolours he has painted are exceedingly charming and possess to the full that delicate sense of form, colour and tone used to express a sympathetic observation of animal life which gives vital interest to his pictures.'

Bibliography: *Studio,* XLIX, 1910.

ALEXANDER, William
1766 (Maidstone) - 1816 (Maidstone)

The son of a coach builder, he was a pupil of Pars and Ibbetson, and studied at the R.A. Schools. He went to China in 1792 as a draughtsman attached to Lord Macartney's Embassy, and some of his best drawings of its progress were used to illustrate Sir George Staunton's account, published in 1797. The other official artist was T. Hickey (q.v.). In 1802 he was appointed Professor of Drawing at the Military College at Great Marlow, a post which he relinquished in 1808 on being appointed Keeper of Prints and Drawings at the B.M. He continued to reuse his Chinese material throughout his career, although later in life he also made many factual drawings of antiquities and some very charming English landscapes.

Published: *Views of the Headlands, Islands etc of China,* 1798. *The Costumes of the Russian Empire,* 1803. *The Costumes of China,* 1805. *Engravings from the Egyptian Antiquities in the B.M.,* 1805. *Picturesque Representations of the Dress and Manners of the Austrians,* 1813. *Picturesque Representations of the Dress and Manners of the Russians,* 1814. *Picturesque Representations of the Dress and Manners of the Chinese,* 1814. *Picturesque Representations of the Dress and Manners of the Turks,* 1814.

Illustrated: Sir G. Staunton: *An Authentic Account of an Embassy,* 1797. Sir J. Barrow: *Travels in China,* 1804. Sir J. Barrow: *Voyage to Cochin China,* 1806. J. Britton: *Architectural Antiquities,* 1805-14.

Examples: B.M.; V.A.M.; Ashmolean; Brighton

A.G.; Fitzwilliam; Greenwich; India Office Lib.; Leeds City A.G.; Maidstone Mus.
Bibliography: *Gentleman's Mag.*, LXXXVI, ii. *Geographical Mag.*, 5 Sept. 1947.

ALEXANDRA, H.M. Queen
1844 (Copenhagen) - 1925 (Sandringham)
Like other dynasties of amateur painters the British Royal Family tended to marry likeminded spouses. In Alexandra, Princess of Denmark, the future Edward VII acquired possibly the best artist of all. She exhibited in an honorary capacity at the R.W.S. from 1880 to 1891, and had she not been royal, she would not have needed the honour.

ALFORD, Marianne Margaret, Viscountess, Lady Marian Alford
1817 (Rome) - 1888 (Ashridge, Berkhamsted)
Daughter of the 2nd Marquess of Northampton, she spent her early life in Italy, coming to England in 1830. In 1841 she married Lord Alford, who died ten years later. She helped to establish the Royal School of Art-Needlework in Kensington and was an accomplished artist in various media, as well as a generous patron.

ALICE Maud Mary, H.R.H. Princess, Grand-Duchess of Hesse
1843 (Buckingham Palace) - 1878 (Hesse)
The third child of Queen Victoria (q.v.). Like her sisters, she was taught by E.H. Corbould (q.v.). She painted rather dainty little figure studies.
Bibliography: C. Bullock: *Doubly Royal*, 1879.

ALISON, Thomas
The son of the Chief Magistrate of Dalkeith, he painted landscapes and portraits in both oil and watercolour. He exhibited at the R.S.A., and twice at the R.S.W., from 1881 to 1899.

He lived at Dalkeith for the most part, and visited Norway.

ALKEN, Henry Thomas
1785 (London) - 1851 (London)
In the naming of their children, the Alken family showed a carelessness of future biographers bordering on the callous. Among the painters there are two Samuels, two or three Seffriens and a Seffrien John, two, if not three Georges, Henry Thomas and Henry Gordon who is also sometimes given as Samuel Henry. Of these, the Samuels, one Seffrien and Henry Gordon are separately noticed.

Henry Thomas was the second son of the elder Samuel, who gave him his first lessons. He also studied with J.T. Barker Beaumont, the miniaturist, whose influence is noticeable in Alken's figure work. In 1801 Alken exhibited miniatures at the R.A. It is possible that he spent a period in the Army, and he may have visited Persia with J.J. Morier. In 1809 he married Maria Gordon at Ipswich, and the following year they went to live in Melton Mowbray. To raise money, he schooled horses and, between 1810 and 1816, he even tried his hand at decorating papier-mâché trays with hunting and coaching scenes. His first prints, which appeared under the pseudonym of 'Ben Tally Ho!', were published in 1813, and his best drawings and prints date from the 1820s and 1830s, after which both his health and the quality of his work declined. His popularity was also falling off, and he died an embittered and penniless man.

He was a meticulous and colourful painter, and of his hunting subjects it was said 'No foxhunter will find matter to cavil at there'. In some ways his prints may be regarded as graphic journalism, illustrating actual events and real characters, but in the best there is a sense of excitement and speed which raises them above mere reporting. In many, even the overtly serious ones, there is a touch of satire. One of his trade marks is to show his characters taking their fences with the right arm raised above the head, flourishing the whip.
Examples: B.M.; V.A.M.; Brighton A.G.; Leeds City A.G.; Leicestershire A.G.; N.G., Scotland.
Bibliography: W. Shaw Sparrow: *H.A.*, 1927. F. Siltzer: *The Story of British Sporting Prints*, 1929. A. Noakes: *The World of H.A.*, 1952. *Queen*, CXVIII, 1905. *Apollo*, XXXVII, 1943. *Country Life*, 9 Oct. 1969.
See Alken Family Tree

ALKEN, Samuel
1756 (London) - 1815 (London)
The eldest son of Seffrien Alken I (c.1717-1782), a carver and gilder, he won a silver medal at the R.A. Schools in 1773, and began his career as an architectural draughtsman, probably intending to practise architecture. Certainly he followed his father as a sculptor for a while, carving capitals and goats' heads for Somerset House in 1783 and 1784. However, his skill as an etcher and aquatinter turned him to fine art. He worked with many of the most celebrated printmakers and artists of the day, including Bartolozzi, Rowlandson and George Garrard and was the first of his family to excel in sporting subjects. He also produced a number of purely topographical drawings and prints, some from the Bristol area.
Published: *A New Book of Ornaments*, 1779.
See Alken Family Tree

ALKEN, Samuel, Yr.
1784 (London) - 1825 (London)
The eldest son of Samuel Alken, with whom, since he hardly ever differentiated his signature, he is often fused or confused. He was also a sporting painter, with an emphasis on fishing subjects. As with the two Henrys, perhaps the only way of telling the work of son

ALKEN, Henry Thomas (1785-1851)
Full Cry. *Pencil and watercolour, 9⅜in. x 13in.*

ALKEN, Samuel Henry Gordon (1810-1894)
Picking up the Scent; Huntsmen at a gate; Taking of Fences; A Regular Surgeon; and Full Cry. *Signed, pencil and watercolour, 9in. x 13in.*

from father is through their lesser quality.
See Alken Family Tree

ALKEN, (Samuel) Henry Gordon
 1810 (Ipswich) - 1894 (London)
Often described as a faker of his father H.T.
Alken's work, he was certainly a close disciple
and was usually content to sign himself 'H.
Alken' *tout court*. He worked in both oil and
watercolour.
See Alken Family Tree

ALKEN, Seffrien, III
 1821 **- 1873 (London)**
A younger son of H.T. Alken, in whose manner
inevitably he worked. He produced some
racing subjects which are of a high quality.
The earlier **Seffrien ALKEN II (1754-
c.1778)**, nephew of Seffrien I, may well have
been a sporting painter, and H.T. Alken's
younger brother **Seffrien John ALKEN
(1796-1837)** certainly was. He shared a studio
with **George ALKEN I (1794-1837)**, another
brother of H.T., whose work is very like his
father's, but his horsemen are often too small.
See Alken Family Tree

ALLAN, Sir Alexander, Bt.
 1764 **- 1820 (Dover)**
After service in the Madras Native Infantry
from 1780, he resigned as a major in 1804. He
became a Director of the East India Company
in 1814. He made many pen and watercolour
drawings of the third and fourth Mysore Wars.
After his return to England he lived in London
and was M.P. for Berwick.
Published: *Views in the Mysore Country*, 1794.
Examples: India Office Lib.

ALLAN, Andrew
 1863 **- 1940**
A painter of landscapes, still lifes, and figure
subjects in watercolour and silver point.
Although he was in Glasgow in 1895, he lived
at Ardrossan, Ayrshire, exhibiting at Glasgow,
with the R.S.W. and elsewhere up to 1935. His
watercolours and illustrations show a *fin de
siècle* French influence.
Examples: Glasgow A.G.

ALLAN, David
 1744 (Alloa) - 1796 (Edinburgh)
He was apprenticed to Robert Foulis, a Glasgow
printer, and was sent to study painting in Rome
in 1764. From 1777 to 1779 he was in London,
and then he returned to Edinburgh, where he
spent the rest of his life, becoming Master of the
Trustees' Academy in 1786. He worked in a
number of media, producing both Italian and
Scottish landscapes, as well as studies of
Edinburgh and Continental characters. He also
made a number of pen and wash illustrations for
Shakespeare and for a life of Mary, Queen of
Scots. In his homely Scottish subjects, he was a
precursor of Wilkie and his school. H.W.
Williams (q.v.) was one of his pupils.

ALKEN, Samuel, Yr. (1784-1825)
Weighing-in. *Signed and dated 1808, pencil and watercolour on thin card, 13⅞in. x 20⅝in.*

Illustrated: A. Ramsay: *The Gentle Shepherd*, 1788.
A. Campbell: *An Introduction to the History of
Poetry in Scotland*, 1798.
Examples: B.M.; Glasgow A.G.; N.G., Scotland;
New York Pub. Lib.
Bibliography: T.C. Gordon: *D.A.*, 1951. *Print
Collectors' Quarterly*, XIV, 1927. *Connoisseur*,
CLXXIII, 1970. Scottish Arts Co., Exhibition Cat.,
1973.

ALLAN, Hugh **1862** **- 1909**
A painter of landscapes and rusticities in oil
and watercolour. He lived in Glasgow and
enjoyed the Clyde and the West coast.

ALLAN, Jessy
The daughter of an Edinburgh banker who was
also the proprietor of the *Caledonian Mercury*,
she was a pupil of A. Nasmyth (q.v.) in 1802.
Her journal in the National Library of Scotland
is most informative as to his methods, but her
own work is probably largely drawn or in oil.
She gave up painting on marriage.

ALLAN, Robert Weir, R.W.S.
 1851 (Glasgow) - 1942 (London)
A landscape and marine painter in oil and
watercolour who moved to London in 1881.
He was elected A.R.W.S. and R.W.S. in 1887
and 1896. Although much of his best work was
painted on the coasts of Scotland, he also
worked in Holland, Belgium, France and Italy.
He visited India from 1890 to 1892 and Japan
in 1907, and he made a world tour in 1900. His
watercolours are generally rather weak in
effect, and tend to be blotty in technique.
Examples: Glasgow A.G.; City A.G., Manchester.
Bibliography: *Studio*, XXIII, 1901. *A.J.*, 1904.

ALLAN, Sir William, R.A., P.R.S.A.
 1782 (Edinburgh) - 1850 (Edinburgh)
The son of a macer in the Court of Session, he
studied at the Trustees' Academy and the R.A.
Schools. In 1805 he went to Russia, staying
there for nine years. He then returned to
Edinburgh, becoming Master of the Academy
in 1820. He was elected R.S.A. and P.R.S.A. in
1829 and 1837, and A.R.A. and R.A. in 1825
and 1835. In 1842 he succeeded Wilkie (q.v.)
as Queen's Limner in Scotland, and in 1844 he
revisited Russia. He painted Russian and
Scottish historical subjects.
Examples: B.M.
Bibliography: *A.J.*, 1849; 1850; 1903. *Connoisseur*,
CLXXXVI, 1973.

ALLASON, Thomas
 - 1852 (? London)
An architect and draughtsman, he was a pupil
of W. Atkinson (q.v.) and entered the R.A.
Schools in 1808. In 1814 he went to Greece as
a draughtsman for Messrs. Spencer Stanhope.
He later became Surveyor to the Stock
Exchange and to other bodies and estates, and
he also designed many villas. He lived in
London and Ramsgate, and his descendants
became both military and landed.
Published: *Picturesque Views of the Antiquities of
Pola in Istria*, 1817.
Illustrated: *The Battle of Platoea*, 1817. *The Actual
State of the Plain of Olympia ...*, 1824.
Bibliography: *Gentleman's Mag.*, 1852, i. *Builder*,
X, 1852.

ALLBON, Charles Frederick
 1856 (Shoreditch)- 1926 (Epping)
An etcher and painter of landscapes and

ALLAN, Sir William (1782-1850)
Tartar Brigands sharing the Spoil. *Pencil and watercolour heightened with gum arabic. 14½in. x 11¾in.*

ALLBON, Charles Frederick (1856-1926)
Off the Dutch Coast. *Signed, pen and ink and watercolour heightened with white, 9½in. x 26in.*

marine subjects in oil and watercolour. He was an A.R.E. from 1887 to 1911. He lived in Croydon and many of his subjects are found on the French and Dutch coasts.

ALLCHIN, William Thomas Howell
1843 (Oxford) - 1883
The organist of St. John's College, Oxford, from 1876 to 1883, he copied still lifes in oil and watercolour, and made spirited but very amateur caricatures of such incidents as Ruskin's road building venture.
Examples: Ashmolean.

ALLEN, George
1798 (Brentford) - 1847
An architect who entered the R.A. Schools in 1818 and exhibited at the R.A. from 1820 to 1840. He was widely employed as a surveyor and worked in Southwark.
Published: *Plans and Designs for the future Approaches to the New London Bridge*, 1827-8.
Bibliography: *Builder*, V, 1847.

ALLEN, Isabella Anne
A number of flower studies by this artist, dated 1829, passed through Sotheby's on 2 February 1973.

ALLEN, Major John Whitacre
A landscape painter who lived in Bath and Cheltenham and who visited Italy and Greece. He exhibited in London from 1859 to 1886, mostly at Suffolk Street and the N.W.S. for which he was an unsuccessful candidate in 1864 and 1867. He was promoted captain in 1865 and major in 1870.

ALLEN, Joseph William
1803 (Lambeth) - 1852
Allen was educated at St. Paul's and worked as an usher at Taunton Academy before taking up painting. He then painted scenery with C. Stanfield (q.v.) at the Olympic Theatre and elsewhere, and exhibited rather grandiose oil

ALLEN, Joseph William (1803-1852)
View of Aberdeen. *Watercolour, signed and dated 1838, 14½in. x 20½in.*

paintings at the R.A. from 1826. He also exhibited at the N.W.S. and became Secretary of the S.B.A. and the first drawing master at the City of London School. His watercolours are rather in the manner of Cox.
Examples: B.M.; V.A.M.
Bibliography: *A.J.,* Oct., 1852.

ALLEN, Thomas John
            1821   - 1846 (London)
A painter of architectural subjects. He shot himself when depressed by the death of a sister.

ALLEN, William Herbert
            1863 (London) - 1943 (Wylye)
A landscape painter in oil and watercolour who studied at the R.C.A. and was made Principal of the Farnham School of Art in 1888. He worked on commission for the V.A.M. and other museums, painting in France and Italy. He was elected to the R.B.A. in 1904 and was active until at least 1929.
Examples: Curtis Mus., Alton.
Bibliography: Curtis Mus., Alton: *Illustrated Handbook to the W.H.A. Bequest,* 1945.

ALLERSTON, John Taylor
A draper, stationer and photographer at Bridlington, who became a professional marine artist in about 1900. He is said to have painted some two thousand local coastal scenes in oil and watercolour.
Examples: Bridlington Lib.; Ferens A.G., Hull.

ALLINGHAM, Helen Mary Elizabeth, Mrs., née Paterson, R.W.S.
            1848 (near Burton-on-Trent) -
            1926 (Haslemere)
The daughter of a doctor, who died when she was

a child, she studied at the Birmingham School of Design and came to London and the R.A. Schools in 1868. She was encouraged in this by her aunt Laura Herford, who had been the first female student at the Schools. There she was

particularly influenced by the work of Birket Foster and Fred Walker (qq.v). She visited Italy in the spring of 1868, and in 1874 she married the Irish poet William Allingham, author of 'Up the airy mountain'. This placed her at the centre of the Cheyne Walk set. She was elected A.R.W.S. in 1875, and when in 1890 full membership was opened to ladies, she was immediately promoted.

Her subject matter is reflected in her husband's poem:

> Four ducks on a pond,
> A grass-bank beyond,
> A blue sky of spring,
> White clouds on the wing:
> What a little thing
> To remember for years
> To remember with tears!

Her colours are always fresh and bright with a predominance of yellow in the palette. Her cottages in Surrey and Berkshire are a little idealised, but less sentimental than those of Foster. Her occasional small portraits are very beautiful indeed.
Illustrated: J.H. Ewing: *A Flat Iron for a Farthing,* 1884. S. Dick: *The Cottage Homes of England,* 1909.
Examples: B.M.; V.A.M.; City A.G., Manchester; Maidstone Mus.; Ulster Mus.
Bibliography: I. Taylor: *H.A.'s England,* 1900. H.B. Huish: *Happy England as painted by H.A.,* 1903. *A.J.,* 1888. *Studio,* Summer No., 1900. Christie's: *Catalogue of the Marley Collection,* 19 Sept. 1991.
See Colour Plate

ALLINGHAM, Helen, Mrs., née Paterson (1848-1926)
The Fields in May. *Signed, water and bodycolour, 12in. x 9⅝in.*

ALLOM, Thomas (1804-1872)
Rouen Cathedral. *Signed and inscribed, watercolour heightened with white, 9¼in. x 13½in.*

ALLOM, Thomas
1804 (London) - 1872 (Barnes)
During a seven year apprenticeship to the architect Francis Goodwin beginning in 1819, he helped draw up the plans for the Kensal Green Cemetery. He entered the R.A. Schools in 1828. Later he was a co-founder of the R.I.B.A. and worked with Sir C. Barry (q.v.) on Highclere and the Houses of Parliament. He travelled widely in Europe, the Near and Far East, drawing houses and landscapes for publication, often by Virtue & Co. and Heath & Co.

He worked in brown wash and in full watercolour, and was essentially a topographer, working neatly, accurately, pleasingly and without great originality.
Illustrated: Fisher: *Constantinople and its Environs,* G.N. Wright: *China in a Series of Views,* 1843. G.N. Wright: *France Illustrated,* 1845. &c.
Examples: B.M.; V.A.M.; Fitzwilliam; Glasgow A.G.; Grosvenor Mus., Chester; N.G., Scotland; Newport A.G., N.G., Tasmania; Queensland A.G., Brisbane.
Bibliography: *A.J.,* 1863. *Builder,* 26 Oct. 1872.

ALLPORT, Henry Curzon
1788 (Aldridge) - 1854 (Paramatta, N.S.W.)
Perhaps the 'Cousin Allport' who gave Cox (q.v.) his first paintbox and helped him to his first scene-painting job in Birmingham, he lived at Aldridge between Lichfield and Birmingham where his parents ran a school for young ladies, and he taught drawing in the latter city from 1808. He exhibited at the R.A. in 1811 and 1812 and at the Oil and Watercolour Society from 1813, to which he was elected in place of Glover in 1818. He showed a few Italian views from 1819, and was re-elected as an Associate of the reconstituted O.W.S. in 1823, but

exhibited for the last time in that year, giving a Lichfield address. Dr. Percy believed that he subsequently went into the wine trade, but this is *ben trovato.* In fact, after a period as a farmer, he went to Sydney in 1839 as agent-steward to the Governor of N.S.W., and he painted landscapes there.

His pupil and niece, **Mary Morton CHAPMAN (1806 Birmingham - 1895)** was also a pupil of J.S. Prout (q.v.) and became a miniaturist in Hobart. Several others of the family became painters.
Examples: B.M.; V.A.M.; Stafford Lib.; Ulster Mus.; Sydney A.G.; Allport Lib. , Hobart; Hobart Mus., Tasmania.

ALMOND, William Douglas, R.I.
1868 (London) - 1916 (London)
An illustrator of Anglo-Scottish parentage, he was on the staff of the *I.L.N.* He also worked for the *English Illustrated Magazine* and the *Studio,* and he exhibited at the R.A., the R.I. and elsewhere from 1886. He was elected R.I. in 1897.

ALPENNY, Joseph Samuel
1787 (Ireland) - 1858 (London)
After studying in London, where he exhibited at the R.A. from 1805 to 1808 and entered the R.A. Schools in 1807, as 'J.S. Halfpenny', he moved to Ireland in 1810. From 1812 he lived in Dublin and used the name Alpenny. He was a prolific exhibitor in Dublin exhibitions, but in about 1824 he returned to London, exhibiting at the R.A. from 1825 to 1853. His work includes portraits, figure and historical subjects and ceremonial pictures in oils and watercolour.
Published: *Alpenny's New Drawing Book of Rustic Figures,* 1825.
Examples: N.G., Ireland.

ALSTON, I   W
A figure and rustic genre painter who was active in Scotland from about 1785 to 1795.

ALTHAUS, Fritz B, later KERR, Fred
c.1865 (London) - 1952
A landscape and coastal painter who first learnt to draw from his mother, an amateur portraitist. He studied under A.H. Haig (q.v.) as well as at St. Martin's School of Art and later Westminster School of Art and the R.I. He exhibited from 1881 and lived in London until 1893 when he moved to Exeter. He painted the moors and coasts of Devon and Cornwall and in Oxford, Cambridge and the Channel Islands. In 1908 he was living in Headingley, and in about 1915 he changed his name, because of the War. As 'Fred Kerr' he became Professor of Art at Leeds University.

AMHERST, Sarah Elizabeth, Countess
1762   - 1838
The daughter of Lord Archer, she married firstly Other Hickman, 5th Earl of Plymouth, and secondly in 1800, **William PITT, 2nd Lord AMHERST.** Amherst led a mission to China in 1816, which failed in its objectives owing to his laudable refusal to kowtow to the Emperor. He was appointed Governor-General of India in 1823, and directed the Burmese War of the following year. In 1826 he was created Earl Amherst and he retired in 1828. Lady Amherst made numerous sketches in India, which she worked up in the de Wint manner on her return to England. The Earl married the widow of the 6th Earl of Plymouth in 1839. He had been a pupil of J.B. Malchair (q.v.). Their daughter, **Lady Sarah PITT (d.1876),** who married Sir John Hay Williams, was also a watercolourist.
Examples: India Office Lib.

ANCRUM, Marion, Mrs. G. Turnbull
An Edinburgh painter of interiors, town scenes and landscapes who was active from about 1885 to 1919. She was particularly fond of Old Edinburgh.
Examples: Edinburgh City Coll.

ANDERSON, John
1835 (Scotland) - 1919
A painter of Warwickshire landscapes in oil and watercolour. He lived in Coventry and exhibited in London between 1858 and 1884. He taught at the Coventry School of Art from 1880 to 1884 and also painted on the Thames, in Devon and in Venice.
Examples: Coventry A.G.

ANDERSON, John Farquharson
A landscape painter who exhibited views, for the most part of Clovelly, at Suffolk Street from 1879 to 1882. In the first year he was living in London and in the last near Dundee.

ANDERSON, Robert, A.R.S.A., R.S.W.
1842 (Edinburgh) - 1885 (Edinburgh)
An engraver and watercolourist who painted landscapes, seascapes and figure subjects. He

exhibited at the R.A. and R.I. from 1880 to 1884 and was elected A.R.S.A. in 1879. He was a founder member of the R.S.W. in 1878.

ANDERSON, William
1757 (Sutherland) - 1837
Originally a shipwright, he came to London and became a painter in both oil and watercolour, exhibiting at the R.A. from 1787 to 1834. He was a close friend of J.C. Ibbetson (q.v.), but does not seem to have been influenced stylistically by him. His drawings 'show the formal vision of the eighteenth century without the crudeness or naïvety of many of the eighteenth century ship painters' (Williams). He specialised in river and harbour scenes, which are usually calm and luminous. His watercolours are generally signed and dated, but his rare monochromes are not. He also produced large numbers of figure sketches and occasional landscapes. In 1825 he published a pamphlet upholding the lawfulness of war.

His son, **(William) Guido ANDERSON (d.1801),** was mortally wounded as a midshipman at Nelson's Battle of Copenhagen. He had exhibited at the R.A. in 1799, when he had also been with the fleet at the Battle of the Nile. There is a sketchbook at Greenwich.
Examples: B.M.; V.A.M.; Fitzwilliam; Greenwich; Ulster Mus.; A.G., S. Australia.

ANDERSON, Will(iam)
A London landscape painter in oil and watercolour who exhibited at Suffolk Street from 1879. His subjects are generally taken from Surrey and Sussex.

ANDOVER, Viscountess, –
see HOWARD, Hon. Frances

ANDREWS, George Henry, R.W.S.
1816 (Lambeth) - 1898 (London)
A professional engineer who painted marine subjects and drew for the *I.L.N.* and the *Graphic.* He exhibited from 1840 until his death, and was elected A.O.W.S. and O.W.S. in 1856 and 1878, becoming Treasurer. He is presumably the artist who accompanied Howard Vyse to Gizeh in 1836 and illustrated his *Operations at the Pyramids of Gizeh,*1840.
Illustrated: J. Corbet Anderson: *English Landscapes and Views*, 1883.
Examples: V.A.M.; Greenwich; Nat. Mus., Wales.

ANDREWS, Henry
c.1810   - 1868
A genre painter, some of whose copies of Watteau subjects were sold as originals. He exhibited from 1827 to 1863, and at his death the *A.J.* remarked: 'Had he been an artist of quality rather than quantity, he might have acquired a good reputation'.

ANDREWS, James, of Olney
1735   - 1817
A monumental sculptor who worked around

ANDERSON, William (1757-1837)
An English Two-decker before the Wind, with other Shipping. *Signed and dated 1806, watercolour, 12½in. x 17½in.*

North Buckinghamshire and Oxfordshire. He taught drawing to the poet William Cowper, who called him 'my Michelangelo'.

ANDREWS, James Pettit, F.S.A.
1737 (nr. Newbury) - 1797 (Hampstead)
Author, antiquarian and draughtsman who painted topographical and marine subjects and was a friend of Grimm and Grose. His wife was a sister of T. Penrose (q.v.). Like the latter he was a militiaman, and he was a magistrate at Queen's Square, Westminster. He built himself a Gothick house, Donnington Grove, near Newbury, but soon sold it. His books are mainly historical. He exhibited with the Society of Artists and the Free Society.
Published: *The Savages of Europe* (trans.), 1764. &c.

ANDREWS, Samuel
c.1767 (Ireland) - 1807 (Patna)
A landscape painter who went to Madras in 1791, and visited Bencoolen in Sumatra between 1794 and 1798. He was in England in 1795. He painted miniature portraits in grisaille, and a set of Sumatran aquatints was published after his watercolours.

ANDREWS, George Henry (1816-1898)
A Dutch Fishing Boat in a Squall. *Signed and dated '51, pencil and watercolour heightened with white, 8½in. x 14¼in.*

ANSELL, Charles (1756-   )
Embarking at Dice Quay for Margate. *Signed with initials and dated 1788, pencil and watercolour with touches of white, 15⅞in. x 20¾in.*

ANELAY, Henry
1817 (Hull) - 1883 (Sydenham)
A landscape and coastal painter who lived at Upper Sydenham from 1848. He exhibited in London and elsewhere from 1845 to 1875 and was an unsuccessful candidate for the N.W.S. in 1859, 1860 and 1869. He was a prolific illustrator, most notably of *Uncle Tom's Cabin,* 1852, and its first Welsh edition in 1880.

ANGAS, George French   1822 (Newcastle-upon-Tyne) - 1886 (London)
The son of one of the founders of South Australia, he travelled widely, in particular visiting the Mediterranean in 1841. He then spent two years in London studying drawing before going to Australia. He settled in Sydney in 1851 as director of the Museum, but returned to England in about 1873. He was the author and illustrator of numerous books.
Published: *A Ramble in Malta and Sicily,* 1842. *Savage Life and Scenes in Australia and New Zealand,* 1847. *The Kafirs illustrated...,* 1849. *Views of the Gold Regions of Australia,* 1851. &c.
Examples: B.M.; Sydney A.G.

ANGELL, Helen Cordelia, Mrs., née Coleman, A.R.W.S.   1847 (Horsham) - 1884 (London)
A flower painter, her early training was in helping her brother, W.S. Coleman (q.v.), in his designs for Minton, and her first exhibited works were at the Dudley Gallery in 1865, again through his influence. W.H. Hunt (q.v.) had already declared that she was his only successor as a painter of flowers and birds. In

1875 she married T.W. Angell, exhibiting thereafter under her married name, and she succeeded Bartholomew (q.v.) as Flower Painter in Ordinary to the Queen. In the same year she was elected R.I., but she resigned three years later, being elected A.O.W.S. in 1879. Her later style is rather looser than in her first works, in which she had aimed at a minute perfection of finish.
Examples: V.A.M.; Exeter Mus.; Stalybridge A.G.

ANGUS, Maria L.
A painter of genre subjects and occasional landscapes who lived in Westminster. She was active at least from 1887 to1912.

ANNESLEY, Rev. and Hon. Charles Francis   1787   - 1863 (Eydon Hall)
A landscape painter, he was the brother of the 10th Viscount Valentia and lived at Eydon Hall, Northamptonshire. His subjects are usually views in Italy, Switzerland and on the Riviera and are strongly drawn, with muted colours. Occasionally his work is a little reminiscent of that of Copley Fielding (q.v.), but he tends to use strong outlines. He became a Fellow of All Souls.
Examples: B.M.; Cardiff Central Lib.

ANSELL, Charles
1756   -
An animal painter and engraver and an illustrator, he was probably studying in Paris in 1778. Two years later he entered the R.A. Schools, and he exhibited at the R.A. in 1780 and 1781. He was still working in 1790. His

figures are not perfectly drawn and show a distant kinship to those of Fuseli (q.v.).
Examples: B.M.

ANSON, Isabella Elizabeth Annabella, née Weld-Forester, Hon Mrs. George
- 1858
A daughter of the 1st Lord Forester, she was a pupil of P. de Wint (q.v.). In 1830 she married Major-General Anson (1797-1857), brother of the 1st Earl of Lichfield, who was C-in-C India. Her brother married M.A. Jervis (q.v.), and her sister was Lady Chesterfield (q.v.).

ANTHONY, Henry Mark
1817 (Manchester) - 1886
A landscape painter in oil and watercolour who was the pupil of his kinsman **George Wilfred ANTHONY (1800-1859),** a Manchester drawing master, landscapist and art critic. He lived in Paris and Fontainebleau from 1834 to 1840, and later visited Ireland and Spain. He absorbed the influence of such French friends as Corot and was approved of by the Pre-Raphaelites.

APPERLEY, George Owen Wynne, R.I., F.S.A   1884 (Ventnor I.o.W.) - 1960 (Tangier)
A descendant of 'Nimrod' the sporting journalist, Apperley had an unhappy childhood in Torquay and at school at Uppingham, since he was himself not sporting. However, Herkomer's school at Bushey was to his taste, and he exhibited at the R.A. from 1905. His first one-man show was in the following year. He married in 1907 and lived in Hampstead, taking twice-yearly landscape classes in Italy, France, Belgium and Holland. He also composed a musical, *The Flying Man,* based on the exploits of Blériot, and himself appeared on the music hall stage. After the death of a daughter, the illness of a son and his own poor health, he moved to Bushey in 1913, the year that he was elected R.I.

In 1916 he was advised to go to Spain for his health, and he never returned. He abandoned his family and lived, first in Granada and then at the Villa Apperley, Tangier, with a Spanish gipsy. He had numerous exhibitions in Spain and was awarded the order of Alfonso X el Sabio in 1945.

His earliest landscapes are a little reminiscent of J.R. Cozens (q.v.). He also painted figures, mythological subjects, landscapes and town views in the typical Herkomer wet style. He was a fine and free draughtsman, and in Spain he learned to convey light and shade excellently.

ARBUTHNOTT, George   c.1803   -
A painter of British and Swiss views, who lived in London and exhibited from 1829 to 1854. He also visited the Rhine and Northern France.
Examples: Edinburgh City Coll.

ARCHER, James, R.S.A
1823 (Edinburgh) - 1904 (Haslemere)
A painter in various media, including

ARDEN, Margaret Elizabeth, Lady (1769-1851)
A Whitethroat. *Signed with initials and dated, 1804, pencil and watercolour, 9in. x 7in.*

ARMOUR, Lt.-Col. George Denholm (1864-1949)
Jorrocks and Pigg. *Signed, pencil, water and bodycolour on linen, 14⅝in. x 12⅞in.*

watercolour and wash, who moved from chalk portraits to literature, history and scripture. He studied at the Trustees' Academy and was elected A.R.S.A. and R.S.A in 1850 and 1858. He moved to London in 1864. He visited the United States in 1884 and two years later went to India. He is said to have been the first Victorian painter to produce portraits of children in period costume.

A second **James ARCHER (b.1850)** entered the R.A.Schools in 1872.
Bibliography: *A.J.*, 1871. J. Ruskin: *Academy Notes*, 1875.

ARCHER, John Wykeham, A.N.W.S.
1808 (Newcastle-upon-Tyne) - 1864 (London)
Apprenticed to the animal engraver John Scott in London, he began his independent career as an engraver in Newcastle where he was in partnership with William Collard, and continued in Edinburgh until 1831. In that year, he returned to London where he worked for the Findens, gradually turning to watercolour painting. He was commissioned by William Twopenny, and later by the Duke of Northumberland, to draw old buildings in London and elsewhere. He also turned his hand to wood-engraving for the *I.L.N.* and to making monumental brasses. He was elected A.N.W.S. in 1842. He and G. Lance (q.v.) married two sisters.
Published: *Views of Old London...*, 1851. *Posthumous Poems*, 1873.
Illustrated: W. Beattie: *The Castles and Abbeys of England*, 1844.

Examples: B.M.; V.A.M.
Bibliography: *A.J.*, 1864.

ARDEN, Edward –
see **TUCKER, Edward, Yr.**
ARDEN, Lieutenant George
c.1792   -   (West Indies)
The eighth son of Rev. John Arden of Longcroft, Staffordshire (1752-1803), he served in the Navy and painted shipping subjects in the manner of D. Serres (q.v.) or W. Anderson (q.v.). His watercolours are small and detailed, in pale colours.

ARDEN, Margaret Elizabeth, Lady
1769   - 1851 (Nork Ho., nr. Guildford)
In youth a pupil of F. Towne (q.v) and in age a pupil and patron of D. Cox (q.v.), she was the daughter of Sir Thomas Spencer Wilson, Bt. of Charlton, Kent. Her mother was a Cheney of Badger Hall, and her sister married the Prime Minister, Spencer Perceval. In 1787 she married George Compton, Lord Arden (1756-1840), whose mother, a sister of two Earls of Northampton, had been created a peeress in her own right. Lord Arden appears to have painted in his youth.

ARMITAGE, Edward, R.A.
1817 (London) - 1896 (Tunbridge Wells)
A historical painter, and a favourite pupil of Paul Delaroche from 1837. He entered the various cartoon competitions for the Houses of Parliament with marked success, and after a year's study in Rome, he began to exhibit at

the R.A. in 1848. He was in the Crimea during the war. He was elected A.R.A. and R.A. in 1867 and 1872. He was a champion of mural painting, and his style is severe and academic.
Illustrated: Baron Bunsen: *Lyra Germanica*, 1868.
Bibliography: J.P. Richter: *Pictures and Drawings selected from the work of E.A.*, 1897. *A.J.*, 1863.

ARMOUR, Lieutenant-Colonel George Denholm
1864 (Waterside, Lanark) - 1949 (Wiltshire)
Educated at St. Andrews University, he studied at the R.A. Schools and became a *Punch* illustrator in 1894. During the First World War he commanded the depot of the Army remount service, and from 1917 to 1919 he served with the Salonica Force. He was awarded the O.B.E. in 1919. His subjects are hunting, shooting and fishing and he illustrated many sporting books. He used much bodycolour and sometimes worked on canvas. He lived in Wiltshire.
Examples: Glasgow A.G.

ARMSTRONG, Fanny
A landscape painter who lived in Oxford and exhibited at the R.I. and Suffolk Street from 1883 to 1890. She visited Italy and also painted in Chester, Surrey and Canterbury and produced genre subjects.

ARMSTRONG, Francis Abel William Taylor 1849 (Malmesbury) - 1920 (Bristol)
A businessman who turned to painting, and studied in Paris and Scotland. He painted landscapes and architectural subjects, and

exhibited in France and Germany as well as in Britain where he became a member of the R.B.A. He provided illustrations for the *A.J.*, *Portfolio* and other art magazines.
Illustrated: R.D. Blackmore: *Lorna Doone*, 1883.
Examples: V.A.M.

ARMSTRONG, Thomas
1832 (Fallowfield, Manchester) - 1911 (Abbots Langley)
A decorative and landscape painter who studied under a Mr. Crazier in Manchester, and in 1853 in Paris, featuring in du Maurier's *Trilby*. He exhibited at the R.A. from 1865 to 1877 and was Director for Art at the V.A.M. from 1881 to 1898. He was in Algeria in 1858 and 1859, and visited Düsseldorf in 1860.

ARMYTAGE, Charles
1835/6 -
A painter of figure subjects who was working between 1857 and 1874. He was the son of an artist and also painted Norman landscapes.
Examples: V.A.M.

ARMYTAGE, Mary Elizabeth, Lady
1772 - 1834
A daughter of O. Bowles (q.v.), she married Sir George Armytage, 4th Bt., in 1791. Like W. Markham (q.v.) and other members of the family, she carried on the traditions of Malchair.
See Bowles Family Tree

ARNALD, George, A.R.A.
1763 (Farndip, Northants) - 1841 (London)
A topographer who was a pupil of William Pether and who exhibited at the R.A. from 1788. He was elected A.R.A. in 1810. In 1798 or 1799 he visited North Wales with J. Varley (q.v.), and in 1828 he was working in France. He also sketched in many parts of the British Isles and Ireland and from 1825 carried out a number of commissions for the Duke of Gloucester. His work is in the tradition of Dayes and early Turner, with thin blue, grey and green washes.
His son, Sebastian Wyndham Arnald (b.1806), and two of his daughters were also artists.
Published: *The River Meuse*, 1828.
Illustrated: T. Wright: *History and Topography...of Essex*, 1836.
Examples: B.M.; Bishopsgate Inst.

ARNOLD, Dr. Joseph
1782 (Beccles) - 1818 (Padang, Sumatra)
A botanist and naval surgeon, he graduated M.D. at Edinburgh in 1807. He joined the Navy in the following year and in 1815 he accompanied a shipload of female convicts to Botany Bay. On the return voyage his ship and journals were burnt and he spent some months with Raffles in Java, reaching home in 1816. He rejoined Raffles in Sumatra in 1818, but died of fever four months later. As well as botanical and entomological drawings he produced rather crude panoramas of coasts and islands as navigational aids. They are in

watercolour, sometimes with pen and ink, and they can be very long.

ARNOTT, Archibald
1803 - 1846 (India)
A surgeon with the Bombay Horse Artillery and the 22nd Native Infantry from 1827 until his death in camp. His accomplished landscapes are in a damp, rubbed and fuzzy style without outlines.
Examples: B.M.

ARNOTT, Elizabeth S.
A landscape and still-life painter who was active in Edinburgh from 1849 to 1879.

ARNOTT, James George McLellan
1855 (Dumfries) - 1923 (Dumfries)
A landscape, portrait and figure painter in oil and watercolour who studied with the local portrait painter J.R. Fergusson before going to Heatherley's in 1873 and on to Antwerp. He worked in London for a while before moving homewards. He was art master at the Benedictine Convent at Maxwelltown from 1890 to 1920.

ARROLL, Richard Hubbard
1853 (Helensburgh) - 1931
The son of a woodcarver, he was educated at Glasgow University. He painted genre and village scenes in oil and watercolour, and lived in Ayr.

ARTAUD, William
1763 (London) - 1823 (London)
The son of a jeweller, he was awarded a premium by the Society of Arts in 1776/7, and entered the R.A. Schools in 1778. There he won silver and gold medals, and in 1795 he was 'sent Abroad' on a travelling scholarship for further study, returning by way of Germany in 1799. He began as a history and biblical painter, but turned more to portraits, occasionally in watercolour. He also made tours of the Midlands turning out portraits, some of which are of fellow artists.

ARUNDALE, Francis Vyvyan Jago
1807 (London) - 1853 (Brighton)
An architect, traveller and topographer. He was a pupil of A. Pugin (q.v.) whom he accompanied to Normandy in 1826. In 1829 he entered the R.A. Schools, and in 1832 he went to Egypt. He stayed in the Near East until 1840, working on Egyptian and Palestinian antiquities and publishing several books on them – see also G.H. Andrews. He finally returned by way of Asia Minor, and most of his winters were spent in Rome. He married a daughter of H.W. Pickersgill, R.A. and is believed to have died of a disease acquired in a Pharaoh's tomb.
Published: *Palladian Edifices in Vicenza*, 1832.
Illustrations of Jerusalem and Mount Sinai, 1837.
Examples and Designs of Verandahs, 1851.
Illustrated: Howard Vyse: *Operations carried out at the Pyramids of Gizeh in 1837*, 1840-2.
Examples: B.M.; Brighton A.G.; Greenwich.
Bibliography: *A.J.*, Feb. 1854. *Builder*, XII, 1854.

ASH, John Willsteed
A landscape and coastal painter working in Warwickshire and elsewhere in the 1890s. He lived in Birmingham and Dudley.

ASHBURNHAM, George, 3rd Earl of, F.S.A. 1760 - 1830
A competent amateur, he married Lady Sophia Thynne, daughter of the 1st Marquess of Bath in 1794, and **Lady Charlotte PERCY (d.1862)** – apparently monogamously – in the following year. The latter was a sister of Lady E.S. Percy (q.v.), and she painted grey wash views in London and doubtless elsewhere.

ASHBURNHAM, George Percy
c.1815 - c.1886
A landscape and architectural painter, he was a grandson of Sir William Ashburnham, 5th Bt. In the 1870s and 1880s he produced very competent copies of Prout's Gothic watercolours.

ASHBY, Henry Pollard
1809 - 1892
A painter of views of Wimbledon and on the south coast, who lived in Mitcham and exhibited at the R.A. from 1835 to 1865. He was the son of Henry, 'Harry', Ashby, Yr. (1778 London - 1847 Plymouth), a portrait and genre painter, and grandson of Harry Ashby, the engraver of banknotes.

ASHFORD, William, P.R.H.A., F.S.A.
1746 (Birmingham) - 1824 (Dublin)
A landscape painter in oil and watercolour who settled in Dublin in 1764. He worked in the Ordnance Department for a while, but soon set up as a professional artist, exhibiting with the Dublin Society of Artists from 1767 to 1780. He first exhibited landscapes in 1772 – until that time he had confined himself to still lifes. He contributed to the R.A. exhibitions at intervals between 1775 and 1811, as well as to the Society of Artists (London) of which he was a Fellow, and the B.I. He worked in conjunction with D. Serres (q.v.) in London for a period in the 1780s, and an exhibition of their works was held in 1790. He later returned to Dublin where, in February 1819, an exhibition of his work was held in the Dublin Society's house in Hawkins Street. He was elected President of the Irish Society of Artists in 1813, and played a large part in the establishment of the R.H.A., becoming its first President in 1823.
Although he was criticised by Anthony Pasquin in 1794 for the weakness of his figure drawing and the greenish tint of his skies, he gained a reputation as the foremost landscape painter of his time in Ireland. Many of his works were engraved. His remaining works were sold by auction in Dublin, 18-21 May 1824.
His son, **Daniel ASHFORD (d.1842)** also exhibited in Dublin.
Examples: N.G., Ireland; Brighton A.G.; Fitzwilliam Mus.; Limerick Mus.

ASHMORE, Charles
1823/4 -
A Birmingham genre painter who was working between 1849 and 1886. He exhibited in London as well as Birmingham, and also painted portraits and rustic subjects.
Illustrated: H. Armitage: *Chantrey Land,* 1910.

ASHPITEL, Arthur, F.S.A.
1807 (Hackney) - 1869
The son of W.H. Ashpitel (q.v.), he was an architect and surveyor as well as an archaeologist, scholar and linguist. He exhibited views and reconstructions of old buildings at the R.A. from 1845 to 1864 and was F.R.I.B.A. In 1853 he was in Italy with D. Roberts (q.v.) visiting Rome and Naples.
Examples: V.A.M.

ASHPITEL, William Hurst
1776 - 1852 (? London)
An architect and draughtsman who was pupil and assistant to Daniel Asher Alexander and George Rennie. He worked in Bath, London and the Home Counties, but retired to his own estate in early life.

ASHTON, Henry
1801 (London) - 1872
An architect and draughtsman who was a pupil of Sir Robert Smirke and worked thereafter for Wyatville (q.v.). He built the stables at Windsor, the kennels at Frogmore, a summer palace for the King of Holland, and the dreary Victorian Victoria Street. He often exhibited designs and views at the R.A.
  A later **Henry ASHTON** painted Indian and Egyptian subjects between 1895 and 1929. He lived at Prestwich.

ASHTON, Julian R
A genre and landscape painter who lived in North London and exhibited in London and Brighton between 1871 and 1879. He then went to Australia. He was perhaps a brother of **G.R. ASHTON** who exhibited watercolours of animals from 1867 to 1877.

ASHWORTH, Susan A
She exhibited fruit and flowers with the Female Artists in 1871, and dead birds and a Dovedale view at Suffolk Street in 1874, from a London address. Despite this, she was a native of Edinburgh, and she succeeded R.S. Lauder (q.v.) as head of the Trustees' Academy.

ASPINALL, J
An artist who exhibited landscapes between 1790 and 1800. In style they are between Towne and Pars, and they are very weak.
Examples: B.M.

ASPINWALL, Reginald
1858 (Preston) - 1921 (Lancaster)
A landscape painter in oil and watercolour who exhibited at the R.A. from 1884 to 1908.
Examples: Lancaster Mus.

ASPLAND, Theophilus Lindsey
1807 (Hackney) - 1890 (Reigate)
The son of a Unitarian minister, he became a pupil of the aquatinter George Cooke, but by 1829 (according to E.W. Cooke, q.v.), he had given up engraving for painting. He worked in Manchester and Liverpool until 1848. In that year he retired to a house on Esthwaite Water and concentrated on painting Lake District views. His work is in the early landscape manner of Cox and Prout, and his washes are sometimes reminiscent of Varley.
Examples: B.M.

ASSHETON, William c.1767 (Cuerdale, Lancashire) - 1833 (Brandon, Warwickshire)
A Lancashire landowner and amateur artist who was educated at Westminster and at Brasenose and Balliol Colleges, Oxford. In 1779 he became a member of the Middle Temple, and until 1786 he lived at Over Norton, Oxfordshire. From June 1783 to November 1784 he made his Grand Tour, travelling extensively in France, Switzerland, Italy, Austria, Germany and Belgium. In Rome he met many artists including Carlo Labruzzi, from whom he took lessons, A. Kauffmann (q.v.), Captain Koehler (q.v.) and J. More (q.v.). In the autumn of 1785 he visited Lisbon. He married in 1786, but separated from his wife in 1804. He was High Sheriff of Lancashire from 1792 and spent the rest of his life on his properties at Cuerdale, Downham and Beaconsfield, travelling and sketching in many parts of England.
  Through his daughters he was connected with the Armytage, Bowles, Holbech and other families of amateur artists.
See Bowles Family Tree.

ASTLEY, Henry
A Liverpool topographer who was working in pen, ink and coloured washes around 1810.

ASTON, Charles Reginald, R.I.
1832 - 1908
The great-nephew of Sir T. Lawrence, he studied architecture, but became a landscape painter in oil and watercolour. He lived in Birmingham for some years around 1850, and travelled widely in Britain as well as to Italy. He exhibited at the R.I., the R.A. and elsewhere in London from 1862, and was a member of the R.I. from 1882 to 1901. He was living in Oxford in 1900.

ATCHERLEY, Ethel
1864 (Eccles) - 1905
A painter of rustic subjects who studied at the Manchester and Lambeth Schools of Art, as well as in Paris. Later she lived in Eccles and Church Stretton, Shropshire, and she exhibited in London between 1895 and 1897. She worked in oil and watercolour.
Examples: City A.G., Manchester.

ATHOW, Thomas
A landscape and portrait painter who exhibited at the R.A. from 1806 to 1822. He also made watercolour copies of Tudor portraits. They are not very good.
Examples: B.M.; Ashmolean; J. Rylands Lib., Manchester.

ATKIN, John
A Hull carrier and amateur artist who was working in the late nineteenth century.
Examples: Hull Central Lib.

ASHFORD, William (1746-1824)
A Mill near Bantry, County Cork. *Signed and inscribed on the reverse, pencil, pen and ink and watercolour, 9½in. x 14½in.*

ATKINS, Samuel (c.1765-?1808)
Bird Watchers on the Coast. Signed, watercolour, 11in. x 15¼in.

ATKINS, Catherine Jane
1846 (London) - 1924 (London)
A genre painter in oil and watercolour who exhibited at the R.A., the R.I. and elsewhere from 1877. She lived in the fashionable parts of London as did her sister, **Emmeline ATKINS (b.1853 London)** who exhibited from 1878 to 1896.

ATKINS, Samuel
c.1765   - ?1808
A marine painter of whom little is known. In 1788 when living off The Strand he advertised: 'Marine Drawing taught in an easy, pleasing and expeditious manner.' He exhibited at the R.A. between 1787 and 1808, and was at sea from 1796 to 1804, visiting the East Indies and the China Coast. He is at his best when working on a small scale, but his work lacks some of the charm of such contemporaries as W. Anderson (q.v.). He often signed with his surname on a buoy or piece of floating wood. Examples: B.M.; V.A.M.; Ashmolean; Ferens A.G., Hull; Greenwich; Leeds City A.G.; Ulster Mus.; A.G., S. Australia.

ATKINS, William Edward
1842/3 (Portsmouth) - 1910 (Portsmouth)
The son of **George Henry ATKINS (1811 Portsmouth - 1872 Portsmouth)**, a marine painter, with whom he published lithographs. He worked in Portsmouth as a ship portraitist and during the 1870s he was correspondent and marine artist for the *Graphic*. In 1864 he painted on the Isle of Wight. He moved to Portsea in 1872 and Southsea in 1878, advertising as a marine painter. He visited America in 1885.

One of his brothers, **Harry Joseph ATKINS (1840 Portsmouth - 1916 nr. Fareham),** was a sailor and proprietor and headmaster of a school in Fareham, and an amateur marine painter in watercolour.
Examples: Brighton A.G.; Greenwich.

ATKINSON, Rev. Christopher
1754 (? Thorpe Arch) - 1795
A younger son of his namesake the rector of Thorpe Arch, York, at least two of his brothers also became clergymen. He was a fellow of Trinity Hall, Cambridge until 1785 when he married a sister of Lord de Tabley (q.v.). He then became rector of Wethersfield, Essex. His watercolours of birds are not only accurate, but pleasing and of high quality. He was the grandfather of the antiquary and author the Rev. John Atkinson (1814-1900), one of whose books was a popular work on birds' eggs and nests.

ATKINSON, George Clayton
1808 (Newcastle-upon-Tyne) - 1877 (Newcastle
A friend and follower of Bewick, who encouraged him both to study natural history and to sketch, he was educated at St Bees, Cumberland and Charterhouse. He worked with his father in the Tyne Iron Co., but kept up his interest in natural history. In 1821 he visited the Hebrides and St Kilda, and he made expeditions to the Shetlands and Iceland in the following two years. Thereafter he lived at West Denton, Wylam and Newcastle. On the second and third expeditions he made his own more than competent drawings, of landscape as well as natural history subjects, but he had H.P. Parker, G. Richardson and the elder T.M. Richardson (qq.v.) work them up with a view to publication with his journals.
Published: *Sketch of the Life and Work of the late Thomas Bewick,* 1831.

ATKINSON, George Mounsey Wheatley
c.1806 (Queenstown) - 1884 (Queenstown)
Of English parentage, he began his naval career as a ship's carpenter, and later became

ATKINSON, Rev. Christopher
(1754-1795)
Study of a Greenshank. *Inscribed on the reverse with the exact life measurements, pencil, pen and brown ink and watercolour heightened with white, 11in. x 8¾in.*

ATKINSON, Rev. Christopher
(1754-1795)
A Merganser. *Inscribed, water and bodycolour, 8⅞in. x 11⅛in.*

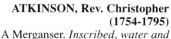

Government Surveyor of Shipping and Emigrants at Queenstown Co. Cork. He taught himself to draw and exhibited marine works at the R.H.A. from 1842.

His eldest son, **George Mounsey ATKINSON (d.1908)** was art examiner at South Kensington for many years. The second son, **Richard Peterson ATKINSON (c.1856-1882)** was a landscape and marine painter living near Cork and the third, **Robert ATKINSON,** was also a marine painter. His daughter, **Sarah, Mrs. DOBBS,** was a Dublin art teacher.
Published: *Sketches in Norway...,* 1852.

ATKINSON, James
1780 (Co. Durham) - 1852
Doctor, journalist and artist of the Afghan Campaign. He was a Civil Surgeon in Bengal from 1805 to 1813, and then Assay Master of the Mint until 1818 when his press career began. In 1823 he founded the *Calcutta Annual Register.* He was appointed Surgeon to the 55th Native Infantry in 1833, and from 1838 to 1841 served in Kabul. He retired to England in 1847.

His wife **Jane ATKINSON** was a pupil of G. Chinnery (q.v.) in Calcutta, and his son **George Franklin ATKINSON (1822-1859)** served with the Bengal Engineers from 1840 until his death, and was the author and illustrator of *Pictures from the North in Pen and Pencil,* 1848; *The Campaign in India, 1857-8,* 1859; and *Curry and Rice,* 1860.
Published: *Sketches of Afghanistan,* 1842. &c.
Examples: India Office Lib.

ATKINSON, John   1863 (Newcastle-upon-
Tyne) - 1924 (Gateshead)
A businessman until 1900 when he attended the Newcastle Art School under W. Cosens Way (q.v.). He exhibited at the R.A., the R.S.A. and elsewhere and was an etcher as well as a landscape and animal painter. Many of his subjects were found near Glaisdale, Yorkshire, where he lived between 1900 and 1914, and he was a close associate of the Staithes Group. He also taught art at Ushaw College and Morpeth Grammar School as well as working for the *Newcastle Journal.* Late in life, he designed many signs for public houses.
Examples: Shipley, A.G., Gateshead; Ulster Mus.
Bibliography: *W&D,* 1991, iv.

ATKINSON, John Augustus, O.W.S.
1775 (London) - c.1833
When nine years old he went to Russia with an uncle, where he was patronised by the Empress Catherine and the Emperor Paul, returning to London after the latter's assassination in 1801. In 1803 he began work on the plates for his *Manners...of the Russians,* and in the same year he exhibited for the first time at the R.A. He was elected both A.O.W.S. and O.W.S. in 1808, and was probably a member of the Chalons' Sketching Club. He resigned from the O.W.S. at the reorganisation of 1812. He remained in London until at least 1818, but little is known of

ATKINS, William Edward (1842/3-1910)
H.M.S. *Victory* at Portsmouth. *Signed, pen and ink and watercolour with scratching, 7in. x 11in.*

his later life. Apart from his Russian scenes, he was chiefly known for spirited battle pieces, many of incidents in the Penisular War. The Duke of Wellington bought a number of these. The figures are strongly drawn in pen, and they are always the centre of interest in his work. He also produced pleasant caricatures in a mildly Rowlandsonian manner.
Published: *A Picturesque Representation of the...Costumes of Great Britain,* 1807. *A Picturesque Representation of the Manners...of the Russians,* 1812.
Illustrated: A Russian edition of *Hudibras,* 1797. Beresford: *The Miseries of Human Life,* 1807. &c.
Examples: B.M.; V.A.M.; Greenwich; Newport A.G.
See Colour Plate

ATKINSON, Robert
1863 (Leeds) - 1896 (Dunedin)
A landscape painter and illustrator, who was a pupil of the portraitist Richard Waller and studied in Antwerp in 1883. He suffered from chest troubles and two years later went to New Zealand for his health. He then moved to Australia where he drew for the *Sydney Bulletin.* In 1889 he returned to Leeds, working as an illustrator for Messrs. Cassells. He moved to Newlyn in 1892, spending the winters of 1892-3 and 1893-4 in Egypt. The following year he went back to New Zealand.
Examples: Leeds City A.G.

ATKINSON, Thomas Witlam
1799 (Cawthorne, Yorkshire) -
1861 (Lower Walmer, Kent)
Architect, traveller and artist, he began work at the age of eight as a farmhand and a bricklayer. When he was about twenty, he spent some

time as a drawing master at Ashton-under-Lyne. In 1827 he set up as an architect in London and in 1835 moved to Manchester. In 1842 he set out for St. Petersburg by way of Hamburg and Berlin. He also visited Egypt and Greece before undertaking a vast journey around Russia, which lasted from 1848 to 1853. Throughout his travels he made hundreds of sketches and watercolours, some of which he used to illustrate his publications. He exhibited at the R.A. from 1830 to 1842.
Published: *Gothic Ornaments selected from the different Cathedrals,* 1829. *Oriental and Western Siberia,* 1858. *Travels in...Amoor,* 1860.
Bibliography: See A.M.W. Stirling: *The Letter-Bag of Lady Elizabeth Spencer-Stanhope,* ii, 1913. *A.J.,* Oct.1861. *Builder,* XIX, 1861.

ATKINSON, William
1775 (Bishop Auckland) - 1839 (Cobham)
An architect who began as a carpenter, was a pupil of James Wyatt, and entered the R.A. Schools in 1796 winning a gold medal in the following year. He was the proprietor of 'Atkinson's Cement' and was architect to the Ordnance Office from 1813 to 1829. He specialised in alterations to country houses, especially in the Scottish baronial style. He was also a botanist and a geologist. One of his pupils was T. Allason (q.v.).
Published: *Picturesque Views of Cottages,* 1805.

AUGUSTA Sophia, H.R.H. Princess
1768 (London) - 1840 (London)
The sixth child of George III, she was, like her sisters, an occasional artist and composer. Her work was in the manner of Cipriani, and she

sometimes produced portraits with thin washes of colour.

Examples: B.M.

Bibliography: D.M. Stuart: *The Daughters of George III*, 1939.

AULD, Patrick Campbell
1813 (Ayr) - 1866

A landscape painter in oil and watercolour who specialised in Scottish subjects and exhibited at the R.A. from 1850 to 1865. In 1851 he was an unsuccessful candidate for the N.W.S. and was living in London. Previously in the 1830s he had lived in Edinburgh, Ayr and Aberdeen, and in the 1860s he returned to Ayr and Aberdeen.

Examples: Aberdeen A.G.

AUMONIER, James, R.A.
1832 (Camberwell) - 1911 (London)

A landscape painter in oil and watercolour, he studied at the Birkbeck Institution, the Marlborough House and South Kensington Schools. He worked as a calico print designer at the beginning of his career, but turned to painting in about 1862. He exhibited at the R.A. from 1870 and was elected A.N.W.S. and N.W.S. in 1876 and 1879. He is known for his green meadows and sheep or cattle. A memorial exhibition was held at the Goupil Gallery, London, in 1912.

Stacy AUMONIER, who also painted late Victorian landscapes, may have been a relation. An exhibition of his work was held at the Goupil Gallery in 1911, and he was a prolific author of short stories. **Louisa AUMONIER** exhibited flower pieces in oil and watercolour from about 1868 to 1900.

Examples: B.M.; Preston Manor, Brighton; Maidstone Mus.

AUSTEN, Henry Haversham Godwin, F.R.S.
1834 (Teignmouth) - 1923 (Godalming)

The surveyor and explorer after whom the mountain K2 is sometimes called. He was at Sandhurst where he was taught drawing by Captain Penley, presumably A.E. Penley (q.v.), and he was commissioned in 1851. He served in the Burmese War of 1852, and from 1856 spent a number of years surveying in Kashmir and among the Karakoram glaciers. In 1863 he accompanied an expedition to Bhutan, and he retired in 1877. His drawings show artistry as well as accuracy.

AUSTEN, James   1765   - 1819

The eldest brother of Jane Austen, he was a pupil of J.B. Malchair (q.v.). His nephew, **Charles Edward Austen LEIGH** also painted.

AUSTIN, H

There is a view of Rotterdam by this artist in the V.A.M. He exhibited in 1833, and he also made figure drawings.

AUSTIN, Samuel (1796-1834)
Carters on a Beach. *Watercolour, 5½in. x 11in.*

AUSTIN, Samuel (1796-1834)
On the Beach, Ostend. *Watercolour, 10½in. x 18in.*

AUSTIN, Samuel, O.W.S.
1796 (Liverpool) - 1834 (Llanfyllin)

After a Charity School education and a period as a bank clerk, he determined to become a professional artist. He took three lessons from P. de Wint (q.v.) and exhibited a local view at the R.A. in 1820. He was a foundation member of the S.B.A. in 1824, and was elected A.O.W.S. in 1827. From 1829 he exhibited views of Holland, Belgium and the Rhine, and from 1830 of Normandy. However, the bulk of his subjects are from Lancashire and North Wales. His style is based on that of de Wint, and he is at his best in conveying atmospheric effects. He was elected to full membership of the O.W.S. on his deathbed in 1834. He had a considerable practice as a drawing master, and left a daughter, **Anna AUSTIN,** also taught by de Wint, whose work is said to be very close to his own. Another of his pupils was Miss A. Swanwick (q.v.).

AUSTIN, Samuel (1796-1834)
Study of Trees. *Watercolour, 17in. x 12in.*

Illustrated: Elliot: *Views in the East*, 1833.
Examples: B.M.; V.A.M.; Accrington A.G.; Ashmolean; Brighton A.G.; Fitzwilliam; Walker A.G., Liverpool; City A.G., Manchester; Castle Mus., Nottingham; Ulster Mus.; Warrington A.G.; Wolverhampton A.G.; N.G. Victoria.
Bibliography: *Connoisseur*, LXXXIV, 1929. Walker A.G.: Exhibition Cat., 1934.

AUSTIN, William
1721 (London) - 1820 (Brighton)

A failed engraver who took up landscape drawing and printselling. He also copied old masters, and may be the artist mentioned by Henry Angelo as a drawing master and political caricaturist. During the 1770s he rivalled M. Darly (q.v.) in the latter capacity, and was known as 'Fox's Fool' for his Whig propaganda. He failed to open a projected Museum of Drawings.

AUSTIN, William Frederick
1833 (Bedford) - 1899 (Reading)

He was in business with his father in Oxford by 1866 under the name 'J. Austin & Son'. They both drew in Wallingford and Wantage. William Frederick made many drawings in Derby, Reading and Norwich, where he lived for some time.

He specialised in drawings of pubs, with which he paid the landlords' bills. His topographical work is primitive in concept, but can be extremely well drawn and shows a good eye for architectural detail. As well as his watercolours, he made a number of pencil portraits.
Examples: Derby A.G.; King's Lynn A.G.; St. Giles's Church Hall, Reading; Reading A.G.

AUTY, Charles

A London painter of genre subjects who exhibited during the 1880s.

AYLESFORD, Heneage Finch, 4th Earl of
1751 (London) - 1812 (Packington)

An enthusiastic amateur artist who was educated at Westminster and at Oxford where he was a pupil of J.B. Malchair (q.v.). He was M.P. for Castle Rising, was elected F.R.S. and to the Dilettanti Society, and toured Italy and Sicily before succeeding to the title in 1777. In a public capacity he was Lord Steward of the Household and Captain of the Yeoman of the Guard. As well as producing numerous pen and wash drawings, he was a talented etcher, and he exhibited at the R.A. from 1786 to 1790. In his earlier years, he remained very much under Malchair's influence. He drew romantic landscapes with castles and other buildings, using brown wash for the foreground and grey for the background, sometimes giving the roofs a touch of pale red. His architectural studies at Packington were made under the guidance of his architect, Joseph Bonomi. It is always difficult to tell his work from that of his numerous kinsfolk and friends who took up

AYLMER, Thomas Brabazon (1806-1858)
Paestum. *Signed and inscribed, pencil and watercolour heightened with white on buff paper, 10¼in. x 14⅝in.*

drawing with his encouragement.

His brothers Edward and Daniel Finch are separately noticed, as is his wife, Louisa, Countess of Aylesford. His third brother **Seymour FINCH (1758-1794)** and his sisters **Sarah Frances, Countess of DARTMOUTH (1761-1838), Maria Elizabeth FINCH (1766-1848)** and **Henrietta Constantia FINCH (1769-1814)** were probably all artists of greater or lesser enthusiasm. The same is true of his children, **Heneage FINCH, 5th Earl of AYLESFORD (1786-1859), Mary FINCH (1788-1823), Daniel FINCH (1789-1868), Elizabeth FINCH (1789-1879), Frances FINCH (1791-1886)** and **Henrietta FINCH (1798-1828)**. Great confusion is obviously possible between the two Daniels, the two Marys and the two Henriettas.
Examples: B.M.; V.A.M.; Ashmolean; Coventry A.G.; Leeds City A.G.; N.G. Tasmania.
Bibliography: *Country Life*, 15 July 1971.
See Aylesford Family Tree.
See Colour Plate

AYLESFORD, Louisa, Countess of
1760 - 1832

The daughter of the 1st Marquess of Bath, she married the 4th Earl of Aylesford (q.v.) in 1781. Horace Walpole wrote of this union: 'Lord Aylesford marries Miss Thynne, or rather her father, for I fancy Bacchus will be better served than Venus.' However, Venus seems to have done well enough, since the Countess produced twelve children, as well as a large number of very competent and attractive botanical watercolours. Many of the latter were in two large albums, originally from Packington, which were broken up in 1973.
See Aylesford Family Tree

AYLING, Albert William
1829 - 1905 (Deganwy)

A painter of landscapes, portraits and country girls, who was brought up in Guernsey where he was a pupil of P.J. Naftel (q.v.). He exhibited from 1853 to 1905, and was an unsuccessful candidate for the N.W.S. in 1857 and for the O.W.S. in 1868. He lived in London and Chester before moving to Liverpool in about 1883, and to Conway in 1886. Many of his landscapes were found in North Wales, and he also painted genre subjects and still lifes, and was a drawing teacher.

AYLMER, Thomas Brabazon
1806 (Limerick) - 1858 (Worthing)

The son of a general, he was a prolific topographical and landscape painter in oil and watercolour. He lived in London and Tunbridge Wells until 1849 when he moved to Weston-super-Mare, later settling in Bath. In 1853 he wrote and illustrated a series of articles for the *A.J.* He exhibited from 1838 to 1855 when he was turned down by the O.W.S., and painted in Belgium, Germany and Italy.

AYRTON, Sophia, née Nicholson

A daughter of F. Nicholson (q.v.) in whose manner she worked. She exhibited from 1800 to 1820.

AYRTON, W J

A landscape painter in oil and watercolour who was living in London when he exhibited at the O.W.S. and Suffolk Street in 1833 and 1834.

B

BABB, Charlotte Elizabeth
1831 -
Having exhibited a Shakespearean subject at the Society of Female Artists in 1857, she studied at Heatherley's. In 1861 she was one of the earliest women to be admitted to the R.A.Schools. She exhibited literary genre and biblical subjects at Suffolk Street, the B.I and elsewhere until 1885.

BABB, John Staines
The brother of C.E. Babb (q.v.), he was a landscape and coastal painter and a designer who lived in Camden and exhibited between 1870 and 1900. Latterly he produced a number of drawings and paintings in the form of Greek friezes.

BACH, Guido Richard, R.I.
1828 (Annaberg) - 1905 (London)
A portrait, figure and genre painter who studied in Dresden and settled in England in 1862. He was elected A.N.W.S. and N.W.S. in 1865 and 1868, and he travelled extensively, visiting Cairo in 1876. His work is often stronger and less sentimental than was usual at the time.
Examples: B.M.

BACH, William Henry, né Back
1809 (London) -
A pupil of T.C. Hofland (q.v.) who became a London painter of Welsh landscapes. He exhibited from 1829 to 1859, and in 1833 briefly joined the N.W.S.

BACK, Admiral Sir George
1796 (Stockport, Cheshire) - 1878
The Arctic explorer. He joined the Navy in 1808 and in the following year was taken prisoner. He remained in France until the beginning of 1814 and taught himself drawing during this time. In the 1820s and 1830s he made a number of polar voyages and explorations both with Franklin and on his own. He was knighted in 1839, and promoted admiral in 1857. He illustrated his *Narratives* with his own dramatic sketches.
Published: *Narrative of a Second Expedition...Polar Sea*, 1828. *Narrative of the Arctic Land Expedition*, 1836. *Narrative of an Expedition in H.M.S. Terror*, 1838.
Examples: B.M.; Greenwich.
Bibliography: C. Stuart Houston (ed.): *Arctic Artist...*, 1994.

BACKHOUSE, Edward
1808 (Darlington) - 1879 (Hastings)
An amateur landscape painter in oil and watercolour. He was a member of a banking family and was brought up in Sunderland. He travelled widely, and his other hobby was natural history.
Examples: Sunderland A.G.

BACKHOUSE, James Edward
1845 (Sunderland) - 1897 (Darlington)
An amateur who was educated at University College, London, before entering the family bank. In 1869 he moved to Croft, while his house at Darlington was being completed. He also had a villa in Italy. He exhibited at the R.I. from 1886 to 1891.
Examples: Darlington A.G.

BACKHOUSE, Margaret, Mrs., née Holden
1818 (Summer Hill, Birmingham) -
The daughter of the Rev. H.A. Holden, she was educated at Calais and studied in Paris under MM. Troivaux and Grenier. She then attended Sass's Academy before marrying. She exhibited from 1846 and was a member of the Society of Female Artists. She painted portraits and genre subjects, with a preference for peasant children. In 1850 she was an unsuccessful candidate for the N.W.S. She was as unsuccessful with the O.W.S. in 1863, but continued to exhibit until 1882, and chromolithographs were made from her work. She lived in Islington.

BACKHOUSE, Mary, Mrs. W.E. Miller
Daughter of M. Backhouse (q.v.), she also painted portraits and genre subjects in oil and watercolour. She married the painter **William Edward MILLER** in about 1881, and she exhibited from 1869. Her husband painted portraits, fruit and figure subjects.

BACON, John Henry Frederick, A.R.A.
1865 (London) - 1914 (London)
An illustrator and painter of portraits and historical subjects in oil and watercolour. He studied at Westminster Art School, exhibited at the R.A. from 1889, and was elected A.R.A. in 1903.
Published: *The King's Empire*, 1906.
Illustrated: C. Squire: *Celtic Myth and Legend...*, 1912.
Examples: B.M.

BACON, Thomas
A topographer and antiquarian who was in Bengal and the Doab, where he drew with Captain Meadows Taylor from 1831 to 1836. He was elected F.S.A. in 1838 and resigned in 1846. In the 1840s he exhibited Italian subjects.
Published: *First Impressions and Studies from Nature in Hindoostan*, 1837. *Oriental Annual*, 1839. *The Orientalist*, 1843.

BADEN-POWELL, Robert, Lord
see **POWELL, Robert BADEN-**

BADESLADE, Thomas
A topographer working in London between 1720 and 1750. He made many drawings of country houses for Harris's *History of Kent* and similar publications. He was also much concerned with the draining of the Fens.
Published: *Thirty-Six Views of... Seats*, 1750. &c.

BADHAM, Edward Leslie, R.I.
1873 (London) - 1944
A landscape painter in oil and watercolour, he studied at the Clapham, Slade and South Kensington Schools, but lived for the most part on the South Coast at St. Leonard's and Hastings. He exhibited at the R.A. from 1898, and was a painting companion of W.T.M. Hawksworth (q.v.). He and his daughter were killed by a bomb.

BAGOT, Richard 1733 - **1819**
The fourth son of the 5th Bt., he exhibited a view of Toulon harbour at the R.A. in 1796. See also Howard, Frances, whom he married in 1783, adding HOWARD to his name.
See Aylesford Family Tree

BAGSHAW, Joseph Richard
1870 - **1909**
A landscape and coastal painter in oil and watercolour. He exhibited at the R.A. and Suffolk Street from 1897, and in 1903 he settled at Whitby.
Examples: B.M.; Pannet A.G., Whitby.

BAILEY, Henry
A landscape painter who lived in London and later at Chelmsford. He was active from about 1879 to 1907 and painted in the Southern counties, Wales and Yorkshire.

BAILEY, John 1750 (Bowes, Yorkshire) - 1819 (Gt. Barrington)
A topographical, agricultural and animal painter who worked at Barnard Castle before becoming land agent for Lord Tankerville at Chillingham. He engraved both his own and other people's drawings as illustrations. He was a friend of T. Bewick (q.v.).
Published: *General View of the Agriculture of the County of Cumberland*, 1794. *General View of the Agriculture of the County of Northumberland*, 1794. *General View of the Agriculture of the County of Durham*, 1797.
Examples: Barnard Castle.

BAILLIE, Caroline
A flower painter who lived in Brighton and

who exhibited there in 1875 and in London in 1872.

BAILLIE, Captain William
1723 (Kilbride, Co. Carlow) - 1810 (London)
Soldier, engraver, connoisseur and occasional painter and draughtsman. After entering the Middle Temple and serving at Culloden and Minden, he gave his true bent free rein on retiring from the army in 1761. He then devoted himself entirely to art, although he held a sinecure as Commissioner for Stamps, and in particular to the various branches of engraving. He is best remembered, or most criticised, for his reworking of Rembrandt's plates. On occasions he made prints from his own drawings.

BAINBRIDGE, Arthur
A landscape painter who lived at Torquay during the 1880s.

BAINES, Henry
1823 (King's Lynn) - 1894 (King's Lynn)
A drawing master at King's Lynn who was a pupil of W. Etty and Sir E.H. Landseer (qq.v.), and studied at the R.A. Schools. He was a prolific painter of local views in oil and watercolour.
Examples: King's Lynn Museum.

BAINES, Thomas
1820 (King's Lynn) - 1875 (Durban)
Elder brother of H. Baines (q.v.); their maternal grandfather was a painter and decorator. After an apprenticeship with a heraldic coach painter, he went to the Cape in 1842 as a marine and portrait painter, and served as artist to the Colonial forces in the Griqua War of 1851-53. In the latter year he accompanied Gregory's North Australia expedition, and thereafter he travelled in Southern Africa. In 1858 he left Livingstone's Zambezi expedition because he had been falsely accused of embezzling paint and canvas. In 1861 he joined Chapman for the journey from Walvis Bay to the Victoria Falls, where he spent twelve days, and he was later employed by the S.A. Gold Fields Exploration Co. in Matabeleland and Mashonaland. He drew the ceremonies at the installation of Lobenguela as Supreme Chief of Matabeleland.
Published: *Journal of a Residence in Africa*, 1961.
Examples: Nat. Archives, Zimbabwe; Nat. Hist. Mus.
Bibliography: J. Carruthers and M. Arnold: *Life and Works of T.B.*, 1995. King's Lynn Mus., Exhibition Cat., 1975.

BAIRD, Nathaniel Hughes John
1865 (Yetholm, Roxburgh) - 1936 (Reading)
An engraver and genre and portrait painter in oil and watercolour, he exhibited at the R.A. and elsewhere from 1883 to 1915. He studied in Edinburgh, London and France. He lived in

BAKER, Oliver (1856-)
A farmyard in November. *Watercolour with scratching out, signed, 11in. x 13½in.*

Devon and Sussex before settling at Reading. He enjoyed rural subjects and horses in particular.
Published: *Antiquities of Exeter*, c.1885.
Illustrated: E.W.L. Davies: *Memoir of the Rev. John Russell*, 1902.

BAKER, Alfred
see BAKER, Richard and BAKER, Samuel Henry

BAKER, Father Anselm   1834-
1885 (Mt. St. Bernard's Abbey, Leics.)
A heraldic painter who trained in Messrs. Hardmans' studios in Birmingham. He became a Cistercian monk in 1857. He painted murals as well as illustrating a number of heraldic publications. His work is signed 'F.A.' (Father Anselm).
Published: *Hortus Animae. Horae Diurnae. Liber Vitae.*

BAKER, Arthur   1844 -
A painter of sporting and rustic subjects in oil and watercolour who entered the R.A. Schools in 1862 and lived in Ongar, London and Tunbridge Wells. He was active from the 1860s to the 1880s, and painted in Scotland and Northern France.

BAKER, Blanche   1844   - 1929
A painter of landscapes and rustic scenes who lived in Bristol and exhibited at the N.W.S. and Suffolk Street from 1869.

BAKER, Henry, 'Harry'
1849 (Birmingham) - 1875
The eldest son and pupil of S.H. Baker (q.v.). He painted landscapes and coastal scenes, often from Devonshire or North Wales, and he exhibited in London and Birmingham from 1866 to 1875. He often used an H.B. monogram.

BAKER, Oliver   1856 (Birmingham) -
The youngest son of S.H. Baker (q.v.), he painted landscapes and etched. Educated at the Bridge Trust School, he exhibited at the R.A. and R.I. as well as in Birmingham from 1874 to 1913. He was a member of the R.B.A., and he lived in Stratford-on-Avon. He also designed silver for Liberty & Co.
Published: *Ludlow Town and Neighbourhood*, 1888. *Jacks and Leather Bottells*, 1921. *In Shakespeare's Warwickshire*, 1937.
Illustrated: A. Hayes: *The Vale of Arden*, 1897.

BAKER, Richard   1823 (Islington) -
An English landscape and gamey still-life painter who worked in Dublin and exhibited at the R.H.A. from 1843 to 1851. He was living in London with his brother in 1861.
His younger brother **Alfred BAKER (b.1825 Islington)** was also an artist and exhibited at the R.H.A. from 1851 to 1854. They were the sons of a military surveyor.

BAKER, Samuel Henry
1824   - 1909
A Birmingham landscape painter who began

BALDOCK, James Walsham (1822-1898)
A rural scene at Barton, Nottinghamshire. *Watercolour, signed and dated 1875, 9in. x 13in.*

his career making magic lantern slides. He studied at the Birmingham School of Design and exhibited with the Birmingham Society from 1848 and at the R.A. from 1875 to 1896. He was a member of the R.B.A. His work is often in the manner of Cox, but he uses an un-Coxlike stipple effect. He signed with initials.

His second son, **Alfred BAKER (1850-1872)** studied at the Birmingham School of Art. His other sons, Harry and Oliver, are separately noticed. For further confusion, **Alfred Rawlings BAKER (b.1865 Southampton)** was active until at least 1923.
Examples: Birmingham City A.G.

BAKER, Thomas, of Leamington
1809 (Birmingham) - 1869
A Midland landscape painter in oil and watercolour who exhibited at the R.A. from 1831 to 1858 and in Birmingham from 1827 to 1873. He was one of the Birmingham family of artists. He lived in Leamington from 1854 to 1862, and many of his landscapes (with cattle) are from the area.
Examples: B.M.; V.A.M.; Coventry A.G.

BALDOCK, James Walsham
1822 (Heeley, Sheffield) - 1898 (Nottingham)
A landscape, sporting and animal painter, and a lithographer and engraver. He began by working on a farm whose owner sent him to have drawing lessons, then for a Worksop painter before setting up on his own. Although something of a recluse, he took an active interest in local art societies.

He brought up his orphaned grandson **Charles Edwin MARKHAM,** who took the additional name of **BALDOCK (1876-1941)** and he too

became an animal and landscape painter.

The elder Baldock worked in oil, watercolour, bodycolour and pencil, and was noted for his forest scenes, horses and hounds.
Examples: Bassetlaw County Lib.

BALDREY, John Kirby   1758 (Norwich) -
1828 (Hatfield Woodside, Hertfordshire)
An engraver and draughtsman who entered the R.A. Schools in 1781, and worked in London and Cambridge to 1810. He produced portraits and landscapes, and exhibited at the R.A. in 1793 and 1794. On his retirement he settled in Hatfield.
Examples: V.A.M.

BALDRY, Alfred Lys
1858 (Torquay) - 1939 (Marlow)
Although a landscape and portrait painter in oil and watercolour, Baldry is best remembered as a writer and critic. He was educated at Oxford and studied at the Royal College of Art and with Albert Moore (q.v.). He exhibited from 1885 and was art critic on the *Globe* and the *Birmingham Daily Post*. He also produced pastels. For a time he lived at Marlow.
Published: *Albert Moore, His Life and Works,* 1894; *Life and Works of Marcus Stone,* 1896; *G.H. Boughton,* 1904; *The Practice of Watercolour Painting,* 1911. &c.

BALDWIN, Robert   - c.1804
An architectural draughtsman who was the son of a builder and became a pupil of the architect Matthew Brettingham. He visited Italy, and exhibited designs and views with the Society of Artists and the Free Society from 1762 to 1783. As an architect he assisted Mylne and George Dance, but later he needed Soane's charity.
Published: *The Chimney-Piece maker's Daily Assistant,* vol ii, 1769. *Plans... of the machines and Centring used in erecting BlackFriars Bridge,* 1787.
Examples: Soane Mus.; Wilts. County Record Office.

BALDWYN, Charles Henry Clifford
1859   - 1943
A painter of birds, landscapes, still life and rusticities in oil and watercolour. He exhibited from 1887, and he lived in Worcester.

BALDWYN, Charles Henry Clifford (1859-1943)
Study of young magpies. *Watercolour, signed and dated 1890, inscribed on reverse, 11in. x 14in.*

BALL, Wilfrid Williams (1853-1917)
Chioggia. *Signed and dated 87, watercolour, 6in. x 9in.*

BALE, Edwin, R.I.
                    1838   - 1923 (London)
A figure and landscape painter who studied at
South Kensington and in Florence. He was Art
Director for Cassells from 1882, and the first
Chairman of the Imperial Arts League. He
exhibited from 1867, and was elected
A.N.W.S. and N.W.S. in 1876 and 1879.
Examples: V.A.M.

BALE, John Edward
An architect from Tunbridge Wells who
exhibited very competent watercolours,
heightened with white and gum arabic, of
church interiors at the R.A. and Suffolk Street
between 1855 and 1859. The subjects were in
Sussex and Wales, and in 1858 he gave a
King's Cross address.

BALFOUR, Alice Blanche
                    1855   - 1936
A granddaughter of the 2nd Marquess of
Salisbury and a sister of the future Prime
Minister, she travelled in South Africa in 1894,
going from Cape Town to Beira by oxwagon.
She was unmarried. Her work is highly
competent and neatly annotated.
Published: *1,200 Miles in a Waggon*, 1895.
Examples: Nat. Archives, Zimbabwe.

BALFOUR, Lady Georgina Isabella –
                    see **CAWDOR**

BALL, Laura Frances, Mrs., née Noel
                    - 1863 (Limerick)
The daughter of A. Noel (q.v.), in about 1807
she married John Ball, a Dublin silk manufacturer, who died in 1810. She exhibited landscapes and portraits at the R.A. as Miss F. Noel
from 1800 to 1805 and in Dublin from 1809 to
1811, and she gave drawing and painting

lessons. She lived in London with her mother
for a time, before marrying Michael Furnell of
Cahirelly Castle, Co. Limerick, in 1820.
Bibliography: *W&D.*, 1987, i.

BALL, Wilfrid Williams
                    1853 (London) - 1917 (Khartoum)
Etcher, landscape and marine painter in
watercolour and oil, he lived in Putney and
worked as an accountant until about 1877,
painting in his spare time. He exhibited
etchings and some pictures at the R.A. from
1877 to 1903. He visited Italy in 1887,
Holland in 1889, Germany in 1890 and Egypt
in about 1893. In 1895 he married and settled

in Lymington. In 1916 he returned to account-
ing and was sent to Cairo, and from there to
Khartoum, to work on military accounts.
   His work is fresh and professional, and
generally on a small scale. Exhibitions were
held at the Fine Art Society in 1899, 1904 and
1912. He illustrated a number of County books.
Examples: V.A.M.; Maidstone Mus.; Newport A.G.
Bibliography: *Studio*, XVI, 1899; XXXI, 1904.

BALLANTYNE, Robert Michael
                    1825 (Edinburgh) - 1894 (Rome)
The author of *The Coral Island* and other
stories for boys, he began his career with the
Hudson's Bay Co., and was also a printer
before turning to literature in 1856. His
watercolours are accomplished, and he
exhibited at the R.S.A. between 1850 and
1885. From about 1880 he lived at Harrow.
Bibliography: *Personal Reminiscences in Book-
Making*, 1893. &c.

BALLINGALL, Alexander
                    c.1850 (?Edinburgh) - ?1910
A coastal painter with a preference for the East
Coast of Scotland and Venice. He was active in
Edinburgh from about 1870 to 1910 and was
painstaking in matters such as rigging.

BALMER, George   1806 (North Shields) -
                    1846 (Ravensworth, Durham)
He began as a decorator in Edinburgh, but
exhibited pictures painted in his spare time. In
1831 he contributed to an exhibition of
watercolours at Newcastle and worked with
J.W. Carmichael (q.v.). He then visited the
Continent before he settled in London as a
professional artist, exhibiting Rhineland and
other scenes and making drawings for the
Findens' *Ports and Harbours of Great Britain*.

BALLINGALL, Alexander
Leith. *Signed, inscribed and dated 1879, watercolour heightened with white, 10¼in. x 27¾in.*

BALMER, George (1806-1846)
Low Tide. *Pencil and watercolour heightened with gum arabic, 6¾in. x 9¾in.*

In 1842 he retired to Ravensworth, Durham.

In his work for engravers he owes much to Turner, in his coastal scenes to Bentley and Carmichael.

Examples: B.M.; V.A.M.; Ferens A.G., Hull; Shipley A.G., Gateshead; Leeds City A.G.; City A.G., Manchester; Laing A.G., Newcastle.

BALMFORD, Hurst
1871 (Huddersfield) -
A portrait and landscape painter in oil and watercolour. He studied at the R.C.A. and Julian's, and became Headmaster of Morecambe School of Art. Later he lived in Blackpool and kept a studio in St. Ives. He exhibited at the R.A. until 1938.

BAMPFYLDE, Coplestone Warre
1720 (Hestercombe, Somerset) -
1791 (Hestercombe)
An amateur topographical draughtsman and caricaturist, he was taught to draw and paint from an early age. He was the son of John Bampfylde, M.P., of Hestercombe, and was educated at Blundell's, Winchester between 1731 and 1737 and St. John's College, Oxford. In the early 1740s he may have made a Grand Tour, and he inherited the estate in 1750. His first known watercolour dates from that year, although he was already a skilled oil painter, collaborating with R. Phelps (q.v.). He exhibited at the S.A., the R.A. and the Free Society between 1763 and 1783. Works by him were engraved by Vivares and Benazech. He occasionally etched landscapes, and made humorous illustrations for *Anstey's Election Ball*, 1776. He made a number of painting tours in England, and was an occasional architect, but his major preoccupation was landscape gardening, at Stourhead and elsewhere as well as Hestercombe. He was a friend and patron of many artists, and was painted by Gainsborough on becoming a major of the Somerset militia.

There are a number of influences to be seen in his drawings, including both G. Lambert and P. Sandby (qq.v)

Examples: B.M.; V.A.M.; Victoria A.G., Bath; Exeter Mus. Stourhead; Whitworth A.G., Manchester.

Bibliography: *Apollo*, XI, 1930. *Country Life*, 27 July 1995. Christie's: Exhibition Cat., July 1995.

BANCROFT, Elias Mollineaux
1846 - 1924
A Manchester landscape painter who also worked in London for a time. He exhibited at the R.A. from 1874 and painted in Wales, Germany and Switzerland. With J.H.E. Partington (q.v.) and others, he set up a Manchester Sketching Club.

His wife **Louisa Mary BANCROFT** was a flower and miniature painter, and an illustrator.

Examples: Darlington A.G.; City A.G., Manchester.

BANGOR, Agnes Elizabeth, Lady
The third daughter of D.M. Hamilton (q.v.), she married the Hon. Maxwell Ward in 1905. He succeeded as 6th Viscount Bangor in 1911, was Speaker of the Senate of Northern Ireland, and died in 1950. She was a talented amateur watercolour painter and draughtswoman.

BANNATYNE, John James, R.S.W.
1836 (Scotland) - 1911
Despite the almost unrelentingly Scottish nature of his landscape watercolours (exceptions are subjects in Surrey and Sussex), Bannatyne lived for a good many years in North London, where he exhibited from 1866. In about 1890 he moved to Glasgow. He was a founder member of the R.S.W.

BANNISTER, Edward
1820 - 1916
Although a member of a Hull family of coal merchants, by 1846 he described himself as an artist. He travelled widely and later moved to Grimsby.

Examples: Ferens A.G., Hull.

BARBER, Charles Burton
1845 (Gt. Yarmouth) - 1894 (London)
A sporting, coaching and figure painter in oil and watercolour, he was also an illustrator for the *Graphic*. He was a favourite of Queen Victoria, and her taste is to be commended. From 1871 to 1873 he lived at Marlow, but otherwise he was based in London.

BARBER, Charles Vincent
1784 (Birmingham) - 1854 (Liverpool)
The elder son of J. Barber (q.v.), he was a friend of Cox, accompanying him on his first trip to Wales in 1805, and he was elected A.O.W.S. with him in June, 1812. He did not, however, become a Member of the Oil and Watercolour Society, although he was an Exhibitor. In 1816 he moved from Birmingham to Liverpool, where he was a teacher, and President of the Liverpool Academy of Arts from 1847 to 1853. He shared Cox's love of North Wales and they often visited Bettws together.

Examples: V.A.M.

BARBER, Christopher
1736 - 1810 (Marylebone)
A painter of miniatures and small landscapes in oil, watercolour and pastel. He was a member of the Incorporated Society and exhibited at the R.A. from 1770 to 1808.

BARBER, Joseph
1757 (Newcastle) - 1811 (Birmingham)
The son of a Newcastle bookseller, he settled as a drawing master in Birmingham where he taught at the Grammar School and gained a considerable reputation. Much of his work consists of small, simple, picturesque landscapes, but he could occasionally be more ambitious, as with some views of North Wales. His best known pupil was David Cox.

Examples: B.M.; V.A.M.; Birmingham City A.G.; Dudley A.G.; Newport A.G.; Ulster Mus.

BARBER, Joseph Vincent
1788 (Birmingham) - 1838 (Rome)
The younger son of J. Barber (q.v.), he was a

painter of landscapes with figures. He was a pupil of his father and spent most of his career in Birmingham. He exhibited in London from 1810, and was Secretary of the Birmingham Academy of Arts in 1814 and a member of the Birmingham Society.

Examples: Birmingham City A.G.; Nat. Lib. Wales.

BARBER, R
In the British Museum are illustrations for Sterne's *Sentimental Journey* bearing this signature and dating from about 1775. They are competent and are in brown wash with touches of colour.

BARBER, Reginald
1853 (Ulverstone) -
A Manchester painter of portraits and genre subjects, sometimes in the manner of A. Moore (q.v.). He entered the R.A. Schools in 1873, and was active at least until 1908, exhibiting at the R.A. from 1885, as well as in Paris and elsewhere.

BARCLAY, Edgar 1842 - 1913
A landscape and figure painter and an etcher, he studied in Dresden in 1861 and Rome in 1874 and 1875. He lived in Hampstead and exhibited frequently at the Grosvenor Gallery between 1878 and 1889.

Published: *Notes on the Scuola di San Rocco*, 1876. *Mountain Life in Algeria*, 1882.

Illustrated: H.D. Barclay: *Orpheus and Eurydice*, 1877.

BARCLAY, Hugh
1797 (London) - 1859 (Paris)
An artist who painted miniature and watercolour copies of Italian pictures, and worked in London and Paris.

BARCLAY, J Edward
A landscape painter in oil and watercolour who exhibited Italian views between 1868 and 1888.

BARCLAY, John Henry
1848 - 1932
A Birmingham solicitor who retired early to paint, settling at Hope Cove, South Devon. He painted landscapes, coasts and shipping. He was capable of very attractive, if un-adventurous, work, which is usually inscribed in pencil. He was prolific, and most of his output was divided among his five nieces.

BARCLAY, John Maclaren, R.S.A.
1811 (Perth) - 1886 (Edinburgh)
A portrait painter who also sketched in watercolour. He exhibited at the R.A. from 1850 to 1875, and was elected R.S.A. in 1871.

Examples: N.G., Scotland.

BARCLAY, William
1850 (Dundee) - 1907
A businessman who took up art criticism and

BARBER, Joseph Vincent (1788-1838)
A Shepherd by a Farm. *Pencil and watercolour heightened with gum arabic, 10⅜in. x 15¼in.*

landscape painting in oil and watercolour. He was particularly noted for his effective skies.

BARDILL, Ralph William
1876 - 1935
Presumably an acolyte of the Huntingdon Frasers (q.v.) at Houghton, where he was working very much in their manner around 1905.

BARDWELL, William
1795 (Southwold) - 1890 (? London)
An architect and designer who exhibited at the R.A. from 1829 to 1845. He was involved in drawing up plans for the improvement of Westminster, and he also worked in Ireland. He lived in Exeter Change in the Strand and, in 1849 when proposing a new sewerage system, his address was in Great Queen Street. He was still in business there at the end of his life, although he was buried at Southwold.

Published: *Temples Ancient and Modern...*, 1837. *Westminster Improvements*, 1839. *Healthy Homes and How to Make them*, 1854. *What a House should be, versus Death in the House*, 1873.

Examples: R.I.B.A.

BARING, Ann c.1758 -
A very competent landscape painter in the Wilson manner in oil, and that of White Abbott in watercolour. She was the eldest daughter of John Baring (1730-1816), a Devonshire businessman and a collateral ancestor of the Northbrook family. She was working in 1791 and painted in Devon and Ireland. Her younger sisters, who may have shared her talent, were **Elizabeth BARING**; **Charlotte BARING**, who married John Jeffrey Short of

Bickham House, Devon, in 1786; and **Margaret BARING (d.1851)**.

Frances Emily BARING (d.1886), daughter of their cousin Henry, painted competent amateur landscapes in the manner of W. Callow (q.v.). In 1830 she married Henry Bridgeman-Simpson of Babworth Hall, Nottinghamshire.

Mary BARING, who painted romantic landscapes in 1794, may also have been a kinswoman.

BARING, Lady Emma –
see CRICHTON, Lady Jane Emma

BARKAS, Henry Dawson
1858 (Gateshead-on-Tyne) - 1924
Shortly after his birth, his family moved to St. Helier. He was educated in Jersey and at Granville in France, and at the age of seventeen entered the Bath School of Art, whence he gained a scholarship to the R.C.A. He taught at the Warrington and Bradford Schools of Art before settling in Reading, where he became Headmaster of the School of Science and Art. In about 1894 he founded another School of Art at Reading, which continued to function until his death. He spent his summer vacations in sketching and experimenting with watercolour, aiming for natural atmospheric effects. His work also included detailed architectural studies. He was a regular exhibitor at the R.A. Summer Exhibitions and, in 1912, an exhibition of his work entitled 'English Pleasure Resorts' was held at the Fine Art Society.

His brother **Herbert Atkinson BARKAS (1870 Jersey - 1939 Reading)** studied under

him at the School of Science and Art, and became a Reading art master. He was for twenty years Headmaster of the Berkshire School of Art, Maidenhead, and also taught art at Eton. There are examples of his work in Reading A.G.
Published: *Art Student's Pocket Manual*, 1892.

BARKER, Benjamin
1776 (nr. Pontypool) - 1838 (Totnes)
A landscape painter who was the younger brother of T. Barker of Bath (q.v.). The family settled in Bath in about 1783. He exhibited in London from 1800 until his death and was a member of the A.A. Benjamin West (q.v.) regarded him as a better and more poetic painter than his brother. He left Bath to live with his daughter at Totnes in 1833.

His watercolours are softly coloured, and he makes great use of umber. His pupils included H.V. Lansdown (q.v.).
Examples: V.A.M.; Victoria A.G., Bath; Grosvenor Mus., Chester; Leeds City A.G.; Newport A.G.

BARKER, Henry Aston
1774 (Glasgow) - 1856 (Bilton, near Bristol)
The younger son of R. Barker (q.v.), he came to London with his father, in 1789, from Edinburgh where he had already made the sketches for their first attempt at a panorama. He studied at the R.A. Schools and made the drawings for their London ventures, and, after his father's death in 1806, carried on the concern. He was a friend of Turner, Ker Porter and, above all, of Girtin (qq.v.), whose own projects in London and Paris he inspired. He sketched in Venice and Naples, showing the results in Dublin in 1823 and 1824.
Bibliography: *Gentleman's Mag.*, 1856, i.

BARKER, John Joseph
A member of the Bath family, he painted landscapes and genre subjects, and exhibited at the R.A. from 1835 to 1863. His colours are fresh and his figures quite well drawn.
Examples: V.A.M.

BARKER, Robert
1739 (Kells, County Meath) - 1806 (London)
A painter of panoramas who, after practising unsuccessfully in Dublin, moved to Edinburgh and set himself up as a portrait and miniature painter. He invented a mechanical system of perspective, which he taught, and in 1787 produced a panoramic view of Edinburgh in watercolour which was exhibited in London the following year. His next panorama, after drawings by his son H.A. Barker (q.v.), was of the Thames and was painted in distemper. All his subsequent panoramas were in oil, and were exhibited in a building constructed by himself in Leicester Place, Cranbourne Street.

His elder son, **Thomas Edward BARKER,** after working with him, started up a rival business in the Strand with R.R. Reinagle (q.v.).

BARKER, Thomas, of Bath (1769-1847)
Men resting under trees, with cattle. *Pen and grey wash, 10½in. x 7¾in.*

BARKER, Thomas, of Bath
1769 (Pontypool, Monmouthshire) - 1847 (Bath)
His family moved to Bath in his youth, and at twenty-one he attracted a rich patron, who sent him to Rome from 1790 to 1793. He was chiefly an oil painter, but occasionally produced large, stiffly drawn and woolly watercolours. He experimented with various washes and generally wiped or scratched out his highlights. His pen and ink drawings are spirited and show a marked Italian influence.
Examples: B.M.; V.A.M.; Haworth A.G., Accrington; Abbot Hall A.G., Kendal; Leeds City A.G.; Ulster Mus.
Bibliography: Sir E. Harington: *A Schizzo on the Genius of Man...*, 1793. *Connoisseur*, X, 1904; XI, 1905.

BARKER, William Dean
A landscape painter who lived at Trefriw on the river Conway, and exhibited from 1868 to 1880. He was living at Plas Celyn in 1886.

BARKWORTH, Emma L
A landscape painter who lived at Tunbridge Wells and was active from at least 1890 to 1900.

BARLOW, Francis
c.1626 (?London) - 1704 (London)
The earliest British sporting painter whose name is known, he worked in oil and pen and wash and was an accomplished etcher. He was apprenticed to 'one Shepherd, a Face-Painter' (William Sheppard, a member of the Painter-Stainers' Company, according to Vertue). He designed ceilings and panels with bird and animal paintings and illustrated an edition of

Aesop's *Fables*, well before which Evelyn could describe him as 'the famous Paynter of fowle Beastes & Birds' (*Diary*, Feb. 16, 1656). He designed the hearse for the funeral of George Monck, Duke of Albemarle in 1670. Laurence Binyon suggested that he probably worked in pure watercolour as well as in monochrome. He spent some of his career in Lincolnshire. Aside from his natural history illustrations, he may claim to be the first English political cartoonist.
Published: *Various Birds and Beasts*, 1710.
Illustrated: E.Benlowes: *Theophila*, 1652. Aesop: *Fables*, 1665.
Examples: B.M.; V.A.M.; Cecil Higgins A.G., Bedford; Leeds City A.G.
Bibliography: E.Hodnett: *F.B., First master of English book illustration*, 1978. *Connoisseur*, XCVIII, 1936. *Apollo*, XIX, 1934; XLI, 1945. *BM Quarterly*, XX, 1955-6.

BARLOW, John 1759 -
There is a naïve and amusing grey wash drawing of a man in the stocks by this artist in the B.M. He entered the R.A. Schools in 1786, and was active at least between 1791 and 1804.

BARLOW, John Noble
1861 (Manchester) - 1917 (St. Ives)
A landscape, coastal and genre painter in oil and watercolour. He studied in Paris, exhibited from 1893 and settled in Cornwall.

BARNARD, Frederick R
1846 (London) - 1896 (Wimbledon)
A genre painter and illustrator from Northumberland, he studied at Heatherley's and the R.A. Schools from 1865, and in Paris. Later he worked in Cullercoats and London. As well as exhibiting at the R.A. from 1858 to 1887, he drew for *Punch* and the *I.L.N.* He painted in both oil and watercolour and was noted for his pure colours. His cartoons are signed with initials. He died in a fire at the house of a friend.
Examples: V.A.M.

BARNARD, George
c.1807 - 1890 (Islington)
An illustrator and drawing master who was a pupil of J.D. Harding (q.v.) and exhibited at the R.A. from 1837 to 1873. He also exhibited at the B.I. and Suffolk Street, and his subjects include views in Switzerland, Wales and Devon. In 1870 he was appointed Professor of Drawing at Rugby.
Published: *The Brunnens of Nassau and the River Lahn*, 1840. Switzerland, 1843. *Handbook of Foliage and Foreground Drawing*, 1853. *The Theory and Practice of Landscape Painting in Water Colours*, 1855. *Drawing from Nature*, 1856. *Barnard's Trees*, 1868.

BARNARD, Katherine, Mrs., née Locking (Edinburgh) -
A landscape painter who exhibited at the R.A.

and R.I. She painted seventy-four pictures of vanishing London for the London Museum. She signed K.B.' or K. Barnard'.
Published: *In a Wynberg Garden*, 1930.
Examples: London Mus.

BARNARD, Rev. William Henry
1767 (Co.Donegal or Co.Derry) - 1818 (Stowe)

A grandson of the Bishop of Derry, Barnard found subjects for his earliest drawings in Ireland, Wales and Oxford. He graduated Bachelor of Civil Laws from Pembroke College, Oxford, in 1797 and thereafter travelled fairly widely, visiting Italy in 1804 and again between 1815 and 1818. He became Rector of Marsh Gibbon and Water Stratford, Buckinghamshire. His drawings can be very striking, but always owe a great deal to Malchair.

His son **Lieutenant-General Sir Henry William BARNARD (1799-1857)** also painted in the same manner.
Examples: Leeds City A.G.; Ulster Mus.; Yale.

BARNES, Joseph H

A painter of sentimental genre subjects and sugary village scenes, he lived in Hammersmith and exhibited for twenty years from 1867. On occasions he could price his watercolours at 100 guineas. In the fashion of the time he was fond of white heightening.

BARNES, Robert, A.R.W.S.
1840 - 1895

A painter of figure and genre subjects, he exhibited at the R.A. and O.W.S. from 1873, and was elected A.O.W.S. three years later. He illustrated a number of books in the 1860s and 1880s.

BARNETT, James D

A painter of French landscapes who lived in Liverpool in the 1840s and at Crouch End until 1892. He exhibited from 1855 to 1872, and also painted in Britain and Germany.

BARNEY, Joseph 1754 (Wolverhampton) - 1827 (? Wolverhampton)

Fruit, flower and occasional classical and literary painter. He was a pupil of A. Kauffmann and A. Zucchi (qq.v.), entered the R.A. Schools in December 1771, when he was stated to be 'aged 17 last July', and won a premium for drawing at the Society of Arts in 1774. Between 1778 and 1781 he assisted Matthew Boulton at Wolverhampton, and from 1793 to 1820 he was drawing master at Woolwich. In 1815 he became Flower Painter to the Prince Regent. He was also concerned in his brother's business of decorating japanned tin trays.

BARNEY, Joseph Whiston
- 1853 (London)

The son of J. Barney (q.v.), he became Fruit and Flower Painter to Queen Victoria. He was living in Greenwich in 1817, Westminster in

BARRALET, John James (1747-1815)
The Wooden Bridge on the Liffey near Luttrellstown. *Signed pen and ink and watercolour, 12⅜in. x 16½in.*

the following year and again in 1851, and at Southampton in the 1830s. He exhibited from 1815 to 1851.

BARNICLE, James

An amateur landscape and coastal painter who lived in London and painted all over Britain and in France and the Channel Islands between 1821 and 1845.

BARR, Major-General William

An amateur painter who served with the Bengal Horse Artillery in India from 1835 to 1859. He made lieutenant-colonel in 1858 and major-general in 1863.
Examples: Nat. Army Mus.

BARRALET, John James
1747 (Dublin) - 1815 (Philadelphia)

A Huguenot, he was trained at the R.D.S. Schools and taught drawing in Dublin before leaving for London in about 1770. In 1773 he opened a Drawing School in James's Street, Golden Square, and in 1777 started up another in St. Alban's Street, Pall Mall. He exhibited at the R.A. from 1770 and the Society of Artists from 1773 to 1780, being elected a Fellow in 1777. He returned to Dublin in 1779 and the following year, with G. Beranger (q.v.), toured Wicklow and Wexford making antiquarian drawings. He was a scene painter for the Crow Street Theatre in 1782, and visited the North in 1787-9, when he taught the Antrim family. He went to America in 1795, and lived in Philadelphia working as a book illustrator. He was a founder of the Society of Artists of the U.S.

According to Pasquin, he drew landscapes in Italian chalk in which he 'affected to imitate Vernet'. He also worked in watercolour, and Williams states that he was 'an inept and heavy handed, if ambitious artist'.
Illustrated: F. Grose: *Antiquities of Ireland*, 1791-95.
Examples: B.M.; Ulster Mus.; H. du Pont Winterthur Mus.

BARRALET, John Melchior
c.1750 (Dublin) - c.1787

The brother of J.J. Barralet (q.v.), he worked in Dublin before moving to London where he taught J. Laporte (q.v.). He exhibited with the Free Society in 1774 and at the R.A. between 1775 and 1787, and was a drawing master, W.F. Wells (q.v.) being among his pupils.

His landscapes, mostly tinted drawings, are taken from London and the South of England.
Examples: B.M.; V.A.M.

BARRATT, Reginald, R.W.S.
1861 (London) - 1917 (London)

An illustrator, landscapist and painter of Oriental scenes, he studied under the architect Norman Shaw and under Bouguereau in Paris. He drew for the *Graphic* early in his career, and travelled widely in Europe, North Africa and the East. He exhibited from 1885, was elected A.R.W.S. and R.W.S. in 1901 and 1913, and was F.R.G.S.
Examples: V.A.M.

BARRAUD, William
1810 (London) - 1850 (Kensington)

Of Huguenot extraction, he was the eldest son

BARRAUD, Charles James (1843-1894)
Lulworth. *Signed, watercolour, size unknown.*

of William Francis Barraud, Prime Clerk in the London Customs House. His grandfathers were Barraud the chronometer maker and Thomas Hull a miniaturist. He was a pupil of A. Cooper (q.v.) and exhibited at the R.A. from 1829. He died of typhoid. He often collaborated with his brother **Henry BARRAUD (1811 London - 1874 London),** who painted portraits, animals and genre and exhibited at the R.A. and elsewhere from 1831 to 1868. These two artists worked mainly in oil.

A younger brother, **Charles Decimus BARRAUD (1822-1897),** became a chemist and emigrated to New Zealand in 1849, where he painted and sketched. In 1877 he published in London a volume of chromolithographs entitled *New Zealand Graphic and Descriptive.*

Francis Philip BARRAUD (1824-1901), another brother, worked almost exclusively in watercolour and was a partner in Lavers and Barraud, stained glass artists. He produced a series of views of colleges, and another of cathedrals.

Other painting members of the family include **Allan F BARRAUD (1847-1913)** and the landscape watercolourist **Charles James BARRAUD (1843-1894),** cousins of William. **Francis James BARRAUD (1856-1924),** son of Henry, was a photographer, the owner of 'Nipper', and thus the artist responsible for *His Master's Voice.* One of his brothers was **Mark Henry BARRAUD (1843-1887),** a scene painter.

Published: H. & W. Barraud: *Sketches of figures and animals,* circa 1850. W. Barraud & T. Fairland: *The book of animals drawn from nature,* 1864.
Examples: V.A.M.
Bibliography: E,M, Barraud: *The Story of a Family,* 1967. A.J., 1850. *British Racehorse,* Sept. 1965. *Country Life,* 25 April 1963 (letters); 21 October 1965.

BARRET, George, R.A.
1732 (Dublin) - 1784 (London)
The son of a clothier, he attended the drawing school in George's Lane, Dublin, supporting himself by colouring up prints for Thomas Silcock. He worked as a drawing master before gaining the patronage of Edmund Burke, who commissioned him to sketch Powerscourt and the Dargle. He moved to London in 1762, and in 1768 was a Foundation Member of the R.A. He was for a while a very fashionable painter, but he was also an improvident man and, towards the end of his life, when he was broken in health

and pocket, Burke again helped by obtaining him the sinecure of Master Painter to Greenwich Hospital.

Although primarily an oil painter, he made a number of 'stained drawings' and had a strong influence on later watercolourists in his romantic representation of English scenery. He gained considerable fame by a continuous view of lakeland scenery which he painted in distemper on the walls of a room at Norbury Park, Surrey.
Examples: B.M.; V.A.M.; Blackburn A.G.; Newport A.G.; Ulster Mus.
Bibliography: T. Bodkin: *Four Irish Landscape Painters,* 1920.

BARRET, George, Yr., O.W.S.
1767 (London) - 1842 (London)
One of the original members of the O.W.S., Barret had exhibited little before 1805, and his professional life seems to have been a struggle from its beginning. He always lived in the Paddington area and never travelled very widely, finding many of his subjects in the Thames Valley and the Home Counties, with a few in Wales. An exception was a tour to Killarney with W.S. Gilpin (q.v.) in 1804. Gradually, he gave up topographical landscapes in favour of Claudian romantic compositions – similar to those of his friend Cristall – with titles such as *Retirement of the Weary Traveller.* A number of his works were engraved for the *Annuals* of the 1820s and 1830s. Like his father before him, he was admired by his colleagues but left his family destitute.
Published: *The Theory and Practice of Water-*

BARRET, George (1732-1784)
Landscape with figures. *Watercolour.*

BARRET, George Yr. (1767-1842)
Keith Bay, Isle of Wight. *Pen and grey ink and watercolour, 5⅜in. x 8¾in.*

Colour Painting, 1840.
Examples: B.M.; V.A.M.; Brighton A.G.; Derby
A.G.; Fitzwilliam; Glasgow A.G.; Leeds City A.G.;
Leicestershire A.G.; City A.G.; Manchester;
Newport A.G.; Richmond Lib.; Southampton A.G.;
Ulster Mus.; Warrington A.G.
Bibliography: *A.J.,* 1898. *Connoisseur,* CV, 1940.
O.W.S. Club, XXVI, 1947; *LII, 1977.*

BARRET, James
c.1765 (London) -
The elder son of G. Barret, R.A. (q.v.), he
painted landscapes in oil and watercolour in
the manner of his father, all over Britain. He
makes a rather lurid use of white heightening
but can be an effective artist. He exhibited at
the R.A. from 1785 to 1819.
Examples: B.M.; Carisbrooke Cas.

BARRET, Mary, O.W.S.   **- 1836**
The daughter of G. Barret, R.A. (q.v.), she was
a pupil of G. Romney (q.v.) and Mrs. Mee, the
miniaturist. Her professional life probably
started in 1797 when she began to send
miniatures to the R.A. She was elected a
Member of the Society of Painters in Water-
Colours on 10 February 1823, and exhibited
birds, fish, fruit and other still-life subjects.
Between that year and her death she lived with
her brother George (q.v.) in Paddington.
   Her sister **Harriet BARRET** was also a still
life painter, represented in the Haldimand
Collection, and a still more obscure member of
the family was **C.P. BARRET,** active in the
1830s and '40s.

BARRETT, John
A landscape painter in watercolour and no

doubt oil, who lived in Plymouth and was
working at least from 1875 to 1895.

BARRETT, Thomas
1845 (Nottingham) - 1924 (Nottingham)
A painter of genre scenes and interiors in oil
and watercolour who taught at the Nottingham
School of Art. He exhibited at the R.A. and the
B.I. from 1883 to 1888, and was an engraver.
Examples: Castle Mus., Nottingham.

BARRINGTON, Hon Sir William Augustus
Curzon   1842 - 1922
A son of the 6th Viscount Barrington, he was a
diplomat, serving in the Argentine and
Paraguay, at Madrid, Vienna and Budapest and
in Sweden. He was made K.C.M.G. in 1901
and retired in 1904. Thereafter he lived in
London. He painted very competent 'water-
colour reconstructions' of ancient Greece and
Rome. They are like woolly Varleys.

BARRON, William Augustus
1751 -
The younger brother of the portrait painter
Hugh Barron, he exhibited from 1764 to 1791
and entered the R.A. Schools in 1770. He was
also a pupil of William Tomkins and won a
premium from the Society of Arts in 1766. He
painted and etched in the Home Counties, and
he was patronised by the Walpoles who found
him a post in the Treasury on which he gave up
painting. On the evidence of the drawing in the
B.M., this was no great loss.
Examples: B.M.

BARROW, Joseph Charles, F.S.A.
- 1804 (London)
An unfortunate business career and similar
marriage led Barrow to become a topographer,
and he held a twice-weekly evening drawing
class at 12 Furnival's Inn Court, Holborn,
employing Francia and J. Varley (qq.v.) as
assistants. He took Varley on a tour to
Peterborough with him in 1797 or 1798. He
redrew some of the sketches of J. Moore (q.v.),
and made a series of views at Strawberry Hill
for Horace Walpole. His style is that of a rather
wooden follower of Sandby. He exhibited at
the R.A. from 1789 to 1802. He never

BARROW Joseph Charles (-1804)
Dover Beach. *Signed, pencil and watercolour, 6in. x 9in.*

recovered from the deaths of his wife and four children, and a spell in the Marshalsea for debt.
Published: *Sixteen Plates... of Churches and other Buildings*, 1790-93.
Examples: B.M.; V.A.M.; Grantham Mus.

BARRY, Sir Charles, R.A., F.R.S.
1795 (London) - 1860 (Clapham)
The architect. He was articled to a firm of surveyors, and from 1817 to 1820 travelled through France, Italy, Greece and Turkey and visited Egypt, Syria, Cyprus, Rhodes, Malta and Sicily. On his return, he set up in practice in London and pioneered the adaptation of the Italian palazzo to English use. In 1836 he won the competition for the new Houses of Parliament, for which he made over eight thousand drawings. He was elected A.R.A. and R.A. in 1840 and 1842, and he was knighted in 1852.

His work is a little stiff with muted colours, and he probably employed other artists to put in his foregrounds and figures.
Examples: B.M.; Hove Lib.; R.I.B.A.
Bibliography: Rev. A. Barry: *Life and Works of Sir C.B.*, 1867. *A.J.*, July, 1860. *Builder*, XVIII, 1860. *R.I.B.A. Trans.*, 1859-60. *Architecture*, 5th ser., iii, 1924-5. *Country Life*, 13 Oct. 1960; 26 August, 4, 11 Sept. 1969.

BARRY, Frederick
A marine, landscape, genre and ornithological painter who lived in London and, from the 1840s, at West Cowes, I.o.W. He exhibited from 1826 to 1860 and was an unsuccessful candidate for the N.W.S. in 1843 and 1846.

BARRY, James
1741 (Cork) - 1806 (London)
The greatest historical painter in Britain during the eighteenth century was the son of a builder and began by copying prints. He moved to Dublin in 1763, where he studied briefly at the R.D.S. and was brought to the notice of Edmund Burke. The latter persuaded him to go to London in 1764, and then, two years later, financed a journey to Rome, via Paris. He returned from Italy in 1770. He was elected A.R.A. and R.A. in 1772 and '73, and was Professor of Painting from 1782 to 1799, when he was ejected from post and Academy for bad temper and language. He died in 'self-imposed poverty' (Waterhouse), but was, none the less, buried in St. Paul's. He disliked painting portraits, but produced them along with landscapes. He left many pen and wash figure, genre and landscape studies. His studio sale was at Christie's, 10/11 April 1807.
Examples: B.M.; R.A.
Bibliography: Fryer: *The Works of J.B.*, 1809. See Crookshank & Glin: *The Painters of Ireland*, 1978. W. Pressley: *Life and Art of J.B.*, 1981.

BARSTOW, Montague
A figure painter in the tradition of A. Moore

BARTON, Lt.-Gen. Ezekial (1781-1855)
Huts in the Indian Jungle. *Pencil, grey and blue washes, 7½in. x 9in.*

(q.v.), he lived in London and exhibited there from 1891 to 1900 and from 1916 to 1919. In 1923 he was living in Monte Carlo.

BARTH, J   S
A painter of Swiss and London views who was working between 1797 and 1809. He aquatinted prints after his own drawings, and also visited Kent, Wales and the South West. He usually painted in bodycolour, but, at its best in pure watercolour, his work can be reminiscent of that of C. Varley (q.v.).
Examples: B.M.; Leeds City A.G.

BARTHOLOMEW, Anne Charlotte, Mrs., née Fayermann
c.1800 (Lodden, Norfolk) - 1862 (London)
An authoress, previously married to Walter Turnbull the popular composer, she married V. Bartholomew (q.v.) as his second wife in 1840. As well as producing plays and poems, she was a miniaturist, exhibiting at the R.A., and, under Bartholomew's influence, she became a flower painter.
Published: *Songs of Azrael*, 1840. *The Ring, or the Farmer's Daughter*, 1845. *It's only my Aunt*, 1850.
Examples: B.M.
Bibliography: *A.J.*, Oct. 1862.

BARTHOLOMEW, Valentine
1799 (Clerkenwell) - 1879 (London)
Although he had some professional instruction at sixteen, Bartholomew was largely self

taught. From 1821 to 1827 he worked for, and lived with, Charles Hullmandel the lithographer, whose daughter, Adelaide, he married in the latter year. He executed a work on flowers for Hullmandel, and in 1826 exhibited a flower piece at the R.A. He was a Member of the N.W.S. in 1834 and 1835, and was elected A.O.W.S. in the latter year. He was appointed Flower Painter to the Duchess of Kent in 1836, and Flower Painter in Ordinary to the Queen in 1837. He lived in London and married as his second wife A.C. Bartholomew (q.v.) in 1840. They were well known for their hospitality to other artists. His models were reared in the conservatory; 'largeness of style' and 'careful execution' were the hallmarks of his style.
Examples: V.A.M.
See Colour Plate

BARTLETT, Richard
An Elizabethan cartographer who produced bird's eye views of towns and castles in Ulster.

BARTLETT, William Henry
1809 (Kentish Town) - 1854 (at sea)
A topographer and traveller who was apprenticed to J. Britton (q.v.) and worked on his publications. He also painted copies of Turner, Girtin, Cotman and others. He exhibited at the R.A. and the N.W.S. from 1831 to 1833. In about 1830 he made a Continental tour and then visited Syria,

Palestine and Egypt. He went to America four times and died between Malta and Marseilles.

His remaining works were sold by Southgate & Barrett of Fleet Street in January 1855.

He should not be confused with the genre painter **William Henry BARTLETT, Yr. (1858-1932)** who was a member of the New English Art Club.

Published: *Walks About Jerusalem*, 1845. *Pictures from Sicily*, 1852. *The Pilgrim Fathers*, 1853.
Examples: B.M.; V.A.M.; Devizes Mus.; Fitzwilliam; Glasgow A.G.; Leeds City A.G.; City A.G., Manchester; Newport A.G.; Ulster Mus.; Worcester City A.G.
Bibliography: W. Beattie: *Brief Memoir of W.H.B.*, 1855. J. Britton: *A Brief Biography of W.H.B.*, 1855. A.M. Ross: *W.H.B., Author and Traveller*, 1973. *A.J.*, Jan. 1855. *Country Life*, 15 Feb. 1968.
See Colour Plate

BARTON, Lieutenant-General Ezekial 1781 - 1855 (Irthlingborough Ho., Northants)
A very accomplished amateur who served in India from 1799, rising to be Colonel of the 46th Bengal Regiment. In 1814 he toured the Upper Provinces taking landscapes in a manner which crossed Towne with the Daniells. His greens are strong and lovely. On other occasions his work is Varley-like.
Examples: B.M.

BARTON, Mary Georgina, 'Molly" 1861 (Dundalk) - 1949 (Bracknell)
Easily confused with her near namesake (*vid.inf.*), Molly Barton was another of the leading Anglo-Irishwomen working in watercolour at the turn of the 20th century. She was the youngest of the seven children of a civil engineer by his first wife. Nine half-siblings followed. In 1895 she moved to England and the Westminster School of Art, and in 1898 she went to study and teach in Rome. From 1900 she exhibited in both Ireland and England, and she was a member of the Watercolour Society of Ireland. She also painted in India, Mexico, Canada, France and Portugal. Latterly she lived at Bracknell, Berkshire.
Published: *Impressions of Mexico with Brush and Pen*, 1911. &c.

BARTON, Rose(mary) Maynard, R.W.S. 1856 (Dublin) - 1929 (London)
The daughter of an Irish solicitor, she lived in Dublin and London and painted town scenes, particularly in London. She exhibited from 1889, and was elected A.R.W.S. and R.W.S. in 1893 and 1911.

Various exhibitions of her work were held in London galleries, including the Japanese Gallery in 1893 and the Clifford Gallery in 1898. She travelled in Europe and Greece and also painted portraits.
Published: *Familiar London*, 1904.
Illustrated: F. Gerard: *Picturesque Dublin*, 1898.
Examples: Ulster Mus.
Bibliography: *W&D*, 1987, i.

BARTON, Rose(mary) Maynard (1856-1929)
Piccadilly. *Signed, watercolour heightened with white, 6in. x 4in.*

BARWELL, John 1798 (Norwich) - 1876
A drawing master who painted portraits, figure subjects, landscapes and architecture. He was a member of the Norwich Society from 1813 to 1833 and exhibited at the R.A. in 1835.

Henry George BARWELL, who was a member of the Norwich Art Circle in 1885, was presumably a relative.

BATCHELDER, Stephen John 1849 - 1932
A painter of the Norfolk Broads. His hallmark is a wherry which almost always appears in the composition.

BATEMAN, Vice-Admiral Charles Philip Butler 1776 (Wormley, Herts.) - c.1857
The son of Captain Nathaniel Bateman, he joined the Navy in 1790, serving in the Channel, the East and West Indies, the North Sea, the Baltic and the Mediterranean. From 1813 he was unemployed, but he continued gently up the promotional ladder.
Examples: Greenwich.

BATEMAN, William 1806 (Chester) - 1833 (Shrewsbury)
An engraver who specialised in views of Chester and who made occasional watercolours.

BATES, David 1840 - 1921
A landscape painter in oil and watercolour who lived in Worcester, in Birmingham from 1884 to 1899, and in Malvern. He exhibited in Birmingham from 1868 to 1907, and at the

BATTY, Lieutenant-Colonel Robert (1789-1848)
Original drawing from *Hanoverian and Saxon Scenery*, 1829.
Pen and brown ink and sepia wash.

R.A. and elsewhere in London from 1872. He painted mostly in the Midlands, but also at times in both Egypt and Switzerland, and he specialised in scenes, notably winter scenes, of cattle and farmworkers.
Examples: Worcester City A.G.

BATH, Elizabeth Marchioness of
– *see* **BENTINCK, Lady E.C.**

BATHURST, Charles
       1790 - 1863
An amateur artist and the son of the Rt. Hon. Charles Bragge (who took the name of Bathurst in 1804). He was educated at Christ Church, Oxford, and lived at Lydney Park, Gloucestershire. His work shows the influence of Malchair, and he drew in London, Oxford, Lancaster, Blenheim and elsewhere.
Examples: Ashmolean; Brighton A.G.

BATLEY, Walter Daniel
    1850 (Ipswich) - 1936 (Ipswich)
The son of a house decorator, he learned to draw and paint while recovering from smallpox, and then trained at the Ipswich School of Art and the R.A. Schools. F.G. Cotman (q.v.) was a fellow student. He moved from Ipswich to nearby Rushmere in 1898, and to Felixstowe in 1921, returning to Ipswich in 1928. Despite this local bias, he did paint elsewhere in England and Wales, and exhibited widely, evolving from a Victorian naturalism to a Whistler and Newlyn inspired impressionism.
There was also a painting **Emily S. BATLEY.**

BATTERSBY, Miss M   **c.1770 -**
A painter of birds, flowers and insects who is probably to be identified with Mary Battersby,

the unmarried daughter of Robert Battersby of Bobsville, Co. Meath. Her known albums of watercolours contain drawings dated from 1804 to 1841, and they are strongly coloured, showing a feel for texture. The models for her birds were generally pets or stuffed specimens.
Examples: R.D.S.; Nat. Lib.Ireland; Ulster Mus.

BATTY, Elizabeth Frances, Mrs. Martineau
The daughter of Dr. Batty (q.v.), she painted landscapes. She exhibited at the R.A. from 1809 to 1816 and visited Italy in 1817. She married Philip Martineau and was the mother of R.B. Martineau (q.v.).
Published: *Views of Italian Scenery,* 1818.

BATTY, John
A landscape painter working at York. He exhibited stained drawings of Yorkshire abbeys and views of the Lake District in London from 1772 to 1788.

BATTY, Dr. Robert
 ?1763 (Kirkby Lonsdale) - 1849 (Hastings)
A surgeon who studied at St. Andrews, practised in London where he edited the *Medical and Physical Journal,* and retired to Hastings. He painted landscapes and marine subjects. He exhibited at the R.A. from 1788 to 1797. His colours are bright and his figures animated. He was the father of E.F. Batty and R. Batty (qq.v.).

BATTY, Lieutenant-Colonel Robert, F.R.S.
    1789 (London) - 1848 (London)
The son of Dr. Batty (q.v.), he was educated at Gonville and Caius College, Cambridge. He entered the Grenadier Guards in 1813, returning to Cambridge on leave to take a degree in medicine. He served in the Peninsular War and at Waterloo, where he was wounded in the hip, and he was promoted lieutenant-colonel in 1828. He produced a series of illustrated memoirs of the campaign, and afterwards worked on a series of views of Europe. He first visited Italy at the age of fifteen, and later toured France in 1819, and Germany in 1820, as well as Belgium, Holland and Wales. He retired in 1839. Redgrave approved of his careful and correct drawings. His wife, Johanna, was a daughter of Sir J. Barrow, recorder of the Macartney Embassy to China.
Published: *A Sketch of the Late Campaign in the Netherlands,* 1815. *An Historical Sketch of the Campaign of 1815,* 1820. *French Scenery,* 1822. *Campaign of the Left Wing of the Allied Army,* 1823. *Welsh Scenery,* 1823. *German Scenery,* 1823. *Scenery of the Rhine, Belgium and Holland,* 1826. *Hanoverian and Saxon Scenery,* 1829. *Six views of Brussels,* 1830. *A Family Tour through South Holland,* 1831. *Select Views of the Principal Cities of Europe,* 1832.
Illustrated: Sir J. Barrow: *The Mutiny and Piratical Seizure of H.M.S. Bounty,* 1876.
Examples: Nat. Mus., Wales; Wolverhampton A.G.
Bibliography: *A.J.,* Jan. 1849.

BAUER, Ferdinand Lucas
1760 (Feldsberg, Austria) - 1826 (Vienna)
In 1786 he was engaged as a draughtsman by John Sibthorp who was passing through Venice on his first journey to Greece. He illustrated Sibthorp's *Flora Graeca* and worked for him as a topographical artist both in Greece and later in England. He drew landscape subjects, sometimes with the Oxford *Almanacks* in mind, although none was used for them. His botanical drawings are conventional, but beautiful, and his sepia and Indian ink views stiff and rather formal. In 1801-5 he was draughtsman for Flinders on the *Investigator,* making 1,541 drawings and sketches, of Antipodean birds, fish and mammals as well as plants. Thereafter he worked in London and Vienna.

His brother, **Frans Andreas BAUER, F.R.S. (1758-1840),** came to England in 1788 and was employed by Sir Joseph Banks as draughtsman to the Royal Botanic Gardens, Kew. He was also Botanic Painter to George III.
Examples: B.M.; Ashmolean; Nat. Hist. Mus.
Bibliography: D. Mabberley: *F.B., the Nature of Discovery,* 1999.

BAXTER, John, Yr.
c. 1738 - 1798 (Edinburgh)
The elder son of the architect and draughtsman John Baxter (c.1700-c.1770), he was, like his father, a protégé of the Clerks of Penicuik. In 1761 he was sent to Rome to study, and he was made a member of the Academy of St. Luke a year before his return in 1767. Thereafter he took over his father's practice. His draughtsmanship benefited from his Roman years.

Although he had a son, John, in the service of the East India Company, the family do not appear to be connected to a second Edinburgh 'John Baxter, junior, Architect', who died in 1837.
Examples: Nat. Lib., Scotland.
Bibliography: *Bull. Sc. Georgian Soc.,* ii, 1973.

BAXTER, Thomas
1782 (Worcester) - 1821 (London)
A porcelain painter at Worcester and Swansea, who entered the R.A. Schools in 1800, and who ran an art school in London from 1814 to 1816 when he returned to Worcester. As well as studies of fruit and of decorative and mythological subjects, he painted portraits and provided drawings for Britton's *Salisbury Cathedral.* He was also an occasional engraver and exhibited at the R.A. from 1802 to 1821.
Published: *An Illustration of the Egyptian, Grecian and Roman Costume,* 1810.
Examples: B.M.; V.A.M.; Worcester City A.G.

BAXTER, William Giles
c.1855 (Ireland) - 1888
After an American upbringing and working for an architect in Manchester, he moved to London where he became a cartoonist for *Judy.* From 1884 to 1886 he produced the drawings for *Ally Sloper's Half-Holiday* (see De Tessier, I.E.).

BAYES, Alfred Walter
1832 (Yorkshire) - 1909 (London)
A genre painter and etcher, he exhibited from 1858. He painted in both oil and watercolour, and his style is that of a meticulous Pre-Raphaelite follower. He illustrated a number of fairy and biblical stories. His maidens tend to look faintly careworn. He was killed by a motor cab.

BAYES, Walter John, R.W.S.
1869 (London) - 1956
The son of A.W. Bayes (q.v.), he was a painter, decorator and scene designer. He was Headmaster at the Westminster Art School, Art Master at Camberwell, and an art critic for the *Athenaeum.* He travelled widely throughout Europe.
Examples: Fitzwilliam; Leeds City A.G.

BAYFIELD, Fanny Jane
A drawing mistress at Norwich, she exhibited flower paintings in London from 1872 to 1897. She was a member of the Norwich Art Circle, and her best known pupil was Sir Alfred Munnings.

BAYLISS, Sir Wyke, F.S.A.
1835 (Madeley, Shropshire) - 1906 (London)
An architect, painter in oil and watercolour and a writer, he was the son and pupil of a drawing master. He studied at the R.A. Schools, worked in an architect's office and lived in Clapham. He exhibited from 1855 and in 1864, after attempting to join the N.W.S., he was elected to the S.B.A. of which he became President in 1888. His subjects are often Gothic church interiors. He was knighted in 1897, and was a lecturer and writer on art.
Examples: City A.G., Manchester; Castle Mus., Nottingham.
Bibliography: *A.J.,* 1906.

BAYNE, James
A landscape painter who was working in Edinburgh in a tight style from about 1867 to 1910.

BAYNES, Frederick Thomas
1824 - 1874
The grandson of J. Baynes (q.v.) and son of T.M. Baynes (q.v.). He lived in London and exhibited fruit and flower subjects from 1833 to 1864, and he was an unsuccessful candidate for the N.W.S. in 1863.
Examples: V.A.M.; Bethnal Green Mus.

BAYNES, James
1766 (Kirkby Lonsdale) - 1837
'A poor nervous creature' but a successful drawing master and landscapist. He studied under Romney and at the R.A. Schools. In 1798 or 1799 he accompanied J. Varley (q.v.) on a sketching tour of Wales, and shortly afterwards he was unmasked by Varley and Nicholson as submitting his own drawings to the Society of Arts for those of his pupils. He was a member of the A.A. and exhibited with the Oil and Watercolour Society until 1820. He was fond of drawing farmhouses, sometimes rather in the manner of Girtin.
Examples: B.M.; V.A.M.; Ashmolean; York A.G.; Whitworth Inst., Manchester.

BAYNES, James (1766-1837)
Norham Castle Overlooking the Tweed. *Watercolour, 13½in. x 19¾in.*

BAYNES, Thomas Mann
1794 - 1854

The son of J. Baynes (q.v.), he was a lithographer. He studied at the R.A. Schools from 1809, and exhibited at the R.A. and the O.W.S. in 1820. He worked in London and Ireland.

Published: *The Parks of London*, 1825.
Examples: B.M.; City A.G., Manchester.

BAYNTON, Henry
1862 - 1926

A landscape painter who lived in Coventry and exhibited at Birmingham in 1883.

Examples: Coventry A.G.

BEACH, Ernest George
1865 (London) -

A landscape, figure and portrait painter in watercolour as well as in oil and pastel. He was educated at Mill Hill School and studied in London and Paris. He lectured on art, lived in Kent, and painted in Holland, Belgium and France. He was still active in 1934.

BEACH, Thomas
1738 (Milton Abbas) - 1806 (Dorchester)

A portrait painter who studied at the St. Martin's Lane Academy, was a pupil of Reynolds and worked in and from Bath. He exhibited from 1772 and was a member of the Society of Artists, but gave up painting around the turn of the century.

Bibliography: F.T. Beach:*T.B.*, 1934

BEALE, James   1798 (Cork) - 1879

A landscape painter who travelled in Europe and North Africa before becoming a shipbuilder. In 1837 he commissioned the first steamships to cross the Atlantic. His partner was R.J. Lecky, husband of S. Lecky (q.v.).

Examples: Cork A.G.

BEALE, Mary, née Cradock, Mrs.
1632 (Barrow, Suffolk) - 1697 (London)

The daughter of the vicar of Walton-upon-Thames, who was an amateur painter, she is said to have been a pupil of Lely, but more probably she took lessons from her father's friend Robert Walker. Certainly she copied Lely and also van Dyck. She married **Charles BEALE,** Lord of the Manor of Walton, Bucks., a notable chemist who manufactured colours, and was a diarist. She painted portraits in oil, watercolour and crayon, and was also a poetess.

They had two sons: **Bartholomew BEALE (1655/6 London - 1709 Coventry),** who began as a portrait painter but turned to medicine, and **Charles BEALE, Yr. (1660 London - 1714 London)** who studied under the miniaturist Thomas Flatman, and assisted his mother. He also painted portraits of his own in various media, but weak eyesight made him give up the profession soon after 1689.

BEAUCLERK, Lady Diana (1734-1808) Caught – Nymph and Cupid. *Signed with initials, and inscribed by a 20th century hand, pencil and watercolour, 11⅝in. x 10¼in.*

BEALE, Sarah Sophia

A painter of modestly priced landscapes and figure subjects which she exhibited at Suffolk Street between 1860 and 1889. She lived in London, with a still more modest sister **Ellen BEALE,** and visited Germany and Paris as well as Harrogate and various parts of the South of England.

BEAN, Anslie H

A landscape and coastal painter who specialised in Italian subjects and exhibited from 1870 to 1886.

BEARDSLEY, Aubrey Vincent
1872 (Brighton) - 1898 (Mentone)

The black and white illustrator. For a time he worked as a city clerk, but on the advice of Burne-Jones turned to art full time. His first illustrations were for Dent's edition of the *Morte d'Arthur,* and he worked for the *Pall Mall Budget, The Yellow Book* and the *Savoy.*

His work has been divided into three phases: first, the romantic and Pre-Raphaelite; second, the decorative and Japanese; and third, the eighteenth century and French. At the time, it was described as 'the mere glorification of a hideous and putrescent aspect of modern life'. Of Wilde's *Salome,* 1894, a newspaper commented: 'As for the illustrations by Mr. Aubrey Beardsley, we hardly know what to say.'

Examples: B.M.; Ashmolean; Cecil Higgins A.G., Bedford; Glasgow A.G.
Bibliography: A. Symons: *A.B.,* 1898. H.C. Marillier: *The Works of A.B.,* 1899, 1901. C.H.C. MacFall: *A.B.,* 1928. A.R. Walker: *How to detect B. Forgeries,* 1950. H. Maas, J. Duncan & W. Good: *The Letters of A.B.,* 1970. B. Reade, *A.B.,* 1987. Tate Gall: Exhibition Cat., 1923-4.

BEARNE, Edward Henry
1844 (Newton Abbot) -

A landscape, genre and portrait painter who studied with T.C.L. Rowbotham (q.v.), entered the R.A. Schools in 1869, and exhibited from 1868 to 1895. He painted in Britain, Italy, Germany, France and Holland, and in 1892 moved from London to Dunster, Somerset. His work is of a very high quality, and an exhibition was held at MacLean's Gallery in 1893.

His wife, **Catherine Mary, née Charlton,** whom he married in 1889, was also a

landscape painter and a Royal biographer.
Illustrated: C.M. *Bearne: Lives and Times of the Early Valois Queens*, 1899.
See Colour Plate

BEATRICE, H.R.H. Princess, Princess Henry of Battenburg 1857 (Windsor Castle) - 1944 (Brantridge Park, Sussex)
The fifth daughter of Queen Victoria (q.v.) and Prince Albert (q.v.), she was a pupil of E.H. Corbould (q.v.), and, with her mother, took lessons from M.A.S. Biddulph (q.v.). She painted landscapes, most notably in Egypt in 1903 and 1904, and was perhaps the best and most serious artist of her family. She was made an Honorary R.I. in 1885, the year of her marriage. She was Governor of the Isle of Wight, succeeding her husband, from 1896.
Bibliography: M.E. Sara: *The Life and Times of H.R.H. Princess B.*, 1945.

BEATTIE, Jane
A floral still-life painter who lived in Edinburgh and exhibited at the R.S.A. from 1844 to 1855.

BEAUCLERK, Lady Diana
1734   - 1808
The eldest daughter of Charles Spencer, 2nd Duke of Marlborough, she married the 2nd Viscount Bolingbroke in 1757. In 1768 she was divorced and, two days later, married Topham Beauclerk. He died in 1780. Reynolds and Walpole were among her admirers, but Johnson thought little of her.
She made seven 'sutwater' designs for Walpole which he hung at Strawberry Hill; and several of her drawings, including a portrait of the Duchess of Devonshire, were engraved by Bartolozzi. She also produced mythological and rustic costume scenes in light colour washes.
Illustrated: Burger: *Leonora*, 1796. *Fables of John Dryden*, 1797.
Examples: B.M.; V.A.M.
Bibliography: B.C. Erskine: *Lady D.B.*, 1903. C. Hicks: *Improper Pursuits*, 2002. *Connoisseur*, VII, 1903. *Antique Collector*, August, 1958.
See Colour Plate

BEAUFORD, William H
1735 (Ireland) - 1819 (Dublin)
An amateur antiquarian draughtsman, working in Dublin. He made an antiquarian tour of the south of Ireland in 1786, and toured Carlow and Wicklow in 1787. Many of his drawings from these and other tours were engraved by James Ford for Ledwich's *Antiquities of Ireland*, 1790. Other drawings were engraved for the *Irish Bards*, and by H. Brocas (q.v.) and S. Clayton for *Anthologia Hibernica*, 1793-4, and Vallencey's *Collecteana de Rebus Hibernicus*. He was one of the founders of the Antiquarian Society.
Published: *The Ancient Topography of Ireland*, 1770. *Druidism Revived*, 1770. *An Essay on the Poetical Accents of the Irish*, 1786.

BEAUMONT, Sir George Howland (1753-1827)
At Lowther. *Inscribed on the reverse and dated 1811, black chalk and grey wash on blue paper, 12in. x 18¾in.*

BEAUFORT, Frances Anne, 'Fanny'
1768   - 1862
Like her brother, W.L. Beaufort (q.v.), she took lessons from N. Pocock (q.v.) and a Miss Simmonds in Bristol, and from F.R. West in Dublin. She became an accomplished flower painter, as well as the fourth wife of Maria Edgeworth's father.
Examples: Huntingdon Lib., California.

BEAUFORT, Rev. William Louis
1771 (Ireland) - 1849
A son of the Rev. Daniel Augustus Beaufort, diarist, mapmaker and Rector of Navan, and a brother of F.A. Beaufort (q.v.). He was rector of Glanmire, and, from 1814, prebendary of Rathcooney, Cork. In 1782 he went to Bristol, where he had lessons from N. Pocock (q.v.) and Miss Simmonds, and then in Dublin he was taught by J.G. Oben/O'Brien (q.v.). He seems to have painted large views, but his artistic career and opus are horribly confused with those of W. Beauford (q.v.).
Further confusion is possible, since he had another sister, **Louisa BEAUFORT (1781-1867)**, author and illustrator of *Essay upon the State of Architecture and Antiquities previous to the landing of the Anglo-Normans in Ireland*, and a brother, the hydrographer **Rear-Admiral Sir Francis BEAUFORT (1774-1857)**, eponym of the Scale and barometer.

BEAUMONT, Sir Albinus
(Piedmont) - 1810
A landscape painter who became a naturalised Englishman. He produced a number of aquatint views of France, Italy and Switzerland from 1787 to 1806. These were usually based on his own rather weak

drawings. He was a tutor to the Duke of Gloucester's children.
Examples: B.M.

BEAUMONT, Alfred
An architect who entered the R.A. Schools in 1831. Later he travelled in Greece, making architectural drawings which he exhibited at the R.A. He became Surveyor to the County Fire Office.
Published: *Hints for Preventing Damage by Fire*, 1835.

BEAUMONT, Sir George Howland, 6th Bt.
1753 (Dunmow, Essex) - 1827 (Coleorton)
In 1762 he succeeded to the baronetcy, and he was brought up in Suffolk by the Rev. Charles Davy, through whom in 1771 he met T. Hearne (q.v.). Both Hearne and J. Farington (q.v.), whom he met two years later, had a considerable influence upon him and they joined him on his honeymoon in the Lake District in 1778. He also studied under Cozens at Eton, and under Malchair at New College, Oxford. He toured Switzerland and Italy with his wife in 1782 and 1783, and made a further visit, or visits, to the Continent from 1819 to 1822, touring Holland, Germany, Switzerland and Italy. He was M.P. for Beeralston from 1790 to 1796. In 1800 he left his house at Dunmow, and, with the assistance of G. Dance (q.v.), began the rebuilding of Coleorton Hall, Leicestershire. There he established a well merited reputation as a patron of artists and writers, befriending Constable, Haydon, Alexander, Edridge, Wordsworth, Coleridge and Scott among many others. His house in Grosvenor Square was also a node point for people from the worlds of art and politics. He

BEAVIS, Richard (1824-1896)
Barges and Tow-horses. *Signed with initials and dated 1869, pencil and watercolour heightened with white, 5in. x 7in.*

was one of the principal founders and benefactors of the National Gallery.

In his drawings he is always old-fashioned in a romantic, eighteenth century manner which shows the influence of Claude and Wilson. His inability to understand the modernism of Constable is well known, as is his dislike of Turner's work. His style is rather woolly, but conveys a sense of the dramatic qualities of landscape. His drawings are generally in pencil and wash. He was a member of O.Bowles' (q.v.) Society of St. Peter Martyr.

An exhibition of his work was held at the Leicester A.G. in 1938.
Examples: B.M.; Glasgow A.G.; Abbot Hall A.G., Kendal; Leeds City A.G.; Leicester A.G.; N.G., Scotland.
Bibliography: W.A. Knight: *Memorials of Coleorton*, 1887. M. Greaves: *Regency Patron, Sir G.B.*, 1966. V.A.M. MSS: *Letters to Dr. T. Monro*, 1808-21, Leicester A.G., Exhibition Cats., 1938; 1953. *Country Life*, 27 Feb. 1969. *O.W.S. Club*, LXII, 1987.

BEAVIS, Richard, R.W.S.
1824 (Exmouth) - 1896 (London)
A landscape and coastal painter who, despite parental opposition, entered the Government School of Design at Somerset House in 1846. Subsequently he worked as designer for Messrs. Trollope, a successful decorating firm, full-time until 1863 and thereafter part-time. He exhibited at the R.A. and elsewhere from 1851, and was elected A.N.W.S. and N.W.S. in 1867 and 1871. He later transferred to the older Society, and was elected A.R.W.S. and R.W.S. in 1882 and 1892. He lived at Boulogne in 1867-8, visiting Holland, and in 1875 he travelled to Egypt and Palestine by way of Venice and Brindisi. He was noted for his atmospheric treatment of his subjects, and he also painted animals and Eastern scenes.

His remaining works were sold at Christie's, 17 February 1897.
Examples: B.M.; V.A.M.; Gray A.G., Hartlepool.
Bibliography: J.H. Hollowell: *A Critical Description... of the Halt of Prince Charles Edward by R. Beavis*, 1881. *A.J.*, 1877.

BECHER, Rear-Admiral Alexander Bridport 1796 - 1876
A surveyor, scientist and amateur artist who, before entering the Hydrographic Office of the Admiralty in 1823, was taught at the R.N.C., Portsmouth by J.C Schetky, served in the West Indies and carried out surveys of the Canadian Lakes, the Azores, a part of the African coast and some of the Cape Verde Islands. From 1820 to 1822 he was in the Pacific and in the latter year he was promoted lieutenant. He worked in the Hydrographic Office until his retirement in 1865, and edited the *Nautical Magazine* from its first issue in 1832 to 1871. He was in the North Sea in 1839 and surveyed the Orkneys in 1847-8. In 1856 he was made a retired rear-admiral. He sketched in Fareham, Wales, Rutland and Scotland.
Published: *Description of an Artificial Horizon*, 1844. *The Landfall of Columbus*, 1856. *Navigation of the Atlantic Ocean*, 1883.
Examples: Greenwich.

BECK, John W
A drawing master at Mussoorie School, India in 1861, he exhibited at the Grafton and New Galleries from 1879 and was on the Consulting Committee of the latter in 1888. He was for a time Secretary of the Grosvenor Gallery.
Examples: India Office Lib.

BECKER, Edmund
Probably an amateur pupil of R. Cooper, Yr. (q.v.) and of German extraction. He seems to

have worked in Rome in about 1780, and in the Lake District and Thames Valley at the end of the 1790s. His style is close to that of T. Sunderland (q.v.), but with a weaker pen line. His drawings are often inscribed with place names and sometimes with colour notes.

He should not be confused with **Ferdinand BECKER** who was active from about 1793 and died at Bath in 1825.
Examples: B.M.; Leeds City A.G.; Nat. Lib. Wales.

BECKER, Harry 1865 - 1928
A landscape painter who was living in Colchester in 1885, London in 1895, and Wenhaston, Suffolk, in 1913.
Examples: B.M.; City A.G., Manchester.

BECKFORD, Commander John Leigh
c.1789 - 1858 (Isle of Wight)
A second cousin of Beckford of Fonthill, he volunteered for the Navy in 1803, served in the Channel until 1807, then in the Mediterranean including the defence of Cadiz, 1810-11. Thereafter he was on the Channel and Scottish stations until 1821 when he went on half-pay. His father lived at Basing Park, Berks., and his mother and wife both came from the Isle of Wight. He lived at Southampton and painted English and Continental views and copies of his contemporaries. His earlier figure drawing is crude. His death certificate gives him the incorrect middle name of Leith.

BECKWITH, Thomas, F.S.A.
1731 (Rothwell, nr. Leeds) - 1786 (York)
A painter of the antiquities of Yorkshire. For a short time F. Nicholson (q.v.) was his pupil. He was working in York from 1765 or earlier, and trained as a house painter.

BEDE, Cuthbert –
see **BRADLEY, Rev. Edward**

BEDFORD, Francis Donkin
1864 (London) -
Possibly the grandson of F. O. Bedford (q.v.), he lived in London, entering the architectural school at the R.A. in 1885. He painted genre scenes, sometimes in imitation of Boucher, and exhibited at the R.A. from 1892. He also made illustrations for children's books, novels and topographical works.

BEDFORD, Francis Octavius
1784 - 1858 (Greenhithe, Kent)
An architectural draughtsman who was in Greece in 1812 drawing the Temple of Diana at Magnesia for the Society of Dilettanti. He later worked as a church architect in London and made topographical illustrations.

His father **John BEDFORD, né Tubb (1741-1805)** was an upholder, but also exhibited architectural drawings, while his son, **Francis BEDFORD, Yr.,** exhibited similar subjects at the R.A. from 1843 to 1849.
Examples: R.I.B.A.; Soane Mus.

BEDFORD, Admiral Sir Frederick George Denham 1838 - 1913
An amateur artist who kept regular albums and diaries. He served as a midshipman in the Crimea, and commanded the Indian trooper *Seraphis* on its voyage to take the Prince of Wales to India in 1875-6. On his return he left for the Pacific on board the H.M.S. *Shah*, where he became engaged in a battle with the Peruvian Ironclad *Huascar*. He was Commander-in-Chief of Capetown in 1892, and of the North American Station in 1899. From 1903 he was Governor of Western Australia.
Published: *The Sailor's Handbook*, 1884. *Life on Board H.M.S. Britannia*, 1890.

BEDFORD, George 1849 - 1920 (Torquay)
After studying at Torquay School of Art and at South Kensington, he returned to Torquay as Headmaster of his old school from 1878 to 1918. He was also Headmaster of Newton Abbot Art School and examiner to the Royal Drawing Society. He lectured on etching and crafts.
Examples: V.A.M.

BEDFORD, John Bates 1823 (Thornhill, Yorkshire) -
A painter of historical and genre subjects and occasional landscapes or garden scenes. He worked in London, studied at the R.A. Schools from 1843 and exhibited at the R.A. and elsewhere from 1848 to 1886. He sometimes used a 'BJB' monogram.

BEECHEY, Admiral Richard Brydges 1808 (London) - 1895 (Southsea)
The second youngest of the eighteen children of Sir William Beechey, R.A. He was an occasional watercolourist but entered the Navy, studying at the R.N. College, Portsmouth, where he may have been taught by J.C. Schetky (q.v.). In 1822 he was posted to the West Indies, and in 1825 he sailed on board H.M.S. *Blossom* to the Pacific, twice visiting the Bering Strait. In 1828 he was sent to the Mediterranean, and in 1835 he joined the survey of Ireland, where he remained for a long time. He was promoted commander in 1846 and captain in 1851.
A watercolour of Macao, dated 1826 and taken from H.M.S. *Blossom*, was in the Chater Collection. He also painted marine subjects in oil.

BEETHAM, William
A portrait painter in watercolour, he lived in Soho and exhibited good Oakley-like, or sub-Richmond, examples between 1834 and 1853.
Bibliography: *Country Life,* 30 November 1989.

BEETHOLME, George Law
A solicitor who exhibited watercolours of Scottish topography from 1847 to 1878. He lived in London.
His son **George Law Francis BEETHOLME** exhibited still lifes of fruit from 1879 to 1904.

BELISARIO, Isaac Mendez (-p.1844)
Cattle, Sheep and Herds. *Signed and dated 1815, watercolour, 12¼in. x 17in.*

BEILBY, William 1740 (?Durham) - 1819 (Nottingham)
The most famous British enameller on glass, he was a son of a Durham goldsmith and brother of the engraver Ralph Beilby, T. Bewick's (q.v.) master. He was also a drawing master and topographer. He was himself taught in Birmingham, and he worked in Newcastle from about 1762 to 1778, then Chelsea, where he kept a school, then Fife and the Nottingham area. In 1778 he was the only drawing master in Newcastle, and in 1785 he produced drawings of Battersea and Chelsea which were aquatinted by Jukes. His brother Thomas and his sister Mary (1749-1797) worked as his assistants. 'Beilby' has become a virtual synonym for enamel decorated Newcastle glass, although glassmaking was an important Tyneside industry and enamelling was also done by others.

BELCHER, Diana, Lady, née Joliffe
A landscape and figure painter who exhibited with the Society of Female Artists in the 1860s. She married Admiral Sir Edward Belcher (1799-1877) in 1830 and had a difficult married life.
Published: *The Mutineers of the Bounty and their Descendants,* 1870.
Bibliography: A.G.K. L'Estrange: *Lady Belcher and her Friends,* 1891.

BELGRAVE, Major-General Dacres Thomas Charles 1847 (Nr. Rugby) - 1930
A landscape painter, he came of a landed, naval and clerical family, and after an education at Eton he inherited Kilworth Close, Leicestershire from his grandfather the Rev. Thomas Belgrave. He was commissioned in the Royal West Kent Regiment in 1866, served in the Sudan in 1885-6 and retired that year as lieutenant-colonel of the regiment. He taught drawing at the R.M.A., Woolwich in the late nineteenth century.

BELGRAVE, Percy
A landscape and genre painter in oil and watercolour who exhibited from 1880 to 1896. He lived in London and painted in the New Forest, on Dartmoor and in Wales.

BELHAVEN and STENTON, Hamilton, Lady c.1795 - 1873
The aunt of J.F. Campbell of Islay (q.v.), she married the 8th baron in 1815. She was a pupil and patron of P. de Wint (q.v.). Her husband's seat was Wishaw, Lanarkshire.

BELISARIO, Isaac Mendez - p.1844 (Jamaica)
A friend and close follower of R. Hills (q.v.). He exhibited from 1815 to 1831, and when Hills left him an annuity in 1842 he was 'of Kingston, Jamaica'. Three sets of aquatints were published after his views. His work is very close indeed to that of his mentor.

BELL, A D
A copyist of Birket Foster (q.v.) – or more probably of chromolithographs after Foster – whose very poor efforts show how good the master was. He was active around 1911.

BELL, Alexander Carlyle
A landscape painter who lived in London and exhibited there and at the R.S.A. between 1847

BELL, Robert Anning (1863-1933)
'The Fainting Dryad.' *Red chalk drawing, signed, 4¾in. x 8in.*

and 1891. His subjects are on the Thames, in Scotland and occasionally North Wales, Worcestershire and Switzerland.

BELL, Arthur George, R.I.
1849 (City of London) - 1916
A landscape painter who lived in Hampstead and London. He exhibited from 1879 and was elected R.I. in 1911. He painted in France and Germany as well as on the Thames, in East Anglia, Devon and the New Forest. He illustrated a number of travel books by Nancy Meugens, whom he later married.

BELL, Sir Charles
1744 (Edinburgh) - 1842 (Worcester)
A surgeon and amateur artist who studied drawing with D. Allan (q.v.). He produced sketchy wash landscape drawings, and etchings. He wrote a number of medical treatises, and his lectures on anatomy influenced his friend D. Wilkie (q.v.).
Examples: B.M.; N.G.Scotland.

BELL, J   H
A portrait painter in the manner of H. Edridge (q.v.), who was working in Bath between 1798 and 1809. He was a pupil of J.S. Copley.
Examples: Victoria A.G., Bath.

BELL, John Anderson
1809 (Glasgow) - 1865
An architect who was educated at Edinburgh University. He studied in Rome in 1829 and 1830, and practised in Birmingham, where he exhibited in 1835, and Edinburgh. He also spent some time in Cambridge. He painted landscapes, sea pieces, Italian churches and Roman ruins, as well as still lifes.
Examples: B.M.; N.G., Scotland.

BELL, John D   - 1910
A marine and coastal painter who was active in Scotland and on the Isle of Man from the 1870s to 1910. He was a founder member of the R.S.W. in 1878 but resigned in 1902. His views of fishing villages are breezy.

BELL, Maria, Lady -
see **HAMILTON, William**

BELL, Robert Anning, R.A.
1863 (London) - 1933
Designer of mosaics and stained glass, sculptor, illustrator and painter in several media, he was apprenticed to an architect and studied at the Westminster School of Art, the R.A. Schools and in Paris under Aimé Morot. He visited Italy and exhibited there and in France as well as London. He was elected A.R.A. and R.A. in 1914 and 1922, and A.R.W.S. and R.W.S. in 1901 and 1904. He was Professor of Design at the R.C.A. from 1918 to 1924, and taught in Glasgow and Liverpool.
    An exhibition of his work was held at the Fine Art Society in 1907.
Examples: B.M.; Cartwright Hall, Bradford; Preston Manor, Brighton; City A.G., Manchester.

BELL, Robert Purves, A.R.S.A.
1841 (Edinburgh) - 1931 (Hamilton)
Son of the engraver Robert Charles Bell (1806-1872), he studied at the R.S.A. Schools and exhibited at the R.S.A. from 1863. He painted portraits, landscapes, flowers, genre and Moorish subjects. He lived variously in Edinburgh, Tayport and Hamilton.

BELL, William H   - c.1902
An Edinburgh landscape painter who exhibited at the R.S.A. from 1885. He lived in London for a while, and later settled at Dumfries. He also visited France.
Published: *Art in Scotland Its Origins and Progress,* 1889. &c.

BELLAIRS, Lieutenant Walford Thomas
c.1794   - 1850
A member of an old Lincoln and Leicestershire family, he was at Greenwich in 1809 and then served on the Channel, West Indian, Mediterranean and North American stations between 1812 and 1819. In 1838 he was posted to the Coast Guard, and in 1842 appointed Admiralty Agent in the Packet Service, which meant that he had to carry official mail from point to point in the Far East. He also painted on the Channel coast, in the West Indies and the Far East, and no doubt elsewhere.

BELLERS, William, Yr.
The son of an artist, he painted and etched

BELLAIRS, Lt. Walford Thomas (c.1794-1850)
Whampoa Pagoda. *Inscribed on the reverse, watercolour, 4¾in. x 7in.*

landscapes in the Lake District, Derbyshire, Hampshire and Sussex. He was working in the second half of the eighteenth century and in the manner of G. Lambert (q.v.). He also painted coastal scenes, and was a printseller in London.

BELSHAW, Frank
c.1850 (Nottingham) - c.1910
A still-life painter in oil and watercolour who exhibited at the R.A. and Suffolk Street in 1881 and 1882.

BENAZECH, Peter Paul
c.1744 (England) - c.1783
A line engraver and landscape draughtsman who was a pupil of F. Vivares (q.v.).
His son, **Charles BENAZECH (1767 London - 1794 London),** travelled to France and Rome. He too was a painter and draughtsman.

BENDIXEN, Siegfried Detlev
1786 (Kiel) - 1864 (London)
A landscape painter, portraitist and printmaker who settled in London in 1832, and exhibited at the N.W.S., the R.A. and elsewhere from 1833 until his death.

BENETT, Newton
1854 (London) - 1914 (Dorchester)
A landscape painter who was the son of a Master in the High Court and a collateral descendant of Sir Isaac Newton. He was a pupil of P.J. Naftel (q.v.), and worked much in the New Forest and Dorset and at Warborough-on-Thames. He used white heightening in his watercolours.
Examples: V.A.M.

BENGER, Berenger 1868 - 1935
A painter of landscapes and town scenes in oil and watercolour. He lived in Liverpool and exhibited at the R.A., the R.I. and elsewhere from 1884. His style is atmospheric and sometimes impressionistic.
William A. Edmund BENGER (d.1915) also painted watercolours.
Illustrated: H.A. Morah: *Highways and Hedges,* 1911.
Examples: Brighton A.G.; Towner Gall., Eastbourne; Glasgow A.G.; Ulster Mus.

BENNET, Julia -
see **GORDON Julia Isabella, Lady**

BENNET, Lady Mary Elizabeth
c.1790 - 1861
A landscape painter who was an enthusiastic pupil of J. Varley (q.v.). She was the youngest daughter of the 4th Earl of Tankerville, of Chillingham Castle, and in 1831 she became the second wife of Sir Charles Lambert Monck, M.P., of Belsay Castle, also in Northumberland.

BENNETT, Harriet Mary
?1852 (Islington) - p.1921
A painter of the highest Victorian genre subjects, who exhibited at the R.A. and the R.I.

BENETT, Newton (1854-1914)
Sandwich, Kent. *Signed with initials and dated 1880, watercolour heightened with white, 9¾in. x 14in.*

from 1877. From about 1881, when she won £100 in a Christmas card competition, much of her time was devoted to designing cards and calendars. These found great favour with Queens Victoria and Alexandra.
She should not be confused with **Frank Moss BENNETT (1874 Liverpool - 1953),** the Cardinal and landscape painter in oil and watercolour, nor with the American naval painter and writer **Frank Marion BENNETT.**

BENNETT, John Martin Wills
?c. 1800 - 1844 (Plymouth)

A painter of portraits, genre subjects and occasional landscape studies in oil and watercolour. He exhibited from 1825 to 1840 and moved from Sheffield to London in about 1830.
An earlier **James BENNETT** exhibited landscapes at the R.A. from 1801 to 1803 and is represented at the Hove Library.

BENNETT, William, N.W.S.
1811 - 1871 (Clapham Park)
A painter of castles and abbeys who may have been a pupil of Cox. He exhibited from 1848, in which year he was elected A.N.W.S.,

BENNETT, William (1811-1871)
Deer in Windsor Great Park. *Watercolour.*

becoming a full member in 1849. He is often listed as 'Yr', and may have been the son of W.J. Bennett (q.v.). On the other hand, his own son exhibited landscapes as **William BENNETT, Jr.** between 1878 and 1887.

His work is often very close to that of Cox in his middle period. His own pupils included A. Williams (q.v.).

Examples: B.M.; V.A.M.; Maidstone Mus.; Sydney A.G.

BENNETT, William James
1787 (London) - 1844 (New York)
Little is known of this artist; even his christian names and the spelling of his surname are in dispute. He was a member of the A.A. and Treasurer during the last two years. In 1820 he was elected A.O.W.S., but resigned in 1825. He seems to have been a talented engraver, and may be identified with the brother-in-law of F. Nash (q.v.) who is said to have fled to America after a banking fraud and become President of the New York Academy. If so, he exhibited a number of Mediterranean views and engraved several plates after his brother-in-law.

A **W.J. BENNETT (b.c.1782)** entered the R.A. Schools in 1801.

Examples: B:M.; Newport A.G.

BENNETT, William Mineard
c.1778 (Exeter) - 1858 (Exeter)
A portrait painter in oil and watercolour and a miniaturist, Bennett was a pupil of Sir T. Lawrence (q.v.). He spent some time in London before moving to Paris, where he practised until 1844, in which year he returned to Exeter. His portraits are much influenced by those of his master.

Examples: Ulster Mus.

BENSON, Charlotte E
1846 (Dublin) - 1893
She attended the R.D.S. Schools, where she won a medal for a still-life drawing. She exhibited landscapes and seascapes at the R.H.A. from 1873 to 1890. She made many sketches while visiting her brother in India. She ran the Ladies' Sketching Club from 1874 until 1888 when it merged with the Dublin Sketching Club.

Her sister **Mary Kate BENSON (d.1921)** was also an artist. She studied at Herkomer's and exhibited with various Irish societies from 1877.

BENT, James Theodore
1852 - 1897
With his wife **Mabel Virginia Anna BENT (1846-1929)** he explored the ruins of Mashonaland at the request of Rhodes and on grants from the R.G.S. and others. There is a collection of their studies and panoramas in the Nat. Archives, Zimbabwe.

BENTHAM, Robert H
1822 - 1900
A landscape painter who lived in Guernsey

and exhibited local, French and Swiss subjects from 1871 to 1874.

Examples: City A.G., Manchester.

BENTINCK, Lady Charles, née Anne Wellesley
- 1875
With her second husband, she was a pupil and patron of de Wint. She was in Italy in 1827. This husband was **Lt.-Col. Lord William Charles Augustus BENTINCK** and they were married in 1816. Her 1806 marriage to Sir William Abdy, 7th Bt., had been dissolved. She was the natural daughter of the Marquess Wellesley.

BENTINCK, Lady Elizabeth, 'Betty', CAVENDISH 1734 - 1825
The eldest daughter of the 2nd Duke of Portland, she and her sisters were pupils of G.D. Ehret (q.v.), who often visited Bulstrode to teach them.

The others were **Henrietta, Countess of STAMFORD and Warrington (d.1827),** and **Lady Margaret Cavendish BENTINCK (d.1756)**. In 1754 she married Viscount Weymouth (1734-1796), who was created

Marquess of Bath in 1789. One of her daughters was Louisa, Lady Aylesford (q.v.), and another, Mary (d.1814), married Osborn Markham, uncle of W. Markham (q.v.). Her third son was the husband of Lady Carteret (q.v.).

BENTLEY, Charles, O.W.S.
1806 (London) - 1854 (London)
A marine artist who was apprenticed to the engraver Theodore Fielding (q.v.). His style was largely moulded by a study of Bonington's work for engravings, and later by his fellow-apprentice and lifelong friend W. Callow (q.v.). He started engraving on his own behalf on the termination of his apprenticeship in 1827, and for some years combined engraving with watercolour painting. He was elected A.O.W.S. in 1834 and O.W.S. in 1843. He was a poor businessman and always in financial difficulties. He died from cholera.

He painted on almost all the British coasts as well as the Channel Islands, and in 1836, 1840 and 1841 he visited Normandy and Paris with Callow. Although he produced subjects which were further afield, these were probably

BENTLEY, Charles (1806-1854)
'A Quiet Smoke.' *Watercolour, dated Oct. 22nd 1853, 11½in. x 8¼in.*

worked up from amateur sketches. His watercolours are done with great verve and his colour comes directly from Bonington. There is sometimes, however, evidence of weak drawing and perspective. On occasions he makes liberal use of bodycolour. His remaining works were sold at Christie's, 15 April 1855.

Examples: B.M.; V.A.M.; Blackburn A.G.; Brighton A.G.; Leeds City A.G.; Newport A.G.; Ulster Mus.

Bibliography: *Walker's Quarterly,* 1 April 1920.

See Colour Plate

BENTLEY, Edward
           1837   - 1882 (Bexley)
A fruity still-life and landscape painter who lived at Bexley and exhibited from 1868. 'Spoils of the Hedgerow' was a favourite title.

BENTLEY, Joseph Clayton
           1809 (Bradford) - 1851 (Sydenham)
The son of a Bradford solicitor, he was a pupil of R. Brandard (q.v.). As an engraver and landscape painter he is often confused with his better-known namesake, Charles. His subject matter is similar, as is his style, although this is rather weaker. They also worked as engravers or illustrators on a number of the same publications, thus adding to the confusion. J.C. Bentley exhibited at the B.I. from 1833 and the R.A. from 1846, as well as at Suffolk Street.

Examples: V.A.M.; Cartwright Hall, Bradford.

Bibliography: *A.J.,* Jan. 1852.

BENTLEY, Richard
           1708 (Cambridge) - 1782 (London)
Son of the controversial Master of Trinity, the judgement that he was 'an accomplished but eccentric man, who achieved nothing signal in life' is only a little unfair. He dabbled in many things, among them architectural designs and illustrations for his friend Walpole. He was generally penurious and lived in the South of France and Jersey before settling at Teddington and later Westminster. From the 1760s, by which time he had quarrelled with Walpole, he attempted playwriting. His drawings for Walpole's edition of Gray's poems have been dismissed as 'showing some cleverness, but are rather grotesque'. However, Gray seems to have liked them. Sir Howard Colvin calls him 'a Georgian Rex Whistler'.

Bibliography: *Builder,* XIX, 1861. *Metropolitan Mus. Studies,* V, i, 1934.

BENWELL, John Hodges
           1764 (Blenheim) - 1785 (London)
A pupil of J. Sanders, Yr. (q.v.), a portrait and genre painter, he studied at the R.A. Schools from 1779, winning a silver medal in 1782. He then became a drawing master in Bath. He was a competent and charming illustrator.

Examples: B.M.; V.A.M.; City A.G., Manchester.

BENWELL, Joseph Austin
A painter of Eastern scenes in oil and

BENWELL, Joseph Austin
Arab caravan. *Watercolour, signed and dated 1868, 17in. x 26in.*

watercolour who spent some years in India and China up to 1856. He was in Egypt and Palestine in 1865-6. He exhibited at the R.A. and the R.I. from 1865 to 1883 and was also a wood engraver.

Illustrated: Raffer: *Our Indian Army.* Capper: *Three Presidencies of India.*

BERANGER, Gabriel
           1729 (Rotterdam) - 1817 (Dublin)
A landscape draughtsman of Huguenot extraction, he came to Dublin in 1750, where he taught drawing and exhibited with the Dublin Society of Artists. In 1773 he made an antiquarian tour of Ireland, and in 1779 toured the west of Ireland with A.M. Bigari (q.v.) and a view to making drawings for the newly formed Antiquarian Society. The next year, together with J.J. Barralet (q.v.), he toured Wicklow and Wexford, and the following year visited Dundalk. He ran a printselling business and, from 1780 to 1789, he had the sinecure of Assistant Ledger Keeper in the Exchequer office.

He was an accurate, if unimaginative, draughtsman. His figures, however, are spirited, and he often included himself in red coat, yellow breeches and cocked hat, measuring-staff in hand. He kept an illustrated itinerary of his tours, which he left, in two volumes ready for publication, to two nieces of his second wife. One of these volumes is now in the R.I.A.

Bibliography: Sir W.R.W. Wilde; *Memoir of G.B.,* 1880.

BERESFORD, Cecilia Melanie
           1840   - 1893
The daughter of a Stafford rector, she was

descended from the 1st Lord Decies. She was a painter of Italian, and occasional Irish, figure subjects. She lived in Tenbury before going to Rome in 1882, and in London after her return ten years later. She exhibited at Suffolk Street and the R.I. from 1865 to 1885. She did not marry.

Examples: V.A.M.

BERESFORD, Colonel Charles Frederick Cobbe   1844   - 1925
A member of the Waterford family. During his career in the Royal Engineers he produced watercolours and drawings in Ireland (1869), Labrador, Bermuda (1870), England (1886) and India (1893). He was still drawing as late as 1923.

Examples: Nat. Army Mus.

BERESFORD, Lady George, née Harriet Schutz   1780   - 1860
The daughter of J.B. Schutz of Gillingham Hall, Beccles, where she had a number of distinguished teachers. C. Varley (q.v.) stayed in 1802 'to teach the ladies', and other masters were J. Varley, W. Payne and W. Crouch (qq.v.). In 1808 she married Lt.-Col. Lord George Beresford, third son of the 1st Marquess of Waterford. He was *custos rotulorum* and colonel of militia for Co. Waterford.

BERRY, Berry Francis
           1854   -
A figure and sentimental genre painter, sometimes with landscape accompaniment. He lived in London and exhibited from 1874, entering the R.A. Schools two years later.

BEST, Mary Ellen (1809-1891)
China Cabinet in the Japanese Palace, Dresden. *Watercolour, 11¼in. x 9¼in.*

BEVAN, William (1817-c.1848)
A Street in an old Town. *Signed, watercolour, 7in. x 5in.*

BERTRAM, Paul, né Pigott
1872 - 1929
The younger son of W.H. Pigott (q.v.), with whom he was not on good terms. He painted landscapes around Sheffield, and sold them as quickly as possible to raise the wind.

BESSBOROUGH, Frederick Ponsonby, 3rd Earl of 1758 - 1844
The son of the 2nd Earl, he succeeded to the title in 1793. He married a daughter of the 1st Earl Spencer and was the father of Lady Caroline Lamb. As Viscount Duncannon he produced a number of views of seats in the 1780s.

BEST, Mary Ellen
1809 (York) - 1891(Darmstadt)
The daughter of a doctor, who was at the centre of the York Lunatic Asylum Scandal and died when she was six, she was a fascinating painter from childhood to middle age, leaving what is in effect a visual autobiography. She was well trained at a school in York run by the drawing master G. Haugh (q.v.) and his wife, and she may well have had lessons from H. Cave (q.v.). She then went south to Miss Shepherd's school at Bromley, after which she attempted to establish a career in York. She had accompanied her parents to Nice, where her father died, and in 1832 she and her mother visited North Wales. In 1834-5 they toured Holland and Germany, and after her mother's death, which left her with independent means, she returned to Germany in 1838 and '39. In 1840 she married Johann Anton Phillip ('Anthony') Sarg, a school teacher and hotel manager of Frankfurt. Thereafter she lived in Germany, making frequent visits to friends and family in England. She had already ceased making any great effort to sell her work, and after her marriage she gradually stopped painting entirely. Her last known work is dated 1860.

She was not interested in landscape or picturesque composition, preferring interiors, town scenes, figures, portraits and still lifes. There is a great clarity to her work, and at times a certain naïvety, and her pictures amount to an invaluable archive detailing the social history, fashions and furnishings of the period in both Britain and Germany.
Examples: V.A.M.; York City A.G.
Bibliography: C. Davidson: *The World of M.E.B.*, 1985.

BESTLAND, Cantlo, otherwise Charles
1763 - c.1837
An etcher and oil painter who entered the R.A. Schools in 1779 and later occasionally produced historical and genre scenes, such as 'The Sailor's Farewell' and 'Return', in watercolour, presumably as preparatory compositions for prints. He entered the R.A. Schools in 1779 as 'Cantlo Bestland' and exhibited from 1783 to 1837.
Examples: N.G., Scotland.

BEUGO, John
1759 (Edinburgh) - 1841
An engraver and friend of Burns. He made watercolours of subjects from Burns as well as engravings for the 1787 edition of the poems. He also painted small wash portraits.
Examples: N.G., Scotland.

BEVAN, Robert Polhill
1865 (Hove) - 1925 (London)
An animal, portrait and landscape painter who studied in Paris. He became Treasurer of the 'London Group'. Early in his career he specialised in scenes of horse sales, and later in Devonshire landscapes.

A memorial exhibition was held at Brighton in August 1926.

BEVAN, William 1817 - c.1848
A drawing master at Hull College from 1842 to 1848, he executed a number of coloured lithographs of local churches. He had been admitted to the R.A. Schools in 1837.

BEVERLY, William Roxby
1811 (Richmond, Surrey) - 1889 (Hampstead)
The son of a family of northern actors called Roxby who took the name of Beverley, or 'Beverly' as the painter usually spelled it, because they liked the town. He began his career as a scene painter and actor for his father in the North. In 1838 he was working in Edinburgh and in 1839 in London. After some time in Manchester, he returned to London in about 1846. In 1851 he visited Switzerland. From 1853 he was scenic director at Covent Garden, and from 1854 to 1884 did a great deal of work at Drury Lane. Between 1865 and 1880 he exhibited marine watercolours at the R.A.

In style he is a follower of Bonington, with a similar liking for beached boats and misty effects. Blues, browns and golden sunsets, usually with touches of red on the figures, are his favourite colours. He was a friend and pupil of C. Stanfield (q.v.). His dashing brown wash sketches can be very free like those of Turner.
Examples: B.M.; V.A.M.; Bridport A.G.; Towner Gall., Eastbourne; Fitzwilliam; Greenwich; Leeds City A.G.; Leicestershire A.G.; Newport A.G.; N.G. of Scotland; Ulster Mus.
Bibliography: *Mag. of Art*, 1889. *Walker's Quarterly*, II; XXI.

BEWICK, Robert Elliot
1788 (Newcastle) - 1849 (Newcastle)
The pupil and only son of T. Bewick (q.v.), he became his father's partner in 1812 and assisted him with the illustrations for Aesop's *Fables*, 1818, and the projected *History of British Fishes*. He took over the business shortly before his father's death. He also made small watercolours of Newcastle buildings.
Examples: B.M.; Laing A.G., Newcastle.

BEWICK, Thomas
1753 (Cherryburn, Northumberland) -
1828 (Gateshead)
The wood engraver and naturalist. He was apprenticed to Ralph Beilby, a copper engraver in Newcastle, whose partner he later became. After a short time in London and Scotland, Bewick returned to Newcastle, where he revived the art of wood-engraving. He produced a number of extremely fine books, and instructed the foremost engravers of the next generation. His health was not good: he had a serious illness in 1812 and, shortly before his death, he passed his business to his son. His drawings are careful and often strongly coloured, as would be expected from an engraver. A loan exhibition of his work was held at the Fine Art Society in 1880. His pupils included L. Clennell (q.v.), J. Nesbit, W. Harvey (q.v.), J. Jackson (q.v.), E. Landells (q.v.), H.F.P.W. Hole, W. Temple, and his son R.E. Bewick (q.v.).

His brother **John BEWICK the elder (1760-1795)**, his nephew **John BEWICK, Yr. (1790-1809)** and his daughter **Jane BEWICK (1787-1881)** were all watercolourists and engravers.
Published: *History of Quadrupeds*, 1790. *History of Birds*, 1797. Aesop's *Fables*, 1818. *Memoir*, 1862.
Illustrated: *Gay's Fables. Select Fables.* Consett: *A Tour through Sweden, Lapland...* &c.
Examples: B.M.; V.A.M.; Fitzwilliam.
Bibliography: J.G. Bell: *A Descriptive and Critical Catalogue...*, 1851. F.G. Stephens: *T.B., Notes on a Collection of Drawings and Woodcuts*, 1881. D.C. Thomson: *The Life and Works of T.B.*, 1882. D.C. Thomson: *The Water-Colour Drawings of T.B.*, 1930. C.M. Weekley: *T.B.*, 1953. V.A.M. MSS: *Letters and Documents. A.J.*, 1903. *Country Life*, 17 Sept. 1970.

BEVERLY, William Roxby (1811-1889)
On the Arun. *Signed with initials, watercolour, 7in. x 12½in.*

BEWICK, William   **1795 (Hurworth) -**
1866 (Darlington, Durham)
No relation of T. Bewick, he was a pupil of B.R. Haydon (q.v.) and produced drawings of antiquities as well as painting portraits and copying old masters in Italy, where he lived for four years in the 1820s. Soon after 1840 his health broke down and he retired to Durham, living at Haughton-le-Skerne.
Examples: B.M.
Bibliography: T. Landseer, *Life and Letters of W.B.*, 1871.

BEWICK, Thomas (1753-1828)
A Vignette. *Watercolour, 3½in. x 4¾in.*

BIDDULPH, General Sir Michael Anthony Shrapnel 1823 - 1904
An artilleryman who entered the army in 1844, was promoted captain in 1850, lt.-col. in 1856 and general in 1886. He served in the Crimea, publishing a set of topographical and panoramic sketches as *The Assault of Sevastopol,* and married the daughter of the Russian commander of Balaklava. He was in India from 1861-85, commanding the Quetta Field Force in the 1878-9 Afghan Campaign. He was one of the RA officers whose work was exhibited at MacLean's Gallery in 1868. In 1879 he showed the Queen what she termed 'his fine sketches', and in the same year he was invested KCB and appointed Groom in Waiting. The Queen also thanked him for giving lessons to herself and Princess Beatrice (q.v.). After his final return from India in 1886 he continued to sketch at Balmoral and elsewhere.

BIDLAKE, Rev. John
1755 (Plymouth) - 1814 (Plymouth)
The Headmaster of Plymouth Grammar School, he was a poet and an amateur artist and encouraged the young S. Prout (q.v.) and B.R. Haydon (q.v.) by taking them on sketching trips. He also taught Sir C.L. Eastlake (q.v.) who painted his portrait in 1813. He was educated at Christ Church, Oxford and was a chaplain to the Prince Regent and the Duke of Clarence. He went blind in 1811 and had to rely on charity during his last years.
Published: *Elegy,* 1788. *Eugenis,* 1799. *Introduction to … Geography,* 1808 &c.
Bibliography: *Gentleman's Mag.,* 1813, i.

BIFFIN, Sarah
1784 (East Quantoxhead, Somerset) - 1850 (Liverpool)
A pupil of W.M. Craig (q.v.) who, being handless and footless, painted miniatures with the brushes held in her mouth. She practised at Brighton, where she lived with her guardian, Mr. Dukes, and at Liverpool, and she received Royal patronage.
Bibliography: *A.J.,* Nov.1850. *Gentleman's Mag.,* xxxiv, 1850.

BIGARI, Angelo Maria (Bologna) -
He left Italy for Ireland, and in 1772 was working as a scene painter for the Smock Alley Theatre, Dublin. He exhibited with the Dublin Society of Artists in 1777, and in 1779 accompanied G. Beranger (q.v.) on his antiquarian tour of Western Ireland. He may have left Ireland thereafter.
Illustrated: F. Grose: *Antiquities of Ireland,* 1791-95.
Examples: R.I.A.

BIGGE, Charles John
1803 (Newcastle) - 1846 (London)
An alderman, and in 1835 Mayor, of Newcastle, he painted landscapes and old

BINGLEY, James George (1840-1920)
'An Oft-read Letter.' *Pencil and coloured washes, signed with initials, 15⅛in. x 11⅜in.*

buildings. He made at least one Continental tour, and he exhibited locally from 1831.

BIGLAND, Mary Backhouse
1844 (Darlington) -
A member of the Backhouse banking family (q.v.), she was a landscape painter who lived in Darlington and also painted in the Home Counties, exhibiting a Surrey view at Brighton in 1875. She also exhibited in London and Newcastle from 1869 and lived in Cheshire for a while. She was active until at least 1893.

BIGOT, Charles
A painter of London views in pen and watercolour, who was working between 1820 and 1850.
Examples: B.M.

BILLING, William Henry
1803 - 1849 (London)
An unsuccessful painter in oil and watercolour, who, according to the *Gentleman's Magazine,* 1849 i, 'for the last

two years had scarcely earned a sufficiency to procure food for himself and his wife'.

BILLINGS, Robert William
1815 (London) - 1874 (London)
A sculptor and architect as well as a landscape and topographical painter. He visited Bath between 1834, in which year he also entered the R.A. Schools, and 1837, painting churches. He exhibited at the R.A. from 1845 to 1872.
Published: *Architectural Illustrations...of Carlisle Cathedral,* 1840. *Architectural Illustrations... of Durham Cathedral,* 1843. *Architectural Illustrations... of Kettering Church,* 1843. *Baronial Antiquities of Scotland,* 1848-52. *The Infinity of Geometrical Design exemplified,* 1849. *The Power of Form,* 1851.
Examples: Victoria A.G., Bath; N.G., Scotland.
Bibliography: *Gentleman's Mag.,* 1851, ii.

BILSTON, S
A prolific architectural painter in Northumbria during the middle of the nineteenth century.

BIRCH, Samuel John Lamorna (1869-1955)
Lamorna Cove. *Signed, inscribed and dated 1946, watercolour, size unknown.*

BIRCH, Samuel John Lamorna (1869-1955)
Seascape Sketch. *Signed and dated 1947, watercolour, 5in. x 6¼in.*

BINGLEY, James George
1840   - 1920 (Norwood)
A landscape painter in oil and watercolour who lived in Godalming, Wallington and Midhurst. He also painted in the West Country and Italy and exhibited at the R.A., the R.I. and elsewhere from 1871. His watercolours are colourful and fairly freely drawn, and he uses white heightening.
Examples: B.M.

BINNY, Graham, R.S.W.
c.1870 (Edinburgh) - 1929
A painter of portraits and figures who lived in Edinburgh, studied in Antwerp, Munich and Paris, and was elected R.S.W. in 1909.

BIRCH, Samuel John Lamorna, R.A., R.W.S.
1869 (Egremont, near Birkenhead) -
1955
Brought up in Manchester, he worked in a mill for some years, selling watercolour sketches made in his spare time. In 1892 he turned to art full time, and moved to Newlyn, Cornwall. Shortly afterwards he went to study in Paris, where he was influenced by Monet and Pissaro. He took the extra name of Lamorna (from the village in which he lived) in order to avoid confusion with Lionel 'Newlyn' Birch. In 1902 he married and settled there permanently. He was elected A.R.A. and R.A. in 1926 and 1934. He travelled widely, reaching Australia and New Zealand, but is chiefly remembered for his views of Cornish woods and streams in oil and watercolour, and for his handling of light and colour.
Examples: B.M.; Towneley Hall, Burnley; Exeter Mus.; Glasgow A.G.; Hove Lib.; Leicestershire A.G.; City A.G., Manchester; Newport A.G.; Nottingham Univ.

BIRD, Edward, R.A.
1772 (Wolverhampton) - 1819 (London)
Apprenticed to a firm of tin and japanware manufacturers at Wolverhampton and Birmingham, he had moved to Bristol and set up a drawing school by 1797. He was self taught and painted portraits, landscapes and historical subjects in oil and watercolour. He exhibited at the R.A. from 1809 and was elected A.R.A. and R.A. in 1812 and 1815. He was appointed Historical Painter to Princess Charlotte. He always painted from the life and often produced Wilkie-like sketches of his friends, who included many of the artists and intellectuals of Bristol. Despite his success he died poor and embittered. A memorial exhibition was held in Bristol in 1820.
Examples: B.M.; Aberdeen A.G.; City A.G., Bristol; Wolverhampton A.G.
Bibliography: *A.J.,* Nov. 1859; 1899.

BIRD, Isaac Faulkner   1802/3   -
A portrait and landscape painter who was working for the most part at Exeter from 1826 to 1861. He entered the R.A. Schools in April, 1831, when he was aged twenty-eight. His work can be free in the manner of Gainsborough, and there are sometimes echoes of J.J. Cotman.

BIRD, John 'of Liverpool'
1768   - 1826 (Whitby)
A topographer who provided drawings for Angus: *Seats of the Nobility,* 1787. He settled in Whitby and encouraged the young G. Chambers (q.v.). His work can be reminiscent of that of R. Dixon (q.v.).
Published: with G. Young: *A Geographical Survey*

BIRD, Edward (1772-1819)
Gypsies. *Inscribed with attribution on old backing, watercolour, 5in. x 7½in.*

BIRTLES, Henry (1838-1907)
The Downs. *Signed and dated 79, pencil and watercolour, 9in. x 6in.*

of the Yorkshire Coast, 1822.
Bibliography: H.C.Marillier: *The Liverpool School of Painters*, 1904. *Gentleman's Mag.*, 1829, i.

BIRKETT, S
A landscape and still-life painter, working in about 1862.

BIRLEY, Ada Kate
A flower painter who lived in Birmingham and exhibited there in 1880 and 1881.

BIRTLES, Henry
    1838 (Birmingham) - 1907
A Birmingham painter of meadows, sheep and cattle who moved to London in 1864. In 1867 he settled at Arundel but kept a studio in Hampstead. He exhibited in Birmingham and London from 1855 to 1900, and was an unsuccessful candidate for the N.W.S. on four occasions from 1863 to 1874.
Examples: Birmingham City A.G.; Glasgow A.G.

BISSCHOP, Catherine Seaton Forman, Mrs., née Swift   **(London) -**
A figure painter, who married a German artist in 1869, and worked in England and on the Continent. She was elected an Honorary Member of the Société des Aquarellists Belges in 1871.

BLACK, Andrew, R.S.W.
    1850 (Glasgow) - 1916 (Glasgow)
After an education in Glasgow and Paris he worked as a designer before turning to painting as a profession in 1877. He was elected R.S.W. in 1884 and exhibited landscapes at the N.W.S. and the R.A. He was a keen yachtsman.

BLACK, James
A painter of small oval portraits in watercolour as well as landscapes in oil paint. He was working in Armagh around 1813.

BLACKBURN, Jemima, Mrs., née Wedderburn   **1823 (Edinburgh) - 1909**
The daughter of the Solicitor General for Scotland and a kinswoman of Clerk of Eldin (q.v.), she showed a precocious talent for drawing birds and animals. She was much influenced by a book of Bewick's. In about 1840 she paid her first visit to London and was encouraged by Landseer and W. Mulready. In 1849 she married Hugh Blackburn, Fellow of Trinity College, Cambridge and later Professor of Mathematics at Glasgow. They travelled widely in Europe and the Middle East, and visited Iceland in 1878. They bought an estate on Loch Ailort in 1854. Thackeray and Ruskin were amongst her fervent admirers, although the latter rather deplored her love of horror.

Her work is extremely accomplished. She had a good visual memory, physical stamina in pursuing her subjects, and a dry wit.
Published: *Scenes from Animal Life and Character*, 1858. *Birds drawn from Nature*, 1862. *A Few Words about Drawing for Beginners*, 1893. *Birds from Moidart*, 1895. &c.
Illustrated: A. White: *The Instructive Picture-Book*, 1859. W.J.M. Rankine: *Songs and Fables*, 1874.
Examples: B.M.

BLACKBURNE, Helena
She exhibited genre and flower subjects (sometimes both at once) and portraits between 1880 and 1899. She lived in West Kensington.

BLACKLOCK, William James
    1816 (London) - 1858 (Dumfries)
The son of a bookseller who returned to his native Cumwhitton, Cumberland, in about 1820. He was apprenticed to a bookseller and printer, and first exhibited in London in 1836. He worked there for about fourteen years to 1850, when he again settled at Cumwhitton. However, his eyes failed and he gave up painting. He also suffered from epilepsy, and he died in a mental institution.

His landscapes, with their Pre-Raphaelite qualities, were admired by such artists as Turner, Roberts and W.B. Scott as well as by Gladstone. He concentrated on the effects of light and cloud and his oil paintings are perhaps better than his watercolours. His figures are generally poor.
    William Kay BLACKLOCK (b.1872), a Sunderland genre painter, was no relation.
Bibliography: *A.J.*, 1856. *Athenaeum*, 1858. *Glasgow Evening News*, July, 1900. *Country Life*, 4 July 1974.

BLACKLOCK, William James (1816-1858)
Cumbrian Fells. *Pencil and watercolour, 5¾in. x 10¾in.*

BLACKLOCK, William Kay (1872-)
A Quiet Read. *Signed and dated 1913, watercolour, 24in. x 19in.*

BLACKWELL, Elizabeth, Mrs.
c.1713 (Aberdeen) -
The daughter of an Aberdeen stocking merchant, in about 1730 she eloped to London with the adventurer Alexander Blackwell. When his attempt to set up as a printer foundered, she secured his release from debtors' prison by drawing medicinal plants. She was encouraged by Sir Hans Sloane and Dr Mead, and engraved and coloured the 500 plates after her own drawings. After the publication of her herbal, little is known of her, although she is said to have been about to join her husband in Sweden at the time of his torture and execution in 1747.
Published: *A Curious Herbal*, 1737, 1739; republished and expanded, 1757-73.

BLAIR, Andrew
1817 (Dunfermline) - 1892
The son of a weaver, he set up as a house-painter, cannily retaining the business throughout his life. He studied at the Board of Manufacturers Schools, and took to painting Highland lochs, primarily in watercolours. Some of these were published by Raphael Tuck. The Trossachs and the neighbourhood of

Oban were favourite areas. He exhibited at the R.S.A. from 1849 to 1891, and was noted for his command of light and shade. His friend, Sir J.N. Paton (q.v.), could 'recall nothing that does not reflect honour on his character'.

BLAIR, Sir Edward HUNTER, 4th Bt.
1818 - 1896
A member of a philoprogenitive and military family. Having served in both the Navy and the 93rd Highlanders, he commanded the Ayrshire Artillery Volunteers. He visited the Cape around 1835. It is likely that other members of his family shared his taste for painting.

BLAIR, John 1850 (Hatton, Berwicksh.) -
1934 (Edinburgh)
An Edinburgh painter active between 1880 and at least 1920. He produced Edinburgh and East Coast views.

BLAKE, Edith, Lady, née Bernal-Osborne
1845 (Newton Anner, Co. Tipperary) -
1926 (Myrtle Grove, Co. Cork)
The elder sister of the Duchess of St. Albans (q.v.), with whom she was taught by T.S. Boys (q.v.) and others. She married Sir H.A. Blake, policeman and colonial governor, in 1874. Their posts were the Bahamas, Newfoundland, Jamaica, Hong Kong and Ceylon, and she specialised in painting flowers and plants. She was also a plant collector and she showed drawings of the flora of the Bahamas at the 1886 Colonial and Indian Exhibition. Two species of native oak in the new Territories were named for the Blakes. She decorated their retirement home, Myrtle Grove, with botanical paintings and illustrations.
Published: *The Realities of Freemasonry*, 1879.
Bibliography: P. Butler: *Irish Botanical Illustrators*, 2000.

BLAIR, John (1850-1934)
Loch Vennacher and Ben Venue. *Signed and dated 1898, and bears inscription, watercolour, 21in. x 29½in.*

BLAKE, Fanny (-1851)
The Bearer of sad Tidings. *Signed and dated 1846, pencil and watercolour, 13½in. x 18½in.*

BLAKE, Fanny   - 1851 (London)
A talented pupil of de Wint who was working between 1812 and 1850. She was the 'accomplished artist, admirable for truth, completeness, and delicacy', behind the exhibition of amateurs in Pall Mall in 1851, as is recorded, with her death, in the *Gentleman's Magazine.*

BLAKE, William
        1757 (London) - 1827 (London)
The son of a hosier, he was apprenticed to James Basire, the engraver, and studied under H. Pars (q.v.) and at the R.A. Schools. In 1780 the R.A. accepted a watercolour by him, and he exhibited eleven more up to 1808. In 1782 he married Charlotte Boucher, who later helped him with his printing. His earliest important patron was Thomas Butts, who bought from him for about twenty years. In 1800 he attracted the notice of that somewhat trying literary patron, William Hayley, and went to live near him at Felpham, Sussex, where he stayed for three years. Thereafter he returned to London and poverty. There was a small exhibition of his work in 1809, but it was not until 1818, when he met John Linnell (q.v.), that he gathered a group of friends and artistic disciples around him. These included J. Varley, S. Palmer, E. Calvert, G. Richmond, F.O. Finch and F. Tatham (qq.v).

Stylistically he owes much to older draughtsmen, such as Stothard, Fuseli and Mortimer, and his effects are largely obtained by a reliance on rhythmically flowing lines. His colours seem to grow stronger throughout his career, and can at times verge on the garish. As Williams says: 'Blake is one of the masters though perhaps rather one of the masters who worked in watercolour than one of the master watercolourists'. He generally signed his drawings either 'W. Blake' or with a monogram. There are however very good forged signatures which are occasionally found on Fuseli drawings. His youngest brother, **Robert BLAKE,** who died in 1787, produced drawings in his manner.
Published: *Songs of Innocence and Experience,* 1789. *The Book of Thel,* 1789. *There is no Natural Religion,* 1790. *Visions of the Daughters of Albion,* 1793. *America,* 1793. *The Book of Urrizen,* 1794. *The Book of Los,* 1794. *Jerusalem,* 1804. &c.
Examples: B.M.; V.A.M.; Aberdeen A.G.; Cecil Higgins A.G., Bedford; Abbot Hall A.G., Kendal; Leeds City A.G.; City A.G., Manchester; Newport A.G.; N.G., Scotland; Southampton A.G.; Tate Gall.; Walsall A.G.
Brief Bibliography: R.L. Binyon: *The Art of W.B.,* 1906. E.L. Cary: *The Art of W.B.,* 1907. G.K. Chesterton: *W.B.,* 1920. G.L. Keynes: *A Bibliography of W.B.,* 1921. D. Figgis: *The Paintings of W.B.,* 1925. A. Gilchrist: *Life of*

W.B., 1942. D. Bindman: *Basan Artist,* 1977. P. Ackroyd: *B,* 1995 &c. Burlington Fine Arts Club, Exhibition Cat., 1876; 1927. Tate Gall., Exhibition Cats., 1913, 2000. N.G., Scotland, Exhibition Cat., 1914. Yale, Exhibition Cat., 1982 &c.

BLAKE, William, of Newhouse
A pupil of J.M.W. Turner (q.v.) who lived in Glamorgan and was active between 1794 and 1798. His landscapes are very green with saw-toothed foliage, and they can be slightly reminiscent of the work of Warwick Smith.
Examples: B.M.

BLAKEY, Nicholas
        c.1710 (Ireland) - c.1778 (Paris)
An Irish book illustrator, who studied and mainly lived in Paris. He illustrated an edition of Pope's works, and together with F. Hayman produced some illustrations of English history, published in 1778. He was already an established portrait painter in 1739, and he may have been in London in 1748.
Illustrated: J. Hanway: *Travels through Persia,* 1753.
Examples: B.M.

BLANCHARD, Beckwith
A drawing master at Hull who was active between 1829 and 1873.

BLAND, John Humphrey
A landscape painter who was living in London in 1863 and Lympton, Devon in 1873. As well as the West Country he painted Yorkshire and Scottish subjects, and he exhibited at the R.A. and elsewhere from 1860 to 1872. He was a pupil of H.B. Carter (q.v.).

BLATCHFORD, Conway
1873 (Bristol) -
A landscape and marine painter in oil and watercolour. He studied at the Bristol School of Art and the R.C.A. and became Headmaster of the Halifax School of Art and Principal of the Newton Abbot School of Art. An exhibition of his work entitled 'Watercolours of the Sea' was held at the Brook Street Gallery in 1922.

BLATHERWICK, Dr. Charles, R.S.W.
- 1895 (Helensburgh)
A doctor and novelist who lived in Highgate and Helensburgh and painted landscapes and genre subjects. He exhibited from 1874. He was a keen founder member of the R.S.W.
Lily BLATHERWICK, R.S.W. (1854-1934), Mrs. A.S. Hartrick, who also painted and lived in Helensburgh, was his daughter. She painted flowers and moved to Gloucestershire on her marriage in 1896. She died in Fulham.

BLAYMIRE, Jonas
- 1763 (Dublin)
A topographical draughtsman who worked as a Surveyor and Measurer in Dublin. In 1738 he was commissioned to make drawings of Irish cathedrals for Walter Harris' edition of *Ware's Works*.
Examples: St. Patrick's Cathedral, Dublin.

BLIGH, Jabez
A painter of wild flowers and, above all, mushrooms, who moved from Worcester to London in the 1860s and then to Gravesend. He was an unsuccessful candidate for the N.W.S. in 1862, and for the O.W.S. in 1890 and '91, and he exhibited in London and elsewhere from 1863 to 1889. His name is sometimes misspelt Bly.
Examples: Worcester City A.G.

BLIGHT, John Thomas
An antiquarian and topographer who worked in Cornwall and on the Isle of Man. He was elected F.S.A. in 1866 and resigned in 1872. By 1883 he was penurious.
Published: *Account of the Exploration of... Treveneague... Cornwall*, 1867.
Illustrated: J.G. Cuming: *The Great Stanley*, 1867.

BLOOMFIELD, John Arthur, 2nd Lord
1802 (Bloomfield Lodge, Tipperary) -
1879 (Ciamhaltha, Tipperary)
and **BLOOMFIELD, Georgiana, Lady**
1822 (Ravensworth) - 1905
Lord Bloomfield was the son of an artilleryman and diplomat who was given an Irish peerage by George IV. The father both studied at and commanded Woolwich, so is likely to have learned to draw. The son was a diplomat from the age of sixteen, serving in Vienna, Lisbon, Stuttgart, Stockholm, St. Petersburg, Berlin and Vienna once more. He succeeded to the Irish title in 1846, and was made a peer of the United Kingdom on retirement in 1871. He painted Tipperary country houses in the 1830s. In 1845 he married the Hon. Georgiana Liddell, sixteenth child and youngest daughter of the 1st Lord Ravensworth. She had been a Maid of Honour, but resigned in that year owing to the ill-health of her parents. While in Waiting she sketched with Lady Canning (q.v.), and like many of her siblings (see Liddell, Hon. Thomas) she had a marked talent for watercolour.
Published: (G.Bloomfield), *Reminiscences of Court and Diplomatic Life*, 1883.

BLORE, Edward, F.R.S., F.S.A.
1787 (Derby) - 1879 (London)
An architectural draughtsman and to some critics a rather uninspired architect, he was the son of Thomas Blore the antiquarian. He drew for various county histories as well as for Britton's *Cathedrals and Architectural Antiquities*. From 1816 he worked on Scott's Gothic rebuilding of Abbotsford. He was Special Architect to William IV and for a while to Queen Victoria, and undertook the completion of Buckingham Palace. He retired as a practising architect in 1849, but continued to draw throughout his long life.
Published: *The Monumental Remains of Noble and Eminent Persons*, 1824.
Illustrated: T. Blore: *History of Rutland*, 1811. Sir J. Hall: *Essay on the Origin...of Gothic Architecture*, 1813. W. Scott: *The Provincial Antiquities and Picturesque Scenery of Scotland*.
Examples: B.M.; R.I.B.A.; Soc. of Antiquaries.
Bibliography: *Proceedings* of the Soc. of Antiquaries, 2nd series, VIII, 1879-81. *A.J.*, 1879. *Builder*, XXXVII, 1879. Nat. Lib. Sc., MSS, correspondence with Sir Walter Scott.

BLUCK, J
An engraver and draughtsman who worked for Ackermann and exhibited at the R.A. between 1791 and 1819. His work is in the eighteenth century topographical tradition.
Examples: Fitzwilliam.

BLUNDEN, Anna E , Mrs. Martino
1829 (London) - 1915
A landscape painter in oil and watercolour, she was brought up in Exeter and worked as a governess in Devon before turning to art. She studied at Leigh's as well as copying at the B.M. and the N.G., and she exhibited from 1853. She was encouraged by Ruskin and the Pre-Raphaelites and soon dropped figures, which she found difficult, from her work. She was on the Continent from 1867 to 1872, when she married Cavaliere Edoardo de Martino (1838-1912). They settled in Birmingham and she exhibited there until 1915.
Examples: Greenock A.G.

BLUNT, Lady Anne Isabella Noel, née King (Lady Wentworth) 1837 - 1917 (Cairo)
The daughter of the 1st Lord Lovelace and granddaughter of Lord Byron, she married Wilfred Scawen Blount of Crabbett, Sussex, in 1869. Ten years later they travelled from Aleppo to the Gulf. Her diaries were published, and she painted straightforward watercolours. She was also an Arabic scholar, a noted horsewoman and a musician. In 1880 she exhibited at the Grosvenor Gallery. She inherited the Wentworth barony in 1917.
Examples: British Lib.

BLUNT, Henry Bala
Probably a pupil of J.D. Harding (q.v.), he sketched in pencil or chalk and clean light washes and was active in the 1830s and 1840s.
Examples: B.M.

BLUNT, James Tillyer
1765 - 1834
An engineer, he served with the Bengal Engineers from 1783 to 1807. He surveyed the Ganges from Cawnpore to Patna, was present at Seringapatam, and thereafter surveyed the Allahabad, Delhi, Hardwar, Lucknow and other areas. He was the brother-in-law of R.H. Colebrooke (q.v.).
Examples: India Office Lib.

BLUNT, John Silvester
1874 (Alderton, Northamptonshire) -
1943
A painter of landscapes and street scenes. He was educated at Denstone College, Staffordshire and lived in Middlesex. He was elected R.B.A. in 1912.

BLUNT, Sir Walter, 5th Bt.
1826 - 1847 (Heathfield Park)
An accomplished artist who inherited the title and family seat, Heathfield Park, Sussex, at the age of fourteen. He was professionally taught, perhaps by W. Callow (q.v.) or another member of the Anglo-French school, and he painted a wide variety of subject matter in watercolour or sepia wash. He worked in Devon, Wales and Derbyshire as well as Sussex, and in 1846 he went to the Alps in search of a cure for consumption. He managed to shoot, and paint, chamois, but died soon after his return. He was a cousin by marriage of Lady A. Blunt (q.v.).
Bibliography: *W&D.*, 1989, i.

BODDINGTON, Harriet Olivia
An amateur painter of figures in landscapes who had a few lessons from W.L. Leitch (q.v.), and occasionally contributed to charity exhibitions.
Published: *Real and Unreal*, 1876.

BODDY, William James
1832 (Woolwich) - 1911 (Acomb)
The son of an architect, he followed the same profession for a while, moving to York in 1853 as assistant to George Jones. However, he soon built up a flourishing practice as a drawing master and exhibited in York and London from 1865 to 1879. A folio of his work was presented to the Princess of Wales in 1900. For the last twenty-five years of his life he lived at Acomb, Yorkshire, and he gave up teaching in 1908.

His landscapes are taken from many parts of Great Britain as well as Switzerland and Normandy.
Published: *Manual for Invalids: Sunday by Sunday*, 1895.
Examples: York A.G.

BODEN, Samuel Standige
1826 (Retford) - 1896
A landscape painter who worked in London. He produced drawings which are very much in the manner of M.B. Foster (q.v.) and sometimes sketched in a freer, de Wint-like style.
Published: *A Popular Introduction to the Study and Practice of Chess*, 1851.
Examples: B.M.

BODICHON, Barbara, Mme., née Leigh Smith
1827 (Watlington, Sussex) -
1891 (Scalands Gate, Sussex)
The foundress of Girton College, and a landscapist. Her grandfather was a patron of Cotman, and her father of W. Henry Hunt (q.v.) whose pupil she was. She became a prolific watercolourist and frequent exhibitor. She had a house in Algiers, where she met her husband, Dr. Bodichon, and another in Cornwall. She was a friend of Brabazon and, with a group of ladies he referred to as his 'harem', often accompanied him on sketching tours. She also visited Canada and America.

Her work is detailed and intense, with a feeling for open-air effects and the handling of flowers. These can be used in the manner of A. Nicholl (q.v.) to form a foreground through which a coastal landscape is seen. There is sometimes an attempt at the detail of the Pre-Raphaelites, who were also her friends.
Bibliography: H. Burton: *B.B.*, 1949. *Apollo*, May 1981. *Country Life*, 2 March 1989.

BOEVEY, Edward Barnston CRAWLEY
1844 - 1888
The fifth son of Sir Martin Crawley-Boevey, 4th Bt., of Flaxley Abbey, Newnham, Gloucestershire, verderer of the Forest of Dean, he served as a lieutenant in the Royal Artillery, and married Katherine Power, the daughter of the vicar of Bramley, Surrey, in 1884. In 1882 he painted the villa at Mentone in which Queen Victoria stayed.

BOISSEREE, Frederick
A painter of Welsh landscapes who lived at Betws-y-coed and was active between 1870 and 1880.

BOITARD, Louis Philippe
c.1720 (France) - 1763 (London)
A pupil of La Fargue, he was brought to London by his father, and settled as an engraver, illustrator and draughtsman. He also worked as a ceramic decorator.
Examples: Yale.

BOLINGBROKE, Minna, Mrs. Watson
1865 (? Docking, Norfolk) -
A watercolourist who was a member of the Norwich Art Circle in 1885. She exhibited in London from 1888 to 1926 and was a member of the R.E. from 1899 to 1930. Her husband was C.J. Watson (q.v.).

BOLTON, Charles Newport
1816 (Ireland) - 1884
An amateur draughtsman who was educated at Oxford. In 1878 he inherited Mount Bolton, Co. Waterford. A volume of his sketches in Killarney and Glengarrif, lithographed by G. Rowe, was published in aid of the Irish Famine Fund, and a second volume containing views of the River Suir was published later. Woodcuts after his drawings appear in the Halls' *Ireland, its Scenery and Character*. He exhibited at the R.H.A. in 1845 and 1846. He was particularly fond of sketching old buildings and heraldic designs.
Illustrated: Hore: *History of Wexford*.

BOLTON, James - 1799 (Halifax)
A naturalist who drew and etched his own illustrations. He was working from about 1775 in the Halifax area. His drawings are in the manner of G.D. Ehret (q.v.) and are sometimes on vellum. He was a pupil of the mezzotinter B. Clawes (d.1782).
Published: *Filices Britannicae*, 1785. *A History of Funguses growing around Halifax*, 1788-91. *Harmonia Ruralis*, 1794-6. *A History of British Proper Ferns*, 1795.
Examples: Fitzwilliam.

BOLTON, John Nunn
1869 (Dublin) - 1909 (Warwick)
The son of **Henry E. BOLTON,** an amateur landscape painter, he trained at the Metropolitan School of Art and the R.H.A., after which he left Dublin to live in Warwick. He exhibited in Dublin, Birmingham and Manchester, and taught for a short time at the Leamington School of Art.

He painted, both in oil and watercolour, landscapes, marine subjects and portraits, as well as miniatures.

BOLTON, William Treacher
1816 - 1884 (Islington)
A painter of town scenes who lived in London and was an unsuccessful candidate for the N.W.S. on four occasions between 1861 and 1872. He exhibited at the S.B.A. from 1857 to 1881 and painted in the Home Counties, West Country, Scotland and Switzerland.

An earlier **T. BOLTON** was a topographer in Yorkshire, working around 1800.
Examples: Victoria A.G., Bath.

BOMFORD, L   G
A painter of Scottish landscapes and views near London in oil and watercolour. He lived in Kilburn and exhibited at the R.A. and Suffolk Street from 1871 to 1882.

BOND, John Linnell
1764 - 1837 (Marylebone)
An architect who studied drawing under J. Malton (q.v.) and entered the R.A. Schools in 1783. He exhibited designs and views at the R.A. from 1782 to 1814. From 1818 to 1821 he travelled in Italy and Greece making topographical and historical, as well as architectural drawings.
Examples: B.M.; British Lib.; R.I.B.A.
Bibliography: *Gentleman's Mag.* 1837. *Literary Gaz.*, 1837.

BOND, John Lloyd
A painter of Welsh landscapes in oil and watercolour who exhibited from 1868 to 1872. He lived in London and Betws-y-coed.
Examples: V.A.M.

BOND, Richard Sebastian
1808 (Liverpool) - 1886 (Betws-y-coed)
A kinsman of W.J.J.C. Bond (q.v.), he studied at Liverpool and lived in Birmingham and at Betws-y-coed. He exhibited in London and elsewhere from 1841 to 1881, and he painted Cox-like landscapes, often with rivers and mills, in oil and watercolour.
Examples: Greenwich.
Bibliography: *The Year's Art*, 1887.

BOND, William John Joseph C – 'Alphabet'
1833 (Liverpool) - 1926 (Formby)
A landscape and marine painter in oil and watercolour, he was apprenticed to a picture restorer and dealer. He lived at Caernarvon and then at Liverpool, where he became a member of the Academy in 1859. His subjects are generally taken from Cheshire, Wales and Anglesey, although he visited Antwerp.

He painted old buildings, harbours and the sea, and was himself a keen sailor. Early in his career he was influenced by the Pre-Raphaelites; later he is closer to Turner.

BONE, Henry Pierce
1779 (Islington) - 1855 (London)
The son and pupil of Henry Bone, R.A., a miniaturist. He entered the R.A. Schools in 1796, and was a member of the A.A. and the Langham Sketching Club, exhibiting enamel portraits and watercolour copies of old masters, usually at the R.A.
Bibliography: V.A.M. MSS.: two letters from J.I. Richards to H.B., 1801.

BONINGTON, Richard Parkes
1802 (Arnold, near Nottingham) -
1828 (London)

His comrade, Delacroix, said of him: 'Other artists were perhaps more powerful or more accurate than Bonington, but no one in the modern school, perhaps no earlier artist, possessed the ease of execution which makes his works in a certain sense diamonds, by which the eye is pleased and fascinated, quite independently of the subject and the particular representation of nature.'

He was the son of **Richard BONINGTON (1768-1835)**, a drawing master and portrait painter and sometime sailor and Governor of Nottingham Gaol. His mother was a teacher, and she probably provided most of his formal schooling. At the end of 1817, or early in the following year, the family moved to Calais, where the father set up in the lace business, and subsequently they settled in Paris. In Calais Bonington took lessons from Francia, thus absorbing the influence of Girtin, and in Paris he studied in the studio of Baron Gros and met the young Delacroix when sketching at the Louvre. He was at the centre of the nascent Romantic Movement, and his first exhibits at the Salon in 1824 caused a sensation. He revisited England in 1825, perhaps touring Scotland as well, and in the following year he exhibited in London, where his reception was rather more reserved. Also in 1826 he paid his homage to La Serenissima, travelling by way of Switzerland and returning by Florence, Turin and the Riviera. In the summer of 1828 he contracted brain fever, and in September he left Paris for the last time, in the hope that the treatment of St. John Long (q.v.) in London might cure him. He was still painting on his death bed.

Despite the shortness of his working life, Bonington is one of the very few English artists to have had a profound effect on Continental painting. The British had not suffered from the stultifying effects of Neo-Classicism to anything like the extent which their French and German contemporaries had. The style was too closely identified with the Imperial propaganda of Napoleon to appeal to his enemies. Thus Bonington was well situated to act as a catalyst to the frustrations of the younger generation of Continental artists. He was also far better placed than his teacher Francia to display the glories of the English watercolour school to an audience who knew little, or nothing of it. His work in oil, superb as it is, should always be seen as the extension of the techniques and genius of a master painter in watercolour.

His work divides into two parts, firstly that of the landscape painter working in the English conventions of the time. His first coastal scenes to be exhibited in London were rightly compared to those of W. Collins (q.v.). Then, in his last years he also proved himself to be the greatest, as well as one of the earliest, of English nineteenth century genre painters. In this he was inspired by the French painters

BONINGTON, Richard Parkes (1802-1828)
The Pont de la Concorde with the Tuileries beyond. *Signed and dated 1827, watercolour, 13in. x 21in.*

BONINGTON, Richard Parkes (1802-1828)
Dunkerque from the sea. *Watercolour.*

of the generation before last, particularly Fragonard, and by Van Dyck. His Venetian scenes and his figures in Valois or Bourbon costume in the parks of Fontainebleau and Versailles are not only charming, but unexpectedly full of life and immediacy.

His influence was not only felt in France during the next half century, but returned to England with the many English artists who were working in Paris, or who visited it in the ten years

following his death. They included his pupil Boys, W. Callow, J.S. Davis, the Fieldings, J. Holland, D. Roberts and D. Cox (qq.v).

Examples: B.M.; V.A.M.; Aberdeen A.G.; Ashmolean; Blackburn A.G.; Fitzwilliam; Glasgow A.G.; City A.G., Manchester; N.G., Scotland; Wallace Coll.

Bibliography: H. Stokes; *Girtin and B.*, 1922. A. Dubuisson and C.A. Hughes: *R.P.B. life and work,* 1924. G.S. Sandilands: *R.P.B.,* 1929. A. Dubuisson: *B,*

BOOTY, Frederick William (1840-1924)
Arabs by Classical Ruins. Pencil and watercolour heightened with white, size unknown.

1927. A. Shirley: *B*, 1940. M. Gobin: *R.P.B.*, 1955. M. Pointon: *The B. Circle*, 1985. M.Cormack: *B.*, 1989. M. Spencer: R.P.B. (unpublished). *A.J.*, May, 1858. *Gaz. des Beaux Arts*, 2nd series, xiv, 1876. *Studio*, XXXIII, 1904. Walpole Society, II, 1913; III, 1914. *Connoisseur*, May 1925. *Burlington Mag.*, III, 1926. Burlington Fine Arts Club: Exhibition Cat., 1937. *Burlington Mag.*, LXXXVIII, 1946. CXXIII, 1981. *Country Life*, 1 March 1962; 22 April 1965. King's Lynn: Exhibition Cat., 1961. Agnew: Exhibition Cat., 1962. Nottingham: Exhibition Cat., 1965. I
See Colour Plates

BONNAR, George Wilmot
1796 (Devizes) - 1836
A wood engraver who produced a number of wash illustrations and worked in London. A pupil was Henry Vizetelly (1820-1894), 'the pioneer of the illustrated press'.
Examples: B.M.

BONNEAU, Jacob, F.S.A.
- 1786 (London)
A landscape painter who came to London in about 1741 with his father, a French engraver. He was a member of the Incorporated Society and a drawing master. He sometimes painted genre subjects.

BONNER, Thomas
1746 (Gloucestershire) -
An engraver and illustrator who made topographical drawings as well as figure subjects for the works of such writers as Shakespeare, Richardson, Smollett and Fielding. He entered the R.A. Schools in 1778 and was working at least until 1807.

His figures are sometimes rather grotesque, and his washes reminiscent of W. Gilpin (q.v.) but with touches of colour.
Illustrated: Collinson: *History of Somersetshire*, 1791. Polwhele: *History of Devonshire*, 1797.
Examples: B.M.

BONOMI, Joseph, Yr.
1796 (Rome) - 1878 (London)
The youngest son of the architect of the same name, and a godson of his cousin A. Kauffmann (q.v.) and of Maria Cosway, he was brought to England at an early age and studied at the R.A. Schools from 1816. He also studied sculpture under Nollekens. He revisited Rome in 1823 and, in the following year, went to Egypt with Robert Hay. He remained there for eight years drawing antiquities and studying the figure and hieroglyphics. In 1833 he was in Sinai and Palestine with F. Arundale (q.v.) and F. Catherwood (q.v.), and he returned to Egypt again for two years from 1842. The remainder of his life was spent in illustrating numerous works on Egypt and as Curator of Sir John Soane's Museum. In 1852 four of his children died within a week, presumably from cholera.

His work is in various media including watercolour, and his figure drawing is particularly impressive.

BOOT, William Henry James, R.I.
1848 (Nottingham) - 1918 (London)
He studied at the Derby School of Art before moving to London, where he contributed to the *Graphic, I.L.N., A.J., Magazine of Art*, and other periodicals. He painted landscapes, including views of Italy and Spain, and exhibited at the R.A. from 1874 to 1884, the R.I. and the R.B.A. In 1884 he became a member of the R.B.A., and later Vice-President.
Published: *Trees and How to Paint Them*, 1883.
Illustrated: R.D. Blackmore: *Lorna Doone*, 1883. G.E.S. Boulger: *Familiar Trees*, 1885.
Examples: Derby A.G.

BOOTH, Rev. Richard Salvey
c.1765 - 1807 (Hastings)
A landscape painter who lived in Folkestone and exhibited at the R.A. from 1796 to 1807. He visited Wales. He died, according to Farington, from a palsy brought on by his father's unexpectedly leaving him a fortune after keeping him on short commons for years. The father was Benjamin Booth, a collector of Wilson's paintings, and his sister Marianne married the magistrate Sir Richard Ford and was the mother of Sir R. Ford (q.v.).

His watercolours can be Dayes-like.
Examples: Newport A.G.; Nat. Lib. Wales.

BOOTH, Lieutenant-Colonel William
A Royal Engineer who was a pupil of P. Sandby (q.v.) at Woolwich. He served at

Gibraltar in 1780 and the Tower of London in 1817. His work is better in the earlier years when the teaching was fresh.

A **William BOOTH,** perhaps the same or his father, had been a minor draughtsman at the Tower in 1767.

Illustrated: J. Heriot: *An Historical Sketch of Gibraltar,* 1792.

Examples: B.M.

BOOTH, William Joseph
1795/6 (London) - 1871 (Torquay)
He studied at the R.A. Schools and visited Italy and Greece before working as surveyor and architect for the Drapers' Company in Ulster from 1822 to 1854. He may also have designed houses on the excellent Lloyd-Baker estate, Clerkenwell. His watercolours of houses and landscapes in Ireland are described by Crookshank & Glin as 'amongst the most memorable, solid, documents of rural Ireland'. He retired to Torquay in 1855.

BOOTHBY, Sir Brooke, 7th Bt.
- 1824
A minor poet and amateur landscape painter, he was one of the Lichfield literary set which revolved around Erasmus Darwin, Anna Seward and R.L. Edgeworth. He perpetrated *The Tears of Penelope.* In 1789 he succeeded to the title and captured an heiress from Hampshire.

BOOTHBY, J.A. –
see under **MILLAIS, W.H.**

BOOTY, Frederick William
1840 (Brighton) - 1924 (Scarborough)
Son of the portrait and landscape painter Edward Booty, he was brought up in Scarborough, where he was perhaps influenced by H.B. Carter (q.v.). He taught at Hull and painted landscapes and marine subjects.

BOREMAN, Zachariah
1738   - 1810
A porcelain decorator at Chelsea until about 1783, then Derby until 1794 when he set up as an outside decorator in London. He produced charming small landscape and topographical black or brown wash drawings, often of Derbyshire subjects.

BORLACH, John C
A Scottish architectural draughtsman employed for many years by James Gibbs (1682-1754), who mentioned him in his will. He prepared twenty engravings of 'Designs of Architecture for Arches or Gates', but they do not appear to have been published. One of his drawings was used in Adam's *Vitruvius Scoticus.*

BORLASE, Captain C
An officer in the Queen's Royal Regiment, he

BOTHAM, William
Nottingham Castle. *Signed and inscribed on the backing, pencil and watercolour, 14½in. x 18¾in.*

produced decorative bird paintings from about 1790 to 1850. He was in Dublin in 1823.

BOSANQUET, Charlotte
1790 (London) - 1852 (London)
She was a member of a large Huguenot family, and her father died when she was ten years old. After the death of her mother five years later, she continued to live in London, making frequent visits to friends and relations at Vintners, near Maidstone; Broxbournbury and Meesdenbury, Hertfordshire; Strood Park, Sussex; and Gabalva, Glamorgan, among other places.

In the Ashmolean is an album of watercolours, mainly dating from the early 1840s, which faithfully portray the interiors of these houses with considerable charm and ability.

Bibliography: *Country Life,* 4 Dec. 1975.

BOSANQUET, John E
A Cork photographer who painted generally naïve local views, mainly in watercolour, and exhibited at the R.H.A. between 1854 and 1861. In Strickland's words: they are 'generally slovenly and of little merit'.

His son, **John Claude BOSANQUET,** active in the 1870s, also painted landscapes.

BOSTOCK, John
1807 (Newcastle-under-Lyme) -
1872 (Kensington)
Bostock, of Kensington, entered the R.A.

Schools in March 1825, aged eighteen. He was elected A.O.W.S. in 1851, but allowed his associateship to lapse in 1855. Between 1835 and 1849 he had produced a number of drawings for the *Annuals,* usually portraits or costume pieces. He exhibited in London from 1826 to 1869.

BOTHAM, William
A topographer and landscape painter who worked in London and Nottingham. He painted in the Girtin manner and exhibited from 1800 to 1830.

Examples: B.M.; Castle A.G., Nottingham; Sheffield A.G.

BOTHAMS, Walter   - c.1925
A painter of rural genre subjects who was living in London in 1882, Salisbury in 1885 and Malvern in 1913. Occasionally during the 1880s and '90s he contributed fishing and architectural illustrations to the *I.L.N.*

Examples: City A.G., Manchester; Salisbury Mus.

BOUGH, Samuel, R.S.A., R.S.W.
1822 (Carlisle) - 1878 (Edinburgh)
A landscape painter who was briefly placed with T. Allom (q.v.) in London to learn engraving. He soon returned to Carlisle and led a wandering life until 1845 when he went to the Theatre Royal, Manchester, as a scene painter. He exhibited at the Royal Manchester Institution, and in Liverpool and Worcester. In

BOUGH, Samuel (1822-1878)
A Royal or Ceremonial Barge approaching a Riverside Castle. *Signed and dated 1878, pencil and watercolour, with touches of bodycolour, 22in. x 33in.*

BOUGH, Samuel (1822-1878)
Highland Landscape. *Pencil and watercolour, 8½in. x 13¼in.*

1848 he moved to the Princess Theatre, Glasgow, and in 1849 to the Adelphi Theatre, Edinburgh. After a quarrel with the manager, he gave up scene painting, and moved to Hamilton for a few years where he practised as a professional landscape painter. He was elected A.R.S.A. in 1856 but did not become a full member until 1875. At this time his work was increasingly sought after, and he became a well established Edinburgh character. Although he travelled widely about Great Britain, his favourite sketching areas were the coasts of the Firth of Forth and Fifeshire. His most typical work is very like that of Cox's late period, although his colours are often thinly painted by comparison. They become fuller, and later he uses bodycolour. His pictures are generally

signed and often dated, but '1857' should always be treated with suspicion since he used this date twenty years later on the grounds that it was said to be 'my best period'.

His brother, **James Walter BOUGH (1828 Carlisle - 1859 Preston)** was also a painter and followed him to Glasgow. However, he was mugged in Manchester and died insane as a result.

Illustrated: R.L. Stevenson: *Edinburgh Picturesque Notes*, 1879.
Examples: B.M.; V.A.M.; Aberdeen A.G.; Dundee City A.G.; Fitzwilliam; Glasgow A.G.; Greenock A.G.; Kirkcaldy A.G.; City A.G., Manchester; Paisley A.G.; N.G., Scotland; Ulster Mus.
Bibliography: S. Gilpin: *S.B.*, 1905. R. Walker: *S.B. and George Chalmers. A.J.*, 1871. *W&D*, 1988, i.

BOUGHTON, George Henry, R.A.
1833 (near Norwich) - 1905 (London)
The son of a farmer, his family emigrated to America in 1839. He returned to Britain for some months in 1853, visiting London, Ireland, Scotland and the Lake District. He then lived and painted landscapes in New York until 1859, when he went to Paris to study. He settled in London permanently in 1861 or 1862 and exhibited at the R.A. from the following year. He visited Norfolk in 1890, Scotland in 1892 and Paris in about 1895, and for a period of some twenty years he was a regular visitor to the Isle of Wight. He was elected A.R.A. in 1879 and R.A. in 1896, and was a member of the R.I. from 1879 to 1885. His early work shows the influence of F. Walker (q.v.), but he

can be oversugared. He was also an illustrator.

His remaining works were sold at Christie's, 15 June 1908.

Examples: V.A.M.; Ashmolean.

Bibliography: *Portfolio*, 1871. *A.J.*, 1899; *Christmas Annual*, 1904.

BOULGER, Thomas

He studied at the R.D.S. Schools, after which he set himself up in Dublin as a painter of portraits, flowers and miniatures, and gave drawing lessons. He exhibited with the Dublin Society of Artists in 1769. In 1788 he was teaching drawing and painting in a school at Portarlington.

BOULTON, Edward Baker
1812 - 1895

A landscape painter who spent a number of years from 1836 in New South Wales as a sheep farmer. On his return to England he settled in Shropshire. He had eighteen children, and Arthur Ransome was a grandson.

BOURNE, Rev. James
1773 (Dalby, Lincolnshire) - 1854 (Sutton Coldfield)

A drawing master who was educated in Louth and who came to London in 1789, where for eighteen months he tried to find employment before moving to Manchester. On his return to London in about 1796 he was taken on by Lord Spencer and the Duchess of Sutherland (q.v.), through whom he may have met Girtin and Turner, and also Sir G. Beaumont (q.v.) with whom he toured Wales in 1800. He first exhibited at the R.A. in that year, and he made regular summer tours, visiting the Lakes in 1789, the West Country in 1799, Lincolnshire in the autumn of 1803, Yorkshire, Surrey and Kent. In 1838 he gave up his profession for the Church, and he left London in 1846.

His style should be unmistakable, but often seems to be mistaken for that of better men. His work is usually in monochrome and is clumsy and without crispness of outline. His habit of using black hatching to indicate the foliage and the details of his foregrounds has a distant kinship with that of Glover.

He was much imitated, not least by his three daughters, **Edmunda BOURNE** (b.1820); **Henrietta** (or **Harriet**) **P. BOURNE**; and **Elizabeth BOURNE (fl.1819-1870).**

Published: *Interesting Views of the Lakes of Cumberland, Westmoreland and Lancashire,* privately printed c.1796, with watercolour illustrations. *A Selection of Views in the County of Lincoln*, 1801.

Examples: B.M.; V.A.M.; City A.G., Birmingham; Brighton A.G.; Dudley A.G.; Fitzwilliam; Hertford Co. Record Office; Hertford Mus.; Hove Lib.; Leeds City A.G.; City A.G., Manchester; Nat. Mus. Wales; Newport A.G.; Glynn Vivian A.G., Swansea; York A.G.

Bibliography: *Connoisseur*, CLXIII, 1966.

BOURNE, Rev. James (1773-1854)
The Ouse Bridge, York. *Signed, inscribed and with address on the reverse, pencil and watercolour, 11¼in. x 15¼in.*

BOURNE, John Cooke
1814 - 1896

A landscape and topographical painter who stood unsuccessfully for the N.W.S. three times between 1866 and 1877. He specialised in railways, especially the Great Western Railway, and was patronised by the Duke and Duchess of Bedford. He lived in London.

Examples: B.M.

Bibliography: *Scotsman*, 18 May 1968.

BOURNE, Samuel
1839 (Totnes) - 1920

An amateur landscape painter who painted in many parts of Britain, as well as on the Continent and in India. He lived in Wapping for a time and exhibited from 1880 to 1898.

Examples: Castle Mus., Nottingham.

BOURNE, John Cooke (1814-1896)
The Smolny Convent and Institute on the Neva, St. Petersburg. *Signed and inscribed on a label, pencil, water and bodycolour, 13in. x 19¾in.*

BOUVIER, Auguste Jules (1824/5-1881)
'Summer.' *Watercolour over traces of pencil, heightened with touches of bodycolour, signed and dated 1864, 10¼in. x 8½in.*

BOUVIER, Agnes Rose, Mrs. Nicholl
1842 (London) - c.1892
The fifth of the six children of Jules Bouvier (q.v.), who taught her. The family spent much time in Germany, Holland and France until the death of her brother James in 1856, when they settled permanently in London. She exhibited a genre subject at Birmingham in 1860. Until the death of her father, for whom she kept house, she exhibited little, but thereafter she was very active, and in 1868 she visited Germany and Venice. In 1874 she married Samuel James Nicholl, an architect. Her favourite subjects were country girls and children.

BOUVIER, Auguste Jules, N.W.S.
1824/5 (London) - 1881 (London)
A son of Jules Bouvier (q.v.), he studied at the R.A. Schools from April 1841, when he was aged seventeen, and in France and Italy. He exhibited in London from 1845, and was elected A.N.W.S. and N.W.S. in 1852 and 1865. He painted portraits and genre subjects in oil and watercolour.
Examples: V.A.M.; Brighton A.G.; Shipley A.G., Gateshead; Maidstone Mus.
Bibliography: *A.J.*, 1881.

BOUVIER, Gustavus Arthur
1844 -
A son of Jules Bouvier (q.v.), he lived in London and painted genre subjects. He exhibited from 1866, the year that he entered the R.A. Schools aged fifteen, to 1884. He translated French books on pastel and enamel painting.

BOUVIER, Joseph Anthony
1826/7 -
Another son of Jules Bouvier (q.v.), he was working in London from 1839 to 1888. In April 1842, aged fifteen, he entered the R.A. Schools. He lived in St. John's Wood and was an unsuccessful candidate for the N.W.S. in 1868. He painted pretty children in oil and watercolour.
Published: *A Handbook for Oil-Painting*, 1885.

BOUVIER, Jules Auguste M Urbain
1800 (Paris) - 1867 (London)
The father of A.R. Bouvier (q.v.), A.J. Bouvier (q.v.), G.A. Bouvier (q.v.), J.A. Bouvier (q.v.) and also of the artists **Julia BOUVIER** and **James Urbain BOUVIER (1831-1856),** who entered the R.A. Schools in 1846. He came to England in 1818 and married a Scotswoman. Thereafter he divided his time between London and the Continent until 1856, when he settled permanently in London. He painted genre subjects and exhibited from 1845 to 1865.
Examples: V.A.M.

BOWDITCH, Sarah, Mrs., later LEE, née Wallis 1791 (Colchester) - 1856 (Erith)
An original and talented painter of fish who used very mixed media including gold and silver with watercolour. The first edition of her *Fresh-Water Fishes* was issued in only 50 copies each illustrated with forty-four original watercolours. She wrote that 'every drawing has been taken from the living fish immediately it came from the water it inhabited.' She was the wife and editor of T.E. Bowditch (1791-1824), the African traveller. In 1814 she tried to join him at Cape Coast Castle, but they missed each other. Subsequently they remained in Africa until 1818, and then they spent about three years in Paris, studying

BOWDITCH, Sarah, Mrs., née Wallis (1791-1856)
A Chub. *Water and bodycolour, further heightened with gum arabic and gold and silver paint, 10¼in. x 13¼in.*

106

Baron Cuvier's collections. In 1822 they travelled to Lisbon, Madeira and the Gambia, where Bowditch died. After her second marriage she became a popular writer and illustrator of scientific works for the young, which she published as Mrs. R(obert) Lee.
Published: *Taxidermy*, 1820. *Narrative of the Voyage &c.*, 1825. *Fresh-Water Fishes of Great Britain*, 1828. &c.
Bibliography: *Gentleman's Mag.*, 1856, ii. *Edinburgh Rev.*, lxii, 1856. *The Field*, 31 Dec. 1887.
Examples: Ashmolean.

BOWEN, Owen   1873 (Leeds) - 1967
A designer, teacher and still-life painter who studied at the Leeds School of Art in 1885 under Gilbert Foster, at whose private school he subsequently taught. As a result of a long illness he gave up teaching and turned to painting still lifes and, later, landscapes in oil and watercolour. He exhibited at Leeds from 1890 and at the R.A. from 1892.
Examples: Leeds City A.G.

**BOWERS, Georgina
**   **1836 (London) - 1912**
The daughter of the Dean of Manchester, she was a caricaturist who copied J. Leech (q.v.) and worked in his style. Despite the discouragement of governesses she drew animals from an early age, and on escape from schooling she studied briefly at the Manchester School of Art. Soon after she began to draw for *Punch*, the *Graphic* and the *Illustrated Sporting and Dramatic News*. She exhibited with the Society of Female Artists in 1862. Between 1862 and 1889, she wrote and illustrated a number of sporting and country books. On marrying she became Mrs. Bowers-Edwards.

BOWERS, Stephen J
A landscape and figure painter who lived at Kew and exhibited at the R.I. and the R.B.A. from 1874 to 1891.

BOWKETT family – *see* **Stuart, C.**

**BOWLER, Henry Alexander
**   **1824 (Kensington) - 1903 (London)**
A landscape and genre painter who studied at Leigh's and the Government School of Design at Somerset House. He was Headmaster of Stourbridge School of Art in 1851, and subsequently taught at Somerset House and worked for the Science and Art Department from 1855 to 1891, from 1876 as Assistant Director. He was Teacher of Perspective at the R.A. from 1861 to 1899, and he exhibited from 1847.
   His wife, **Ellen Anne BOWLER,** painted landscapes.
Examples: V.A.M.
Bibliography: *A.J.*, 1908.

**BOWLES, Oldfield, F.S.A.
**   **1739   - 1810 (Testwood, Southampton)**
A 'most accomplished country Squire' and

BOWERS, Stephen J.
A Country Lane. *Signed, watercolour, 4in. x 6½in.*

enthusiastic amateur painter. He was probably at Eton 1753-1758, and went up to Queen's College, Oxford, in the latter year. An obituary calls him 'The Patron and example of excellence in the Fine Arts, and equally distinguished by his amiable qualities in civil and domestic life'. Through Thomas Price, Wilson's pupil, who stayed with him at North Aston, Oxfordshire, he became a close follower of the master. He was also an amateur actor, and a leading light of the convivial

Society of St. Peter Martyr, whose other members were his son **Charles Oldfield BOWLES (1785-1862),** a marine artist and, like his father, a colonel of militia, A. Phipps, Sir G.H. Beaumont, B. West, J. Farington, G. Dance and T. Hearne (qq.v.). He was also a patron of J.B. Malchair (q.v.) and a member of his circle. Several of his descendants inherited his enthusiasms.
Bibliography: See Farington's *Diaries*.
See Bowles Family Tree

BOWLES, Charles Oldfield (1785-1862)
Royal Yacht George at Holyhead Aug. 10. 1821. *Inscribed, watercolour, 8⅜in. x 12¾in.*

BOYCE, William Thomas Nicholas (1858-1911)
'Running for Home.' *Watercolour, signed and dated 1909, 24in. x 33½in.*

BOWYER, Robert
1758   - 1834 (Byfleet, Surrey)
Possibly a pupil of John Smart, he was appointed Painter in Water Colours to George III and Miniature Painter to the Queen. He exhibited at the R.A. from 1783 to 1828.
Illustrated: D. Hume: *History of England*, 1800.
Examples: B.M.

BOX, Alfred Ashdown
(Manningtree) - ?1927
A landscape painter who was educated and worked in Birmingham. He was an organist at St. Thomas's Church there. He exhibited in Birmingham and Manchester from 1879 to 1910. He signed 'A. Ashdown Box', presumably to differentiate himself from another landscape painter, **Alfred BOX**, who may have been a relative and was working in Herefordshire in 1881.

BOXALL, Sir William, R.A., F.R.S.
1800 (Oxford) - 1879 (London)
A painter of portraits and religious subjects in oil and watercolour who entered the R.A. Schools in 1819. He was in Italy for about two years from 1827 and was elected A.R.A. and R.A. in 1852 and 1863, retiring in 1877. He was appointed Director of the N.G. in 1865, when he gave up his successful portrait practice. He was knighted in 1871.

His work in watercolour can be free in the best manner of J. Absolon (q.v.). His remaining works were sold at Christie's, 8 June 1880.
Examples: Ashmolean.
Bibliography: *A.J.*, 1880.

BOYCE, George Price, R.W.S.
1826 (London) - 1897 (London)
An artist who was closely linked with the Pre-Raphaelites. He was trained as an architect, entering the R.A. Schools in 1848, but after meeting Cox in the following year he abandoned this career and took up painting, having independent means to support himself. He was always drawn to architectural subjects, which he executed with an exactitude which shows the influence of his Pre-Raphaelite friends. He exhibited at the R.A. between 1853 and 1861 and, in 1864, he was elected A.O.W.S., becoming a full Member in 1877. The diary which he kept between 1851 and 1875, and which was published by the O.W.S. in 1941, provides many valuable insights into the workings of the Pre-Raphaelite group.

The correctness of his style is saved from pedantry by the mellow, harmonious colours he used, of which a favourite was plummy red. He was a friend of J.W. North (q.v.), and their work is similar.
Examples: B.M.; V.A.M.; Ashmolean; Fitzwilliam; N.G. Scotland; Stalybridge A.G.
Bibliography: *Architectural Review*, 1899. O.W.S. Club, XIX, 1941 (Diary). Tate Gall., Exhibition Cat., 1987. *W&D*, 1987, iii.
See Colour Plate

BOYCE, William Thomas Nicholas
1858 (Blakeney) - 1911
The son of a shipowner who took his family to South Shields, he worked as a draper before turning professional artist. Much of his life was spent in Durham and his subjects are generally marine.

Three of his sons, out of thirteen children, **Herbert Walter BOYCE (1883-1946)**, **Albert Ernest BOYCE (1886-1952)** and **Norman Septimus BOYCE (1895-1962)**, were also marine and landscape watercolourists.
Examples: Laing A.G., Newcastle; South Shields Pub. Lib. and Mus.; Sunderland A.G.

BOYD, Alexander Stuart, R.S.W.
1854 (Glasgow) - 1930 (New Zealand)
An illustrator and painter of street scenes. He worked for *Punch*, the *Graphic*, and other magazines, and exhibited at the R.A. and the R.I. from 1884 to 1887. He emigrated to New Zealand in 1914. He used the pseudonym 'Twym'.
Published: *Glasgow Men and Women*, 1905.
Illustrated: C. Blatherwick: *Peter Stonnor*, 1884.
Examples: Glasgow A.G.

BOYD, Alice 1825 (Penkill) - 1897 (Penkill)
A landscape and subject painter in oil and watercolour who inherited a love of sketching from her mother. For a time she lived in Newcastle where she was encouraged by W.B. Scott (q.v.), and in 1865 she retired to Penkill Castle, Ayrshire, which she decorated.

She exhibited at the R.S.A., the R.A., the Dudley Gallery and elsewhere.
Published: *Robin's Christmas Song*.
Examples: Ayr Lib.; Penkill Cas.

BOYD, Edward Fenwick
1810 (Newcastle) - 1889 (Leamside, Durham)
The son of a banker he was educated locally and at Edinburgh University before becoming a mining engineer. He was an acquaintance of T. Bewick (q.v.) and of E. Swinburne (q.v.), who persuaded his father to let him have lessons from T.M. Richardson (q.v.). He was an enthusiastic sketcher of Northumbrian views.

BOYD, Dr. Michael Austin
- 1899
A doctor who lived in Kingstown and Dublin, and painted landscapes. He was a frequent exhibitor with the Watercolour Society of Ireland.

BOYD, Walter Scott c.1858 -
A Glasgow artist who moved to England in the 1880s, and then to Dolgelly in about 1899. He exhibited at the R.A. four times, and also showed a view of Smethwick at the Birmingham Society in 1881.

BOYLE, Rear-Admiral Courtney Edmund
William   1800   - 1859
Son of a vice-admiral and nephew of the 8th Earl of Cork, he was a pupil of H. Bright (q.v.), as was his cousin Lord Dungarvan (q.v.). He was promoted captain in 1830.
Examples: Nat. Army Mus.

BOYLE, Hon. Mrs. Eleanor Vere
1825 (Auchlunies, Kincardine) - 1916 (Brighton)

The youngest daughter of Alexander Gordon of Ellon, she married the Hon. and Rev. Richard Boyle, Rector of Marston Bigott, Somerset, in 1845. She had no formal training, but was encouraged and advised by Boxall and Eastlake, and from 1851 she published a long series of children's books under the initials 'E.V.B.'.

Her style is reminiscent of that of C. Green and Sir J. Gilbert (qq.v.).

Published: *Child's Play,* 1851. *A Children's Summer,* 1852. &c.

BOYLE, James
1872 (Stockport) - 1935

A talented amateur landscape painter. His family moved to Perth, where he studied art before becoming manager of Pullars of Perth. He was a member of the local art club and taught evening classes. He exhibited local views from about 1904.

BOYNE, John
1750 (Co. Down) - 1810 (London)

A caricaturist who was taken to London at the age of nine by his father, a joiner, and apprenticed to the engraver William Byrne. He left to join a company of strolling players, returning in 1781. Thereafter he set up a drawing school, but he was too lazy to make a great success of it. He worked, rather weakly, in the manner of Rowlandson.

Examples: B.M.; V.A.M.; Fitzwilliam.

BOYS, Thomas Shotter, N.W.S.
1803 (Pentonville) - 1874 (London)

In 1817 Boys was apprenticed to George Cooke, the engraver and father of E.W. Cooke (q.v.). In 1823, on the expiry of his indentures, he went to Paris where he worked, first as an engraver, then as a lithographer and water-colourist, in close contact with Bonington. His pupils in Paris included W. Callow (q.v.) and A. Poynter (q.v.). He returned to London in 1837 and continued his lithographic work, being the virtual inventor of chromo-lithography. He was elected A.N.W.S. and N.W.S. in 1840 and 1841, but hardly attended a meeting for the next three years in consequence of a 'domestic affliction'. In 1847 he joined W. Oliver (q.v.) in his criticism of the Society, afterwards becoming a most assiduous member. Despite the brilliance of his watercolours and the fame of his lithographs, Boys' career faded away after the early 1840s. He found new subjects in Germany, North Wales and the West Midlands, but was also scraping work for architects and tinting backgrounds for lesser men. By 1871 illness rendered him utterly 'inable' to work.

He was primarily an architectural painter, admiring only Girtin of his predecessors. The accuracy of his portraits of buildings and his

BOYLE, Hon. Mrs. Eleanor Vere (1825-1916)
The Sunbeam stole in to kiss him. *Pencil and watercolour heightened with white, 6in. x 5¼in.*

BOYNE, John (1750-1810)
The Country Chronicle – a Scene in the Hen and Chickens, 1808. *Signed, inscribed and with address on the original backing, watercolour, 22¾in. x 28¾in.*

BOYS, Thomas Shotter (1803-1874)
Calais Harbour. *Pencil and watercolour, 3⅞in. x 9⅞in.*

BOYS, Thomas Shotter (1803-1874)
The Duke's Bedroom at Apsley House. *Signed and dated 1852, pencil and watercolour, 12¼in. x 16⅞in.*

BRABAZON, Hercules Brabazon (1821-1906)
Crossing the Desert. *Signed with initials, pencil, water and bodycolour, 7in. x 9½in.*

skill in composition have seldom been bettered. In his French years he used all the tricks that distinguish the Bonington circle, thumb prints, scraping and so on. He also produced a group of watercolours following Bonington's costume pieces, which feature Watteau-like figures at Versailles. Later he turned to landscapes without buildings, and in the striking colour and power of his studio works showed himself to be a major High Victorian watercolourist.

Published: *Picturesque Architecture in Paris, Ghent, Antwerp, Rouen, &c.,* 1839. *Original Views of London as it is,* 1842.

Examples: B.M.; V.A.M.; Aberdeen A.G.; Ashmolean; Cecil Higgins A.G., Bedford; Brighton A.G.; Grosvenor Mus., Chester; Fitzwilliam; Leeds City A.G.; Walker A.G., Liverpool; Laing A.G., Newcastle; Newport A.G.; Castle Mus., Nottingham; Shrewsbury Mus.; Tate Gall.; Ulster Mus.

Bibliography: E. Beresford Chancellor: *Original Views of London &c.,* 1926. E. Beresford Chancellor: *Picturesque Architecture in Paris &c.,* 1928. J. Roundell: *T.S.B.,* 1974. *Connoisseur* LX, 1921. *Walker's Quarterly,* XVIII, 1926. *Architectural Review,* LX, 1926.

See Colour Plate

BRABAZON, Hercules Brabazon, né Sharpe   1821 (Paris) - 1906 (Oaklands)
The second son of Hercules Sharpe, he was educated at Harrow, Geneva and Cambridge. On leaving Cambridge, where he read mathematics, he determined to become an artist and spent three years in Rome, studying under J. D'Egville (q.v.) in 1847 and later under A.D. Fripp (q.v.). On the death of his elder brother, he inherited the Brabazon estates (and name) in Ireland and in 1858, on the death of his father, Oaklands, Sussex, and lands in Durham. In Ireland he was an absentee, and in England a vicarious landlord, leaving the estate management to his brother-in-law and nephew. He spent his summers in England and winters in France, Spain, Italy or Germany; after 1867 he included North Africa and the Nile on his itineraries, and in 1870 he went to India. It was not until 1891 that this consummate amateur became known to a wide public. In that year he was elected to the N.E.A.C., and in the following December he was unwillingly persuaded by Sargent and other artists to allow a Brabazon Exhibition to be mounted at the Goupil Gallery. In old age he found himself, as a result, at the forefront of the modern movement. His last three years were largely spent at Oaklands, going through his portfolios and signing his works.

He was most influenced by Turner, Cox, Müller and de Wint among his predecessors, and by Velasquez among oil painters. The essences of his style are simplicity and a mastery of colour. He is the continuer of Turner's late 'impressionist' period, concerned with the feel of a place rather than a topographical exactitude. He was a musician as well as an artist, and his career has been summed up by Sir Frederick Wedmore as 'A country gentleman who at seventy years old made his debut as a professional artist and straightway become famous'.

An exhibition of his work was held at Leighton House in 1971.

Examples: Oaklands, Sedlescombe, near Battle, Sussex; B.M.; V.A.M.; Ashmolean; Cecil Higgins A.G., Bedford; Cartwright Hall, Bradford; Brighton A.G.; Towner Gall., Eastbourne; Fitzwilliam; Hove Lib.; Leeds City A.G.; Leicestershire A.G.; City A.G., Manchester; Newport A.G.; Nottingham Univ.; N.G., Scotland.

Bibliography: Mrs. H.T. Combe: *Notes on the Life of H.B.B.*, 1910. D.S. MacColl: *The Study of B.*, 1910. Sir F. Wedmore: *H.B.B.*, 1910. C. Lewis Hind: *H.B.B.*, 1912. *Studio*, XXXV, 1905. *A.J.*, 1906. *Antique Collector*, Oct. 1962; March 1974. Chris Beetles Gall., London, Exhibition Cat., 1989.

See Colour Plate

BRACEBRIDGE, Selina, 'Sigma', Mrs., née Mills
1797 (Bisterne, Hants) - 1874

The youngest daughter of William Mills, M.P. of Bisterne, she was the favourite pupil of S. Prout (q.v.). In 1824 she married Charles Bracebridge (d.1872) of Atherstone Hall, Coventry, and they went to Italy and Germany . They made their first visit to the Near East in 1833, and were in Sweden in 1840 and the Pyrenees in 1842. From 1846 they were friends and supporters of Florence Nightingale, whom they took to Italy in 1847 and Egypt and Greece in 1849-50. They then accompanied her to Scutari in 1854-5. Mrs. Bracebridge's work is sometimes reminiscent of that of E. Lear (q.v.), and at others that of W. Page (q.v.). Her nephew was the 1st Lord Hillingdon.

Published: *Panoramic Sketch of Athens*, 1836

'BRADDON, Paul'

The *nom de plume* of James Leslie Crees who spent a considerable part of his life in the neighbourhood of Hull, where he made large watercolour copies of old prints. He also made a number of drawings of cathedrals. His colour and his subject matter show the influence of Paul Marny (q.v.), the French watercolourist.

Examples: V.A.M.; Birmingham Lib.; Doncaster A.G.; Ferens Gall. and Central Lib., Hull; Leeds City A.G.; Johnson Birthplace Mus., Lichfield.

Published: *Nooks, Corners and Crannies of Old Birmingham*, 1893.

BRADFORD, Louis King, A.R.H.A.
1807 (Dublin) - 1862 (Dublin)

He entered the R.D.S. Schools in 1824 and first exhibited at the R.H.A. in 1827. He exhibited at the S.B.A. in 1854, and was elected A.R.H.A. in 1855. Until 1838 his work consisted entirely of landscapes in oil and watercolour, but after this date he also painted genre and literary subjects.

BRADFORD, Rev. William (1780/1-1857)
Pass near Villa Franca. *Pen and black ink and watercolour, 7¾in. x 11⅝in.*

BRADFORD, Rev. William
1780/1 - 1857

A Chaplain of Brigade to the British army in the Peninsula 1808-9. He had been educated at St. John's College, Oxford, and in 1811 the Duke of Norfolk presented him to the living of Storrington, Sussex. He was also Chaplain in Ordinary to the King, and later to the Queen. His Iberian watercolours are weakly in the Sandby tradition, but they are still pleasing, and interesting as the account of an eyewitness.

Published: *Sketches... in Portugal and Spain...*, 1809.
Examples: Nat. Army Mus.

BRADLEY, Basil, R.W.S.
1842 (Hampstead) - 1904 (Hampstead)

A landscape, genre and sporting painter who studied at the Manchester School of Art. He exhibited, mostly at the O.W.S., from 1866 and was elected Associate and Member in 1867 and 1881. He visited New South Wales. He was a son of W. Bradley (q.v.).

Examples: B.M.; Haworth A.G., Accrington; City A.G., Manchester; Sydney A.G.

BRADLEY, Rev. Edward
1827 (Kidderminster) - 1889 (Lavington, near Grantham)

Humorist, author and illustrator, he was educated at University College, Durham, and ordained deacon in 1850. He was curate of Glatton, Huntingdonshire from 1850 to 1854;

BRADLEY, Basil (1842-1904)
Milking. *Signed, pen and watercolour heightened with white, 24in. x 44in.*

Leigh, Worcestershire from 1854 to 1857; Bubbington, Staffordshire from 1857 to 1859; he was rector or Vicar of Denton, near Peterborough from 1859 to 1871; Stretton, near Oakham from 1871 to 1883, and Lavington (or Lenton) from 1883. His best known work, with his own illustrations, was *The Adventures of Mr. Verdant Green, an Oxford Freshman*, 1853-6. As well as illustrations, he painted watercolours of his churches, which can be a little dull. They are signed with his *nom de plume*, 'Cuthbert Bede'.

Confusingly his son, **Cuthbert Edward BRADLEY (1861-1943)**, painted sporting subjects. He was self taught, and lived in Lincolnshire, having married Lucy Heathcote of Folkingham in 1895.

Examples: B.M.; Brighton A.G.

BRADLEY, Gordon
A member of the N.W.S. in 1834, he lived in London and exhibited at the R.A. and elsewhere from 1832. He may have taught drawing at Eton around 1840, but by 1846 he had forfeited his membership of the N.W.S. and was bankrupt.

BRADLEY, John Henry
1832 (Hagley, Worcestershire) -
A landscape and coastal painter, he was a pupil of D. Cox (q.v.) and J. Holland (q.v.). He lived in Leamington and London and, in 1869, in Florence. He exhibited in London and on the Continent from 1854, and was an unsuccessful candidate for the N.W.S. on several occasions from 1865 to 1879. He exhibited in Birmingham until 1896.

BRADLEY, Mary
A flower painter who exhibited at the R.A. in 1811.
Examples: V.A.M.

BRADLEY, Robert
1813 (Nottingham) - c.1880
He was for many years landlord of the 'Lord Belper', Nottingham. He painted local scenes in oil and watercolour until his intemperate habits brought his artistic career, and shortly afterwards his life, to an untimely end.
Examples: Derby A.G.; Castle Mus. Nottingham.

BRADLEY, William
1801 (Manchester) - 1857 (Manchester)
An errand boy who, at the age of sixteen, set up in a Manchester warehouse as a 'portrait, miniature and animal painter and teacher of drawing'. He was largely self taught, with advice from Mather Brown. He came to London in 1823, and first exhibited in that year with the encouragement of Lawrence. In 1833 he revisited Manchester and worked in the studio of C. Calvert (q.v.), whose daughter he married. He returned finally to Manchester in 1847, but by this time he was in poor health.

BRANDARD, Robert (1805-1862)
A Duckpond by a Farm. *Signed, watercolour, 11in. x 16in.*

BRANDARD, Robert (1805-1862)
Selling Fish and Oysters in Drury Lane. *Signed and dated 1830, pencil and watercolour heightened with white, 12¼in. x 8⅝in.*

William BRADLEY, Yr., who lived in London and at Maidenhead, exhibited landscapes, river scenes and flowers from 1872 to 1889, was his son, as was B. Bradley (q.v.).
Examples: B.M.; City A.G., Manchester; Sydney A.G.
Bibliography: A.J., 1857.

BRAGG, Edward 1785 - 1875
There are views of Battersea in the V.A.M. by this artist.

BRAGG, John

A Birmingham coastal and landscape painter who was active between 1880 and 1889.

He was presumably related to the figure painter Henry BRAGG who was working in Birmingham in 1814, and to the figure, portrait and genre painter **Charles William BRAGG** who exhibited there and in London from 1852 to 1887.

BRANDARD, Edward Paxman
1819 - 1898

The brother of R. Brandard (q.v.), he was an engraver and collaborated with Queen Victoria (q.v.) on a view of Balmoral. He also painted rustic scenes and biblical subjects.

BRANDARD, Robert
1805 (Birmingham) - 1862 (London)

He came to London in 1824 and studied engraving under Edward Goodall for a year before turning professional. Although primarily an engraver, working on such publications as Turner's *Picturesque Views in England and Wales,* 1838, he painted watercolours, and was an occasional exhibitor at the R.A. and the N.W.S. and elsewhere. His drawing is good, as is to be expected, but his colour can be overdone and his compositions rather awkward.

Examples: B.M.; V.A.M.; Blackburn A.G.; Fitzwilliam.

Bibliography: *A.J.,* Feb.1862.

BRANDLING, Henry Charles
1819 -

He entered the R.A. Schools in 1844, and was elected A.O.W.S. in June 1853. However, he only exhibited six views of Nüremberg, one of Glasgow Cathedral and an historical scene in Durham Cathedral before allowing his associateship to lapse in 1857. He may have exhibited portraits at the R.A. from 1847 to 1850. He lived in London. In 1848 he published a series of lithographic views in Northern France. The watercolours for these are close in style to S. Prout (q.v.).

Illustrated: W.W. Collins: *Rambles beyond Railways,* 1852.

BRANDOIN, Michel Vincent Charles
1733 - 1807

A Swiss artist who worked and taught in England at least from 1768 to 1772, enrolling at the R.A.Schools in 1770. Like S.H. Grimm (q.v.) he forms one of the valuable links between the English and Swiss watercolour schools in the late eighteenth century.

Examples: B.M.; Aberdeen A.G.

Bibliography: Walpole Society, XXIII, 1935.

See Colour Plate

BRANEGAN, John F

Probably an Irishman, he was a landscape painter. He was working in Dublin in 1841, and later visited many parts of the British Isles including the Isle of Man, Rochester, Scotland in 1857 and Norfolk in 1871. He exhibited at the R.A. and Suffolk Street from 1871 to 1875, and at that time lived in London. His drawing is good and his colours are effective.

BRANGWYN, Sir Frank William (1867-1956)
Italian fishermen. *Watercolour, signed with initials.*

BRANGWYN, Sir Frank William (François Guillaume), R.A.
1867 (Bruges) - 1956 (Ditchling)

Painter, designer, etcher, lithographer and watercolourist, in the early part of his career he worked for his friend W. Morris (q.v.) and then went to sea and travelled in Europe, the Near East and South Africa. He exhibited at the R.A. from 1885, and elsewhere, and settled in Hammersmith in 1896. In 1924 he moved to Ditchling, and he was knighted in 1941. The Brangwyn Museum was opened in Bruges in 1936, and a memorial exhibition was held at the Fine Art Society in 1958.

He was much influenced by the Newlyn School in his early days, and was at the centre of the Art Nouveau movement. His watercolours emerge from greyness to full colour in the course of his career.

Examples: B.M.; Aberdeen A.G.; Blackburn A.G.; Brighton A.G.; Bruges; Darlington A.G.; Dundee City A.G.; Fitzwilliam; Glasgow A.G.; Harrogate Mus.; Leeds City A.G.; Maidstone Mus.; Newport A.G.

Bibliography: P. Macer-Wright: *B a Study of Genius.* V. Galloway: *Oils and Murals of B.* W. Shaw-Sparrow: *F.B. and His Work,* 1910. H. Furst: *The Decorative Art of F.B.,* 1924. *A.J.,* 1903, *Studio,* 1924; 1928. *Apollo,* XLI, 1945. *Country Life,* 24 Oct. 1952. O.W.S. Club, XLIII, 1968.

BRANWHITE, Charles, A.O.W.S.
1817 (Bristol) - 1880 (Westfield Park, Clifton)

The second son of N.C. Branwhite (q.v.), he began his career as a sculptor and as a painter in oil, and was a pupil of his father and of W.J. Müller (q.v.). It was he who carved Müller's memorial in Bristol Cathedral. He was elected A.O.W.S. in 1849 and was a regular exhibitor for the rest of his life. He remained in Bristol throughout his life and was a close friend of his fellow townsmen F. Danby and S.P. Jackson (qq.v.). He sketched well in watercolour, but 'was so lavish in the use of bodycolour that many of his drawings may be regarded as works in distemper' (Roget). Some of his best landscapes suggest his passion for fishing. He was the father of C.B. Branwhite (q.v.)

His remaining works were sold at Christie's, 15 April 1882.

Examples: B.M.; V.A.M.; Bristol City A.G.
Bibliography: *A.J.,* 1880.

BRANWHITE, Charles Brooke
1851 (Bristol) - 1929 (Bristol)

The son of C. Branwhite (q.v.) under whom he studied before going to South Kensington. He lived in Bristol and painted West Country landscapes in oil and watercolour

BREE, Rev. William Thomas (1754-1822)
Maxstoke Priory, Warwickshire. *Watercolour heightened with gum arabic, 10in. x 14in.*

BREE, Rev. William Thomas (1754-1822)
Maxstoke Priory, Warwickshire. *Watercolour heightened with gum arabic, 10in. x 14in.*

BRANWHITE, Nathan Cooper
1775 (Lavenham, Suffolk) - 1857 (Bristol)
The father of C. Branwhite (q.v.), R. Müller (q.v.), and the portrait painter and engraver **Nathan BRANWHITE (1813-1894)**, he painted miniatures and watercolour portraits, and he exhibited at the R.A. from 1802 to 1828. He was the son of Peregrine Branwhite of Lavenham, Suffolk, a friend of Gainsborough.

BRAY, Lieutenant Gabriel
1750 - 1823 (Charmouth, Devon)
An amateur topographer and marine painter who lived in Deal during the second half of the eighteenth century. A view of the fleet at Portsmouth painted by him in 1773 was presented to George III. In the same year he was commissioned as a naval lieutenant. He served first on the *Pallas*, making two voyages to West Africa and Jamaica, 1775-6, and later on the *Sprightly* (1779) and *Nimble* (1782) cutters. His *Pallas* album at Greenwich shows him to be a good on-the-spot man, influenced by P. Sandby (q.v.), presumably through J. Cleveley, Yr. (q.v.). His caricature work is like early J. Nixon (q.v.).
Examples: B.M.; V.A.M.; Greenwich.
Bibliography: *The Mariner's Mirror*, LXXXI, i, 1995.

BRAY, Joel   1787   - 1846 (Chelsea)
A London surveyor who was President of the Surveyors' Club in 1835. In the 1820s he produced a volume of watercolour designs for villas, some of which he marked as built, presumably as a pattern book. They are competent and pleasing examples of their kind.

BREANSKI *see* De Breanski

BREE, Rev. William Thomas
1754   - 1822
The rector of Allesley, near Packington Park, the seat of Lord Aylesford (q.v.), by whom he was clearly influenced. His accomplished watercolours, usually in low tones of grey and green, also show slight influences of Grimm, Rooker and Nattes. He is particularly good at rendering the stonework of his buildings.
Published: *The Plain Reader's Help in the Study of the Holy Scriptures,* 1821.
Examples: B.M.; Coventry A.G.

BRENAN, John
c.1796 (Fethard, Co. Tipperary) - 1865
He entered the R.D.S. Schools in 1813, after which he worked first as a heraldic and later as a landscape painter in Cork. He exhibited at the R.H.A. between 1826 and 1864, and his views are taken from Cork and the South. He gave D. Maclise (q.v.) some of his first lessons in drawing.
His son, **James Butler BRENAN, R.H.A. (1825-1889)**, was a portrait painter in Cork. Another son, **John J. BRENAN**, trained in London, after which he returned to Cork and spent his time painting in the backgrounds to his brother's portraits.

BRENNAN, Michael George
1839 (Castlebar) - 1871 (Algiers)
A landscape painter who studied at the R.D.S. Schools, the Hibernian Society and then at the R.A. Schools from 1860. He worked in Italy and North Africa as well as Ireland.

BRENTON, Captain Edward Pelham
1774 (Rhode Island) - 1839
The younger brother of Sir J. Brenton (q.v.), he

also painted marine subjects. He entered the Navy in 1788 and was promoted commander in 1802 and captain for his gallantry under the batteries of Martinique in 1808. He went on half-pay in 1813 and devoted much of his time to writing, good causes and also temperance societies.

Published: *Naval History of Great Britain*, 1823. &c.

Examples: Greenwich.

BRENTON, Vice-Admiral Sir Jahleel, Bt.
1770 (Rhode Island) - 1844
The elder son of an American loyalist, under whom he served for two years from 1781 before being educated at Chelsea and in France. He rejoined the Navy in 1787. In 1803 he was forced to surrender the *Minerve* frigate, but was exchanged in 1806. He was tried and acquitted for the loss, and thereafter served in the Mediterranean, most notably in a gallant but misjudged action off Naples in 1810. He was created a baronet in 1812. Between 1813 and 1821 he was commissioner for the dockyards at Port Mahon and Cape Town. In 1831 he was appointed Lieutenant-Governor of Greenwich Hospital. He became increasingly religious and published a number of tracts and pamphlets. His watercolour subjects, naturally enough, are mostly naval.

His sister, **Mary BRENTON**, was also a watercolour painter.

Examples: Greenwich.
Bibliography: *Apollo*, CII, 1975.

BRETT, John Edward, A.R.A.
1831 (Bletchingley) - 1902 (Putney)
A landscape and coastal painter, he worked extensively in watercolour in his early years, but almost entirely in oil after 1870. He was a son of an army vet, and was brought up in Dublin and from 1846 in and around Maidstone. In 1851 he was taught by J.D. Harding (q.v.) and soon after encountered the writings of Ruskin. He lived in London and visited Italy for the first time in 1858. On his second visit he stayed in Florence from November 1861 to March 1862, and he also spent the winters of 1862-3, 1863-4 and 1864-5 in Italy. Every summer from the 1860s he took his family to the coast, Cornwall, Wales or Scotland, and he was a keen sailor. He was much influenced by W. Henry Hunt (q.v.) and the Pre-Raphaelites, contributing to their exhibition at Russell Place in 1857. His early work is in the Pre-Raphaelite manner; later it becomes more impressionist in feeling. There is often a strong geographical element. He was described by Ruskin as 'one of my keenest-minded friends' – they quarrelled later – and was elected A.R.A. in 1886. The eccentricity of his domestic arrangements (as his Putney house was one of the first in London to boast central heating, he preferred to paint in the nude) may well have prevented his attainment of the full Academic honour.

BREWER, Henry Charles (1866-1943)
Durham. *Signed and inscribed, watercolour, 19in. x 25in.*

His sister, **Rosa BRETT (1829-1882,)** exhibited fruit, flowers, animals and landscapes at the R.A. from 1858 to 1881.
Examples: Ashmolean; Birmingham City A.G.; Brighton A.G.; Fitzwilliam; Maidstone Mus.; Whitworth Inst., Manchester.
Bibliography: *A.J.*, 1902. *Burlington Mag.*, CXV, Feb. 1973. (Rosa Brett), *Burlington Mag.*, Oct. 1984. N.G. Wales: *Exhibition Cat.*, 2001.

BRETT, Joseph William
An artist who painted views on the Thames in 1830.
Examples: B.M.

BRETT, Admiral Sir Peircy
1709 - 1781 (Beckenham)
The son of a master in the Navy, he served as a volunteer and midshipman and was promoted lieutenant in 1734. He served on Anson's circumnavigation, capturing and painting Paita in Ecuador in 1742, and returned as captain of the *Centurion* in 1744. In the following July he commanded the *Lion* in the action with the French ship *Elisabeth* which proved so damaging to the attempt of the Jacobites. He fought at Finisterre in 1747, and was knighted in 1753 as commander of the Royal yacht. He served on the commission to examine the state of the port of Harwich in 1754, was at Quebec with Anson in 1758-9 and promoted admiral in 1778. He is said to have painted the designs for the porcelain service presented to Anson by the merchants of Canton.
Examples: Greenwich.
Bibliography: *Gentleman's Mag.*, 1781, ii.

BREWER, Henry Charles, R.I.
1866 - 1943
A landscape and architectural painter and engraver who studied at the Westminster School of Art. He exhibited at the R.A. and the R.I. as well as in Australia and New Zealand, and exhibitions of his work were held at the Fine Art Society in 1908 and 1911. He visited Tangier in 1910. He was the son of H.W. Brewer (q.v.), and in 1885 he accompanied his aunt to Germany to illustrate her articles on the toy manufacturers for *The Girl's Own Paper*. He was also a protégé of Mrs. Henry Wood.

BREWER, Henry William
1836 - 1903
A painter in the manner of S. Prout (q.v.), and an illustrator, he was a son of the historian J.S. Brewer. He was educated at Oxford, trained under Hardwick, William Warren and C. Stanfield (q.v.) and lived in London. He exhibited at the R.A. and elsewhere from 1858, and was an unsuccessful candidate for the N.W.S. in 1869. He was a contributor to *The Builder*, the *Graphic* and the *Daily Graphic*, making numerous Continental tours. He sometimes collaborated on illustrations with T.S.C. Crowther.
Illustrated: H.A. Cox: *Old London Illustrated*, 1921.

BREWER, John James
Castle of Grignan (after M.V.C. Brandoin). *Extensively inscribed on the reverse and dated 1793, pen and black ink and watercolour heightened with touches of white, 10⅞in. x 17in.*

BREWER, John
1764 (Madeley, Shropshire) - 1816 (Derby)
A landscape and porcelain painter. In 1795 he moved to Derby to work for Duesbury and, at the same time, gave drawing lessons and kept open studio to potential buyers. His landscapes are of good quality.

His brother, **Robert BREWER (1775 Madeley - 1857 Birmingham)**, came to Derby to join him at the porcelain works, and took over after his death. He painted landscapes in oil and watercolour, and his wife Mary was a miniature painter.
Examples: Derby A.G.

BREWER, John James
A grey wash draughtsman who made copies of the work of M.V.C. Brandoin (q.v.) around 1793.

BREWTNALL, Edward Frederick, R.W.S.
1846   - 1902
A landscape painter in oil and watercolour who exhibited from 1868, and was elected A.R.W.S. and R.W.S. in 1875 and 1883. He was also a member of the S.B.A. from 1882 to 1886.
Examples: V.A.M.; City A.G., Manchester.

BRICKDALE, Eleanor FORTESCUE-, R.W.S.   **1871   - 1945**
An illustrator, designer and painter of genre and historical subjects in oil, chalk and watercolour. She studied at the Crystal Palace School of Art and the R.A. Schools, and exhibited at the R.A. from 1896. She was elected A.R.W.S. and R.W.S. in 1902 and 1919. Her work is a continuation of the Pre-Raphaelite tradition, with its minuteness of detail and jewel-like colours. A loan exhibition was held at Leighton House in 1904.

Her brother, **Sir Charles FORTESCUE-BRICKDALE (1857-1944),** exhibited a landscape at the R.I. in 1887.
Published: *E.F.B.'s Golden Book of Famous Women,* 1919.
Examples: Birmingham City A.G.; Brighton A.G.; Leeds City A.G.
Bibliography: Studio, XIII, 1898; XXIII, 1901. A.J., 1905. Ashmolean, Exhibition Cat., 1972.

BRIDDEN, Rev. John
Eight volumes of topographical watercolours by this artist, mostly of churches, were sold by Sotheby's in 1929. He was working in Gloucestershire, Hampshire, Herefordshire, Hertfordshire, Lancashire and Lincolnshire between 1782 and 1791.
Examples: Co. Record Office, Lincoln.

BRIDELL, Frederick Lee
1831 (Southampton) - 1863
Mainly a portraitist and copyist of old masters, he also painted landscapes, usually Continental. He exhibited at the R.A. from 1851 to 1862. His remaining works were sold at Christie's on 26 February 1864.

His wife, **Eliza Florence BRIDELL-FOX, née Fox (b.1825 Hackney),** exhibited portraits and genre subjects at the R.A. from 1859 to 1871. The majority of both husband and wife's work is in oil. After his death she visited Algiers, and in 1871 she married her cousin George Edward Fox.
Examples: Shipley A.G., Gateshead.
Bibliography: *A.J.,* 1864. *Apollo,* Aug. 1974.

BRIDGES, James 1802   - 1865
A landscape and portrait painter who lived in Oxford. He travelled in Italy, Sicily and Germany and exhibited at the R.A. from 1819 to 1853. He worked in oil and watercolour, and he lived with his brother **John BRIDGES (b.1805),** who painted similar subjects and was active from 1818 to 1854. They both entered the R.A. Schools in 1821, and one of

BREWTNALL, Edward Frederick (1846-1902)
A Christmas Whist Party. *Watercolour, signed and dated 1893, 14in. x 21in.*

them was appointed landscape drawing master at Woolwich from 1838 and superannuated in 1864. James' watercolours show the influence of J. Varley (q.v.), and his figures are generally poor.

Examples: B.M.; Grundy A.G., Blackpool.

BRIDGFORD, Thomas, R.H.A.
1812 (Lancashire) - 1878 (Dublin)
His family moved to Ireland in 1817 and in 1824 he entered the R.D.S. Schools. He first exhibited at the R.H.A. in 1827, and was elected an Associate in 1832. In 1834 he went to London where he practised as a portrait painter. He was a friend of D. Maclise (q.v.), and his work was admired by Thackeray. He returned to Dublin in 1844 and was elected R.H.A. in 1851. He taught drawing at Alexandra College and elsewhere.

As well as painting portraits and genre in oil, he made small, rather stiff, portraits in pencil and watercolour.

Examples: N.G., Ireland; R.H.A.

BRIERLY, Sir Oswald Walters, R.W.S.
1817 (Chester) - 1894 (London)
A marine painter who was the son of a doctor and amateur artist, and who studied at Sass's School and at Plymouth. In 1841 he set out to sail round the world, but settled in Auckland. He then made two surveying cruises on the Australian coast, and returned home in 1851 by way of New Zealand and the Pacific coasts of North and South America. He accompanied the British fleet to the Baltic on the outbreak of the Crimean War in 1854, and then went to the Black Sea. From this time he was a favourite of the Royal Family, accompanying the Duke of Edinburgh to Norway and the Mediterranean as well as round the world in 1867-8. He was with the Prince of Wales in Egypt, Turkey and the Crimea in 1868. He was an A.N.W.S. from 1840 to 1843, and was elected A.R.W.S. in 1872 and a full member in 1890. He was appointed Marine Painter to the Queen in 1874 and was knighted in 1885.

His paintings of contemporary marine subjects can be fine and atmospheric. His later historical subjects, in particular the Armada, are less so. An exhibition of his work was held at the Pall Mall Gallery in 1887.

Published: *The English and French Fleets in the Baltic 1858.*
Examples: Greenwich; Sydney A.G.: Portsmouth City Mus.
Bibliography: *A.J.*, 1887.

BRIGGS, Ernest Edward, R.I., R.S.W.
1865 (Broughty Ferry) - 1913 (Dunkeld)
A landscape and portrait painter who trained as a mining engineer before studying at the Slade and in Italy. He exhibited at the R.A. and the R.I. from 1889, and was elected R.I. in 1906. Various exhibitions of his work were held at the Fine Art Society, including one of specifically Highland subjects in 1908.

BRIERLY, Sir Oswald Walters (1817-1894)
The Morning Gun. *Pencil and watercolour, 11in. x 15in.*

Published: *Angling and Art in Scotland*, 1908; *The Two Rivers*, 1912.
Examples: Leeds City A.G.

BRIGHT, Henry
1810 (Saxmundham) - 1873 (Ipswich)
A landscape and marine painter who was the son of a clockmaker and was apprenticed to a chemist in Norwich. However, his indentures were transferred to A. Stannard (q.v.), and he also took lessons from J.B. Crome (q.v.) and J.S. Cotman (q.v.). He moved to Paddington in 1836 and lived in or near London until 1858, building up a highly successful practice as a drawing master. He exhibited in London from 1836, was a member of the N.W.S., from 1839 to 1845, and of the Graphic Society. He exhibited at Norwich from 1848. In 1858 he returned to his brother's house, Park Lodge, Saxmundham; two years later he moved to

BRIGHT, Henry (1810-1873)
Hever Castle, Kent. *Pencil and watercolour, 13in. x 19½in.*

Redhill, and he may have lived in Maidstone after 1865. For the last five years of his life he settled in Ipswich. He made regular sketching tours both in Britain and abroad, visiting Wales and Sussex before 1838, Devon, Cornwall and Monmouth before 1844, Yorkshire by 1846, Oxfordshire by 1847 and Kent in 1847, Cumberland in 1850 and Scotland and the North several times in the 1850s and 1860s. Abroad he certainly visited the Alps in 1849, the Rhine in 1851 and Paris in 1853 and 1855, and he probably travelled more widely.

His early watercolours are fine uncluttered examples of the later Norwich style, and his pencil drawings show a strong sense of line and composition. His later works, by which he is best known, are executed in a variety of media, with crayon and bodycolour coming to predominate; they are often on tinted paper and sometimes verge on the gaudy.
Published: *Drawing-Book of Landscapes*, 1843. &c.
Examples: B.M.; V.A.M.; Bridport A.G.; Brighton A.G.; Dudley A.G.; Leeds City A.G.; Newport A.G.; Castle Mus., Norwich; Glynn Vivian A.G., Swansea; Gt. Yarmouth Lib.
Bibliography: *A.J.*, Nov. 1873; *Walker's Quarterly*, I, i, 1920. Castle Mus., Norwich, Exhibition Cat., 1973. J. Walpole: *Art and Artists of the Norwich School*, 1997.

BRIGHT, Henry Barnabus, Yr., 'Harry'
1846 (Lambeth) - 1897 (Kingston)
The son of an eccentric painter of anthropomorphised frogs, **Henry Barnabus BRIGHT (1824-1876),** he became a rather sentimental bird painter and was active between 1867 and 1892 or later. Occasionally he produced free sketches in the manner of E. Alexander (q.v.). These are much more interesting than the general run of his robins and wrens.
Published: *Birds and Blossoms*, 1879; *A.B.C. of Pretty Birdies*, 1896, 1902. &c.
Examples: Ashmolean.

BRIGHTWELL, Cecilia Lucy
1811 (Thorpe, Norfolk) - 1875 (Norwich)
An etcher and authoress who was a pupil of J.S. Cotman (q.v.). Her father, a solicitor and Mayor of Norwich, had scientific tastes, and she helped with and illustrated his natural history writings. She herself wrote religious-minded biographies for the young. A number of her prints were also published.

BRIGHTY, George M   1788   -
A portrait painter who entered the R.A. Schools in 1808, and exhibited at the R.A. and the B.I. from 1809 to 1827. His drawing is good and he uses thin washes of colour.
Examples: B.M.; Brighton A.G.

BRINSON, John Paul
1870 (Cheltenham) - 1927
The founder and secretary of the British Watercolour Society, he was a landscape painter

and also worked in pastel. He exhibited from 1895 to 1918 and lived in Reading. He was a pupil of the younger D. Cox (q.v.) and a friend of L.B. Bruhl (q.v.). He was also a magician.

BRISBANE, Rear-Admiral Sir Charles
c.1769   - 1829
The son of an admiral under whom he served from 1779 at Cape St. Vincent, Gibraltar and in the West Indies. In 1793 he fought at Toulon and in Corsica with Nelson, like him losing an eye. In 1796 his Nelsonian disregard of orders led to the capture of the Dutch fleet at Saldanha Bay, and thereafter he served on the Cape Station until 1798. He was off Brest in 1801 and then in the West Indies. In 1806 he was involved in a number of actions, some of which he sketched, off Havana, and in the following year he captured Curaçao and was knighted. He was governor of St. Vincent from 1809 until his death.
Examples: Greenwich.

BRISTOL, Admiral Augustus John Hervey,
3rd Earl of   1724   -1779 (London)
The son of Lord Hervey of Ickworth and grandson of the 1st Earl of Bristol, he entered the Navy in 1736. He served first in the Mediterranean and then, having married the notorious Elizabeth Chudleigh in 1744, in the West Indies. In 1746 he was off Cherbourg, and for most of the next ten years in the Mediterranean. He was with the Channel Fleet, 1759-61, and in the West Indies again 1761-2, participating in the attacks on Martinique and Havana. This was really the end of his active service, although in 1763 he was briefly C-in-C, Mediterranean. From 1757 until he succeeded to the peerage in 1775 he was an M.P. In the latter year he was promoted to Admiral. He produced both landscape and marine drawings.

BRISTOW, Edmund
1787 (Eton) - 1876 (Eton)
Predominantly a sporting and animal painter in oil, he lived at Eton and Windsor, where his patrons (in so far as he allowed himself to be patronised) included William IV. His water-colours tend to be in the eighteenth century tradition. He was the son of a heraldic painter and a friend of Sir E. Landseer (q.v.).
Bibliography: *A.J.*, 1876.

BRISTOW, S
A landscape and topographical painter who was active between 1778 and 1780, and sketched in South Wales.
Examples: Newport A.G.

BRITTAN, Charles Edward
1837 (? Cornwall) - 1888
A West Country artist who painted landscapes and cattle and exhibited at the S.B.A. in 1858.
He is easily confused with his son, **Charles Edward BRITTAN, Yr. (b.1871 Plymouth),**

who lived near Princetown, Dartmoor, and illustrated an edition of *Lorna Doone* in 1911 and A. Vowles' *The Lorna Doone Country*, 1925. Exhibitions of his work, including views of Dartmoor in 1901 and Perthshire in 1902, were held at the St. James's Galleries, and Ackermann's held an exhibition entitled 'Arran and the Western Isles' in 1913.
Examples: Plymouth A.G.

BRITTON, John F.S.A.
1771 (Kingston St. Michael, Wiltshire) -
1857 (London)
The topographer and antiquarian. He was the son of a shopkeeper and small farmer, and was apprenticed to the landlord of a Clerkenwell tavern. He progressed to cellarman and became a hop merchant. By this time he had met, and collaborated on a ballad with, Edward William Brayley, and in 1801 their *Beauties of Wiltshire*, the first of twenty-six county volumes, appeared. By 1804 the authors had travelled some 3,500 miles in their researches. Britton gave up his full-time connection with the project after the publication of Volume VII. Subsequently he published his own *Architectural Antiquities of Great Britain*, 1805-14, and *Cathedral Antiquities of England*, 1814-35. For all these works as well as other publications such as *Specimens of Gothic Architecture*, 1823-5, *Architectural Antiquities of Norway*, 1825, *Public Buildings of London*, 1825-8, *History...of the...Palace...of Westminster*, 1834-6, (again with Brayley), and *Architectural Description of Windsor*, 1842, he commissioned illustrations from the best topographical draughtsmen of the day, and himself did some of the drawings. His work is in the tradition of Dayes and the Bucklers, and is usually soft in colour and on a small scale.
Published: *Autobiography*, 1850. &c.
Examples: B.M.; Ashmolean; Devizes Mus.
Bibliography: *R.I.B.A. Papers*, 18567; *A.J.*, Feb. 1857.

BROADBELT, W
A bird painter in water and bodycolour who was working about 1785. F. Nicholson (q.v.) had a friend of this name in Knaresborough.

BROCAS, Henry   1762 (Dublin) - 1837
A landscape painter and engraver who worked for several Dublin periodicals. He was appointed Master of the Landscape and Ornament School of the R.D.S. in 1801, which post he held until his death. His work includes portraits, topographical views and occasional political caricatures as well as landscapes. Occasionally he painted in oil.
Examples: N.G.I.; Nat.Lib.I.
Bibliography: *Dublin Historical Record*, XVII, i, 1961.

BROCAS, Henry, Yr.
1798 (Dublin) - 1873
The fourth son of H. Brocas (q.v.), he was, like

BROCAS, William (c.1794-1868)
The Liffey near Dublin. Signed and inscribed on the mount, watercolour heightened with touches of white, 11½in. x 19½in.

his father, a landscape painter and engraver. He etched a series of twelve *Views of Dublin* after drawings by his brother S.F. Brocas (q.v.) which were published in 1820. He exhibited at the R.H.A. periodically between 1828 and 1872, and in 1838 succeeded his father as Master of the Landscape and Ornament School of the R.D.S. He drew and engraved portraits and caricatures as well as topographical works, and he retired in 1854.
Examples: B.M.; Nat.Lib.I.

BROCAS, James Henry
c.1790 (Dublin) - 1846 (Cork)
The eldest son of H. Brocas (q.v.), he attended the R.D.S. Schools and settled in Cork in about 1834.
He painted landscapes, portraits and animals, and made etchings.
Examples: B.M.

BROCAS, Samuel Frederick
c.1792 (Dublin) - 1847 (Dublin)
The second son of H. Brocas (q.v.). He won three medals from the R.D.S. Schools, after which he practised in Dublin as a landscape painter in oil and watercolour. He exhibited at the R.H.A. between 1828 and 1847, and was a member of the Society of Irish Artists. Twelve of his drawings of Dublin were engraved by his brother H. Brocas, Yr. (q.v.) in 1820 as part of a projected general topography of Ireland.
Examples: B.M.; V.A.M.; N.G., Ireland.

BROCAS, William, R.H.A.
c.1794 (Dublin) - 1868 (Dublin)
The third son of H. Brocas (q.v.), he exhibited portraits and figure subjects as well as occasional landscapes at the R.H.A. between 1828 and 1863. He was on the Continent in 1840. He was President of the Society of Irish Artists, and was elected Associate and Member of the R.H.A. in 1854 and 1860. He etched caricatures for James Sidebotham, and made etchings after Hogarth's engravings.
Examples: N.G.I.

BROCK, Charles Edmund, R.I.
1870 (London) - 1938
A prolific illustrator and portraitist, he was educated in Cambridge. He worked on many popular editions, such as Lamb's *Essays* and Dent's edition of Jane Austen's works. He was elected R.I. in 1909. He also drew for *Punch* and the *Graphic*.

BROCK, Henry Matthew, R.I.
1875 (Cambridge) - 1960
The younger brother of C.E. Brock (q.v.), he was also a prolific illustrator in black and white and colour. He was educated in Cambridge, and he worked for *Punch* as well as on Dent's *Essay Series* and other popular classics. He also made spirited landscape sketches for his own pleasure. He was elected R.I. in 1906.
A third brother was **Richard Henry BROCK** who was active in the first quarter of the twentieth century.

BROCKEDON, William, F.R.S.
1787 (Totnes, Devon) - 1854 (London)
After attempting his father's watchmaking trade, Brockedon moved to London and the R.A. Schools in 1809. He exhibited portraits and sculpture from 1812. In 1815 he made his first Continental visit, travelling through France and Belgium, and he was in Italy in 1821 and 1822. He became a member of the Academies of Florence and Rome. In 1830 he assisted in the founding of the R.G.S., and in 1831 founded the Graphic Society. He was also an inventor, improving steel pens, and in 1843 patenting his 'artificial plumbago for lead pencils', said to be the best black lead of the day.
His landscapes, often views in Italy, are sometimes brightly coloured and are usually well drawn.
Published: *Illustrations of the Passes*, 1827-9. *Journals of Excursions in the Alps*, 1833. *Road Book from London to Naples*, 1835. *Italy, Classical, Historical and Picturesque*, 1842-4.
Examples: B.M.; V.A.M.

BROCKY, Charles (Karoly), A.N.W.S.
1807 (Temeswar, Hungary) - 1855 (London)
A Hungarian who worked as strolling player, cook, barber and painter in Vienna and Paris before being brought to London by Munro of Novar. He exhibited portraits and classical subjects at the R.A. from 1839 to 1854 and also at the N.W.S., and he built up a successful practice as a drawing master. He also made watercolour copies of old masters. In 1854 he was elected A.N.W.S. However, clothed sitters came to bore him, and he turned to nudes, for which he found little market.
Examples: B.M.; V.A.M.
Bibliography: N. Wilkinson: *Sketch of the Life of C.B. the Artist*, 1870. J. Szentkláry, *B.K., festömüvészélete*, 1907.

BROKE, Sir Arthur De Capel, 2nd Bt.
1791 (London) -
1858 (Oakley Hall, Northamptonshire)

BROMLEY, (Valentine) Walter (Lewis) (1848-1877)
'The Greatest of these is Charity.' *Watercolour and bodycolour, signed and dated 1875, 16½in. x 23in.*

The eldest son of Sir Richard de Capel Brooke, he graduated from Magdalen College, Oxford, in 1813. He travelled widely, particularly in Northern Europe. He also entered the army, and was promoted major in 1846. In 1829 he succeeded his father. He was an original member of the Travellers' Club, and in 1821 founded the Raleigh Club, which later became part of the Royal Geographical Society. In 1843 he was made Sheriff of Northamptonshire. The rest of the family spelled themselves 'Brooke'.
Published: *Travels through Sweden, Norway and Finmark to the North Pole in the Summer of 1820,* 1823. *A Winter in Lapland and Sweden...,* 1827. *Winter Sketches in Lapland...,* 1827. *Sketches in Spain and Morocco,* 1837.

BROMLEY, John
A draughtsman who was working in London from 1784 to 1796.
BROMLEY, (Valentine) Walter (Lewis), A.N.W.S.   **1848 (London) - 1877 (Fallows Green, near Harpenden)**
The son of William Bromley, a genre painter and great-grandson of the engraver William Bromley (q.v.), he also painted genre and historical subjects in oil and watercolour. He entered the R.A. Schools in 1869, and later worked for the *I.L.N.* and as a book illustrator, accompanying Lord Dunraven to America in 1875 to illustrate *The Great Divide.* He also painted views. He was elected A.N.W.S. in 1868 and lived in St. John's Wood. He seems to have preferred to use his middle Christian name.

His wife, **Alice Louisa Maria BROMLEY, née Atkinson,** was a landscape painter.
Examples: Shipley A.G., Gateshead.
Bibliography: *A.J.,* 1877.

BROMLEY, William, A.R.A.
1769 (Carisbroke) - 1842
An engraver and occasional draughtsman. He was apprenticed to a London engraver named Wooding and elected an associate engraver of the R.A. in 1819. He was much employed by the B.M. engraving the Elgin Marbles, and he also made figure and portrait drawings. He was the great-grandfather of V.W.L. Bromley (q.v.).

BROOK, Walter Harvey
1864 (York) - 1943 (York)
An architect who was an assiduous and very competent amateur painter in oil and watercolour. He trained in London. He made an extended tour of the Antipodes between 1883 and 1887, visiting Java, St. Paul in the far South, Australia and New Zealand, and returning by Colombo and Aden. He was again in Australia, and probably New Zealand, in 1890, when he also visited Venice. In 1906 he went to South Africa by way of the Canaries and St. Helena. In between these extensive travels he painted in Northern France as well as Yorkshire and later Cornwall.

He was a notable archaeologist in his native county, and unpaid keeper of medieval sculpture in the Yorkshire museum. It is no surprise that he enjoyed painting cathedral interiors as well as landscapes.

There was also a painting **Percy BROOK** active in Yorkshire from about 1894 to 1916. His work has been described as 'hazy and ethereal'.
Examples: York City A.G.
Bibliography: Ferens A.G., Hull: *Exhibition Cat.,* 1976.

BROOKBANK, W   H
Presumably a son of Mary Scott (q.v.), he lived in Brighton and London and exhibited flowers in 1847, as well as landscapes at Suffolk Street from 1864 to 1883.

BROOKE, A   Newton
A landscape and coastal painter who was working in Devon in 1883.
Examples: V.A.M.

BROOKE, Rev. John
c.1802   - c.1881
A pupil of de Wint who matriculated at B.N.C., Oxford in 1821 and was ordained in 1826. From 1831 to 1847 he was vicar of Shifnal, Shropshire, and on retirement he lived at Haughton Hall, Shifnal. It is probable that he shared some of the interests of his neighbour Rev. J.L. Petit (q.v.). He sketched in North Wales.

BROOKE, Leonard Leslie
1863   - 1940
He was educated at Birkenhead School, and studied at the R.A. Schools, winning the Armitage Medal in 1888. Thereafter he became an illustrator and landscape painter, exhibiting at the R.A. and the R.I. from 1887. He illustrated Andrew Laing's *The Nursery Rhyme Book* and other works, and he lived in London and at Steventon in Berkshire.
Published: *Johnny Crow's Garden,* 1903; *L.B.'s Children's Books* 1907-22.
Examples: City A.G., Manchester.

BROOKE, William Henry, A.R.H.A.
1772 (Dublin) - 1860 (Chichester)
He was the grandson of **Robert BROOKE** a portrait painter in Co. Cavan, and son of **Henry BROOKE (1738-1806),** a historical and biblical painter in London and Dublin and a drawing master. He trained under S. Drummond (q.v.) and established himself as a portrait painter. He was elected A.R.H.A. in 1828, but most of his career was in England.

As an illustrator he was much influenced by his friend T. Stothard (q.v.). He produced both landscape and figure drawings, the former freely sketched in pen and ink with clear, fairly bright washes. His pretty figures are very close to those of Stothard. He sometimes inscribed in a characteristic, flowing hand.
Illustrated: T. Moore: *Irish Melodies,* 1822. Keightley: *Greek and Roman Mythology,* 1831.
Examples: B.M.
Bibliography: B.Stewart & M.Cutten: *Chichester Artists,* 1987.

BROOKE, William Henry (1772-1860)
Crafts: Shipbuilding; Blacksmithing; Turning; Basket-making; Spinning.
Pencil, pen and brown ink and watercolour, each 2¼in. x 2¾in.

BROOKES, Warwick, of Manchester
        1808 (Salford) - 1882 (Manchester)
He worked in a calico print works before studying at the Manchester School of Design under John Zephaniah Bell. In 1840 he became the head designer to the Rossendale Printing Company and retained the position for twenty-six years.

He produced figure subjects and landscapes and became known to a wider public with the Manchester Exhibition of 1857. In 1866 he contributed illustrations to *A Round of Days* and in 1868 he became a member of the Manchester Academy.
Illustrated: J. Brown: *Marjorie Fleming*, 1884. T. Letherbrow: *W.B.'s Pencil Pictures of Child Life*, 1889.
Examples: B.M.; V.A.M.; City A.G., Manchester.

BROOKING, Charles
        1723 (Deptford) - 1759 (London)
Brooking's father, also Charles (died 1758), had been a ship's painter at Plymouth, cartographer in Dublin and decorator at Greenwich. The son was brought up in the dockyard at Deptford and may have been to sea. He painted marine subjects from an early age but died of consumption before his reputation was well established. He also suffered from unscrupulous dealers, one of whom is said to have removed the signatures from his works. His drawings, usually in monochrome, are very attractive, and many were engraved.

An exhibition of his oil paintings, drawings, and engravings was held by the Paul Mellon Foundation in 1966 in association with the Aldeburgh Festival and Bristol City A.G.
Illustrated: J.Ellis: *The Natural History of the Corallines*, 1755.
Examples: B.M.; V.A.M.; Yale.
Bibliography: D.Joel: *C.B. and the 18th Century British Marine Painters*, 2000. St. Barbe A.G., Lymington: *Ex. Cat.*, 2001.

BROUGH, Robert Barnabas
        1828 (Monmouthshire) - 1860
A writer and journalist who worked as a portrait painter from an early age and, while still in his teens, started up a satirical paper in Liverpool. He and his brother William produced satires and burlesques for the London stage. He used the *nom de plume* 'Papernose Woodensconce'.

        Robert BROUGH (1872 Invergordon - 1905 nr. Sheffield), an Aberdeen oil painter who was killed in a railway accident, produced a number of bold watercolours of Paris and elsewhere.

BROWN, Agnes Mary
A landscape, church and flower painter who lived in Birmingham and exhibited there from 1867 to 1886.

BROWN, Alexander Kellock, R.S.A., R.I., R.S.W.
        1849 (Edinburgh) - 1922 (Lamlash, Arran)
A landscape and flower painter in oil and watercolour who was educated at the Haldane Academy, Glasgow, and studied at Heatherley's and the Glasgow School of Art. Later he worked as a calico designer. He exhibited at the R.S.A. from 1871, and the R.A. and R.I. from 1873. He was elected A.R.S.A. and R.S.A. in 1892 and 1908, and R.I. in 1916.
Examples: Glasgow A.G.
Bibliography: *A.J.*, 1901; 1904; 1909. *Studio*, 1917-18.

BROWN, Alfred J   WARNE
        1854   - 1915 (Shifnal)
A coastal and landscape painter who exhibited at the R.A., the R.I. and elsewhere from 1884. An exhibition of his work was held at the Fine Art Society in 1905. He lived in Ealing until 1894, when he moved to Ruan Major on the Lizard. Many of his subjects are taken from Cornwall. His name is sometimes spelt with a final 'e'.

BROWN, David
A landscape painter who began his career painting signs. At the age of thirty-five, he worked under Morland (q.v.) as a copyist. He later set up as a drawing master in the country. He exhibited ten landscapes at the R.A. from 1792 to 1797, and he may have been in Liverpool between 1811 and 1822. The bulk of his work was probably in oil.

BROWN, Edward Archibald
        1866 (Ancaster Hall, Lincs.) - 1935
A landscape and animal painter who lived in Hertford and Bedford and exhibited at the R.A. from 1900. He also painted, infrequently, in oil, and his animals are poorly drawn.
Examples: Hertford Mus.

BROWN, Ford MADOX-
1821 (Calais) - 1893 (London)
Trained in Belgium, he began his career in Antwerp and Paris and in 1845 he spent some months in Rome. In 1848 he took Rossetti as a pupil, thus coming into contact with the Brotherhood. He never formally joined them but the exchange of influence between them was marked. He was not a very popular painter, and also quarrelled with the artistic establishment. He taught at the Camden Town Working Men's College from 1854, and from 1861 to 1874 was a leading designer for Morris and Co.
Examples: B.M.; V.A.M.; Ashmolean; Cecil Higgins A.G., Bedford; Cartwright Hall, Bradford; Maidstone Mus.; City A.G., Manchester.
Bibliography: F.M. Heuffer: *Memoir of M.B.*, 1896. H.M.M. Rossetti: *F.M.B.*, 1901. *A.J.*, 1873, 1893. Birmingham City A.G., Exhibition Cat., 1939 and supp.

BROWN, Frederick
1851 (Chelmsford) - 1941
A landscape and genre painter in oil and watercolour, he studied at South Kensington, and in Paris in 1883. He taught at the Westminster School of Art from 1877 to 1892 and was Slade Professor from 1892 to 1918.
   An exhibition of his Isle of Wight views was held at the Goupil Gallery in 1920.
Bibliography: *A.J.*, 1893. *Studio*, XXXVII, 1906; XLIV, 1908. *Burlington Mag.*, LXXXII, 1943.

BROWN, James Michael
1853   - 1947
A genre painter who worked in Edinburgh and exhibited at the R.A., the R.I. and elsewhere from 1880. His watercolours would be unlikely to aid digestion.

BROWN, John
1752 (Edinburgh) - 1787 (Leith)
He studied at the Trustees' Academy, Edinburgh, and was a pupil of A. Runciman (q.v.). He went to Italy in 1771 and stayed there for ten years or more, visiting Sicily among other places. He was not really a watercolourist, but his drawings are very much in the manner of Fuseli (q.v.), of whose circle in Rome he was a member. He did sometimes use sepia wash and may have used colour. He returned to Edinburgh in or after 1781, but died (on a subsequent return from London by sea) before he could establish any great reputation.
   His monogram J.B. can sometimes look deceptively like Blake's. W.Y. Ottley (q.v.) was his pupil.
Examples: B.M.; N.G., Scotland; N.P.G., Scotland.
Bibliography: J.M. Grey: *J.B., the Draughtsman*, 1889. *Country Life*, 12 Aug. 1971.

BROWN, Major-General John
A landscape, marine and town painter who painted in monochrome and full colour, and worked in Hampshire, the Isle of Wight, Ireland and Scotland between 1792 and 1820.
Examples: Nat. Lib., Scotland.

BROWN, John
An architect who was County Surveyor of Norfolk from about 1835. He exhibited at the R.A. from 1820 to 1844. As an architect he specialised in churches, and as an artist in church interiors. His drawing is good, and his detail exact and pleasing.

BROWN, Lancelot, 'Capability'
1715 (Harle-Kirk, Northumberland) - 1783 (Hampton Court)
The landscape gardener and architect whose work included the remodelling of the grounds at Kew, Blenheim and Nuneham Courtenay, and buildings at Croome. The preparatory drawings which he made, often on a large scale, are typical of the tinted manner, with careful and conventional outlines and grey, green and blue washes.
Examples: Heveningham Hall, Suffolk.
Bibliography: D. Stroud: *C.B.*, 1950; 1975.

BROWN, Oliver MADOX-
1855 (Finchley) - 1874
The son of F. Madox-Brown (q.v.), he showed great promise and strong individuality both as an author and a watercolourist. He first exhibited at the Dudley Gallery when he was fifteen, and at the R.A. the following year. His subjects include scenes from *The Tempest* and *Silas Marner*. His own first novel, *Gabriel Denver*, was published in 1873. He died of blood poisoning following gout.
Published: *Gabriel Denver*, 1873. *The Dwale Bluth*, 1876.
Examples: City A.G., Manchester.

BROWN, Peter
A flower painter in water and bodycolour who was a member of the Incorporated Society, and exhibited there and at the R.A. from 1766 to 1791. He was appointed Botanical Painter to the Prince of Wales.
Published: *Nouvelles Illustrations de Zoologie*, 1776.
Examples: B.M.

BROWN, Richard
An 'Architect and Professor of Perspective', probably from Devon, who exhibited designs and landscapes at the R.A. from 1804 to 1828. He worked as an architect at Norwich in 1829, on Holland House in 1831, and on the Independent Chapel at Topsham in 1839 – described by Colvin as 'a feeble Gothic structure' – and he seems to have moved back to Devon from London.
Published: *Principles of Practical Perspective...*, 1818. *Domestic Architecture...*, 1842, *Sacred Architecture...*, 1845. &c.

BROWN, Thomas Austen, A.R.S.A., R.I., R.S.W. 1857 (Edinburgh) - 1924 (Boulogne)
The son of a drawing master, he studied at the R.S.A. Schools before moving to London. He was elected A.R.S.A. in 1889, and was a member of the R.I. from 1888 to 1899. He lived in Boulogne for many years and his paintings, which are in many styles, and coloured woodcuts, won medals at several Continental exhibitions.
Published: *Bits of Chelsea*, 1921 (lithographs).
Examples: B.M.; V.A.M.; N.G., Scotland.

BROWN, Vandyke
A Shrewsbury artist who painted landscapes, street scenes and buildings and was active between 1819 and 1840. In the 1880s, someone of this name edited the periodical *The Berkshire Bell and Counties Review*.
Examples: Shrewsbury Lib.

BROWN, William
A drawing master and topographer who worked in Norfolk and Durham. A print was made from one of his drawings by Jukes and Sarjent in 1809. His style is reminiscent of that of J. Farington (q.v.), and he uses grey and brown washes.
   His son, **Forster BROWN (d.1878)** also taught drawing at Durham and at Sunderland.
   He may be identifiable with **William BROWN (1778-1851)**, an architect and timber merchant from Mendham, Norfolk, who spent his last years in an asylum.
Examples: B.M.

BROWN, William Beattie, R.S.A.
1831 (Haddington) - 1909 (Edinburgh)
A painter of the Highlands in oil and watercolour. He studied at the Trustees' Academy and was elected R.S.A. in 1884.
   His son **William Beattie BROWN, Yr.,** painted similar subjects from the 1890s until about 1915.
Bibliography: *A.J.*, 1904; 1909.

BROWN, William Fulton, R.S.W.
1873 (Glasgow) - 1905 (Glasgow)
A genre painter who was the nephew and pupil of the Scottish artist D. Fulton (q.v.). He also studied at the Glasgow School of Art.
Examples: Glasgow A.G.; Paisley A.G.

BROWNE, Alexander
An artists' colourman and teacher of drawing at 'The Sign of the Pestel and Mortar', an apothecary's shop in Long Acre. He was one of the first people to prepare water-based colours professionally for others. He gave drawing lessons to Mrs. Pepys (q.v.) in 1665. His partner in 1675 was Arthur Tooker, a stationer, publisher, bookseller, colourman and print seller.
   There was a Scottish herald-painter of the same name active between 1660 and 1677.
Published: *Ars Pictoria*, 1669; (revised edition, 1675).
Bibliography: Modern Language Ass. of America (N.Y.), LV, 1940.

BROWNE, Charles Henry
A painter of fruit, flowers and figures, who lived in Shrewsbury and London. He exhibited during the 1860s and was twice turned down by the N.W.S. and once by the O.W.S. He was presumably a son of P. Browne (q.v.).

BROWNE, E F
A North-eastern landscapist of the late nineteenth century.

BROWNE, George Henry
1805 - 1892 (Blackheath)
A landscape, history and stormy marine painter who lived in Greenwich, Camberwell and Blackheath. He exhibited from 1836 to 1885, mostly watercolours. He painted in (or off) Wales, Sussex and Surrey. Wrecks and lifeboats were favourite subjects.

BROWNE, George Ulick –
see SLIGO, 6th Marquess of

BROWNE, Gordon Frederick, R.I.
1858 (Banstead, Surrey) - 1932
The younger son of H.K. Browne (q.v.), he was an illustrator and worked on editions of Shakespeare, Scott and Defoe. He lived in Richmond, Surrey, and was elected R.I. in 1896.
Examples: Doncaster A.G.; Hove Lib.
Bibliography: *Studio*, Special Winter No., 1901.

BROWNE, Hablot Knight, 'Phiz'
1815 (Kennington) - 1882 (Brighton)
The ninth son of a merchant, he was educated in Suffolk and apprenticed to Finden the engraver. As soon as he was out of his articles, he set up as a painter and attended life classes in St. Martin's Lane. His first illustrations for Dickens appeared in 1836, with *Sunday as it is, by Timothy Sparks* and *The Pickwick Papers*. In 1837 he visited Flanders with Dickens, and the following year they went to Yorkshire. Although best known as an illustrator, he exhibited both in oil and watercolour. Apart from his work with Dickens, his most popular illustrations were for the works of Charles Lever, in which he was greatly helped by his passion for horses and hunting. In 1867 he became paralysed but continued to work at drawing and etching until his death. In 1880 he moved to Brighton.
Examples: B.M.; City A.G., Manchester; Portsmouth City Mus.
Bibliography: F.G. Kitton: *Phiz, a Memoir*, 1882. D.C. Thompson: *Life and Labours of H.K.B.*, 1884. S.M. Ellis: *Mainly Victorian*, 1924. *Country Life*, 10 June 1965.

BROWNE, James Denis Howe
1827 -
A grandson of the Earl of Altamont, and great-nephew of the 1st Marquess of Sligo, he lived in London for a while, but was seated at Claremont House, Co. Mayo. He went to Mont

BROWNE, Thomas Arthur (1872-1910)
'The Queue for Aladdin.' *Watercolour, signed, 14in. x 20¼in.*

Blanc with E.A. Goodall (q.v.) in 1852, and subsequently produced a volume of ten lithographs.
It is unlikely that he was the **T.D.H. BROWNE** who exhibited an Asia Minor view at the S.B.A. in 1863 and a figure subject two years later. This painter also showed biblical and historical figure subjects at the R.A. and the B.I.
Bibliography: *Country Life*, 27 April 1961.

BROWNE, James Loxham
A landscape and flower painter who visited North Wales and exhibited at the R.B.A. in 1892 and 1893 and the R.A. from 1894. He lived in Hampstead.

BROWNE, Philip
A landscape, sporting, still-life and genre painter in oil and watercolour who lived in Shrewsbury. He exhibited in London and Birmingham from 1824 to 1868, and was an unsuccessful candidate for the N.W.S. in 1841 and the O.W.S. on occasions from 1826 to 1858. His landscapes are sometimes Claudian or Barretlike in composition, but their style and technique owe more to J. Varley (q.v.). He sketched in Wales and Holland, and in his later years he concentrated on painting fruit.
Examples: Ashmolean.

BROWNE, Thomas Arthur, R.I.
1872 (Nottingham) - 1910 (London)
A black and white illustrator who also worked in watercolour and pastel and painted in Holland, Spain, China and Japan as well as Britain. He was apprenticed to a firm of lithographers in Nottingham, and came to London in 1895. He exhibited at the R.A. from

1898 to 1901, in which year he was elected R.I., and he was a member of the R.B.A. from 1898. He established a printing business in Nottingham under the name 'Tom Browne Ltd.'
Published: *Tom Browne's Clyde Sketch Book*, 1897; *Tom Browne's Annuals*, 1904-5. &c.
Examples: Castle Mus., Nottingham.
Bibliography: A.E. Johnson: *'T.B.'*, 1909.

BROWNE, William Henry James
- 1872
Son of the Dublin Harbourmaster, he joined the navy and served on the Ross Arctic expedition of 1848-9, and again on H.M.S. *Resolute* in 1850-1. He painted sets for the 'Royal Arctic Theatre' (where his fellow Irishman G.F. Mecham (q.v.) was an actor), and later produced an Arctic panorama in London.

BROWNING, Robert Wiedemann Barrett, 'Pen' 1849 (Florence) - 1912
The only child of the poets, he became a genre painter in oil and watercolour and was also a sculptor. He studied in Antwerp and Paris and exhibited in London from 1878. He was also instructed by Sir J.E. Millais (q.v.). Later he lived at Venice and Asolo.

BROWNLOW, Emma, Mrs. Emma Brownlow King
1832 (London) - 1905 (Kent)
A daughter of John Brownlow (c.1800-1874), a foundling who became secretary to Thomas Coram's Foundling Hospital, she was primarily an oil painter who utilised the family background for subject matter. She tended to

draw out her compositions and sometimes used watercolour sketches to provide her with landscape backgrounds to genre subjects. She visited France and Switzerland in the 1850s, and in 1863 she and a sister spent two months in France, for the most part in Brittany which provided her with many subjects thereafter. In 1867 she made an unfortunate marriage to a singer, and although she was the main bread-winner for her children, she did not exhibit after 1877. The last decades of her life were peripatetic, including residences in Kent, the Isle of Wight, London, New Zealand in 1888-9, the Isle of Wight again, Bradford-on-Avon, Bournemouth, Australia and New Zealand once more in the mid-1890s, returning by way of Ceylon in 1901. It would be surprising if she did not at least sketch during these later years.

Examples: Thomas Coram Foundling Hospital.
Bibliography: P. Gerrish Nunn: *Victorian Women Artists,* 1987.

BROWNLOW, Sophia, Countess
c.1775   - 1814
The younger daughter of the virtuoso Sir Abraham Hume, and sister of Lady Farnborough (q.v.). She married John Cust, 2nd Baron and 1st Earl Brownlow, and she painted landscapes.

BROWNSWORD, Harry A
c.1850 (Nottingham) - c.1910
The son of a Nottingham silk merchant, he was an amateur artist. He exhibited at the R.A. and Suffolk Street between 1889 and 1892, and painted in oil and watercolour

BRUCE, Harriet C
A coastal landscape, still-life and figure painter who lived in Edinburgh and Lochgilphead, Argyllshire. She exhibited at the R.S.A. and elsewhere from 1876 to 1899.

BRUCE, James
1730 (Kinnaird, Stirlingshire) -
1794 (Kinnaird)
A discoverer of the source of the Blue Nile, and an antiquarian draughtsman, he was educated at Harrow and dabbled with the cloth, the law and the wine trade before discovering his true bent while visiting Spain in the 1750s. He was appointed Consul at Algiers with a commission to study the architectural remains. Before his arrival there in 1763 he spent six months in Italy, drawing at Paestum and then engaging an Italian draughtsman, Luigi Balugani, whose work he was later accused of appropriating. In fact the two made a tour through Barbary in 1765, after Bruce's resignation as Consul, and it is difficult to tell the *camera obscura* drawings of the one from the other.

After a shipwreck he made his way from Benghazi to Crete and Syria and then to Egypt. He arrived in Abyssinia in 1769 and for the

BUCK, Adam (1759-1833)
Mrs. Forster of Dublin. *Inscribed, watercolour, 8in. x 5in.*

next three years was embroiled in the politics and civil wars of that country. He returned through Nubia and Egypt and reached Marseilles in 1773. He returned to England a year and a half later, but then retired to his Scottish estate in pique at his poor reception. He died from falling down the stairs. Some of the Barbary drawings are in the Royal Collection. His figures can sometimes be Sandby-like.
Published: *Travels,* 1790.
Examples: B.M.

BRUETON, Frederick
A painter of portraits, figures and coastal subjects in oil and watercolour who lived at Brighton, Bridgwater and Paignton. He was active at least from 1897 to 1911.

BRUHL, Louis Burleigh
1861 (Baghdad) - 1942
Educated in Vienna, he specialised in landscape painting in oil and watercolour. He was President of the British Watercolour Society and a member of the R.B.A., and he

lived in Watford.
Published: *A China Dish; Landscape,* 1929.
Illustrated: A.R.H. Moncrieff: *Essex,* 1909.
Examples: Newport A.G.

BRUMMELL, George Bryan, 'Beau'
1778 (Westminster) - 1840 (Caen)
Educated at Eton, he spent a year at Oriel College, and held a cornetcy in the 10th Hussars from 1794 until 1798 when the regiment was ordered to Manchester. He ruled London society until his debts and his quarrel with the Prince Regent (q.v.) drove him to Calais in 1816. He was consul at Caen from 1830 to 1832, and in 1835 he was imprisoned for debt. He died insane. He painted landscapes which may owe a little to F.L.T. Francia (q.v.), and figures which are in the tradition of R. Westall (q.v.).

BRYDALL, Robert
1839 (Glasgow) - 1907
A painter of British and Continental landscapes who studied and taught at the

Glasgow School of Art. He worked in both oil and watercolour and exhibited from the 1860s.

His wife, **Mrs. Robert BRYDALL,** was also a watercolour painter.

Published: *Art in Scotland – Its Origins and Progress*, 1889. &c.

BRYANT, John

A crude painter of ships and figures who was active between 1764 and 1791.

BRYANT, Joshua

A landscape draughtsman and engraver who was working between 1795 and 1810.

BUCK, Adam 1759 (Cork) - 1833 (London)

A portrait and miniature painter, he was the son of Jonathan Buck, a Cork silversmith, and had acquired a good reputation locally before coming to London in 1795. His portraits, often of children, were popular and he was a successful teacher. Many of his works were engraved. He exhibited at the R.A., S.B.A. and the B.I.

His work is usually elaborately drawn in pencil and washed in clear, thin colours with a concentrated finish on the head of the sitter. He made occasional illustrations, as for an edition of Sterne's *Sentimental Journey.*

His sons, **Alfred BUCK and Sidney BUCK,** carried on their father's profession in London. His younger brother, **Frederick BUCK (1771-1840),** was a miniature painter in Cork.

Published: *Paintings on Greek Vases*, 1811.

Examples: B.M.; Ashmolean; Fitzwilliam; City A.G., Manchester; Ulster Mus.

Bibliography: *Apollo*, XXXVIII, 1943.

BUCK, Samuel 1696 - 1779 (London)

An engraver and topographical draughtsman, he produced more than five hundred prints of the remains of abbeys, castles, &c., as well as more extensive views of towns. From 1711 to 1726 he engraved his own works, after which his brother, **Nathaniel BUCK,** worked with him on both the drawings and engraving until 1753. They generally travelled around the country each summer, making drawings which they engraved during the winter. Samuel exhibited at Spring Gardens in 1768 and 1774, and at the R.A. the following year.

Their drawings are mostly done in Indian ink with grey or brown wash. They have the crude and rather stiff appeal of the earlier generation of Dutch topographical artists working in this country. The styles of the brothers are much the same, although that of Nathaniel is perhaps rather looser. The drawings often bear fake signatures.

Published: The complete works were republished as: *Buck's Antiquities...*, 1774.

Examples: B.M.; Greenwich; N.G., Scotland; R.I. Wales, Swansea.

See Colour Plate

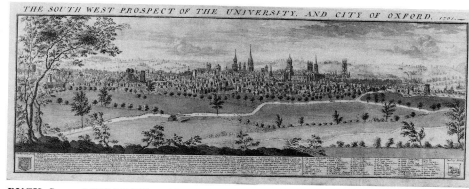

BUCK, Samuel (1696-1779) and BUCK, Nathaniel (-?1753)
South West Prospect of the University and City of Oxford. *Signed, extensively inscribed and dated 1731, black ink and grey wash. 11¾in. x 30¾in.*

BUCK, William

An amateur artist in watercolour and pen and black ink. In 1876 he was in the Isle of Wight where he made many coastal sketches, often on tinted paper, and he was on the Thames in 1877 and 1878. He has a fine sense of space and distance and sometimes uses a *pointilliste* technique. His colours are clear, and the details are well drawn.

Examples: Ashmolean; Carisbrooke Castle; Reading A.G.

BUCKLE, Mary

A landscape painter working in about 1817. She may have visited North Wales, or she may have copied the views of others. She worked in pencil and wash.

BUCKLER, John, F.S.A. 1770 (Calbourne, Isle of Wight) - 1851 (London)

The antiquarian draughtsman. He was articled to a Southwark architect, Charles Thomas Cracklow, and practised as an architect until 1826 when he handed over his practice to his son, J.C. Buckler (q.v.). He worked for Sir R.C. Hoare (q.v.) in Wiltshire, Lord Grenville in Buckinghamshire, Dr. Whitaker in Yorkshire, H.S. Pigott in Somerset and W. Salt in Staffordshire. He exhibited at the R.A. from 1796 to 1849. At the end of his life, he estimated he had made more than 13,000 drawings.

Examples: B.M.; V.A.M.; Ashmolean; Bristol City A.G.; Grosvenor Mus., Chester; Coventry A.G.; Devizes Mus.; Co. Record Office, Hertford;

BUCKLER, John (1770-1851)
Stourhead. *Signed and dated 1840, watercolour, 12in. x 16in.*

BUCKLER, John Chessell (1793-1894)
St. Katherine's Priory, Gloucester. *Signed and dated 1819, inscribed on the reverse, watercolour, 6in. x 8½in.*

BUCKLER, John Chessell (1793-1894)
North-East view of Woodstock with the roofs of Blenheim. *Signed, inscribed and dated 1821 below the mount, pencil and watercolour, 9⅜in. x 15⅛in.*

Lambeth Lib.; Newport A.G.; Cas. Mus., Norwich; William Salt Lib., Stafford; Taunton Mus.; Wakefield City A.G.; York A.G.
Bibliography: C.A. Buckler: *Buckleriana*, privately printed, 1886. Bodleian Lib., MSS. *Gentleman's Mag.*, 1852, i. *Builder*, X, 1852.

BUCKLER, John Chessell
1793   - 1894
The eldest son of J. Buckler (q.v.), to whose architectural practice he succeeded in 1826. He too painted topographical subjects in a manner so close to that of his father that only the signature distinguishes between them. His work is very rarely exciting, but always worthy. Essentially, they both belong to the eighteenth century tradition.

In his turn, J.C. Buckler's son, **Charles Alban BUCKLER (1824-1904)** joined the family business. Later he worked at the College of Heralds.
Published: *Views of Cathedral Churches in England*, 1822. *Historical and Descriptive Account of the Royal Palace at Eltham*, 1828. *Remarks upon Wayside Chapels*, 1843. *History of the Architecture of the Abbey Church at St. Albans*, 1847. *Description of Lincoln Cathedral*, 1866.
Examples: B.M.; Ashmolean; Bristol City A.G.; Bowes Mus., Durham; Fitzwilliam; Usher Mus., Lincoln; City A.G., Manchester; Cas. Mus., Norwich; Richmond Lib.; Southwark Lib.; William Salt Lib., Stafford; Wakefield City A.G.
Bibliography: *Jackson's Oxford Journal*, 1894. *Drawings of Oxford* (Bodleian), 1951. *A.J.*, 1894.

BUCKLER, William
1814 (Newport, Isle of Wight) - 1884
Nephew of J. Buckler (q.v.), he studied at the R.A. Schools and exhibited watercolour portraits at the R.A. from 1836 to 1856. In about 1848 he settled at Emsworth and took up entomology. This gradually became his main interest, and, with the meticulousness that characterises the family, he made at least five thousand drawings of larvae as well as writing articles and books.
Published: *The Larvae of the British Butterflies and Moths*, 1886-1901.
Examples: B.M.; Nat Army Mus.

BUCKLEY, Charles Frederick
1812   - 1869 (London)
A landscape painter who came to London, probably from Cork, in about 1840. He painted in Hampshire, the Isle of Wight, the Lake District, North Wales, Yorkshire, Derbyshire and Ireland, and he exhibited at the R.A. and R.B.A. from 1841 to 1869. He was an unsuccessful candidate for the N.W.S. in 1844. He was a prolific painter, and his work is pleasing if of no great originality.
Examples: V.A.M.; Cape Town Mus.; Derby A.G.; Glasgow A.G.; Leeds City A.G.

BUCKLEY, John Edmund
1824   - 1876 (London)
Probably the brother of C.F. Buckley (q.v.), with whom he was living in 1843. He painted landscapes and Tudor and Stuart scenes, and exhibited at the R.B.A. from 1843 to 1861. He had been in Bootle in 1840, perhaps on his way from Ireland, and was still active in 1873.

In the 1850s there was also a **Henry BUCKLEY** active as an artist in London.
Examples: V.A.M.; Brighton A.G.

BUCKLEY, John
A miniaturist, portrait and landscape painter who moved from Cork to London in about 1835. He was perhaps related to the other painting Buckleys.

BUCKLEY, William
A landscape. architectural, miniature and genre painter who exhibited at the R.B.A. from 1840 to 1845. At that time he was living

BUCKLEY, Charles Frederick (1812-1869)
Santa Maria della Salute and the Dogagna, Venice. *Signed, pencil and watercolour heightened with white and with stopping out, 7¼in. x 10⅛in.*

in Kensington. He painted in the Isle of Wight and on the Wye, probably with C.F. Buckley (q.v.), and in Essex and Kent.

BUCKMAN, Edwin, A.R.W.S.
1841 - 1930
A painter of domestic and street scenes and figure subjects. He lived in London and Birmingham, and was in Jersey in 1875. He was elected A.R.W.S. in 1877, and a member of the Birmingham Society in 1890. His pupils included Queens Alexandra and Mary.
Bibliography: *Studio*, XVIII, 1900.

BUCKNALL, Ernest Pile
1861 (Liverpool) -
A landscape painter who exhibited at the R.A., the R.I. and the R.B.A. from 1885. An exhibition of his work was held at the Burlington Gallery in 1888, and he was still painting in 1919.

BUCKNER, Richard
1812 (Royal Arsenal, Woolwich) -
1883 (Westminster)
An immensely popular portrait and genre painter in oil and watercolour who fell into total obscurity after his death, remaining there for many years. The family came from Chichester, where he was brought up. He was in the army for a short period, and then worked in Rome from 1820 to 1840. On his return he was highly

successful in London, exhibiting at the R.A. from 1842 to 1877. Sales of his work were held at Christie's, 22-24 February 1873 and 31 July 1877. Du Maurier, who understood such matters, deprecatingly described him as 'the only

Victorian artist to be accepted as a gentleman'.
Examples: B.M.
Bibliography: B.Stewart & M.Cutten: *Chichester Artists*, 1987. *A.J.*, 1859. *Apollo*, Feb. 1977. *W&D*, 1988, ii. *Antique Collector*, April, 1989.

BUCKLEY, John Edmund (1824-1876)
Old Rivals. *Signed and dated 1865, water and bodycolour, 17in. x 26½in.*

BULLEID, George Lawrence (1858-1933)
'At the Fountain.'. *Watercolour over traces of pencil, signed and dated 1921, 17¾in. x 11¾in.*

BULMAN, Job (1745-1818)
Ruins by a Bridge. *Bears fake signature 'N. Pocock', pen and ink and watercolour, approx. 9in. x 12in.*

BUDD, George   (London) -
A hosier who turned to art and painted landscapes, portraits and still lifes. He taught drawing for some years at Dr. Newcombe's School at Hackney. He drew the executions of Lords Kilmarnock and Balmerino in 1746, and was working around 1750. The bulk of his work is probably in oil.

BUGLER, Abel
An artist who made drawings of churches, some of which were published as prints in about 1850.

BULLEID, George Lawrence, A.R.W.S.
1858 (Glastonbury) - 1933
Suitably, in view of his birthplace, he painted mythological subjects as well as figures and still lifes in oil and watercolour. The son of a solicitor, he exhibited from 1884 and was elected A.R.W.S. in 1889. He lived in Bath, and according to *Studio* his work is 'possessed of classic charm'.
Examples: Preston A.G.
Bibliography: *Studio*, XXXVII, 1906.

BULLER, Susannah, Lady, née Yarde
c.1747   -
The daughter and heiress of Francis Yarde of Churston Ferrers and Ottery St. Mary, Devon, she was a pupil of F. Towne (q.v.) and painted landscapes. In 1763 she married the judge Francis Buller, who was created a baronet in 1790 and died in 1800. Her niece by marriage married A. Champernowne (q.v.), and her grandson was created Lord Churston.

BULLOCK, George
A painter and decorator at Bridlington, who made a number of local views in watercolour in about 1900.

BULMAN, Henry Herbert
1871 (Carlisle) - 1928 (London)
A landscape painter in oil and watercolour, who also produced portraits, genre and flower subjects. He lived in London and exhibited from 1899. He was a member of the Langham Sketching Club and the R.B.A. His landscapes in Westmorland and Cumberland can be impressive.
Examples: V.A.M.

BULMAN, Job
1745   - 1818 (Cox Lodge, Newcastle)
A banker and an amateur artist who is said to have been a friend of P. Sandby (q.v.), by whose topographical style he was certainly much influenced. He visited Scotland, Cumberland, the Isle of Man, Suffolk, Sussex, Cornwall, the Wye Valley and Yorkshire, as well as painting in his native North-East.
  His work is generally rather crude and heavy in handling, although he can rise to slightly better things.
Examples: B.M.; Christchurch Mus., Ipswich; Leeds City A.G.; Nat. Lib., Wales.
Bibliography: *W&D*, 1988, i (Editorial).

BULWER, Rev. James
1794   - 1879
An amateur landscape painter of high quality,

he was educated at Jesus College, Cambridge, from 1815 and was ordained in 1818. He married the daughter of an Irish barrister, and from 1823 was Perpetual Curate of Booterstown, Dublin. From 1833 to 1848 he was Minister of York Chapel and Curate of St. James's, Westminster, and from 1848 until his death Rector of Stody with Hunworth, Norfolk. He was a pupil and friend of J.S. Cotman (q.v.), and his son, **J.N. BULWER,** also made Cotman copies.
Published: *Views of Madeira*, 1825-26. *Views of Cintra in Portugal. Views in the West of England.*
Examples: B.M.; N.G., Washington.
Bibliography. J. Walpole: *Art and Artists of the Norwich School*, 1997.

BUNBURY, Henry William
1750 (Suffolk) - 1811 (Keswick)
An amateur caricaturist who was educated at Westminster and St. Catherine's College, Cambridge, Bunbury studied drawing at Rome while on the Grand Tour. He married in 1771 Catherine Horneck, Goldsmith's 'Little Comedy', who acted with him in amateur productions at Wynnstay. For these he designed invitation cards, and P. Sandby (q.v.) the scenery. He was a friend of West, Walpole, Goldsmith, Garrick and Reynolds, and was appointed equerry to the Duke of York in 1787. He was colonel of the West Suffolk Militia. He exhibited at the R.A. in an honorary capacity between 1780 and 1808. His wife died in 1798, and he then retired to Keswick.
  He produced many caricature drawings which

BULWER, Rev. James (1794-1879)
Leigh Woods, near Bristol. *Inscribed, watercolour with stopping out, 8in. x 12in.*

BUNBURY, Henry William (1750-1811)
Courier François. *Signed, inscribed and dated 1769, pencil, pen and ink and grey wash, 11¾in. x 17½in.*

were often etched, or otherwise reproduced, by professional artists. These include two strip cartoons published in 1787, *A Long Minuet, as Danced at Bath* and *The Propagation of a Lie.* His humour is social rather than political. His Shakespearian figure subjects, perhaps inspired by the Wynnstay productions, are like those of Lady D. Beauclerk (q.v.).

Several members of his family, including his second son, **Sir Henry Edward BUNBURY (1778-1860),** the soldier and military historian, produced drawings very much in his manner.

Published: As 'Geoffrey Gambado': *An Academy for Grown Horsemen,* 1787.

Examples: B.M.; V.A.M.; Ashmolean; Greenwich; N.G., Scotland.

Bibliography: *Country Life,* 19 February, 1943 (letters).

BUNCE, Myra Louisa
1854 (Aston) -
A landscape, coastal, still-life and flower painter, she was the elder daughter of the Editor of the *Birmingham Post.* She painted in oil and watercolour, and in Cornwall and Wales, and exhibited in Birmingham and London from 1873 to 1910.

Her sister, **Kate Elizabeth BUNCE (1858-1927),** studied at the Birmingham School of Art, painted portraits, genre subjects, flowers and church interiors and was influenced by the Pre-Raphaelites.

BUNDY, Edgar, A.R.A., R.I.
1862 (Brighton) - 1922 (Hampstead)
A genre and historical painter in oil and watercolour who was largely self-taught, but encouraged by A. Stevens (q.v.). He was also a member of the Langham Sketching Club. He exhibited at the R.A. from 1881 and was elected R.I. in 1891, becoming Vice President, and A.R.A. in 1915.

Examples: Blackburn A.G.; Towneley Hall, Burnley; Shipley A.G., Gateshead.
Bibliography: *A.J.,* 1897; 1900; Summer No., 1900; 1905; 1909.

BUNNEY, John Wharlton
1828 (London) - 1882 (Venice)
A painter of Venetian scenes in oil and watercolour who was an unsuccessful candidate for the N.W.S. in 1862, when living in Kentish Town. He exhibited at the R.A. from 1873 to 1881 and an exhibition of his work was held at the Fine Art Society in 1883.
Examples: Maidstone Mus.

BUNNEY, Sydney John
1877 - 1928
A Coventry topographer who studied at the Art School and worked as a cashier at the Auto-Machinery Co. He made more than five hundred pencil and watercolour drawings of local buildings.
Examples: Coventry A.G.

BUNTING, Thomas
1851 (Aberdeen) - 1928
A painter of Aberdeen and Perthshire landscapes and rivers. He was a pupil of the itinerant painter James Winkley, and exhibited

BUNDY, Edgar (1862-1922)
An interior scene. *Watercolour, signed and dated 1892, 19in. x 26in.*

BURDETT, Major Peter Perez (c.1734-1793)
The Margrave of Baden's Yacht (?). *Signed and inscribed, pen and ink and watercolour, 14in. x 18in.*

from 1874. In 1885 he was a founder of the Aberdeen Society of Artists.
Examples: Aberdeen A.G.

BURBANK, James M
1805 - 1873
An animal and bird painter in oil and watercolour who entered the R.A.Schools in 1822. He was a member of the N.W.S. in 1833. He exhibited at the R.A. and elsewhere from 1825 to 1872. He travelled in America.

He lived in Camberwell, where he shared an address with **Miss L. BURBANK.** She exhibited fruit, flowers and birds' nests from 1826 to 1842 at the R.A., the N.W.S. and Suffolk Street.

BURCHETT, Arthur
A genre painter in oil and watercolour who lived in Hampstead and was working between 1874 and 1913.
Examples: Preston Manor, Brighton.

BURD, Laurence
A Shrewsbury estate agent who painted landscapes and exhibited in Birmingham from 1848 to 1870. He painted views of Gibraltar in 1851 and 1852, on the South Coast from 1872, in Yorkshire from 1885 and in Wales from 1892 to 1898.

BURDER, William Corbett
A painter who lived in Clifton and exhibited in London in 1859. He painted Welsh landscapes. In subject handling and writing his work can be very like that of W.J. Müller (q.v.).
Published: with others: *The Architectural Antiquities of Bristol,* 1851. *The Meteorology of Clifton,* 1863.
Examples: V.A.M.

BURDETT, Major Peter Perez
c.1734 (?Eastwood, Essex) -
1793 (Karlsruhe)
The grandson of the Rev. Peter Perez, vicar of Eastwood, from whom he inherited a small estate, he was a man of many talents. In the early 1760s he was in Derby working as a cartographer, and his 1:1 scale map of the county won him a premium from the Society of Arts on its publication in 1767. He was closely involved with Wright of Derby, for whom he sold pictures and from whom he borrowed money which was not always repaid. He features, sketching, in Wright's *A Philosopher giving a Lecture on the Orrery.* In 1768 he moved to Liverpool, where he combined cartographic projects with other artistic ventures. He was a friend of J.H.Mortimer (q.v.), and in 1771 he published the first aquatint to be printed in England, after a Mortimer painting. Whether he actually invented or modified the technique is not clear, and

whether he did so before or after C.F. Greville (q.v.) had purchased or learned it from Le Prince is equally obscure, but it seems that he sold his process to P. Sandby (q.v.) for £40 when in need of funds. Other schemes, some of which were successful, involved him with Josiah Wedgwood, Frederick the Great, George Parry, the ironmaster for the Coalbrookdale Company, M.'A'. Rooker (q.v.) and Benjamin Franklin – who remarked that the colonies were not yet ready for Burdett. He was a skilled draughtsman, and noted for his expertise in perspective, which led to his election as first President of the Liverpool Society of Arts. He also exhibited at the S.A. in London. Various cartographic schemes turned in his hand, and in 1775 he took service with the Margrave of Baden, leaving a wife and considerable debts behind him. With the rank of major he was in charge of the survey of the Margravate, and he founded a school of mathematicians and surveyors. At this time he also built a yacht, no doubt for the Margrave, and his watercolours of it on the slips show how well he had profited from his associations with Liverpool and Sandby.
Bibliography: P.Laxton & J.B.Harley: *A Survey of the County Palatine of Chester by P.P.Burdett, 1777,* 1974. J.Egerton: *Wright of Derby,* 1990. D.N.B., *Missing Persons,* 1993.

BURGESS, Henry William (c.1792-1844)
Fishing. *Watercolour, 4in. x 6in.*

BURGESS, Henry William (c.1792-1844)
A young Fisherman with his Donkey. *Pencil and watercolour, 5in. x 3in.*

BURGESS, Adelaide
1844 (Bedminster) - 1894 (Leamington)
The relationships between the various members of the Burgess family are very difficult to elucidate and the problem is further complicated by unrelated artists of the same name. Adelaide was a daughter of J. Burgess, Yr. (q.v.) She lived in Leamington and exhibited genre subjects from 1857 to 1872.
Examples: V.A.M.
Bibliography: *A.J.*, 1859.

BURGESS, Henry William
c.1792 (London) - 1844 (London)
The youngest son of W. Burgess (q.v.) and the father of J.B. Burgess (q.v.), he exhibited landscapes from 1809 to 1844 and was appointed Landscape Painter to William IV in 1826. He was also a drawing master at Charterhouse from about 1823 to 1840, and he lived in London.

He was the father of **Hugh Gilbert BURGESS (1823-1848)** who died in St. Kitts.
Published: *Views of the General Character and Appearance of Trees...* 1827.
Examples: B.M.; Leeds City A.G.
Bibliography: *Connoisseur*, June 1947.

BURGESS, James Howard
1817 (Ulster) - 1890
A landscape and miniature painter who worked in Belfast, Carrickfergus and Dublin. He exhibited at the R.H.A. from 1830, and he was no relation to any of the English artists.
Illustrated: Hall: *Ireland, its Scenery and Character*, 1841.
Examples: Ulster Mus.

BURGESS, John, Yr., A.O.W.S.
1814 (Birmingham) - 1874
The son of J.C. Burgess (q.v.), he was of artistic stock on both sides, and became a painter after an early flirtation with the sea. In about 1833 he went to Italy via Normandy and Paris, and stayed there until 1837. At this period he was attempting to become a figure painter, but soon turned to landscape, where his true talent lay. On his return he made sketching tours in Devon, Surrey and the Thames Valley, and in 1840 settled in Leamington, buying the teaching practice of the widow of D. Dighton (q.v.). In 1851 he

was elected A.O.W.S. He is at his best when using a pencil, and his architectural sketches made on the spot have been favourably compared to those of S. Prout (q.v.) and H. Edridge (q.v.).

His sister, **Jane Amelia BURGESS (b.1819/20)**, worked as a governess and exhibited flower subjects in 1843 and 1844. In the latter year, she was an unsuccessful candidate for the N.W.S.

Frederick BURGESS (1825-1892), who was an unsuccessful candidate for the N.W.S. in 1869, lived in London, Leicester, Malvern and Leamington, and exhibited landscapes at

BURGESS, James Howard (1817-1890)
On the Isle of Arran. *Signed, water and bodycolour, 14½in. x 26¾in.*

BURGESS, John, Yr. (1814-1874)
Rochester. *Pencil, 2½in. x 4½in.*

the R.A. until 1892, was a son either of H.W. or of J.C. Burgess (qq.v.). He was evidently prosperous, dying at Burgess Hall, Finchley.

In 1852 there was also a painting **Alfred BURGESS** in Leicester.
Examples: V.A.M.; Haworth A.G., Accrington; Fitzwilliam; Nottingham Univ.
Bibliography: *Walker's Quarterly*, IV, 16, 1925.

BURGESS, John Bagnold, R.A.
1829 (Chelsea) - 1897 (London)
The son of H.W. Burgess (q.v.), he was trained by Sir W.C. Ross the miniaturist. He went to Leigh's School and in 1849 to the R.A. Schools. He began as a portrait and genre painter, but from 1858 devoted himself to Spanish subjects, visiting Spain annually for thirty years. He also crossed to Morocco at least once. He was elected A.R.A. and R.A. in 1877 and 1888.

He left a vast number of sketches and watercolours which were usually made in preparation for his oil paintings. His remaining works were sold at Christie's, 25 March 1898.
Examples: Worcester City A.G.
Bibliography: *A.J.*, 1880; 1898.

BURGESS, John Cart, N.W.S.
1788 (London) - 1863 (Leamington)
The second son of W. Burgess (q.v.), he painted flowers and landscapes, exhibiting at the R.A. from 1812. In 1825 he married a daughter of Anker Smith and became a drawing master, with Royal pupils.
Published: *A Practical Treatise on Flower Painting*, 1811. *Useful Hints on Drawing and Painting*, 1818. An Easy Introduction to Perspective, 1828.
Examples: B.M.; Newport A.G.
Bibliography: *A.J.*, April, 1863.

BURGESS, Thomas, Yr.
1784 (London) - 1807 (London)
The eldest son of W. Burgess (q.v.), he exhibited historical subjects from 1778 to 1791 and landscapes from 1802 to 1806 at the R.A. He also made pencil and wash drawings of stormy beach scenes, which are slightly reminiscent of those of L. Clennell (q.v.).

The earlier **Thomas BURGESS** (c.1730-1791 London), grandfather of this one, was the second student to be enrolled at the R.A. Schools. Later he set up the Maiden Lane School, which merged with the St. Martin's Lane Academy, where he is said to have taught Gainsborough.
Published: *Principles of Design in Architecture*, 1809.
Examples: B.M.

BURGESS, William
1749   - 1812 (London)
A conventional topographical draughtsman. His drawings are outlined with a fine pen and rather timidly tinted, often in greys and blues. He visited South Wales and the Wye in 1785. He is chiefly notable as one of the first of the artistic dynasty. He was the son of the earlier Thomas, and the father of T., J.C., and H.W. Burgess (qq.v).
Examples: B.M.; Newport A.G.

BURGESS, William, of Dover
1805 (Canterbury) - 1861 (Dover)
Unrelated to the London and Leamington Burgesses, he was a schoolfriend of T.S. Cooper (q.v.) in Canterbury, where he had drawing lessons. He was apprenticed to his uncle, a coach builder and painter, and undertook the redecoration of the local theatre. In 1827 he went to Dover with Cooper, and they pressed on to Calais and Belgium. Leaving Cooper, he went back to coachpainting. He exhibited landscapes at the R.A. and Suffolk Street from 1838 to 1856, and visited London in about 1840 and perhaps Edinburgh in 1850. He then settled in Dover as a drawing master.

Although Cooper praises his early landscape work, there is sometimes something rather awkward in the perspective of his drawings.
Published: *Dover Castle, A.D. 1642*, 1847.
Examples: B.M.; V.A.M.

BURGESS, William, of Dover (1805-1861)
A Brewer's Dray. *Watercolour, 11⅜in. x 16⅞in.*

BURLINGTON, Dorothy, Countess of
1699 - 1758

The daughter and co-heiress of William Savile, Marquess of Halifax, she married Richard Boyle, the architect and 3rd Earl of Burlington. She was a patroness of musicians, drew in crayon, and was said to have a genius for caricature. It would be surprising if she had not tried to produce at least wash drawings.

BURLISON, John
c.1812 (? Eggleston) - p.1846

A son of the clerk of the works to the architect Bonomi in Durham, by whom he also was employed before working for a builder in Darlington. In the 1840s he probably accompanied his younger brother, the oil painter Clement Burlison (1815 Eggleston - 1899 Durham), on a tour to Italy.

BURN, Gerald Maurice
1862 (London) -

A painter and etcher of architectural subjects, he produced both oils and watercolours. He was educated at University College School, London and studied at South Kensington, in Cologne, Düsseldorf, Antwerp and Paris. He lived in Amberley, Sussex, and also painted maritime subjects.

Examples: Portsmouth City Mus.

BURN, Henry   ? 1807 (Birmingham) -
1884 (Melbourne, Australia)

The son of a varnish maker, he was apprenticed to an artist, perhaps S. Lines (q.v.). He was probably a teacher, and exhibited once at the R.A. in 1830, as well as locally. He travelled extensively around England until 1852, when he sailed from Liverpool, arriving in Melbourne in January 1853. There he painted and lithographed topographical subjects, but he was not greatly appreciated, dying in the Benevolent Asylum.

BURN, Thomas F
(Northumberland) -

A landscape and coastal painter who was living in London in 1861, and exhibited at the B.I. in 1867. He worked in Lancashire, Yorkshire, the Isle of Wight, Boulogne and Italy, and also painted on the Thames.

Examples: B.M.

BURNET, James M
1788 (Musselburgh) - 1816 (Lee, Kent)

The brother of J. Burnet (q.v.), he was apprenticed to a woodcarver and studied at John Graham's Evening Academy in Edinburgh. In 1810 he joined his brother in London and fell under the influence of Wilkie and the Dutch Masters. He exhibited at the R.A. from 1812, taking his subjects from rural Battersea and Fulham. He was noted for his careful study of nature and his strong colours.

Examples: B.M.; V.A.M.

BURNET, John, F.R.S., H.R.S.A.
1784 (Musselburgh) - 1868 (Stoke Newington)

The son of the Surveyor-General of Excise for Scotland, he was apprenticed to the engraver Robert Scott, and he studied at the Trustees' Academy at the same time as Wilkie (q.v.). In 1806 he moved to London and concentrated on engraving, often after Wilkie. He exhibited genre and historical works from 1808 to 1862. Like his brother James (q.v.), he painted many landscapes with cattle. He visited Paris in 1815.

Published: *Practical Hints on Composition,* 1822. *Practical Hints on Light and Shade,* 1826. *Practical Hints on Colour,* 1827. *An Essay on the Education of the Eye,* 1837. *Hints on Portrait-Painting,* 1850. *Turner and his Works,* 1852. *Progress of a Painter in the Nineteenth Century,* 1854.

Examples: B.M.; V.A.M.; Aberdeen A.G.; N.G., Scotland; Wolverhampton A.G.

Bibliography: *A.J.,* 1850; 1868.

BURNETT, William Hickling
1808 -

An architectural and landscape painter who lived in London and visited Italy, Egypt, Spain, Tangier and Scotland. In the admissions list of the R.A.Schools for 1829 his name is given as 'Stickling'. He published fourteen views of Cintra in 1836, and exhibited at the R.A. from 1844 to 1860. His colours and details are clear and precise.

BURNEY, Rev. Charles Parr
1785 - 1864

A grandson of Dr. Burney, the musical historian, he took over his father's school at Greenwich in 1813. He was an author and occasional landscape painter.

BURNEY, Edward Francis
1760 (Worcester) - 1848 (London)

A cousin of Fanny Burney, for whose *Evelina* he produced an illustration. He came to London in 1776, where he lived with his uncle Dr. Burney and studied at the R.A. Schools. He exhibited at the R.A. from 1780 to 1803. In 1784 he designed large illustrations for Dr. Burney's volume for the Handel Commemoration in Westminster Abbey; these show his talent for arranging complicated figure groupings. He made a number of charming designs and vignettes, as well as his well-known large satirical watercolours. He designed scenes for the lids of snuff boxes, and for the last forty years of his life worked almost exclusively as a book illustrator, illustrating the works of such poets as Langhorne and Young. These drawings are often in grey wash, with light overcolouring. His caricatures can be splendid things, owing their composition to Hogarth and some of the figure drawing to Fuseli, as well as to Stothard's illustrations.

Examples: Brighton A.G.

See Colour Plate

BURNS, Robert
1869 (Edinburgh) - 1941 (Edinburgh)

A figure, landscape and portrait painter who studied at South Kensington and, from 1890 to 1892, in Paris. He exhibited at the R.S.A. from the latter year and was elected A.R.S.A. in 1902, resigning in 1920. He was influenced by the Russian Ballet and by Vorticism, and he designed stained glass and painted murals. Despite his illustrative work, watercolour and drawing was secondary to painting and design in his career.

Published: *Scots Ballads by Robert Burns,* Limner, 1939.

Illustrated: *The Song of Solomon.*

Examples: Aberdeen A.G.; N.G., Scotland.

Bibliography: *Studio,* LXXXI, 1921. Fine Art Soc., Exhibition Cat., 1978. Bourne Fine Art, Edinburgh, Exhibition Cat., 1982.

BURR, A   Margaretta HIGFORD, née Scobell

A traveller and amateur artist who married Daniel Higford Burr, M.P., of Aldermaston Park, Berks., in 1839. In that year they visited Spain, Portugal and Italy, and in 1844 they went to Egypt, Palestine and Constantinople. Two years later they returned to the Nile, reaching a point some two hundred miles below Khartoum.

A number of her sketches were published by the Arundel Society, others were exhibited for charity. Her Aldermaston recipe for venison pasty appears in *The Cookery Book of Lady Clark of Tillypronie,* 1909.

Bibliography: *A.J.,* 1859.

BURR, George Gordon
1862 (Aberdeen) -

A painter of Aberdeen streets and houses who was working in about 1894. His watercolours are sometimes on a large scale.

Examples: Aberdeen A.G.

BURR, John, A.R.W.S.
1831 (Edinburgh) - 1893 (London)

A genre and portrait painter in oil and watercolour who studied at the Trustees' Academy. He moved to London in 1861 and is said to have studied at 'Mr. Emblin's Academy' at Leytonstone, Essex. More probably he taught there. He exhibited at the R.A., the O.W.S. and elsewhere from 1862, and was elected A.R.W.S. in 1883. He was also a member of the R.B.A. Christie's held a sale of his work in April 1883.

Examples: B.M.

Bibliography: *A.J.,* 1869.

BURRARD, Admiral Sir Charles, Bt.
1793 - 1870

Burrard went to sea at twelve, served through the Napoleonic wars, and in 1808 was in the Baltic on board the *Victory,* under Vice-Admiral Sir James Saumarez. He was promoted captain in 1822, rear-admiral in

1852, vice-admiral in 1857, and admiral in 1863 while on half-pay, and he retired to his seat at Lyndhurst.

His early works at sea are reminiscent of N. Pocock (q.v.). His New Forest landscapes are freer and more colourful, and were probably influenced by W.S. Gilpin (q.v.), who was for a time a neighbour.

Burrard married Louisa (c.1801-1885), sister of M. Lushington (q.v.), had six daughters, and on his death the baronetcy became extinct.

His nieces **Harriet and Mary Anne BURRARD** were pupils of W. Gilpin (q.v.).
Bibliography: *Country Life*, 27 Feb. 1948; 18 June 1948; 7 July 1960.

BURRELL, Frances, Lady, née Wyndham
c.1786 - 1848
The eldest sister of the 1st Lord Leconfield, she married Sir Charles Burrell, 3rd Bt., M.P. in 1808. She was a pupil of H. Bright (q.v.). Her daughter-in-law was H.K., Lady Burrell (q.v.).

BURRELL, Henrietta Katherine, Lady, née Pechell - 1880
The daughter of Admiral Sir G.B. Pechell, she was a pupil of P. de Wint (q.v.) before her marriage in 1856 to the 4th Burrell baronet.

BURRINGTON, Arthur Alfred, R.I.
1856 (Bridgwater) - 1924 (Lake Garda)
A painter of landscapes, portraits, figures, genre and flower subjects, who studied at South Kensington and the Slade before going on to Rome and Paris, where his masters included Cipriani, Julian and Bonnat. He exhibited in London from 1880 and was elected R.I. in 1896. He also exhibited in France, Tasmania and America. Early subjects were found in Brittany, Switzerland and Algiers as well as in Britain. He lived in the West of England, and then settled at Menton on the Riviera.
Examples: Victoria A.G., Bath; A.G. of New South Wales, Sydney.
Bibliography: E. Magagiyo: *A.B., le Peintre-Poète*, 1925. *Bulletin* de la Soc. d'Art Mentonnais, June 1993.

BURT, Albin Robert
1784 - 1842 (Reading)
Is there a Youth who his Adora loves?
Whose every step his partial eye approves?
Till Time shall place her on the Bridal Throne
Let BURT portray the charmer – Lover's own...
(Llwyd)
Burt started his career as an engraver under Robert Thew and Benjamin Smith, and later turned to portraiture, exhibiting at the R.A. in 1830. As well as young ladies, he painted Reading dignitaries, and he had a good eye for detail.

His son, **Henry W. BURT**, was also a portrait painter, and opened a drawing school in Reading in about 1830. He sometimes painted small, full-length figures, using a miniaturist's technique. The work of father and son is very similar.

His daughter Emma married John White, a Reading artist.

C.T. Burt (q.v.) may have been another of his eight children.
Examples: Reading A.G.

BURT, Charles Thomas
1823 (Wolverhampton) - 1902
A Birmingham artist who may have been a son of A.R. Burt (q.v.) and who studied under S. Lines (q.v.) and painted in Wales, the Orkney Islands, Worcestershire, Somerset, Yorkshire and Derbyshire. He exhibited at the R.A., B.I., R.B.A. and elsewhere, and was a member of the Birmingham Society of Artists from 1856.

He worked in oil and watercolour, the latter rather in the manner of D. Cox (q.v.), whose friend and pupil he was.

BURTON, Sir Frederick William, R.H.A., R.W.S., F.S.A.
1816 (Corofin House, Co. Clare) - 1900 (London)
The son of Samuel Frederick Burton, an amateur landscape painter in oil, he trained under the Brocas brothers (q.v.) in Dublin. He first exhibited at the R.H.A. in 1837, in which year he was elected A.R.H.A., becoming a full Member two years later. He began by painting portraits in watercolour or chalk, and miniatures, but soon moved to genre pictures. He made several visits to Germany and lived in Munich for seven years from 1851. During this time he paid yearly visits to London, where he exhibited his German drawings. He was elected A.O.W.S. and O.W.S. in 1855 and 1856. In 1869 he resigned, but was made Honorary Member in 1886. He was one of the founders of the Archaeological Society of Ireland, and was elected F.S.A. in 1863. In 1874 he was appointed Director of the N.G., and gave up painting to devote his time to improving the Gallery's collection of old masters. He was knighted on his retirement in 1894.

A memorial exhibition of his work was held at the N.G., Ireland a few months after his death. A sale of his drawings was held at Christie's on 21 June 1901.
Examples: B.M.; V.A.M.; Ashmolean; N.G., Ireland; City A.G., Manchester.
Bibliography: *A.J.*, 1859. *W&D*, 1987, iv.

BURTON, John
An actor and landscape painter who specialised in moonlight scenes and copies of Gainsborough. In 1792 he published *Cottages from Nature in watercolour painting*, and he exhibited from 1769 to 1789. He had a painting daughter and, perhaps, a son.

BURTON, William Paton, R.S.W.
1828 (Madras) - 1883 (Cults, Aberdeen)
After an education in Edinburgh, he worked for a short while for David Bryce, the architect. He then turned to landscape painting and exhibited frequently at the R.A. and Suffolk Street from 1862 to 1880. He painted views in England, Holland, France, Italy and Egypt. He was an unsuccessful candidate for the N.W.S. on several occasions from 1867, when he moved to Witley in Surrey, to 1872. He was elected R.S.W. in 1882, and also had a base at Cults, near Aberdeen.
Examples: B.M.; V.A.M.; Aberdeen A.G.; City A.G., Manchester; Newport A.G.

BURTON, William Shakespeare
1830 (London) - 1916 (Lee, Kent)
A Pre-Raphaelite follower, best known for *The Wounded Cavalier* which was exhibited at the R.A. in 1856. He studied at the R.A. Schools, gaining a gold medal in 1851. He hardly worked during the 1880s and 1890s, but resumed in about 1900. He was primarily an oil painter, but occasionally worked in watercolour.
Bibliography: V. Paton: *An Artist in the Great Beyond, Messages from a Father*, 1925.

BURY, Thomas Talbot
1811 (London) - 1877 (London)
An architect and topographer who produced Parisian views for A.C. Pugin (q.v.) between 1828 and 1831. They are somewhat in the manner of W. Callow (q.v.). He also worked in London and Liverpool.
Published: *Remains of Ecclesiastical Woodwork*, 1847. *Rudimentary Architecture*, 1849.
Examples: B.M.; City A.G., Manchester.

BUSH, Flora, Mrs., née Hyland
(Bethersden, Kent) -
Unsurprisingly a flower painter, she studied at South Kensington. She married Reginald Edgar James Bush, R.E., A.R.C.A. (1869-1956), Principal of the Bristol School of Art, and lived in Bristol from 1889 to 1929.

BUSHBY, Thomas
1861 (Eccleshill, near Bradford) - 1918 (Carlisle)
A landscape painter who started work in a woollen mill at the age of ten. At fourteen he became a pupil teacher, and was then apprenticed to a lithographer. He also took drawing lessons at the Mechanic's Institute. After four years in London he moved to Carlisle in 1884 and worked as a designer. He was encouraged by the Earl of Carlisle (q.v.), and frequently sketched in Norway, France, Switzerland, Holland and Italy.

He was in some ways a topographer, but his work can show a Pre-Raphaelite precision of detail.
Examples: Carlisle City A.G.

BUSHE, Laetitia   **- 1757**
An Irish amateur artist who painted naïve landscapes and miniatures in Ireland, as well as a watercolour panorama of London. She was a daughter of Arthur Bushe of Dangan, Co. Kilkenny, and was active from at latest 1731. She was very sociable, and a friend of Mrs. Delany, but smallpox and straightened finances spoiled her chances on the marriage market. She visited London and Bath in 1743, and perhaps on other occasions.
Illustrated: R.Barton: *Lectures on Natural Philosophy…* 1751; *Some Remarks on the County of Kerry,* 1751.

BUSS, Robert William
            1804 (London) - 1875 (Camden Town)
After an apprenticeship to his father, an engraver and enameller, he studied under G. Clint (q.v.). For some years he painted only theatrical portraits, but later he turned to historical and conversation pieces, which he exhibited at the R.A., the B.I. and Suffolk Street from 1826 to 1859. For some time he was editor of *The Fine Art Almanack.* He was also a successful illustrator, notably of the novels of F. Marryat (q.v.), and of *The Pickwick Papers.* His landscapes are Callow-like, and he was the father of *the* Miss Buss.
Examples: B.M.; Fitzwilliam; Newport A.G.
Bibliography: *A.J.,* 1874; 1875.

BUSSEY, Reuben
            1818 (Nottingham) - 1893
The son of a corkcutter, he learned the trade in Nottingham and also studied art under Thomas Barber and John Rawson Walker before being sent to study in London, where he spent much time sketching in the Tower. His father's death caused him to return to Nottingham and corkcutting. In middle age, however, he retired to devote himself to painting. His subjects are chiefly taken from Bailey's *History of Nottinghamshire,* Shakespeare and the Bible.
A memorial exhibition was held at the Castle Mus., Nottingham, in 1894.
Examples: Castle Mus., Nottingham.

BUTLER, Elizabeth Southerden, Lady, née Thompson, R.I.
            1846 (Lausanne) - 1933
A battle painter on an heroic scale. She and her sister, the poet Alice Meynell, were brought up abroad, and she studied at South Kensington from 1866, in Florence in 1869, and in Rome. She first exhibited at the R.A. in 1873 and was elected R.I. the following year. She married Lt.-Gen. Sir W.F. Butler in 1877, and they spent their honeymoon in Kerry. She was a Roman Catholic and sketched peasants and chapels. She was the best man among Victorian battle painters, and as well as her battle scenes, which show a Pre-Raphaelite exactness of detail, she sketched landscapes and life in Palestine, Egypt, South Africa, Italy and Ireland.
Published: *Letters from the Holy Land,* 1903. *From*

BUTLER, Mildred Anne (1858-1941)
A Lady painting. *Watercolour, 10½in. x 7in.*

Sketchbook and Diary, 1909. *An Autobiography,* 1923.
Examples: B.M.; City A.G., Manchester.
Bibliography: *A.J.,* 1874; 1876; 1905. *Art Annual,* 1898. *Studio,* 1898. *Country Life,* 21 Nov. 1952. Nat. Army Mus., Exhibition Cat., 1987.

BUTLER, Canon George
            1819 (Harrow) - 1890 (London)
An amateur painter, he was the son of the headmaster of Harrow. He was educated there, at Cambridge and Oxford, and became a don. He was ordained in 1854 and was installed at Winchester in 1882. He lectured on art at Oxford and was later principal of colleges at Cheltenham and Liverpool. His wife came from Northumberland, and for a time they lived at Ewart Park.

BUTLER, Mary E
A flower painter who exhibited at the R.A., the R.I. and elsewhere from 1867. By 1909 she was living in Natal.
Examples: V.A.M.

BUTLER, Mildred Anne, R.W.S.
1858 (Kilmurry, Co. Kilkenny) - 1941
A landscape, genre and animal painter, she studied at the Westminster School of Art and under Frank Calderon. She was also a pupil of Norman Garstin at Newlyn. She was elected A.R.W.S. in 1896. Her work is in the Cox tradition.
Her father, **Captain Henry BUTLER (1805-1881)** painted animals and weird jungles in the Cape, West Indies and Brazil during an army career.
Examples: Tate Gall.; Ulster Mus.
Bibliography: A.Crookshank: *M.A.B.,* 1992. Christie's, Sale Cat., 13 Oct. 1981.
See Colour Plate

BUTLER, Samuel
            1835 (Langar, Notts.) - 1902
The author, lawyer, painter and theorist. He studied under F.S. Cary and at Heatherley's on his return from farming in New Zealand in 1865, and he put painting first among his careers between 1869 and 1875. He illustrated a number of his writings, and his watercolours are sometimes ahead of their time, being reminiscent of the style of Muirhead Bone. Among his literary theories was one that the *Odyssey* was written by a Sicilian lady.
Examples: B.M.
Bibliography: E. Shaffer: *Erewhons of the Eye, S.B.,* 1988.

BYRNE, Anne Frances (1775-1837)
Wild Flowers. *Watercolour heightened with white, signed, 7½in. x 10in.*

BYRNE, John A. (1786-1847)
Twickenham. *Watercolour, signed, 7⅜in. x 10¼in.*

BYRON, Frederick George (1764-1792)
Breakfast at Breteuil. *Pen and grey ink and watercolour, 12½in. x 18½in., mounted with a cut-out figure.*

BUTTERSWORTH, Thomas
1768 (Isle of Wight) - 1842 (Greenwich)
A marine painter who had been a sailor and who lived in London. He was active between 1798 and 1827, and was appointed Marine Painter to the East India Company. He specialised in the naval battles of the Napoleonic Wars.
Examples: B.M.; Greenwich.

BUXTON, Albert Sorby
1867 (Mansfield) - 1932
The first head of the Mansfield Art School, he was the town's topographer, antiquarian and historian. He presented his collection of watercolours to the Mansfield A.G.
Published: *Mansfield a Hundred Years Ago. Mansfield in the Eighteenth Century.*
Examples: Mansfield A.G.

BYRNE, Anne Frances, O.W.S.
1775 (London) - 1837 (London)
The eldest daughter of William Byrne (1743-1805), the engraver, and sister of J. Byrne (q.v.), she began her career as a teacher, but soon turned to a full-time practice of art. She was the first lady Associate in 1805, and Member in 1821, of the O.W.S. She retired during the 'oil invasion' of 1812 to 1819, but was a regular exhibitor both before and after until her retirement in 1834. She was the first to break the Society's initial ban on flower painters, and she remained faithful to the genre throughout her career, with an occasional bird or nest in her later years. From 1808 she lived near Fitzroy Square.
The second daughter **Mary BYRNE (1776-1845)** was a pupil of the miniaturist Arland and married James Green (q.v.). She was the mother of B.R. Green (q.v.). She exhibited miniatures and copies at the R.A. from 1795 to 1835.
Another painting sister was **Elizabeth**

BYRNE who exhibited English and Continental landscapes between 1838 and 1849. She lived with J. Byrne (q.v.).
Examples: V.A.M.
Bibliography: O.W.S.Club, XLVIII, 1973.

BYRNE, John, A.O.W.S.
1786 (London) - 1847 (London)
The only son of William Byrne, like his sisters Letitia and Elizabeth he began life as an engraver, both assisting his father and on his own account by, for example, producing plates for Wilde's *Cathedrals*. He left engraving for landscape painting and was elected A.O.W.S. in 1827. After 1832, he travelled extensively in France and Italy, but largely remained faithful to the Home Counties and Wales for his subject matter. He visited the West Country in 1844 and Yorkshire in 1845, and he very occasionally attempted subjects from Roman history.
Examples: V.A.M.; Laing A.G., Newcastle; Richmond Lib.
Bibliography: O.W.S. Club, XLVIII, 1973.

BYRNE, Letitia
1779 (London) - 1849 (Marylebone)
A daughter of William Byrne, the engraver, she exhibited views in Derbyshire, Wales and France from 1799 to 1848.
Illustrated: P. Amsinck: *Tunbridge Wells*, 1810.
Examples: B.M.; Doncaster A.G.
Bibliography: O.W.S. Club, XLVIII, 1973.

BYRNE DE SATUR, Edmond Ribton
1840 - 1885 (Highgate)
An Irish painter of domestic subjects and views around Highgate where he was living during the period from 1878 to 1885 when he exhibited in London. He also exhibited at the R.H.A. in 1882 and 1885. He enjoyed gardens and evidently liked cats. His death is registered under the names 'Edmund Ribbon B. De Satur'.

BYRON, Frederick George
1764 - 1792 (Bristol Hot Wells)
Several members of the Byron family painted, usually caricatures, including the poet's father, **Captain John BYRON (1756-1791),** and his cousin, F.G. Byron. The latter exhibited with the Society of Arts in 1791. His work is rather in the manner of H.W. Bunbury (q.v.), but his drawing is poor.
Examples: B.M.

BYRON, Rev. and Hon. Richard
1724 (Newstead Abbey) - 1811 (Haughton-le-Skerne)
The third son of W., Lord Byron (q.v.), he was educated at Westminster and Christ Church, Oxford, obtaining his BA in 1747. In 1758 he became vicar of Eglingham, Northumberland, moving to Ryton, Durham in 1769, and to Haughton-le-Skerne in 1795. He had considerable industrial and business interests, particularly in coal, and in Canada. He seems to have accompanied his brother, Captain John Byron, to Louisburg in 1760 as a naval chaplain, and four years later he obtained a vast land grant in Nova Scotia. His brother was made Governor of Newfoundland in 1769.
He inherited his facility with pen and pencil from his father, and although his watercolours of MicMac Indians are a little crude, they are important and detailed records. His reputation as an artist was high in his day and circle.
His son Rear-Admiral **Richard BYRON (1769-1837)** was probably also a painter.

BYRON, William, 4th Lord
1669 - 1736 (Newstead Abbey)
Gentleman of the Bedchamber to Prince George of Denmark, and an amateur watercolourist. He was a pupil of P. Tillemans (q.v.), whom he employed to make drawings at Newstead Abbey. He inherited the title in 1695.

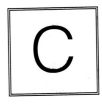

CADENHEAD, James, R.S.A., R.S.W.
1858 (Aberdeen) - 1927 (Edinburgh)
A landscape painter in oil and watercolour who was educated at the Dollar Institute and Aberdeen Grammar School, and who studied at the R.S.A. Schools and in Paris under Duran. He exhibited at the R.S.A. from 1880 and was elected A.R.S.A. and R.S.A. in 1902 and 1921. He was also a founder of the N.E.A.C. and a printmaker.
Examples: Aberdeen A.G.; Dundee City A.G.; City A.G., Manchester.
Bibliography: *Studio,* X, 1897; XXXV, 1905; Special No., 1907; LVIII, 1920.

CADOGAN, Lady Augusta Sarah
1811 - 1882
A painter of landscapes and figure subjects, she was a daughter of the 3rd Earl Cadogan and was a lady-in-waiting to the Duchess of Cambridge.

CADOGAN, General the Hon. Sir George
1814 - 1879
A brother of A. and H. Cadogan (qq.v.), he produced impressive watercolours of life in the Crimean trenches, which have been described as 'one of the most accomplished and detailed artistic records of the Crimean War'. He also painted watercolour portraits. He was a liaison officer with the Sardinian Army, and in later life he was military attaché at Florence, where two of his daughters married Italian officers.
Examples: Nat Army Mus.
Bibliography: R. Pearman: *The Cadogans at War.*

CADOGAN, Lady Honoria Louisa
1813 - 1904
The third child of the 3rd Earl Cadogan (1783-1864) for whom she and her sister Lady A. Cadogan (q.v.). kept house after, and perhaps effectively before, the death of their mother in 1845. In 1842-4 both sisters had been with their father in Rome pursuing archaeological interests, and on their return they published a book of engravings for the benefit of the Chelsea Infant School. During this Italian visit Lady Honoria sometimes produced three watercolours a day. She enjoyed architectural details, church interiors, street scenes and processions as well as larger landscapes. In later years she was often in Belgium, France and Switzerland as well as Italy, to which she returned frequently. In Britain Cowes was regularly visited, and she also ventured to Jersey, and recorded events such as the Great Exhibition as well as the houses of her family and friends.

It seems more than likely that she was

CAFFIERI, Hector (1847-1932)
Two children on a seashore. *Watercolour, signed, 20½in. x 13¾in.*

influenced by G.B. Campion (q.v.), whom she may have met through her brother G. Cadogan (q.v.).
Bibliography: *Country Life,* Jan. 16, 1992.

CAFE, James Watt
1857 (London) - 1939
Probably the younger son of T. Cafe, Yr. (q.v.), he painted cathedrals and other architectural subjects, such as the Radcliffe Camera, in oil and watercolour.
Examples: Salisbury Mus.

CAFE, Thomas, Yr.
1820/1 (Hammersmith) - 1909 (London)
The nephew of T.S. Cafe (q.v.), he painted topographical and landscape subjects and exhibited at the R.A. and at Suffolk Street between 1844 and 1868. He spent some years in Edinburgh between about 1838 and 1845, and sketched in Scotland with W.L. Leitch (q.v.).
Examples: Richmond Lib.

CAFE, Thomas Smith
1793 - 1843 (Marylebone)
A landscape, portrait, architectural and marine

painter who entered the R.A.Schools in 1812 and exhibited between 1816 and 1840. He lived in Kilburn and St. John's Wood and often worked at Hastings.
Examples: B.M.; Towner A.G., Eastbourne.

CAFE, Thomas Watt
1856 (London) - 1925 (Florence)
The elder son of T. Cafe, Yr. (q.v.), he painted landscapes and genre subjects and exhibited from 1876, although he entered the R.A. Schools only in 1879. He lived at St. John's Wood and later in Italy.

CAFFIERI, Hector, R.I.
1847 (Cheltenham) - 1932
A landscape, flower and sporting painter who studied in Paris before working in London and Boulogne. He seems to have covered the Russo-Turkish war of 1877-8 and to have lived in London from 1882 to at least 1901. In Boulogne he painted the fisherfolk. He was a member of the R.B.A. and was elected R.I. in 1885, retiring in 1920.

An exhibition of his work was held at the Continental Gallery, London, in 1902.

CAHILL, Richard Staunton
1829 - 1904
A figure painter in oil and watercolour who trained at Leigh's school, entered the R.A. Schools in 1852 and exhibited at the R.H.A. from 1851 and in London from 1853 to 1887. He lived in Ireland a well as London, and many of his subjects were Irish.

CAHUSAC, John Arthur, F.R.S., F.S.A.
1802 - 1866 (Hampstead)
A painter of fruit, figure subjects and portraits who entered the R.A. Schools in 1821 and exhibited from 1827 to 1853. A portrait drawing by him was engraved and published in 1818, and he was a member of the N.W.S. from 1834 to 1838. At that time he lived in Pentonville and described himself as a 'Professor of Figure Drawing'. He was elected F.S.A. in 1840.

CAIL, William   1779 (Carlisle) -
The son of an innkeeper, he was possibly a pupil of R. Carlyle (q.v.). He toured the south of Scotland in 1792 and seems to have left Carlisle soon afterwards. He specialised in landscape and topography.

A William Cail published *The Collier's Wedding* in 1829, under the *nom de plume* 'Edward Chicken'.
Examples: Carlisle City A.G.

CAIRNS, John
A painter of coasts, particularly those of Arran, North-east Scotland and Holland, in both oil and watercolour. He lived in Edinburgh, and was active between about 1845 and 1867. He also visited France. His style was suited to the harsh lights of the North Sea.
Examples: N.G. Scotland; Paisley A.G.

CALCOTT, J
A Portsmouth painter of landscapes and coasts who was active in the 1860s.
Examples: Portsmouth City Mus.

CALDECOTT, Randolph, R.I.
1846 (Chester) - 1886 (St. Augustine, Florida)
The son of an accountant, he became head boy of King Henry VIII's School, Chester, where he won a drawing prize. Despite this early evidence of his aptitude, he was set to work as a banker, firstly in Whitchurch, Shropshire, and then in Manchester, developing his true talent by doodling. Between 1866 and 1869 drawings of his were published in local papers, and, encouraged by this success, he moved to London in 1872, determined on becoming an artist. Drawings were accepted by *London Society* and other papers, and he studied in the studio of the sculptor Dalou. His first major successes were the illustrations for Washington Irving's books, *Old Christmas and Bracebridge Hall* in 1875 and 1876. He was then encouraged by Edmund Evans (q.v.), the publisher, to illustrate children's books. In

CALLCOTT, Sir Augustus Wall (1779-1844)
View in a North Italian Town. *Signed, watercolour, 4¾in. x 5½in.*

1878 his first two, *The House that Jack Built* and *John Gilpin,* were instantly popular. In all he produced sixteen books of this kind.

He exhibited finished watercolours at the R.A. from 1872 to 1885 and was elected R.I. in 1882. He also occasionally produced sculpture. In 1885 he went to America to escape the English winter, as his health had been weak for a long time. He died while engaged on a series of sketches of American life.

He was a highly original artist with a keen eye for the eccentricities of English country life. His colours are applied in flat washes, and the seeming spontaneity of his pen outline is the result of long practice and great thought. As he said, he 'studied the art of leaving out as a science', believing that 'the fewer the lines, the less error committed'. The influence of this discipline is plain not only in his own work, but also in that of later artists such as Phil May and Cecil Aldin.
Examples: B.M.; V.A.M.; Ashmolean; Cecil Higgins A.G., Bedford; Grosvenor Mus., Fitzwilliam; Newport A.G.; Ulster Mus.; Walsall A.G.
Bibliography: H.R. Blackburn: *R.C.,* 1886. M.G. Davis, *R.C.,* 1946. R. Engen: *R.C., Lord of the Nursery,* 1975. *A.J.,* 1886. *Gaz. des Beaux Arts,* 1886. *Apollo,* XLIII, 1946.

CALDWELL, Edmund
1851 - 1930 (London)
An animal painter and sculptor, and an occasional landscape painter, he lived in London and was active at least from 1880.

CALDWELL, Commander James Thomas
- 1849 (Paris)
A grandson of an admiral, he became a naval officer, serving on the Far East station from 1842 to 1849. There he produced rough chunky watercolours of Eastern scenes rather in the manner of Chinnery (q.v.). He was promoted commander in 1844, but died of cholera.

CALEY, George Allison
A pupil of J. Glover (q.v.), who was working in 1837.

CALLANDER, Adam
c.1760 - c.1812
A landscape painter who exhibited from 1780 to 1811. His subjects are taken from Scotland and Wales, as well as being the fruits of more extensive travels, such as a visit to Tenerife. Waterhouse, following the R.A., spells him with a middle 'a', but McEwan gives 'Callender'.

CALLCOTT, Sir Augustus Wall, R.A.
1779 (Kensington) - 1844 (Kensington)
He began his career as a musician, but then became a pupil of Hoppner, studied at the R.A. Schools, and turned firstly to portraiture and then to landscape and seascape painting. He was a member of Girtin and Francia's sketching club and was elected A.R.A. and R.A. in 1806 and 1810. He visited France and Holland before 1827, and in that year he married and made his first visit to Italy. Thereafter Continental subjects form the

CALLOW, John (1822-1878)
Criccieth Castle. *Watercolour over traces of pencil, signed, inscribed and dated July 3rd '63, 9in. x 19¼in.*

CALLOW, John (1822-1878)
In the Bay of Biscay. *Signed, watercolour, 11in. x 17in.*

majority of his exhibited work. From 1837, when he was knighted, he also exhibited figure subjects in oil. In 1849 he was appointed Conservator of the Royal Pictures. In his own time he was classed in the same category as his friend Turner, and although this was obviously to overestimate his abilities, he could be a very pretty and able draughtsman. He is at his best with coastal scenes, either in sepia or in full colour. His remaining works were sold at Christie's, 8-11 May 1845, and 22 June 1863.

His wife **Maria, Lady CALLCOTT (1785-1842)** was the daughter of Rear-Admiral Dundas, with whom she went to India in 1808. She married Captain Graham in the following year and returned to England in 1811. They went to South America in 1821, but the captain died off Cape Horn. She married Callcott in

1827. They spent much time in Italy, and she made many competent watercolours and drawings, some of which are in the B.M. She was the author of *Journal of a Residence in India*, 1812; *Letters on India*, 1814; and *Little Arthur's History of England*.
Examples: B.M.; V.A.M.; Cartwright Hall, Bradford; Leicestershire A.G.
Bibliography: J. Dafforne: *Pictures by Sir A.W.C.*, 1875. R.B. Gotch: *Maria, Lady C.*, 1937. *A.J.*, 1845; Jan. 1856; April, 1860; 1866; 1896. *Portfolio*, 1875.

CALLCOTT, William James
A marine painter who lived in Regent's Park and Putney and who worked from 1843 to 1896. His subjects are often on the North Sea coasts and he also visited Plymouth. He painted in oil and watercolour and was an

unsuccessful candidate for the N.W.S. in 1856, 1868 and 1874, and for the O.W.S. in 1876. In the 1880s he was painting scenery for the Theatre Royal, Haymarket, sometimes with J. Absolon (q.v.) providing figures.

CALLENDER, Adam –
see CALLANDER, Adam

CALLENDER, H   R
A friend and follower of F. Nicholson (q.v.).

CALLOW, George Dodson
A landscape and marine painter in oil and watercolour who worked between 1858 and 1873. His style is reminiscent of that of T.B. Hardy (q.v.).

The marine painter **James W. CALLOW** seems to have been his brother, but they do not appear to have been related to the more famous family.

CALLOW, John, O.W.S.
    1822 (Greenwich) - 1878 (Lewisham)
A pupil of his brother William, who took him to Paris in 1835, where he studied and ultimately took over the drawing practice, returning to England in 1844. He was elected A.N.W.S. in 1845, but resigned in 1848 and joined the O.W.S. the following year. From 1855 to 1861 he was Professor of Drawing at the R.M.A., Addiscombe, after which he became joint Master of Landscape Drawing with A.E. Penley (q.v.) at the R.M.A., Woolwich, resigning in 1865. In 1875 he was appointed Professor at Queen's College, London; at the same time he kept up a large and profitable private practice.

His style is largely based on that of his brother, and he excelled in coastal scenes. His subjects were taken from the coasts of England, Wales, Normandy and the Channel Islands. He also painted landscapes in North Wales from 1861, Scotland from 1862 and the Lakes from 1864. He occasionally painted in oil. Like his brother, he was a firm believer in the use of pure watercolour rather than heightening with bodycolour.

His executors held sales of his drawings at Christie's, 24 June and 18 December 1878 and 7 April 1879.
Examples: B.M.; V.A.M.; Glasgow A.G.; Gray A.G.; Hartlepool; Leeds City A.G.; Newport A.G.; N.G. Ireland; Birmingham City A.G.; Beecroft A.G., Westcliffe-on-Sea; York City A.G.
Published: with R.P. Leitch: *Easy Studies in Water-Colour Painting*, 1881.
Illustrated: V. Foster: *Painting for Beginners*, 1884.

CALLOW, William, R.W.S.
1812 (Greenwich) - 1908 (Great Missenden)
The son of a builder, who encouraged his early artistic efforts, he was employed by Theodore Fielding (q.v.) in 1823 and formally articled to him two years later. A fellow apprentice was C. Bentley (q.v.) who gave him his first painting

CALLOW, William (1812-1908)
Venice from the Dogana at the entrance to the Grand Canal. *Watercolour, signed and dated 1846, 12⅞in. x 18⅞in.*

lessons. Callow worked for Thales Fielding (q.v.) between 1827 and 1829, when he went to Paris where he worked for the Swiss artist Osterwald, as well as for Newton Fielding (q.v.). He returned to London for six months but in 1831 was back in Paris where he shared a studio with T.S. Boys (q.v.) and thus came under the influence of Bonington (q.v.). In 1834 he took over the studio from Boys and built up a large and profitable teaching practice among the French nobility, including the duc de Nemours, the Prince de Joinville and the Princess Clementine, sons and daughter of King Louis Philippe. At this period he began the series of long walking and sketching tours which he made during his holidays. He visited the South of England in 1835, the South of France in 1836, Switzerland and Germany in 1838, Italy in 1840, Normandy in 1841, the Rhine and Moselle in 1844, Holland in 1845, Germany, Switzerland and Venice in 1846, and Coburg, Potsdam and Berlin in 1862. His final visit to Italy was made in 1892. Between the earlier tours he also revisited England. In 1838 he was elected A.O.W.S. and this encouraged him to leave Paris in 1841 and to set up as a drawing master in London. Here again he built up a large practice, and his pupils included Lady Beaujolais Berry, Lady Stratford de Redcliffe and Lord Dufferin (q.v.). He continued to work as a drawing master until 1882. In 1848 he was elected O.W.S. and he served the Society well throughout his life, acting as Trustee and as Secretary from 1865 to 1870. In 1855 he moved from London to Great Missenden where he lived until his death.

Callow could be said to have started at the height of his powers and to have declined gradually throughout his very long working life. In his earlier work the influence of Boys and Bonington is very marked, and he often uses the tricks and mannerisms of the older men, even to stopping out lights with a finger or thumb. The decline in quality becomes evident after about 1850. It is worth noting, too, that at about this date, he changes his neat and precise signature for a sloppy, backwardsloping one. He begins to grow overambitious and to work on too large a scale. His attitude to nature is always that of the topographer, although his marine subjects, which owe something to

CALLOW, William (1812-1908)
A View of Shakespeare Cliff from Dover Beach. *Signed with initials, watercolour, 6⅛in. x 10in.*

CAMERON, Sir David Young (1865-1945)
A Scottish River at Evening. *Signed, pen and black ink and watercolour, 10in. x 16in.*

Bentley, show a greater freedom. Throughout his career, his draughtsmanship is exact, but his sense of composition, which was unerring at first, grows less sure. Even though he was carried away by a fussy attention to detail and over-variety of colour, he continued all his life making small, more effective drawings for his own pleasure.
Published: *An Autobiography* (ed. H.M. Cundall), 1908.
Examples: B.M.; V.A.M.; Aberdeen A.G.; Ashmolean; Blackburn A.G.; Cartwright Hall, Bradford; Bridport A.G.; Grosvenor Mus., Chester; Coventry A.G.; Bowes Mus., Durham; Towner A.G., Eastbourne; Exeter Mus.; Fitzwilliam; Glasgow A.G.; Greenwich; Inverness Lib.; City A.G., Manchester; N.G., Scotland; Newport A.G.; Beecroft A.G., Southend; Stalybridge A.G.; Ulster Mus.; Worcester City A.G.
Bibliography: H.M. Cundall: *W.C.,* 1908; J. Reynolds: *W.C.,* 1980; *Walker's Quarterly,* XXII, 1927. O.W.S. Club, XXII; LVI.
See Colour Plate

CALVERT, Charles, Yr.
1785 (Glossop Hall, Derby) - 1852 (Bowness, Westmorland)
The son of his namesake, the Duke of Norfolk's agent, who was an amateur artist, he was a cotton merchant before turning to art. He taught both oil and watercolour and painted landscapes. He was a founder of the Royal Manchester Institution and father-in-law to W. Bradley (q.v.). During his last years he was confined to bed, where he still endeavoured to paint.
Examples: V.A.M.; City A.G., Manchester.
Bibliography: *A.J.,* May, 1852.

CALVERT, Edward
1799 (Appledore) - 1883 (London)
After a period in the Navy, he studied under James Ball and A.B. Johns at Plymouth. In 1824 he moved to London and entered the R.A. Schools. He became one of 'The Ancients', Blake's disciples, and was a frequent visitor to Shoreham. He exhibited at the R.A. from 1825 to 1836 as well as at the S.B.A. Thereafter he devoted most of his time to producing woodcuts. He attended the Life Academy in St. Martin's Lane, where he became a close friend of Etty (q.v.). To improve his knowledge of anatomy he sketched at St. Thomas's and St. Bartholomew's Hospitals during the cholera epidemic of 1830. He made several visits to Wales, the first in 1835, and in 1844 he toured Greece, returning by way of Venice, the Rhine and Antwerp. In 1851 he moved from Paddington to Hampton Court, and finally, in 1854, to Hackney. His woodcuts, oil paintings and watercolours alike are imbued with the arcadian spirit of Greece; the Welsh landscape also had a profound influence on him.
Examples: B.M.; Exeter Mus.
Bibliography: S. Calvert: *Memoir of E.C.,* 1893. R.L. Binyon: *The Followers of William Blake,* 1925. R. Lister: *E.C.,* 1962. *Print Collector's Quarterly,* XVII, ii. 1930. *West Country Mag.,* 1946.

CALVERT, Edwin Sherwood, R.S.W.
1844 (England) - 1898 (Glasgow)
A Glasgow School follower of Corot who began by painting coasts and harbours. Later he concentrated on landscapes from Northern France and he also visited Italy in 1877. He exhibited at the R.A. from 1878 to 1896 and used a subdued palette.

CALVERT, Frederick **- c.1845**
Originally from Cork – an aquatint of a Cork subject after a drawing by him is dated 1807 – he exhibited with the Dublin Society of Artists and the Hibernian Society in 1815, and left for England soon afterwards. There he exhibited between 1827 and 1844 and contributed antiquarian articles and illustrations to the *Archaeological Journal.* He also published a series of lithographs, *Studies of Foreign and English,* in 1824.
Published: *The Interior of Tintern Abbey. Lessons in Landscape Colouring &c.*
Illustrated: W. West: *Picturesque Views in Staffordshire and Shropshire,* 1830. J. Pigot: *Pigot's Coloured Views. The Isle of Wight...,* ?1847.
Examples: V.A.M.; Ashmolean; Chelsea Lib.; Dudley A.G.; Richmond Lib.

CALVERT, John Smales
1836 (Staithes) - 1926 (Middlesbrough)
A schoolmaster and painter of landscapes and architectural subjects he was the son of a railway engineer. He taught in Middlesbrough, where he became Director of Education. He painted locally and in France, Belgium, Norway and Germany.
Examples: Middlesbrough A.G.

CALVIN, William
1752 (Penrith) - 1830
A landscape and decorative painter who was the son of a house painter. He drew for T. Pennant's *Tour of Scotland,* 1769, and later

CAMERON, Katharine (1874-1965)
The Legend of the Christmas Rose. *Signed with initials and inscribed, watercolour, 7¾in. x 11in.*

worked for the Earl of Lonsdale.

His sister, **Ann CALVIN, (1747 Penrith - c.1785 London),** painted birds and flowers.

CAMERON, Sir David Young, R.A., R.S.A., R.W.S., R.S.W.
1865 (Glasgow) - 1945 (Perth)
The great etcher, and a fine painter in oil and watercolour. He was the son of a minister and of **Margaret Johnston CAMERON, née Robertson (1839-1924),** a talented amateur watercolourist, and he trained at the Glasgow School of Art during a brief stint in commerce. He also studied in Edinburgh and exhibited from 1886. His first etchings date from the following year. He was elected R.W.S. in 1915 and R.A. in 1920. He declined the Presidencies of both the R.A. and the R.S.A., but accepted a knighthood in 1924. It took him some time to find his own style, and it is at its best and most original in his monumental etchings of Highland landscapes. There is much of the etcher in his watercolour work, but the style is not unsympathetic to the medium, with spare drawing and thin but powerful washes of colour.
Examples: B.M.; V.A.M.; Nat. Gall., Scotland.
Bibliography: A.M.Hind: *The Etchings of D.Y.C.,* 1924. B. Smith: *D.Y.C. The Visions of the Hills,* 1992. *Studio,* XXXVI, 1905; 1919. *A.J.,* 1901; 1909. *Apollo,* Oct.1929. O.W.S. XXVII, 1949. Scottish Arts Co., Exhibition Cat., 1965. Fine Art Society, Edinburgh, Exhibition Cat., 1990.

CAMERON, Hugh, R.S.A., R.S.W.
1835 (Edinburgh) - 1918 (Edinburgh)
A portrait and genre painter who studied at the Trustees' Academy. He exhibited in Scotland from 1854 and was in London between 1876 and 1888. Thereafter he spent his summers at Largs and his winters in Edinburgh. He visited the Riviera in about 1880. He was elected A.R.S.A. and R.S.A. in 1859 and 1869 and R.S.W. in 1878. He specialised in children and crones.
Examples: Paisley A.G.

CAMERON, Katharine, Mrs. Kay, R.S.W.
1874 (Glasgow) - 1965 (Edinburgh)
The sister of D.Y. Cameron (q.v.), she too was an excellent etcher and a painter. She studied at the Glasgow School of Art, was elected R.S.W. in 1897, and in 1902 went to the Académie Calarossi in Paris. Although her landscape style is obviously derived from that of her brother, it is impressive enough to be appreciated for itself. Her flower studies are lovely – as she said 'there is nothing so inspiring as painting flowers'. In 1928 she married the connoisseur and collector Arthur Kay, H.R.S.A. (1861-1939). He was the author of *Treasure Trove in Art,* 1939, for which she designed the cover and jacket.
Illustrated: L. Chisholm (ed.): *In Fairyland,* 1904. C. Kingsley: *The Water-Babies,* 1905. F. Grierson: *Haunting Edinburgh,* 1929. &c.
Bibliography: B. Smith: *D.Y. Cameron The Visions of the Hills,* 1992. *A.J.,* 1900. *Scots Pictorial,* 18 Oct. 1919. *International Studio* (New York), LXXV, 1922. *Walker's Monthly,* April 1930. *Glasgow Herald,* 6 March 1959. *Scottish Field,* CVI, Oct. 1959. *Scottish Art Review,* XIII, i, 1971.

CAMPBELL, Alexander
1764 (Tombea, Loch Lubnaig) - 1824 (Edinburgh)
Musician, author, landscape painter and caricaturist, he was the son of a carpenter. The family settled in Edinburgh where the poverty-stricken father died. However, Campbell studied music with Tenducci before teaching it to boys like Walter Scott. For a while he studied medicine, but then he turned to writing, and in the 1790s he published some of his own Highland views 'drawn on the spot'. He was also known for a caricature of J. Kay (q.v.), who replied in kind. He travelled widely in Scotland collecting specimens of minstrelsy, but by the end of his life he was reduced to copying manuscripts for his old pupil Scott and others.
Published: *A Journey from Edinburgh through parts of North Britain,* 1802. &c.
Examples: N.G.Scotland.

CAMPBELL, Caecilia Margaret, Mrs. Nairn   1791 (Dublin) - 1857 (Battersea)
The daughter of J.H. Campbell (q.v.) who gave her lessons, and in whose style she worked. She exhibited in Dublin from 1809, and between 1826 and 1847 sent views, particularly of Killarney and Wicklow, to the R.H.A. In 1826 she married George Nairn, A.R.H.A., an animal painter in oil. Her son, John Campbell Nairn (b.1831) copied and restored his father's pictures. She painted in both oil and watercolour and also made wax models of flowers.

Her daughter **Anna Langley NAIRN** was a designer for the Belleek porcelain factory during the 1840s.

CAMPBELL, John Henry (1757-1828)
The Island of Lambay from Malahide. *Watercolour, signed, inscribed and dated 1805, 4¼in. x 6in.*

CAMPBELL, Charlotte, Elizabeth and Georgiana – *see* **CAWDOR**

CAMPBELL, James
A painter of landscapes, portraits and genre subjects in oil, watercolour and sepia wash. He lived in Glasgow, exhibiting there and in Edinburgh from 1853 to 1896.

CAMPBELL, John Francis, of Islay
1822 - 1885 (Cannes)
The eldest son of W.F. Campbell of Islay, he was educated at Eton and Edinburgh University. He held a number of official and courtly posts such as Groom in Waiting, Secretary to the Lighthouse Commission and Secretary to the Coal Commission, but his most important work was as a writer and folklorist. He travelled on the Continent in the 1840s, visiting Italy in 1841 and 1842, Spain in 1842, Germany in 1846 and France in 1848, and he went to America in 1864. Much of his time was spent in the Western Highlands and on Islay collecting traditional tales and songs. He illustrated a number of his books, as well as making landscape and topographical sketches.
    His aunt was Lady Belhaven (q.v.).
Published: *Popular Tales of the West Highlands,* 1860-2. *Life in Normandy,* 1863. *Frost and Fire with Sketches,* 1865. *A short American Tramp in the Fall of 1864,* 1865. *Leabhair na Fenine,* 1872. *Thermography,* 1883. &c.
Examples: N.G., Scotland.
Bibliography: *Athenaeum,* 1885, i 250. *Academy,* 1885, XXVII, 151.

CAMPBELL, John Henry
1757 (Dublin) - 1828
A landscape painter in oil and watercolour, he was trained in the R.D.S. Schools and exhibited in the opening exhibition of the R.H.A. in 1826 and again in 1828. His views appear to be taken entirely in Ireland: Dublin and Wicklow in particular. His drawing is good, if conventional, and his colouring strong. He was the father of C.M. Campbell (q.v.).
Examples: B.M.; V.A.M.; Nat. Mus., Ireland; Ulster Mus.

CAMPBELL, John Hodgson
1855 (Newcastle-upon-Tyne) - 1927 (Whickham, nr. Gateshead)
The son of an artist, he studied in Edinburgh and later worked as a portrait painter in Newcastle. He was a member of various local literary and artistic clubs and also painted large numbers of landscapes in watercolour.
Examples: B.M.; Shipley A.G., Gateshead; Laing A.G., Newcastle; S. Shields A.G.

CAMPION, George Bryant, N.W.S.
1796 - 1870 (Woolwich)
A prolific topographical, genre and coastal painter who taught drawing at the R.M.A. Woolwich between 1841 and 1870. He exhibited from 1829 and joined the N.W.S. in 1834 when he was living in Pentonville. He generally worked on grey or light brown paper and often used a combination of chalk and watercolour rather in the manner of Henry Bright (q.v.). As a result of his employment, many of his drawings contain soldiers. He had a wide influence, not only on his military pupils, but also on their families.
Examples: B.M.; Ashmolean; Brighton A.G.; Towner A.G., Eastbourne; Greenwich; Newport A.G.
Bibliography: *Walker's Monthly,* 87-88, Mar.-Apr., 1935.

CAMPION, George Bryant (1796-1870)
The Thames at Richmond, Surrey.

CARELLI, Gabriel (1821-1900)
The Albert Memorial. *Signed and inscribed, watercolour, 9in. x 16¾in.*

CANNING, Charlotte, Countess
1817 - 1861 (Calcutta)
The elder daughter of Lord Stuart de Rothesay and sister of Lady Waterford (q.v.), with whom she was a pupil of W. Page, J.D. Harding and W.L. Leitch (qq.v), the last of whom she introduced to Queen Victoria (q.v.). In 1835 she married Charles, later 2nd Viscount and Earl (1859), Canning, and she was a Lady of the Bedchamber to the Queen from 1842 to 1855, accompanying her on the visits to Louis Philippe and Belgium in 1843 and to Gotha in the following year. She also recorded the early years of Balmoral and the building of Osborne House. Canning was appointed Viceroy of India in 1855, and the rest of her life was spent there, travelling widely and writing graphic accounts of the Mutiny to the Queen. Her landscapes and small flower studies were admired by Ruskin who maintained that of the two sisters 'Lady Canning was the colourist'. Her work is, however, much the less original, although still thoroughly competent.
Bibliography: A.J.C. Hare: *The Story of Two Noble Lives*, 1872. V. Surtees: *C.C.*, 1975. *Country Life*, 4 April 1957; 14 Aug. 1997. Harewood House, Exhibition Cats., 1996, 1997. Holburne Mus., Bath, Exhibition Cat., 1997.

CANNON, William
b.1840 (? Newcastle) -
A pupil of T.B. Hardy (q.v.), he worked mainly as a marine painter on the coast of France and Italy. He was awarded a gold medal in Paris in 1877, and he was painting at least until 1901, when he was working on the Medway.

CAPELL, A
A bird painter working in 1766.

CAPELL, Lady Mary
1723/4 - 1782
The youngest daughter of the 3rd Earl of Essex. With her sisters (one of whom was Charlotte, Countess of Clarendon), she was a pupil of the flower painter G.D. Ehret (q.v.). Her botanical drawings are in both bodycolour and watercolour. In 1758 she married Admiral the Hon. John Forbes.

CAPON, William
1757 (Norwich) - 1827 (Westminster)
The son of an artist, who taught him portrait painting. His talent, however, was more for architecture, so he was articled to Novozielski and worked at the Italian Opera House and Ranelagh Gardens. In 1794 he built a theatre for Lord Aldborough in County Kildare. Thereafter he was chiefly connected with Kemble as a scene painter at Drury Lane. He also undertook architectural (and theatrical) work in Bath in 1807 and he was appointed draughtsman to the Duke of York in 1804. He produced a number of watercolour views of London and exhibited at the R.A. and elsewhere from 1788 to 1827. He was a friend and sketching companion of J. Carter (q.v.), especially around the Palace of Westminster and the Abbey.
Examples: B.M.; Victoria A.G., Bath; Guildhall Lib.; Westminster Lib.
Bibliography: *Gentleman's Mag.*, 1827. *Mag. of Art*, XVIII, 1894-5.

CARDONNEL, Adam de
– *see* **LAWSON, Adam de CARDONNEL**

CARELLI, Gabriel(e) Mariano Nicolai
1821 (Naples) - 1900 (London)
The son of Raphael Carelli, special artist to the 6th Duke of Devonshire, Carelli settled in England, dropped the final 'e' from his first name, married an Englishwoman and took British nationality. He travelled widely in Europe, North Africa, Turkey and Palestine. He was an unsuccessful candidate for the N.W.S. in 1866, when he was living at Kenilworth, and he exhibited at the R.A. from 1874. He was a favourite of Queen Victoria.
Gonsalvo CARELLI (1818 Naples - 1900 Naples), who lived with him for a time, was an elder brother. **Conrad H.R. CARELLI (1869-1956 London)** was the son of Gabriel, studied at Julian's in Paris and also travelled widely. He held a number of spring exhibitions at Menton. His style is rather looser than that of his father, whose eye for colour and detail was superior.

CAREY, Joseph Carey
1859 (Belfast) - 1937
A fine, if very slightly naïve, painter of watercolour land- and seascapes, he trained at the Belfast printer Marcus Ward & Co. before setting up his own business as an illuminator of addresses and illustrated books. He was a member of the Belfast Ramblers Sketching Club. He painted throughout Ireland, and also in the West of Scotland, and he had a liking for wild scenery, although, according to Crookshank and Glin, his cottages are somewhat banal. He used white heightening, and his style did not develop over the years. He signed 'Jos.Carey'.
His brother, **John CAREY (c.1860-1943)** was a genre painter in watercolour.

CAREY, General Peter
1774 (Guernsey) - 1852 (Southampton
A landscape painter who was a pupil of J.

CARLAW, John (1850-1934)
Sunday Morning Gallop. *Watercolour, signed, 12¼in. x 19¼in.*

Farington (q.v.) in 1791, entered the R.A. Schools in the following year and exhibited at the R.A. in 1795. J.G. le Marchant (q.v.) was his brother-in-law and his father-in-law was General Hewett, Commander-in-Chief in India, whom he served there as military secretary from 1807 to 1812, and subsequently in Ireland. He was a most competent watercolourist, and he also painted in the Lake District, Devon, the Channel Islands, France, Switzerland and Germany.

CARFRAE, J
A landscape painter who exhibited at the R.A. in 1787 and was working in Scotland as late as 1799.
Examples: B.M.; N.G., Scotland.

CARLISLE, George Howard, 9th Earl of (1843-1911)
The River Mouth, Tangier. *Numbered 9 and inscribed on the reverse, watercolour heightened with white, 10½in. x 14½in.*

CARLAW, John, R.S.W.
1850 (Glasgow) - 1934 (Helensburgh)
He was a designer at the Saracen Foundry, Glasgow, before retiring at an early age to devote himself to painting. He worked mainly in watercolour and was elected R.S.W. in 1885. Later in life he lived at Helensburgh.
William CARLAW, R.S.W. (1847-1889), by whom there is a watercolour in Glasgow A.G., and who exhibited there in 1878, was his brother, and **Effie CARLAW** who exhibited in 1886, presumably a sister.

CARLILL, Stephen Briggs
1859   - 1903 (South Africa)
A master at the Hull School of Art and an examiner for the Department of Science and Art, he entered the R.A. Schools in 1886 and exhibited at the R.A. and R.I. from 1888. Later he went to farm in South Africa where he was 'killed by Kaffirs'.
Published: with A. Woodruff: *Rural Rambles*, 1889.
Examples: V.A.M.

CARLINE, George Francis
1855 (Lincoln) - 1920 (Assisi)
A painter of landscapes, genre subjects and portraits in oil and watercolour, he was the son of a solicitor, but descended from a distinguished family of masons, architects and sculptors in Lincoln and Shrewsbury. He studied at Heatherley's, in Antwerp and in Paris, and he exhibited in London from 1886. He lived in Oxford for some years, becoming Secretary of the Oxford Art Society; later he lived in Hampstead. Fifty-nine of his pictures were shown at the Dowdeswell Galleries in 1896 and he was elected R.B.A. in 1904.
In the Leicestershire A.G. is an example of the work of his son **Sydney William CARLINE (1888 London - 1929)**, who painted landscapes and portraits.
Illustrated: A. Lang: *Oxford*, 1915.
Examples: V.A.M.
See the Hayward and Carline Family Tree in Colvin, p.484.

CARLISLE, George James Howard, 9th Earl of, H.R.W.S.
1843 (London) - 1911 (Brackland, Surrey)
An amateur painter in oil and watercolour who was educated at Eton and Trinity College, Cambridge, studied at South Kensington and exhibited from 1868. He was a Liberal MP before succeeding to the title in 1889. His London house was decorated by Morris and Burne-Jones, and after he inherited the title in 1889, he entertained a wide circle of literary and artistic friends at Naworth Castle, Cumberland. Perhaps under the influence of his wife, he was a militant temperance campaigner. He travelled widely in Europe and visited Africa and the West Indies. He was an Honorary R.W.S. and Chairman of the Trustees of the N.G. His watercolours are brightly coloured and not particularly detailed,

in the contemporary Italian manner.
Published: *A Picture Songbook,* 1910.
Examples: B.M.
See Chambers Family Tree

CARLISLE, John Percy

A landscape painter who lived in London and Dorking and later at Keats Cottage, Hampstead. He exhibited from 1866 to 1916 and painted in Devon, Wales, Scotland and Guernsey, as well as in the South of England.

CARLYLE, Robert
1773 (Carlisle) - 1825 (Carlisle)

A landscape and architectural painter, he was the son of a sculptor. He won a silver medal from the Society of Arts in 1792 for drawings of Carlisle Cathedral. In 1801, according to Farington, he was in Edinburgh as a pupil of A. Nasmyth (q.v.). He supplied illustrations for Britton's *Beauties* and ran successful drawing classes. In 1808 he drew up plans for the rebuilding of the city, unexecuted, and in 1822 he was one of the founders of the Carlisle Society. At the time of his death he was working on a series of views of Dovedale, Matlock, the Scottish Lochs, Cumberland, Westmorland and North Wales. He was also a poet and published *De Vaux or the Heir of Gilsland,* 1815. He was a topographer, and his work is usually outlined in pen. His pupils included his nephews George and Robert, W. Cail (q.v.) and M.E. Nutter (q.v). His work was much copied.
Illustrated: W. Hutchinson: *History of Cumberland,* 1794.
Examples: Carlisle City A.G.; Carlisle Lib.

CARMICHAEL, John Wilson
1799 (Newcastle) - 1868 (Scarborough)

After a period at sea and an apprenticeship to a ship builder, Carmichael became a pupil of the elder T.M. Richardson (q.v.). From 1838 to 1862 he sent oil paintings and watercolours for exhibition at the R.A. and elsewhere in London, and in about 1844 he moved there himself. He visited Holland and Italy and went to the Baltic as a war artist for the *I.L.N.* during the Crimean War. In about 1862 he left London in poor health and settled in Scarborough.

He is a clean workman and the freedom which he sometimes attains in his finished work is based on careful observation and drawing. This is in part due to his early

---

CARMICHAEL, John Wilson (1799-1868)
Sunderland Old Pier. *Signed with initials, pencil and watercolour, 8in. x 12¼in.*

CARMICHAEL, John Wilson (1799-1868)
The Hospital Ship *Belisle* receiving cattle in Faro Sound. *Extensively inscribed on the reverse and dated June 5, 1855, pencil and watercolour, 10in. x 14in.*

CARLISLE, John Percy
Coastal Natives. *Signed and dated 1870, pencil, water and bodycolour, 17½in. x 26½in.*

CARPENTER, William Hookham (1818-1899) *Martinique. Signed, inscribed and dated 1859, pencil and watercolour, 9in. x 13¾in.*

association with J. Dobson (q.v.) the architect of Newcastle, for whose plans he provided the figures and often the colour. He is chiefly known as a marine painter, and this tends to obscure the quality of his town scenes. His sea pieces show practical experience and a strong feeling for the elements.

His remaining works were sold at Christie's, 24-5 November 1870. He has sometimes been misnamed James, perhaps by confusion with an Edinburgh contemporary, **James F. CARMICHAEL**, who exhibited for twenty years from 1833.

Published: *The Art of Marine Painting in Watercolours*, 1859. *The Art of Marine Painting in Oil Colours*, 1864.
Examples: B.M.; V.A.M.; Brighton A.G.; Darlington A.G.; Shipley A.G., Gateshead; Greenwich; Laing A.G., Newcastle; Newport A.G.; Sunderland A.G.; Ulster Mus.
Bibliography: D.Villar: *J.W.C.,* 1995. *A.J.,* July, 1868. Laing A.G., Newcastle, Exhibition Cat., 1968.

CARPENTER, A   R
A landscape and coastal painter who painted in oil and watercolour and exhibited at Birmingham from 1868 to 1890.

CARPENTER, John
A painter of shipping in brown wash who was working in 1827. He is perhaps identical to the watercolour portraitist working in the 1840s.
Examples: V.A.M.

CARPENTER, Margaret Sarah, Mrs., née Geddes   1793 (Salisbury) - 1872 (London)
The elder daughter of Captain Geddes of Edinburgh, a relative of A. Geddes (q.v.), she took lessons from a Salisbury drawing master,

and copied paintings from Lord Radnor's collection at Longford Castle, before establishing herself in London as a portraitist in 1814. In 1817 she married William Hookham Carpenter, later Keeper of Prints and Drawings at the B.M. She exhibited at the R.A. and elsewhere from 1818 to 1866. As well as portraits she made landscape studies in watercolour. She was the mother of W.H. Carpenter (q.v.), and her sister married W. Collins, R.A. (q.v.). A second sister was C.E. Gray (q.v.).
Examples: B.M.; V.A.M.
Bibliography: D.C. Whitton: *The Grays of Salisbury,* 1975. *A.J.,* Jan. 1873.

CARPENTER, Mary
1807 (Exeter) - 1877 (Bristol)
A philanthropist, she was the daughter of the Unitarian Lant Carpenter who gave her a wide classical, scientific and artistic education. After a brief period as a governesss, she involved herself with the running of schools in the most deprived areas of Bristol, and in organising conferences on education, prisons and women's work. Until 1866 she had not travelled far beyond the British Isles, but a long sympathy for India led to her first visit to Bombay, Madras and Calcutta. She made three more visits to the Sub-continent, in 1868-9, 1869-70 and 1875-6, and also visited Darmstadt in 1872 at the invitation of Princess Alice (q.v.) and America and Canada in 1873. She managed to find time to sketch pleasing and more than competent, if conventional, landscapes.
Published: *Reformatory Schools for the Children of the Perishing and Dangerous Classes...* 1851; *Six Months in India,* 1868; &c.

Bibliography: J.E. Carpenter: *Life and Work of M.C.,* 1879. *Theological Review,* Apr.,1880.

CARPENTER, Percy
1820   - 1895
The younger son of M.S. Carpenter (q.v.), he entered the R.A. Schools in 1838, and later painted in India and the Far East, exhibiting during the 1840s and 1850s. He illustrated a book on hog hunting and covered other aspects of Anglo-Indian life.
Examples: India Office Lib.
Bibliography: D.C. Whitton: *The Grays of Salisbury,* 1975.

CARPENTER, William Hookham, yr.
1818 (London) - 1899 (Forest Hill)
The son of M.S. Carpenter (q.v.), he spent many years in India, accompanying the 1855 Afghan expedition, and he drew and etched Oriental ladies and landscapes. He also sketched in the Scilly Isles. His work can be reminiscent of that of J.D. Harding (q.v.). An exhibition of his Indian subjects was held at South Kensington in 1881. In 1859 he visited a brother in Barbados, and he was in Boston, U.S.A., for some time from 1862.
Examples: B.M.; V.A.M.; Ashmolean.
Bibliography: D.C. Whitton: *The Grays of Salisbury,* 1975.

CARPENTER, William John
An architectural and figure painter who lived in London and exhibited at the R.I. and Suffolk Street from 1885 to 1895.

CARR, Frances
A pupil of Cox at Kennington, she made a sketching tour of the Rhine. She was perhaps the Frances Susanna Carr who published *Genevive: a Tale,* 1826. Her sister-in-law was Mrs. Jane Carr, the daughter of John Allnutt the collector, who herself left many watercolours to the V.A.M.

CARR, Sir John
1772 (Devonshire) - 1832 (London)
A gossip and traveller who was called to the bar but did not practise because of poor health. The success of his first *Tour* led to a long series, and after the Irish one he was knighted by the Viceroy, the Duke of Bedford. He was satirised by Walter Scott and others, and Byron begged to be omitted from the account of Spain. He also published poetry. His illustrations are much in the manner of the landscape and topographic work of J. Nixon (q.v.), although they are not as accomplished as Nixon's at his best.
Published: *The Stranger in France. A Tour from Devonshire to Paris,* 1803. *A Northern Summer, or Travels around the Baltic,* 1805. *The Stranger in Ireland,* 1805. *A Tour through Holland,* 1807. *Caledonian Sketches,* 1808. *Descriptive Travels in Spain,* 1811.
Examples: B.M.

CARR, or KERR, Johnson
                    1743   - 1765
An apprentice, copyist and assistant in
Wilson's studio from about 1758 to 1763.
He won several prizes for drawing, and
naturally he concentrated on landscape.

CARR, Rev. William Holwell
        1758 (Exeter) - 1830 (London)
A landscape painter in the manner of J.
Bourne (q.v.), he held the living of
Menheniot, Cornwall, *in absentio* from
1792. He was the son of Edward Holwell,
an apothecary, married Lady Charlotte
Hay and took the additional name of Carr
in 1798 in consequence of an inheritance
from her uncle. He exhibited at the R.A.
from 1797 to 1820, but was best known
as a connoisseur and patron.
Examples: B.M.

CARRICK, Robert, R.I.
1829 (Western Scotland) - 1905
A landscape and genre painter somewhat
in the manner of the Pre-Raphaelites. He
had moved to London by 1848 when he
was elected A.N.W.S. He was elected
N.W.S. in 1850 and also exhibited at the
R.A. from 1853 to 1880.
Examples: City A.G., Manchester.
Bibliography: *A.J.*, 1859.

CARRICK, Thomas Heathfield
1802 (Upperly, Carlisle) - 1875 (Newcastle)
A chemist and self-taught miniaturist, he
worked at Carlisle, Newcastle and in London.
He exhibited at the R.A. from 1841 to 1866
and also produced larger portraits and hand-
coloured photographs.
Examples: V.A.M.; Laing A.G., Newcastle; Nat.
Lib. Wales.

CARROLL, Michael William
A general artist and engraver active in Hull
from 1795 to 1807. He painted portraits and
landscapes in various media, and he may be
identifiable with the William Carroll, an
Irishman, who exhibited Irish views at the
R.A. from 1790 to 1793 when living in
London.

CARRUTHERS, William –
                    see **AFFLECK, William**

CARSE, Alexander
        c.1770 (Edinburgh) - 1843 (Edinburgh)
After establishing a reputation in Edinburgh
where he was painting views as early as 1796,
he moved to London in 1812 and exhibited at
the R.A. and the B.I. He returned to Edinburgh
in about 1820. He was best known for his
drawings and paintings of Scottish domestic
life, and scenes from Burns and his own
unpublished poems. In his genre subjects he
forms a link between Allan and Wilkie.
    He was probably the father or brother of the

CARRICK, Robert (1829-1905)
'The Anglers.'. *Watercolour, signed, 8¼in. x 6¼in.*

oil painter **William CARSE** who was working
between 1818 and 1845, and fairly certainly
the father of **James Howe CARSE (1819-
1900).**

Examples: B.M.; Fitzwilliam; N.G., Scotland.
Bibliography: *Portfolio*, 1887.

CARTER, Ellen, Mrs., née Vavasour
        1762 (York) - 1815 (Lincoln)
She was educated at a convent in Rouen
and married Rev. John Carter, later
Headmaster of Lincoln Grammar School.
She provided illustrations for periodicals
such as *Archeologia* and the *Gentleman's
Magazine* and was particularly noted for
her figure drawing.

CARTER, Henry Barlow
1795 (Scarborough) - 1867 (Torquay)
A marine and landscape painter who
served in the Navy and lived in
Plymouth, Newington and Hull before
settling in Scarborough in the 1830s. He
remained there teaching drawing until
1862 when he retired to Torquay. His
style is derived from that of Turner, and
his palette and subject matter are limited,
his penchant being for a yellow-green
and for wrecks and storms. At some point
he took lessons from P. de Wint (q.v.),
and he owned examples of his work.
    His sons J.N. Carter (q.v.) and **Vandyke
CARTER** were also artists. **Matilda
Austin CARTER (b.1842)** who was an
unsuccessful candidate for the N.W.S. on
several occasions from 1868, and who
lived in Torquay, was probably a daughter,
and R.H. Carter (q.v.) possibly another son.
Examples: B.M.; V.A.M.; Derby A.G.; Greenwich;
Hull Mus.; Leeds City A.G.; Maidstone Mus.;
Wakefield City A.G.; York A.G.

CARTER, Henry Barlow (1795-1867)
Whitby from the Lighthouse. *Watercolour, signed, 7in. x 9½in.*

CARTER, Lt. Col. John Money (1811/12-1888)
The Heathfield Memorial, Gibraltar. *Watercolour, 12in. x 16in.*

CARTER, Lt. Col. John Money (1811/12-1888)
Rosia Bay, Gibraltar, and the South Barracks. *Watercolour, 11¾in. x 15¼in.*

CARTER, Hugh
1837 (Birmingham) - 1903 (London)
A topographer and genre and portrait painter who studied promiscuously at Heatherley's, under Alexander Johnston, J.W. Bottomley, F.W. Topham and J. Phillip, and at Düsseldorf under von Gebhardt. He exhibited in London and Birmingham from 1859 and was elected A.N.W.S. and N.W.S. in 1871 and 1875, resigning in 1899. A memorial exhibition was held at Leighton House in 1904.
Examples: V.A.M.
Bibliography: *Studio*, XXIV, 1902.

CARTER, John, F.S.A.
1748 (London) - 1817 (London)
An architectural draughtsman and writer, he was the son of a marble carver and was trained as a surveyor and mason. In 1774 he began to draw for the *Builder's Magazine*, and he continued to do so until 1786. In 1780 he was employed by the Society of Antiquaries as a draughtsman, and he was elected F.S.A. in 1795. Also in 1780, he began to work for Richard Gough, one of his most important patrons. Others included the Earl of Exeter, Horace Walpole, Sir H.C. Englefield (q.v.) and Sir R.C. Hoare (q.v.). Between 1798 and 1817 he published a series of papers entitled 'Pursuits of Architectural Innovation' in the *Gentleman's Magazine* which were an attack on overzealous restoration as carried out by Wyatt and others, and they provoked stormy scenes among the Antiquaries. He had a small practice as an architect. His style is close to that of J. Varley (q.v.) in his early years, and by the 1790s he had abandoned the old topographical tradition of careful pen outlining. His foliage is rather flat with a number of sloping curved lines and much stopping out. W. Capon (q.v.) was a neighbour and sketching companion about Westminster, as was, according to Britton, a young female servant who dressed in boy's clothes.

His collection, including his remaining works, was sold at Sotheby's, 23-5 February 1818.
Published: *The Scotch Parents, or, the Remarkable Case of John Ramble written by himself*, 1773. *Specimens of Ancient Sculpture and Painting*, 1780-94. *Views of Ancient Buildings in England*, 1786-93. *The Ancient Architecture of England*, 1795-1814. &c.
Examples: B.M.; V.A.M.; St. Alban's Abbey; Victoria A.G., Bath; Bodleian Lib.; Canadian Centre for Architecture, Montreal; Durham Cath. Lib.; Exeter Mus.; R.I.B.A.; Westminster Lib.
Bibliography: *Gentleman's Mag.*, 1817, ii; 1818, i; 1822, i. *Builder*, VIII, 1850. *Harlaxton Symposium*, 1985, 1986.

CARTER, Lieutenant-Colonel John Money
1811/12 - 1888 (Brentford)
Commissioned ensign in the 1st Royal Regiment of Foot in 1832, he served as a captain in Gibraltar from 1839 — when he showed four oil paintings at the R.S.A. — to early 1846, when he returned to England and went on half-pay. He was made up to lt.-col. in 1858, selling his commission in 1862, and he lived in Monmouth and perhaps London. He first exhibited watercolours in 1842, with very competent views of the Rock, and he continued to show Welsh and Scottish subjects and still lifes in London until 1865. He has a good feel for heat and distance, and his figures and buildings can be impressive.
Bibliography: *W&D*, 1986, iv.

CARTER, Joseph Newington
1835 (Scarborough) - 1871
A son of H.B. Carter (q.v.) whose style and subjects he inherited. He entered the R.A. Schools in 1855, but otherwise lived at Scarborough and Torquay. He exhibited in London from 1857 to 1860.
Examples: B.M.; York A.G.

CARTER, Owen Browne
1806 (London) - 1859 (Salisbury)
A Winchester architect who spent some time in Cairo in the early 1830s where he made many architectural and topographical drawings. Thereafter he worked in Hampshire both as an architect and an antiquary, illustrating his own writings. His topographical works show a strong drawing line, and he generally uses light washes.
    The architect G.E. Street (q.v.) was a pupil.
Published: *Picturesque Memorials of Winchester*, 1830. *Some Account of the Church at Bishopstone*, 1845.
Illustrated: R. Hay: *Illustrations of Cairo*, 1840.
Examples: B.M.
Bibliography: R. Freeman: *The Art and Architecture of O.B.C.*, 1991. *Gentleman's Mag.*, 1859, i. *Wilts. Archaeological Mag.*, XL, 1918-19.

CARTER, Richard Harry, R.I.
1839 (Truro) - 1911 (Sennen)
Possibly a son of H.B. Carter (q.v.), he painted Cornish landscapes. He exhibited from 1864 and turned to oil painting later in life.
Illustrated: J.T. Tregallas: *Peeps into the Haunts and Homes of Cornwall*, 1879.
Examples: Maidstone Mus.

CARTER, William
A Leeds landscape and coastal painter who exhibited in London from 1836 to 1876. It is possible that he was a relative of or perhaps even the same as the Carter mentioned in the biography of G. Chambers (q.v.) as working in Whitby and Stockington in the early 1830s. He went to London in 1835 and was believed to have cut his throat there.
Examples: V.A.M.

CARTERET, Mary Ann, Lady, née Masters
1777 (Cirencester Abbey) - 1863 (London)
An amateur painter in oil and watercolour, she married Lord John Thynne (1772-1849), later 3rd and last Lord Carteret, in 1801. She produced portraits, landscapes in the Aylesford manner and copies of old masters. Her mother-in-law, Lady E. Bentinck (q.v.), and at least two sisters-in-law, Lady Aylesford (q.v.) and Lady M. Markham, were flower painters.

CARTWRIGHT, Frederick William
A landscape painter who lived in Brixton and Dulwich and exhibited from 1854 until 1894. He worked in both oil and watercolour and painted in North Wales, Devon, Surrey, on the South Coast and on the Continent.
Examples: Exeter Mus.

CASSIE, James (1819-1879)
Dundee. *Signed and dated 1862, watercolour, 5in. x 9in.*

CARTWRIGHT, Joseph
1789 (Dawlish) - 1829 (London)
A marine painter who worked for the Navy as a civilian. On the British occupation of the Ionian Islands he was appointed paymaster-general at Corfu where he spent several years. On his return to England he became a professional artist, exhibiting at the R.A., the B.I. and with the S.B.A. of which he was elected a member in 1825. He was appointed Marine Painter to the Duke of Clarence in 1828. He shows a firm grasp of drawing, accuracy in nautical detail and a good sense of composition. His palette is made up of harmonious blues, greys and greens with the occasional touch of plummy red.
Published: *Views in the Ionian Islands*, 1821.
Examples: B.M.; V.A.M.; Greenwich.

CARVER, Robert
c.1730 (Dublin) - 1791 (London)
The son and pupil of Richard Carver, a historical and landscape painter. He began his career by exhibiting small watercolours in Dublin and painting scenery for Cork and Dublin theatres. Garrick was impressed by his work and invited him to Drury Lane where he met with considerable acclaim. He moved to Covent Garden with Springer Barry and there worked with J.I. Richards (q.v.). He exhibited landscapes in oil and watercolour with the Incorporated Society from 1765 to 1790, being elected a Fellow in 1773, Vice-President in 1777 and President in 1787. He also exhibited with the Free Society, and at the R.A. in 1789 and 1790.
    The techniques of scene painting are evident in his watercolours. He shows considerable skill in conveying atmospheric effects. E. Garvey (q.v.), his pupil, thought that he painted best 'the dashing of the sea waves upon a flat shore, or upon rocks – the colour so

true – the water so transparent' (Farington, *Diaries*, III, p.48). He signed his works 'R.C.' as did R. Crone (q.v.).

CARWITHAM, Thomas
A pupil and imitator of Sir J. Thornhill (q.v.), he made wash drawings of classical myths and architectural ornament.
Published: *The Description and Use of an Architectonick Sector*, 1723.
Examples: V.A.M.

CASEY, William Linnaeus
1835 (Cork) - 1870 (London)
The son of a gardener, he was a portrait and genre painter who trained at the Cork School of Design and at Marlborough House. In 1854 he was appointed second master at the Limerick School of Art, and later he set up as a drawing master in London, his pupils including some of the Royal children. He was Master of the St. Martin's Lane Academy for a time.
Examples: V.A.M.

CASHIN, Edward
An Irishman who painted views of Bristol for G.W. Braikenridge. His style is inspired by the seventeenth century Dutch painters and in particular by Jan van der Heyden. He was in Bristol from 1823 to 1826.
Examples: V.A.M.; Bristol City A.G.

CASLEY, William 1867 - 1921 (Penzance)
A landscape and marine painter who exhibited from 1890 to 1920. In 1891 he was living at The Lizard.

CASSIE, James, R.S.A., R.S.W.
1819 (Keith Hall, Aberdeen) -
1879 (Edinburgh)
An accident lamed him in early life and made him turn to painting as a career. He was a pupil

CATTERMOLE, George (1800-1868)
Putney Bridge. Signed with initials, pencil and watercolour, 11in. x 18¼in.

of J. Giles (q.v.) and lived in Aberdeen until 1869 when he was elected A.R.S.A. and went to live in Edinburgh. He was elected R.S.A. in 1879. Early in his career he mainly painted landscapes in the manner of Giles, but gradually he found his subjects more on the coast and among the fisherfolk. He also painted portraits, animals and domestic subjects. His style is broad and he avoids over-elaboration of detail and composition.
Examples: Aberdeen A.G.
Bibliography: *A.J.*, 1879.

CATESBY, Mark, F.R.S.
1682 (Sudbury) - 1749 (London)
One of the great English naturalists, Catesby was a son of a Suffolk lawyer and a member of the Jekyll family. An uncle introduced him to the naturalists John Ray and Samuel Dale, which probably influenced the course of his career. In 1712 he went to Williamsburg, Virginia, where his sister was settled, remaining in North America until 1719. The collection of plants and the drawings that he brought back caught the attention of Sir Hans Sloane and other patrons, who helped him to a second expedition to Carolina between 1722 and 1726. This time he concentrated on birds as well as botany, and drew previously undrawn mammals and reptiles. He also studied marine life off Florida and the Bahamas. The rest of his life was spent in preparing his great *Natural History,* with upwards of 100 plates, drawn and coloured by himself or by G.D. Ehret (q.v.) who helped with the second volume. The secretary of the Royal Society described it as: 'the most magnificent work I know since the Art of printing has been discovered'. That Catesby was a copyist of earlier men such as J. White

(q.v.), and an original artist, in water and bodycolour, does not detract from the value of his work as a naturalist.

The original drawings were bought by George III and remain at Windsor.
Published: *The Natural History of Carolina, Florida, and the Bahama Islands,* 1731, 1743.
Bibliography: H.McBurney: *M.C.'s Natural History of America, the watercolours from the R.Lib., Windsor Castle,* 1997.

CATHERWOOD, Frederick
1799 (London) - 1854 (at sea)
An archaeological draughtsman and railway engineer, he was a pupil of the architect Michael Meredith. From 1821 to 1825 he toured Italy, Greece and Egypt. In 1831 he returned to the Nile with Haig's expedition. He visited Palestine and Syria with F.V.J. Arundale (q.v.). In 1836 he set up in New York as an architect and in 1839 went to Central America to record the Mayan antiquities. It was at this time that he worked on the railways. He visited England in 1853 and was drowned on the return voyage.
Published: *Views of Ancient Monuments in Central America,* 1844.
Examples: B.M.
Bibliography: V.W. von Hagen: *F.C., Architect,* 1950.

CATLOW, George Spawton
A landscape painter who lived in Leicester and exhibited at the R.A. and the R.I. from 1884 to 1916. He was painting at Runswick Bay, Yorkshire, in 1907.

CATTERMOLE, Charles, R.I.
1832   - 1900
The son of R. Cattermole (q.v.) and the nephew of G. Cattermole (q.v.), whose subject matter he adopted. In 1851 he was admitted to the architectural school at the R.A., and he exhibited from 1858. He was elected A.N.W.S. and N.W.S. in 1863 and 1870, serving as Secretary for many years. He was also the Secretary of the Artists' Society at Langham Chambers. Although his landscape work is not

CATTERMOLE, George (1800-1868)
A Blasted Heath. Signed with monogram, watercolour, 4in. x 6in.

as good as that of his uncle, his Civil War and Stuart hunting scenes, especially when on a small scale, are often very pretty indeed.

Illustrated: E.M.Lawson: *Records and Traditions of Upton-on-Severn*, 1869. E.M. Lawson: *The Nation in the Parish*, 1884.

Examples: B.M.; V.A.M.; Leicestershire A.G.; Paisley A.G.; Royal Shakespeare Theatre, Stratford; Sydney A.G.

Bibliography: *W&D*, 1991, i.

CATTERMOLE, George
1800 (Dickleburgh, Norfolk) - 1868 (London)

The youngest brother of R. Cattermole (q.v.), his artistic career began as an architectural draughtsman for J. Britton (q.v.), with whom he was placed at the age of fourteen. He first exhibited at the R.A. in 1819 and was elected A.O.W.S. in 1822 but, allowing his Associateship to lapse, had to be re-elected in 1829, becoming a full Member in 1833. During the 1820s he shifted the emphasis of his art from the architecture of old buildings to the historical figures with which he peopled them. His early reading is said to have been Scott. In 1830 he toured Scotland making illustrations for the *Waverley Novels* and his works are to art what Scott's were to literature. He refused to take pupils, however eminent, and also refused a knighthood in 1839, but was an intimate of the Blessington-d'Orsay circle and a member of the Athenaeum and the Garrick. In 1852 he resigned from the O.W.S. and spent his last years in an unsuccessful attempt to establish himself as an oil painter.

Cattermole's figure subjects, despite the characteristically sketchy handling, won even Ruskin's approval, and his pure landscapes that of Cox, for whose work they are sometimes mistaken. His remaining works were sold at Christie's, 9 March 1869.

His eldest son, was **Ernest George CATTERMOLE (1841-1863)** who showed artistic promise before joining the 22nd Punjab Infantry. The second was L. Cattermole (q.v.); and the youngest, **Sidney William George CATTERMOLE (1858-1915),** was also a painter of animals, especially dogs.

Published: *Cattermole's Portfolio*, 1845.

Illustrated: R. Cattermole: *The Great Civil War*, 1841-5.

Examples: B.M.; V.A.M.; Haworth A.G., Accrington; Ashmolean; Blackburn A.G.; Grundy A.G., Blackpool; Cartwright Hall, Bradford; Brighton A.G.; Devizes Mus.; Dudley A.G.; Exeter Mus.; Ferens Art Gallery, Hull; Glasgow A.G.; Leeds City A.G.; Maidstone Mus.; City A.G., Manchester; N.G., Scotland; Newport A.G.

Bibliography: A.J., July, 1857; Sept. 1868; March, 1870. O.W.S. Club, IX, 1932. *W&D*, 1990, iv; 1991, i.

CATTERMOLE, Leonardo Forster George
1843 - 1895 (Peckham)

A pupil and assistant to his father G. Cattermole (q.v.), Leonardo was an admirable painter of horses, as well as a figure

CATTERMOLE, Charles (1832-1900)
The Casting of Perseus. *Signed and dated '63, watercolour, 29½in. x 23¼in.*

CATTERMOLE, George (1800-1868)
The Armoury at Haddon Hall. *Inscribed on label, pencil and watercolour heightened with white, 5¾in. x 8¾in.*

draughtsman and a caricaturist. He exhibited from the 1870s, and was also a comic poet, but the weight of his father's reputation combined with his own given name proved too much, and he died in an asylum.

Published: *Odds and Ends*, 1886
Illustrated: *Sir F. Fitz Wygram: Horses and Stables.*
Bibliography: *W&D*, 1991, i.

CATTERMOLE, Rev. Richard
1795 (Dickleburgh) - 1858 (Boulogne)
The eldest brother of G. Cattermole (q.v.), he began his career as an architectural draughtsman, working for such publications as Pyne's *Royal Residences* and Britton's *Cathedral Antiquities of Great Britain*. He also exhibited with the Oil and Watercolour Society in 1814. His subjects were generally cathedrals, which was probably no coincidence, since he abandoned art for the Church, taking a B.D. at Cambridge in 1831. He was minister of the South Lambeth Chapel from 1844 and vicar of Little Marlow from 1849. He published many devotional, literary and historical works, including *The Book of the Cartoons of Raphael*, 1837. His drawing style is close to that of his brother.
Examples: B.M.
Bibliography: *W&D*, 1990, iv.

CATTON, Charles, R.A.
1728 (Norwich) - 1798 (London)
Apprenticed to a London coachpainter, he later set up on his own and became Coach-Painter to George III. He studied at the St. Martin's Lane Academy and was a Foundation Member of the R.A. He had previously exhibited with the Incorporated Society. In 1784 he was Master of the Painter-Stainers' Company.
Examples: V.A.M.; N.G., Scotland.

CATTON, Charles, Yr.
1756 (London) - 1819 (New Paltz, N.Y.)
The son and pupil of C. Catton (q.v.), he also studied at the R.A. Schools, and he became a scene painter and animal artist. He also sketched for the topographic publishers and presumably maintained some connection with his father's native Norwich, since a small watercolour of the town by him was engraved for Walker's *Copper-plate Magazine* in 1792. He exhibited at the R.A. from 1775 to 1800. In 1793 he worked with E.F. Burney (q.v.) on a series of designs for Gay's *Fables*. In 1804 he emigrated to America where he lived on a farm on the Hudson River. His style is sometimes close to that of Dayes, with careful architectural drawing and freely applied colour washes.
Published: *Animals drawn from Nature*, 1788.
Examples: B.M.; V.A.M.; Ashmolean.

CAULFIELD, Mrs.
A Dublin lady renowned for her skill with the needle. She also worked as a modeller, and painted flowers, birds and genre subjects in oil

and watercolour. She was active in the late eighteenth century.
Bibliography: Rev. J.Campbell: *Philosophical Survey of the South of Ireland*, 1778.

CAUTLEY, George
1807 - 1880
A painter of Near Eastern subjects.

CAUTY, Horace Henry
1846 - 1909
A painter of landscapes, figure and illustrative subjects, together with occasional portraits, for the most part in watercolour. He exhibited from 1867 and became Curator of the R.A. Schools, at which he had studied from 1861.

He shared addresses in London and Sutton with **Horace Robert CAUTY**, who was presumably a brother rather than a son, since he exhibited watercolour landscapes and coastal subjects from 1870. Many of his subjects are found in Devon and Cornwall, and both Cautys visited Scotland.

CAVE, Henry   1779 (York) - 1836 (York)
A York topographer, working somewhat in the manner of the elder T.M. Richardson, he was the fourth son of William Cave, an engraver under whom he studied. In 1801 he was admitted a Freeman of York and described on the roll as an engraver. In 1821 he was elected a Chamberlain of the city. He taught drawing, and his favourite subjects were the monastic ruins and the coast of his native county. He painted in oil and watercolour, and he also made Indian ink copies of old masters in private collections for engraving. He exhibited at the R.A. and the B.I. from 1814 to 1825.

His elder brother, William Cave, Yr., and several other members of the family, were engravers.
Published: *The Antiquities of York*, 1813.
Examples: Dundee A.G.; York City A.G.

CAVE, James
An architectural and landscape painter who worked in Winchester and exhibited from 1801 to 1817. He was unconnected with the York family of artists.
Illustrated: J. Milner: *History of Winchester*, 1801.
Examples: B.M.

CAVENDISH, Lady Catherine Susan
– *see* CHESHAM, Lady

CAVENDISH, Hon. Susan Frederica
1843 - 1906
A painter of town scenes, landscapes and country houses, she was the youngest daughter of the 3rd Lord Waterpark. Her mother was a Lady of the Bedchamber, and she stayed at Osborne in 1869. She never drew with a pencil, and used a wet technique.
Bibliography: A.M.W. Stirling: *Life's Little Day*, 1924.

CAW, Sir James Lewis, H.R.S.A.
1864 (Ayr) - 1950 (Lasswade)
An artist and connoisseur who was educated at Ayr Academy and studied at Glasgow, Edinburgh and on the Continent. From 1895 he was the Curator of the Scottish N.P.G. and from 1907 Director of the N.G., Scotland.
Published: *Sir Henry Raeburn*, 1901. *Scottish Portraits*, 1903. *Scottish Painting*, 1908. *National Gallery of Scotland*, 1911. *William McTaggart*, 1917.
Examples: N.G., Scotland.

CAWDOR
Several members of this family were amateur artists, of some quality. They include **John CAMPBELL, 1st LORD CAWDOR, F.R.S., F.S.A. (c.1754-1821)**; his sons **John Frederick CAMPBELL, 1st EARL CAWDOR, F.R.S. (1790-1860)**, and Rear-Admiral the **Hon. George Pryse CAMPBELL (1793-1858)**; his daughters-in-law **Elizabeth THYNNE, LADY CAWDOR (d.1866)**, and **Charlotte GASCOIGNE**; his granddaughters **Lady Georgiana Isabella BALFOUR of BALBIRNIE (1820-1884)**, and **Elizabeth Lucy, Lady DESART (d.1898)**. The last three, at the least, were pupils of H. Bright (q.v.).

CAWSE, John
1779 (London) - 1862 (London)
A portrait and history painter in oil and watercolour, he studied at the R.A.Schools and exhibited at the O.W.S., the R.A. and elsewhere from 1801 to 1845. In the B.M. there is a pen drawing in the manner of Rowlandson.

His daughter **Clara Libana CAWSE (b.c.1819 Islington)** exhibited literary and genre subjects and portraits in watercolour at the R.A. and Suffolk Street between 1841 and 1867.
Published: *The Art of Painting in Oil*, 1840.

CAZALET, Captain Charles Henry
1818 (India) - 1860 (Kamptee)
The son of Anglo-Indian parents, he was educated in Paris and Southampton, and in 1837 he was commissioned as an ensign in the 29th Madras Native Infantry. He was promoted lieutenant in 1840 and captain in 1848. His watercolour of Penang Harbour dated 1856 is illustrated in a letter to *Country Life*, 22 February 1973.

CHAIGNEAU, Henry   c.1760 -
A landscape painter who entered the R.D.S. Schools in 1776. He exhibited until 1780, after which his name does not appear. There is a drawing signed 'Thes. Heny. Chaigneau' at the N.G.I. This may be by Theophilus Chaigneau, son of David Chaigneau, M.P. for Gowran, who may be identical with the above. If so, he was the brother of Peter Chaigneau, secretary of the R.D.S. A drawing dated 1792 was sold

by Robinson & Fisher on 5 May 1932. It was stiff and Malton-like.

CHALLIS, Ebenezar
1806 - 1881 (Islington)

A painter of British, and later French, abbeys and castles. He lived in Islington and was active from about 1846. He also engraved plates after D. Roberts (q.v.), T. Allom (q.v.) and others for the *A.J.* and similar publications.

CHALMERS, George Paul, R.S.A., R.S.W.
1833 (Montrose) - 1878 (Edinburgh)

A portrait, and later landscape, painter who moved to Edinburgh in 1853 to study under Scott Lauder (q.v.) at the School of Design. He exhibited at the R.S.A. from 1863 and was elected A.R.S.A. and R.S.A. in 1867 and 1871. Previously he had worked for a ship chandler and as a grocer. In 1862 he sketched in Brittany with J. Pettie (q.v.) and John Graham, and in 1874 he toured France, Belgium and Holland with Joseph Farquharson. He also painted genre subjects and was influenced by Rembrandt and Wilkie (q.v.).
Bibliography: A. Gibson: *G.P.C.*, 1879. E. Pinnington: *G.P.C. and the Art of his Time*, 1896. *Portfolio*, 1877; 1880; 1887. *A.J.*, 1878; 1897. *Studio*, 1907.

CHALMERS, J

A scene painter working in Dublin and Cork between 1801 and 1820. In 1819 he was appointed Drawing Master at the Cork Institution, and he exhibited landscapes.

CHALMERS, Roderick
c.1685 - p.1746

Ross Herald in Scotland, he drew and painted figures and landscapes. He was related to Jamesone and the Alexanders, and a member of a family of baronets which lost all but the title for Jacobite sympathies. His son was the portrait painter Sir George Chalmers, Bt. (c.1720-1791).
Examples: N.G.Scotland.

CHALMERS, William A
1768 - 1798

A painter of architectural and theatrical subjects who lived and worked in London and appears to have died young. He exhibited at the R.A. from 1790 to 1798, and studied at the R.A. Schools from 1792.

CHALON, Alfred Edward, R.A.
1780 (Geneva) - 1860 (London)

The son of a Huguenot refugee from Geneva who settled in Kensington, and the younger brother of J.J. Chalon (q.v.). The brothers, both unmarried, lived in Kensington for the rest of their lives. A.E. Chalon entered the R.A. Schools in 1797. He became a member of the A.A. in 1807, resigning in 1808 to found the Sketching Society with his brother and F.

CHALON, Alfred Edward (1780-1860)
A Country House. *Signed and dated 1831, watercolour with scratching out, 6in. x 8in.*

Stevens (q.v.). He exhibited at the R.A. from 1810 and was elected A.R.A. and R.A. in 1812 and 1816.

He is the better known of the two brothers and enjoyed the greater success during his lifetime. His graceful portraits, usually about fifteen inches high, typify early Victorian art. His portrait of the young Queen was reproduced on numerous early issues of colonial stamps, and he was appointed Painter in Water Colours to the Queen. He also painted many historical and literary subjects in oil, and like his brother, caricatures in brown wash.
Illustrated: L. Fairlie: *Portraits of Children of the Nobility*, 1838. M. Gardiner: *The Belle of a Season*, 1840. S. Uwins: *A Memoir of Thomas Uwins*, 1858.
Examples: B.M.; V.A.M.; Ashmolean; Blackburn A.G.; Leeds City A.G.; N.P.G.; Castle Mus., Nottingham; Ulster Mus.
Bibliography: *A.J.*, 1860; Jan. 1862; 1899. V.A.M., MSS correspondence with J. Constable.

CHALON, John James, R.A., O.W.S.
1778 (Geneva) - 1854 (London)

A landscape and genre painter in oil and watercolour, and the elder brother of A.E. Chalon (q.v.), he entered the R.A. Schools in 1796 and exhibited his first picture at the R.A. in 1800. In December 1805 he was one of the first Associates elected by the O.W.S., and he became a full Member in 1807. He was elected A.R.A. and R.A. in 1827 and 1841. In 1816 he exhibited his best known work in oil, 'Napoleon on the Bellerophon', at the R.A. In 1819 or 1820 he visited Paris and produced a set of lithographs, published in 1822, entitled

24 Subjects exhibiting the Costume of Paris. He is said to have had an extensive practice as a drawing master.

His favourite sketching grounds were the Thames and Wye Valleys and the South Coast. Many of his drawings contain elements of caricature, and his pure caricatures are more accomplished than those of his brother. They are often executed in freely handled brown wash.
Published: *Sketches of Parisian Manners*, 1820.
Examples: B.M.; V.A.M.; Maidstone Mus.; Richmond Lib.
Bibliography: *A.J.*, 1854; Jan.1855.

CHAMBERLAIN, Dawson J

A land and seascape painter who was active in Glasgow at least between 1887 and 1912. He exhibited at the R.S.W. as well as the Glasgow Institute.

CHAMBERLAYNE, Lieutenant Henry
1796 - 1844

The son of Sir Henry Chamberlayne, consul-general at Rio de Janeiro from 1815 to 1829, he painted panoramic Brazilian views which are lightly coloured and annotated.
Published: *Views and Costumes of ...Rio*, 1822.

CHAMBERLAYNE, General William John
1821 (Charlton, Kent) - 1910 (Torquay)

The son of the vicar of Charlton, he joined the army and later wrote that 'my profession has taken me to the least frequented parts of the world, and has afflicted me with a deal of idle time. This I have endeavoured to kill with

CHAMBERS, George (1803-1840)
Tilbury. *Signed, inscribed and dated 1838, pencil and watercolour, 6½in, x 11¾in.*

pencil, brush and pen'. Professionally he rose to the command of two West Indian regiments and in 1881 to the rank of lt.-general. He also served in West Africa and Mauritius. He retired to Torquay in 1882, and there he painted and wrote poetry.

While some of his landscapes and views in the British Isles and the tropics are not so far removed from those of military contemporaries and men of the next generation such as L.G. Fawkes or H.M. Sinclair (qq.v), there is often a phantasmagoric element in his work which chimes with the Victorian love of ghouls. His background and early admiration for J. Martin (q.v.) is seen in illustrations to *Paradise Lost* and other religious subjects, and further parallels can be made with Caspar David Friedrich, or even F. Towne (q.v.).

His elder daughter, **Charlotte Hannah CHAMBERLAYNE (1861 Jamaica - 1947 Torquay),** often portrayed in his work, inherited his talent.
Published: *The Tropic Bird*, 1878. *The Enchanted Land*, 1892.
Examples: V.A.M.
Bibliography: W. Drummond, London:Exhibition Cat., 1978.
See Colour Plate

CHAMBERS, George, O.W.S.
1803 (Whitby) - 1840 (Brighton)
The second son of a Whitby sailor, he went to sea at the age of ten. His first artistic work was decorating the brig *Equity* on which he served a five year apprenticeship. Freed from his indentures, he spent three years with a house and ship painter at Whitby. His first important commission came from Christopher Crawford, the landlord of the Waterman's Arms, Wapping, for whom he painted a 'Prospect of Whitby', which inspired further commissions

for ship portraits. Crawford also helped him to go on a number of sketching voyages around the coasts and to work on T. Horner's (q.v.) Panorama in Regent's Park. After a period as a scene painter, he set up as a marine artist and soon gained commissions from naval men and the Sailor King himself because of the accuracy of his nautical detail. His health being poor, he returned to Whitby for a while and in 1833 spent some time in Sussex. At about this time he turned from oil painting to the more subtle medium, and he was elected A.O.W.S. and O.W.S. in 1834 and 1835. In 1837 he visited Whitby, and in 1838 he went to Holland with his pupil J.C. Gooden-Chisholm (q.v.). Thereafter his health collapsed entirely, and Crawford sent him to Madeira, but he died at Brighton on his return.

He can be one of the most poetic of British marine artists, and his stylistic epitaph was written by his friend Sidney Cooper: 'His painting of rough water was truly excellent, and to all water he gave a liquid transparency that I have never seen equalled…his ships are all in motion.'

His remaining works were sold at Christie's, 10 February 1841.
Examples: B.M.; V.A.M.; Exeter Mus.; Ferens A.G., Hull; Greenwich; Leeds City A.G.; Newport A.G.; Portsmouth City Mus.; Wakefield City A.G.
Bibliography: Anon: *Memoir of G.C.,* 1837. J. Watkins: *Life and Career of G.C.,* 1841. A. Russett: *G.C.,* 1996. O.W.S. Club, XVIII, 1940.

CHAMBERS, George William Crawford
1830   - ?c.1900 (? Trinidad)
The elder son of G. Chambers (q.v.), he was educated at Sandgate and Christ's Hospital. He became a marine painter in his father's manner and exhibited at the R.A. from 1850 to 1861. He painted on the South and East Coasts, the

Thames and in Holland. He seems to have left England, perhaps for South America, some time after 1863, and according to one unsubstantiated account he was killed in a riot at Trinidad.

His brother, William Henry Martin Chambers (b.1832) may also have painted.
Examples: Greenwich; Gray A.G., Hartlepool.

CHAMBERS, John
1852 (South Shields) - 1928
A landscape, architectural and portrait painter who worked for the Tyne Pilotage Service before studying in Paris. His subjects are usually found in North Shields, where he lived, and on the Tyne.
Examples: Laing A.G., Newcastle.

CHAMBERS, Sir John Harcourt and Family   – *see* Appendix III

CHAMBERS, Richard Edwards Elliot
1863   - 1944
Owing to the disgraceful behaviour of a cousin and ultimate inheritor, who might plead senility, and his solicitors, whose only refuge can be the 'Nüremberg Defence', the bulk of the work of this Anglo-Irish painter, photographer and prolific letter writer has been destroyed.

Chambers was a member of the family of Fostertown, near Trim, and he later lived at Barnstaple and Lyme Regis. His importance was not so much as an artist – his work is competent but rather primitive – but as a recorder of California, Colorado and New Mexico in the 1880s. Luckily, some examples of his work escaped the vandals.

CHAMBERS, Thomas
1828   - 1910 (York)
A Scarborough marine painter who had an unsuccessful career until 1879 when he gave up art for the millinery business and moved to York. He died rich.

CHAMBERS, Thomas King
1818   - 1889
A leading West End doctor and senior consultant physician to St Mary's Hospital and the Lock Hospital, Chambers was chosen to accompany the Prince of Wales to Rome in 1859. He was recommended as possessing 'a mass of much general information', but was 'by no means disinclined to impart it to others'. The party returned by way of Gibraltar and Spain, and Chambers painted landscapes, which perhaps owe something to J.D. Harding (q.v.). He held the post of Honorary Physician to the Prince until his death.

CHAMPAIN, Colonel Sir John Underwood BATEMAN
1835 (London) - 1887 (San Remo)
The son of Col. Agnew Champain, he took the additional name of Bateman in 1872. He was

educated at Cheltenham, the Edinburgh Military Academy under Sir H. Yule (q.v.), Addiscombe and Chatham. He was commissioned in the Bengal Engineers in 1853 and promoted full colonel in 1882. He was knighted in 1885. He served with distinction and sketched during the Indian Mutiny, and in 1862 he accompanied Col. Patrick Stewart on a survey to trace a possible line for the first telegraph across Persia to link India and the Home Country. In 1866 he was in Iraq and the following year in St. Petersburg. Thereafter he made repeated visits to India, Turkey, Persia and the Gulf, winning the admiration of the Shah. In 1873 he won a gold medal at the Albert Hall Exhibition with a Persian landscape, and an example of his work is given in *Country Life,* 19 June 1975.
Illustrated: Sir F. Goldsmid: *Telegraph and Travel.*

CHAMPERNOWNE, Arthur
1769 - 1819
The owner of Dartington Hall, his name was originally Harrington. He was a pupil of Francis Towne (q.v.) and painted Devonshire views. He was a Dilettante from 1798 and an M.P. His collection was sold by Christie's in June 1820.
His wife, **Louisa CHAMPERNOWNE**, a member of the Buller family, was also a sketcher and later members of the family were patrons and pupils of de Wint (q.v.).

CHANDLER, Rose M
A genre painter who lived in Haslemere and exhibited at the R.I. and Suffolk Street from 1882 to 1891.

CHANNING, William
A scene painter at the Theatres Royal Manchester and Edinburgh. In the the former place, around 1845, he taught S. Bough (q.v.) who repaid him by support in his old age. He made many careful topographical sketches of Edinburgh, as well as drawings of military and other costumes for use in the theatre. He died at Leith in or after 1860.
Examples: Edinburgh City Lib.

CHANTREY, Sir Francis Leggatt, R.A.
1781 (Norton, Derbyshire) - 1842 (London)
Of the Bequest. He was a sculptor, but at the beginning of his career he took portraits in miniature and pencil, and later he became a keen landscape sketcher, visiting France, Holland and Italy. He was elected A.R.A. and R.A. in 1816 and 1818 and was knighted in 1835. His landscape drawings are often in thick pencil with thin blue, green and pink washes.
Published: *C's Peak Scenery,* 1885.
Examples: B.M.
Bibliography: G. Jones: *Sir F.C.,* 1849. J. Holland: *Memorials of Sir F.C.,* 1851. A.J. Raymond: *Life and Work of Sir F.C.,* 1904.

CHAPMAN, Abel
1851 (Sunderland) - 1929 (Northumberland)
A cousin of J. Crawhall (q.v.), and a natural history writer, he often illustrated his books with drawings and watercolours. He lived at Houxty, near Wark, from 1898 until his death. He published a number of bird books and illustrated the works of others on big game hunting and kindred subjects.
Published: *Retrospect: Reminiscences, 1851-1928,* 1928. &c.
Examples: Hancock Mus., Newcastle.

CHAPMAN, Mary Morton –
see ALPORT, Henry Curzon

CHAPMAN, William
1817 (Sunderland) - 1879
A successful engraver who had studied under William Miller in Edinburgh, he spent the latter part of his life in York, where he made many watercolours of both buildings and landscapes. He may be the R. William Chapman who stood for the N.W.S. in 1858 and the O.W.S. 1859-61.
Examples: B.M.; Leeds City A.G.; Laing A.G., Newcastle; York City A.G.

CHAPPELL, Reuben
1870 (Hook, Yorkshire) -
1940 (Par, Cornwall)
By the age of twenty he had set himself up as a ship painter at Goole, much of his work being commissioned by the masters and crews of Danish ships. In 1904 he moved to Cornwall on account of his health, where he remained for the rest of his life. He never exhibited and supported his family entirely by commissions. During the War he made watercolour plans for improvements in ship construction which were considered by the Ministry of Defence. He did little work after 1930.
His merchant coasters are usually depicted broadside and under sail. The majority of his work is in watercolour, brightly coloured and technically accomplished. He also painted occasional landscapes. Before about 1908 he usually signed 'R. Chappell, Goole', later he signed 'R. Chappell', 'R.C.' or, very rarely, 'R.C.G.' He kept regular diaries of his commissions. He is represented in many Continental collections, especially in Denmark, and exhibitions of his work were held at the Bristol City A.G. and Greenwich in 1970.
Examples: Kronberg Mus., Elsinore; Greenwich; Ferens A.G., Hull; Marstal Mus.; Amts Mus., Svendborg.
Bibliography: *Sea Breezes,* Feb. 1948.

CHARLES, W.
A marine and landscape painter who exhibited at Suffolk Street in 1870 and 1871 and was still active three years later.

CHARLEVILLE, Catherine Maria, Countess of **1762 - 1851**
A daughter of T.T. Dawson, she was educated

at the Collège Royale de Toulouse between 1778 and 1781, and in 1787 she married James Tisdall of Co. Louth. Widowed, she married Lord Tullamore in 1798, and eight years later he was created Earl of Charleville. She was a noted intellectual and drew in pencil, watercolour and gouache and a romantic manner. She and her husband built Charleville Forest, a Gothick castle.

CHARLTON, Mary Catherine
– see under BEARNE, Edward Henry

CHARLTON, John, R.I.
1849 (Bamburgh) - 1917 (Lanercost)
A painter of portraits, battles and landscapes and an illustrator, Charlton began his career in a Newcastle bookshop. Later he entered the School of Art under W.B. Scott (q.v.) and then South Kensington. He exhibited at the R.A. for the first time in 1870 and moved to London permanently. He worked for some years in the studio of J.D. Watson (q.v.), concentrating on figure painting. He also drew for the *Graphic* and produced grand ceremonial pictures and military subjects.
Published: *Twelve Packs of Hounds,* 1892.
Illustrated: H.A. Macpherson: *Red Deer,* 1896.
Examples: V.A.M.; Shipley A.G., Gateshead; Gray A.G., Hartlepool; Laing A.G., Newcastle; S. Shields A.G.

CHARLTON, William Henry
1846 (Newcastle-upon-Tyne) - 1918
A landscape and coastal painter in oil, watercolour and chalk, he studied under C. Richardson (q.v.) and at the Académie Julian in Paris. His watercolours are often on a small scale.
Examples: B.M.; Laing A.G., Newcastle.

CHARTERIS, Captain the Hon. Frederick William **1833 - 1887**
The youngest son of the 9th Earl of Wemyss, he was a captain in the navy. Since the family properties included seats in Peebles, Haddingtonshire and Perth as well as Gloucestershire, it is not surprising that he exhibited Scottish subjects at the Grosvenor Gallery from 1878 to 1882. He married Lady L. Charteris (*vide infra*) in 1864.

CHARTERIS, Lady Louisa, née Keppel
1836 -
The daughter of the 6th Earl of Albemarle, she married Captain the Hon. F.W. Charteris (q.v.) in 1864. As a widow she lived in London. In 1910 the Fine Art Society held an exhibition of her watercolours of the Riviera, Italy and Scotland.

CHASE, Frank M
A London landscape painter who exhibited at the R.A. from 1875. He painted in Venice and Switzerland as well as in Britain. He was presumably a son of J. Chase (q.v.).

CHESHAM, Francis (1749-1806)
The Battle of the Nile. *Watercolour, 10in. x 16in.*

CHASE, John, N.W.S.
1810 (London) - 1879 (London)
A pupil of Constable who also studied architecture, he exhibited landscapes and views of churches from 1826 and was a member of the N.W.S. from 1834. His first wife, **Mary Ann CHASE, née Rix,** was elected to the N.W.S. in 1835 and exhibited until 1839.
Published: *A Practical Treatise on Water Colours,* 1863.
Examples: V.A.M.; Sydney A.G.
Bibliography: *A.J.,* 1879.

CHASE, Marian Emma, R.I.
1844 (London) - 1905 (London)
The second daughter of J. Chase (q.v.) by his second wife Georgiana Ann, née Harris. She was taught by her father and by M. Gillies (q.v.) and exhibited at the R.A., the N.W.S. and elsewhere from 1866. She was elected A.N.W.S. and N.W.S. in 1875 and 1879. In 1888 she was awarded the silver medal of the Royal Botanical Society. She painted genre subjects as well as flowers. She appears to have gone abroad only once, with her father in about 1876.
Her sister **Jessie CHASE** was also a watercolour painter.
Examples: V.A.M.; Aberdeen A.G.
Bibliography: *Queen,* 87, 15 Feb. 1890; *St John's Wood, Kilburn and Hampstead Advertiser,* 29 Aug. 1901; 23 Mar. 1905.

CHATELAIN, John Baptist Claude
1710 (London) - 1771 (London)
A draughtsman and engraver of Huguenot descent whose real surname was Philippe. French authorities claim that he was born and died in Paris and that he served in the French Army. He worked for Boydell and exhibited engravings at the Free Society from 1761 to 1763. He lived in Chelsea and produced views of London as well as of the Lake District and copies after Italian artists. The topographical drawings which he made for prints are usually much more free than his finished wash or chalk drawings, which tend to be formal and with a strong conventional outline. His colour washes are very limited, usually no more than browns, greys or blues. F. Vivares (q.v.) was probably his pupil.
Examples: B.M.; V.A.M.

CHATTOCK, Richard Samuel
1825 (Solihull) - 1906 (Clifton)
A landscape painter in oil and watercolour and an etcher, he was educated at Rugby, and worked in Birmingham, Solihull and the Black Country. He exhibited at the R.A. and the R.I. from 1865 and was an R.P.E. as well as a member of the Birmingham Society.
Published: *Wensleydale,* 1872. *The Black Country,* 1878. *Practical Notes on Etching,* 1883.
Illustrated: W.W. Wood: *Sketches of Eton,* 1874.

CHAWNER, Thomas
1775 - 1851 (London)
An architect and draughtsman, he was a pupil of Sir J. Soane and entered the R.A. Schools in 1797. Ultimately he became Joint Architect and Surveyor under the Commissioners of Woods and Works, retiring in 1845. His architectural work was mostly in London and Surrey, and he lived in both.
Examples: B.M.

CHEARNLY, Anthony
An Irish amateur draughtsman and collector of antiquarian drawings. He was active from around 1740. Two views by him of his house, Burnt Court, County Tipperary, and a view of Ardfinnan Castle appear in Grose's *Antiquities of Ireland.* He also made illustrations for Smith's *History of Waterford* and *History of Cork* and for Ledwich's *Antiquities.* His brother Samuel (d.1746) had been an amateur architect, and in 1791, perhaps on his own death, his son and namesake inherited Salterbridge, Co.Waterford, serving as High Sheriff in 1809.

CHENEY, Harriet 1810 -1852
The sister of de Wint's patrons, Edward Cheney (1803-1884) and **(Robert) Henry CHENEY (1801-1866)** of Badger Hall, Shropshire, she was a pupil of the artist, although her work is not usually in his style. She was active in about 1815 and a print dedicated to Sir Joseph Banks was published from her drawing of a bust of Euripides. Her eldest brother Henry was a pupil as well as patron of de Wint, and was probably the most accomplished artist of the family. He and Edward, who drew in pen and ink only, travelled extensively in Italy during the 1820s and '30s. There they saw much of T.H. Cromek (q.v.), as well as the leading members of Anglo-Italian society. They also drew in England and Wales.

CHERON, Louis
1655 (Paris) - 1725 (London)
The son of Henri Chéron, a miniaturist, he visited Italy, returning to Paris in 1687, and left France finally in 1695 as a result of the Revocation of the Edict of Nantes. In England he worked as a painter of murals, but the competition was too great for him, and he turned to book illustrations. His drawings are generally in black chalk and light brown wash with a characteristic knobbly outline, and his subjects were biblical and mythological. He also illustrated an edition of Milton in 1720. Two of his sisters, Elisabeth Sophie and Marianne, were miniaturists.

CHESHAM, Catherine Susan, Lady
c.1795 - 1866
A pupil, patron and collector of P. de Wint (q.v.), she was the eldest daughter of the 9th Marquess of Huntly. Her sister-in-law was Catherine, Marchioness of Huntly (q.v.). In 1814 she married the Hon. Charles Compton Cavendish, a younger son of the 1st Cavendish Earl of Burlington. In 1858 he was raised to the peerage as Lord Chesham.

CHESHAM, Francis
1749 - 1806 (London)
An engraver who made prints after P. Sandby (q.v.), G. Robertson (q.v.) and others. His engravings are in the manner of Vivares (q.v.), and his own drawings are in thin washes with the tight, spindly pen-line of an eighteenth century

print maker. They are rather Dutch in feeling.
Examples: B.M.

CHESTERFIELD, Anne Elizabeth, Countess of c.1803 - 1885
The eldest daughter of the 1st Lord Forester, and a sister-in-law of M.A. Jervis (q.v.), a fellow pupil of H. Bright (q.v.). Her sister was I.E.A. Anson (q.v.), and she married the 6th Earl of Chesterfield in 1830.

CHILDE, Elias 1778 - 1862
Primarily a landscape and coastal painter in oil, he was also an occasional exhibitor with the O.W.S. and the N.W.S. He was active from 1798 to 1848 and painted much in Sussex, Kent and on the Thames. He became a member of the S.B.A. in 1825.

His brother, James Warren Childe (1778-1851), was a miniaturist.

CHILDS, George 1798 - 1875
A painter of landscapes and rustic genre subjects in oil and watercolour who exhibited at the R.A. and Suffolk Street between 1826 and 1873 and stood for the N.W.S. unsuccessfully in 1839 and 1841. He was also a lithographer.
Published: *A New Drawing-Book of Figures. The Little Sketch Book. Childs' Drawing-Book of Objects. English Landscape Scenery and Woodland Sketches.*

CHINNERY, George 1774 (London) - 1852 (Macao)
The landscape and portrait painter. He entered the R.A. Schools and first exhibited at the R.A. in 1791. In 1796 he went, by way of Bristol, to Dublin, where he had influential relatives. The following year he was appointed director of life classes at the Dublin Society, and in 1799 he married. In 1800 he reorganised the moribund Society of Artists in Ireland and became its Secretary. In 1802 he abandoned his family, returned briefly to London and sailed to Madras. In 1807 he moved to Calcutta and from 1808 to 1812 was in Dacca, where he gave lessons to his friend Sir C. D'Oyly (q.v.) and others. From 1812 to 1823 he had a studio in Calcutta, and in 1823 he was in Serampore. In 1825, to escape debts and his wife, who had rejoined him, he moved to Macao. The rest of his life was spent in Macao, Hong Kong and Canton. The ban on European women in Canton enabled him to evade his wife when she again attempted to follow him.

Throughout his career he was highly thought of as a portrait painter, in oil and miniature, but today he is most remembered for the innumerable pencil sketches, wash drawings and finished watercolours which he made on the China Coast. His subjects are old buildings, junks and crowds of coolies in the streets. There are also many drawings for his portraits of European and Chinese merchants, most notably his patrons, Messrs. Jardine and Matheson and the great Hou Qua. He had many followers, both European and Chinese, but it is usually possible to tell his work from theirs. His sketches are often annotated in

CHILDS, George (1798-1875)
The Dover to Folkestone Railway. *Watercolour with scratching out heightened with bodycolour, signed and dated 1850, 19¾in. x 28½in.*

shorthand, and his figures are beautifully drawn, often with large foreheads and a stocky build. His palette is muted, and his handling atmospheric.

He was not, as is often claimed, of Irish birth, nor was he a member of the R.H.A. which was founded in 1823, twenty-one years after his departure from Ireland. The persistent claim that he was elected to it in 1798 *(sic)* is probably due to a confusion with the Society of Artists in Ireland.
Examples: B.M.; V.A.M.; Ashmolean; Greenwich; Leeds City A.G.; N.G., Scotland.
Bibliography: J.J. Cotton: *G.C.*, 1852. H. & S. Berry-Hill: *G.C.*, 1963. P. Conner: *G.C.*, 1993. *China Journal*, VIII, 1928. Tate Gall.: Exhibition Cat., 1932. *Country Life*, 30 May 1936. Arts Council: Exhibition Cat., 1957. *Connoisseur*, CLXXV, 1970.
See Colour Plate

CHIPP, Herbert
A landscape painter who lived in Ely and exhibited at the R.I., Suffolk Street and in Birmingham from 1877 to 1885. He sketched in the Channel Islands. He was also a devotee of lawn tennis.
Examples: Ulster Mus.

CHISHOLM, Alexander, F.S.A., A.O.W.S. 1792 (Elgin) - 1847 (Rothesay)
He was apprenticed to a weaver at Peterhead, but taught himself to draw both there and in Aberdeen. In about 1812 he went to Edinburgh, where he won the patronage of the Earls of Buchan and Elgin and taught drawing at the R.S.A. Schools. He married one of his private pupils, **Susanna Stewart**

CHISHOLM, née Fraser, and in 1818 moved to London and set up as a portrait painter. He gradually turned from portraits to subject pictures and from oil to watercolour, and he was elected A.O.W.S. in 1829. From about 1832 he concentrated largely on historical and literary subjects. He made a number of illustrations for the *Annuals* and for the *Waverley Novels,* and his work resembles that of T. Uwins (q.v.) or J.W. Wright (q.v.). He died on the Isle of Bute while making portrait studies for an ambitious picture of the Evangelical Alliance, and he left a large family of impecunious daughters. His name is sometimes spelt, wrongly, with a final 'e'.
Examples: B.M.; V.A.M.

CHISHOLM, James Chisholm GOODEN- - p.1875
A pupil of G. Chambers (q.v.), whom he accompanied on a number of yachting and sketching trips on the Thames in 1837 and 1838. In the latter year they also visited Holland. In the summer of 1858 he was on the Thames again, this time with E. Duncan (q.v.). He was also a friend of W.J. Müller (q.v.), and he exhibited from 1835 to 1865.
Published: *The Thames and Medway Admiralty Surveys,* 1864.
Examples: V.A.M.; Newport A.G.

CHOWNE, Gerard Henry Tilson 1875 (India) - 1917 (Macedonia)
The son of Colonel W.C. Chowne, he was educated at Harrow and studied at the Slade under Professor Brown. He painted

CHURCHYARD, Thomas (1798-1865)
Fishing Boats at Southwold, 1849. *Pencil and watercolour, 4¼in. x 7¼in.*

landscapes, portraits and flowers and was a member of the N.E.A.C. In the First World War he served as a captain in the East Lanarkshire Regiment, and he died of wounds. His work is free, impressionistic and pleasing.
Examples: V.A.M.; City A.G., Manchester; Ulster Mus.

CHRISTEN, Sydney Mary, Mme.
- c.1935
An Irishwoman who married the Swiss-born painter and teacher Rodolphe Christen (c.1859-1906), and they settled in Aberdeenshire in 1902. She painted watercolour landscapes and still lifes and wrote a biography of her husband.
Published: *Rodolphe Christen: An Artist's Life,* 1910.
Examples: Ulster Mus.

CHUBB, John
1746 (Bridgwater) - 1818 (Bridgwater)
The son of a wine and timber merchant, he passed virtually all his life in his native town. At thirteen he did visit London, wishing to become a 'limner', but his father persuaded him to return to a sinecure in his business. He produced

hundreds of watercolours, principally good Bunbury-like caricatures of his neighbours and friends. He was much involved in politics in the Whig interest, and he became a friend of Fox and Coleridge. He often satirized the clergy. He also wrote verse and enjoyed music. His wife was Mary Witherell from Wells, and they had two sons and a daughter.
Examples: Admiral Blake Mus., Bridgwater.
Bibliography: *Country Life,* 7 Dec. 1989.

CHURCH, Sir Arthur Herbert, F.R.S., F.S.A.   1834 (London) - 1915
An occasional painter, who was educated at King's College, London, and Lincoln College, Oxford, and was Professor of Chemistry at Cirencester from 1863 to 1879 and the R.A. from 1879 to 1911. He wrote on chemistry, precious stones, English porcelain and other subjects and exhibited infrequently between 1854 and 1870.
Examples: V.A.M.

CHURCHYARD, Thomas
1798 (Melton) - 1865 (Woodbridge)
An enthusiastic amateur painter and a good but

unenthusiastic country lawyer, Churchyard was educated at Dedham Grammar School and lived an uneventful life at Woodbridge. He visited London and Bury St. Edmunds occasionally, but for the most part painted the fields and rivers about his home. There his friends and fellow 'Wits of Woodbridge' included the poets Edward Fitzgerald and Barton. He may well have known Constable and G. Frost (q.v.). He exhibited in London from 1830 to 1833 and in Norwich in 1829 and 1852.

The quality of his work varies, but his watercolours are almost always charming. In his earlier days he based his style on that of Crome and his Norwich followers, later he was a devoted disciple of Constable.

His daughters, and probably his sons, were also painters, and their work can be similar to his. They were **Thomas CHURCHYARD, Yr. (b.1825); Ellen CHURCHYARD (1826-1909); Emma CHURCHYARD (1828-1878); Laura CHURCHYARD (1830-1891); Anna CHURCHYARD (1832-1897); Elizabeth CHURCHYARD (1834-1913); Harriet CHURCHYARD (1836-1927); Catherine CHURCHYARD (1839-1889)** and **Charles Isaac CHURCHYARD (1841-1929).**
Examples: B.M.; V.A.M.; Ashmolean; Dundee City A.G.; Fitzwilliam; Christchurch Mansion, Ipswich; Maidstone Mus.; Castle Mus., Norwich.
Bibliography: D. Thomas:. *T.C. of Woodbridge,* 1966. W. Morfey: *Painting the Day, T.C.,* 1986. R. Blake: *The search for T.C.,* 1997. Christchurch Man., Exhibition Cat., 1998.

CIPRIANI, Giovanni Battista, R.A.
1727 (Florence) - 1775 (Hammersmith)
The pupil of an English painter in Florence called Hugford, Cipriani went to Rome in 1750 and came to England in 1755 on the persuasion of Sir William Chambers and Joseph Wilton. In 1758 he was appointed teacher of drawing in the shortlived school set up by the Duke of Richmond in his private gallery in Whitehall. He studied at the St. Martin's Lane Academy and was one of the Foundation Members of the R.A. in 1768. His drawings, in pencil, black or red chalk or pen and grey wash, are generally much more attractive and stronger than his pure watercolours. These represent the classical Italian tradition in its extreme decadence, but his little cherubs are sometimes pretty, according to Williams. He had a fairly wide influence, and it is often difficult to differentiate between his work and that of Hamilton, Kauffmann and Mortimer. His remaining works were sold at Christie's, 22 March 1786.

His son, **Captain Sir Henry CIPRIANI (1762 London - 1843 Brighton),** occasionally painted watercolours.
Examples: B.M.; V.A.M.; Fitzwilliam.

CLACK, Thomas
1830 (Coventry) - 1907 (Hindhead)
The son of a schoolmaster in whose

CIPRIANI, Giovanni Baptista (1727-1775)
Design for an Overdoor. *Pen and ink and watercolour, 4in. x 12¼in.*

establishment he was educated, he lived in Coventry for much of his life. In 1884 he was a master at the National Art Training School at Marlborough House, teaching painting and free-hand drawing of ornament, the figure and anatomy. He exhibited at the R.A. from 1851 to 1891.

Examples: V.A.M.; Coventry A.G.

CLARK, Christopher, R.I.
1875 (London) - 1942
A painter and illustrator of military and historical subjects. He was elected R.I. in 1905. He lived in London and King's Langley, Hertfordshire. From 1917 to 1919 he served with the RNVR.

Published: *British Soldiers, 1550-1906*, 1907. &c.
Illustrated: R.D. Blackmore: *Lorna Doone*, 1912. Sir H.J. Newbolt: *Tales of the Great War*, 1916.

CLARK, Ernest Ellis
1870 - 1932 (Derby)
An oil and watercolour painter who studied at the Derby School of Art and became a designer at the porcelain works. Later he taught at the School of Art and was a member of the Derby Sketching Club. He exhibited locally from 1893.

Published: *A Handbook of Plant-Form for Students of design*, 1904.
Examples: Derby A.G.

CLARK, George
A painter of local seats who lived at Scaldwell, Northamptonshire, and was active around 1850.

A Glasgow based **George CLARKE** exhibited a Scottish subject at the R.S.A. in 1847.

CLARK, James, R.I.
1858 (West Hartlepool) - 1943 (Reigate)
A landscape, flower and portrait painter and biblical illustrator, who studied locally, at South Kensington and in Paris. He worked in Chelsea and West Hartlepool and also made frescoes and stained glass designs and painted in oil and pastel.

Examples: Shipley A.G., Gateshead; Gray A.G., Hartlepool; Laing A.G., Newcastle.

CLARK, John Heaviside, 'Waterloo'
1771 - 1863 (Edinburgh)
A landscape painter and book illustrator who was working in London from 1802 to 1832. Prior to this, he was the 'I. Clark' whose name appears on a number of excellent aquatinted views of Aberdeen and other Scottish cities. He is likely to have been the son of the earlier I. Clark, aquatinter and engraver, who was living in Edinburgh in 1773-4. He was evidently a sound businessman, earning his nickname by going to the field of Waterloo immediately after the battle, and prints were published profitably from his sketches. He also painted marine subjects. His Myriorama

CLARK, John Heaviside, 'Waterloo' (1771-1863)
Mackerel Fishing. *Watercolour with pen and grey ink, 5¼in. x 7in.*

toys, published in 1824 and 1825, are delightful.

Published: *Practical Essay on the Art of Colouring and Painting Landscapes*, 1807. *Field Sports Etc. of the Native Inhabitants of New South Wales*, 1813. *Practical Illustration of Gilpin's Day*, 1824.
Examples: Glasgow A.G.; Greenwich; Maidstone Mus.

CLARK, Joseph
1835 (Cerne Abbas) - 1926 (Ramsgate)
A still-life painter who studied at Leigh's School and exhibited at the N.W.S. and elsewhere from 1857. At one time he lived in Ramsgate.

His nephew, **Joseph Benwell CLARK (1857-1938)** was also a painter in oil and watercolour, and an illustrator. He was a co-founder of the School of Animal Painting in 1894.

Bibliography: *A.J.*, 1859; 1860; 1863; 1869.

CLARK, Thomas, A.R.S.A.
1820 (Whiteside, Stirling) - 1876 (Dunderach, Aberfoyle)
A landscape painter who injured his shoulder during his schooldays at Dollar, making him a cripple for life. He studied at Edinburgh and was elected A.R.S.A. in 1865. Although he often spent the winters in the South, his subjects are chiefly Scottish.

Bibliography: *A.J.*, 1877.

CLARKE, Rev. Edward Daniel
1769 (Willingdon) - 1822 (London)
A traveller, antiquary and mineralogist. He

was educated at Tonbridge Grammar School and Jesus College, Cambridge, and worked as a tutor which gave him the opportunity to travel. In 1791 he toured Great Britain and, in 1792-3, Italy. His most ambitious journey took place from 1799 to 1802 when he visited Scandinavia, Russia, Siberia and the Caucasus, Turkey, Cyprus, Rosetta, Palestine, Greece and France. He was a keen, if envious, disciple of Elgin in the collecting of antiquities. On his return much of his time was taken up with writing and with scientific experiments. He was ordained in 1805 and held the livings of Harlton and Yeldham, Essex. His drawings were used to illustrate his *Travels* and are of a fairly high quality.

His wife, **Angelica CLARKE, née Rush,** also painted.

Published: *Travels in Various Countries...* 1810-15. &c.
Bibliography: W. Otter: *The Life and Remains of the Rev. E.D.C.*, 1824.

CLARKE, George – *see* CLARK, George

CLARKE, George Row
1830 -
A landscape painter who stood unsuccessfully for the N.W.S. in 1871 and 1873 and exhibited there and elsewhere from 1858 to 1888. He had studied architecture at the R.A. Schools from 1848, and he lived in London, although many of his subjects were found in the Midlands or Wales, and he also visited Belgium and Germany towards the end of his career.

CLAUSEN, Sir George (1852-1944)
A view across a field. *Watercolour, signed, 8½in. x 11¼in.*

CLARKE, Theophilus, A.R.A.
1776 - 1831
A student at the R.A. Schools and under John Opie, he exhibited at the R.A. from 1795 to 1810. He was elected A.R.A. in 1803, and his name remained on the list until 1832. He exhibited portraits, landscapes, fishing and domestic subjects and painted in both oil and watercolour.

CLARKSON, George Henry
A landscape painter who was also a sculptor and worked in enamels. He was active in Sunderland in the early years of the twentieth century.

CLAUSEN, Sir George, R.A., R.W.S.
1852 (London) - 1944 (Newbury)
The son of a Danish sculptor, he studied at South Kensington and in Paris. He visited Holland and Belgium in 1876, the year of his first R.A. exhibit, and was influenced by the Hague School as well as by his French contemporaries. He was a member of the R.I. from 1879 to 1888, transferring to the R.W.S. in the following year and becoming a full member in 1898. He was elected A.R.A. and R.A. in 1895 and 1908 and was knighted in 1927. From 1904 to 1906 he was Professor of Painting at the R.A. and later he was Director of the Schools. He was a keen exponent of *plein air* painting, and he spent much time on the farms of Essex. His work captures atmosphere rather than detail.
Published: *Six Lectures on Painting*, 1904. *Aims and Ideals in Art*, 1906.
Examples: B.M.; V.A.M.; Aberdeen A.G.; Cecil Higgins A.G., Bedford; Blackburn A.G.; Fitzwilliam; Glasgow A.G.; Leeds City A.G.; City A.G., Manchester; N.G., Scotland; Newport A.G.; Ulster Mus.
Bibliography: D. Hussey: *G.C.*, 1923. *A.J.*, 1890. O.W.S. Club, XXIII. Bradford A.G.: Exhibition Cat., 1980.

CLAXTON, Adelaide, Mrs. Turner
1835 (London) - 1908 (Litchfield)
An illustrator and humorous artist. As a child she was taken to Australia and the Far East by her father, Marshall C. Claxton (1813 Bolton - 1881 London), a figure painter who took the first exhibition of pictures to be shown in Australia. Although she copied at South Kensington and studied briefly at Carey's, she had little training and first exhibited in 1863. She made many copies of her most popular works. As well as genre subjects, she specialised in ghosts. She married George Gordon Turner in 1874.
Her elder sister **Florence Ann CLAXTON, later Mrs. Farrington,** was also an illustrator until her marriage in 1868. She was the author of *Milly Moss*, 1862, illustrated by E.C. Clayton (q.v.).
Published: *A Shillingsworth of Sugar-Plums*, 1867. *Brainy Odds and Ends*, 1900.

CLAYTON, Alfred Bower
1795 (London) - 1855 (Everton)
An architect who originally intended to be a painter and studied under W. Etty (q.v.). Later he was in the offices of D.R. Roper and William Smith. where he worked in the Greek Revival style. He visited the Mediterranean in 1820 and chiefly worked in London and, from 1837, Manchester. He exhibited designs for houses and churches at the R.A. from 1814 to 1837. He also painted historical subjects and made prints. He died from shock after falling from a building.
Examples: R.I.B.A.
Bibliography: *Builder*, XIII, 1855.

CLAYTON, Eleanor, 'Ellen' Creathorne, Mrs. Needham c.1832 (Dublin) -
The descendant of an artistic family, she became a novelist and illustrator. She studied briefly at the N.G. and the B.M. She made a number of humorous drawings for magazines, including *Judy,* and in the early 1870s did a great deal of commercial painting, Valentines, calendars and so forth.
Published: *Notable Women*, 1859. *Queens of Song,* 1863. *Cruel Fortune,* 1865. *Repenting at Leisure,* 1873. &c.
Illustrated: F. Claxton: *Miss Milly Moss,* 1862.

CLAYTON, John
1728 (Edmonton) - 1800 (Enfield)
A still-life painter who was trained as a surgeon, but soon turned to art, painting in both oil and watercolour. He exhibited from 1761 with the Free Society and with the Incorporated Society from 1767. His studio, with many of his best works, was destroyed in the Covent Garden fire of March 1769. After this he virtually gave up painting for gardening and music, although he exhibited once more, in 1778.

CLAYTON, Joseph Hughes
A painter of beach and coastal scenes who was working about 1900. He used white heightening.

CLEGHORN, John; and CLEGHORN, John, Yr.
The father was an engraver and draughtsman of landscapes and figures. He lived in Islington and exhibited from 1818 to 1828. The son, who produced landscapes and natural history subjects, moved from Islington to Fulham. He exhibited from 1840 to 1881, and a number of his subjects were taken from the area around Dorking.
There was also a painting **T. CLEGHORN** in the family.

CLENNELL, Luke
1781 (Ulgham, Northumberland) - 1840 (Newcastle)
The coastal and landscape painter. After working for his uncle, a tanner, he was apprenticed to T. Bewick (q.v.) in 1797 and became a very talented wood engraver. In 1804 he moved to London, where he continued to work as an engraver until 1810, painting on his own account at the same time. He was a member of the A.A. from 1810 to 1812 and exhibited at the R.A. and the Oil and Watercolour Society. After completing his most ambitious work, 'The Banquet of the Allied Sovereigns in the Guildhall', he became insane

in 1819, as did his wife, a daughter of Charles Warren the engraver, soon afterwards. In his more lucid moments thereafter he wrote strange poems and made weird drawings. From 1831 he was almost entirely confined to an asylum.

His earliest watercolours are in the contemporary style of S. Prout and J. Cristall (qq.v.). Later he excelled in painting rapid action with a strong feeling for the elements. Although he sometimes painted pure landscapes and figure subjects, he is at his best with beach and coastal scenes in which the fishermen of his native north-east battle stolidly against wind and spray.

Examples: B.M.; V.A.M.; Dundee City A.G.; Greenwich; Laing A.G., Newcastle; Newport A.G.; Ulster Mus.

CLERIHEW, William
A topographer and landscape painter who worked in the Near East, India and Ceylon in the 1840s and 1850s.

CLERK, Sir John, 2nd Bt. of Penicuik, F.R.S., F.S.A.
1676 (Penicuik) - 1755 (Penicuik)
Judge, antiquary and enthusiastic amateur artist. During a Grand Tour, which ended in 1699, he took lessons from one of the Mieris family at Leyden, probably Willem (1662-1747) – which would make him a great-grandson of Rembrandt by artistic genealogy – and he made many hundreds of drawings. He was a Scottish M.P. from 1702 to 1706, served on the Commission for the Union and sat in the first Parliament of Great Britain. He was raised to the bench in 1708 and succeeded to the baronetcy and estate in 1722. He was a friend and correspondent of R. Gale (q.v.) and a patron of Allan Ramsay. J. Clerk of Eldin (q.v.) was his seventh son. He wrote a number of learned and legal treatises. Colvin gives his date of birth as above, although others have offered 1684.
Bibliography: ed. P. Willis: *Furor Hortensis*, 1974. Scottish Hist. Soc., XIII, 1892. *Burlington Mag.*, March, 1969. Scottish Record Office, Clerk family papers (and drawings at Penicuik).

CLERK, John, of Eldin
1728 (Penicuik) - 1812 (Eldin)
An amateur artist and etcher who was the seventh son of Sir John Clerk of Penicuik. After a successful business career in Edinburgh he retired in 1773 and settled at Eldin, just outside the city, where he developed his artistic and scientific interests. He is best known for an essay he wrote on naval tactics which aroused great controversy. In 1753 he had married Susannah Adam, sister of the architects, and their son became the judge, Lord Eldin. He drew for most of his career, and in about 1770, encouraged by his friend P. Sandby (q.v.), he took up etching. A collection of his prints was presented to the King by the Earl of Buchan in 1786. His etchings were published by the Bannatyne

CLENNELL, Luke (1781-1840)
Fishermen returning. *Watercolour.*

Club in 1825 (twenty-eight plates) and 1855 (eight plates).

His drawings, which include both landscapes in the Edinburgh area and portraits, are generally in monochrome or low colour with firm pen outlines.

His son **John, Lord ELDIN (1757-1832)** was also an amateur draughtsman, as was his brother **Sir George CLERK-MAXWELL of Penicuik (1715-1784)** who etched a number of Scottish views.
Examples: B.M.; N.G., Scotland.

CLEVELEY, John, Yr.
1747 (Deptford) - 1786 (London)
The twin son of **John CLEVELEY (c.1712 Southwark - 1777 Deptford)**, a shipwright and painter of Deptford, he attracted the notice

CLEVELEY, John, Yr. (1747-1986)
Eddystone Lighthouse. *Watercolour, 7½in. x 10in.*

of P. Sandby (q.v.), then at Woolwich, who gave him lessons. He first exhibited in 1767, and in 1772 he was draughtsman to Sir Joseph Banks' expedition to the Hebrides, Orkneys and Iceland. He has been said to have accompanied Phipps' expedition of the following year in search of a northern route to India, which got little further than Spitzbergen. In fact, his only part was to work up drawings brought back by Midshipman Philippe d'Auvergne, future duc de Bouillon. However, he may have travelled more widely, possibly to Ireland and Portugal. He also worked up the drawings of his brother **James CLEVELEY (b.1752)** who sailed as a carpenter on Captain Cook's third voyage. Occasionally he made topographical drawings and painted in oil as well as in watercolour. His father signed 'I. Cleveley' and until 1777 the son 'Jno. Cleeley Junr.'

Examples: B.M.; V.A.M.; Greenwich.

CLEVELEY, Robert
1747 (Deptford) - 1809 (Dover)
The twin brother of John Cleveley, Yr. (q.v.) who transmitted Sandby's influence to him. He too first exhibited in 1767. He held civilian appointments as clerk and purser with the Navy, serving on the North American station and on the royal yacht taking the Duke of Clarence to Prussia in1783. This may have led to his appointments as Marine Draughtsman to the Duke and Marine Painter to the Prince of Wales. He often worked on a very large scale for a watercolourist, and he produced drawings of London and elsewhere in which a topographical element is added to the nautical. The influence of E. Dayes (q.v.) as well as that of Sandby is sometimes evident. He died as a result of a fall from a cliff.

Examples: B.M.; Brighton A.G.; Greenwich; Portsmouth City Mus.; Richmond Lib.

CLEYN, Francis
c.1582 (Rostock) - 1658
A tapestry designer and book illustrator who worked in Denmark and Italy before settling in England in 1625. He designed for Mortlake, and both designs and illustrations are known in pencil, grey and brown wash. Classical and biblical subjects are treated with high emotion.

CLIFF, William, F.R.S.
1775 - 1849
A topographer who worked in the London area. When in full colour his work can be rather gaudy, and his underdrawing, sometimes in charcoal, is weak.

Examples: B.M.

CLIFFORD, Edward
1844 (Bristol) - 1907
A painter of landscapes, portraits and historical subjects in oil and watercolour. He studied at the Bristol School of Art and at the R.A. Schools from 1865, and he exhibited in London from 1886. He visited Italy, India and the East. He was particularly noted for his portraits of the aristocracy and for his religious and philanthropic work late in life.

Bibliography: *The Times*, 20 Sept. 1907.

CLIFFORD, Edward Charles, R.I.
1858 - 1910 (London)
An illustrator and figure painter who exhibited from 1891 and was elected R.I. in 1899. He was Secretary of the Artists' Society and the Langham Sketching Club and one of the Principals of the Berry Art School. He provided illustrations and essays for the *A.J.* and similar magazines.

Published: *Trees and Tree Drawing*, 1909.

CLIFFORD, Major-General the Hon. Sir Henry Hugh, V.C.
1826 (Irnham Hall, Newark) - 1883 (Ugbrooke, Devon)
The third son of the 7th Lord Clifford of Chudleigh. Much of his childhood was spent in Rome with his maternal grandfather, Cardinal Weld. He was educated at Stonyhurst (formerly a Weld seat) and the University of Fribourg and was commissioned in the Rifle Brigade in 1846. He served in the Kaffir War and through the Crimea, winning the V.C. at Inkerman. In 1856 he joined his father in Rome, but was posted to China in the following year. He returned to England as a lieutenant-colonel and held various appoint-ments on the staff. He was also appointed ADC to the Duke of Cambridge in 1870. Thereafter his only active service was a year at the Cape in 1879-80. After the death of his nephew he lived at Ugbrooke, the family seat.

His sketches, made at least from the Crimea until the end of his life, are amateur but competent, and sometimes show the influence of Varley and Prout.

Hugh Charles, 7th Lord CLIFFORD (1790-1858) and his brother and sisters had been taught by some of the leading water-colour painters of the time, including Towne, Payne, Varley and Prout. The siblings, who may have left drawings, were: **Charles CLIFFORD** of Irnham Hall (1797-1870); **Christine CLIFFORD,** who died a nun in 1857; and **Mary Lucy CLIFFORD, Lady Stourton (d.1882).** Their father, **Charles, 6th Lord CLIFFORD (1759-1831)** painted romantic scenes in grey wash.

Examples: Nat. Army Mus.

Bibliography: *Henry Clifford, V.C.: His Letters and Sketches in the Crimea*, 1956.

CLIFT, William, F.R.S.
1775 (Burcombe) - 1849 (London)
A naturalist and landscape painter, he was the youngest child of a poor Cornish family. He was at school in Bodmin, where his drawings came to the notice of the Gilbert family who sent him to the physician John Hunter as an apprentice. He made anatomical drawings for Hunter, and after the latter's death in 1793, was curator of his collections. This left him time to paint and draw.

CLINT, Alfred
1807 (London) - 1883 (London)
The younger son and pupil of G. Clint (q.v.), he was primarily an oil painter, but he also produced landscapes, port and coastal scenes and portraits in watercolour. He exhibited from 1828, was Secretary of the S.B.A. from 1858 and President from 1870. He also made a brief appearance as a member of the N.W.S. in 1833. Many of his subjects were found on the South Coast and in the Channel Islands. His remaining works were sold at Christie's, 23 February 1884.

Published: *Landscape from Nature*, 1855. *Guide to Oil Painting*, c.1885.

Illustrated: G.J. Bennett: *The Pedestrian's Guide through North Wales*, 1838.

Examples: B.M.

Bibliography: *A.J.*, 1854; 1868.

CLINT, George
1770 (London) - 1854 (London)
A portrait painter and engraver, he was educated in Yorkshire and apprenticed to a fishmonger. However, after a quarrel with his master, he became a decorator, working at Westminster Abbey and elsewhere in London. Later he took up miniature painting and then tried larger portraits in oil and watercolour. He made copies of prints after Morland and Teniers and painted leading actors and actresses in scenes from their plays. He was elected A.R.A. in 1821 but resigned in 1836. He produced both engravings and mezzotints.

Of his five sons it is probable that **George CLINT, Yr.** was the eldest. He drew Yorkshire coast scenes at the end of the century and is represented in the Bridlington Library. **Scipio CLINT (1805-1839),** another son, was a medallist and sculptor.

Examples: B.M.

Bibliography: *A.J.*, July, 1854. J. Walpole: *Art and Artists of the Norwich School*, 1997.

CLIVE, Lady Charlotte Florentia
– *see under* **POWIS, H.A., Countess of**

CLIVE, Lady Harriet –
see **WINDSOR, Lady**

CLOUGH, Tom 1867 - 1943
A landscape painter in oil and watercolour who lived in Bolton and North Wales.

CLOVER, Joseph
1779 (Aylsham, Norfolk) - 1853
A portrait painter in oil and watercolour who worked in Norwich and London and was taught by John Opie and influenced by Lawrence. He studied at the R.A. Schools from 1806, exhibited at the R.A. and the B.I. from 1804 to 1836, and his works comprise a

COCKBURN, Major-General James Pattison (c.1779-1849)
Distant view of Greenwich. *Watercolour, 12½in. x 19½in.*

valuable catalogue of the features of the painters of the Norwich School.
Examples: Castle Mus., Norwich.
Bibliography: J. Walpole: *Art and Artists of the Norwich School,* 1997.

CLOWES, Harriett Mary
A painter of church interiors and exteriors and landscapes in Scotland and on the Rhine. She was working at least between 1847 and 1861 and sometimes collaborated with **E.A. CLOWES.**

COBBETT, Edward John
                                  1815 (London) - 1899
A landscape and genre painter who was a pupil of J.W. Allen (q.v.). He exhibited at the R.A. from 1833 to 1880 and was a member of the R.B.A.
Bibliography: *A.J.,* 1859; 1860.

COCHRANE, Helen Lavinia, Mrs., née Shaw   1868 (Bath) - 1946
A painter of romantic landscapes and Venetian scenes, she was educated at Clifton High School and studied at the Liverpool and Westminster Schools of Art and in Munich. She lived in Italy and, during the First World War, was in charge of military hospitals at Menton and Sargens.

COCKBURN, Edwin
                  1813/14   - 1873 (Edmonton)
A painter of domestic genre and landscapes who was a pupil of J. Jackson (q.v.). He was working from 1835 to 1870 and painted at Whitby early in his career, becoming a friend of G. Chambers (q.v.). He lived in London. His paintings were sold at Foster's, London, on 18 March 1874.
Examples: B.M.

COCKBURN, Major-General James Pattison c.1779   -1849 (Woolwich)
A pupil of P. Sandby (q.v) at Woolwich, which he entered in 1793 and left in 1795 to serve at the capture of the Cape of Good Hope. He was in India in 1798 and at Copenhagen as a captain in 1807. He also visited Canada. He was Director of the Royal Laboratory, Woolwich, from 1838 to 1846, in which year he was promoted major-general. After the peace of 1815 he was stationed for a time at Malta, whence he made a number of visits to Italy and Switzerland, resulting in several publications. His drawings, often in greys, greens and blues, can be charming and of high quality. A number of prints were made from them.
Published: *Swiss Scenery,* 1820. *Views in the Valley of Aosta,* 1822. *Views to Illustrate the Simplon Route,* 1822. *Views to Illustrate the Mont Cenis Route,* 1822. *Pompeii Illustrated,* 1827.
Examples: B.M.

COCKERELL, Charles Robert, R.A.
                  1788 (London) - 1863 (London)
An architect and archaeologist, he was the second son of Samuel Pepys Cockerell and was educated at Westminster. He worked for his father for about five years, during which time he toured Wales and the West Country. In 1810 he went to Turkey and Greece, where he was one of the discoverers of the Aegina marbles with J. Foster (q.v.) and Baron Heller. In 1811 and 1812 he toured the country of the Seven Churches and the Ionian Islands. After visiting Malta, Sicily and Albania, he returned to Greece in 1813. He wintered in Rome in 1815-16 and reached England in 1817. Thereafter he concentrated on his architectural

practice. He was elected A.R.A. and R.A. in 1829 and 1836 and was appointed Professor of Architecture in 1840, retiring in 1857. Not only was he an excellent architectural draughtsman, but his figures and landscapes are of a high order.
Published: *The Antiquities of Athens &c.,* 1830. *The Temple of Jupiter Olympus at Agrigentum,* 1830. *The Iconography of the West Front of Wells Cathedral,* 1851. *The Temples of Jupiter Panhellenus, &c.,* 1860.
Examples: B.M.; V.A.M.; R.I.B.A.; Haddo House, Aberdeen.
Bibliography: D. Watkin: *The Life and Work of C.R.C.,* 1974. *A.J.,* Nov. 1863. *Gentleman's Mag.,* 1863. *Builder,* XXI, 1863. R.I.B.A. *Transactions,* 1863-4; N.S. VI, 1890. R.I.B.A. *Journal,* 3rd series, VII, 1899-1900; XVIII, 1911; XXXVII, 1930. *Architectural Review,* XII, 1902; XXIX, 1911.

COCKING, Thomas
The personal servant and draughtsman to F. Grose (q.v.). It is probably impossible to distinguish the work of man and master. Pierce Egan in his *Sporting Anecdotes* says: 'The Captain had a funny fellow of the name of Tom Cocking, one after his own heart, as an amanuensis, and who was also a draughtsman of considerable merit'. He accompanied Grose to Scotland and Ireland and was active from as early as 1766 to 1791.
Examples: R.I.A.

COCKRAM, George, R.I.
                  1861 (Birkenhead) - 1950
A painter of mountains and coasts who studied at the Liverpool School of Art from 1884 and in Paris in 1889. He exhibited at the R.A. from 1883 and was elected R.I. in 1913. He lived in Liverpool until 1890 and thereafter in North Wales, at Conway and in Anglesey. His subjects were predominantly Welsh, but in his later years he also painted in Venice.
Examples: Christchurch A.G, N.Z.; Walker A.G., Liverpool.

COCKRAN, Jessie
A fruit painter who exhibited with the Society of Female Artists in 1875.

CODRINGTON, Lady Georgiana Charlotte Anne Somerset   - 1884
The second daughter of the 7th Duke of Beaufort, she married C.W. Codrington, M.P., in 1836. Their seat was Dodington Park, Gloucestershire, and their son was created baronet in 1876. She was a very competent artist, producing interiors at Badminton in the 1850s. They are in a clean, strongly drawn style.

COKE, Lady Anne –
                  see **LEICESTER, Countess of**

COLE, Edward S
A painter of French domestic and architectural

COLE, George Vicat (1833-1893)
Stoke, near Arundel. *Signed with monogram and dated 1869, watercolour, 11¼in. x 18in.*

subjects who lived in London and Richmond, exhibiting from 1837 to 1868 and standing unsuccessfully for the N.W.S. in 1858.

COLE, George Vicat, R.A.
1833 (Portsmouth) - 1893 (London)
The son and pupil of **George COLE (1810-1883)**, a landscape painter who is represented by a fine watercolour in the Portsmouth City Museum, his first exhibited works were views in Surrey and on the Wye which were shown at the B.I. and the S.B.A. in 1852. In the following year he toured Germany with his father, and then he set himself up as a drawing master in London. From 1863 until 1867 he lived at Holmbury Hill, Surrey, and thereafter in Kensington. He was elected A.R.A. and R.A. in 1870 and 1880. At this period he also broadened his scope by painting in the Thames Valley and Sussex, and after 1888 found many subjects in the Pool of London.

Cole was primarily an oil painter, and his best work in both oil and watercolour was done in his earlier Surrey period, when he showed a meticulous craftsmanship and an understanding of the effects of sunlight. When there is no other clue, it is possible to give an approximate date to his works by the signature. Until 1854 he signed in full, then Vicat Cole *tout court* until 1870, after which he used a 'V.C.' monogram.

His son **Rex Vicat COLE (1870-1940)** was also a landscape painter. He was a co-founder of the Byam Shaw (and Vicat Cole) School of Art.
Examples: B.M.; V.A.M.; Cartwright Hall, Bradford; Portsmouth City Mus.
Bibliography: R. Chignell: *Life and Works of V.C.,* 1898. *A.J.,* 1870; 1893; 1909.

COLE, Sir Henry
1808 (Bath) - 1882 (London)
The son of an army officer, he was educated at Christ's Hospital from 1817 and in 1823 entered the Record Commission under Sir Francis Palgrave. He also studied under Cox and exhibited at the R.A. On the setting up of the Record Office in 1838, he was made one of the senior assistant-keepers. Through his work he developed an interest in medieval art, and he learnt engraving and later etching. Under the name of 'Felix Summerly' he wrote illustrated guide books and books for children. He became a member of the Society of Arts in 1846 and was chairman in 1851 and 1852. He was also on the Committee for the Great Exhibition in 1851. Until his retirement in 1873 he was much involved with the Schools of Design, of which he became Secretary, and with the formation of the South Kensington Museums, of which he was the first Director. He also proposed the plans for the Albert Hall. For the rest of his life he continued to take an interest in projects for artistic reform. From 1876 to 1879 he lived in Birmingham and Manchester, returning to London in 1880. He was made K.C.B. in 1875. Fifty-eight volumes of his diaries, dating from 1822 to 1882, are in the V.A.M.
Examples: V.A.M.

COLE, or COLL, Sir Ralph, 2nd Bt.
1625 (?Kepyer) - 1704
The friend of F. Place (q.v.) he painted portraits in oil and miniature, engraved and made wash drawings. He inherited Brancepeth Castle and a fortune from his father, but spent so much on art and artists, including several Italians whom he retained, that by 1701 the

castle had to be sold. He was, however, buried there. He took lessons from Van Dyck, was painted by Lely and scraped a mezzotint of Charles II. He was also an M.P. and a colonel of militia.

COLE, Thomas William
1857 - c.1915
The headmaster of the Ealing School of Art, he painted landscapes, architectural, fruit and flower subjects.

COLEBROOKE, Lieutenant-Colonel Robert Hyde 1762 - 1808 (Bhagalpur)
A soldier and surveyor who served in the Mysore War and was Surveyor-General of India from 1800 until his death. He was a keen observer and an enthusiastic draughtsman.
Published: *Twelve Views of Mysore,* 1794.
Examples: B.M.

COLEMAN, Frank R
A painter of landscapes and rural genre subjects in oil and watercolour. He lived in Bradford and exhibited from 1880 to at least 1895.

COLEMAN, Rebecca
c.1840 (Horsham) -
The sister of W.S. Coleman and Mrs. Angell (qq.v.). With her brother's encouragement she spent a few months at Heatherley's, but found the life of an artist difficult. She taught English in Germany for three years, returning on the outbreak of the Austro-Prussian War in 1866. Thereafter she took to painting seriously, producing portraits, figure and genre subjects, as well as making a name for herself as a designer of heads on pottery.

COLEMAN, William Stephen
1829 (Horsham) - 1904 (London)
The brother of Mrs. Angell and R. Coleman (qq.v.), he was trained as a surgeon before he turned to art. He exhibited between 1865 and 1879, producing landscapes with figures, rather in the manner of M.B. Foster (q.v.), classical figure subjects akin to those of A. Moore (q.v.) – but often with strangely childish heads set on more mature near-naked bodies, and pastels – oil paintings and etchings. He was a keen naturalist, making illustrations for books and for the *Illustrated London Almanack,* and designing a heading for the *Field.* Until 1881 he was on the committee of the Dudley Gallery, and he designed tiles for Minton.
Published: *Our Woodlands, Heaths and Hedges,* 1859. *British Butterflies,* 1860.
Examples: V.A.M.; Grundy A.G., Blackpool.
Bibliography: *A.J.,* 1904.

COLERIDGE, Frederick George
c.1840 (?Glasgow) - 1925
A great-great nephew of the poet, he joined the King's Own Borderers in 1856, retiring as a

captain in 1865. He served in India during the Mutiny, fighting at Cawnpore, Lucknow and elsewhere and being mentioned in despatches. In 1861 and '62 he was in the West Indies, where he painted, and on retirement he became a professional landscape painter, living at Twyford, Berkshire, for the rest of his life. He exhibited from 1866 to 1925. As well as the Thames Valley he painted Norman and Italian subjects.

Examples: Laing A.G., Newcastle.

COLEY, Hilda

A flower painter who was working in Birmingham in about 1805.

COLKETT, Samuel David
1800 (Norwich) - 1863 (Cambridge)

A pupil of J. Stark (q.v.), he lived in London from 1828 to 1836, when he returned to Norwich and set up as a drawing master and also in business as a picture dealer and restorer. From 1843 to 1853 he lived at Great Yarmouth and, for the last ten years of his life, in Cambridge. He often produced copies of Stark's work.

His daughter Victoria became Mrs. Harry T. Hine (q.v.).

Examples: B.M.; Castle Mus., Norwich.

Bibliography: W.F. Dickes: *The Norwich School*, 1905. J. Walpole: *Art and Artists of the Norwich School*, 1997.

COLERIDGE, Frederick George (c.1840-1925)
Eton from the River. *Signed, watercolour, 6in. x 8½in.*

COLLET, John
c.1725 (London) - 1780 (Chelsea)

A caricaturist, he was a pupil of G. Lambert (q.v.) and studied at the St. Martin's Lane Academy. He first exhibited with the Free Society in 1761, and last appeared there, posthumously, in 1783. He inherited 'a genteel fortune', and lived in Chelsea. A large number of prints were made from his drawings and published by such leading figures as Carington Bowles, Smith and Sawyer, and Boydell.

His caricatures owe much to Hogarth, but have not his moral force. Both they and his landscape and figure drawings are rather clumsy and generally have a thick black pen outline. His colour can be harsh, and the whole effect is rather stiff, although not devoid of charm.

Examples: B.M.; V.A.M.; Leeds City A.G.

COLLIER, Alexander

A landscape painter in oil and watercolour who worked in London and Southampton and exhibited from 1870 to 1882.

COLLIER, Emily E

A painter of children and domestic subjects who was working from about 1879 until well into the twentieth century. She exhibited at the R.I. and Suffolk Street as well as with the Society of Female Artists, and she lived in Kent and Sussex.

COLLIER, Thomas, R.I.
1840 (Glossop) - 1891 (Hampstead)

The landscape painter. He was the best and most important of the inheritors of the traditions of Cox and de Wint. He studied at the Manchester School of Art, and from 1864 to 1869 he lived at Betws-y-coed, which remained a source of inspiration to him

COLLET, John (c.1725-1780)
The Proposal. *Pen and ink and grey wash, 5⅞in. x 7⅛in.*

COLLIER, Thomas (1840-1891)
Southwold. *Signed, pencil and watercolour, 9¼in. x 14in.*

throughout his career. He first exhibited in London in 1863, and he moved there in the hope of election to the O.W.S. However, he was turned down twice and turned to the N.W.S., being elected Associate unanimously in 1870 and a full member two years later. In 1879 he built himself a large house and studio in Hampstead. He continued to visit many parts of the country on sketching tours, especially Wales and East Anglia. His health was always weak, and it cannot have been helped by his habit of working out of doors in all weathers. He died young and comparatively unnoticed by the artistic

establishment, although in 1878 his first exhibit in Paris, a view of Arundel Castle from the Park, had won him the Legion of Honour.

J. Orrock (q.v.), who had first met with his work in Birmingham in 1868, called him 'a master in our English School', and 'the finest of sky painters, especially of rain and cumulus clouds, while possessing more mastery of direct modelling and pearl-grey shadows than any of our brotherhood'. Orrock, along with his other friends, E.M. Wimperis, C. Hayes and R. Thorne Waite (qq.v) also paid him the flattery of imitation.

Collier's subjects, moor and downland, tend

to be repetitive, but this is partly because the quality of his work is so consistent.
Examples: B.M.; V.A.M.; Aberdeen A.G.; Williamson A.G., Birkenhead; Birmingham City A.G.; Towneley Hall A.G., Burnley; Guildhall; Harrogate A.G.; Leeds City A.G.; Walker A.G., Liverpool; City A.G., Manchester; N.G., Ireland; Nat. Mus., Wales; Laing A.G., Newcastle; Castle Mus., Nottingham; Oldham A.G.; Lady Lever A.G., Port Sunlight; Salford A.G.; Sheffield A.G.; Stoke A.G.; Ulster Mus.; Wakefield City A.G.
Bibliography: A. Bury: *The Life and Art of T.C.,* 1944. G. Emslie: *A Countryman's Anthology,* 1944. O.W.S. Club, LV, 1980.

COLLIER, Thomas Frederick
1823 - 1885 (London)
A landscape painter who entered the R.D.S. Schools in 1848. He exhibited at the R.H.A. from 1850 and also at the R.A. in 1856, 1857 and 1860. From 1853 he taught at the Cork School of Design, becoming Headmaster in 1860. He became an alcoholic, and was forced to leave the School a few months after his promotion. He also left his wife and children, and may have moved to England, where he exhibited until 1874.

He painted town views and landscapes, some with rather awkward figures, and also produced still lifes in the manner of Clare.

His son **Bernard COLLIER** occasionally exhibited at the R.A. and Suffolk Street in the 1880s, and taught for a time at Hereford and at the Canterbury School of Art founded by T.S. Cooper (q.v.).
Examples: B.M.; V.A.M.; Ashmolean; Newport A.G.

COLLING, James Kellaway
An architectural and landscape painter who was active in Norfolk and elsewhere between 1844 and 1889.
Published: *Gothic Ornaments,* 1846-50. *Details of Gothic Architecture,* 1851-6. *Art Foliage,* 1865. *Examples of English Medieval Foliage,* 1874. *Suggestions in Design,* 1880.

COLLINGS, Albert Henry, R.I.
1858 (London) - 1947
A figure, portrait and genre painter who lived in London.

COLLINGS, Charles John
1848 (Devonshire) - 1931
A landscape painter working rather in the Barbizon manner, he first exhibited in 1887. A number of one-man and other exhibitions were held in London prior to 1910 when he moved to Canada, settling in British Columbia. Thereafter he painted the Rockies.

He has a highly original broad sweeping style and a strong sense of form and design and atmospheric effect. His deep admiration for Cotman is shown in his work.
Examples: Fitzwilliam.
Bibliography: *Apollo,* LIV, 1951.

COLLING, James Kellaway
Waterloo Bridge and the Shot Towers. *Signed with monogram and dated 1889, pencil and watercolour heightened with white, 11⅝in. x 20¾in.*

COLLINGS, Samuel   - 1793 (Soho)

A landscape painter and caricaturist. He provided Rowlandson with drawings for prints, including satires on *Johnson's Tour to the Hebrides* and *Goethe's Sorrows of Werter*. He also contributed humorous drawings and verses to *The Wit's Magazine*. He exhibited at the R.A. between 1784 and 1789.

Published: *Picturesque Beauties of Boswell*, 1786.
Examples: B.M.

COLLINGWOOD, William, R.W.S.
1819 (Greenwich) - 1903 (Bristol)

A landscape painter, he was the son of an architect and a pupil of J.D. Harding and S. Prout (qq.v) as well as of his cousin W.C. Smith (q.v.). From about 1856 he made his name as an Alpine painter. Much of his working life was spent in Liverpool, where he was a lay preacher for the Plymouth Brethren.

His son was William Gersham Collingwood (1854-1920), Ruskin's disciple and secretary.

Examples: V.A.M.; Ashmolean.

COLLINS, Charles
c.1680 (Ireland) - 1744

A painter of still lifes and especially of birds in water and bodycolour. He was working in Dublin in the 1720s and 1730s. In the catalogue of the collection of Sir Gustavus Hume, which was sold in Dublin in May 1786, 'two pictures, most admirably executed, one of live fowl, the other of a dead hare, &c., by an Irish master, Collins' are recorded.

Examples: B.M.; Leeds City A.G. Yale

COLLINS, Charles, II   - 1921

A prolific painter of landscapes and rustic genre subjects in oil and watercolour. He was active from about 1867 and lived in South London and Dorking. Most of his views are in the South, but he also worked in Scotland.

COLLINS, Charles Allston
1828   - 1873 (London)

The second son of W. Collins (q.v.), he studied at the R.A. Schools from the age of fifteen, sketched with Millais, and joined the Pre-Raphaelites. He exhibited at the R.A. from 1847 to 1855, when he gave up painting for literature. He married Kate Perugini (q.v.), a daughter of Charles Dickens.

Examples: B.M.; Ashmolean.
Bibliography: *A.J.*, 1859; June 1873; 1904.

COLLINS, George Edward
1880 (Dorking) - 1968

An etcher and illustrator. He was educated at Dorking High School and studied at the Epsom and Lambeth Schools of Art. He was interested in natural history and illustrated an edition of Gilbert White's *Selborne* in 1911. He was art master at his old school and later at the Royal Grammar School, Guildford, and he lived at Gomshall.

COLLINS, William (1788-1847)
A Boy with a Boat-hook. *Pencil and watercolour on light fawn paper, 10¼in. x 9⅛in.*

COLLINS, Thomas
1838   - 1894 (W. Bromwich)

A painter of flowers, still lifes and landscapes who lived in Birmingham. He exhibited both there and in London from 1857 to 1893.

COLLINS, William, R.A.
1788 (London) - 1847 (London)

The son of an Irish author who wrote a biography of Morland (q.v.). Collins watched Morland painting, and his enthusiasm encouraged his father to send him to the R.A. Schools in 1807. By 1812 he had established himself as a painter of landscapes and genre scenes. In 1815 he visited the Norfolk coast, where he stayed with the family of J. Stark (q.v.); in 1817 he went to Paris and in 1828 visited Holland and Belgium. In 1836 he went to Italy, where he stayed until 1838. He visited Germany in 1840 and the Shetlands in 1842. In between these journeys he made numerous sketching tours in England and Scotland. He was elected A.R.A. in 1814 and R.A. in 1820. In 1840 he was appointed Librarian, but he resigned after two years. In 1822 he married the sister of M.S. Carpenter (q.v.), and he was a lifelong friend of Linnell (q.v.).

In both subject matter and style he resembles Mulready, being a careful and pretty draughtsman, if a little dull. His landscapes are generally freer and can be very attractive. Again, like Mulready, he made watercolour versions of some of his best known oil paintings.

He was the father of Wilkie Collins, who wrote his biography, and of C.A. Collins (q.v.), the painter and author.

Examples: B.M.; V.A.M.; Towner Gall., Eastbourne; N.G., Scotland; Newport A.G.
Bibliography: W.W. Collins: *Memoirs of the Life of W.C.*, 1848. *Athenaeum*, 20 February 1847. *A.J.*, May, 1855; 1859; 1899.

COLLINS, William Wiehe, R.I.
1862 (London) - 1951

A painter of military subjects and street scenes, he was the son of an Army doctor and was educated at Epsom College. He was elected R.I. in 1898 and in the First World War saw service in the Dardanelles and in Egypt, which provided him with subjects. Later he lived in Wareham, and Bridgwater, Dorset.

Exhibitions of his work were held at the Fine Art Society in 1901 and the Abbey Gallery in 1927.

Published: *Cathedral Cities of Spain*, 1909. *Cathedral Cities of Italy*, 1911.
Illustrated: G. Gilbert: *Cathedral Cities of England*, 1905. R.H. Cox: *The Green Roads of England*, 1914.

COLLINSON, James
1825 (Mansfield, Nottingham) - 1881 (London)

An original Pre-Raphaelite Brother who

COMPTON, Edward Theodore (1849-1921)
An Alpine lake scene. *Watercolour, signed and dated 1886, 7¾in. x 12½in.*

studied at the R.A. Schools and was engaged to Christina Rossetti in 1849-50, when he resigned from the Brotherhood and retired to become a monk at Stonyhurst. Later he returned to London and painted pretty genre subjects in oil and occasionally watercolour. He exhibited from 1847 and his work can be like that of W. Henry Hunt (q.v.) without the high finish.

Examples: Ashmolean.
Bibliography: *Apollo*, XXXI, 1940.

COLLYER, Herbert H
1863 (Leicestershire) - 1947 (Mapperley, Nottingham)
He moved to Nottingham at the age of thirty and became a member of the Nottingham Society of Artists. He was associated with the firm of Tom Browne Ltd., Colour Printers, founded by T.A. Browne (q.v.). He was an amateur and painted local scenes, particularly gardens.

Another talented amateur landscape painter was **William COLLYER,** who was painting in Cyprus in the 1880s.

COLMAN, Samuel
?1816   - 1894
A painter of primitive, visionary watercolours who was the eleventh son of the Norfolk mustard family. One of his nephews was created a baronet in 1907, and he himself married a Norfolk Bowles.

He should not be confused with the Bristol romantic painter of the same name, who was active from 1816 to 1840, nor with their American namesake of the Hudson River School (1832-1890).

COLQUHON, Lieutenant-Colonel James
1835   - 1883
The son of the author of *The Moor and the Loch,* and a nephew of the 4th baronet of Luss, his army career was spent in the Highland Borderers and the 4th Dragoon Guards. He served and drew in the Crimea and, in 1879, in Afghanistan.
Examples: Nat. Army. Mus.

COMBER, Mary E
A painter of mossy banks and blossoms in the manner of W. Cruickshank (q.v.). She lived in Warrington and was active in the 1880s.

COMPTON, Edward Theodore
1849 (London) - 1921 (Tutzing, Bavaria)
An active climbing and painting member of the Alpine Club. During the First World War he was nominally interned, after which he attempted to work as an art correspondent near the Italian frontier, but was refused a permit. He lived for most of his life in Austria and Germany, sending contributions to London exhibitions, including the R.A. from 1879. After his seventieth birthday he climbed the Gröss Glockner. His work is generally delicate both in colour and feeling.

His son, **Edward Harrison COMPTON (1881 Feldenfing, Bavaria - 1960)** followed in his footsteps and exhibited with him at the Fine Art Society in 1907 and 1909.
Illustrated: T. Compton: *A Mendip Valley*, 1892. J.F. Dickie: *Germany*, 1912. G.W. Bullett: *Germany*, 1930.
Bibliography: E.W. Bredt: *Die Alpen und ihre Maler*, 1910. S. Wichmann: *E.T.C. und E.H.C., Maler und Alpinisten*, 1999. *A.J.*, 1907.

COMPTON, Lady Frances Elizabeth
1791   - 1883
The only daughter of the 9th Earl and 1st Marquess of Northampton (d.1828), Lady Frances was a pupil of J.C.Nattes (q.v.). In 1829 she married Charles Scrase Dickins, and they lived at West Stoke, near Chichester, until

CONDY, Nicholas (1793-1857)
A Boathouse in Bigbury Bay, near Plymouth. *Watercolour over pencil, 4¾in. x 6in.*

he inherited Coolhurst, near Horsham, in 1843. She produced views around her childhood home Castle Ashby, sometimes working alongside Nattes.
Examples: Northamptonshire Record Office.

CONDER, Charles Edward
1868 (London) - 1909 (Virginia Water)
A painter of landscapes in oil and charming fan designs, often on silk, in watercolour. He was brought up in India and went to Australia in 1885. There he worked for the *Illustrated Sydney News* and studied at the Melbourne Art School. In 1890 he went to Paris and Julian's, and in 1897 he settled in London. He was elected to the N.E.A.C. in 1901, and he gave up painting because of poor health, in 1906.
Examples: B.M.; Aberdeen A.G.; Cecil Higgins A.G., Bedford; Cartwright Hall, Bradford; Fitzwilliam; Glasgow A.G.; Leeds City A.G.; City A.G., Manchester; N.G., Scotland; Ulster Mus.
Bibliography: F.G. Gibson: *C.C.*, 1914. J. Rothenstein: *The Life and Death of C.C.*, 1938. *A.J.*, 1909. Tate Gall., Exhibition Cat., 1927.

CONDY, Nicholas
1793 (Withiel, Cornwall) - 1857 (Plymouth)
After service in the Peninsula, Condy retired as a half-pay lieutenant in 1818 and became a professional artist in Plymouth. Between 1830 and 1845 he occasionally exhibited at the R.A., the B.I. and Suffolk Street.

His works are mainly small watercolours on tinted paper, usually about 5in. x 8in. They are executed in water and bodycolour, often with rather garish reds and greens. They are somewhat impressionistic in technique and can be very appealing.

His son, **Nicholas Matthews CONDY (1818 Plymouth -1851 Plymouth)** was also a marine painter and teacher at Plymouth. There are examples of his work at Exeter Mus. and Greenwich.
Published: *Cothele... the seat of the Earl of Mount-Edgecumbe*, 1850.

CONEY, John
1786 (London) - 1833 (Camberwell)
A topographical draughtsman and engraver who was apprenticed to an architect but never practised. He exhibited ten works at the R.A. between 1805 and 1821. From 1815 to 1829 he drew and engraved a series of exterior and interior views of English Cathedrals and Abbeys, and from 1829 to 1832 he was engaged in similar work on Continental Cathedrals, Town Halls and the like. He also engraved for C.R. Cockerell (q.v.) and Sir John Soane.

He is best on a small scale; his larger works are poor in detail.
Published: *A Series of Views... of Warwick Castle*, 1815. *The Beauties of Continental Architecture*, 1843. &c.
Illustrated: Sir W. Dugdale: *Monasticon Anglicanum*, 1846.
Examples: B.M.; V.A.M.; Ashmolean.

CONDY, Nicholas Matthews (1818-1851)
Shipping. *Watercolour with rubbing out, 3½in. x 5in.*

CONNOLLY, John
An Irish landscape painter, working in the early nineteenth century. He also produced several lithographs, both after his own drawings and those of other artists.

CONRADE, Alfred Charles
1863 (Leeds) - 1955 (Heywood)
A very fine traditional architectural painter who studied in Düsseldorf, Paris and Madrid. He travelled widely in Europe and visited Japan. He was chief artist at the White City from 1911 to 1914, and he lived in London, Kingston-on-Thames and Manchester.
Examples: B.M.

CONROY, Lady Alicia, née Parsons
1815 - 1885
The daughter of the 2nd Earl of Rosse, she married Sir Edward Conroy, Bt. in 1837. She painted both landscapes and witty commentaries on the local society around Birr.
Examples: Birr Castle, Co. Offaly.

CONRADE, Alfred Charles (1863-1955)
Cleopatra. *Signed, pen and ink and watercolour, 11in. x 18in.*

CONSTABLE, John (1776-1837)
Landscape sketch with bridge and trees. *Watercolour.*

CONSTABLE, John, R.A.
1776 (East Bergholt, Suffolk) -
1837 (Hampstead)
By the time he left Dedham Grammar School between sixteen and seventeen, Constable was already determined on becoming an artist, but at his father's insistence he worked for a while in the family watermills. He early acquired his first patron, Sir G. Beaumont (q.v.), who introduced him to the works of Claude and, later, Girtin. From 1795, when he paid a visit to London, he was also aided by J.T. Smith (q.v.), who helped him with his artistic education thereafter by letter. In 1799 he finally abandoned milling and was admitted to the R.A. Schools. In 1801 he visited Derbyshire, in 1803 he made a voyage from London to Deal and in September and October, 1806, he made a tour of the Lake District, visiting J. Harden (q.v.). In 1809, with the encouragement of Farington, he stood for, but failed to gain, election as A.R.A. He was finally elected in 1819, and to full membership in 1829. In 1811 he first visited Salisbury, and the area became, with Sussex and Hampshire, one of his favourite sketching grounds. He stayed with Beaumont at Coleorton Hall, Leicestershire, in 1823, and visited Brighton annually between 1824 and 1828. He was at Arundel in 1834 and 1835. Otherwise his life was uneventful; despite the influence which his pictures had on the Continent from 1824, he never went abroad himself.

Even his large and formal studio drawings show an unexpected spontaneity of handling, and in the best of his pencil drawings and watercolour sketches there is a freedom that is far ahead of his time. These sketches, like his cloud studies, whilst only intended as rough notes, convey a strong atmosphere and sense of locality. Many of these characteristic and most remarkable watercolours date from the last decade of his life.

His children all drew to some degree. They were **John Charles CONSTABLE (1817-1841); Maria Louisa CONSTABLE (1819-1885); Charles Golding CONSTABLE (1821-1879)**, who served in the Indian Navy and sketched in the East, the Mediterranean and widely in Britain; **Isobel CONSTABLE (1822-1888)**, who painted studies of shells; **Emily CONSTABLE (1825-1839); Alfred Abram CONSTABLE (1826-1853)** and **Lionel Bicknell CONSTABLE (1828-1887)**.
Published: *Various Subjects of Landscape characteristic of English Scenery,* 1830-32.
Examples: B.A.; V.A.M.; Ashmolean; Cecil Higgins A.G., Bedford; Birmingham City A.G.; Blackburn A.G.; Brighton A.G.; Exeter Mus.; Leeds City A.G.; City A.G., Manchester.
Bibliography: C.R. Leslie: *Memoirs of the Life of J.C., R.A.,* 1843. S.J. Key: *J.C., his Life and Work.* J.C. Holmes: *C.,* 1902. J.D. Linton: *C's. Sketches,* 1905. A. Shirley: *J.C.,* 1944. A.G. Reynolds: *C., the Natural Painter,* 1965. F. Constable: *J.C.,* 1975. I. Fleming-Williams: *C. Landscape Watercolours and Drawings,* 1976. *A.J.,* Jan. 1855; 1903. O.W.S. Club, XII, 1935; LXI, 1986. *Country Life,* 1 May 1937; 16 April 1938; 10 March 1955. *Connoisseur,* CXXXVIII, 1956. A.G. Reynolds: Cat. of the Constable Collection at the V.A.M. 1960. Tate Gall., Exhibition Cat., 1976.
See Colour Plates

CONYERS, C., H., M., and S.
– see NEWDIGATE, Sir Roger

COOK, Charles A
A landscape painter who was active in Kent, Sussex and East Anglia in the 1890s. He

CONSTABLE, Lionel Bicknell (1828-1887)
Poplars at Dedham. *Pencil and watercolour with gum arabic and scratching, 4¾in. x 6½in.*

COOK, Ebenezer Wake (1843-1926)
Sorrento, Italy. *Watercolour, signed and inscribed on reverse, 21½in. x 32in.*

painted on Skye in the late 1870s and visited Rome in 1891. He lived at Blackheath, and might perhaps be identifiable with Sir Charles Archer Cook (1849-1934), the legal writer and Chief Charity Commissioner.

COOK, Ebenezer Wake
1843 (Maldon, Essex) - 1926 (London)
A landscape painter who studied in Paris and exhibited at the R.A. from 1875 to 1910 as well as at the R.I. He took his subjects from Italy and the Lakes, Switzerland, Yorkshire and the Thames Valley. His work is pretty but oversweet and detailed, and his colours are bright. He was a spiritualist.
Published: *Anarchism in Art and Chaos in Criticism,* 1904. *Retrogression in Art and the Suicide of the Royal Academy,* 1924.
Examples: V.A.M.; Shipley A.G., Gateshead; Melbourne A.G.; Sydney A.G.
Bibliography: *Studio,* XXVIII, 1903.

COOK, Edward Dutton
1829 (London) - 1883 (London)
An author, playwright and dramatic critic, he studied painting under Charles Rolt and for a time worked for *Punch* as a wood engraver.

COOK, Henry   1819   - 1890
A landscape painter who studied in London and Rome and settled in Italy in 1859. He travelled in the Near East, painted battles for Napoleon III and the King of Sardinia, and also wrote on art. There was a London exhibition of his views in Greece, Italy, the Ionian Islands and Scotland in 1856, and he showed North Italian subjects at the Grosvenor and Egyptian Galleries in 1883. He was sometimes known as 'Henrico'. Later in life he returned to London, where he won the patronage of Queen Victoria.
Published: *Scenery of Central Italy,* 1846
Bibliography: *Athenaeum,* 5 July 1856.

COOK, Herbert Moxon
1844 (Manchester) - c.1920
A landscape painter in oil and watercolour who exhibited at the R.A., the R.I. and elsewhere from 1868. He lived in London and later in his career at Prestatyn, North Wales. He also painted a great deal in the Highlands and on Arran.
Examples: Manchester City A.G.

COOK, Richard, R.A.
1784 (London) - 1857 (London)
A historical painter who studied at the R.A. Schools. He first exhibited at the R.A. in 1808 and was elected A.R.A. in 1816 and R.A. in 1822. As well as his work in oil he was a book illustrator and made many tinted pencil sketches of figures, furniture, arms and the like.
His remaining works, including sketches, were sold at Christie's, 1 June 1857.
Illustrated: Sir W. Scott: *The Lady of the Lake,* 1810.
Examples: B.M.; Swansea A.G.

COOK, Samuel, of Plymouth, N.W.S.
1806 (Camelford, Cornwall) -
1859 (Plymouth)
He received a rudimentary education and at the age of nine was apprenticed to a local firm of woollen manufacturers. At the same time he was painting sign boards and the like. Once out of his articles he moved to Plymouth and eventually set up as a house painter. In his spare time he made sketches of the coast and quays. He was an unsuccessful candidate for the N.W.S. in 1843 but was elected Associate and Member in 1849 and 1854. In the former year he was in Ireland.
Examples: B.M.; V.A.M.; Exeter Mus.; Shipley A.G., Gateshead.
Bibliography: *A.J.,* 1861.

COOK, William, of Plymouth
Probably the son of S. Cook (q.v.), he painted repetitive views of the Cornish coasts. They are usually signed with initials and are painted in a very characteristic range of greens and pinks. He exhibited in London and in the 1870s.

COOKE, Edward William, R.A., F.R.S.
1811 (London) - 1880 (Groombridge, Kent)
The son of the engraver George Cooke, he was already making wood engravings of plants for publication by the age of nine. Some of these were used to illustrate Loudon's *Encyclopedia of Plants,* and others Loddidge's *Botanical Cabinet.* He married Loddidge's daughter in

COOKE, Edward William (1811-1880)
St. Mary-le-Strand. *Water and bodycolour, 6¼in. x 4⅝in.*

COOKE, Isaac (1846-1922)
A Fruit Porter. *Signed and dated 1918, black chalk and watercolour, 10in. x 6in.*

1840. In about 1825 he met C. Stanfield (q.v.), and sketched boats after him. He began to study architecture under A. Pugin (q.v.), but gave up this to pursue his interest in ships. Between 1825 and 1831 he made a series of drawings of the building of the new London Bridge, and also made studies of antiquities at the B.M. In 1826 he sketched on the Norfolk coast at Cromer, in 1830 he went to Normandy and between 1832 and 1844 he visited Belgium and Holland several times, as well as France, Scotland, Ireland and elsewhere. In 1845-6 he was in Italy and later he travelled in Spain, North Africa, Germany, Denmark and Sweden. He was elected A.R.A. in 1851 and R.A. in 1864.

His drawing is of a very high quality, and he made many careful pencil studies. His full watercolours are rarer but also impressive. Occasionally he painted small figure studies of fisherfolk, and he also produced humorous drawings and etchings. He was meticulous in recording both his life, in diaries, and work, in ledgers, both of which survive.

His remaining works were sold at Christie's, 22 May 1880.

Two of his sisters, **Harriette COOKE** **(1815-1898)** and **Georgiana Eglinton, Mrs. WARD (1822-1861)**, were very sound pencil draughtswomen. The latter illustrated her brother-in-law N.B. Ward's *On the Growth of Plants*, 1852, along with E.W. Cooke.
Examples: B.M.; V.A.M.; Ferens A.G., Hull; Glasgow A.G.; Greenwich; Leeds City A.G. (with Cotman); Wakefield A.G.
Bibliography: J. Munday: *E.W.C.*, 1996. *A.J.* 1869; 1880.

COOKE, George
1781 (London) - 1834 (Barnes)
The engraver, and father of E.W. Cooke (q.v.). Occasionally he painted landscapes and architectural subjects in wash.

His brother **William Bernard COOKE (1778-1855)** was also an engraver and painter of landscapes.
Examples: B.M.

COOKE, Isaac
1846 (Warrington) - 1922
A landscape painter in oil and watercolour who exhibited in London and elsewhere from 1879. He was a member of the R.B.A. from 1896 to 1915 and of the Liverpool Academy and Water-Colour Society. He lived in Cheshire.
Bibliography: *Studio*, XXIV, 1901.

COOKE, William Cubitt
1866 (London) - 1951
A landscape and figure painter and book illustrator who was apprenticed to a chromolithographer. He studied at Heatherley's and the Westminster School of Art and exhibited from 1890. He worked for the *I.L.N.* and the *Graphic* and lived in London and Stroud.

COOKSEY, Mary Louise Greville
1878 (Birmingham) -
An 'ecclesiastical artist' and figure and landscape painter in watercolour and oil. She studied at the Leamington and Liverpool Art Schools and South Kensington, and she won a travelling scholarship to Italy. She lived at Freshfield, Lancashire.

COOLEY, Thomas
1740 (England) - 1784 (Dublin)
An architect who had been apprenticed to a carpenter. He won a Premium at the Society of

Arts in 1753, and in 1769 he won the competition to build the Royal Exchange in Dublin. His other buildings include a tower at Armagh Cathedral and the Newgate Prison in Dublin. He was working on the Four Courts at the time of his death. As well as architectural designs, which he exhibited with the Free Society from 1765 to 1768, he painted landscapes.

His grandson **Thomas COOLEY, A.R.H.A (1795-1873)**, was deaf and dumb but none the less made a career as a portrait painter in Dublin and London, where he entered the R.A. Schools in 1812. He also drew pen and ink genre subjects.

COOPER, Abraham, R.A.
1787 (London) - 1868 (Greenwich)
A painter of sporting and battle pictures, he was largely self taught except for a few lessons from Benjamin Marshall. At the age of thirteen he was working at Astley's Circus and soon afterwards for Meux the brewer. He first exhibited at the B.I. in 1814 and he was elected A.R.A. and R.A. in 1817 and 1820. Among his pupils were the elder Herring and William Barraud (qq.v.). He was primarily an oil painter.

His son, **Alexander Davis COOPER (b.1820)**, who entered the R.A. Schools in 1837 and exhibited from that year until 1888, painted animals, landscapes, portraits and literary genre subjects. His wife painted fruit, flowers and figures. Both worked primarily in oil paint. J.D. Watson (q.v.) was a pupil and friend. Another son was **(Edward Mallinson) Alfred William COOPER (b. 1830)**, who entered the Schools in 1848 and was still active in 1901.
Examples: B.M.
Bibliography: *A.J.*, 1863; 1869. *Apollo*, May, Sept., 1949. *Country Life*, Dec. 19, 1968.

COOPER, Alfred Heaton
1863 (Nr. Bolton) - 1929 (Ambleside)
A landscape and still-life painter and illustrator who lived at Ambleside. He exhibited in London from 1885 and was the father of **William Heaton COOPER (b.1903)**, who painted similar subjects and portraits.

COOPER, Duncan Elphinstone
?1810 - 1904 (London)
A farmer and topographer who arrived in Victoria, Australia, in 1842 and remained there until 1855. He was described as 'an amateur of some accomplishment' and 'a well-connected and evidently fairly affluent bachelor'. He was the first to paint the Victorian interior and he also visited Tasmania, where he gave lessons and lectures.

COOPER, Edwin W
1785 (Beccles) - 1833 (Beccles)
An animal painter who was the son of **Daniel COOPER**, who taught drawing at Bury

COOPER, Richard, Yr. (1740-1820)
Near Tivoli. *Signed, watercolour, 13⅞in. x 24¾in.*

School. He worked at Norwich, Newmarket and Cambridge and specialised in horse portraits. He also painted stalking and genre subjects.
Examples: B.M.; V.A.M.; Castle Mus., Norwich. J. Walpole: *Art and Artists of the Norwich School*, 1997.

COOPER, Emma, Mrs., née Wren
1837 (Buntingford, Hertfordshire) -
A bird and flower painter, she married C.B. Cooper on leaving school in 1858 and only took to art seriously in 1865. She was a friend of the Coleman family (q.v.), who encouraged her to study at Heatherley's. During the 1870s she obtained a great reputation as a successor to 'Bird's Nest' Hunt (q.v.) and as an illuminator. Inevitably, wrens were a favourite subject.
Published: *Plain Words on the Art and Practice of Illumination*, 1868.

COOPER, Frederick Charles
1819/20 (Nottingham) - 1883 (Epping)
After setting up as an artist in Nottingham, he moved to London, where he exhibited at the R.A., the B.I. and Suffolk Street from 1844 to 1868. In 1849 he was sent out to record the excavations of Sir Henry Austen Layard at Nineveh. The two did not get on, and Layard seems to have taken credit for some of Cooper's better work. Cooper also visited Trebizond, and in the 1860s he painted in Brittany. While he chiefly exhibited figure subjects and interiors, in oil as well as watercolour, his landscapes are effective, although in them the figures can be shaky.
Illustrated: H.A.Layard: *Nineveh and Babylon*.

COOPER, George
An architectural draughtsman who also exhibited English and Continental topo-

graphical drawings at the R.A. from 1792 to 1830. He published two sets of architectural engravings in 1807, and he provided many drawings for W.M. Wade's *Walks in Oxford*, 1817.

He is not to be confused with his namesake, a Gloucester statuary mason and occasional architect who was active from at least 1811 to 1838. Neither is to be identified with their further namesake, the Canterbury carver and gilder who was active from at least 1818 to 1851.
Published: *Architectural Reliques...*, 1807. *Designs for the Decoration of Rooms*, 1807.
Examples: B.M.; Soane Mus.

COOPER, Richard, Yr.
1740 (Edinburgh) - 1820
The son of **Richard COOPER (1705-1764)**, the engraver and occasional watercolourist. The younger Cooper studied in London and Paris and went to Italy in about 1770. He may have stayed there at least until 1776, but had certainly returned by 1778, when he exhibited Roman and Italian views at the R.A. Thereafter he shows a penchant for the Richmond and Kew area. He lived for some time in Edinburgh and in the 1780s was drawing master at Eton. He later taught the Princess Charlotte. His drawings are usually in pen or pencil and wash, often a distinctive yellow-brown wash, but occasionally he produced pure watercolours. He was fond of small, strongly contrasted areas of light and shade, outlined in pen, giving a mottled, sunlit effect, which may have been imitated from Canaletto, whose drawings and etchings he may well have seen at Windsor Castle.
Examples: B.M.; V.A.M.; Aberdeen A.G.; Fitzwilliam; Leeds City A.G.; N.G.Scotland; N.G.Ireland.

COOPER, Thomas Sidney (1803-1902)
Goats. *Signed, pencil and watercolour with scratching out, 6¼in. x 9½in.*

COOPER, Thomas George
1829   - 1896 (W. Ham)
A landscape and rustic genre painter, he was a son of T.S. Cooper (q.v.). He visited North Wales and Osborne, Isle of Wight, with his father in 1848, and he exhibited from 1868 to 1896. He worked in both oil and watercolour.

COOPER, Thomas Sidney, R.A.
1803 (Canterbury) - 1902 (near Canterbury)
The landscape and cattle painter. He studied at the B.M. with G. Richmond (q.v.) and Catterson Smith as fellow pupils, and won a place at the R.A. Schools which he was unable to take up. He then taught at Canterbury, and, in 1827, went to France with W. Burgess (q.v.) and on to Brussels on his own, where he remained until the revolution of 1830. He was strongly influenced by his friend Verboekhoeven. In 1829 he toured the Meuse towns with Captain Hotham (q.v.), a pupil, and in 1830 paid a brief visit to Holland. He returned to London in 1831. He exhibited at the R.A. from 1833, was elected A.R.A. and R.A. in 1845 and 1867, and from 1847 collaborated on a number of oil paintings with F.R. Lee (q.v.). He visited the Isle of Wight in 1839, and again, on a commission from the Queen, in 1848. In that year he also visited North Wales. Other sketching grounds included Liverpool, Norfolk and Devon. In the 1860s he moved back to Canterbury and in about 1869 set up an Art School and Gallery. He made visits to Switzerland in 1879 and to Skye in 1882 or 1883.

His works, which are repetitive, with their groups of cattle or sheep often set on the Canterbury marshes, have been extensively faked, both in his lifetime and subsequently.

Many of the earliest frauds were taken from the lithographs which were issued in the 1840s.

In London his pupils included the daughters of Lords Liverpool, Fitzwilliam and Stourton (Mrs Brand), and the daughter of Dr Stephen Lushington.
Published: *T.S.C's Drawing Book of Animals and Rustic Groups,* 1853. *My Life,* 1890.
Examples: B.M.; V.A.M.; Aberdeen A.G.; Haworth A.G., Accrington; Blackburn A.G.; Brighton A.G.; Exeter Mus.; Leeds City A.G.; Maidstone Mus.; City A.G., Manchester; Newport A.G.
Bibliography: E.K. Chesterton: *T.S.C.,* 1902. *A.J.,* 1849; 1861; 1902.

COOPER William Sidney
1854 (Canterbury) - 1930 (Chesterfield)
The second son of T.S. Cooper (q.v.), he painted landscapes and cattle and he exhibited at the R.A. from 1871 to 1908. He entered the R.A. Schools in 1872.
Examples: Maidstone Mus.

COPE, Charles   - 1827
An amateur artist who lived in Wakefield and Leeds. He was a friend of West and Turner, and the father of C.W. Cope (q.v.); his wife also painted rustic subjects. She died in about 1812, and he after a coach accident.
Published: *Views of Bolton Abbey and its Environs,* 1822.
Examples: Leeds City A.G.

COPE, Charles West, R.A.
1811 (Leeds) - 1890 (Bournemouth)
A historical painter and the son of C. Cope (q.v.), he studied at Sass's School in 1827 and entered the R.A. Schools in 1828. In 1832 he

visited Paris and in 1833 set out for two years in Italy. He had been a friend of the patron John Sheepshanks from childhood and was introduced by him to G. Richmond and R. Redgrave (qq.v), with whom he sketched. He was a founder of the Etching Club, and he was elected A.R.A. and R.A. in 1843 and 1848. He was much taken up with fresco painting for the Houses of Parliament, and he visited Italy in 1845 in order to study the art. In 1876 he represented the R.A. at the Centennial Exhibition in Philadelphia. In 1879 he settled in Maidenhead.

His work in watercolour, apart from studies and sketches, consists of Leighton Leitch-like landscapes and illustrations.

One of his sons was **Sir Arthur Stockdale COPE, R.A. (1857-1940),** the portrait painter.
Examples: B.M.; Ashmolean; Leicestershire A.G.
Bibliography: C.H. Cope: *Reminiscences of C.W.C.* 1889. *A.J.,* 1859; 1869; 1890. *Journal of the Warburg Inst.,* 1954.

COPLAND, Charles
At Greenwich there are forty pencil and watercolour sketches of St. Helena, Bombay and the East by this artist. They appear to have been drawn in about 1810.

COPPIN, Daniel
1771   - 1822
A Norwich landscape painter in oil and occasionally in watercolour. He exhibited copies of Barker of Bath at the Norwich Society from 1805 to 1816 and was President in the latter year. He visited Paris in 1814 with Crome, and his daughter became E. Stannard (q.v.).
Bibliography: J. Walpole: *Art and Artists of the Norwich School,* 1997.

CORBAUX, Marie Françoise Catherine Doetter, 'Fanny', N.W.S.
1812 (Paris) - 1883 (Brighton)
She studied at the N.G. and the B.I. and in 1827 her watercolours received silver medals from the Society of Arts. In 1830 she was elected an honorary member of the S.B.A., where she exhibited small oil paintings, and in 1839 a member of the N.W.S. She was well known as a biblical critic and writer. As well as figure studies in watercolour she painted miniatures.

Her sister **Louisa CORBAUX, N.W.S. (b.1808)** exhibited children and animals from 1828 to 1881 at the R.A., the S.B.A., and the N.W.S., of which she was elected a member in 1837.
Illustrated: T. Moore: *Pearls of the East,* 1837. T. Moore: *Cousin Natalia's Tales,* 1841.
Examples: B.M.

CORBET, Matthew Ridley, A.R.A.
1850 (S. Willingham, Lincolnshire) - 1902 (London)
A portrait and landscape painter in oil and watercolour who was intended for the Army,

but turned to art. He was educated at Cheltenham and studied under Davis Cooper, at the Slade and the R.A. Schools from 1872. In 1880 he went to Rome for three years, studying under Giovanni Costa. He exhibited from 1875 to 1902, gradually turning from portraits to landscapes. He was elected A.R.A. in 1902.

Examples: V.A.M.

Bibliography: *A.J.,* 1902. *Studio,* XXV, 1902. *Mag. of Art,* XXVI, 1902. Stoke-on-Trent A.G.: Exhibition Cat., 1989.

CORBOULD, Alfred Chantrey
1852 - 1920

The son of A.H. Corbould (q.v.), he was a painter of horses, portraits, rustic genre and sporting subjects, and he worked for *Punch* and exhibited from 1878 at Suffolk Street, the R.I. and elsewhere.

An earlier **Alfred CORBOULD,** who exhibited sporting subjects and horse portraits in the 1830s seems to have been a nephew of R. Corbould (q.v.).

Bibliography: G.C.B. Poulter: *The Corbould Genealogy,* 1935.

See Corbould Family Tree

CORBOULD Alfred Hichens
1821 - 1874

One of the youngest sons of H. Corbould (q.v.), he married Mary, a sister of C.S. Keene (q.v.) and was the father of A.C. Corbould (q.v.). He was himself a pupil of J.S. Cotman (q.v.) at King's College School. Much of his work was in oil and was exhibited at the R.A., but he also produced watercolour sketches and perhaps portraits.

Bibliography: G.C.B. Poulter: *The Corbould Genealogy,* 1935

See Corbould Family Tree

CORBOULD, Aster Richard Chilton
1811 (London) - 1882 (London)

The eldest painting grandson of R. Corbould (q.v.) he painted genre and rustic subjects and equestrian portraits. Many of his subjects, in oil and watercolour, were taken from the Highlands. He lived in Kensington, but probably a little less grandly than his cousin Edward (q.v.).

Bibliography: G.C.B. Poulter: *The Corbould Genealogy,* 1935.

See Corbould Family Tree

CORBOULD, Edward Henry
1815 (London) - 1905 (Kensington)

Eldest son of Richard Corbould (q.v) and a grandson of Richard Corbould (q.v.). His younger brothers were Francis John (1819 - 1884), a sculptor, and the twins Henry Heath and Alfred Hichens, born in 1821. H.H. Corbould became a surgeon. All four were educated at King's College School where the younger brothers were taught drawing by J.S. Cotman (q.v.). E.H. Corbould was taught by

his father and at Henry Sass's school before entering the R.A. Schools in 1834. In that year he won a gold medal at the Society of Arts with a watercolour, but his prize entries in the following two years were models. Thereafter he largely abandoned sculpture. With rare exceptions he worked in watercolour, or at least claimed to. In fact, at least from 1851 when he contributed one of the few paintings shown at the Great Exhibition, he often used the 'new silica colour and a glass medium' invented ten years previously by Thomas Miller of Long Acre. He exhibited at the N.W.S. from 1837, being elected a member in the same year. In 1861 he resigned over financial mismanagement, but returned after failing to win election to the 'Old' Society. He finally retired from active membership in 1898. In 1840 he drew the portrait of the Queen for the Penny Black, and he designed stamps for Trinidad, Mauritius, Ceylon and Van Diemen's Land. In 1842 his 'The Woman taken in Adultery' was bought by the Prince Consort, who subsequently presented a number of his works to the Queen, and in 1851 he was appointed 'instructor of historical painting' to the Royal Family. Corbould was married three times; his children included Jemima, who married F.J.Wyburd (q.v.), and two granddaughters became miniaturists, Mrs Eveline Corbould-Ellis and Mrs Weatherley. By the mid-1870s Corbould's historical paintings were out of fashion, and the Queen noted in her Journal that she 'thought him much aged and altered'. He was a prolific book and magazine illustrator, working on many standard 19th century editions, such as the 'Abbotsford' Waverley Novels (Cadell, 1841-6), Black's edition of the same (1852-3), Spenser's *Faerie Queen* and Chaucer's *Canterbury Tales* (Routledge, 1853).

See Corbould Family Tree

See Colour Plate

CORBOULD, Henry, F.S.A.
1787 (London) - 1844 (Robertsbridge, Sussex)

The third son of R. Corbould (q.v.), he became a figure draughtsman and illustrator. He studied at the R.A. Schools, gaining a silver medal, and first exhibited at the R.A. in 1807. A major part of his work was as a book illustrator, but he was also employed for some thirty years in drawing the marbles at the B.M.

He was the father of E.H. Corbould (q.v.); Francis John Corbould, a sculptor; Henry Heath Corbould, a surgeon; and his twin A.H. Corbould (q.v.).

Illustrated: W. Camden: *History of England.* A. Lefanu: *Rosara's Chain &c.,* 1815; F. Burney: *Cecilia,* ?1825; D. Defoe: *Robinson Crusoe,* 1860.

Examples: B.M.; Leeds City A.G.

Bibliography: G.C.B. Poulter: *The Corbould Genealogy,* 1935.

See Corbould Family Tree

CORBOULD, Richard (1757-1831)
A Valetudinarian (for The Spectator). Pen and grey ink, grey wash, 3½in. x 2¾in.)

CORBOULD, Richard
1757 (London) - 1831 (Highgate)

The youngest son of **George CORBOULD (1725-1766),** an artist and engraver who moved from Suffolk to London. Although chiefly a book illustrator, Richard painted, both in oil and watercolour, portraits, landscapes, still life, history, copies of old masters, and miniatures on ivory, porcelain and enamel, and he exhibited from 1776 to 1817. He was a pupil of R. Marris (q.v.), and he also etched. Much of his work was for publishers, including Cooke, whose pocket editions of English Classics, upon which he worked, appeared from 1795 to 1800. He also produced charming drawings for J. Parsons' *Select British Classics,* 1793-4, which reproduced stories, essays and letters from such early eighteenth century periodicals as *Tatler, The Spectator* and *The Guardian.* These drawings were exhibited by Spink, London, in 1984. Corbould was left handed.

H. Corbould (q.v.) was his youngest son, the others being Richard Thomas Corbould (1783-1865), father of A.R.C. Corbould (q.v.); and **George Thomas CORBOULD (1786-1846),** an artist-engraver.

Examples: B.M.; V.A.M.

Bibliography: G.C.B. Poulter: *The Corbould Genealogy,* 1935.

See Corbould Family Tree

CORBOULD, Walter Edward
1860 -

The son of Dr H.H. Corbould, and a grandson of H. Corbould (q.v.), he painted genre subjects in oil and watercolour.

Bibliography: G.C.B. Poulter: *The Corbould Genealogy,* 1935.

See Corbould Family Tree

CORNISH, Hubert (1778-1823)
Mr. Birch's Garden House at Barraset. *Inscribed on the reverse, pencil and watercolour, 15⅝in. x 21⅛in.*

CORDEN, William, Yr.
1819 (Derby) - 1900
The son of William Corden, miniature painter, copyist and china decorator, he too was a copyist as well as a landscape and portrait painter. The father worked for George IV and William IV at Windsor, and the son copied oil portraits for Queen Victoria. He also coloured photographs of watercolours by such Royal favourites as C. Haag (q.v.). In 1844 he painted a series of watercolours of Coburg and Windsor for Prince Albert.

CORDINER, Rev. Charles
1746 - 1794 (Banff)
An antiquary and the episcopalian minister at Banff from 1769. His first published work was in the form of a series of letters to T. Pennant (q.v.), and the second was illustrated with engravings by P. Mazell (q.v.). His talent for landscape drawing was inherited by at least one of his eight children, J. Cordiner (q.v.).

CORDINER, Rev. James
1775 (Banff) - 1836 (Aberdeen)
The third son of C. Cordiner (q.v.) he was educated at Banff and Aberdeen University. In 1797 he was appointed to the Military Orphan Asylum, Madras, and chaplain to the 80th Foot at Trincomalee. About a year later he went to Colombo with the 51st Foot and became principal of all the schools on the island. He returned to Britain in 1804 and was a Minister at Aberdeen from 1807 to 1834. Although his

Description includes an account of the expedition to Kandy in 1803, he did not actually accompany it. The book is illustrated from his original drawings.
Published: *A Description of Ceylon*, 1807; *A Voyage to India*, 1820.
Bibliography: *Aberdeen Journal*, 20 Jan. 1836.

CORNER, Frank William
1873 (North Shields, Northumberland) - 1928 (North Shields)
A town and coast painter who frequently exhibited in Northumbrian exhibitions. He was also an etcher.
Examples: Laing A.G., Newcastle; Sunderland A.G.

CORNER, Sidney
A London landscape and figure painter who exhibited at Suffolk Street from 1838 to 1849. In 1847 he was an unsuccessful candidate for the N.W.S. and in 1864 he applied, with equal lack of success, for the Keepership of the Society.
Published: *Rural Churches*, 1869. *The Earl's Path*, 1875.

CORNISH, Hubert
1757 Teignmouth - 1823
The eighth son of Dr. James Cornish, a medical practitioner and the Collector of Customs at Teignmouth. He was an amateur artist and musician, and professionally an attorney at Exeter. Between 1793 and 1798 he was in India as private secretary to his brother-

in-law the Governor-General Sir John Shore, later 1st Lord Teignmouth. His views are really very good, and suggest that he may have been taught by R.Marris (q.v.) He travelled widely with Shore. Between June and August 1798 they were on St Helena. On his return to England he produced a panorama of Sidmouth, where he had a house in 1805, engraved and published in 1815. His sister Charlotte, Lady Teignmouth (d.1834) may have shared his talent. Certainly two of her grandsons, the 4th and 5th Lords Teignmouth (qq.v) did so. Captain T. Hastings (q.v.) was acquainted with him.
   Hubert CORNISH, II (1778 -1832, Black-hall) also painted shipping and landscapes. He was the elder Hubert's nephew, and he too went to India, as a Civil Servant, in 1797. In the same year he survived the massacre in Benares. Later he became a judge in Bengal, and in 1830 he retired to his estate at Totnes.
Examples: India Office Library.

COSTELLO, Dudley
1803 (Sussex) - 1865 (London)
After Sandhurst he became an ensign in the 34th Regiment of Foot, later serving with the 90th Foot in North America and the West Indies. He retired on half-pay in 1828 and went to Paris, where he worked with his sister **Louisa Stuart COSTELLO (1799-1870)** copying illuminated manuscripts. She was a pleasing miniaturist. On his return to London in 1833, he became a journalist and novelist.
Published: *A Tour through the Valley of the Meuse*, 1846. *Piedmont and Italy from the Alps to the Tiber*, 1859-61.

COSWAY, Richard, R.A.
1740 (Oakford, Devon) - 1821 (Edgware, Middlesex)
A portraitist in watercolour, oil and miniature, he showed an early inclination towards art and was sent to London, where he studied at Shipley's Academy and under Hudson. In 1755 he won his first premium from the Society of Arts. On leaving Shipley, Cosway taught at Pars' drawing school, painted shop signs and 'not always chaste' snuff box lids. He was also a picture dealer. In 1769 he entered the R.A. Schools, and he was elected A.R.A. and R.A. in 1770 and 1771. In 1781 he married **Maria Louisa Caterina HADFIELD, later Baroness Cosway (1760-1838)**, herself an artist and one of the best known faces of the period. They visited Paris and Flanders together, but later separated. Cosway enjoyed the patronage of the Prince of Wales, the Duchess of Devonshire and other leaders of fashion. Like many artists of the time, he had leanings towards mysticism. Despite the war, Maria Cosway copied at the Louvre, and ran a school for girls at Lyon, until eventually she returned to nurse her husband through his last years. She then settled in Italy.

COSWAY, Richard (1740-1821)
The Countess of Hopetoun with her daughters Jasmin and Lucy.
Pencil and watercolour, 9¼in. x 5⅝in.

and he made many watercolours during the tour. He was elected R.I. in 1882 and an exhibition of his work 'Around London' was held at the Dowdeswell Galleries in 1888. His watercolours vary in quality. They can be very impressive with strong drawing and bright colours.

Examples: Ashmolean; Castle Mus., Norwich.
Bibliography: *Studio*, XLVII,1909. J. Walpole: *Art and Artists of the Norwich School*, 1997.

COTMAN, John Joseph
1814 (Great Yarmouth) - 1878 (Norwich)
The second son of J.S. Cotman (q.v.) and the most original of his children. In 1824 the family moved to Norwich, and he was apprenticed to his uncle, a haberdasher. His first sketches were made with his friends J. Geldart (q.v.) and Arthur Dixon. In 1834 he went to London with his father, where he helped to teach at King's College and studied at the B.M. and N.G. In the summer he had a holiday at Cromer and in 1835 he returned to Norwich, the more practical and tractable Miles Edmund taking his place with their father. From 1849 to 1851 he lectured at the Thorpe Institute and in the latter year also at Yarmouth. In about 1852 Miles Edmund came to live with him at Thorpe-by-Norwich. In 1858 he moved back to the centre of Norwich. He was always mentally unstable, alternating periods of depression and lassitude with bursts of work. His personal life was also erratic.

His work is hot and bright, in some ways a cross between the styles of his father and Samuel Palmer. He was an inveterate sketcher and liked red outlines.

Examples: B.M.; V.A.M.; Fitzwilliam; Gt. Yarmouth; Castle Mus., Norwich.
Bibliography: *A.J.*, 1878. J. Walpole: *Art and Artists of the Norwich School*, 1997.

He usually painted small, full-length figures, sketchily executed, with the exception of the head and hands, which are highly finished.

Examples: Blenheim Palace; B.M.; Ashmolean; Exeter Mus.; Fitzwilliam.
Bibliography: G.C. Williamson: *R.C., his Wife and Pupils*, 1897. Nat. Port. Gall.: Exhibition Cat, 1995.

COTMAN, Frederick George, R.I.
1850 (Ipswich) - 1920 (Felixstowe)
A landscape, portrait and genre painter in oil and watercolour, he was the nephew of J.S. Cotman (q.v.). He studied at the R.A. Schools from 1868 and exhibited from 1871. He assisted Leighton for a time. He went to the Mediterranean with the Duke of Westminster, who had commissioned portraits from him,

COTMAN, John Joseph (1814-1878)
Whitlingham Church. *11¾in. x 20in.*

COTMAN, John Sell (1782-1842)
A Ruined Aqueduct. *Pencil and watercolour, 9¼in. x 14¼in.*

COTMAN, John Sell
1782 (Norwich) - 1842 (London)
He was educated at Norwich Grammar School, where he was encouraged to draw by the enlightened Headmaster, Dr. Forster. After a brief period in his father's drapery business he went to London in 1789, finding employment with Ackermann and earning the patronage of Dr. Monro (q.v.). Monro's classes provided one link with Girtin (q.v.), and Cotman also became a member of the Francia/Girtin sketching club, although probably not until the very end of Girtin's life. In 1800 he made a sketching tour to Bristol and Wales, again meeting Girtin, whose work at this time his closely resembles. In 1801 he visited South Devon, and in 1802 he made another Welsh tour with P.S. Munn (q.v.). His most important summer sketching tours were in 1803, 1804 and 1805, when he visited his most influential patrons, Mr. and Mrs. Francis Cholmeley of Brandsby Hall, Yorkshire. These visits provided Cotman with his inspiration for the next five years at least, and resulted in the Greta drawings which are perhaps the greatest in his career. He seems to have gone home to Norwich at some point in each year and in 1803 he had briefly tried to set up a drawing practice there. At the end of 1806 he did indeed return to Norwich, where he joined the Norwich Society and attempted to become a portrait painter. He stayed in Norwich until 1812, when he moved to Yarmouth to take over Crome's functions as supplier of architectural drawings to Dawson Turner, and teacher to his daughters. From 1824 to 1833, having escaped from Turner's benevolent but exacting patronage, he lived in Norwich again, but in the latter year he was elected Professor of Drawing at King's College, London, where he based himself for the rest of his life. It is worth

noting that he and his sons were very keen yachtsmen.

The most important works undertaken for Turner were the result of three journeys to Normandy in 1817, 1818 and 1820. The drawings done on these trips were the finest series of architectural wash drawings ever done by an English artist. Throughout his life, with the possible exception of the Yorkshire period, Cotman was subject to violent bouts of depression, and an inability to bear opposition, which led to a suppression of the stylistic

individuality of his children, including **Anne COTMAN (1812-1862)** and his pupils. In fact, he used his children as a sort of factory to produce drawings for his Circulating Library, through which he hired out drawings for amateurs to copy, and later for his classes at King's. Often these works are indistinguishable from his own, and are even signed by him. After the Greta drawings, in which his preoccupation was with pattern, flat areas of colour and clear-cut form to build up a fresh and vital whole, he gradually fell into a hardness and stylisation which can become unattractive, despite his technical brilliance. This is especially true in the 1830s, when he attempted garish blue and gold historical paintings in a search for popular success. Of his late works, only those from his last Norfolk visit in 1841 have anything of the poetry and harmony of his best period. These were done entirely for his own pleasure, and provide a fitting end to his career. In his maturity, by the boldness of his colour and the simplicity of his subject matter and composition, he was more advanced in spirit than many who came after him. In some works it seems almost as if a pointillist painting had been vastly magnified, leaving only a few large dots to convey the relevant impression.

His remaining works were sold at Christie's, 18-19 May 1843.

Examples: B.M.; V.A.M.; Ashmolean; Blackburn A.G.; Brighton A.G.; Dudley A.G.; Ferens A.G., Hull; Fitzwilliam; Glasgow A.G.; Inverness Lib.; Abbot Hall A.G., Kendal; Leicestershire A.G.; City A.G., Manchester; N.G., Scotland; Newport A.G.; Castle Mus., Norwich; Glynn Vivian A.G., Swansea; Wakefield A.G.; Nat. Mus., Wales; Gt. Yarmouth; York A.G.

COTMAN, John Sell (1782-1842)
The Crystal Pool. *Inscribed by W. Munn, pencil and grey wash, 8¾in. x 12¾in.*

Bibliography: W.F. Dickes: *The Norwich School,*
1905. S.D. Kitson: *Life of J.S.C.,* 1937. V.G.R.
Reinacker: *J.S.C.,* 1953. H.L. Mallalieu: *The
Norwich School,* 1975. M. Rajnai: *J.S.C.,* 1982.
A.W. Moore: *J.S.C.,* 1982. Burlington Fine Arts
Club: Exhibition Cat., 1888. N.G.: Exhibition Cat.,
1922. *Connoisseur,* 1923. *Studio* Special No. 1923.
Walker's Quarterly, V., 1926. Walpole Soc., 1926,
1927. Norwich Castle: Exhibition Cat., 1927.
O.W.S. Club, VII, 1929. Whitworth Inst.,
Manchester: Exhibition Cats., 1927, 1937.
Burlington Mag., LXXXI, July, 1942; LXXXVII,
August, 1945; CXIV, November, 1972. N.Yorks. Co.
Record Office, *Publication No. 22,* 1980. Arts
Council: Exhibition Cat., 1982. J. Walpole: *Art and
Artists of the Norwich School,* 1997.
See Colour Plates

COTMAN, Miles Edmund
1810 (Norwich) - 1858 (Norwich)
He was the eldest son of J.S. Cotman (q.v.),
from whose influence he never escaped. On
his father's appointment as drawing master to
King's College, London, in 1834, he took over
the teaching practice in Norwich. However, in
1836 he changed places with his brother, John
Joseph, as assistant to his father, whom he
succeeded in 1843. He exhibited in London
between 1835 and 1856. Towards the end of
his life his health broke down and he returned
to Norfolk, where he continued to teach.

Primarily a marine painter, his style is a
weaker version of that of his father. His work
is skilful and can be pleasing and even
impressive, but it lacks originality. The effect
is often hard and dry.
Examples: B.M.; V.A.M.; Ashmolean; Fitzwilliam;
Greenwich; City A.G., Manchester; N.G., Scotland;
Castle Mus., Norwich; Southampton A.G.; Gt.
Yarmouth.
Bibliography: *Walker's Quarterly,* 1927. J. Walpole:
Art and Artists of the Norwich School, 1997.

COTTON, R   C
An artist working in the Lake District in about
1800. He was probably an amateur, using
pencil, thin washes and pen overdrawing. He
also employed a convention of foliage drawing
similar to that of J. Powell (q.v.).

In the Richmond Lib., Surrey, there is a
topographical drawing, dating from about
1812, by **Charles COTTON.**

Barbara COTTON was a good botanical
painter, working in the 1820s. There are
examples at Kew.
Examples: B.M.

COTTRELL, Henry J
An architectural painter in oil and watercolour,
who lived in Birmingham and exhibited there
between 1878 and 1884. He was probably
related to the Birmingham landscape painter
and engraver **Arthur Wellesley
COTTRELL,** who exhibited there and in
London from 1872 to 1913.
Examples: Birmingham City A.G.

COUTTS, Hubert (1851-1921)
The Paps of Jura. *Signed, watercolour with scratching out, 11½in. x 17¾in.*

COULDERY, Thomas W
Presumably one of several sons of the animal
painter Horatio Henry Couldery (b.1832), or
his artist brother Bertram Allen Couldery
(b.c.1838). He lived in Lincoln's Inn and
exhibited genre subjects and rusticities at the
R.A., the N.W.S. and Suffolk Street during the
1880s and 1890s.

COUSEN, John   1804   - 1880
A landscape painter who exhibited at the R.A.
in 1863 and the following year.

He lived at Norwood, South London, as did
Charles COUSEN (c.1821-1889), who
exhibited a watercolour portrait at Suffolk
Street in 1848.

COUSINS, Samuel, R.A.
1801 (Exeter) - 1887 (London)
A mezzotint engraver and occasional
watercolourist, he was trained at the Society of
Arts and apprenticed to S.W. Reynolds (q.v.),
whose partner he later became. His early
patrons included Captain Bagnall and Sir T.
Dyke Acland (q.v.). In about 1825 he set up
business on his own and in 1826 he visited
Brussels. In 1825 he was also elected A.R.A.,
and he became an 'academician-engraver' in
1855. His earliest works were pencil copies of
engravings, and later he made landscape and
portrait watercolours.
Examples: B.M.
Bibliography: G. Pycroft: *Memoir of S.C.,* 1887.
A.C. Whitman: *S.C.,* 1904.

COUTTS, Hubert, R.I., né Tucker
1851 (Wandsworth) - 1921 (Windermere)
A Lake District painter who exhibited from
1874 and was elected R.I. in 1912. He was the

third son of E. Tucker (q.v.) and, to avoid
confusion with his brethren, in 1893 he
changed his name from Hubert Coutts Tucker.
He also painted among the Western Isles of
Scotland, and he can be impressive, both with
weather effects and the textures of stone
cottages or lichen.

COVENTRY, James
A landscape painter who exhibited
watercolour views of Wales, the Lakes and
Scotland at Suffolk Street and elsewhere from
1854 to 1861. He lived in Bloomsbury and
Islington.

COVENTRY, Robert McGowan, A.R.S.A.,
R.S.W.   1855 (Glasgow) - 1914 (Glasgow)
A marine painter in oil and watercolour who
studied in Glasgow and Paris and exhibited in
London from 1890. He specialised in North
Sea fishing scenes and Dutch harbours, and
was elected A.R.S.A. in 1906. He painted in
Scotland, Holland and Belgium.
Examples: Glasgow A.G.
Bibliography: *Studio,* XXV, 1902; XXVII, 1903;
XXXVII, 1906; XXXVIII, 1906; XXXIX, 1907.

COWELL, Major-General Sir John
Clayton   1832   - 1894
A Royal Engineer who was a pupil of G.B.
Campion (q.v.) at Woolwich. He was
commissioned second lieutenant in 1850 and
served in the Baltic and Crimean campaigns.
There he corrected Simpson's drawings of
fortifications, and his lucid account of the
battles so impressed the Queen that he was
made governor and tutor to Prince Alfred in
1856. He accompanied his charge on H.M.S.
Euryalus in 1858 and to the Mediterranean. He

was appointed KCB in 1865 and Master of the Royal Household the following year. In 1892 he was made Lt.-Governor of Windsor Castle.

His Crimean drawings clearly show the influence of his master.

COWEN, William
1797 (Rotherham, Yorkshire) - 1861
A landscape painter whose early drawings gained him the patronage of Earl Fitzwilliam, who paid for him to travel through Switzerland and Italy. The sketches he made on his journey provided him with material throughout his career. He exhibited in London from 1823 until his death. In 1840 he went to Corsica, and in 1843 published a series of twelve etchings of the island. These were later used as illustrations for his book *Six Weeks in Corsica*, 1848. After his return he lived in London. He was very much a topographer.
Published: *Six Views of Woodstone Hall*, 1851.
Examples: B.M.; Kensington & Chelsea Lib.

COWHAM, Hilda, Mrs. Lander
1873 - (London) 1964
One of the first lady artists to work for *Punch*, she studied at the Lambeth School of Art and exhibited with the R.W.S. She was the creator of the 'Cowham Kid'. She lived in London and Guildford.
Examples V.A.M.
Bibliography: *Studio*, III, 1894.

COWPER, Frank Cadogan, R.A., R.W.S.
1877 (Wicken Rectory, Northamptonshire) - 1958 (Cirencester)
A portraitist and romantic subject painter in watercolour and oil. He was educated at Cranleigh and studied at the St. John's Wood School of Art and at the R.A. Schools. He was elected A.R.W.S. and R.W.S. in 1904 and 1912, and A.R.A. and R.A. in 1907 and 1934. He also painted landscapes, and he lived in Guernsey and later in Gloucestershire.
Bibliography: *Studio*, XXVII, 1903; XLI, 1907; XLIV, 1908. *A.J.*, 1904; 1905. *Record of Art*, 1912. *The Times*, 24 Jan. 1912. *I.L.N.*, 25 May 1912. Barbican A.G., London, Exhibition Cat., 1989.

COWPER, William
A landscape painter, probably amateur, who visited Switzerland in 1778 and worked up his sketches in 1793. He was perhaps a relative of the 2nd Earl Cowper.

His namesake the poet is known to have had drawing lessons and to have produced slightly naïve landscapes.

COX, Alfred Wilson
1829 (Nottingham) - 1888 (Liverpool)
A Nottingham artist and photographer, he painted landscapes and portraits in oil and watercolour. He exhibited at the R.A. and Suffolk Street from 1868 to 1886.

His daughter, Louisa, was a miniaturist.
Examples: Castle Mus., Nottingham.

COX, David (1783-1859)
Can Office, North Wales. *Inscribed on the reverse, monochrome washes, 6½in. x 9in.*

COX, David (1783-1859)
A Bridge. *Pencil and watercolour, 8⅞in. x 13⅜in.*

COX, David, O.W.S.
1783 (Deritend, Birmingham) - 1859 (Birmingham)
After the briefest of educations, Cox was put to work in his father's smithy, but was encouraged to paint by his cousin Allport, possibly H.C. Allport (q.v.), and sent to J. Barber (q.v.) for drawing lessons. Thereafter he was apprenticed to a toymaker until 1800, and then became a scene painter under de Maria at the Birmingham Theatre. He went to London in 1804, where he continued to work in theatres as well as selling sepia drawings to dealers. In 1808 he married Mary Ragg, his landlady's daughter, who encouraged him to take pupils, and they set up house at Dulwich.

Cox was always willing to take advice and instruction – as late as 1840 he took lessons in oil painting from the young W.J. Müller (q.v.) – and at this period was a pupil of J. Varley (q.v.), whose landscape formulae influenced his work for many years. He visited Wales in 1805 and 1806 and paid regular visits to his parents in Birmingham. He was an exhibitor with the A.A. from 1809 to 1812, and President in 1810. On the collapse of the Association he was elected A.O.W.S. and he became a full member of the reconstituted O.W.S. in 1820. When living in Dulwich his pupils included Lady Arden (q.v.), Lady Burrell, Lady Sophia Cecil, Lady Gordon (q.v.), the Hon. Misses Eden, Miss Tylney Long and Colonel the Hon. Henry Windsor, later 8th Earl of Plymouth (q.v.). He was drawing master at the Military College at Farnham in 1814, after which he moved to Hereford and taught at a number of schools in the area. He also continued to take private pupils, among them J.M. Ince (q.v.). In 1816 he toured the valley of the Wye, in 1818 North Wales and in 1819 was in Bath and Devonshire. The first of his Continental visits was with his son to Belgium and Holland in 1826. His other two visits abroad occurred in 1829, when he went to Paris, and 1832, when

COX, David (1783-1859)
A distant view of Harlech. *Inscribed and perhaps signed on the reverse, watercolour, 8in. x 10½in.*

COX, David (1783-1859)
Warping in to Calais Pier. *Signed and dated 1832, watercolour with scratching out, 7¼in. x 10¼in.*

COX, David (1783-1859)
Yews in the Churchyard at Betws-y-coed. *Black chalk and watercolour, size unknown.*

he was on the coast at Dieppe and Boulogne. In 1826 he returned to London, where he lived until 1841. During this time he sketched in Yorkshire in 1830, Derbyshire in 1831, 1834, 1836 and 1839, Wales in 1837, Kent in 1838 and Lancashire in 1840. In 1841 he returned to Birmingham, where he lived for the rest of his life. For the first four years of this period he usually paid a visit to his son in London each summer before sketching in Yorkshire, in 1842, or Derbyshire and North Wales. However, after staying at Betws-y-coed in 1844 with H.J. Johnson (q.v.), he was won over almost exclusively to North Wales.

Stylistically, his work can be divided into three major periods. The first, which lasted until about 1820, saw him gradually introducing clean and low-toned washes of colour into his largely monochrome drawings. The influence of Varley and Barber is strong throughout, although, especially at the beginning, his works are very close to those of Cotman, Prout and Girtin in the same period. During the second period (1820-1840) he fully mastered the use of colour, although he always used a limited palette with blue gradually predominating; and, in his Continental drawings, often with a splash of bright green as a highlight. During his last twenty years he achieved a freedom and a breadth in his painting which is a direct forerunner of Impressionism. These pictures are, as he said, 'the work of the mind, which I consider very far before portraits of places'. It was at this time that he was so complimented for his painting of wind and atmospheric effects. The rough paper

which he preferred and had sent especially from Dundee is still known as 'Cox Paper' although the modern version is far too pink.

His remaining works were sold at Christie's, 3-5 May 1873. His main professional pupils included W. Bennett, D.H. McKewan and his son, D. Cox, Yr. (qq.v).
Published: *Treatise on Landscape Painting and Effect in Watercolour,* 1813. *Progressive Lessons on Landscape for Young Beginners,* 1816. *A Series of Progressive Lessons,* c.1816. *The Young Artist's Companion,* 1825.
Examples: B.M.; V.A.M.; Aberdeen A.G.; Haworth

A.G., Accrington; Ashmolean; Birmingham City A.G.; Blackburn A.G.; Cartwright Hall, Bradford; Bridport A.G.; Brighton A.G.; Bury A.G.; Grosvenor Mus., Chester; Coventry Mus.; Doncaster A.G.; Dudley A.G.; Exeter Mus.; Ferens A.G., Hull; Fitzwilliam; Glasgow A.G.; Greenwich; Hartlepool A.G.; Hove Lib.; Abbot Hall A.G., Kendal; Leeds City A.G.; Leicestershire A.G.; City A.G., Manchester; N.G., Scotland; Newport A.G.; Nottingham Univ.; Southampton A.G.; Ulster Mus.; Wakefield A.G.; Nat. Mus., Wales; York A.G.
Bibliography: N.N. Solly: *D.C.,* 1873. W. Hall: *D.C.,* 1881. F.G. Roe: *D.C.,* 1924. F.G. Roe: *Cox the Master,* 1946. T. Cox: *D.C.,* 1947; 1954. C.A.E. Bunt: *D.C.,* 1949. *A.J.,* 1859; Feb. 1860; 1898; 1909. Burlington Fine Arts Club, Exhibition Cat., 1873. *Gentleman's Mag.,* March, 1878. Birmingham City A.G., Exhibition Cat., 1890. *Studio,* XXXIV, 1905. *Connoisseur,* May, Jul., 1905. O.W.S. Club, X, 1933. *Antique Collector,* Oct. 1959.

COX, David, Yr., A.R.W.S.
1809 (Dulwich) - 1885 (Streatham)
His choice of career was largely predestined, although he may have spent a brief time in the Navy, and he accompanied his father on many sketching tours, including the visit to Belgium and Holland in 1826. He first exhibited at the R.A. in 1827, thereafter helping his father in the teaching practice until 1841, when he took over the business. He was briefly a member of the N.W.S. and, from 1848, A.O.W.S. Like his father, he drew much inspiration from North Wales; other subjects were taken from Scotland, the Lakes, the Home Counties and Devon, and there is evidence of a visit to Grenoble in about 1853 and Switzerland in 1869. His works are often but poor reflections of his father's genius, although at his best he is a very pretty and competent artist.
Examples: B.M.; V.A.M.; Ashmolean; Coventry Mus.; Greenwich; Hove Lib.
Bibliography: *A.J.,* 1886. O.W.S. Club, LX, 1985.

COZENS, Alexander (1717-1786)
Goats and Trees. *Ink and wash, 6½in. x 8¼in.*

COX, Dorothy, Mrs. Lewis
1882 -
A landscape, marine and architectural painter who exhibited widely in the early years of the twentieth century. She lived at Shoreham.
Examples: Brighton A.G.

COZENS, Alexander
1717 (?Kazan, Russia) - 1786 (London)
The 'Blotmaster-General to the Town' or 'Sir Dirty Didgit' was the son of one of Peter the Great's English shipbuilders. He was sent to England in 1727, to study painting, returning to Russia around 1740, and he had journeyed to Rome by 1746. There he worked for a time in Claude Joseph Vernet's studio and sketched in both City and Campagna. He was in London soon afterwards and built up a highly successful practice as a drawing master. He taught at Christ's Hospital from 1749 to 1753 and at Eton from about 1763. He may also have given lessons for a time in Bath. From 1778 to 1784 he taught Princes William and Edward. Also in about 1778 he came into contact with his great patron and friend, William Beckford. Other notable pupils included Lady Amabel Polwarth (*see* de Grey), the Grimston family and their friends around York, and Sir James Grant and his circle in Scotland.

The great success of Cozens as a drawing master lay partly in his 'blots', which became fashionable, as did Gainsborough's 'moppings and grubbings' or, later, Payne's stylised manner. He must also have been an inspiring teacher, since Mrs. Harcourt, later Countess of (q.v.), wrote that she spent six hours a day following his methods. These are described in full in the *New Method* which is reprinted in Oppé.

As well as the blots, Cozens painted more conventional watercolours and wash drawings, and a few oil paintings and magnificent oil sketches on paper. In all his work he shows the powerful romanticism which attracted Beckford to him.

Published: *An Essay to Facilitate the Inventing of Landskips, intended for Students in the Art*, 1759. *A Treatise on Perspective and Rules for Shading by Invention*, 1765. *The Shape...of Trees...*, 1771. *The various Species in landscape &C.*, c.1775. *Principles of Beauty relative to the Human Head*, 1778. *A New Method*, 1785. &c.
Examples: B.M.; V.A.M.; Aberdeen A.G.; Ashmolean; Cartwright Hall, Bradford; Ferens A.G., Hull; Fitzwilliam; Leeds City A.G.; N.G., Scotland; Yale.
Bibliography: A.P. Oppé. *A. and J.R.C.*, 1952. K.Sloan: *A. and J.R.C.*, 1986. Burlington Fine Arts Club, Exhibition Cat., 1916. *Burlington Mag.*, 1919. *Print Collectors' Quarterly*, VIII, 1921. Graves A.G., Sheffield, Exhibition Cat., 1946. Tate Gall., Exhibition Cat., 1946. *Connoisseur*, CXIX, 1947. Whitworth Inst., Manchester, Exhibition Cat., 1956. O.W.S. Club, XLIV, 1969. Mellon Center, Yale, Exhibition Cat., 1980.

COZENS, Alexander (1717-1786)
Footpads in a Forest. *Ink and washes, 11½in. x 15½in.*

COZENS, John Robert
1752 (London) - 1797 (London)
The son of A. Cozens (q.v.) and his wife, a daughter of the engraver John Pine, and an early inspiration to Girtin and Turner, Cozens is perhaps the most poetic of English painters. Comparatively few details of his life are known. He exhibited for the first time in 1767 and helped his father in his practice. In 1768 he visited a Pine uncle in Suffolk, and in 1772 he paid a brief visit to Matlock. He visited Italy twice, first in 1776 with Payne Knight, from whom he parted in Rome, staying until 1779, and secondly with Beckford in 1782, returning towards the end of the following year. Despite the evidence of numerous

COZENS, John Robert (1752 -1797)
Monte Circeo from Terracina between Rome and Naples. *Watercolour, signed on the original mount, 12⅛in. x 18in.*

CRAIG, William Marshall (c.1765-c.1834)
A Ruined Castle. *Pencil and watercolour, 16¾in. x 13in.*

sketches and finished drawings, Beckford regarded him as lazy. Towards the end of his life he is said to have visited the Lake District, probably with his pupil T. Sunderland (q.v.). He died mad, under the care of Dr. Monro (q.v.).

Constable said of him that he was 'all poetry, the greatest genius that ever touched landscape', and this was achieved by a very limited palette, usually blues, greys and greens, the simplest of compositions and occasionally (in the earlier works) faulty drawing. There is a grandeur and simplicity about his best work which appeals directly to the heart. A sale was held at Christie's in 1805.
Examples: B.M.; V.A.M.; Aberdeen A.G.; Ashmolean; Cecil Higgins A.G., Bedford; Birmingham City A.G.; Blackburn A.G.; Brighton A.G.; Leeds City A.G.; City A.G., Manchester; Ulster Mus.; Yale.
Bibliography: A.P. Oppé: *A. and J.R.C.*, 1952. K. Sloan: *A. and J.R.C.*, 1986. *Studio*, LXIX, 1917. Burlington Fine Art Club, Exhibition Cat., 1923. *Country Life*, 30 Nov. 1935; 11 March 1971. Walpole Society XXIII, 1935, LVII, 1995. Whitworth Inst., Manchester, Exhibition Cat., 1937; 1956. V.A.M.,

Exhibition Cat., 1971. Mellon Center, Yale, Exhibition Cat., 1980. Tate Gall.: Exhibition Cat., 2002.
See Colour Plates

CRACE, Frederick
1779 (London) - 1859 (London)
Commissioner of sewers, architectural decorator and collector of maps and views of London, Crace is most remembered as a patron of such artists as T.H. Shepherd (q.v.). His ambition was to have a painting of every noteworthy building in the metropolis, and he drew many himself. This remarkable archive is now in the B.M.
Examples: B.M.; Brighton A.G.

CRADOCK, Marmaduke
c.1660 (Somerton, Somerset) - 1716 (London)
After serving an apprenticeship with a London housepainter, he turned to painting animal and bird studies and still lifes, often on commission from dealers. Some of his groups of birds were engraved and published in 1740-3 by Josephus Sympson.
Examples: B.M.

CRAIG, James
1744 (Edinburgh) - 1795 (Edinburgh)
One of the architects of the Edinburgh New Town, and an architectural draughtsman. He was the son of a merchant and a nephew of the poet James Thomson. His schemes were strictly geometric, and luckily he failed to carry through a further plan for the remodelling of the Old Town.

A **John CRAIG** of Edinburgh painted landscapes and marine subjects in the early nineteenth century.

CRAIG, William
1829 (Dublin) - 1875 (Lake George)
A landscape painter who entered the R.D.S. Schools in 1847 and first exhibited at the R.H.A. in the same year. He continued to exhibit there until 1862, and the following year went to America, where he exhibited Irish as well as American views and became a founder member of the American Society of Watercolour Painters.

His work deteriorated in the latter part of his career as he painted almost exclusively for 'auction-dealers'.
Examples: N.G., Ireland; New York Hist. Soc.

CRAIG, William Marshall
c.1765 (?Edinburgh) - c.1834
Probably the brother of J. Craig (q.v.), he was an illustrator, miniaturist, engraver and painter in oil, as well as a watercolour painter of rustic subjects in the manner of R. Westall (q.v.). He was a frequent exhibitor at the R.A. from 1788 and elsewhere, and from 1810 to 1812 he was a member of the A.A. He was obviously a favourite with the Royal Family, for he was Painter in Watercolours to Queen Charlotte, Miniaturist to the Duke and Duchess of York, and taught the Princess Charlotte. He lived in Manchester during the early part of his life and moved to London in about 1790. Many of his drawings were done for wood engravers and they are usually colourful and highly finished in a somewhat pointillist fashion. They are also usually on a small scale.
Examples: B.M.; V.A.M.; N.G., Scotland; Newport A.G.; Castle Mus., Nottingham.
Bibliography: *The Collector*, XI, Dec. 1930.

CRAMPTON, Sir John Fiennes Twistleton, Bt.
1805 (Dublin) -
1886 (near Bray, Co. Wicklow)
A diplomat who was at Eton from 1820 and whose career began at Turin in 1826. He was transferred to St. Petersburg in 1828, Brussels in 1834, Vienna in 1839 and Berne in 1844. His most important post was Washington, where he served from 1845 to 1856, when he was declared *persona non grata* for recruiting troops for the British Army in defiance of American law. Diplomatic relations were broken off, and there was even talk of war. He was sent to Hanover in 1857 and to St. Petersburg again the following year. His last

post was Madrid from 1860 to 1869, after which he retired to his seat in Ireland, Bushey Park, where he died.

He painted freely, rather in the manner of Cox, as well as producing more careful, lightly coloured, drawings, and some caricature doodles in pen and ink.

His sister, **Selina CRAMPTON (1806-1876)**, also painted and often visited him *en poste*.

Examples: B.M.

CRANE, Walter, R.W.S.
1845 (Liverpool) - 1915 (Horsham, Sussex)
The son of **Thomas CRANE (1808 Chester - 1859 London)**, a miniaturist and watercolour portrait painter, and brother of **Lucy CRANE (1842-1882)**, authoress, critic and occasional artist. There are examples of Thomas's work in the Grosvenor A.G., Chester.

Walter Crane was best known as a designer and a prolific illustrator and also as a teacher. His family moved first to Torquay, and in 1857 to London where he was apprenticed to W.J. Linton (q.v.) and studied at Heatherley's. From 1867 he worked for the Dalziels, for *Once a Week* and for *Fun*. In 1869 he sketched at Betws-y-coed, and in 1871 he married and went to Italy for two years. He revisited Italy in 1881 and the winter of 1883-4. He was a member of the R.I. from 1882 to 1886, but resigned to join the older Society, and was elected A.R.W.S. and R.W.S. in 1888 and 1889. In this period he became increasingly involved with W. Morris (q.v.) and socialism. He visited Greece in 1888, Bohemia and Italy in 1890 and in 1891 America. He was in Hungary in 1894 and Normandy and the Channel Islands in 1896.

His illustrations for children's books bid fair to equal the appeal of those of K. Greenaway (q.v.), but his touch is a little heavier.

His son **Lionel Francis CRANE (b.1876 London)** studied architecture under Reginald Blomfield and Ernest George. He worked in America, Ireland and Italy.

An earlier **W. CRANE** of Chester published a series of views of Snowdonia in 1830.

Published: *An Artist's Reminiscences*, 1907.

Examples: B.M.; V.A.M.; Aberdeen A.G.; Ashmolean; Cecil Higgins A.G., Bedford; Dundee City A.G.; Fitzwilliam; Glasgow A.G.; City A.G., Manchester; N.G., Scotland.

Bibliography: P.G. Konody: *The Art of W.C.*, 1902. I. Spencer: *W.C.*, 1975. *A.J.*, 1901; 1902. *Country Life*, 4 May 1935. Yale Univ. Lib., XXXI, 3, 1957. *W&D*, 1989, ii. G. Smith and S. Hyde: *W.C., Artist, Designer and Socialist*, 1989.

CRANSTONE, Lefevre James
1821/2 -
A landscape and genre painter who lived in Hemel Hempstead, entered the R.A. Schools in 1840 and exhibited in London from 1845 to 1867. He sketched in Scotland, Berkshire, Nottingham and Kent as well as in Hertford-

CRANE, Walter (1845-1915)
Watercolour, signed and dated 1885.

shire, and he also lived in Birmingham. In 1859 he went to America, by way of Ireland and Nova Scotia, to visit relatives. He toured widely, making many sketches of Wild West towns, and returned to England the following year. Shortly afterward he emigrated to Australia. He uses pale colours, and his work is very delicate and pretty.

Published: *Fugitive Etchings*, 1849.

Examples: Boston Mus.; Indiana Univ. Lib.

CRANSTOUN, James Hall
1821 (Edinburgh) - 1907 (Perth)
A Perthshire landscape painter in oil and watercolour. He studied at the Slade and thereafter lived in Perth.

Examples: Dundee City A.G.

CRAWFORD, Edmund Thornton, R.S.A.
1806 (Cowden, near Dalkeith) -
1885 (Lasswade)
A marine and landscape painter who was briefly apprenticed to a housepainter in Edinburgh before entering the Trustees' Academy where he became the friend and disciple of William Simson (q.v.). Although one of the first Associates of the R.S.A., he failed to exhibit until 1831 and was not re-elected until 1839. He was elected R.S.A. in 1848. He made several visits to Holland which provided him with material which he worked up for many years afterwards. He taught painting for a while, and left Edinburgh for Lasswade in 1858.

His most typical subjects are coastal and river scenes on the Scottish and North-east coast and in Holland. The influence of the Dutch masters can be seen in his picturesque style. His watercolours are often on light brown paper and show a free use of bodycolour.

Bibliography: *Portfolio*, 1887. *Studio*, 1907.

CRAWFORD, Thomas Hamilton, R.S.W
1860 (Glasgow) - 1933
A painter of portraits and architectural subjects in oil and watercolour, and an etcher. He was the son of a sculptor and studied with Herkomer (q.v.) as well as at the Glasgow and Edinburgh Schools of Art. He was elected R.S.W. in 1887. In 1893 he went to London, later moving to Berkhamsted, Hertfordshire, and he worked both in Britain and on the Continent, with churches as favourite subjects.

Illustrated: R.L.Stevenson: *A Picturesque Note*.

CRAWHALL, Joseph, Yr.
1821 (Newcastle-upon-Tyne) -
1896 (Paddington)
The son of his namesake, an amateur artist, Crawhall worked in the family ropery business. He was a close friend of C.S. Keene (q.v.), providing him with ideas and preliminary sketches for his *Punch* cartoons. He also wrote and illustrated a number of books and was secretary of the Newcastle Arts Club.

Published: *The Compleatest Angling Book That Ever was Writ*, 1859. &c.

Examples: B.M.; Glasgow A.G.

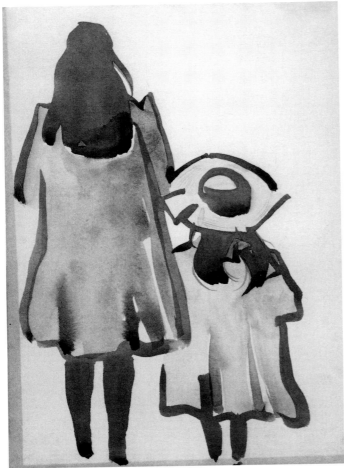

CRAWHALL, Joseph, III
Back View of Two Children. *Watercolour, 10in. x 7in.*

CRAWHALL, Joseph, III, 'Creeps', R.W.S.
1861 (Morpeth) - 1913 (London)
The animal painter in oil and watercolour and son of J. Crawhall (q.v.), who gave him his earliest lessons and insisted that he work from memory without corrections. He was educated in Newcastle and at King's College School, London, subsequently studying for two years in Paris. On his return he went to Scotland and became a leader of the Glasgow School. He was in Lincolnshire in the summer of 1882. Later he spent much of his time in Tangier, drew bullfights in Spain, and finally settled in Brandsby, Yorkshire.

He was a perfectionist in his work, destroying anything which did not please him. He was a friend of E.J. Alexander (q.v.) and like him was influenced by the prevailing Japanese styles.
Examples: V.A.M.; Newport A.G.
Bibliography: A. Bury: *J.C., the Man and the Artist*, 1958. V.Hamilton: *J.C.*, 1990. *A.J.*, 1905; 1906; 1911. *Studio*, III; XLVII; LVI. O.W.S. Club, XXIII, 1945. *Country Life*, 2 April 1948; 1 May 1969. *Apollo*, LXVI, 1957.

CREALOCK, Lieutenant-General Henry Hope   1831   - 1891 (Mayfair)
After an education at Rugby, he joined the Army in 1848, serving in the Crimea, China in 1857-8, the Indian Mutiny, St. Petersburg and Vienna, and in Zululand in 1879. He was promoted lieutenant-general in 1884. There are a number of his drawings in the B.M., and he also produced watercolours of dogs, figures and landscapes.
Illustrated: Anon: *Wolf-Hunting and Wild Sport in Lower Brittany*, 1875. G.J.W. Melville: *Katerfelto*, 1875. W.D.B. Davenport: *Sport*, 1885.
Examples: B.M.; Nat. Army Mus.

CREASY, John L
A marine and landscape painter who lived and taught in Greenwich. He was active from 1797 or before, exhibited from 1800 to 1828, and his speciality was portraits of East Indiamen, often seen from three positions. He was not connected to the architect, antiquarian and sanitary engineer, Edward Cresy (*sic*) of Dartford (1792-1858). However, his father was presumably also a painter, since he sometimes signed himself 'jun'. His work can be of a high quality.
Examples: Greenwich.

CREE, Edward Hodges
1814 (Devonport) - 1901 (?London)
A surgeon, he entered the Navy in 1837 and the following year served in the Mediterranean. In 1839 he sailed to China on board the H.M.S. *Rattleship*, in which he took part in operations connected with the first China War of 1840-42. He was involved in affrays with pirates in Borneo in 1845. After

CREASY, John L.
A Mountainous Landscape. *Signed and dated 1797, pencil and watercolour, 6in. x 10in.*

1850 he served in the Baltic and Black Sea, in China again and on the Home and Lisbon Stations. In 1855 he was present at the capture of Sebastopol and Kinburn. Several of his drawings of the China War were lithographed for the *I.L.N.* He was a pupil of one of the Schranz family in Malta and of R.H.C. Ubsdell, and he met Chinnery. His journals were published in 1981.

CREES, James Leslie –
see **BRADDON, Paul**

CRESWICK, Thomas, R.A.
1811 (Sheffield) - 1869 (London)
A landscape painter in oil and watercolour and a book illustrator. He studied under J.V. Barber (q.v.) in Birmingham, and moved to London in 1828, when he first exhibited at the R.A. He was elected A.R.A. in 1842 and R.A. in 1851. In 1837 he visited Ireland, producing many charming drawings. He was one of the first members of the Etching Club.

In his larger paintings, particularly his oils, he often worked in collaboration with figure and cattle painters such as Ansdell, Cooper, Elmore and Frith. He preferred to work directly from nature, which gives his paintings freshness linked with a careful reflection of English landscape. His foliage was praised by Ruskin.

His collection of English pictures, together with one hundred of his own sketches was sold at Christie's, 7 May 1870.
Examples: B.M.; Brighton A.G.; Glasgow A.G.; Leicestershire A.G.; City A.G., Manchester.
Bibliography: *A.J.*, May, 1856; Feb. 1870; 1906; 1908.

CREW, John Thistlewood
1810/11   -
An architect and painter who was active from about 1830 to 1860. He was a pupil of E. Blore (q.v.), was in Paris in 1831, and entered the R.A. Schools in 1834. Sometimes his work is a little reminiscent of that of W. Payne (q.v.). He was probably the architect employed to enlarge Caversham Park, Oxon., in about 1841.

CRICHTON, Lady (Jane) Emma, née Baring 1854 -1936 (Hampshire
The daughter of the 1st Earl of Northbrook, Governor General of India, who was a widower, and for whom she acted as hostess. She was made both a C.I. and a C.B.E. Northbrook was a friend of E. Lear (q.v.), who went to India at his behest and greatly influenced Lady Emma's watercolours. She married Col. the Hon. Sir Henry Crichton (1844-1922, a son of the 3rd Earl of Erne, in 1890, and they lived at Netley Castle, Hants. As well as Indian subjects she painted in Britain, France, Italy, the Netherlands, Algiers, Portugal and elsewhere, and she was active until at least 1921.

CRISTALL, Joshua (1768-1847)
Ladies of Fashion or Fantasy. *Signed, pencil, pen and brown ink and watercolour, 6⅝in. x 9⅛in.*

CRIDDLE, Mary Ann, Mrs. Harry, née Alabaster, A.O.W.S. 1805 (Holywell, Flint) - 1880 (Addlestone, near Chertsey)
The daughter of an amateur caricaturist, she was educated at Colchester. She was at first discouraged from drawing by her mother, but in 1824 she was allowed to take lessons from Hayter, which she did until 1826. Until 1846 she worked in oil but, being of poor health, she found watercolour more appealing thereafter. At this time she took some lessons from S. Setchel (q.v.), and she entered a cartoon for the Houses of Parliament competition in 1847, a literary subject, as were most of her works. In 1852 she nearly lost her sight from attempting miniature painting and in 1861 she moved from London to Addlestone. From 1849 until just before her death she was an A.O.W.S. Although her subjects were often taken from Spenser, Milton, Thomson, Dickens, Tennyson and George Eliot or from the New Testament, she did virtually no work as an illustrator.
Illustrated: *The Misses Catlow: The Children's Garden*, 1865.

CRISTALL, Joshua, P.O.W.S.
1768 (Camborne, Cornwall) - 1847 (London)
The son of a Scottish sea captain and merchant and a Cornishwoman, he was brought up in Rotherhithe. His father, wishing to make a businessman of him, found him various jobs in the china trade, and later as a copying clerk and calico printer at Old Ford. In the last job he was befriended by J.S. Hayward (q.v.), with whom he later collaborated on panoramas and in 1803 joined 'The Brothers'. However, being determined to become an artist, he turned down an offer of the management of a china seller's business. He appears to have been largely self taught, despite a period spent at the R.A. Schools, and by 1795 was trying to support himself entirely by painting. In 1802 he sketched in North Wales, where he met C. and J. Varley, and T. Webster (qq.v) with whom he was nearly lynched as a French spy. He returned to Wales with C. Varley in 1803, meeting W. Havell (q.v.), with whom and the Varley brothers he was a founder member of the O.W.S. two years later. His life for the next

CRISTALL, Joshua (1768-1847)
Aber Ilan. Signed, inscribed and dated 1802, pen and brown ink and watercolour on paper watermarked 1799, 7½in. x 12¼in.

twelve years, although a constant struggle against poverty, was apparently uneventful. His wife, whom he married in 1812, ran a school at Paddington. He visited the Lakes, was in Scotland in the summer of 1818, and often stayed at Hastings and on the Isle of Wight. He was President of the O.W.S. in 1816 and 1819 and again from 1821 to 1831. In 1823 he moved to Goodrich on the Wye, where he lived until 1841. He was driven back to London by the death of his wife and the breakdown of his own health. In his last years he was an active member of the Sketching Society, and attempted to win popularity through portrait painting.

His early style shows an affinity with those of his younger contemporaries, Prout and Cox. By 1810, however, his initial simplicity has given place to a more sentimental approach. His charming sketches of country boys and girls have been tidied up in the studio and his landscapes have acquired the romantic patina of a Barret or Finch. Occasionally though, in his last years, his landscape drawings escape from these conventions, as do his sketches and flower studies, which seem to have been done for his own gratification. Some of these, initialled, J.C., are over enthusiastically given to Constable.

Examples: B.M.; V.A.M.; Haworth A.G., Accrington; Glasgow A.G.; Gloucester City A.G.; Abbot Hall A.G., Kendal; Leeds City A.G.; Newport A.G.; Portsmouth City Mus.; Walsall A.G.; Ulster Mus.
Bibliography: W.G.S. Dyer: *J.C., Cornish Painter*, 1958. J. Tisdall: *J.C., In Search of Arcadia*, 1996. O.W.S. Club, IV, 1926; L, 1975 . V.A.M., Exhibition Cat., 1975. *W & D*, 1988, iv.
See Colour Plate

CROCKER, Philip
A topographer who was active in Somerset and Wiltshire in the first quarter of the nineteenth century.

CROCKET, Henry Edgar, R.W.S.
1874 (London) - 1926
A landscape painter who studied at South Kensington and the Académie Julian. He exhibited from 1900 and was elected A.R.W.S. and R.W.S. in 1905 and 1913. He lived at Lewes.

CROFT, Arthur
1828 - 1902 (Wadhurst)
A landscape and genre painter who painted in Wales, Switzerland in 1871, Algeria in 1881, and the U.S.A. and New Zealand. He exhibited at the R.A. and elsewhere from 1868 and was an unsuccessful candidate for the N.W.S. on several occasions between 1862 and 1873. From 1890 he lived at Wadhurst, Sussex. Much of his work is not particularly distinguished, but he was admired by his fellow members of the Alpine Club.
Examples: V.A.M.

CROFT, John Ernest
A cattle painter in oil and watercolour who lived in Tunbridge Wells and exhibited from 1868 to 1873.
A **Miss Marian CROFT** of Bayswater exhibited landscapes from 1869 to 1882. She was the daughter of an ivory carver, and she became a member of the Society of Female Artists.
Examples: V.A.M.

CROKE, Sir Alexander 1758 (Aylesbury) -
1842 (Studley Priory, Bucks.)
A lawyer, author, antiquarian and amateur landscape painter. He was educated at Burton, Buckinghamshire, and Oriel College, Oxford, and and was called to the Bar in 1786. From 1801 to 1815 he sat as judge in the Vice-Admiralty Court at Halifax, Novia Scotia, and he was knighted on his return. Thereafter he resided at Studley, the family seat, and devoted himself to antiquarian and artistic pursuits. His major work was a history of the Croke family, and he also wrote on legal and religious subjects.

CROME, John
1768 (Norwich) - 1821 (Norwich)
A landscape painter and the lynch-pin of the Norwich School and Society which he helped to found in 1803. With the exceptions of a brief period in London and a visit to Paris in 1814, Crome's life was almost entirely spent in Norfolk.

Although his most important work is in oil, Crome was a drawing master for much of his career, and he left a number of impressive watercolours. They are modelled on the style of the Dutch masters but adapted to East Anglia. The composition is often flat, the colours sometimes bright and the drawing broad rather than crisp. It is difficult to be precise about his watercolours, since his work is often confused with that of his followers and vice versa. A memorial exhibition was held at Norwich Castle in October 1821.

Three of his sons, J.B. Crome (q.v.), **Frederick James CROME (1796-1831)** and **William Henry CROME (1806-1873)** and one daughter, **Emily CROME (1801-1833)**, became artists.
Examples: B.M.; V.A.M.; Blackburn A.G.; Cartwright Hall, Bradford; Donaster A.G.; Castle Mus., Norwich.
Bibliography: J. Wodderspoon: *J.C. and his Works*, 1876. W.F. Dickes: *The Norwich School*, 1905. R.H. Mottram: *J.C. of Norwich*, 1931. D. and T. Clifford: *J.C.*, 1968. H.L. Mallalieu: *The Norwich School*, 1975. Norwich Castle: Exhibition Cat., 1927. Country Life, 15 August 1968. J. Walpole: *Art and Artists of the Norwich School*, 1997.

CROME, John Berney
1794 (Norwich) - 1842 (Great Yarmouth)
The eldest son of J. Crome (q.v.), he was educated at the Norwich Grammar School, of which he became Captain. He sketched with his father as a boy and, in 1816, visited Paris with George Vincent. In 1819 he became President of the Norwich Society and helped to end the secession. He was also appointed Landscape Painter to the Duke of Sussex. He built up a good practice and reputation, but also debts, and was declared bankrupt in 1831. In 1833 he moved to Yarmouth.

He is best known for his moonlight scenes and his Cuyp-like landscapes.
Examples: B.M.; City A.G., Manchester; Castle

CROME, John (1768-1821)
Raglan Castle. *Grey wash, 11⅛in. x 9⅜in.*

Mus., Norwich.
Bibliography: W.F. Dickes: *The Norwich School,* 1905. *Art Union,* 1842; 1843. J. Walpole: *Art and Artists of the Norwich School,* 1997.

CROMEK, Thomas Hartley, A.N.W.S.
1809 (London) - 1873 (Wakefield)
The son of R.H. Cromek, the engraver, who died when he was three, Cromek was a pupil of J. Hunter, a portrait painter at Wakefield, and J. Rhodes (q.v.) at Leeds. He became a landscape and topographical painter, and he lived on the Continent, primarily in Rome, where he was successful both as a teacher and in selling his work, from 1831 to 1849. He also painted in Belgium, Germany and Switzerland, and in 1834 visited Corfu, Albania and Athens. He returned to Athens for two months in 1844, but Garibaldi's threatened assault on Rome finally drove him home. He was elected A.N.W.S. in 1850, but never thrived after his return to England and was reported to be 'in a helpless condition' in 1871. His work is colourful and sometimes striking, although his drawing is not always perfect. He can convey a marvellous simplicity and grandeur of composition.
Published: *A Manual of Hebrew Verbs,* 1850; *Memorials of the Life of R.H. Cromek,* 1862.
Examples: B.M.; Fitzwilliam; Harewood Ho.; Whitworth, Manchester; Wakefield City A.G.
Bibliography: Harewood Ho., *Exhibition Cat.,* 1999.

CROMPTON, James Shaw, R.I.
1853 (Bootle) - 1916 (Hampstead)
An illustrator who was a pupil of J. Finnie

(q.v.) and studied at Heatherley's. He exhibited from 1882, was elected R.I. in 1898 and was Chairman of the Langham Sketching Club. He painted genre subjects.
Examples: V.A.M.; Maidstone Mus.

CRONE, Robert c.1718 (Dublin) - 1779
A Wilson pupil who was working in Rome in 1755. His drawings are closely based on those of his master, but without their freedom and spirit.
He signed 'R.C.' as did R. Carver (q.v.).
Examples: B.M.

CRONSHAW, James Henry
1859 (Accrington) -
A landscape and flower painter who studied at South Kensington. He was an art master at Accrington and Slough, before becoming Headmaster of the Ashton-under-Lyne School of Art. He was still active in 1927.

CROSBY, Charles James
1809 (Nottingham) - 1890 (Ireland)
An amateur artist who worked in the Inland Revenue Office, Somerset House, for many years. He retired to paint in Ireland. His work consists of small watercolours and pencil drawings.

CROSBY, William
1830 (Sunderland) - 1910 (Sunderland)
An artist in oil and watercolour who exhibited landscapes, portraits, coastal, animal and genre subjects at the R.A. from 1859 to 1873. Early in his career he studied for three years at Antwerp.

CROSSE, Lawrence c.1650   -1724
A miniaturist who was a pupil of Samuel Cooper. He also made watercolour copies of old masters.

CROSSE, Richard
1742 (Knowle, Devon) - 1810 (Knowle)
The deaf and dumb miniaturist. He also painted larger portraits in watercolour. He was a member of the Free Society, exhibiting there from 1760, and at the R.A. from 1770 to 1795.
A fifteen year old R. Crosse entered the R.A. Schools in 1794.

CROTCH, Dr. William
1775 (Norwich) - 1847 (Taunton, Somerset)
At the age of four he was already performing in London on the organ and piano, and was famous as the 'Musical Child'. By eleven he was in Cambridge studying music and two

CROTCH, Dr. William (1775-1847)
Westminster Abbey. *Signed with initials and inscribed and dated 1809, pencil and watercolour, 3⅜in. x 6in.*

CROTCH, Dr. William (1775-1847)
Woodland near Windsor. *Watercolour over pencil, lengthily inscribed, dated July 28, 1832, 5½in. x 7½in.*

years later he settled in Oxford, where he met J.B. Malchair (q.v.). In 1790 he was appointed organist of Christ Church, where he remained until about 1807, and in 1797 he became a Professor of Music. In about 1810 he moved to London where he continued his musical career, becoming the first Principal of the Royal Academy of Music. At the same time he was an etcher and talented amateur watercolourist. His drawings owe a great deal to Malchair, with their underpainting of dark grey and light washes of limited colours on top. They often have notes on the reverse, giving atmospheric and other information. Many of them were done between 1832 and 1842 at Windsor and on holiday at Budleigh Salterton and Brighton. According to his friend Samuel Wesley he was left-handed in youth, but 'later may properly be styled ambidexter'.

His son **William Robert CROTCH (1799-1877)** also drew.
Examples: Ashmolean; Brighton A.G.; Grosvenor A.G., Chester; Fitzwilliam; N.G., Scotland.
Bibliography: *Country Life*, 30 Jan. 1948.

CROUCH, William
An obscure but prolific watercolour painter who was active between 1817 and 1840. He painted small romantic subjects of ruins in Italianate landscapes. Stylistically, they fall between the work of F.O. Finch (q.v.) and that of W.M. Craig (q.v.).
Examples: B.M.; Ashmolean; Leeds City A.G.; Newport A.G.

CROWE, Eyre, A.R.A.
1824 (London) - 1910 (London)
The son of E.E. Crowe, historian and journalist, he studied under William Darley and in Paris under Delaroche. He was at the R.A. Schools from 1845 and was secretary to his cousin Thackeray for a time. He lived in America from 1852 to 1857. He exhibited from 1846 to 1904 and was elected A.R.A. in 1875.

His subjects are often historical, but sometimes contemporary social comment.
Published: *With Thackeray in America*, 1893.
Examples: Ashmolean.
Bibliography: *A.J.*, 1864; 1868; 1904.

CROWTHER, John
An architectural and genre painter who exhibited at the R.A. from 1876 to 1898. He also exhibited at the Royal Pavilion Gallery, Brighton, in 1875 from a London address and worked well into the twentieth century.
Illustrated: E.B. Chancellor: *Lost London*, 1926 (painted c.1879-1887).

CROXFORD, William Edwards
A marine painter who was working between 1871 and at least 1905. He lived in Brentford, Hastings and Newquay and sometimes used the name 'William Croxford Edwards'.

CROZIER, George
1846 (Manchester) - 1914 (Prestwich)
The son of Robert Crozier (1815-1891), President of the Manchester Academy and a genre and portrait painter, he was encouraged

CROWE, Eyre (1824-1910)
Meifod, Montgomeryshire. *Signed with initials and dated April 26th 1849, pencil and coloured washed heightened with white on Whatman Turkey Mill paper dated 1847, 8in. x 9¾in.*

CRUIKSHANK, George (1792-1878)
Gnomes being captured by a stork. *Watercolour, signed, 2¾in. x 9in. A very untypical example.*

to study natural sciences by Ruskin and produced scientific drawings. Between 1869 and 1890 he applied to join the R.W.S. almost yearly, but was always rejected. He lived in Westmorland and Lancashire and also painted in Ireland and Scotland, Norway, France, Italy and Greece. His sister, **Anne Jane CROZIER,** exhibited domestic subjects at the N.W.S. and elsewhere from 1868 to 1886.

CROZIER, Robert
A marine painter in oil and watercolour who exhibited from 1836 to 1848 and was living in London in 1846. Many of his subjects were taken in the Thames estuary or at Boulogne. He is easily confused with his namesake, the Manchester genre and portrait painter (1815-1891).

CRUICKSHANK, Francis
A painter of watercolour portraits, including one of Audubon, and studies of peasants and fruit. He was based in London and Edinburgh, and was active at least from 1845 to 1881.

CRUICKSHANK, Frederick
1800 (Aberdeen) - 1869
A genre and portrait painter who was a pupil of Andrew Robertson, the miniaturist. He exhibited at the R.A. and elsewhere from 1822 and worked in Scottish country houses.
Examples: V.A.M.; Greenwich; City A.G., Manchester.

CRUICKSHANK, William
?1813   - ?1896 (Auckland)
A follower of W. Henry Hunt (q.v.) whose career was mostly spent in South London and who was active at least from 1866 to 1890. He was a painter of still lifes and above all of birds' nests on mossy banks.
He is presumably not to be confused with his near namesake, the nephew of G. Cruikshank, who was born at Broughty Ferry in 1848, studied at Heatherley's and entered

the R.A. Schools in 1870. The latter went to Canada and the United States, dying in Kansas City and 1922.
Examples: Brighton A.G.

CRUIKSHANK, George
1792 (London) - 1878 (London)
A caricaturist, he was the second son of I. Cruikshank (q.v.) and brother of I.R. Cruikshank (q.v.). He was largely self taught and published his first etching aged about twelve. His career began with political and social caricatures which carried on the tradition of Gillray. These included stock subjects such as the career of Napoleon and the loves of the Prince Regent, and one, 'Banknote not to be Imitated', 1818, is credited with encouraging the liberalisation of the hanging laws. From 1819 he turned more and more to book illustration and by the 1830s this had become his main business. In 1836 his connection with Harrison Ainsworth and with Dickens began, and his drawings for these two authors are among his best – although his claims to have supplied some of their better known plots cannot be taken too seriously. From 1847 he concerned himself more and more with teetotal propaganda, the most effective being *The Bottle,* 1847, and *The Drunkard's Children,* 1848. To Dickens's disgust, he even used fairy stories as temperance tracts. He continued both to draw and paint until the last year of his life. His home lives were complex, and provide a measure of Victorian morality.
As well as an etcher and watercolourist, he was a competent oil painter, and exhibited regularly at the R.A. His lack of academic training shows in his weakly drawn horses and women. His touch is surer with men, however, and his long skeletal villains with their satanic grins are as good as a signature. His handling of crowd scenes is particularly good.
Examples: V.A.M.; Coventry Mus.; City A.G., Manchester; Newport A.G.; Portsmouth City Mus.

Bibliography: G.W. Reid: *Descriptive Cat. of the Works of G.C.,* 1871. W. Bates: *G.C.,* 1878. D. Jerrold: *Life of C.,* 1822-3. L. Grego: *C's Watercolours,* 1904. A.M. Cohn: *G.C., Catalogue Raisonné,* 1924. R.L. Patten: *G.C.'s Life, Times and Art,* 2 vols., 1992, 1996. *A.J.,* 1878. Arts Council, Exhibition Cat., 1974.

CRUIKSHANK, Isaac
1764 (Edinburgh) - 1811 (London)
A Lowland Scot who was not only a caricaturist but also a painter of sentimental genre scenes. His father, a Jacobite who had fought at Culloden, had been a professional artist for a time and Cruikshank followed him at an early age. He exhibited at the R.A. in 1789, 1790 and 1792, and the majority of his political and social prints are dated from 1790 to 1810. He worked as an illustrator for Laurie

CRUIKSHANK, Isaac (1764-1811)
The Soldier's Farewell. *Pen and black ink and watercolour, 9½in. x 7⅛in.*

CUMBERLAND, George (1752-1848)
The Entrance to Mr. Praed's Tin Mine at Trevethow. *Watercolour, 5¼in. x 9in.*

and Whittle.

His drawings sometimes bear fake Rowlandson signatures but these need cause little confusion since his line is smoother and more flowing. The predominating colours are usually blues and greys, with touches of red.
Examples: B.M.; V.A.M.; Fitzwilliam; Greenwich.
Bibliography: F. Marchmont: *The Three Cs*, 1897. E.B. Krumbhar: I.C. *Catalogue Raisonné*, 1966. *Burlington Mag.*, April 1928.

CRUIKSHANK, Isaac Robert
1789 (London) - 1856 (London)
The elder son of I. Cruikshank (q.v.), he went to sea on an Indiaman before setting up as a miniaturist and caricaturist. Like his brother George, he turned to book illustration, and they sometimes worked in collaboration. The most successful of their books, with text by Pierce Egan, was *Life in London*, 1821, which was a best seller and was turned into a play.

His style is akin to that of his brother, by whom he is overshadowed.
Examples: B.M.; Huntingdon Mus., California.
Bibliography: F. Marchmont: *The Three Cs*, 1897. W. Bates: *G.C., the Artist, the Humorist and the Man, with some account of his brother Robert*, 1878.

CRUISE, John
A landscape and subject painter who won the first prize for drawing at the R.D.S. Schools in 1814. He exhibited at the R.H.A. from 1827 to 1830, and in 1832 he came to London where he exhibited at the R.A. and the B.I. His name does not appear after 1834.
Examples: St. Patrick's Cathedral, Dublin.

CUBLEY, William Harold
1816   - 1896 (Newark)
A Newark art master and landscape painter in oil and watercolour. His best known pupil was Sir William Nicholson. He exhibited at the R.A. and Suffolk Street from 1863 to 1878. He also took portraits.
Published: *A System of Elementary Drawing*, 1876.
Examples: Castle Mus., Nottingham.

CUIT, George 1743 (Moulton, Yorkshire) -
1818 (Richmond)
A landscape and portrait painter who was sent to Italy in 1769 where he remained until 1775. On his return he was in London for a while and exhibited at the R.A., but within two years he returned to Richmond. There he worked for Lord Mulgrave, for whom he produced a set of views of Yorkshire ports visited by Captain Cook. He also made many landscape drawings in bodycolour which are bright and attractive, but a little naïve in detail.
Examples: B.M.; Newport A.G.

CUITT, George
1779 (Richmond, Yorkshire) -
1854 (Masham)
The only son of G. Cuit (q.v.), he was an etcher and painter, and taught drawing at Richmond, and at Chester from about 1804 to about 1820. He then returned to the Richmond area and built a house at Masham, where he lived for the rest of his life. He painted watercolour views at Farnley, in the Lake District and elsewhere. They are often variations on the themes of green and grey, giving an aquatint-like effect. Like his father's bodycolour work,

Cuitt's watercolours are more naïve in detail than a longer view would suggest.

He added the second 't' to his name to distinguish himself from his father, but on the evidence of late twentieth century catalogues, the ploy failed.
Published: *Saxon Buildings of Chester*, 1810-11. *History of Chester*, 1815. *Yorkshire Abbeys*, 1822-5. *Wanderings and Pencillings among the Ruins of Olden Time*, 1848.
Examples: B.M.; Leeds City A.G.; Laing A.G., Newcastle; Newport A.G.

CUMBERLAND, George
1752   - 1848
A miniaturist, landscape and figure painter, as well as a poet and art critic, he was a friend of Blake, who engraved some of his designs, of Lawrence and of Stothard. He exhibited at the R.A. from 1773 to 1783 and settled in Bristol in about 1808. There he helped other artists and sketched with them regularly, working rather in the manner of his friend Linnell (q.v.). He was also an etcher and lithographer.
Examples: B.M.; V.A.M.; City A.G., Bristol.
Bibliography: *The Book Collector*, Spring 1970. British Lib., MSS correspondence.

CUMING, J   B
A painter of portraits and landscapes which are in the arcadian vein of F.O. Finch (q.v.) or G. Barret, Yr. (q.v.). He was working in 1812.

Richard CUMING (b.c.1776) painted landscapes and topographical subjects and exhibited from 1797 to 1803. He entered the R.A. Schools in 1794 and was still active in 1806.
Examples: B.M.

CUMMING,   Constance   Frederica
GORDON-   1837 (Altyre) - 1924
The twelfth child of Sir W.G. Gordon-Cumming, a philoprogenitive patron and amateur painter, she became a traveller and a watercolourist. In 1868 she went to India, where she travelled in the North for a year before returning to Europe. From 1872 she spent two years in Ceylon, and thereafter she visited Fiji, New Zealand, Tahiti, Japan, Hawaii, North America and China. Her later years were spent teaching a version of braille to Chinese peasants. Her work is well drawn, strong and colourful, much as she must have been herself.
Published: *From the Hebrides to the Himalayas*, 1876. *Two Happy Years in Ceylon*, 1892. *Memories*, 1904. &c.

CUMMING, Wiliam Skeoch
1864 (Edinburgh) - 1929
A portrait and military painter, and a tapestry designer for Lord Bute's Corstorphine studios. He studied at the Edinburgh School of Art and the R.S.A. Schools. He served and sketched in the Boer War, and also commemorated slightly earlier Scottish military involvements, such as

CUMMING, Wiliam Skeoch (1864-1929)
Men from the 92nd Gordon Highlanders. *Watercolour, signed and dated 1886, 17¾in. x 25¾in.*

the Afghan War. He exhibited at the R.S.A from 1885 to 1928, and also at the R.A. in 1903 and 1904. His work is generally colourful and bold, and the military subjects could be described as Norie in more realised landscape settings.

His wife, **Belle Skeoch CUMMING (1888-1964),** was a figurative and landscape painter in watercolour.
Examples: City of Edinburgh Collection.

CUNDELL, Henry   1810   -
A landscape and marine painter who lived in London and exhibited at the R.A. from 1838 to 1858. His early work in brown wash and full colour is reminiscent of that of T.S. Boys (q.v.).
Examples: B.M.

CUNDY, Thomas, Yr.
1790   - 1867 (Bromley)
The eldest son and pupil of his namesake the architect, with whom he visited Rome in 1816. On his father's death in 1825 he took over the practice, succeeding also to the surveyorship of the Grosvenor estates in London. In due course he was aided and succeeded by **Thomas CUNDY III (1820-1895).** He also visited Greece and Constantinople, and toured France and Lombardy in 1863, Geneva in 1865 and Scotland in 1869. Betweenwhiles he sketched landscapes and views throughout England in various media.

Bibliography: *Builder,* XXV, 1867. *Building News,* Aug. 30, 1867.

CUNNINGHAM, Georgina, Mrs.
A genre painter who lived in Putney and exhibited from 1888.

CUNNYNGHAME, D
A topographer who was working in Edinburgh in 1782. Many of the family of the Cunnynghame baronets of Milncraig were named David.
Examples: N.G., Scotland.

CURNOCK, James Jackson
1839 (Bristol) - 1891
The son of James Curnock (1812-1870), a portrait painter, he painted lakes and mountains, particularly in North Wales. He was a pupil of his father and lived in Bristol, exhibiting in London from 1873 to 1889. Towards the end of his life he also painted in oil.
Examples: Bristol City A.G.; Reading A.G.

CURREY, Fanny W   - 1912
The daughter of the agent of the Devonshire estates at Lismore, she became a landscape and flower painter. She was active from about 1858, was a founder of the Irish Amateur Drawing Society (which became the Watercolour Society of Ireland) in 1870, and visited France in 1879. She also visited North Wales

and exhibited in London from 1880.
Published: *Prince Ritto,* 1877.

CURTIS, John Digby
c.1775 (Newark) - 1837
A topographer who worked from Newark in oil and watercolour. He sometimes worked up the drawings of others, but his own touch is uncertain.

CURZON, R. –
see **TEYNHAM, H.G.R-C., Lord**

CUST, Mary Anne, the Hon. Lady
1799/1800   - 1882 (Birkenhead)
The only child of L.W. Boode, she married the youngest son of the 1st Lord Brownlow in 1821. She was a pupil and patron of P. de Wint (q.v.). Her husband (1794-1878) was an equerry to Prince Leopold, the future King of the Belgians, and Master of Ceremonies to Queen Victoria. He was created a baronet in 1876.

CUSTARD, Henry Marsh
1806/7   - 1895 (Yeovil)
A landscape and figure painter who lived in Yeovil and exhibited in London from 1856 to 1860. He was an unsuccessful candidate for the N.W.S. in 1863. The initial 'A' given him in previous editions seems to have been a misreading from the manuscript minutes of the society.

DADD, Frank, R.I.
1851 (London) - 1929
Nephew of R. Dadd (q.v.) and brother-in-law
and cousin of K. Greenaway (q.v.). He is best
known for his black and white illustrations,
but was also a very competent painter in oil
and watercolour. He studied at the R.C.A. and
the R.A. Schools from 1871. He drew for the
I.L.N. from 1878 to 1884 and thereafter for the
Graphic. In the latter year he was elected R.I.
He sometimes initialled his watercolours,
which can lead to confusion with the work of
F. Dillon (q.v.). He exhibited at the R.A.from
1878 to 1912.
Illustrated: J.H. Newman: *Lead Kindly Light,* 1887.
G.M. Fenn: *Dick O' the Fens,* 1888. G.R. Sims: *Nat
Harlowe, Mountebank,* 1902.
Examples: B.M.; Exeter Mus.
See Colour Plate

DADD, Richard   **1817 (Chatham) -**
1886 (Broadmoor, Berkshire)
The son of a Chatham chemist and businessman. Dadd was educated at the grammar
school and took drawing lessons at William
Dadson's Academy. He also studied the
picture collection at Cobham Park and
sketched in the Kentish countryside, as well as
on the Medway. In 1834 the family moved to
London, where his father set up as a carver and
gilder. This led to friendships with a number of
artists, including D. Roberts and C. Stanfield

DADD, Richard (1817-1886)
'The Music Lesson or the Governess – A Sketch.'
Watercolour heightened with bodycolour, on grey paper, signed,
inscribed and dated 1855, 20¼in. x 7in.

DADD, Richard (1817-1886)
Studies of Eastern Heads. *Pen and brown ink and watercolour heightened with gum arabic. 7in.
x 10in.*

(qq.v.), who recommended him to the R.A.
Schools, which he entered in January 1837.
The visitors who taught him there included D.
Maclise, W. Mulready, W. Etty and Stanfield
himself. His taste for fairy painting was
encouraged by Henry Howard, who was
Professor of Painting at the time. His co-
students and friends included W.P. Frith, J.
Phillip, A. Egg, A. Elmore, E.M. Ward and
H.N. O'Neil, who shared his ideals and called
themselves 'The Clique'. In 1840 he won a
medal for the best life drawing. He began to
exhibit portraits and landscapes at the S.B.A.
in 1837, and the B.I. in 1839. At about this
time he was commissioned to decorate Lord
Foley's house in Grosvenor Square with
scenes from Tasso's *Jerusalem Delivered* and
Byron's *Manfred.*
  In July 1842 he left England with his patron
Sir Thomas Phillips for a tour of Italy, Greece
and the Middle East. They visited Venice,
Bologna, Corfu, Athens, Smyrna,
Constantinople, Halicarnassus, Lycia, Rhodes,
the Lebanon, Damascus, Palestine and Cairo.
They sailed up the Nile, and returned home by
way of Malta, Naples and Rome. By this time
Dadd was convinced that he was pursued by

devils, one being Sir Thomas and another the Pope, whom he considered assassinating. Although he was obviously mad by his return the following May, the full danger was not realised despite drawings of his friends with their throats cut. On 28 August he murdered his father in Cobham Park. He fled to France, and was arrested two days later after attacking a stranger in a diligence. He was extradited in 1844 and admitted to Bethlem Hospital, Southwark. There he was treated by Dr. Edward Thomas Monro, son of T. Monro (q.v.), who may have encouraged him to take up painting again. In 1853 Dr. W.C. Hood was appointed resident physician, and he became a great collector and admirer of Dadd's work. In 1864 he was moved to the new hospital at Broadmoor, where he died.

Although his style has a kinship both with the Pre-Raphaelites and the Fuseli/Blake tradition, it cannot be strictly classified. His watercolours are generally not as precise as his oils, although in both media, and increasingly towards the end of his life, he can work with the exactitude of the miniaturist. He has a very personal, *pointilliste* method of painting the sea. His colours are usually soft, clear and cold, and some of his later drawings are almost monochromes in greys and blues. Many of his asylum works, such as the series to 'Illustrate the Passions', are pedantically inscribed with dates and times.

Illustrated: S.C. Hall, *Book of British Ballads*, ?1843.
Examples: B.M.; V.A.M.; Bethlem Hospital, Beckenham; Cecil Higgins A.G., Bedford; Fitzwilliam; Laing City A.G., Newcastle; Newport A.G.
Bibliography: D. Greysmith: *R.D.*, 1973. P. Allderidge: *R.D.*, 1974. *Art Union*, 1843; 1845. *A.J.*, 1864. *Sotheby's Year Book*, 1963-4. Tate Gall., Exhibition Cat., 1974, and MS poem.

DADD, Stephen Thomas
1858 (Poplar) - 1917 (Hackney)
Nephew of Richard and younger brother of F. Dadd (q.v.), he trained as a wood engraver under his distant cousin John Greenaway, the father of Kate. As a watercolourist he specialised in domestic and genre subjects. His son, Stephen Gabriel Dadd, was a sculptor and was killed in the First World War, and he himself seems to have given up work in about 1914.

DADE, Ernest
1865 (Scarborough) - 1935 (London)
A genre, marine and landscape painter in oil and watercolour who exhibited from 1886. He lived in Chelsea in 1887 and 1888 and then returned to Yorkshire. He specialised in subjects on the Yorkshire and East Anglian coasts. He sometimes signed 'Ernst'.
Published: *Sail and Oar*, 1933.
Examples: V.A.M.; Greenwich; London Mus.

DADE, Ernest (1865-1935)
Cottages and Haystacks. *Signed and dated 92, pencil and watercolour, 6in. x 9in.*

DAGLEY, Richard
c.1765   - 1841
An orphan and educated at Christ's Hospital, where he was taught by B. Green (q.v.), Dagley was apprenticed to a jeweller, for whom he painted ornaments. He was a friend of Henry Bone, the enamel painter, and designed medals as well as painting in watercolour. For a while he taught drawing in Doncaster, but returned to London in 1815 where he worked as a book reviewer and an illustrator. He exhibited at the R.A. and elsewhere from 1784 to 1833.
Published: *Gems selected from the Antique*, 1804.
Illustrated: I. D'Israeli: *Flimflams*, 1805.

DAHL or DALL, Nicholas Thomas, A.R.A.
**   - 1776 (London)**
A Dane who settled in London in the 1740s or '50s. He was a scene painter at Covent Garden, and he was an impressive topographer, as in the drawings of Hackfall, Yorkshire, formerly in the Oppé Collection, which are dated 1766. He was elected A.R.A. in 1771. His penwork can be rather fussy.

DALE, Henry Sheppard
1852 (Sheffield) - 1921
In 1872, while at London University, he exhibited a view of Scarborough at the S.B.A. He visited Venice, and painted in Devon, exhibiting again in 1885-6. He was a *Graphic* illustrator and an etcher, and also showed at the R.I. and the R.A.

DALGLEISH, William
1857 (Glasgow) - 1909 (Glasgow)
A landscape painter in oil and watercolour who exhibited at the R.A. and in Glasgow. He studied locally and also produced marine subjects.
Examples: Paisley A.G.

DALTON, Richard, F.S.A.
1715 (Deane, Cumberland) - 1791 (London)
He studied in Dublin and Rome and from 1749 travelled with Lord Charlemont to Sicily, Greece, Constantinople and Egypt. On his return he became Librarian and Keeper of the Pictures to George III. He was sent to the Continent to buy pictures on several occasions and in 1763 persuaded Bartolozzi to come to England from Venice. He was a member of the Incorporated Society and became Antiquarian to the R.A.

His drawings are weak, although interesting as the earliest of Near Eastern antiquities.
Published: *A Selection from the Antiquities of Athens*, 1751.
Examples: Soane Mus.
Bibliography: Stanford & Finopoulos (eds): *The Travels of Lord Charlemont in Greece*, &c., 1984.

DALZIEL, Edward Gurden
1849 (London) - 1889
The eldest son of Edward Dalziel (1817-1905), the wood engraver, he exhibited genre subjects from 1869 to 1882. He also painted rather Pre-Raphaelite landscape studies.
Bibliography: *The Brothers Dalziel...*, 1901.

DALZIEL, Thomas Bolton Gilchrist Septimus
1823 (Wooler, Northumberland) - 1906
The seventh and youngest of the sons of

DANBY, Francis (1793-1861)
The Avon Gorge, looking towards the Severn and Cook's Folly. *Signed, pencil and watercolour, 10½in. x 16¾in.*

Alexander Dalziel, and an uncle of E.G. Dalziel (q.v.), he was the best draughtsman among them. He joined his brothers George, Gilbert, Edward and John in the family engraving firm in 1860. As well as wood engraving he painted figures and landscape in watercolour and charcoal.
Illustrated: *Arabian Nights*, 1864. *Pilgrim's Progress*, 1865. *Bible Gallery*, 1990. &c.
Bibliography: *The Brothers Dalziel A Record of Work, 1840 1890*, 1901. Sotheby's Belgravia, Sale Cat., 1978.

DANBY, Francis, A.R.A.
1793 (Nr. Killinick, Wexford) -
1861 (Exmouth)
Danby's family moved to Dublin during the 1798 rebellion and there he studied at the R.D.S. and under J.A. O'Connor (q.v.). In 1813 he accompanied O'Connor and G. Petrie (q.v.) to London, and settled in Bristol, having run out of funds on the return journey. He visited Norway and Scotland before 1817. In 1824 he moved to London and was elected A.R.A. the following year. Domestic troubles drove him abroad in 1829 and he lived on the Continent, mostly on the Lake of Geneva, until 1841. He then took a house in Lewisham, and in 1847 settled permanently in Exmouth.

His subjects are very varied, from pure landscapes and marine paintings to visionary masterpieces reminiscent of Martin, and history and genre pictures. His watercolours and drawings are usually but small expressions of his painting in oil.
Examples: B.M.; V.A.M.; City A.G., Bristol; Ulster Mus.
Bibliography: E. Adams: *F.D.*, 1973. E. Malins and

M. Bishop: *James Smetham and F.D.*, 1974. *A.J.*, 1855; 1861. *Cornhill Mag.*, 1946. Arts Council: Exhibition Cat., 1961.
See Colour Plate

DANBY, James Francis
1816 (Bristol) - 1875 (London)
Eldest son of F. Danby (q.v.), he shared his family's Continental travels until 1841. He first exhibited at the R.A. in 1842. His thoroughly competent work is in the poetic manner of his father, but without great originality, and he shows a penchant for sunsets. He seems to have visited Ireland and was an occasional exhibitor at the R.H.A. from 1849 to 1871.
Bibliography: *A.J.*, 1859; 1876.

DANBY, Thomas, R.H.A., R.W.S.
1817 (Bristol) - 1886 (London)
The second son of F. Danby (q.v.), he left England with his family in 1829 and during several years spent in Paris became adept at copying old masters in the Louvre, where he also fell under the influence of Claude. Later, the family moved to Switzerland, and Swiss and Italian lake scenes appear regularly among his subjects. The family returned to England in 1841 and Danby first exhibited at the R.A. in 1843. He was elected R.H.A. in 1860. It was not until 1866 that he finally turned to watercolour as his principal medium, but he quickly adapted himself to it, and within a year was unanimously elected A.O.W.S. He became a full member in 1870. He was twice married, firstly to the daughter of the landlord of the inn at Capel Curig, which was one of his favourite sketching grounds. In his last years his subjects were drawn almost exclusively from South Wales. His style is generally unlike his father's, being close to that of his friend (and ultimate stepfather) P.F. Poole (q.v.). His remaining works were sold at Christie's, 17-18 June 1886.
Examples: B.M.; V.A.M.; Cartwright Hall, Bradford; Ulster Mus.
Bibliography: *A.J.*, 1886.

DANCE, George, Yr., R.A., F.R.S., F.S.A.
1741 (London) - 1825 (London)
The fifth and youngest son of George Dance, Surveyor to the City of London, who trained him as an architect and sent him to study in France and Italy with his brother N. Dance-Holland (q.v.). He returned at the end of 1764. He was a member of the Incorporated Society, first exhibiting in 1761, and a Foundation Member of the R.A., serving as Professor of Architecture from 1798 to 1806, without, however, giving any lectures. Among his buildings as an architect – he succeeded his father in 1768 – were All Hallows, London Wall, Newgate Prison and St. Luke's Hospital.

DANBY, Thomas (1817-1886)
Boating at Oystermouth, South Wales. *Watercolour, signed and dated 1885. 10½in. x 20½in.*

DANCE, George, Yr. (1741-1825)
Portrait of Joseph Hodgkinson. *Pencil, 8¼in. x 6in., signed and dated July 3, 1803.*

DANIELL, Rev. Edward Thomas (1804-1842)
Djebel Serbal. *Inscribed and dated June 19 1841, pen and ink and watercolour, 13⅛in. x 19⅝in.*

He produced many portraits in chalk as well as in the manner of Downman, and like his elder brother, Dance-Holland, he was a caricaturist working in grey wash.
Published: *A Collection of Portraits sketched from the Life,* 1811.
Examples: B.M.; V.A.M.; Ashmolean; City Record Office; R.I.B.A.; Soane Mus.
Bibliography: D. Stroud: *G.D., Architect,* 1971. G. Teyssot *Citté utopia... G.D. il giovane,* 1974. *Gentleman's Mag.,* 1825, i. *Builder,* V, 1847. R.I.B.A. *Journal,* 3rd ser., LIV, 1947. Geffrye Mus., London: Exhibition Cat., 1972.

DANIELL, Rev. Edward Thomas
1804 (London) - 1842 (Adalia)
The son of a former Attorney-General of Dominica, he was born in London and brought up at the family's Norfolk home. He attended the Grammar School, where he was taught drawing by Crome. He went to Balliol in 1823, but showed a strong interest in artistic matters during the vacations, visiting Linnell in London and frequenting Joseph Stannard's Norwich studio. In 1831 he was ordained and spent two years in a Norfolk curacy, but then he moved to London and fully entered into the artistic life of the capital. In 1840, however, he was so impressed by Robert's Egyptian drawings that he went to Egypt and Sinai in 1841, then joined the Lycian expedition and died of fever in Asia Minor. He was a master of etching and dry point, and his watercolours are far from the laboured productions of so many amateurs. On the contrary, they have been well described as 'the perfection of free sketching'.

DANIELL, Rev. Edward Thomas (1804-1842)
Nablus. *Inscribed, pencil, pen and ink and watercolour, 13⅛in. x 19⅜in.*

Examples: B.M.; V.A.M.; Castle Mus., Norwich.
Bibliography: R.I.A. Palgrave: *E.T.D.,* 1882. F.R. Beecheno: *E.T.D.,* 1889. W.F. Dickes: *The Norwich School,* 1905. H.L. Mallalieu: *The Norwich School,* 1975. J. Walpole: *Art and Artists of the Norwich School,* 1997.

DANIELL, Samuel
1775 (Chertsey) - 1811 (Ceylon)
The younger brother of W. Daniell (q.v.), he was probably the most talented of the family. He was educated at the East India College, Hertford, where he was taught by T. Medland (q.v.). He was also Medland's private pupil in

DANIELL, Thomas, R.A. (1749-1840)
View of the Temple at Permador. *Inscribed on reverse 'Hindoo Temple at Permadod, April 11th 1792', pencil, grey and pink washes, 14¾in. x 21¾in.*

London. He exhibited for the first time at the R.A. in 1792. In 1799 he sailed for the Cape, where he attached himself to the Governor's suite. In October 1801 he set out as a secretary and draughtsman to an expedition to Bechuanaland, then unvisited by Europeans. After numerous hardships and adventures he was back in the Cape in April 1802, and the following year he returned to England. In 1805 he left for Ceylon. There again he made a friend of the Governor, who appointed him to the entirely honorific post of 'Ranger of the Woods and Forests'. He remained on the island until his death.

In his work, both finished watercolours and sketches, he breaks away from the largely topographical tradition of his family and the eighteenth century methods which satisfied his uncle Thomas. His figure drawing is quite the best of the family. The published plates from his work were engraved by his brother.

Published: *African Scenery and Animals*, 1804. *Scenery &c. of Ceylon*, 1808.

Illustrated: Sir J. Barrow: *Account of Travels into the Interior of South Africa*, 1806. Sir J. Barrow: *A Voyage to Cochin China*, 1806.

Examples: B.M.; V.A.M.

Bibliography: T. Sutton: *The Daniells*, 1954.

See Colour Plate

DANIELL, Thomas, R.A.
1749 (Chertsey) - 1840 (London)
The son of an innkeeper, he was apprenticed to a coach-painter and then worked for C. Catton (q.v.) in the same line. He first exhibited at the R.A. in 1772 and entered the R.A. Schools in the following year. At this time he was painting flowers, landscapes, portraits and caricatures, and he worked in Buckinghamshire, Oxfordshire, Somerset and Yorkshire. In 1785 he left for India with his sixteen-year-old nephew William (q.v.), travelling by way of Madeira, the Cape, Java and the China coast. They spent two years in Calcutta and in 1788-9 undertook the outward leg of their North Indian tour, reaching Srinagar in Garwhal, the first Europeans to do so. On the return journey they spent a year with S. Davis (q.v.) at Bhagalpur, and they reached Calcutta again in the autumn of 1791. There they held a successful lottery of the one hundred and fifty or so pictures resulting from the tour, and they sailed to Madras the following March. In April 1792 they set out on a southern tour reaching Cape Comorin and Ceylon. After a second lottery they sailed to Bombay and to Muscat. There they heard of the outbreak of war with France, and they returned to Bombay. Late in 1793 they set out for home, again travelling by the China coast, where they joined Lord Macartney's convoy. They reached Spithead in September 1794.

Thereafter, much of Thomas's time was taken up with the publication of *Oriental Scenery*, and with the architectural projects to which it gave rise at Melchet and Sezincote. The original plans for Brighton Pavilion were also influenced by his work. He was elected A.R.A. and R.A. in 1796 and 1797, and he exhibited for the last time in 1830. He visited Devon, and Wales in 1807, with William, and lived in London.

His watercolours are those of an eighteenth century topographer, with careful drawing sometimes done with the aid of a *camera obscura*, a ground of grey wash, and light local colours. His work is fresh, but careful, and as Colonel Grant said: 'A good Thomas Daniell is, in short, a very fine thing.'

Published: with W. Daniell: *Oriental Scenery*, 1795-1808. With W. Daniell: *A Picturesque Voyage to India by Way of China*, 1810.

Examples: B.M.; V.A.M.; Victoria Memorial Hall, Calcutta; Ferens A.G., Hull; Fitzwilliam; India Office Lib.

Bibliography: T. Sutton: *The Daniells*, 1954. M. Shellim: *The Daniells in India*, 1970. Walpole Society, XIX, 1931. *Walker's Quarterly*, 356, 1932. *Country Life*, 23 Jan. 1958. *Journal of the R.I.B.A.*, Sept. 1960. *Apollo*, Nov. 1962. *Connoisseur*, CLII, 1963. Journal of the Royal Society of Arts, Oct. 1962.

DANIELL, William, R.A.
1769 (Chertsey) - 1837 (London)
The son of the elder brother of T. Daniell (q.v.), who had inherited the family inn, the Swan at Chertsey. His training was of the most practical nature, as his uncle's assistant in India from 1785 to 1794. For details of their voyaging, many of which are taken from William's journals, see the previous notice. By the time of their return to England, William was not only a proficient draughtsman, but was perfecting himself in the art of aquatinting. After the publication of the first series of *Oriental Scenery*, nearly all the family plates were engraved by William, whatever the attribution on them.

From 1802 to 1813 much of his time was taken up with a series of views of London and another of the London Docks. He was elected A.R.A. and R.A. in 1807 and 1822. He refused the post of draughtsman to an Australian expedition, the job going to his brother-in-law W. Westall (q.v.), and instead made numerous tours in England and Scotland. His *Voyage Round Great Britain* occupied him from 1813 to 1823. In 1813 he went from Land's End to Holyhead and in 1814 from Holyhead to Creetown. Both of these tours were with Richard Ayton, who wrote the text for this part of the work. In 1815 he completed the Scottish coasts on his own. He did no more fieldwork until 1821 and may have visited the Continent in the interim. In 1821 he went from St. Andrews to Southend, in 1822 from Sheerness to Torquay, and in 1823 from Torquay to Land's End. He visited Ireland in 1828, probably with a similar project in mind, and he was in France in 1833.

He was a superb aquatinter, and his watercolours advanced in style and quality after his return to England. On tour he made small wash sketches, producing larger, coloured versions in the studio. Perhaps his best work is among the Scottish views for the *Voyage*, and the English scenes of the Windsor and Eton series. In these, his restrained colours capture the atmosphere perfectly, while his Indian works rely almost entirely on accurate draughtsmanship and the interest of the subjects. His work lacks the originality promised by that of his brother Samuel (q.v.), but it should not be dismissed in the scornful manner of many of his artistic contemporaries. It is topography at its best. His marine work, too, is excellent.

His daughter was S.S. Gent (q.v.).

Published: with T. Daniell: *Oriental Scenery,* 1795-1808. With T. Daniell: *A Picturesque Voyage to India by the Way of China,* 1810. *Interesting Selections from Animated Nature,* 1807-12. *A Familiar Treatise on Perspective,* 1810. *A Voyage Round Great Britain,* 1814-25. *Illustrations of the Island of Staffa,* 1818. After S. Daniell: *Sketches of the Native Tribes… of Southern Africa,* 1820. *Views of Windsor, Eton and Virginia Water,* 1827-30.

Examples: B.M.; V.A.M.; Aberdeen A.G.; Cecil Higgins A.G., Bedford; Brighton A.G.; Exeter Mus.; Ferens A.G., Hull; Fitzwilliam; Glasgow A.G.; Greenwich; India Office Lib.; Leeds City A.G.

Bibliography: T. Sutton: *The Daniells,* 1954. M. Shellim: *The Daniells in India,* 1970. *Connoisseur,* CLII, 1963.

See Colour Plate

DANSON, George
1799 (Lancaster) - 1881 (London)

A scene painter, who also produced landscapes and town views in oil and watercolour, usually on a large scale. He exhibited at the R.A. and elsewhere in 1823 to 1848.

Examples: V.A.M.

DARBY, Mary, Mrs., née Boyle
c.1800 - 1869

The wife of the Rev. C.L. Darby of Leap Castle and Kells Priory, Kilkenny. She met E. Lear (q.v.) at her brother-in-law's parish near Knowsley, and her Irish and English landscapes were strongly influenced by him. She toured France, Belgium and Switzerland in 1850.

Examples: Indianapolis Mus. of Art.

DARCY, Laura

A painter of moralities and gardens in watercolour and oil who exhibited at the R.A., the N.W.S. and Suffolk Street for ten years from 1881. Her addresses, in Blackheath, West London and Wadhurst, Sussex may indicate that she was a governess.

DARLY, Matthias

An engraver, artists' colourman, caricaturist and drawing master who worked in London and Bath from the 1740s to about 1780. He published some of Bunbury's earliest works and engraved most of the plates for Chippendale's *Director,* as well as producing some three hundred of his own caricatures and painting landscapes and marine subjects. These last may have been in bodycolour. He was influential as a designer and publisher of designs, styling himself 'Teacher and Professor of Ornament'.

DANIELL, William (1769-1837)
Arundel Castle from the Park. *Pencil and brown wash heightened with white, 6½in. x 9½in.*

His wife **Mary DARLY** was a printseller and also a caricaturist, with a shop in Leicester Fields from c.1756 to 1777.

Published: *A New Book of Chinese, Gothic and Modern Chairs,* 1751. With G. Edwards: *New Book of Chinese Designs,* 1754. *The Ornamental Architect, or Young Artist's Instructor,* 1770. &c.

Bibliography: See P. Ward-Jackson: *English Furniture Designs,* 1958. See E. Harris: *British Architectural Books and Writers,* 1990.

DARRELL, Sir Harry Verelst, 2nd Bt.
1768 - 1828 (India)

A Bengal merchant. Either he or his son, **Sir Harry Francis Colville DARRELL (1814-1853),** who lived in Richmond, Surrey, painted a number of views in Sicily. The son also worked in India around 1840.

DARVALL, Henry 1828/9 -

An English painter of literary genre subjects and occasional landscapes who studied at the R.A. Schools from 1847 and exhibited in London from the following year. About twenty years later his career took a violent change of direction when he settled in Venice. La Serenissima provided his subject matter thenceforward, until at least 1889.

DASHWOOD, Selina Georgiana, Mrs.Watson
c.1834 (Shenley, Herts) - 1879

An amateur artist who sketched in Scotland in 1851. She was a member of the Kirtlington family of baronets, and married the Rev. G.W. Watson in 1854.

Her kinswoman **Susan Alice DASHWOOD (b.c.1853)** painted effective interiors of Kirtlington Park, Oxon, in a rather thick watercolour style, over pencil and using white heightening. She has a squirly monogram.

DASHWOOD, Rev. Henry
c.1801 - 1846

A younger brother of Sir G.H. Dashwood of West Wycombe. He was at Eton from 1814, where he painted and was an exact contemporary of Sir G. Beaumont's namesake and heir.

DAVENPORT, John

An artist working in the Crimea in 1855.

DAVEY, Robert - 1793 (London)

A drawing master who taught at a school for young ladies in Queen's Square and painted portraits. He succeeded G. Massiot (q.v.) as assistant drawing master at Woolwich in 1780 and was killed by robbers near the Tottenham Court Road.

A **William DAVEY** made a very competent topographical watercolour of Exeter Cathedral in the 1790s. Both it and a print after it are in Exeter Mus.

DAVIDSON, Alexander, R.S.W.
1838 - 1887

A genre painter in oil and watercolour and an illustrator who studied in Glasgow and exhibited in London from 1873. He was fascinated by Bonnie Prince Charlie, and illustrated an edition of Scott's *Waverley Novels* – as did an earlier **Alexander DAVIDSON,** perhaps his father, who exhibited at the R.S.A. between 1834 and 1842. The younger Davidson lived in Stirling and Glasgow, and was elected R.S.W. in 1883.

DAVIDSON, Charles (1824-1902)
Rocky Coast. *Watercolour, 9in. x 12¾in.*

DAVIDSON, Caroline
A very competent artist who visited Ramsgate in 1838. Her style is close to Cox, her colours strong, and she shows a good understanding of skies and light.
Examples: Ashmolean; Blackburn A.G.

DAVIDSON, Charles, R.W.S.
1824 (London) - 1902 (Falmouth)
A landscape painter who studied under J. Absolon (q.v.). He lived at Bletchingley and Redhill and sketched in Surrey, Kent and Yorkshire. He was elected Associate and Member of the N.W.S. in 1847 and 1849 but moved to O.W.S. in 1855, becoming a full member in 1858. He exhibited some eight hundred watercolours in London from 1844 but, as he rarely signed, much of his work may have been reattributed. He was a friend of Linnell, Varley and Palmer, and his daughter Annie Laura married F.M. Holl (q.v.).

His son **Charles Topham DAVIDSON (b.1848)** exhibited coastal views, often in Scotland, Cornwall and Wales, and occasionally in Ireland, from 1870 to 1902. He left the family home in Redhill for London in about 1873.
Examples: V.A.M.; Blackburn A.G.; Brighton A.G.; Reading A.G.

DAVIDSON, George Dutch
1879 (Goole, Yorkshire) - 1901 (Dundee)
An illustrator of Scottish extraction who studied at Dundee from 1897. In 1899 he went to Italy by way of London and Antwerp, returning in 1900. There was a memorial exhibition in Dundee in 1901, and a memorial volume was published the following year. He

was one of the most notable of the Scottish Symbolists.
Examples: Dundee City A.G.
Bibliography: *Mag. of Art,* 1904. *Scottish Art Review,* n.s. XIII, 4, 1972.

DAVIES, Edward, R.I.
1841 (London) - 1912 (London)
A landscape painter in oil and watercolour who lived in Leicester. He also painted in

Scotland, Wales and the Isle of Man. He exhibited from 1880.

Presumably he should be identified with **Edward DAVIES, R.I.,** whose dates are given as 1841 to 1920, and who was elected in 1896. He is said to have moved from London to Leicester at the age of twenty-four, and to have begun painting under the influence of Cox. North Wales was a favourite sketching ground.
Examples: Leicestershire A.G.

DAVIES, Henry Casson (or Casom)
1821   - 1868
A drawing master at Hull College in 1851, he seems to have spent some time in Australia.

DAVIES, John
1796   - 1865 (Woodford, Essex)
An artist and architect who was in Italy in 1820 and 1821. He was probably a pupil of the architect George Maddox and worked in the Home Counties and London, exhibiting at the R.A. from 1819 to 1853. His buildings were also mostly in or near London.

DAVIES, Norman Prescott, F.R.S.
1862 (Isleworth) - 1915
A miniaturist, portrait and genre painter who worked in Isleworth and Central London in the 1880s and 1890s, and later at Radway, Warwickshire. He studied at South Kensington, the City and Guilds and Heatherley's.
Illustrated: B. Davies: *The Vicar's Pups,* 1900.

DAVIES, Lieutenant-General Thomas
1737   - 1812 (Blackheath)
He served in the Royal Artillery, being promoted major in 1782, lieutenant-colonel

DAVIES, Edward (1841-1912)
Haymakers. *Signed, watercolour, 7in. x 11in.*

DAVIES, Norman Prescott (1862-1915)
'All Hands to the Pump.' *Watercolour, signed and dated 1891, 10¼in. x 13¼in.*

DAVIS, John Scarlett (1804-1845)
The Entrance Steps at the Tuileries. *Signed, inscribed and dated 1831, pencil, pen and brown ink and brown wash on buff paper, 8⅝in. x 6¼in.*

1783, colonel 1794, major-general 1796 and lieutenant-general 1803. He sketched in Wales, North America, the West Indies and elsewhere. He produced a panoramic view of New York in about 1760. It is a little primitive but very pleasing. He also painted at Gibraltar in 1782. His picturesque figures, introduced as onlookers, may be a little out of scale.

DAVIS, Edward Thompson
1833 (Worcester) - 1867 (Rome)
A genre painter who studied at the Birmingham and Worcester Schools of Design under J. Kyd (q.v.). He exhibited at the R.A. in 1854, when living in Worcester, and in 1856, giving a London address. He was a friend of the Rossettis.

He is a pleasing and competent painter of subject pictures with titles such as 'Granny's Spectacles' and 'The Little Pegtop'. His people are chubby and carefully drawn with free washes.
Examples: Ashmolean.
Bibliography: *Country Life*, 30 Nov. 1989.

DAVIS, Frederick
A landscape painter who lived in Colchester and London and was active from 1853. He painted in Southern England, Wales and Ireland.
Arthur Alfred DAVIS and **Miss C.L. DAVIS** lived with him in the 1870s and 1880s. The former painted metropolitan genre scenes, and the latter landscapes.

DAVIS, Frederick William, R.I.
1862   - 1919
A Birmingham genre painter in oil and watercolour. He was elected R.I. in 1897 and was also a member of the Birmingham Society. He first exhibited there in 1887.
Examples: Preston Manor, Brighton.

DAVIS, Lieutenant-Colonel Henry Samuel
An Irish officer with the 52nd Regt., he retired as lieutenant-colonel in 1851. He exhibited West Indian sketches in 1845 and American and Irish views at the R.H.A. in 1833, 1835 and 1843. He also painted historical subjects.

DAVIS, Henry William Banks, R.A.
1833 (Finchley) - 1914 (Rhayader, Radnor)
A sculptor, landscape and animal painter in oil and watercolour who exhibited from 1853 and was elected A.R.A. and R.A. in 1873 and 1877.

DAVIS, John Philip, 'Pope'
1784 (Ashburton, Devonshire) - 1862
Primarily a portraitist and painter of large subject pictures in oil. Although he exhibited at the R.A. from 1811, like his friend Haydon he was its persistent attacker. He went to Rome in 1824, returning to London by 1826. Graves claims that he exhibited until 1875. This is unlikely since his last book gives his date of death as 28 September 1862.
Published: *Facts of Vital importance relative to the Embellishment of the House of Parliament*, 1843. *The Royal Academy and the National Gallery*, 1858. *Thoughts on Great Painters*, 1866.

DAVIS, John Scarlett (1804-1845)
The Pavillon de Flore. *Pen and ink and watercolour, 8in. x 6¼in.*

DAVIS, John Scarlett
1804 (Leominster) - 1845 (London)
The son of a silversmith, he studied under Witherington, Lawrence and the mezzotinter Charles Turner before attending the R.A. Schools from 1820 to 1822. He may also have had lessons from Cox at Hereford with his friend J.M. Ince (q.v.). He also spent some time at the Louvre. He became a fine architectural draughtsman, with a liking for church interiors, and he exhibited in London

from 1825. He lithographed twelve heads after Rubens and, in 1832, some views of Bolton Abbey. After 1830 he travelled in Italy, Spain, France and Holland. His clear style is close to that of Bonington, for whom he has sometimes been mistaken, and it also forms a bridge to the architectural work of D. Roberts (q.v.).

Examples: B.M.; V.A.M.; Ashmolean; Fitzwilliam; Hereford A.G.

Bibliography: *Connoisseur*, 1912. Hereford A.G., Exhibition Cat., 1937. O.W.S. Club, XLV, 1970.

DAVIS, Joseph Lucien, R.I.
1860 (Liverpool) - 1951 (Ashford)

The son of the Irish landscape painter William Davis (1813 Dublin - 1873 London), he was principal social artist on the *I.L.N.* for twenty years. He had studied at the R.A. Schools from 1877; on his retirement he became art master at St. Ignatius College, North London. He exhibited abroad as well as from 1878 at the R.A. and R.I., to which he was elected in 1893.

DAVIS, Richard Barrett
1782 (Watford) - 1854 (Middx.)

An animal painter who studied under Bourgeois and Beechey as well as at the R.A. Schools and possibly with Evans of Eton. He exhibited from 1802. His father had been Huntsman to the Royal Harriers, and he was appointed Animal Painter to the King in 1831.

His brother **William Henry DAVIS (c.1795-1885)** painted similar subjects.

DAVIS, Samuel
1757 (West Indies) - 1819

Davis went to India in 1780 and travelled fairly widely, penetrating as far as modern Bhutan. He became Accountant-General in Bengal. Between July 1790 and July 1791 he was visited by Thomas and William Daniell (qq.v.) at Bhagalpur, and Thomas may well have given him some lessons. William later aquatinted some *Views of Bootan*, 1813, after his drawings. In 1795 he was made judge and magistrate of Benares, and in 1799 he defended his house singlehanded against the forces of Wazir Ali. He was then posted to Calcutta until his return to England in 1806. Thereafter, he was a Director of the East India Company. On the whole his style is close to that of Thomas Daniell.

Illustrated: Turner: *Account of an Embassy to the Court of Teshwo Lama in Tibet*, 1800.

Examples: B.M.; V.A.M.; R.G.S.; Victoria Memorial Hall, Calcutta.

Bibliography: T. Sutton: *The Daniells*, 1954.

DAVIS, Valentine 1784 - 1869 (Islington)

An architectural draughtsman and perhaps an architect who worked in London, although he is also said to have 'built Portleven Harbour'. He was the son of the proprietor of Davis's Wharf, Horselydown, and was employed by Rennie and others. At the R.A. he showed a view of the wharf as well as designs for villas.

Examples: R.I.B.A. (incl. MS note).

DAVISON, Nathaniel c.1730 - 1780

Presumably a member of the distinguished and extensive Northumbrian family. He was active in the area in the 1760s, using white heightening and annotating his work.

DAVISON, William, II 1789 -

A portrait and landscape painter in oil and watercolour who entered the R.A.Schools in 1812 and exhibited at the B.I. and the R.A. from 1813 to 1843.

An architectural draughtsman of this name, **William DAVISON, I,** was active from about 1797 to 1825. He worked in London and published *A Series of Original designs for Shop-Fronts*, 1816.

DAVISON, William, III
1798 - 1870 (Sunderland)

An accomplished amateur marine, coastal and landscape painter who lived at Sunderland and Hartlepool. He was a friend of T. Bewick (q.v.), and he occasionally exhibited locally from 1829.

DAVY, Charles R 1800 (London) -

An artist who was working from 1856 or earlier. He painted landscapes in brown wash and pencil, reminiscent of Munn, and worked in Somerset, Cornwall, Bath, the Wye Valley, Yorkshire and around London. He is probably to be identified with the Charles Davy whose principal career was as a colourman.

Published: *Mechanical Drawing for Beginners*, 1891.

DAVY, Henry - 1832/3

An architect and landscape painter who published sets of etchings of Suffolk antiquities and seats in 1818 and 1827. He lived in Ipswich. His collection and remaining works were sold by Deck of Ipswich, 16 April 1833.

DAWE, Philip c.1740 - c.1785

The mezzotint engraver and humorous draughtsman. He was the son of a City merchant and was articled to H.R. Morland. He is said to have worked for Hogarth in about 1760, but Waterhouse makes this a different **Philip DAWES.** He exhibited at the S.A. in 1767 and in the first exhibition of the R.A. two years later.

He was the father of **George DAWE, R.A. (1781 London - 1829 London),** the portrait painter and biographer of George Morland; also of Henry Dawe (1790 London - 1848 Windsor), an engraver, and Philip Dawe, Yr. (b.1794), a painter.

DAWS, J

An early nineteenth century marine painter.

DAWSON, Henry
1811 (Hull) - 1878 (Chiswick)

A landscape and marine painter who was put to work at an early age in a Nottingham lace

factory. In 1835 he set up as a professional artist painting anything that offered and in 1838 he took twelve lessons from W.H. Pyne (q.v.). He moved to Liverpool in 1844 where he studied at the Academy and rapidly found patrons. However his income was small, and he settled in Croydon in 1850. He was encouraged by Ruskin, but regularly 'skied' at the Academy, and in the south of England his work did not find popularity until the very end of his life. He was an unsuccessful candidate for the N.W.S. in 1870.

His early work is in the tradition of Wilson. Later he was influenced by Turner. His watercolours are generally only sketches for oil paintings but a number were engraved for Bulmer's *East Riding of Yorkshire*.

Examples: Ferens A.G., Hull; Castle Mus., Nottingham.

Bibliography: A. Dawson: *The Life of H.D.*, 1891. *A.J.*, 1879. *Portfolio*, 1879.

DAWSON, Nelson, R.W.S.
1859 (Lincolnshire) - 1941 (London)

A marine and landscape painter who exhibited in oil and watercolour at the R.A. and R.I. from 1885. His subjects were mainly on the Cornish coasts. From 1895 both he and his wife, Edith, largely abandoned painting for metalwork.

Illustrated: E.V. Lucas: *A Wanderer in London*, 1906.

Examples: City A.G., Bristol.

Bibliography: *Studio* Special Nos. 1898; 1901.

DAWSON, Robert
1776 - 1860 (Woodleigh, Devonshire)

A topographical draughtsman who joined the Ordnance Survey of Great Britain in 1794. In 1802 he transferred to the Corps of Surveyors and Draughtsmen at the Tower of London, where he acted as drawing master to officers of the R.E. and the Q.M.G.'s department. From 1810 he also taught at the R.M.A., Addiscombe.

He had a keen eye for the artistic use of light and was said to have helped to bring the 'sketching and shading of Ordnance plans to the degree of perfection afterwards attained'.

His son Lieutenant-Colonel **Robert Kearsley DAWSON, R.E. (1798-1861)** worked on the Scottish and Irish Surveys and superintended the government survey of cities and boroughs for the first Reform Bill. He kept a detailed journal in Scotland, where he was accompanied by A.W. Robe (q.v.).

DAWSON, William

A painter of rather primitive landscapes and town scenes who was working in Exeter from the 1830s until at least 1864. Railway bridges were a speciality.

Examples: Exeter Mus.

DAY, Charles William - 1859 (Portsea)

A miniaturist and painter in oil and

watercolour, who won a prize at the S.S. in 1815, and exhibited landscapes and portraits between 1821 and 1859. In 1854 he was living or staying at Deal, but for the most part he gave London addresses. He travelled extensively, visiting the West Indies, Florence, and Egypt in the 1830s, and he may have served in the navy. It is possible that he was a son of Charles Day of Bibis Hall, Southampton, and if so he was a member of a distinguished and extensive naval family.

Published: *The Art of Miniature Painting*, 1852. *Five Years Residence in the West Indies*, 1852.

Examples: B.M.

DAY, William   1764 (London) - 1807

An amateur landscape painter, geologist and mineralogist who worked as a linen draper in London until about 1804, when he inherited a Sussex estate. He made a number of sketching tours with his friend J. Webber (q.v.), including visits to Derbyshire in 1789 and to North Wales in 1791. He exhibited at the R.A. from 1782 to 1801. He was self taught, but his style was greatly influenced by Webber, whose practice of making detailed pencil drawings on the spot, and colouring them later, he followed. His earlier rather dull colours became increasingly delicate and subtle. His finest works are those in which his passion for geology shows itself in craggy mountains and rocks. His latest recorded works, dated 1805, are mainly in pen or pencil and wash and taken from Hampshire, Sussex and the Isle of Wight.

Examples: B.M.; Derby A.G.

Bibliography: *Connoisseur*, CLXXIV, 1970.

DAY, William Cave
1862 (Dewsbury) - 1924

A genre and landscape painter in oil and watercolour who studied in Paris and at Herkomer's school at Bushey. He lived in Harrogate, painting locally, and later in Cornwall. He was elected to the R.B.A. in 1903.

DAYES, Edward
1763 (London) - 1804 (London)

Dayes studied printmaking under William Pether, the mezzotinter, and produced prints, miniatures, oil paintings and book illustrations as well as his better known watercolours. He entered the R.A. Schools in 1780, and exhibited at the R.A. from 1786 until his suicide. He also exhibited at the Society of Artists, and was appointed Designer to the Duke of York. He had a number of pupils and apprentices, including Girtin (q.v.), whom he is supposed to have had gaoled. He was largely employed as a topographer, and travelled throughout Britain. After 1790 he visited the northern counties on a number of occasions, and some of his best works are of northern subjects. He was also employed in working up, or redrawing, the sketches of lesser men and amateurs such as J. Moore (q.v.).

DAYES, Edward (1763-1804)
Lympne Castle, Kent. *Signed and dated 1791 on the mount and inscribed on the reverse, pencil and watercolour, 5½in. x 8½in.*

DAYES, Edward (1763-1804)
The Royal Exchange, London. *Watercolour and pencil on card, signed and dated 1795, also inscribed on reverse, 8in. x 6¼in.*

DEANE, William Wood (1825-1873)
Santa Maria della Salute, Venice. *Watercolour heightened with white, signed and dated 1866, 16in. x 24in.*

His style had a great influence on the young Turner and Girtin, and it is sometimes difficult to tell which of the three is the author of a particular work. He is particularly fond of producing what are, in effect, blue monochromes, in which he uses Prussian blue and brown Indian ink over light pencil. When he uses a pen, it is in the neat manner of the eighteenth century tinted drawings. Occasionally he worked on larger and more ambitious watercolours, such as his Buckingham House, St. James's Park in the V.A.M., in which the crowded figures are elegant, graceful and full of life. His purely topographical drawings tend to be rather more woolly in effect.
Published: *Instructions for Drawing and Colouring Landscape*, 1805. *Professional Sketches of Modern Artists*, 1805. *The Works of the late E.D.*, 1805.
Examples: B.M.; V.A.M.; Haworth A.G., Accrington; Blackburn A.G.; Cartwright Hall, Bradford; Brighton A.G.; Ferens A.G., Hull; Fitzwilliam; Greenwich; Leeds City A.G.; Leicestershire A.G.; City A.G., Manchester; Whitworth Gall., Manchester; Newport A.G.; Nottingham Univ.; N.G., Scotland; Stalybridge A.G.; Ulster Mus.; Nat. Lib. Wales.
Bibliography: V.A.M. MSS., documents including a work diary, 1798-1801. O.W.S. Club, XXXIX; LXII, 1987.

DEACON, Augustus Oakley
1819 (London) - 1899
An art teacher in Derby who helped to establish the School of Art, and taught privately. He later moved to the South Coast to devote himself to his own painting of landscapes and churches, but shortly afterwards went blind.

Published: *Elements of Perspective Drawing*, 1841.
Examples: Derby A.G.; Derby Borough Lib.

DEACON, James c.1728 - 1750 (London)
A miniature and portrait painter in colour and grey wash. He died of gaol fever while attending the Old Bailey as a witness. This outbreak, which claimed at least one judge, was known as the 'Black Assizes'.
Examples: B.M.

DEAKIN, Peter 1830 - 1899
A landscape painter in oil and watercolour who lived in Birmingham and Hampstead. He exhibited from 1855 to 1879 and was an unsuccessful candidate for the N.W.S. in 1868 and 1873 and for the O.W.S. during the '70s. He was a sketching companion, and later executor, of his friend Cox, whose manner he followed.
His wife **Jane DEAKIN** also painted watercolours, exhibiting between 1861 and 1884. She was a member of the Society of Female Artists.
Examples: V.A.M.

DEALY, Jane Mary –
see **LEWIS, Jane Mary, Lady**

DEAN, Frank 1865 (Headingley) - 1947
A painter of landscape and genre subjects who studied at the Slade and from 1882 to 1886 in Paris. He returned to Leeds in 1887. He also painted in India and Ireland, and visited Egypt in 1894 and Switzerland in 1912.
An exhibition of his views of Northern and Central India was held at the Fine Art Society in 1910.

Bibliography: *Studio*, XXXIX, 1907; XLIX, 1910. *The Year's Art*, 1913.

DEANE, Dennis Wood 1820 -
Elder brother of W.W. Deane (q.v.), he painted scenes from Spanish and Italian history and from Shakespeare. He entered the R.A. Schools in 1837, and exhibited at the R.A. from 1841 to 1868.
Bibliography: *A.J.*, 1859; 1860.

DEANE, John Wood
A merchant seaman who was present at the surrender of the Cape of Good Hope in 1803. He became a cashier in the Bank of England. A coloured etching from his sketch of the surrender was published in June 1805. He was an accomplished amateur watercolourist.
His wife was from Barnstaple, Devon, was named Glasse, and also painted. Two of their sons are separately noticed.

DEANE, William Wood, O.W.S.
1825 (Islington) - 1873 (Hampstead)
The third son of J.W. Deane (q.v.) he was articled to Herbert Williams, an architect, in 1842, entered the R.A. Schools in 1844, and became an Associate of the R.I.B.A. in 1848. He travelled on the Continent, mostly in Italy, with his brother Dennis from 1850 to 1852 and continued to practise as an architect and architectural draughtsman until about 1856, then gradually turning to painting. He made sketching tours in Normandy in 1856, Belgium in 1857, and to Whitby in 1859 and Cumberland in 1860. He became an Associate and Member of the N.W.S. in 1862 and 1867 and transferred to the O.W.S. in June, 1870. He continued to visit the Continent, concentrating on France, Spain, which he visited in 1866 with F.W. Topham (q.v.), and Italy. He married the sister of the architect George Aitchison, A.R.A. He was noted for catching the atmosphere of the countries which he painted, and his Venetian scenes have been compared to those of J. Holland and even Turner. However, he could be overlavish in the use of bodycolour.
Examples: B.M.; V.A.M.; Wakefield A.G.
Bibliography: *A.J.*, March, 1873.

DE BREANSKI, Alfred
1852 - 1928 (Greenwich)
A landscape painter in oil and watercolour who lived in Greenwich. He studied at St Martin's and in Paris with Whistler, and specialised in Welsh and Highland scenes. He also painted on the Thames, exhibiting from 1869.
His son **Alfred Fontville DE BREANSKI** (1877-1955) exhibited a view of Fiesole at the R.A. in 1904. He was mostly an oil painter, producing flower pieces and landscapes in his father's manner. He sometimes called himself 'Alfred Fontville' and at others 'Gustave Courtier'.

DE BREANSKI, Gustave
c.1856 - 1898
Probably the brother of A. de Breanski, whose style and subject matter he echoed. He exhibited from 1877 to 1892, and also painted marine subjects.

DE CORT, Henry Francis (Hendrik Frans)
1742 (Antwerp) - 1810 (London)
After studying in Antwerp under W. Herreyns and H.J. Antonissen, he was in Paris from about 1780 to 1788, moving to England in the following year. He travelled widely in England, especially the West, and exhibited in London from 1790.

He was a landscape painter specialising in views of towns. He produced many brown wash drawings, and among his pupils was G.H. Harlow (q.v.).
Examples: Glynn Vivian A.G., Swansea.

DE FLEURY, James Vivian
A landscape and marine painter who was working in London and exhibited between 1847 and 1868. He travelled in Brittany, Switzerland and Northern Italy, where he made a speciality of Venetian views which are cool and competent. He also painted in Kent and Guernsey, and he moved from Fulham to Notting Hill.
Bibliography: A.J., 1860.

DE GREY, Amabel, Countess, née Yorke
1750 - 1833
The daughter of the Earl of Hardwicke, she married Viscount Polwarth (1750-1781) in 1772. Her mother was Marchioness Grey and Baroness Lucas in her own right as heiress to the last non-Royal Duke of Kent, and in 1797 Lady Polwarth inherited the Lucas barony and was created Countess de Grey. She was a good landscape painter and produced engravings from her drawings.

Her great-niece and successor, **Anne Florence, Baroness LUCAS (1806 - 1880 Westminster)** drew classical subjects in brown wash, really rather well. She was the daughter of the 2nd Earl de Grey, and married the 6th Earl Cowper in 1833.

D'EGVILLE, James T   Hervé
1806 - 1880 (London)
The son of a ballet master settled in London, he entered the R.A. Schools in 1823 and was a pupil of A. Pugin (q.v.). He exhibited English and Continental landscapes from 1826, was in Rome for some years about 1840, and was elected N.W.S. in 1848. With F.T. Rochard (q.v.) he prepared the French versions of their exhibition catalogues. He was a successful drawing master, H.B. Brabazon (q.v.) being among his pupils.
Examples: V.A.M.

DE LA COUR, F   J
An Irish painter who was working in a sub-

DE CORT, Henry Francis (1742-1810)
Stourhead. *Signed and inscribed on the reverse, pencil and brown washes, 27in. x 19¼in.*

Nicholson manner in about 1830 around Cork.
In 1818 a **B. DE LA COUR (b.c.1795)** entered the R.A. Schools, and by 1822 he was painting portraits in London and the manner of A. Buck (q.v.). In 1825 and 1830 he signed clean and competent views of houses belonging to the Benson family in London and Kent.
Examples: B.M.; V.A.M.

DELACOUR, William
c.1700 - 1768 (Edinburgh)
A Frenchman who was appointed the first drawing master at the Board of Manufacturers' School in Edinburgh in 1760. He painted landscapes and portraits and did decorative work. His eight annual *Books of Ornament* established him as one of the foremost Rococo furniture designers of the day. He had moved from London, where in 1745 he advertised as teaching 'Ladies and Gentlemen to paint in Crayons and Watercolours', to Dublin, and then to Edinburgh in 1757. There he died of 'old age'.
Published: *Book of Ornament,* 8 vols., 1741-9.

Bibliography: *The Scottish Bookman,* I, v, 1936. *Country Life,* 24 May 1962. *Bulletin* of the Sc. Georgian Soc. 1972, i.

DE LACY, Charles John
c.1860 (Sunderland) - 1936 (Cheam)
A marine painter in the manner of Wyllie, who was working from 1885. He was the son of a painter, music teacher and photographer, and he trained as an engineer and served in the army and navy before turning to art. He was an illustrator for *I.L.N.* and other magazines.
Illustrated: A.O. Cooke: *A Book about Ships,* 1914. J.S. Margerison: *Our Wonderful Navy,* 1919.

DELAMERE, Henrietta Elizabeth, Lady, née Williams Wynn   - 1852
The youngest daughter of Sir W. Williams Wynn (q.v.), she was presumably a pupil of P. Sandby (q.v.), and she painted landscapes and figures. In 1810 she married Thomas Cholmondley of Vale Royal, Chester (1767-1865), who was created Lord Delamere in 1821.

DELAMOTTE, William Alfred (1775-1863)
Bristol. *Signed and dated 1800, watercolour, approx. 14in. x 20in.*

DE LA MOTTE, Edward
1817 - 1896 (Farnham)
Presumably a son or nephew of W. Delamotte (q.v.), he taught drawing at Harrow from 1870 to 1880 and thereafter at Sandhurst.

DELAMOTTE, Philip Henry
1822 - 1889 (Bromley, Kent)
The son of W.A. Delamotte (q.v.) he was a very active photographer from 1848 or even earlier, as well as an artist working much in his father's manner. He was Professor at King's College London from 1855 to 1879 and exhibited at the R.A. from 1861 to 1876.
Published: *The Art of Sketching from Nature*, 1871. *Drawing Copies*, 1872. *Trees*, 1886. &c.
Illustrated: C.H. Hartshorne: *A Guide to Alnwick Castle*, 1865. Sir H. Lyle: *A History of Eton College*, 1875. G. White: *The Natural History of Selborne*, 1875. M.O. Oliphant: *The Makers of Florence*, 1876.
Examples: B.M.

DELAMOTTE, William Alfred
1775 (Weymouth) - 1863 (Oxford)
A drawing master and landscapist, Delamotte won the patronage of George III when a boy at Weymouth, and he was placed under B. West (q.v.) and at the R.A. Schools in 1794 at the King's instigation.

His career was largely spent in Oxford, where he inherited Malchair's drawing practice, and in the Thames Valley. In 1803 he was appointed drawing master at the R.M.A., Great Marlow. In 1805 he was one of the first Associates elected to the O.W.S., but retired after three years. He seems to have visited Paris in 1802, and often returned to the Continent after 1819. Although his earliest works are sometimes said to be close to those of Girtin, his style shows very little change or development throughout his long life. His drawings show the conscientious handling of a drawing master, with careful outlinings in soft pencil or pen, and thin, even washes of gentle colour. They are often fairly exactly inscribed and dated. His remaining works were sold at Sotheby's, May 1864.

His brother **George Orleans DE LA MOTTE** was also a landscape painter, and taught at Sandhurst and Reading.
Published: *Thirty etchings of rural subjects*, 1816. *Illustrations of Virginia Water*, 1828. *Original views of Oxford*, 1843. *An Historical Sketch...Hospital of St. Bartholomew*, 1844.
Illustrated: W.H. Ainsworth: *Windsor Castle*, 1843. G.T. Fisher: *Smokers and Smoking*, 1845.
Examples: B.M.; V.A.M.; Ashmolean; Cartwright Hall, Bradford; Brighton A.G.; Canterbury Cathedral Lib.; Fitzwilliam: Greenwich; Reading A.G.; Ulster Mus.; Weymouth Lib.

DELL, John Henry
1830 - 1888 (Kingston)
A painter of figures, cows and landscapes in oil and watercolour. His work tends to be small and detailed. He lived in London and later at New Malden, Surrey.

His sister **Etheline E. DELL** painted similar subjects and unsuccessful sirens between the 1850s and 1890s.
Bibliography: *The Year's Art*, 1889.

DELL, Etheline E. (fl.1850s-1890s)
'A Surrey Cornfield.'. *Pencil and coloured washes, signed, 8½in. x 9⅝in.*

DE LOUTHERBOURG, Philip James (1740-1812)
Bolney, Sussex. *Signed, pen and ink and watercolour, 10⅜in. x 16⅞in.*

DE LOUTHERBOURG, Philip James, R.A.
1740 (Strasburg) - 1812 (Chiswick)
The son of a miniature painter, he studied at Strasburg and Paris under Vanloo and Casanova, being elected to the Académie Royale in 1767. He travelled in Switzerland, Germany and Italy, coming to England in 1771. He worked for Garrick at Drury Lane and Covent Garden until 1785. He exhibited at the R.A. from 1772, being elected A.R.A. in 1780 and R.A. in 1781. In 1782 he visited Switzerland and in 1793 he and Gillray accompanied the Duke of York's Netherland expedition. In his later years at Chiswick he became a mystic and faith healer.

As an oil painter, he specialised in battle pictures and many of his drawings and watercolours are sketches for these. He also made theatrical portraits, marine drawings in wash, 'banditti' subjects, which are reminiscent of Mortimer, and rather weak topographical watercolours. A number of drawings attributed to him are, in fact, by Gillray, dating from their joint commissions. He was the painter and proprietor of the 'Eidophusikon', a Panorama in which theatrical lighting and gauze veils gave the illusion of movement and atmospheric effects.
Examples: B.M.; V.A.M.; Fitzwilliam; Greenwich; Nat. Lib. Wales.

DENHAM, John Charles
The Treasurer of Girtin and Francia's sketching club, 'The Brothers', which met for the first time on 20 May 1799, and an honorary exhibitor at the R.A. from 1796 to 1858. He was a friend of Constable, and his work can approach that of C. Fielding (q.v.). He lived in Chelsea, where his wife, a daughter of Sir Thomas Bell, died in 1849.
Examples: Soane Mus.

DENNING, Stephen Poyntz
1795   - 1864 (Dulwich)
A portrait painter who was a pupil of the miniaturist J. Wright. He was Curator of the Dulwich Museum from 1821 and exhibited at the R.A. from 1814 to 1852. In that year a Rev. S.P. Denning was appointed Head Master of Worcester Cathedral School. They were presumably not identical, since there is no mention of taking the cloth in the *Athenaeum* obituary notice, which describes Denning as 'an able watercolour painter and a very skillful copyist'.
Examples: N.P.G.; Fitzwilliam.
Bibliography: *A.J.*, 1864. Athenaeum, 1864.

DENNISTOUN, William
1838   - 1884 (Venice)
A landscape and architectural painter in oil and watercolour who trained as an architect, was first President of the Glasgow Art Club in 1867 and exhibited in London from 1880. He settled in Italy and was in Capri in 1878.
Examples: Glasgow A.G.

DENYER, Alfred
A painter of river landscapes, especially around Bedford where he lived, and views of Lincoln. He exhibited at Suffolk Street between 1882 and 1894 and also painted in Somerset and Sussex.

DENYER, Edwin Ely
c.1840   - p.1905
A landscape painter who was head of the Hartlepool School of Art until 1905.
Examples: Gray A.G., Hartlepool.

DERBY, Alfred Thomas
1821 (London) - 1873 (London)
He was educated in Hampstead and studied at the R.A. Schools from 1837, beginning his career as a portrait painter and illustrator of Scott. Later he helped his father W. Derby (q.v.) to make watercolour copies and thereafter concentrated on portraits and figure subjects in watercolour. He exhibited from 1839 to 1872. His remaining works were sold at Christie's, 23 February 1874.
Examples: V.A.M.; N.G., Scotland.

DERBY, William
1786 (Birmingham) - 1847 (London)
A copyist who learnt drawing from J. Barber (q.v.) and came to London in 1808. He worked as a portrait painter and miniaturist as well as copying pictures until 1825, when he took over the drawing for Lodge's *Portraits of Illustrious Personages of Great Britain* from W. Hilton, R.A. (q.v.). This was completed in 1834. He was partially paralysed in 1838 and thereafter was assisted by his son, A.T. Derby (q.v.). As well as copying from Landseer and

DETMOLD, Edward Julius (1883-1957)
Gurnard and Pike. *Watercolour, 12in. x 20½in.*

older masters he produced still lifes and painted in oil. He exhibited from 1811 to 1842. In his copies he catches the spirit of the originals as well as providing faithful reproductions.
Examples: B.M.; V.A.M.; Greenwich.

DE ROS, Charlotte, Lady
                    1769   - 1831
The daughter of the Hon. Robert Boyle-Walsingham, she married Lord Henry Fitzgerald, third son of the 1st Duke of Leinster (and elder brother of Lord Edward). In 1806 she inherited the barony of de Ros and took the name. She produced landscape and architectural drawings, and in 1786 she decorated a room in her house at Thames Ditton in black Japanwork.

DE SATUR, Edmund Ribbon Byrne
  see **BYRNE DE SATUR, Edmond Ribton**

DE TABLEY, Sir John Fleming Leicester, Bt., 1st Lord 1762 (Tabley House, Cheshire) -
                    1827 (Tabley House, Cheshire)
A pupil of Marras, T. Vivares (q.v.) and P. Sandby (q.v.), Leicester was educated at Trinity, Cambridge. From 1784 he travelled in France and Italy, sketching with Sir R.C. Hoare (q.v.). On his return he built up a fine collection of British art, which was open to the public at his London house from 1818. In 1805-6 he helped to found the B.I. He was M.P. for Yarmouth, Isle of Wight, in 1791, for Heytesbury, Wiltshire, in 1796 and for Stockbridge, Hampshire, in 1807. He was a friend of George IV (q.v.), W.R. Fawkes and other patrons. He was created Lord de Tabley in 1826.

As well as his watercolour sketches, he made lithographs and occasionally painted in oil.

DE TESSIER, Isabelle Emilie
            1851 (Paris) -
An actress and humorous · illustrator who worked under a number of *noms d' artistes* including 'Marie Duval' and 'The Princess of Hesse-Schartzbourg'. She worked for several English magazines including *Judy* from 1869 when it was taken over by her husband, Charles H. Ross. She took on the drawing of

Ross's character 'Ally Sloper' both in *Judy* and in a series of comic strip books. When *Ally Sloper's Half-Holiday* was founded as a penny weekly in 1884, W.G. Baxter (q.v.) took over the illustration. For a time she was the only comic draughtswoman in Europe.

DETMOLD, Charles Maurice
            1883 (Putney) - 1908 (Ditchling)
Twin brother of **Edward Julius DETMOLD (1883-1957),** with whom he worked closely. They studied in the Zoological Gardens and

DEVIS, Anthony (1729-1817)
Landscape with men fishing. *Pencil and wash, 8in. x 5¼in.*

exhibited at the R.A. from their fourteenth year. They worked together illustrating books of fish and birds and producing drawings and etchings.

A joint exhibition of their work was held at the Fine Art Society in 1900.

Illustrated: R. Kipling: *The Jungle Book*, 1903. &c.

Examples: B.M.; V.A.M.; Fitzwilliam.

Bibliography: *The Artist Engraver*, 1904. *Studio*, XXX, 1904; XXXIII, 1905; XXXVIII, 1906; LI, 1911; LVII, 1913. A.J., 1908. *Die Graph. Kunste*, XXXIII, 1916.

DEVIS, Anthony
1729 (Preston, Lancashire) - 1817 (Albury, nr. Guildford)

The younger half-brother of **Arthur DEVIS (1712 Preston - 1787 Brighton)** the portrait and landscape painter, he was working in London in the early 1740s, although he later returned to Preston for a time. He exhibited at the R.A. and the Free Society between 1761 and 1781 and then retired from professional practice. From 1780 until his death he lived at Albury House near Guildford. He may have visited Italy in 1783-4 with William Assheton of Cuerdale Hall (q.v.), who seems to have been one of his pupils. He also travelled fairly extensively in Britain, probably visiting Scotland early in his career and returning often to the Lakes, Yorkshire and Glamorgan. He may have made a number of country house views in 1783 and 1784 for Wedgwood's Russian Service. His most easily recognisable mannerism is his representation of leaves by a series of banana-like loops. His sheep, of which he was fond, are also characteristic with their long, sticklike legs. He used a number of media, even bodycolour, but most frequently

DEVIS, Anthony (1729-1817)
Distant View of Dover. *Pen and grey ink and grey wash, 14½in. x 20½in.*

employed pen and grey-blue washes.

On the whole, his earlier drawings are the stronger and more imaginative; in his middle years they show Italian influence with strong shadows of Indian ink; towards the end they are pretty, but weaker and often circular in shape.

He is sometimes confused with his nephew **Thomas Anthony DEVIS (1757 London - 1810)**, who won a silver medal at the R.A. Schools in 1778, and the work of a nephew-in-law, R. Marris (q.v.), is also very close to his in style.

Examples: B.M.; V.A.M.; Aberdeen A.G.; Ashmolean; Grundy A.G.; Blackpool; Dudley A.G.; Towner Gallery, Eastbourne; Fitzwilliam; Abbot Hall A.G., Kendal; Leeds City A.G.; Leicestershire A.G.; City A.G., Manchester; Newport A.G.; Castle Mus., Norwich; Ulster Mus.; York A.G.

Bibliography: S.H. Pavière: *The Devis Family of Painters*, 1950. Walpole Society, XXV, 1937. Harris A.G., Preston: Exhibition Cat., 1937; 1956.

DEVOTO, John

A 'Frenchman of Italian parents', he was a scene painter at a number of London theatres including Lincoln's Inn Fields and Goodman's Fields from about 1719. His drawings, which are often brightly coloured and spirited, include designs for wall decorations and cartouches as well as stage settings. He was still active in 1776, and also engraved plates for books such as F. Tolson: *Hermathenae*, c.1740.

Examples: B.M.

See Colour Plate

DE WESSELOW, Lieutenant Francis Guillemand Simkinson
1819 - 1906

As a naval lieutenant he was officer in charge of the observatory at Hobart, Tasmania during the 1840s. He was an inveterate landscape painter, and was one of the artistic set around J.S. Prout (q.v.). He had returned by 1849 when he made the first of many Continental tours. He also painted extensively around the British Isles.

Examples: Tasmania A.G.

DEVOTO, John
Design for a Façade with the Royal Coat of Arms. *Pen and brown ink, grey, brown and blue washes, 6in. x 8¼in.*

DE WINT, Peter (1784-1849)
Lincoln Castle from the Cathedral. *Pencil and watercolour, 12¾in. x 19¼in.*

DE WILDE, Samuel
1751 (Holland) - 1832 (London)
Brought to England as a very young child he was baptised in London by his widowed mother, apprenticed to a Soho woodcarver and entered the R.A. Schools in 1769. His artistic career began with a series of mezzotint portraits issued under the pseudonym of 'Paul' from about 1770. He began to exhibit at the S.A. in 1776 and the R.A. in 1782. These early works were generally portraits and 'banditti' pictures in oil. From 1795 his attention was caught by the stage and he began to produce the long series of theatrical portraits which occupied the rest of his life. These portraits are usually in soft pencil or crayon with light washes of watercolour. They are delicate and spirited. He occasionally used a reed pen. His work is usually signed with the initials 'S.D.W.' and dated.
Examples: B.M.; V.A.M.; Ashmolean; Newport A.G.; The Garrick Club.
Bibliography:Nottingham A.G.: Exhibition Cat., 1971.

DE WINT, Peter, O.W.S.
1784 (Stone, Staffordshire) - 1849 (London)
The fourth son of a Dutch-American father and a Scottish mother, he took his first lessons from the Stafford drawing master B. Rogers (q.v.), and in 1802 he was apprenticed to J.R. Smith (q.v.). A fellow apprentice was his friend and future brother-in-law W. Hilton (q.v.), who introduced him to Lincolnshire, which became his favourite sketching ground. In 1806 de Wint's indentures were cancelled and he made the acquaintance of Dr. Monro, through whom

DE WINT, Peter (1784-1849)
Still Life. *Pencil and watercolour, 14in. x 11½in.*

DE WINT, Peter (1784-1849)
Haymaking near Cookham. *Inscribed on the reverse, pencil and watercolour, 9½in. x 18⅛in.*

he came under the influence of the work of Girtin. He was also advised by John Varley, his near neighbour. In 1809 he became a student at the R.A. and the next year he married Harriet Hilton. He first exhibited at the R.A. in 1807, appeared briefly at the O.W.S. in 1810 and 1811, and finally rejoined the reorganised society in 1825. With the sole exception of a visit to Normandy in 1828, his travels were confined to England and Wales. Each summer he would stay with one of his patrons, who included the Earl of Lonsdale at Lowther Castle; the Earl of Powis; the Marquis of Ailesbury; the Clives of Oakley Park, Ludlow; the Heathcotes of Connington Castle; Mr. Cheney of Badger, Shropshire; Walter Ramsden Fawkes of Farnley Hall, Yorkshire; Mr. Champernowne of Dartington, Devon; Mr. Ellison of Sudbrooke Holme, Lincolnshire; and Colonel Greville Howard of Castle Rising, Norfolk. He also sketched in the valleys of the Trent and the Thames, where he was probably acquainted with the Havell family of Reading. Throughout his life he had many amateur pupils, whose style is very close to his own. In particular, drawings by his daughter, Helen, Mrs. Tatlock (q.v.), can be deceptively like his.

In his landscapes, chiefly of river and harvesting scenes, he is very fond of the shallow broad panorama, often enclosed by sombre masses of woodland, and he also frequently uses a St. Andrews Cross composition. The trees are built up in several layers of superimposed blues and greens becoming darker in tone. There is much brown, green and orange in his work, but this predominance may be due to fading, from which the drawings have often suffered badly. In particular, his skies are now often pink or non-existent. Although he could be rather woolly, his best is very impressive indeed. Towards the end of his life his style becomes freer, and the effect is closer to the sketchiness of his pencil drawings. He rarely, if ever, signed his works, and signatures or initials should be treated with suspicion. His remaining works were sold at Christie's, 22-28 May 1850.

Examples: B.M.; V.A.M.; Aberdeen A.G.; Ashmolean; Ferens A.G., Hull; Grundy A.G., Blackpool; Brighton A.G.; Towner Gall., Eastbourne; Fitzwilliam; Abbot Hall A.G., Kendal; Leeds City A.G.; Leicestershire A.G.; Usher A.G., Lincoln; City A.G., Manchester; Newport A.G.; Castle Mus., Norwich; Ulster Mus.; York A.G.

Bibliography: W. Armstrong: *P. de W.,* 1888. A. de Wint: *A short memoir of P. de W.,* 1900. A.P. Oppé: *The watercolours of Turner, Cox and de W.,* 1925. M. Hardie: *P. de Wint,* 1929. B.S. Long: *List of Works exhibited by P. de W. AJ.,* 1898. *Studio,* 1903; 1917; 1919; 1922. O.W.S. Club I,1923. *Connoisseur,* XCIII, 1934. Usher A.G., Lincoln: Catalogues, 1937; 1942; 1947. *Apollo,* XXVI, 1937. *Antique Collector,* April, 1949. *Country Life,* 1 July 1949. *Antique Collecting,* May 1999.

See Colour Plate

DE WINT, Peter (1784-1849)
A Distant View of Ripon. *Watercolour, 8in. x11¾in.*

DIBDIN, Thomas Richard Colman (1810-1893)
Arras. *Signed, inscribed and dated 1872, watercolour, 21in. x 30in.*

DIBDIN, Charles

An amateur landscape painter who worked in the Lake District. It is probable that this artist is the dramatist and songwriter Charles Dibdin (1745 Southampton - 1814 London) who had three illegitimate sons, one of whom was the father of T.R.C. Dibdin (q.v.).

Another of his grandsons, **Henry Edward DIBDIN (1813-1866),** was not only a fine musician, but also a skilled artist and illuminator, and he exhibited at the R.S.A. between 1843 and 1854.
Examples: V.A.M.

DIBDIN, Thomas Richard Colman
1810 (Betchworth, Surrey) - 1893 (London)

A painter of landscapes and town scenes, he was the grandson of C. Dibdin (q.v.), the actor and dramatist. He worked as a clerk in the G.P.O. for a time and exhibited from 1831. His subjects, which are sometimes in the middle manner of W. Callow (q.v.), are often found in the towns of Northern France, Belgium and Germany. In 1851 he exhibited a panorama of Indian scenes, based on other peoples' sketches, and he also produced a London series. These are like W.H. Hunt's work of the1820s.
Published: *A Guide to Water-Colour Painting,* 1859.
Examples: B.M.; V.A.M.; Ashmolean; Gloucester City A.G.; Hove Lib.; Leicestershire A.G.; Nottingham Univ.; Portsmouth City Mus.; Sydney A.G.

DICKINS, Lady Frances Elizabeth
– *see* COMPTON, Lady Frances Elizabeth

DICKINSON, Arthur

A landscape painter working around 1880. His subjects are in the South of England, and his prices were very modest.

DICKINSON, John Reed

A London painter of landscapes, genre and Breton peasant subjects. He exhibited from 1870 to 1881, and between 1869 and 1873 he was unsuccessful several times as a candidate for the N.W.S. He was perhaps a son of W.R. Dickinson (q.v.).

DIBDIN, Thomas Richard Colman (1810-1893)
Village street with figures. *Watercolour and bodycolour, signed and dated 1863.*

DICKINSON, Lowes Cato
1819 (Kilburn) - 1908 (Hanwell)

The son of Joseph Dickinson, a London lithograph publisher, with whom he worked. With the help of Sir R.M. Laffan he spent three years in Italy and Sicily from 1850. Later he taught drawing at the Working Men's College with Rossetti and Ruskin and, in 1860, helped to found the Artists' Rifle Corps. He exhibited portraits, including one of Queen Victoria, from 1848.

Published: *Letters from Italy,* 1850-1853, 1914.
Examples: B.M.; V.A.M.; Fitzwilliam.

DICKINSON, William Robert

A landscape and rustic painter who lived in London and was active from about 1836 to 1882. Many of his subjects are Breton. He may have been the father of J.R. Dickinson (q.v.).

DICKSEE, Sir Francis Bernard, 'Frank', P.R.A., R.I. 1853 (London) - 1928 (London)

The son of the genre and portrait painter **Thomas Francis DICKSEE (1819-1895)**, he studied at the R.A. Schools from 1870 to 1875 where he was influenced by Leighton and Millais. He began his career as a book and periodical illustrator, but soon became a fashionable portraitist. He was elected A.R.A. in 1881, R.A. in 1891, and P.R.A. in 1924, and he was knighted in the following year. He was a Trustee of the B.M. and N.P.G.

Illustrated: H. Longfellow: *Evangeline,* 1882.
Examples: B.M.; V.A.M.; City A.G., Manchester; Newport A.G.; Royal Shakespeare Theatre, Stratford.
Bibliography: E.R. Dibdin: *F.D.,* 1905. *Mag. of Art,* 1887. *A.J.,* 1897; 1901; 1902; 1904; 1905; 1906; 1908; 1909. *Studio,* XXIII, 1901. *Art Annual,* Christmas No., 1905. *Country Life,* 31 Jan. 1985.

DIGHTON, Denis
1792 (London) - 1827 (St. Servan, Brittany)

A son of Robert Dighton (q.v.), he studied at the R.A. Schools. He won the patronage of the Prince of Wales, which gained him a commission in the 90th Regiment. He resigned on his marriage, and in 1815 was appointed Military Draughtsman to the Prince, sometimes making professional tours abroad. He exhibited at the R.A. from 1811 to 1825.

He is at his best with soldiers and uniforms and is in some ways the most serious painter of his family. His handling of watercolour is delicate and his detail accurate.

His wife **Phoebe DIGHTON, née Earl,** was a still-life painter, exhibiting from 1820 to 1835. She was appointed Flower Painter to the Queen, and until about 1830 she taught drawing in Leamington. Her work is Dutch in inspiration and is rather flat. She later married a Mr. Macintyre and was still active in 1854, but her teaching practice was taken over by J. Burgess, yr. (q.v.).

Examples: B.M.; V.A.M.; Canterbury Mus.; Nat. Army Mus.; Nottingham Univ.

DIGHTON, Richard (1795-1880)
A Shopkeeper. *Pencil and watercolour heightened with gum arabic,
9⅞in. x 6⅝in.*

DIGHTON, Richard
1795 (London) - 1880 (London)

A son of Robert Dighton (q.v.), he specialised in rather stilted semi-caricature full or three-quarter length portraits in profile. They are often of racing and hunting personalities. He worked in Worcester, Cheltenham, Stoke and London.

Another brother, **Joshua DIGHTON,** also produced sporting caricatures from the 1820s to the 1840s.

Richard's son **Joshua DIGHTON, II (1831 Worcester - 1908 Kingston)** was active from about 1860. He also specialised in sportsmen, and he lived in Hammersmith, Merton and Wimbledon.

Examples: B.M.; N.P.G.; Ashmolean; Greenwich.
Bibliography: *Antique Collector:* Mar. 1983, (R. and J, II).

DIGHTON, Robert
1751 (London) - 1814 (London)

The son of John Dighton, a London printseller, he became a portrait painter, caricaturist, etcher and drawing master. He began to exhibit in 1769 and entered the R.A. Schools in the following year. His working life was spent in London, although his subjects include views at Brighton and elsewhere. In 1806 he was discovered to have stolen and sold a number of prints from the B.M., leaving copies in their place.

His work includes theatrical and legal portraits as well as more elaborate social satires. His figures and faces are rather stylised. His drawing and colour have been called harsh (Williams), but are always strong and accomplished and he shows a good eye for detail. He generally signed 'R. Dighton' in contrast to his son Richard, who signed in full.

DIGHTON, Robert (1751-1814)
South View of the Church of St. Pancras, Middlesex. *Inscribed, and with the address of Carington Bowles, on the reverse, pen and black ink and watercolour, 10¼in. x 15½in.*

DIGHTON, Robert (1751-1814)
Margaret Nicholson attempting to assassinate George III. *Signed and indistinctly inscribed, pen and black ink and watercolour, 10½in. x 14¼in.*

Examples: B.M.; V.A.M.; Ashmolean; Fitzwilliam; City A.G., Manchester; Newport A.G.; N.G., Scotland.
Bibliography: D.Rose: *Life, Times and Recorded Works...*, 1981. *Apollo,* XIV, 1931. *Print Collectors' Quarterly,* XIII, i and ii. Sotheby's: Sale Cat., 23 Feb. 1978.

DIGHTON, Robert, Yr.
c.1786   - 1865 (Southsea)
The eldest son of Robert Dighton (q.v.), he joined the London Volunteers and the Norfolk Militia, before fighting in the Peninsula and being wounded at Bayonne with the 38th Regiment. He retired on half-pay in 1816, but rejoined in 1829 and served with the 16th Lancers in India. A number of his Peninsular drawings were worked up by his brother Denis, but he appears not to have painted after 1815.

DIGHTON, William Edward
1822   - 1853 (Hampstead)
A landscape painter who studied under W.J. Müller (q.v.) in Bristol and F. Goodall (q.v.) in London and exhibited from 1845. He moved to London from Bristol with Müller in 1839, and made an extended tour of Egypt and Palestine, from which he returned only in the year of his death. He was Trustee of the Clipstone Street Society.
There is a feeling of de Wint in much of his work, and like E.T. Daniell (q.v.) he favoured panoramic views.
Examples: B.M.; V.A.M.

DILLON, Frank, R.I.
1823 (London) - 1909 (London)
A landscape painter and traveller who was a pupil of J. Holland (q.v.) and studied at the R.A. Schools. After some topographical work including two plates for *Apsley House and Walmer Castle*, he travelled extensively especially in Egypt, where he was sharing a studio with Lundgren and Boyce in 1861. In 1865 he was in Ravenna, again with Lundgren. He was a friend of Mazzini, and of Hungarian revolutionaries. He also visited Spain, Madeira and Japan. He was elected R.I. in 1882. An exhibition of his Japanese work was held by Messrs. Agnew in 1877, and his remaining works were sold at Christie's, 21 January 1911.
His early work is tight and precise in the manner of T.S. Boys (q.v.). Later, via that of T.M. Richardson, Yr. (q.v.), his style becomes very free.
Published: *Sketches in the Island of Madeira*, 1850.
Examples: V.A.M.
Bibliography: *A.J.,* 1909.

DINGLE, Thomas, Yr.
The son of a landscape painter, he too painted landscapes with sheep and cattle, around 1880.

DITCHFIELD, Arthur
1842 (London) - 1888

DILLON, Frank (1823-1909)
Apsley House. *Signed, pencil and watercolour, 10in. x 15in.*

A landscape painter in oil and watercolour who studied at Leigh's and the R.A. Schools which he entered in 1861. He exhibited from 1864 to 1886 and his subjects are taken from Spain, Italy and North Africa as well as the Thames and Cornwall.
Examples: V.A.M.
Bibliography: *A.J.*, 1908. Stoke-on-Trent A.G., Exhibition Cat., 1989.

DIXEY, Frederick Charles
- p.1920
A painter of marine and Thames subjects in oil and watercolour who was working from 1877 to 1891.
Examples: Richmond Lib.

DIXON, Charles Edward, R.I.
1872 (Goring) - 1934 (Itchenor, Sussex)
The son of **Alfred DIXON**, a figure painter working from the 1860s to the 1890s, he became a marine painter. He first exhibited at the R.A. at the age of sixteen and in 1900 was elected R.I. He worked as an illustrator for *The Graphic* and other periodicals and was a member of the Langham Sketching Club. Himself a keen yachtsman, he generally painted contemporary shipping subjects, although occasionally he attempted vast watercolours of naval history. His style is a blend of freedom and accuracy. If at times he could be crude, he was never as crude as his modern faker or fakers.
Illustrated: C.N. Robinson: *Britannia's Bulwarks*, 1901.
Examples: V.A.M.; Aberdeen A.G.; Greenwich;

Grundy A.G., Blackpool; Newport A.G.; Portsmouth City Mus.
Bibliography: *Antique Collector*, Mar. 1990.

DIXON, George Pelham
1859 (Tynemouth) - 1898 (S. Shields)
A self-taught landscape and marine painter who was the son of a librarian. He became a headmaster at Leeds and in Derbyshire, and he taught art privately. His views are often vignettes.
Examples: S. Shields A.G.

DIXON, Grace Charlotte, Mrs., née Cowell

A copyist and painter of portraits, religious and historical subjects, sometimes on ivory. She was active from about 1851 to 1875. In 1852 she married **F.H. DIXON**, who painted similar subjects, and they lived in London and Leamington.

DIXON, John
In the Ashmolean are landscapes with the signature 'J.Dixon' which are dramatically lit and have Rowlandson figures. It might be possible to identify the artist with the **John DIXON** who was clerk and draughtsman to the architect James Wyatt from about 1772 to 1796, or with his nephew **Joseph DIXON**.

DIXON, John, II
1835 (Newcastle) - 1891 (London)
A painter of marine and coastal subjects who exhibited between 1879 and 1887. He was a civil engineer and ironmaster, and he moved to London in 1867 where he enjoyed considerable success. He was responsible for the transhipping of Cleopatra's Needle from Alexandria. Late in life he went to South Africa, but he returned to die in Croydon.

DIXON, John Turnbull
1844 (Rothbury) - p.1921
A draper who worked in the family business at Rothbury. He made line drawings to illustrate his brother's books, and he also painted marine and landscape subjects in oil and watercolour.
Illustrated: D.D. Dixon: *The Vale of Whittingham;* D.D. Dixon: *Upper Coquetdale.*
Examples: Cragside, Rothbury.

DIXON, Otto Murray 1885 -1917
An excellent painter of birds and wildlife in the Thorburn mould.

DIXON, Percy, R.I. 1862 - 1924
A landscape painter who lived in London and later Bournemouth. He was elected R.I. in

DIXON, Charles Edward (1872-1934)
The Liner she's a Lady. *Signed and dated 1920, watercolour, 27in. x 53in.*

DIXON, Robert (1780-1815)
Outside a Country Inn. *Pen and ink and monochrome wash, size unknown.*

DIXON, Robert
1780 (Norwich) - 1815 (Norwich)
He was a scene painter at the Norwich Theatre as well as a teacher of drawing. For the first five years of the Norwich Exhibitions he was a regular contributor, and he was elected Vice-President in 1809. His watercolours vary greatly in style from weak imitations of J.S. Cotman or Girtin to far more impressive productions which are close to Crome. He is chiefly notable for his soft ground etchings, which are among the best prints produced by the Norwich School.
Published: *Norfolk Scenery,* 1810-1811.
Examples: B.M.; V.A.M.; Leeds City A.G.; Castle Mus., Norwich.
Bibliography: W.F. Dickes: *The Norwich School,* 1905. J. Walpole: *Art and Artists of the Norwich School,* 1997.

DIXON, Samuel   (Dublin) - 1769 (London)
The brother of John Dixon, an engraver working in Dublin and London, Samuel produced bird and flower miniatures in bas-relief which were hand-coloured in bodycolour. In 1756 he went to London, and on his return two years later he set up a textile printing business. He again lived for a short while in London from 1765, returning to Dublin in 1768, in which year he exhibited three flower pieces in watercolour at the R.D.S.
Among his assistants were Gustavus Hamilton and James Reilly, who became miniaturists.

DOBBIN, John
1815 (Darlington) - 1888
A landscape painter who travelled in Holland, France, Spain and Germany as well as working in Scotland, Yorkshire and the North-east. He exhibited at the R.A. and the S.B.A. from 1837 to 1884, and his works usually included well-drawn ancient buildings. He also painted in oil and designed mosaics.
Examples: V.A.M.; Cartwright Hall, Bradford; Darlington A.G.; Shipley A.G., Gateshead.

DOBSON, Henry John, R.S.W.
1858 (Inverleithen) - 1928
A Scottish genre painter who worked in Edinburgh and Kirkcudbright. He visited America in 1911. His work has been described as energetic and luminous.

DOBSON, John
1787 (Chirton, North Shields) -
1865 (Newcastle-upon-Tyne)
After an apprenticeship to David Stephenson, the leading Newcastle architect of the day, Dobson took lessons from J. Varley (q.v.) and set up in his home town. He made sketching tours in England and France and made stage designs. To his architectural skill are due the buildings and streets which made Newcastle one of the most beautiful towns in the North. Owing to the improving zeal of a developer and the corrupt enthusiasm of local authorities comparatively little of his work now remains. However, the Laing Art Gallery retains many of his plans – some coloured by T.M. Richardson or J.W. Carmichael (qq.v.) – as a memorial to the past splendour of the city, and the more recent barbarity of (some of) its inhabitants.
Examples: B.M.; Laing A.G., Newcastle; Soc. of Antiquaries; Warrington Mus.
Bibliography: M.J. Dobson: *A Memoir of J.D.,* 1885. *J.D. Architect and Landscape Gardener.* L. Wilkes: *J.D.,* 1980. T. Faulkner and A. Greg: *J.D., Newcastle Architect,* 1987. *Builder,* XXIII, 1865. *Newcastle Daily Journal,* 16 Jan. 1865.

DOBSON, Robert
A landscape painter in oil and watercolour who lived in Birkenhead,and who painted in Lancashire and Cheshire from the 1850s to the 1880s. He also produced scenes in the Liverpool docks.

DOBSON, William Charles Thomas, R.A.,
R.W.S.   1817 (Hamburg) -
1898 (Ventnor, Isle of Wight)
A pupil of Edward Opie, Dobson entered the R.A. Schools in 1836 and thereafter taught at the Government School of Design. He was Headmaster at the Birmingham School from 1843 to 1845, when he went to Italy. He then spent several years in Germany, where he came under the influence of the Nazarenes. He was elected A.R.A. and R.A. in 1860 and 1871 and Associate and Member of the O.W.S. in 1870 and 1875.
On his return from Germany he devoted himself to biblical subjects in oil and water-colour. His work is simple, if sentimental, and he strongly objected to the use of bodycolour.
Examples: V.A.M.
Bibliography: *A.J.,* 1859; May, 1860.

DOCHARTY, Alexander Browlie
1862 (Glasgow) - 1940
A landscape painter who specialised in Highland and Scottish coastal scenes in oil and watercolour. The latter can be very pretty indeed. He studied in Paris and exhibited at the R.A. from 1882. He lived in Kilkerran, Ayrshire, but travelled on the Continent, especially to Venice.
Examples: Glasgow A.G.
Bibliography: *Studio,* XXXI, 1904. *A.J.,* 1909.

DODD, Arthur Charles
He worked in Tunbridge Wells and exhibited between 1878 and 1890. He painted landscapes and farmyard scenes, mostly in oil. According to the family he was unrelated to the other Tunbridge Dodds.

DODD, Barrodail Robert

An engraver who signed a watercolour of Newcastle-upon-Tyne in 1825. He was also a canal and railway engineer, painted portraits and was a copyist.

DODD, Charles Tattershall
1815 (Tonbridge) - 1878 (Tunbridge Wells)

A landscape painter who exhibited from 1832. In 1837 he was appointed drawing master at Tonbridge School and he held the post until his death. As well as views and lithographs of the area, he painted in Sussex and Wales.

His son **Charles Tattershall DODD, Yr. (1861-1951)**, also drawing master at Tonbridge School, painted landscapes and architectural subjects at the end of the nineteenth century. **Joseph Tattershall DODD,** who painted in Spain, was presumably another son.
Examples: V.A.M.

DODD, Daniel

A portrait painter in oil, pastel and wash, and an illustrator, he was a member of the Free Society, with whom he exhibited from 1761 to 1780. He provided grey wash illustrations for the Bible, Harrison's series of *Novelists,* and Raymond's *History of England,* as well as making drawings of fashionable life.
Examples: B.M.

DODD, Joseph Josiah
1810 (Tonbridge) - 1894

A landscape painter and topographer who worked in Cheshire. He also produced Parisian views in about 1835. Although his work is very competent, it can have a slightly primitive air. At other times it harks back to F. Towne (q.v.). He was the brother of the elder C.T. Dodd (q.v.).
Examples: Grosvenor A.G., Chester; City A.G., Manchester.

DODGSON, George Haydock, O.W.S.
1811 (Liverpool) - 1880 (London)

He was intended for an engineer and apprenticed to George Stephenson between 1827 and 1835; however, a series of accidents and over-exertions turned him to painting. After a sketching tour of Wales, Cumberland and Yorkshire, he moved to London in 1836, making sketches of St. Paul's, the Abbey and other public buildings. By 1842 he had turned more to landscape and joined the N.W.S., from which he resigned in 1847, and he joined the O.W.S. the following February. He worked for the *Cambridge Almanack* and the *I.L.N.* In the 1850s and early 1860s he sketched on the Thames – in 1858 with Fripp and Field – and thereafter much in the Whitby area where he was friendly with the Weatherill family (q.v.). From 1875 he also visited the Gower Peninsula. His subjects have been described as being divided between *L'Allegro* and *Il Penseroso,* at least until 1860, after which they became more directly topographical. His style

DODGSON, George Haydock (1811-1880)
A Lock Gate. *Signed and dated 1861, and inscribed on the reverse, watercolour, 8¼in. x 17¾in.*

was affected by a shaking hand which led to a spotting technique in powerful colours, which he often worked on very wet paper.
Published: *Illustrations of the Scenery on the Line of the Whitby and Pickering Railway,* 1836.
Examples: B.M.; V.A.M.; Leicestershire A.G.; Maidstone Mus.
Bibliography: *A.J.,* 1880. *Athenaeum,* 1880.

DODSON, George J.

A painter of South Coast scenes who lived in Kingston-on-Thames and London. He was active at least from 1893 to 1899.

DODWELL, Edward, F.S.A.
1767 (Dublin) - 1832 (Rome)

An archaeologist and draughtsman who was educated at Trinity College, Cambridge, and who visited Greece in 1801 and 1805-6, the second time as a French prisoner on parole. He spent most of the remainder of his life in Italy. He made some four hundred, often quite large, drawings in Greece and illustrated his publications.
Published: *Alcuni Bassi rilievi della Grecia,* 1812. *A Classical and Topographical Tour through Greece,* 1819. *Views in Greece,* 1821. *Views and Descriptions of Cyclonian or Pelasgic Remains...,* 1834.

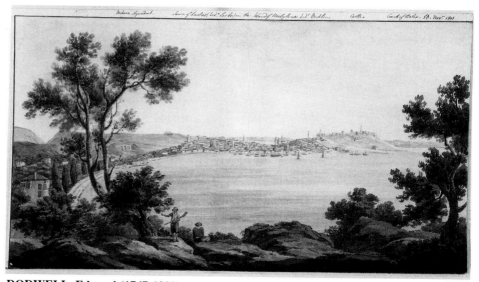

DODWELL, Edward (1767-1832)
Mitilini, on the Island of Lesbos. *Signed with initials, pedantically inscribed and dated 'Nov 1801', pencil and watercolour, 10in. x 17½in.*

DONALDSON, Andrew (1790-1846)
Crawford Castle, Arran beyond. *Pencil and watercolour heightened with white, 15½in. x 20½in.*

DOLAN, Peter
A London painter who stood unsuccessfully for the O.W.S. in 1873, and exhibited a view of Mapledurham at Brighton in 1875. He also painted costume subjects.

DOLBY, Edwin Thomas
A painter of churches who lived in London and was a candidate for the N.W.S. several times between 1850 and 1864. He was still active in the mid-1870s.
Published: *A Series of…views…during the Russian War,* 1854. *D's Sketches in the Baltic,* 1854.
Illustrated: E.H. Nolan: *Great Britain as it is,* 1859.

DOLBY, Joshua Edward Adolphus
    1811   - 1881 (London)
A landscape sketcher who worked in France, Holland, Switzerland and Italy between 1837 and 1875, as well as at Eton.

DOLLMAN, John Charles, R.W.S.
    1851 (Brighton) - 1934 (London)
A black and white artist who turned to colour, painting in watercolour and in oil, in 1901, and at the same time moved from the R.I. to the R.W.S. He lived in London and studied at South Kensington and the R.A. Schools from 1870. He painted historical genre and animal subjects. An exhibition of his works was held at the F.A.S. in January 1906.
    Ruth DOLLMAN painted weak but pretty landscapes in Sussex at the beginning of the twentieth century, and an exhibition of her works was held at the Leicester Galleries, April-May, 1904. There is a watercolour by

Charles DOLLMAN in Newport A.G.
Published: *The Legend of the Devil's Dyke,* 1868.
Illustrated: J.M. Brown: *In the days when we went Hog-Hunting,* 1891.
Examples: Glasgow A.G.; City A.G., Manchester.

DONALD, John Milne
    1817 (Nairn) - 1866 (Glasgow)
A landscape painter in oil and watercolour who was apprenticed to a Glasgow house painter. He then studied in Paris in 1840 and worked for a London picture restorer before returning to Glasgow. He exhibited in London from 1844 to1847.
Bibliography: *Portfolio,* 1887.

DONALD, Thomas William, 'Tom', R.S.W.
    1853 (Glasgow) - 1883
A landscape painter who worked in the Highlands and on the West Coast. He was a founder member of the R.S.W.

DONALDSON, Andrew
1790 (Comber, nr. Belfast) - 1846 (Glasgow)
Landscape and architectural painter in oil and watercolour who went to Glasgow and worked in a cotton mill at an early age. After an accident he turned to painting and concentrated on village scenes. He sketched in England and Ireland, and gave drawing lessons.
Examples: Glasgow A.G.

DONALDSON, Andrew Benjamin
    1840 (London) - 1919
A painter of landscapes, historical and religious subjects. He studied at the R.A.

Schools, visited Italy in 1864 and lived in London where he exhibited from 1861 to 1898, and later at Lyndhurst. He was responsible for the murals once on the staircase of the St. Pancras Station Hotel.
Examples: V.A.M.

DONALDSON, James H
A painter of still lifes and occasional landscapes who was active from about 1883 to at least 1892. He lived at Scarborough and visited Brittany.

DONALDSON, John, F.S.A.
    1737 (Edinburgh) - 1810 (Islington)
An etcher, miniaturist, caricaturist and figure painter, he was the son of a glover. He worked as a porcelain painter at Worcester and moved to London in 1762. He was a member of the Incorporated Society and exhibited from 1761 to 1791, and he was elected F.S.A. in 1771.
Published: *The Elements of Beauty,* 1780. *Poems,*1784.
Examples: B.M.

DONNE, Colonel Benjamin Donisthorpe Alsop   **1856 (London) - 1907 (Isleworth)**
The elder son of B.J.M.Donne (q.v.), he became a professional soldier and served in Jamaica in 1878, Cyprus between 1880 and 1882, and Egypt and the Sudan from 1882 to 1885, as well as India and South Africa. He was an assiduous landscape painter and also sketched in Italy, Germany, Greece and at home. He was the author of the first English book published in Cyprus. His work is bright and freely drawn, and after his return to England he painted old ships. He was also a conscientious letterwriter and keeper of diaries.
Published: *Records of the Ottoman Conquest of Cyprus,* 1885. *Colloquy and Song,* 1898.
Examples: Fitzwilliam; Army Regular Commissions Board, Westbury, Wiltshire.
Bibliography: A. Harfield (ed.): *The Life and Times of a Victorian Officer,* 1986

DONNE, Benjamin John Merifield
    1831   - 1928
A self-taught painter of landscapes, coastal and occasional classical subjects. Several exhibitions of his work, which is free and atmospheric, were held at the Dowdeswell Galleries, London, in the 1880s. He lived at Crewkerne, Somerset, and was the father of B.D.A. Donne and H.R.B. Donne (qq.v.).
    His daughter **Anna Jane Merifield DONNE (b.1855)** was also a talented watercolour painter.
Examples: B.M.; Exeter Mus.

DONNE, Colonel Henry Richard Beadon
    1860 (Crewkerne) - 1949 (Honiton)
A landscape painter like his father and brother, he was commissioned in the Norfolk Regiment and served with the 1888-9 Burma expedition,

on the North-West Frontier in 1897 and on the Tirah expedition in 1897-8. From 1907 he was Assistant Adjutant-General at Headquarters, and he was appointed C.B. in 1908. He was active until at least 1939.

DONNELLY, William A
A Dumbartonshire painter of birds, landscapes, seascapes and figure subjects who exhibited in Glasgow in the 1860s.

DONOWELL, John
An architect and a topographical and architectural draughtsman in the manner of the Maltons. He proposed to issue a series of engravings of Oxford in 1754, and eight prints were issued in the following year. He exhibited in London from 1761 to 1786. In the 1750s and 1760s he was probably working as draughtsman and clerk of the works at West Wycombe. A friend of Sir Francis Dashwood commented: 'I believe the man is honest & does to the best of his Abilities, but these I am afraid from the experience I have had of him are not very extensive'. In the 1770s and '80s he was surveyor for the Earls of Salisbury in London and at Hatfield.
Examples: B.M.
Bibliography: *Country Life*, 5 March 1948 (letters); 1 Dec. 1983.

DONTHORN, William John
1799 (Swaffham) - 1859 (Hastings)
An architect who was a pupil of Wyatville from 1817-20, and thereafter built Greek Revival houses and rectories in Norfolk. He was a member of the Norwich Society from 1815 and exhibited at the R.A. from 1817 to 1853. He was a founder of the R.I.B.A.
Examples: R.I.B.A.
Bibliography: *Ecclesiologist*, III, 1843. *Builder*, II, 1844; XVII, 1859. *Gentleman's Mag*, 1846, ii; 1859, ii. *Architectural Hist.*, XXI, 1978.

DORRELL, Edmund
1778 (Warwick) - 1857 (London)
He began exhibiting at the R.A. in 1807 and was elected A.O.W.S. in 1809, but resigned in 1812. He concentrated upon cottages, trees and river banks in the Home Counties, but also produced similar subjects from Monmouthshire and South Wales. From 1819 to 1836 he exhibited with the S.B.A., but throughout his career only eighty-four exhibits are recorded in all. He married a Miss Robson, possibly a relative of the artist. His style is pleasant but rather indefinite.
Examples: V.A.M.; Coventry Mus.; Fitzwilliam.

D'ORSAY, Count Alfred Guillaume Gabriel   1801 (Paris) - 1852 (Dieppe)
The son of a Napoleonic general and a Princess of Würtemburg, d'Orsay reluctantly entered the French Army after the Restoration. He was in England for the Coronation of George IV. In 1823 he was persuaded by the

DORRELL, Edmund (1778-1857)
Beach at Tynemouth. *Watercolour.*

Earl and Countess of Blessington to resign his commission and to join them on a tour of Italy. In Genoa he took a portrait of Byron. He briefly married the Blessington's daughter but they were almost immediately separated and in 1831 he came to England with his widowed mother-in-law. For the next twenty years he and Lady Blessington were at the centre of a brilliant social, intellectual and artistic circle, after which he found himself deeply in debt and constantly pursued by bailiffs. In 1849 he retired to Paris, where he set up a studio and was appointed Director of Fine Arts by Louis Napoleon. He was a sculptor and a painter, but is best known for his small sketches in profile of his most distinguished contemporaries.

DORRELL, Edmund (1778-1857)
A Forest Scene. *Watercolour. 8½in. x 10⅞in.*

These are excellent likenesses, usually in pen and ink or soft pencil with touches of colour, but they are a little naïve in comparison with similar works by his friends Landseer and Wilkie.
Examples: B.M.; V.A.M.
Bibliography: *A.J.*, Sept. 1852.

DOUGLAS, Allen Edmund
1835 (Clones, Co. Monaghan) - 1894 (Warrenpoint)

A doctor who was trained at Edinburgh and practised at Glasslough and for twenty-five years at Warrenpoint. He drew and painted as a hobby, and spent his holidays sketching in the Mourne Mountains. His other interests included carving, modelling and antiquarian studies.

DOUGLAS, Hon. Caroline Lucy
see SCOTT, Caroline Lucy, Lady

DOUGLAS, Rev. James, F.S.A.
1753 (London) - 1819 (Preston, Sussex)

After an adventurous career including service in the Austrian army and the Leicester Militia, he went up to Peterhouse, Cambridge, and was ordained. He was rector of Litchborough, Northamptonshire, from 1787 to 1799; of Middleton, Sussex, from 1799 to 1803; and vicar of Kenton, Suffolk, thereafter. He painted portraits in oil and miniature and is said by Henry Angelo to have been a caricaturist.
Published: *On the Urbs Rutupiae of Ptolemy*, 1780. *Travelling Anecdotes through various parts of Europe*, 1782. *A Dissertation on the Antiquity of the Earth*, 1785. *Discourses on the influence of the Christian Religion*, 1792. *Nenia Britannica; or, a Sepulchral History of Great Britain*, 1793.
Bibliography: See: H. Angelo: *Reminiscences*, 1830.

DOUGLAS, James
1858 (Dundee) - 1911 (Liff, nr. Dundee)

A landscape painter who lived and studied in Edinburgh. He exhibited at the R.I. in 1885, worked at Rothenburg, Germany between 1895 and 1897, and visited Paris in 1900. He was elected to the R.S.W. in that year but was struck off the roll in 1907, and thereafter was confined because of mental illness. He was a close friend of T.M. Hay (q.v.). Many of his drawings were reproduced as postcards.
Examples: Dundee City A.G.

DOUGLAS, John
1867 (Kilmarnock) - 1936 (Ayr)

A Scottish landscape painter in oil and watercolour. He first tried the life of a draper in Edinburgh and spent some years in the United States. On his return, he studied at the Glasgow School of Art and later lived in Ayr. Sir John Lavery was a close friend.

DOUGLAS, Lady –
see HAMILTON, Duchess of

DOUGLAS, William
1780 (Glenbervie) - 1832 (Edinburgh)

A miniaturist who also painted occasional landscapes and animal subjects, as well as larger portraits with the heads, at least, in watercolour. He was a Douglas of Glenbervie, and his patrons included the Duke of Buccleuch. He exhibited in Edinburgh from 1808 to 1816, and in the following year he was appointed Miniature Painter to Princess Charlotte.
His elder daughter, most confusingly named **Archibald Ramsey DOUGLAS (1807 Edinburgh - 1886 Edinburgh)**, was also a miniaturist.

DOUGLAS, William
1784 (Kirkudbright) - 1821 (London)

The nephew of his namesake the 1st baronet, whose heir he hoped to be, he was educated at Edinburgh High School and Trinity, Cambridge, and became an advocate. In 1807 and 1812 he failed to be elected to Parliament for his local seat, but in the latter year he secured Plympton, which he held until 1816. He was a travelling and sketching companion of H. 'G'. Williams (q.v.)

DOUGLAS, Sir William Fettes, P.R.S.A.
1822 (Edinburgh) - 1891 (Newburgh, Fife)

The son of an amateur artist, he worked in a bank until 1847 when he spent a few months at the Trustees' Academy. He exhibited at the R.S.A. from 1845, being elected A.R.S.A. and R.S.A. in 1851 and 1854. In 1859 he made his first visit to Italy; previously his sketching had been done in England and Scotland with the Faeds and A. Fraser (qq.v). He was curator of the N.G., Scotland from 1872 until 1882, when he was elected P.R.S.A. and was knighted.
His early work is a mixture of landscape and Pre-Raphaelite subject painting. Later he turned almost entirely to small landscapes in watercolour.
Examples: V.A.M.; Aberdeen A.G.; Ashmolean; Dundee City A.G.; Glasgow A.G.; N.G., Scotland.
Bibliography: J.M.Gray: *Sir W.F.D., P.R.S.A.*, 1885. *A.J.*, 1869; 1891; 1892; 1906.

DOUGLASS, Richard

A landscape painter who lived near Regent's Park and exhibited at Suffolk Street, the R.I. and the Grosvenor Gallery between 1875 and 1890. He painted in Wales, along the South coast and in Windsor Great Park.

DOW, Alexander Warren
1873 (London) - 1948

A painter of landscapes, towns and still lifes in watercolour, he was educated at the Leys and Clare College, Cambridge. He was a pupil of Brangwyn and Garstin and studied in Paris. He exhibited at the R.A., R.I. and elsewhere and for a time worked as art critic for *Colour*. He also etched, and painted in oil.

DOW, Thomas Millie, R.W.S.
1848 (Dysart) - 1919 (St. Ives)

A landscape, still-life, historical and classical figure painter in oil, pastel and watercolour. He studied in Paris under Gérôme and Duran, after first trying the law. On his return to Scotland he was elected R.S.W. in 1885, and was grouped with the Glasgow School. He had a studio in that city until he moved to St. Ives in 1895. In Paris he was influenced by Stott of Oldham, but his work tends to greater abstraction. From about the time of his move to Cornwall, he also moved from flowers to figures. He was a keen traveller and spent winters in Canada, Italy and Tangiers.
Bibliography: N. Garstin: *The Work of T.M.D.*, (?). *Studio*, V, 1895; X, 1897, XXXIII, 1905. *A.J.*, 1904; 1905.

DOWELL, Charles R   R.S.W.
- 1935

A Glasgow-born portrait, marine, landscape and still-life painter in watercolour and oil. He studied with Fra Newbery (q.v.) and in Rome, and was elected R.S.W. in 1933. He enjoyed the East coast of Scotland and also produced interiors and silhouettes.

DOWNIE, Patrick, R.S.W.
1854 (Greenock) - 1945

A postman turned ship painter. He studied in Paris and exhibited from 1885. He lived in turn in Greenock, Paisley, Glasgow and Skelmorlie, Argyll. His exhibited at the R.S.A. from 1885 and the R.A. from 1887. His subjects are clippers and square-riggers and his paint is liberally mixed with nostalgia.
John Patrick DOWNIE, R.S.W. (1871 Glasgow - 1945 Edinburgh) painted interiors, fishermen and genre.
Examples: Pailsey A.G.; Glasgow A.G.

DOWNING, H   E   - 1835

A painter of landscapes and town views, he was a Foundation Member and first Secretary of the N.W.S. He is presumably the 'H.E. Dowing' who taught drawing in Lambeth in 1828, and he also lived in Camden Town. His first initial is sometimes wrongly given as 'M'. His style is a rather sloppy version of that of Prout, and he exhibited from 1827 to 1833.
Examples: B.M.

DOWNMAN, John, A.R.A.
1750 (probably Ruabon, Wales) - 1824 (Wrexham)

He came to London in his youth, studying under B. West (q.v.) and at the R.A. Schools, first exhibiting in 1768 with the Free Society and in the following year at the R.A. He was elected A.R.A. in 1795. In November 1771 he set out for Italy with Wright of Derby (q.v.), arriving in Rome in March 1774, by way of Lyons, Nice, Turin, Verona, Venice and Florence. He may have visited Naples, and he returned to England in 1775. He was in Cambridge from 1777 to

1778, and then he remained in London until 1804, when he moved to East Malling, Kent. In 1806 he was at Plymouth, and in 1807 and 1808 at Exeter, returning to London again in 1809. In 1812 he made a tour of the Lake District, and in 1817 settled at Chester.

He is perhaps the most important watercolour portraitist of the late eighteenth century. The most characteristic of his portraits are small ovals, although he occasionally worked on a much larger scale. His works (and his sitters) are pretty and delicate, usually done in light watercolour over black chalk or charcoal. He sometimes even applied the colour for the faces to the back of the paper to give a softer effect. He often wrote comments on the sitters underneath his characteristic mounts. Downman's rare landscape drawings, so far as they are known, come from the Italian journey and the Lake District tour. Of these, the more impressive are the Italian drawings, despite a rather fussy pen line, over which are laid light washes, chiefly of pale grey and yellow green. They are not highly finished and have the vigour of on-the-spot sketches.

Examples: B.M.; V.A.M.; Cecil Higgins A.G., Bedford; Exeter Mus.; Fitzwilliam; Greenwich; City A.G., Manchester.

Bibliography: *Connoisseur*, Extra Number, II, 1907. *B.M. Quarterly*, Sept. 1940.

DOWSON, Russell
- *see under* **ENFIELD, Anne**

DOYLE, Charles Altamont
1832 (London) - 1893 (Crighton Institute, Dumfries)
Fourth son of J. Doyle (q.v.). At the age of nineteen he entered the Edinburgh Office of Works, where he remained for most of his life. He frequently exhibited watercolours and pen and ink studies at the R.S.A. and produced illustrations for the London Society in 1862, 1863 and 1864, as well as for humorous books. He died of epilepsy in a lunatic asylum. He was the father of Sir Arthur Conan Doyle.
Bibliography: J. Maas (ed):*The Doyle Diary*, 1978. V.A.M., Exhibition Cat., 1984.

DOYLE, Henry Edward, R.H.A.
1827 (Dublin) - 1892 (Dublin)
Third son of J. Doyle (q.v.). After training in Dublin, he moved to London and worked as a draughtsman and wood-engraver for *Telemachus, Punch* and *Fun*. He was Commissioner for Rome in the London International Exhibition of 1862. In 1864 he decorated the chapel of the Dominican Convent at Cabra, near Dublin. From 1869 until his death he was Director of the N.G.I. and his work in improving the collection, particularly with regard to the portraits, gained him a C.B. in 1880. He was elected A.R.H.A. and R.H.A. in 1872 and 1874, and he occasionally exhibited portraits and religious subjects in oil and watercolour.
Examples: N.G.I.
Bibliography: V.A.M.: Exhibition Cat., 1984.

DOWNMAN, John (1750-1824)
A Rocky Stream in Italy. *Pen and black ink and watercolour, 14½in. x 19¼in.*

DOWNMAN, John (1750-1824)
Portrait study of Mrs. Mitchell. *Coloured chalks, 7in. x 5½in.*

D'OYLY, Sir Charles, 7th Bt. (1781-1845)
Lion Shoot at the Cape. *Inscribed 'Cape Town' and dated 1st June 1832, watercolour, 11½in. x 16¾in.*

DOYLE, James William Edmund
        1822 (London) - 1892 (London)
Eldest son of J. Doyle (q.v.), he started life as a painter but soon turned to historical research. He made drawings to illustrate his publications.
Published: *A Chronicle of England*, 1864. *Historical Baronage of England*, 1886.

DOYLE, John, 'H.B.'
        1797 (Dublin) - 1868 (Kensington)
He studied under the landscapist Gabrielli, the miniaturist Comerford, and at the R.D.S. He moved to London in 1821 and exhibited portraits at the R.A., but having little success he turned to caricature lithography. His series of nine hundred and seventeen plates, which appeared from 1829 to 1851, over the signature H.B., provide a political and social history of the period. The signature originated JD over JD

Thackeray said of him in 1840, 'You never hear any laughing at H.B., his pictures are a great deal too genteel for that'. There is none of the zestful savagery of Gillray, and the drawing is closer to H. Alken than to Rowlandson. Despite its high quality, his work marks the beginning of the long decline of political caricaturing.
Examples: B.M.
Bibliography: *A.J.*, 1868. V.A.M., Exhibition Cat., 1984.

DOYLE, Richard
        1824 (London) - 1883 (London)
The second son of J. Doyle (q.v.) who educated him and taught him to draw at home. By the age of fifteen he had developed a remarkable skill as a draughtsman and at nineteen he was a regular contributor to *Punch,* for which he worked from 1843 to 1850. Thereafter he concentrated on book illustration and watercolour painting.

As Dobson says: 'in Oberon's court he would at once have been appointed sergeant-painter,' for the majority of his designs are of 'elves and fays and gnomes' often with backgrounds taken from the moors and woods of Devon and Wales. His *Punch* series

Manners and Customs of ye Englyshe, drawn from ye Quick and the later *Bird's-eye Views of Society* which he contributed to the *Cornhill Magazine* are an equally charming commentary on a more substantial society. A collection of his drawings was exhibited at the Grosvenor Gallery in 1881.
Examples: B.M.; V.A.M.; Cartwright Hall, Bradford; Fitzwilliam; N.G., Ireland; Newport A.G.; Ulster Mus.
Bibliography: D. Hambourg: *R.D.*, 1948. R. Engen: *R.D.*, 1983. V.A.M.: Exhibition Cat., 1984.

D'OYLY, Sir Charles, 7th Bt.
        1781 (Calcutta) - 1845 (Livorno)
After an education in England, D'Oyly returned to India in the Company's Service in 1798. He was in Calcutta until 1808 when he became a Collector in Dacca, where he had lessons from Chinnery. He returned to Calcutta in 1818, became opium agent at Behar in 1821, commercial agent at Patna in 1831 and senior member of the Board of Customs in 1833. In 1824 he initiated an art society, entitled 'The United Patna and Gaya Society' or 'Behar School of Athens' which local residents as well as officers posted nearby were urged to join. In 1832 and 1833 he made a tour of the Cape. He returned to England in 1838 and spent most of the remainder of his life in Italy.

His work is often on a small scale, and brightly coloured. He also made numerous pen and ink drawings. Occasionally, as at the Cape of Good Hope, he tried humorous sketches in pen and wash, but his figure drawing is poor. He published *The Feathered Game of Hindostan*, 1828, and *Oriental Ornithology*, 1829, in conjunction with Christopher Webb

D'OYLY, Major-General Sir Charles Walters, 9th Bt. (1822-1900)
Government House, Calcutta. *Signed and dated 1855, water and bodycolour, 13¼in x 19⅝in.*

Smith, who drew the birds.
Published: *Antiquities of Dacca*, 1814-1815. *Tom Raw, the Griffin: a Burlesque Poem*, 1828. *Indian Sports*, 1829. *The Costumes of India*, 1830. *Sketches on the New Road in a journey from Calcutta to Gyah*, 1830.
Illustrated: Capt. T. Williamson: *The European in India...*, 1813.
Bibliography: *Connoisseur*, CLXXV, 1970.
See D'Oyly Family Tree

D'OYLY, Major-General Sir Charles Walters, 9th Bt. 1822 - 1900
Son of Sir J.H. D'Oyly, 8th Bt, and M. D'Oyly (q.v.) he was quite as competent an artist as one would expect for a member of this family. During the Mutiny he fought at Punniar and charged with the Caribineers at Gungari. He was an A.D.C. to Lord Dalhousie, the Governor-General between 1852 and '56. In the following year he served in the Gwalior campaign, and two years later again he was in Ceylon. In later life he was a Dorset J.P.

His wife, **Elinor, Lady D'OYLY, née Scott (d.1914)**, was also an artist.
See D'Oyly Family Tree

D'OYLY, Elizabeth Jane, Lady, née Ross 1789 - 1875 (Blandford)
The second wife of Sir C. D'Oyly (q.v.), whom she married in India in 1817, and whose manner she imitated closely. She was also a pupil of Chinnery.
See D'Oyly Family Tree

D'OYLY, Sir Hastings Hadley, 11th Bt. 1864 (Calcutta) - 1950
The son of the 10th Bt. and a daughter of Sir F. Halliday, Lieutenant-Governor of Bengal, he became a commissioner at Port Blair in the Andaman Islands, where he painted landscapes. He was a captain both in the Territorials and the Behar Light Horse.
See D'Oyly Family Tree

D'OYLY, Mary, Lady, née Fendall 1794 - 1886
The daughter of the Hon. John Fendall, a member of the Supreme Council of Calcutta, she became the second wife of **Sir John Hadley D'OYLY (1794-1869)** in about 1834. He succeeded his brother Charles (q.v.) as 8th Bt. in 1845. She painted Indian scenes and landscapes. Inevitably, her husband also painted.
See D'Oyly Family Tree

DRAKE, Nathan, F.S.A. 1728 (Lincoln) - 1783 (York)
A drawing master and portrait painter who was the son of a minor canon of Lincoln. He settled in York in 1750 and two years later advertised as a teacher of watercolour painting. His charge was an entrance fee of 1gn., and 2gns. per quarter. He was a kinsman of Francis Drake, author of *Eboracum*, was himself elected F.S.A. in 1771, and was the father of two noted surgeons.

D'OYLY, Sir Hastings Hadley, 11th Bt. (1864- 1950)
Triumphal Arch (? Calcutta). *Pencil and watercolour, signed with initials, inscribed on reverse 'for Papa from Hadley'. 9in. x 14in.*

DRAPER, Charles F
A landscape and coastal painter who came from Guernsey but also lived on Jersey and in London. He exhibited at Suffolk Street and the N.W.S. between 1871 and 1887, and he visited the North of England and the Lakes.

DRUMMOND, Lady E.C. –
see under **PERCY, Emily**

DRUMMOND, James, R.S.A. 1816 (Edinburgh) - 1877 (Edinburgh)
The son of a merchant, he first worked as a draughtsman for Captain Brown, author of works on ornithology. He taught drawing briefly before entering the Trustees' Academy under Sir W. Allan (q.v.). He first exhibited at the R.S.A. at the age of eighteen, being elected A.R.S.A. in 1845 and R.S.A. in 1852. In 1868 he was appointed Curator of N.G., Scotland.

His main works, other than portraits and landscapes, are large scenes from Scottish history, which show great attention to antiquarian detail. He is easy to confuse with Julian Drummond (q.v.), but did not produce the watercolours of fishermen and peasants.
Illustrated: J. Anderson: *Ancient Scottish Weapons*, 1881.
Examples: V.A.M.; Blackburn A.G.; N.G., Scotland.
Bibliography: *A.J.*, 1877. Cannongate Tolbooth Mus., Edinburgh, Exhibition Cat., 1983.

DRUMMOND, John Murray 1803 (Edinburgh) - 1889
The eldest son of Admiral Sir Adam Drummond of Megginch and Lady Charlotte Murray, he was educated at Corsham, near

Bath, and at Edinburgh High School. In Edinburgh he studied art under A. Nasmyth (q.v.), and on going up to Sandhurst in August 1818 he wrote home, 'I like all the studies here very much, except landscape drawing, for I think the professor does not teach so well as Mr. Nasmyth'. In 1821 he went to Fontainebleau, and in 1822 was commissioned in the Grenadier Guards and posted to Dublin. He retired from the Army in 1838. He was a cousin of the Duke of Atholl, and served in his army, as well as taking part in the Eglinton Tournament.

He was a prolific amateur artist, and he painted for Queen Victoria at Osborne. The watercolours, which form the larger part of his work, are of a higher quality than the oil paintings.

DRUMMOND, Julian 1824 -
A son of S. Drummond (q.v.), he entered the R.A. Schools in 1843. Either he, or a son, was the Julian E. Drummond who was a genre and landscape painter working in London and Brighton from the 1880s to at least 1903. This one produced portraits and landscapes, and was the author of a long series of rather sickly and loosely drawn watercolours of the heads and shoulders of fishermen and peasants.

At a similar time **J. Nelson DRUMMOND** was at work in London and Rye.

DRUMMOND, Samuel, A.R.A. 1765 (London) - 1844 (London)
The son of an active Jacobite, he ran away to sea for some years, and then returned to England in about 1786. He began by drawing crayon

DUDLEY, Robert Charles (1826-1900)
Tell's Chapel, Lake Lucerne. *Signed and dated 1876, and signed and inscribed on a label,*
pencil and watercolour heightened with white and gum arabic, 13in. x 20in.

portraits, and worked for several years for the *European Magazine.* He turned to oil painting and exhibited at the S.A. from 1790 and the R.A. from 1791, being elected A.R.A. in 1808. He later became Curator of the Painting School.

He was mainly a portrait painter, also producing landscapes in Wilson's Italian manner, naval and biblical scenes, and illustrations from poetry.

He had five painting, or miniature painting, daughters and three sons: **Samuel DRUMMOND, Yr. (b.1807)**, entered the R.A. Schools in 1822; **Eliza A. DRUMMOND** exhibited at the S.B.A. between 1825 and 1843; **F. Ellen DRUMMOND** exhibited 1836-1860; **James DRUMMOND** exhibited 1839-1872; **Rose Emma DRUMMOND** was active between 1815 and 1835; and **Rose Myra DRUMMOND** exhibited under the Christian name Myra from 1833 to 1849. Samuel Drummond's first wife **Mrs. V.E. DRUMMOND** exhibited only in 1829. Julian Drummond is noticed above.
Examples: B.M.

DRUMMOND, William
A portrait painter working in 1849. Perhaps he may be identified with the student who won prizes at the R.D.S. in 1826 and 1827 and who published lithographs in Dublin. He (or one of them) was in London from 1830 to 1838 and in 1843.

DRURY, Susanna, Mrs. Warter
- 1775/6
The sister of the Dublin miniature painter, Franklin Drury (d.1771), she painted landscapes in England and Ireland between about 1733 and 1770, and occasionally made book illustrations. She made two drawings of the Giant's Causeway, which were turned into popular engravings by Vivares. These drawings are in bodycolour on vellum and were shown at the R.D.S. exhibition of 1858.
Examples: Ulster Mus.

DU CANE, Ella Máry 1874   -1943
A daughter of Sir C. Du Cane of Braxted Park, Essex, and a granddaughter of Lord Chancellor Lyndhurst (the son of J.S. Copley). She became a landscape and flower painter and an illustrator. Both Queen Victoria and Edward VII were admirers of her flowers.

DUCKETT, Isabella, Lady
The daughter of Lieutenant-General Sir Lionel Smith, Governor of Jamaica, she married Sir G.F. Duckett, Bt. in 1845. She was a pupil of one of the Schranzs (the Maltese family of artists) and of one of the Earps (the Brighton family of painters). She exhibited birds and flowers from 1867 and for a time painted in oil as well as watercolour.

DUDLEY, Robert Charles
1826   - 1900
A marine, portrait and landscape painter in oil and watercolour and a lithographer. He studied at the R.A. Schools from 1848, worked in Spain, Tangiers and Venice as well as in England, exhibited at the R.A. in 1865, and elsewhere from 1853. He illustrated popular history books, the Bible and Army and Navy *Almanacks.*

Illustrated: W.H.Russell: *A Memorial to the Marriage of the Prince of Wales...,* 1864.

DUDLEY, Thomas
A Hull landscape and coastal painter, who was the son of a musician and taught by a Mr. Dodd. He became a drawing master himself and exhibited in York and elsewhere from 1879 to 1910. He painted in Durham, the Lake District and Cornwall as well as in Yorkshire.
Examples: V.A.M.; Ferens A.G., Hull.

DUFF, John Robert Keitley, R.I.
1862 (London) - 1938 (London)
Trained as a barrister, he was educated at Bishop's Stortford, and Sidney Sussex College, Cambridge, before studying at the Slade under Legros. He painted in watercolour, pastel and oil, was an R.E., and exhibited from 1891. He was elected R.I. in 1913, and he sometimes used a 'JRD' monogram.

DUFFERIN AND AVA, Frederick Temple, 1st Marquess of 1826 (Florence) - 1902
Statesman, diplomat and watercolour painter. He was the son of the 4th Lord Dufferin of Clandeboye, near Belfast, whom he succeeded in 1841. He was educated at Eton and Christ Church, Oxford, and was a pupil of W. Callow (q.v.). He was a lord-in-waiting, 1848-52 and 1854-58, and commissioner in Syria in 1860-61. He was then Secretary of State for India, 1864-66, and War in 1866, Chancellor of the Duchy of Lancaster, 1869-72, Governor-General of Canada, 1872-78, ambassador to Russia, 1879-81, and Turkey, 1881-84, Commissioner in Egypt, 1882-83, Viceroy of

India, 1884-86, ambassador to Italy, 1888-91, to France 1891-96, and Lord Warden of the Cinque Ports. He was also Lord Lieutenant of his native County Down. He was made an Earl in 1850 and advanced to Marquess in 1888.

DUFFIELD, Mary Ann, Mrs., née Rosenberg, R.I. 1819 (Bath) - 1914
A daughter of T.E. Rosenberg (q.v.), she married W. Duffield (q.v.) in 1850. She won a silver medal from the Society of Arts in 1834 and exhibited flower pieces of a high quality from 1848 to 1912. She was elected to the N.W.S. in 1861.
Published: *The Art of Flower Painting*, 1856.
Examples: V.A.M.
See Colour Plate

DUFFIELD, William
1816 (Bath) - 1863 (London)
A still-life painter in oil and watercolour, he studied under G. Lance (q.v.) in London, at the R.A. Schools from 1836, and in Antwerp under Baron Wappers. He then returned to Bath. He specialised in food paintings, occasionally turning to flowers, sometimes in collaboration with his wife (q.v.). He died of an infection caught from a dead stag which he was painting in his studio.
Bibliography: *A.J.*, 1863.

DUFFIELD, William Laud 1850 -
The son of M.E. and W. Duffield (qq.v), he entered the R.A. Schools in 1867 and exhibited figures and landscapes in the 1870s and '80s. He visited Egypt in 1880.

DUGGAN, Patrick
An Irish landscape painter. He gained prizes at the R.D.S. Schools in 1815 and 1818. Portraits by him of Oliver J. Dowel Grace and his wife Frances, as well as Irish castles and buildings, are engraved in *Memoirs of the Family of Grace*.
Illustrated: Hardiman: *History of Galway*, 1820.

DUGMORE, John, of Swaffham
1793 - 1871 (Swaffham)
A topographer who was a protégé of the Keppel family, one of whom he accompanied on a Grand Tour of Germany and Italy. He also drew in Scotland.

His style is old-fashioned, harking back to the traditions of the eighteenth century. Some of his drawings were lithographed by Hullmandel.

DUGUID, Henry G
A drawing master and music teacher in Edinburgh, he painted landscapes and old buildings and was working between 1828 and 1860. In 1851 he made a two-sheet aquatint panorama of Edinburgh from the Calton Hill, and another of his views of Edinburgh was engraved by C. Rosenberg.
Examples: N.G., Scotland. S.N.P.G. Edinburgh City Coll.

DUFF, John Robert Keitley (1862-1938)
Kandersteg. *Signed with monogrammatic signature, pencil and watercolour, 14in. x 18in.*

DU MAURIER, George Louis Palmella Busson, R.W.S.
1834 (Paris) - 1896 (London)
The pen and ink illustrator and novelist who was the chief *Punch* caricaturist from 1864. He studied in Paris and Antwerp between 1856 and 1860 and published his best known novel, *Trilby*, in 1894. His watercolours were all produced between about 1880 and 1889, when he gave up because of eyestrain. They are almost all family portraits or copies of *Punch* drawings.
Examples: B.M.; Cartwright Hall, Bradford; City A.G., Manchester; Portsmouth City Mus.; N.G., Scotland; Ulster Mus.
Bibliography: T. Martin Wood: *G du M.*, 1913. D. du Maurier: *The Young G. du M.*, 1951. L. Ormond: *G. du M.*, 1969. *A.J.*, 1896.

DUNBAR, Sophia, Lady
c.1820 - 1909
The daughter of George Orred of Tranmere Hall, Cheshire, she married Sir Archibald Dunbar, Bt. of Northfield, Elgin, in 1840. She took lessons from J. le Capelain (q.v.) and exhibited in London and Edinburgh from 1863. She painted landscapes in Scotland, Algeria with Mme. Bodichon (q.v.), Corsica, the Riviera, Spain and the New Forest.

An exhibition of her work was held at the Aberdeen A.G. in 1989.

DUNBAR, W
A painter of still lifes, churches and ruins who was living in Andover from 1834 to 1851. Perhaps he is to be identified with the **W. Nugent DUNBAR,** who exhibited Roman views and

figures in 1839, or with **W.J. DUNBAR,** who showed a view of Stonehenge in 1845.

DUNCAN, Allan 1844 (London) -
A son of E. Duncan (q.v.), who lived with his father in Hampstead while exhibiting from the 1860s to the '80s. He painted in Wales and Cornwall and on the Thames.

DUNCAN, Edward, R.W.S.
1803 (London) - 1882 (London)
Duncan was apprenticed to the Robert Havells, elder and younger, the aquatint engravers, and his first independent practice as an artist was engraving coaching and marine prints for such publishers as Fores. He was not himself a sailor, and his introduction to marine painting was through William Huggins, whose pictures he engraved and whose daughter, Bertha, he married. He began to exhibit in 1830 and became a member of the N.W.S. in 1834. In 1847 he resigned, to become an Associate of the O.W.S., of which he was elected a member in 1849. His sketching tours were generally confined to the southern counties and the Bristol Channel, although in 1840 he sailed across to Holland. In the early 1850s he went to the Channel Islands and in 1865 he visited Italy. He also made occasional visits to Scotland and Wales. His subjects are divided between the coastal scenes, for which he is best known, and landscapes, most often in the Thames Valley. In his marine painting he often depicts rough and breezy weather and is at his most successful with wrecks, rescues and lifeboats. He was also at home with beachcombers and fisherfolk. In contrast, his Thames views are peaceful in the

DUNCAN, Edward (1803-1882)
Estuary scene with children and fisherfolk. *Watercolour, 13½in. x 19in.*

extreme, with punts, cattle, sheep and perhaps a distant church tower as the main points of interest. He employed strong blues and greens and was not afraid of white heightening. His drawing is generally good, perhaps as a result of his training as an engraver.

His remaining works were sold at Christie's, 1883 and 11 March 1885.
Published: *Advanced Studies in Marine Painting.* 1889. *British Landscape and Coast Scenery,* 1889.
Examples: B.M.; V.A.M.; Haworth A.G., Accrington; Blackburn A.G.; Cartwright Hall, Bradford; Ferens A.G., Hull; Glasgow A.G.
Bibliography: *A.J.,* 1882; 1883. *Walker's Quarterly,* XIII, 1923. O.W.S. Club, VI, 1928; LX, 1985; O.W.S. Club, LX, 1985.

DUNCAN, Lieutenant-Colonel John
c.1760 - ?1803
An artilleryman who was a pupil of P. Sandby (q.v.) at Woolwich. He was commissioned second lieutenant in 1780 and promoted lieutenant-colonel in 1798.

DUNCAN, John
c.1846 (Newcastle) - p.1898
The son of a taxidermist, he preserved birds in oil and watercolour. He was also a lithographer, a draughtsman and a glass painter. He studied under W.B. Scott (q.v.) and worked at a glasshouse. For some ten years from about 1888 he drew birds for the *Newcastle Weekly Chronicle,* and some of these drawings were reused elsewhere.

DUNCAN, Lawrence
1835/6 (London) -
A son of E. Duncan (q.v.) he entered the R.A. Schools in 1854, and lived in Long Ditton and London to at least 1890. He exhibited genre subjects and British and Breton landscapes from 1860 to at least 1891.

DUNCAN, Thomas, A.R.A., R.S.A.
1807 (Kinclaven, Perthshire) -
1845 (Edinburgh)
A portrait and history painter who studied at the Trustees' Academy, of which he later became Master. He was Professor of Colour and subsequently of Drawing at the R.S.A. He painted mainly in oil and was elected R.S.A. in 1829 and A.R.A. in 1843.

DUNCAN, Walter, A.R.W.S.
1847 (London) - 1932 (Richmond, Surrey)
A son of E. Duncan (q.v.), he entered the R.A. Schools in 1865, lived in Hampstead in the 1880s, Central London from 1890 to 1895, and thereafter in the southern suburbs. He was working from 1869 to 1906 and was elected A.O.W.S. in 1874. He painted marine, Indian and historical subjects, some with an excess of bodycolour.

DUNDAS, Adela, 'Ada'
1840 (Edinburgh) - 1887
The daughter of the Registrar-General for Scotland, she was a protégée of J. Ruskin (q.v.), who arranged for her to become a pupil

of another protégé, William Ward. She suffered from curvature of the spine and needed constant attention, but despite this she travelled through France, Switzerland and Italy, 1861-62. She only actually met Ruskin late in life, visiting Brantwood in 1884, but earlier he had called her the wisest 'of his stranger correspondents'.
See Colour Plate

DUNDAS, Agnes
A painter of birds and dogs in oil and occasional landscapes in watercolour, she lived in London and exhibited between 1863 and 1884. Her landscape watercolours and nature studies are excellently drawn, with strong, clear colours.

DUNDAS, James
An artist who painted landscapes and figure studies in England and on the Continent between 1846 and 1868.

DUNGARVAN, Charles, Viscount
1800 - 1834
The eldest son of the 8th Earl of Cork. Like his cousin C. Boyle (q.v.) he was a pupil of H. Bright (q.v.).

DUNKARTON, Robert John
1744 (London) - 1811
A mezzotint engraver of portraits who also worked occasionally in watercolour. He was a pupil of Pether and won a Premium at the

Society of Arts in 1762. Later he portrayed both politicians and beauties. Early in his career he aspired to being a painter.

DUNMORE, Charles Adolphus, 7th Earl of
1841 - 1907

A captain in the Scots Fusilier Guards and Hon. Colonel of the 1st Cameron Highlanders, he was a lord-in-waiting to the Queen, 1874-80, and Lord Lieutenant of Stirlingshire. His seat was on the Isle of Harris. He was an F.R.G.S. and in 1894 he showed his watercolours of an expedition through Kashmir, Western Tibet, Chinese Tartary and Russian Turkestan at the Fine Art Society.

DU NOYER, George Victor
1817 (Dublin) - 1869 (Co. Antrim)

A topographical draughtsman of Huguenot parentage. He studied in Dublin under G. Petrie (q.v.), who procured for him a job on the Ordnance Survey. In about 1844-5 he was teaching drawing at St. Columba's College, Stackallan, afterwards working with the Geological Survey of Ireland. He exhibited at the R.H.A. from 1841 to 1863 and in 1859 was elected a member of the Royal Irish Academy. He was also a member of the Kilkenny Archaeological Society. He died of scarlet fever while working on a revision of the Geological Survey in the North of Ireland.

Illustrated: Hall: *Ireland, its Scenery and Character,* 1841. Portlock: *Geological Report on Londonderry, Tyrone and Fermanagh.*
Examples: R.I.A.; University Coll., Dublin. N. Botanical Gdns., Dublin.

DUNSTALL, John - 1693

A 'small professor and teacher of drawings' in the Strand during the 1660s, he also described himself as a 'School Master in Blackfriars'. He may have come from Sussex, and he certainly painted views there. They are old-fashioned, using opaque colours on vellum. The figures are rather primitive, but the whole effect is charming. In the B.M. is his undated manuscript *The Art of Delineation, or Drawings. In 6 Books.*

Published: *A Book of Flowers, Fruits, Beastes, Birds and Flies exactly drawn,* 1620.
Examples: B.M.
Bibliography: M. Clarke. *The Tempting Prospect,* 1981.

DUNTHORNE, James, Yr.
c.1758 (Colchester) - c.1793

The son of **James DUNTHORNE (1730-1815)**, a portrait and miniature painter known as the 'The Colchester Hogarth'. He was a crude but amusing caricaturist working a little in the manner of Rowlandson, and he exhibited at the R.A. from 1783 to 1794. Usually he worked on a comparatively large scale, painting local social gatherings. His drawing 'Ague and Fever' was etched by Rowlandson.

This family should not be confused with the John Dunthornes, father and son, who lived at East Bergholt and were plumbers, glaziers and amateur artists. The elder **John DUNTHORNE (1770-?1848)** was a friend of Constable, and his son **John DUNTHORNE, Yr. (1798-1832)** became Constable's assistant and exhibited at the R.A. from 1827 to 1832.

A link may exist between the families, and it is possible that the elder John was a son or nephew of the elder James.

Bibliography: W. Gurney Benham: *The Ds of Colchester,* 1901.

DUPPA, Brian Edward
c.1803 (Hollingbourne Ho., Kent) - 1866

A portrait and figure painter who was working in oil, watercolour and London from the 1830s to the 1850s.

He was a collateral descendant of his namesake, Charles II's tutor the Bishop of Winchester, and a distant relative of **Richard DUPPA, F.S.A. (1770-1831)**, the author and draughtsman, who had studied in Rome and illustrated some of his own books on botanical, artistic and political subjects.

DURRANT, Captain

A pleasing landscape and picturesque feature painter, rather in the uncaricatured manner of J. Nixon (q.v.). He was active in the 1820s.

DUTTON, Thomas Goldsworthy
1819/20 - 1891 (Wandsworth)

The lithographer of shipping subjects, which he also painted in oil and watercolour. He was living in Wandsworth in 1862 and '63 when he was an unsuccessful candidate for the N.W.S. He had a feeling for the texture of water, rubbing and dragging to imitate spray.

Examples: The Old Customs House, Lymington.

DUVAL, Marie –
see DE TESSIER, Isabelle Emilie

DYCE, Rev. Alexander
1798 (Edinburgh) - 1869 (London)

An amateur artist and cousin of W. Dyce (q.v.), he graduated from Exeter College, Oxford, in 1819. He held two curacies between 1822 and 1825, when he moved to London and devoted himself to literary studies. He edited Shakespeare and Beaumont and Fletcher. He painted flowers and butterflies.

Examples: V.A.M.; N.G.

DYCE, William, R.A., A.R.S.A.
1806 (Aberdeen) - 1864 (Streatham)

During his education at Marischal College, Aberdeen, he taught himself to paint, selling his pictures in order to raise the money to go to London. He briefly attended the R.A. Schools before going to Rome, in the autumn of 1825, for nine months. In 1826 he revisited Aberdeen, and returned to Rome in 1827, remaining until late 1828. While there he developed the style which later became known as Pre-Raphaelitism. Although this won him a following among foreign artists, it was little appreciated at home, and he virtually gave up painting in favour of science on his return. However, in 1830 he moved to Edinburgh and was encouraged to take up portraiture. He remained in Edinburgh for about seven years, becoming Fellow of the Scottish Royal Society in 1832 and A.R.S.A. in 1835. For a time he travelled on the Continent preparing a report on Schools of Design at Somerset House. In 1843 and 1844 he was Inspector of Provincial Schools, and then became Professor of Fine Arts at King's College, London. He was elected A.R.A. in 1844 and R.A. in 1848. At this time, feeling deskbound and in need of new inspiration, he attended life classes at Taylor's in St. Martin's Lane.

He provided one of the most successful frescoes for the House of Lords, 'The Baptism of Ethelbert', having revisited Italy to study the technique. He painted many other frescoes and also worked as a stained glass and coin designer and an etcher.

In watercolour, as in oil, his colour is bright and clear, and his detail essentially Pre-Raphaelite. In contrast to his scholarly oil paintings, his watercolours are often of landscapes and old buildings, and were done more for his own pleasure.

His son, **J. Stirling DYCE (d.c.1900)** painted landscapes in Scotland, England and France in a Pre-Raphaelite manner.

Illustrated: Sir T.T. Lauder: *The Morayshire Floods,* 1830. *Highland Rambles,* 1837.
Examples: B.M.; V.A.M.; Aberdeen A.G.; Ashmolean; Fitzwilliam; Owen's College, Manchester; N.G., Scotland.
Bibliography: M. Pointon: *W.D.,* 1979. *A.J.,* Oct. 1860; April 1864; 1865. Aberdeen A.G., Exhibition Cat., 1964. *Country Life,* 13 August 1964. *Burlington Mag.,* CV, Nov. 1963.

DYER, Rev. John
1699 (Aberglasney, Carmarthen) - 1758 (?Kirkby-on-Bane, Lincs.)

'Dyer's longer poems are now unreadable, though there is still some charm in *Grongar Hill* and some shorter pieces' (Leslie Stephen). He is probably best known by the sonnet addressed to him by Wordsworth. Before taking the cloth in 1741 Dyer had been a pupil of Jonathan Richardson and had toured England, Wales and Italy as an itinerant poet and painter. In Italy he caught malaria, and after his return he could not find success with the brush. He held a number of livings in Leicestershire and Lincolnshire and spent much on building. W. Gilpin (q.v.) was among his critics.

Published: *Grongar Hill,* 1727; *Ruins in Rome,* 1740; *The Fleece,* 1757; *Collected Poems,* 1761.

DYSON, John William
1855 (Wharfdale) - 1916 (Newcastle)

An architectural draughtsman and a landscape and figurative painter in oil and watercolour. He was trained at Bishop Auckland and worked at Newcastle.

EADIE, John
A Glasgow painter of coastal subjects in watercolour, and occasionally oil, he exhibited locally between 1877 and 1894.

James EADIE, also of Glasgow, exhibited genre subjects and landscapes in Glasgow and at the R.S.A. between 1856 and 1863.

Robert EADIE, R.S.W. (1877 Glasgow - 1954) painted portraits in watercolour and was elected R.S.W. in 1916. He studied in Glasgow, Munich and Paris and served in the Royal Engineers during the First World War.

EAGLES, Lieutenant Edward Bampfylde - 1866 (Dover)
A marine and shipping artist who was in the West Indies in 1805 and was promoted first lieutenant in the Royal Marine Artillery in 1807. He was placed on half-pay in 1816. He was the brother of J. Eagles (q.v.) and a cousin of C.W. Bampfylde (q.v.). Many of his drawings are in pen and ink, but he also worked in full watercolour.
Examples: Greenwich.

EAGLES, Rev. John
1783 (Bristol) - 1855 (Bristol)
A Wykehamist who made a tour of Italy and then returned to Wadham and to take orders. He began as curate of St. Nicholas, Bristol, and then became vicar of Halberton, Devon, from 1822; of Winford, Bristol, from 1835; and of Kinnersley, Hertfordshire, returning to Bristol in 1841. He was a member of Danby's Sketching Club and an etcher. His style is old-fashioned in the manner of Claude and the Poussins, and his drawings are mostly in monochrome. He is best remembered as an art critic, writing for *Blackwood's*. It was his attack which roused Ruskin 'to the height of black anger' in the defence of Turner. He was a candidate for the O.W.S. in 1824, but was excluded as an amateur.
Published: *The Sketcher*, 1856.
Examples: City A.G., Bristol.

EARL, William Robert
A coastal, landscape and rustic genre painter who exhibited from 1823 to 1867. He lived in South London and worked on the South Coast and in North Wales. He also produced views of the parks of Lords Yarborough and Farnborough.

EARLE, Augustus
1793 (London) - 1838 (London)
The son and nephew of American artists, he studied at the R.A. Schools, and then travelled from about 1813, visiting the Mediterranean, Africa and the U.S.A. He spent six months shipwrecked on Tristan da Cunha, travelled around South America and went on to New

EAGLES, Rev. John (1783-1855)
A cart in a landscape. *Watercolour, 6½in. x 10in.*

Zealand, Australia and India, returning to England by way of France. Later he was draughtsman to H.M.S. *Beagle* for some time until 1832. On returning to London he painted portraits, but died of 'asthma and debility'.

He exhibited at the R.A. from 1806 to 1815 and from 1837 to 1839. As well as topographic work, he produced caricatures, portraits and genre drawings, some of which were worked up by D. Dighton (q.v.).
Published: *Views of New South Wales*, 1830. *A Narrative of a Nine Months' Residence in New Zealand*, 1832.
Examples: B.M.
Bibliography: J. Hackforth-Jones: *A.E. Travel Artist*, 1980.

EARLE, Charles, R.I.
1832 - 1893 (London)
A landscape painter who worked in England,

Wales, Germany, Italy and France and lived in London. He exhibited at the R.A. and elsewhere from 1857 to 1893 and was elected R.I. in 1882. He had a penchant for rather violent colouring.

EARP, Henry 1831 - 1914 (Brighton)
The Earps of Brighton, like so many of the dynasties of English watercolourists, are veiled in obscurity. They were landscape and coastal painters. They were prolific, but for the most part their work is undistinguished. Henry exhibited in London from 1871 to 1884 and specialised in cattle.

Frederick EARP (1827-1897) was presumably his elder brother. There are examples of his work at Greenwich and Hove Lib. Other painters of the name, and probably the family, include **Edwin EARP**, who was active about 1900; **George EARP**, who was

EARLE, Augustus (1793-1838)
H.M.S. Beagle, January 1832, Porto Praya, Island of St. Jago. *Pencil, watercolour and pen wash on paper, 7¾in. x 17in.*

active from at least the 1850s and living in Brighton in 1874, and whose work is represented in the Carlton Mus., Nottinghamshire; **Vernon EARP,** who lived in London and exhibited in Manchester in 1900; and **William Henry EARP** who also lived in Brighton. An earlier **George EARP** was working in Brighton c.1833, and was perhaps Henry's father.

Examples: Brighton A.G.

EAST, Sir Alfred, R.A., F.R.S.
1849 (Kettering) - 1913 (London)
A landscape painter in oil and watercolour, who began his working life in his brother's factory. In about 1872 he was in Glasgow on business and attended the School of Art. Thereafter he studied in Paris, and in about 1883 he settled in London. He was discovered by Leighton and was elected R.I. in 1887, resigning in 1898. He was elected A.R.A. and R.A. in 1899 and 1913. He was knighted in 1910. He travelled widely, visiting Japan in 1889 as well as Morocco, Spain, Italy and France, where he was influenced by the Barbizons. He was President of the R.B.A. and also produced etchings.

Published: *Brush and pencil notes in landscape,* 1914. *A British Artist in Meiji Japan* (ed. Sir H. Cortazzi),1991.

Examples: B.M.; V.A.M.; Haworth A.G., Accrington; Ashmolean; Dudley A.G.; Towner Gall., Eastbourne; A. East Gall., Kettering; Leeds City A.G.; Newport A.G.; Wakefield A.G.

Bibliography: Sir H. Cortazzi (ed): *A British Artist in Meiji Japan,* 1991. *Studio,* VII, 1896; XXXIV, 1905; XXXVII, 1906; XL, 1907. *Chronique des Arts,* 1913. *Connoisseur,* XXXVII, 1913. Laing A.G., Newcastle, Exhibition Cat., 1914. Fine Art Soc., London, Exhibition Cat., 1991.

EASTLAKE, Caroline H
A flower painter who lived at Plymouth and exhibited from 1868 to 1873.
Examples: V.A.M.

EASTLAKE, Charles Herbert
A landscape painter who studied in Antwerp and Paris and visited Japan. He exhibited at the R.A. and the R.I. from 1889 and was active until about 1930. Both he and Caroline H. Eastlake (q.v.) had Plymouth connections and thus may well have been related to Sir C.L. Eastlake (q.v.). He also lived in South London.
Examples: V.A.M.
Bibliography: *Studio,* XXXVI, 1906; XXXVIII, 1906.

EASTLAKE, Sir Charles Lock, P.R.A.
1793 (Plymouth) - 1865 (Pisa)
A historical, genre and portrait painter in oil and watercolour who was educated at Plympton Grammar School under J. Bidlake (q.v.) and took lessons from S. Prout (q.v.). He spent a term at Charterhouse, but left in January 1809 to become a pupil of Haydon – like Prout, a former pupil of Bidlake – also

EARP, Henry (1831-1914)
Cattle and drover in a hilly landscape. *Watercolour, signed and dated 1899, 10¼in. x 14¼in.*

entering the R.A. Schools under Fuseli. In 1813 he painted several portraits in Plymouth and in the following two years visited Calais and Paris. He made several sketches of Napoleon on the *Bellerophon* and the sale of the resulting picture enabled him to go to Italy in 1816. He remained there until 1830, only revisiting England briefly in 1820 and after his election as A.R.A. in 1828. He also visited Greece, Sicily and Malta in 1818 and toured Holland, Belgium and Germany in 1828. He visited Vienna *en route* for England in 1830 in which year he was elected R.A. He was Librarian of the R.A. from 1842 to 1845 and Keeper of the National Gallery from 1843 to 1847. He was elected P.R.A. in 1850 and appointed Director of the N.G. in 1855. He made a number of journeys to buy pictures in Europe and it was on one of these that he died. Christie's held a studio sale on 14 December 1868.

He married **Elizabeth RIGBY (1816-1893)** in 1849. She was a daughter of Dr. Edward Rigby of Norwich and a pupil of J.S. Cotman (q.v.). She was a noted writer of articles on artistic and literary subjects and travelled widely both before and after her marriage. Her drawing is well disciplined and reminiscent of her master.

Examples: B.M.; Exeter Mus.; Newport A.G.
Bibliography: Lady Eastlake: *A Memoir of Sir C.L.E.,* 1869. C. Monkhouse: *Pictures by Sir C.L.E.,* 1875. D. Robertson: *Sir C.E. and the Victorian Art World,* 1978. *Fraser's Mag.,* 1838. *A.J.,* Oct. 1855; Feb. 1866.

EASTWOOD, Francis Hurst
1855 (Huddersfield) - p.1902
A painter of landscapes, old buildings and young ladies, who lived in London and was active at least between 1875, when he entered the R.A. Schools, and 1902. He visited Italy in about 1879 and later Algiers.

EASTWOOD, Walter
1867 (Rochdale) - 1943
A Lancashire painter who studied at the Heywood School of Art and lived at Lytham St. Annes, where he was first President of the Art Society.
Examples: Grundy Gall., Blackpool; Harris Gall., Preston.

EBDON, Christopher
1744 (Durham) - 1824 (Durham)
The son of a cordwainer, he was apprenticed to James Paine, the architect, and was in Italy in 1766. He exhibited views and architectural designs at the Society of Artists from 1767 to 1783 and worked as a draughtsman for Soane in 1791 and 1792. He designed the Freemasons' Lodge, Elvet, Durham in 1810.
Bibliography: *Gentleman's Mag.,* 1824, ii. Soane Mus., MSS correspondence. Walpole Soc. XXXXII. *Burlington Mag.,* Aug. 1990.

EBSWORTH, Joseph Woodfall
1824 - 1908
A landscape painter and lithographer who studied at the Trustees' Academy under Sir W. Allan (q.v.) and David Scott. He painted in Italy and England as well as producing

EDRIDGE, Henry (1769-1821)
Furness Abbey. *Watercolour, signed and dated 1814.*

architectural views of Edinburgh. He gave up painting for the Church in about 1860.
Examples: Huntly Ho., Edinburgh.

EDDINGTON, William Clarke
A landscape painter who lived in Worcester and exhibited from 1861 to 1885. He was an unsuccessful candidate for the N.W.S. and O.W.S. between 1862 and 1871. His work can be in the manner of M.B. Foster (q.v.), but with poor figures. He sometimes signed with initials.
Examples: V.A.M.; Reading Mus.

EDEN, Sir William, 7th and 5th Bt.
1849 (Windlestone, Durham) -
1915 (London)
Soldier, boxer, gardener, M.F.H. and amateur artist, he had lessons from S.T.G. Evans (q.v.) at Eton and he succeeded to the baronetcies in 1873. He and Whistler played the title roles in the 'Bart and Butterfly' lawsuit of 1875. He visited Egypt, India, Japan and the U.S.A. and exhibited in London and Paris. His style approaches the modern tradition of Rothenstein and Muirhead Bone.
   Another landscape painting **William EDEN** was active in Liverpool and London from 1866. This was not the baronet's father, although he had also been an amateur. Furthermore, his uncle **Lt.-Gen. George Morton EDEN (1806-1862 Berne)**, painted, having been a pupil of P. de Wint (q.v.).
Bibliography: J.A.McN. Whistler: *Eden versus Whistler, the Baronet and the Butterfly, A Valentine with a Verdict*, 1899. Sir T. Eden: *The tribulations of a Baronet*, 1933. L. Wilkes: *The Aesthetic Obsession*, 1985. *A.J.*, 1905; 1906; 1908.

EDGE, John William
c.1805 - c.1870
A marine painter who exhibited with the N.W.S. and was working between 1827 and 1834. He was a fellow apprentice of the Fieldings with W. Callow (q.v.) and C. Bentley (q.v.) until 1825, and in 1835 he accompanied Callow on his first walking tour.

EDGELL, Vice-Admiral Henry Edmund
1809 - 1876
A prolific sketcher who entered the Navy in 1821 and was stationed in Scotland in 1823. He then spent three years on the North American, West Indian, Home and Mediterranean stations and was promoted lieutenant in 1828. In 1831 he went to China on the *Imogene,* after which he was stationed in Spain and the Mediterranean. He was promoted captain in 1845 and was in the East again from 1855 to 1860.
Examples: Greenwich; Raffles Mus., Singapore.
Bibliography: *I.L.N.,* 19 Feb. 1876.

EDMONSTON, Samuel
1825 (Edinburgh) - 1906
A painter of portraits, marine and rural genre subjects in watercolour and chalk. He studied at the R.S.A. Schools and exhibited in London in 1856 and 1857 as well as in Edinburgh. Late in life he emigrated to the U.S.A.
Examples: N.G., Scotland.

EDMONSTONE, Robert, H.R.S.A
1794 (Kelso) - 1834 (Kelso)
A painter of children, portraits and genre subjects, occasionally in watercolour. He

moved from Edinburgh to London in about 1819 and studied with G.H. Harlow (q.v.) and at the R.A. Schools. He visited Italy in the early 1820s and again in 1831-32, catching fever. He returned home by way of London.

EDRIDGE, Henry, A.R.A.
1769 (Paddington) - 1821 (London)
After an apprenticeship to William Pether, he attended the R.A. Schools, where he won the approval of Reynolds. He began his career as a miniaturist, often drawing portraits of his friends and fellow artists such as Dr. Monro, Girtin, and Hearne with whom he made a number of sketching trips. He was best known as a portraitist and specialised in small full or three-quarter length drawings, usually with the sitter rather formally posed against a park or landscape. They are generally done with blacklead pencil and a little flesh colour applied to the face and hands. Charming though these can be, his landscape and architectural work is on the whole more interesting. As F.G. Stephens writes: 'Edridge's landscapes often remind us of de Wint's, and they have more colour than Girtin's, less delicate mystery and variety than Turner's, and they are only a little less masculine and studious than Hunt's'. In 1817 and 1819 he visited the North of France, and his knotty pencil drawings, sometimes with watercolour, of Gothic buildings, predate those of Prout's later style, which they probably inspired. He was elected A.R.A. only a few months before his death, presumably in recognition of his eminence as a portraitist.
Examples: B.M.; V.A.M.; Fitzwilliam; Greenwich; Leeds City A.G.; City A.G., Manchester; N.G., Scotland; Ulster Mus.
Bibliography: V.A.M.; MSS Letters to Dr. Monro, 1808-21. *Antique Collector,* Aug. 1972.

EDWARD VI, H.M. King
1537 (Hampton Court) - 1553 (Greenwich)
The only legitimate son of Henry VIII, he reigned from 1547. His father employed various Flemish painters, such as Vincent Volpe (q.v.) and John Luckas, who made topographical drawings in watercolour, usually of castles and fortifications. Edward may have been taught by one of these artists, and there is a watercolour of Windsor Castle from the Park by him on the endpaper of a miniature Bible, which once belonged to his sister Queen Elizabeth, and is now in the B.M.

EDWARDES, Hon. Elizabeth
1840 - 1911
The daughter of the 3rd Lord Kensington, she painted Windsor and the Thames. The family seat was St. Bride's Castle, Pembrokeshire, and she lived, unmarried, in London.

EDWARDS, Edward, A.R.A.
1738 (London) - 1806 (London)
A friend and follower of P. Sandby (q.v.),

EDRIDGE, Henry (1769-1821)
Portrait of a boy and girl. *Pencil and watercolour,*
signed and dated 1811, 12in. x 9in.

Edwards attained neither the fame nor the prosperity of the greater artist. He began by providing designs for furniture-makers, including his father. In 1759 he worked as a student at the Duke of Richmond's Gallery, and shortly afterwards he opened his own evening drawing school, while still himself studying at St. Martin's Lane. He began to work for Boydell in 1763 and first exhibited at the R.A. in 1771. He was elected A.R.A. in 1773. In 1775, with the help of Robert Udney, he went to Italy, returning in the following year. Later he worked as a decorator, as well as providing drawings for Horace Walpole up to 1784. In 1787, after failing to be elected to the Chair of Perspective at the Academy, he took a post as scene-painter at the Newcastle theatre. Many of his best topographical drawings are of Northumbrian subjects, but he regarded himself as an exile and was happy to return to London on winning the election in the following year. He retained the post until his death.

His topographical style is very close to that of Sandby, with careful and conventional outlines (sometimes etched) and even washes, often with a predominance of blue. He also did portrait drawings and pen and wash studies of classical figures for book illustrations, as well

as drawings for furniture and architectural detail. He generally signed with initials, and these are almost identical with the monogram of Edward Eyre (q.v.)
Published: *A Short History of the Hurricane,* 1781. *Anecdotes of Painters...,* 1808.
Examples: B.M.; V.A.M.
Bibliography: *Country Life,* 7 June 1930.

EDWARDS, Rev. Edward
1766   - 1849
A Norfolk vicar who was largely responsible for the foundation of King's Lynn Museum in 1844. The Museum now houses a collection of his local views, mostly in pen and wash. Britton used some of them for his *Beauties.*

EDWARDS, Edwin
1823 (Framlingham) - 1879 (London)
An etcher and landscape painter, who, in 1860, gave up a flourishing bar practice to become a professional artist. His earlier works were watercolours, but later, under the influence of Fantin Latour and other Frenchmen, he turned to oil painting. He was a lover of coastal scenes, especially in Cornwall and Suffolk, where he had a house at Dunwich, as well as of views on the Thames and of old towns. He

and his wife were close friends of C.S. Keene (q.v.) and of the poet Edward Fitzgerald.
Published: *Old English Inns,* 1873-81.
Examples: Castle Mus., Nottingham.
Bibliography: D. Hudson: *Charles Keene,* 1947.

EDWARDS, George F.R.S., F.S.A.
1694 (Stratford, Essex) - 1773 (Plaistow)
A naturalist who became librarian to the Royal College of Physicians. He served an apprenticeship in London, after which he spent a month in Holland. In 1718 he visited Norway, where he was taken up as a suspected spy, and in 1719 and 1720 he travelled through France. On his return he began making wash drawings of animals. He revisited Holland in 1731. His *Uncommon Birds* was used as a source book for Chelsea figures, and he was an inspirer of the vogue for chinoiserie. In 1750 he won the gold medal of the Royal Society and was later elected a Fellow. He was elected F.S.A. in 1752, and in 1764 he retired to Plaistow. Shortly before his death, his collection of drawings was bought by the Earl, later Marquess, of Bute.
Published: *Natural History of Uncommon Birds,* 1743-47. *History of Birds,* 1743-51. With M. Darley: *New Book of Chinese Designs,* 1754. *Gleanings of Natural History,* 175864. *Essays of Natural History,* 1770. *Elements of Fossilogy,* 1776.
Examples: B.M.; V.A.M.
See Colour Plate

EDWARDS, George Henry
A painter of architectural subjects, particularly churches, and landscapes, who lived in London and was active from about 1837 to 1847.

EDWARDS, George Henry, II
1859   - 1918
A genre and fairy painter in oil and watercolour who exhibited from 1883. He lived in London and also painted amusing and attractive envelopes.

EDWARDS, James
1832 (Quorndon, Leics.) - 1888 (Nottingham)
A Nottingham landscape painter who exhibited at the R.A. in 1868.
Examples: V.A.M.

EDWARDS, Jessie A
A painter of genre subjects and gardens who lived in Chelsea and exhibited at Suffolk Street between 1864 and 1879.
Near neighbours were **Kate J. EDWARDS,** who showed a genre subject in 1879, and **Louisa EDWARDS,** who showed flowers and figures in 1884 and 1885.

EDWARDS, Mary Ellen, Mrs. Staples
1839 (Kingston-upon-Thames) - c.1910
A prolific book illustrator who specialised in the homely. She worked for the *Graphic, I.L.N., Good Words, Cornhill Magazine* &c. She exhibited at the R.A. from 1862 to 1908,

using her maiden name until 1869, then Mrs. Freer until 1872, when she became Mrs. Staples. She lived in Chelsea and Essex before moving to Shere, Surrey, in 1892.
Examples: Ulster Mus.
Bibliography: *Studio*, Special Winter No., 1897-98.

EDWARDS, Rev. Pryce Carter
c.1810 - c.1840
A Welsh follower of J.S. Cotman (q.v.), who lived in Bath and was working between 1830 and 1840. His drawings are mostly in brown wash but occasionally in full watercolour, and are strongly reminiscent of Cotman's Greta period. His humans and cattle are distinctly Cubist.
Examples: Nat. Mus., Wales.
Bibliography: *Apollo*, XXVII, 1938.

EDWARDS, Sydenham Teast
1768 (Usk) - 1819 (Brompton)
A draughtsman of flora and fauna who exhibited at the R.A. from 1792 to 1814. He provided illustrations for Rees's *Cyclopaedia*, the *Sportsman's Magazine*, &c. Although he has traditionally been given the apposite middle name 'Teak', his memorial stone in Chelsea Old Church declares otherwise. It also proclaims that: 'as a faithful Delineator of Nature, few equal'd, none excel'd' him'.
Published: *Cynographia Britannica*, 1800-5. *New Flora Britannica*, 1812.
Examples: B.M.; V.A.M.

EDWARDS, William Henry
A painter of floral still lifes and occasional landscapes. He exhibited at the R.A. and the S.B.A. from 1793 to 1850 and was an unsuccessful candidate for the N.W.S. in 1843. He lived in Hammersmith, and he sometimes produced Swiss subjects.
His wife, **Mrs. W.H. EDWARDS**, exhibited a still life at the S.B.A. in 1847.
Published: *The Young Artist's Guide to Flower Drawing, and painting in Watercolours*, 1820.

EDWARDS, William Croxford
see CROXFORD, William Edward

EGERTON, Hon. Alice Mary
c.1830 - 1868
The daughter of the 1st Lord Egerton of Tatton, she married R. Cholmondeley of Condover Hall, Shropshire, in 1867 and died in childbirth the following year. She painted Civil War subjects and possibly portraits from at least 1849.

EGERTON, Lord Francis –
see ELLESMERE, Earl of

EGERTON, Jane Sophia –
see SMITH, William Collingwood

EGGINTON, Wycliffe, R.I.
1875 (Edgbaston) - 1951
A landscape painter in the Collier tradition who worked in Ireland and England, and

especially on Dartmoor. He exhibited from 1910 and was elected R.I. in 1912. In 1927 he was living in Teignmouth.
Examples: Aberdeen A.G.; Feaney A.G., Birmingham; Exeter Mus.; City A.G., Manchester; Plymouth A.G.

EGLEY, William
1798 (Doncaster) - 1870 (London)
A miniaturist who occasionally painted on a larger scale. He exhibited at the R.A. from 1824 to 1870 and was noted for his portraits of children. He moved from Doncaster to Nottingham to London and was the father of W.M. Egley (q.v.).
Bibliography: *A.J.*, July, 1870.

EGLEY, William Maw
1826 - 1916
The son of W. Egley (q.v.), he became a genre painter. He first exhibited at the R.A. in 1843 and from that year until 1855 he concentrated on book illustrations. For the next seven years, probably under the influence of his friend W.P. Frith (q.v.), he painted scenes from contemporary life and thereafter eighteenth century costume subjects. He worked in both oil and watercolour.
Examples: B.M.; V.A.M.; Fitzwilliam.
Bibliography: V.A.M. MSS diaries.

EHRET, Georg Dionysius
1708 (Erfurt) - 1770 (London)
A natural history draughtsman and a friend of Linnaeus, Ehret first came to England in 1735, settling permanently the next year after a visit to Holland. His approach is that of a scientist rather than a decorative artist. He often worked on vellum and used bodycolour as well as watercolour.
Examples: V.A.M.; Ashmolean; Kew; Nat. Hist. Mus.; R.H.S.
Bibliography: Linnaean Soc.: *Proceedings*, 1894-5.

ELEY, Mary
A genre painter who exhibited genre subjects, sometimes on Oriental themes, at the R.A. and Suffolk Street between 1874 and 1897. She lived in London.

ELFORD, Sir William, Bt.
1749 (Bickham, Devon) - 1837 (Totnes)
A partner in a Plymouth bank, he was Mayor of Plymouth in 1797 and M.P. from 1796 to 1806. From 1807 to 1808 he was M.P. for Rye. He was also Lieutenant-Colonel in the South Devon Militia and served in Ireland during the 1798 rebellion. He was created a baronet in 1800 and lived the later part of his life at the Priory, Totnes, where he took an active part in local affairs. A member of a wide literary and artistic circle, he was himself an artist, exhibiting at the R.A. from 1774 to 1837. He often made presents of his pictures and drawings to his friends, including the Prince Regent.
Examples: B.M.

ELGOOD, George Samuel, R.I.
1851 (Leicester) - 1943
A landscape painter and gardener, he was educated at Bloxham and studied at South Kensington. He lived near Leicester and near Tenterden, Kent, and specialised in painting formal gardens and architecture in England, Italy and Spain. He was elected R.I. in 1882. Various exhibitions of his views of gardens were held at the Fine Art Society. He was a brother-in-law of J. Fulleylove (q.v.).
Thomas Scott ELGOOD, by whom there are three watercolours in the Darlington A.G., may have been a relation. He was living in Birmingham in 1879.
Published: *Some English Gardens*, 1904. *Italian Gardens*, 1907.
Examples: Preston Manor, Brighton; Maidstone Mus.; Wakefield A.G.
Bibliography: *Studio*, V, 1895; XIII, 1898; XIX, 1900; Summer No., 1900. XXV, 1902; XXXI, 1904; XLIII, 1908. *A.J.* 1906.

ELGOOD, J.
A draughtsman and caricaturist working in the late eighteenth and early nineteenth centuries.

ELIZABETH, H.R.H. Princess, Landgravine of Hesse-Homburg
1770 (Buckingham House) - 1840 (Frankfurt)
Seventh child of George III and Queen Charlotte, she married the Hereditary Prince of Hesse-Homburg in 1818, and remained in that state until his death in 1829, when she moved to Hanover. She revisited England in 1831 and spent many winters in Frankfurt.
Her early enthusiasm for drawing earned here the nickname of 'The Muse'. The first series of engravings after her drawings *The Birth and Triumph of Cupid* was published in 1795. Later publications included *Cupid turned Volunteer*, 1804 and *The Power and Progress of Genius*, 1806, the profits from which provided dowries for virtuous girls. She continued to produce similar subjects in Germany.
Examples: B.M.
Bibliography: Mrs. E.T. Cook: *Royal Elizabeths*, 1928. D.M. Stuart: *The Daughters of George III*, 1939.

ELLESMERE, Francis Egerton, né Leveson-Gower, 1st Earl of
1800 (London) - 1857 (London)
The younger son of the Duchess-Countess of Sutherland (q.v.), and the nephew of the Earl of Bridgewater from whom he inherited the great collection of paintings and a fortune. He was himself a notable patron and collector, and was President of the British Association. He was educated at Eton and Christ Church, and served briefly in the army before election to the House of Commons in 1822. He held a number of government offices and succeeded to his uncle's possessions (and surname) in

1833. He spent the winter of 1839 cruising in the Eastern Mediterranean, and thereafter built a gallery for the public display of the collection at Bridgewater House. He was created Earl of Ellesmere in 1846. He was also a poet and writer on a variety of topics, and his wife Harriet Greville, was an authoress. As well as Near Eastern subjects, he drew English houses, sometimes in pencil and wash.
Published: *Mediterranean Sketches,* 1843. &c.
Illustrated: H. Egerton: *Journal of a Tour in the Holy Land…,* 1841.

**ELLICOMBE, General Sir Charles Grene
1783 (Alphington, Devon) - 1871 (Worthing)**
The elder son of the rector of Alphington, he was a topographer. On leaving Woolwich in 1801 he was commissioned in the Royal Engineers and spent the next eighteen months in Portsmouth. He was then sent to Ceylon, where he remained until 1807. He served next at Chatham and in the North, and, from 1811 to 1814, in the Peninsula. In 1813 he was promoted lieutenant-colonel, becoming full colonel in 1830 and major-general in 1841. From 1821 to 1842 he was Inspector-General of Fortifications in London. He was appointed Colonel-Commandant of the Royal Engineers in 1856, was promoted full general in 1861 and knighted in the following year. On his retirement he settled at Worthing. His brother married Eliza, daughter of J. Swete (q.v.).
Examples: B.M.

**ELLIOTT, Rev. Anthony Lewis
c.1847 - 1909**
An amateur artist who graduated from Trinity College, Dublin in 1869. He held various appointments in Dublin, becoming a Canon of Christ Church Cathedral in 1905.

**ELLIOTT, Captain Robert James, F.S.A.
1791 - 1849 (London)**
A naval officer who cannot have been the **Robert ELLIOTT** who exhibited views of Canada and Jamaica at the R.A. from 1784 to 1789. Robert James Elliott entered the Navy in 1802, serving at Portsmouth and Halifax, visiting Chile, and making lieutenant in 1808. He was wounded at Batavia and remained in the East Indies until 1814. He was then promoted commander, and mostly served ashore. He was an active promoter of a Sailors' Home in the Port of London. His sketches of India, Canton and the Red Sea made between 1822 and 1824 were worked up for publication by S. Prout and C. Stanfield (qq.v.).
Illustrated: E. Roberts: *Views in the East,* 1830-33.
Examples: Portsmouth City Mus.

**ELLIOTT, Robinson
1814 (South Shields) - 1894 (South Shields)**
A painter of landscapes, portraits, coastal and genre scenes in oil and watercolour. He attended Sass's Academy and on his return to the North-East set up the first art class in South Shields. He exhibited at the R.A. from 1844 to 1881. He was also a poet.
Published: *Treasures of the Deep,* 1894.

ELLIS, Major-General Sir Arthur Edward Augustus 1837 (Gibraltar) - 1907
As equerry to the Prince of Wales from 1867 he may have started the fashion for illustrated envelopes among Royal servants, and in fact, he is probably the master of this esoteric subsection of the English School of watercolours. His comic figures are really very good indeed. He was a son of Col. the Hon. A.F. Ellis. From Sandhurst he went to the Crimea, and he was A.D.C. to Lord Elphinstone, Governor of Bombay, from 1858 to 1860. In 1866 he accompanied the Prince to Russia, and wrote up and illustrated the trip. He was promoted colonel in 1878 and major-general in 1885. He was knighted in 1897, and was Sergeant-at-Arms in the House of Lords from 1898 1901.
Illustrated: Lord Suffield: *Memoirs,* 1913.
Bibliography: D. Swales: *Hand Illustrated Postal Envelopes,* 1996. See *Country Life,* 26 April 1990 for illustration (wrongly attrib.).

**ELLIS, Edwin John
1841 (Nottingham) - 1895**
A marine and landscape painter who moved to London after working in a lace factory and studying under Henry Dawson. He exhibited from 1865 to 1891 and became a member of the S.B.A. in 1875. His favourite subjects were found on the coasts of Yorkshire, Cornwall and Wales. His work can be free in the later manner of Napier Hemy (q.v.), although his colour tends to be brighter. He was also a poet and book illustrator.
Examples: V.A.M.; Maidstone Mus.; City A.G., Manchester; Castle Mus., Nottingham.
Bibliography: *A.J.,* 1895.

**ELLIS, Tristram James
1844 (Great Malvern) - 1922**
Probably a relative of E.J. Ellis (q.v.), he worked as an engineer on the District and Metropolitan Railways before studying art in Paris. He travelled in Syria in 1880, produced a number of Norwegian views around 1893 and visited Cyprus in 1879, and Egypt, Cyprus, Turkey and Russia in 1896 and 1898. He was a book illustrator, and at one time P. May (q.v.) shared a studio with him.
Published: *On a Raft, and through the Desert,* 1881.
Bibliography: *Portfolio,* 1879. *A.J.,* 1884. *Studio,* Summer No., 1902.

ELLIS, William 1747 (London) - 1810
An engraver who was a pupil of W. Woollett (q.v.) and worked from his own topographical drawings as well as those of the Sandbys, Hearne and others. His work is in the manner of S.H. Grimm (q.v.).
Illustrated: D. Lyson: *Environs of London,* 1844.
Examples: B.M.

**ELLIS, William Webb
c.1750 (Cambridgeshire) - 1785 (Ostend)**
Educated at Cambridge and St. John's Hospital, he accompanied Captain Cook's last voyage to the Pacific as surgeon's second mate on the *Discovery.* His prospects of a naval career were blighted by the publication of his unofficial account of the voyage in 1782. He was accidentally killed in a fall from a mast. His drawings are of two kinds: detailed studies of flowers, fish and birds, and topographical views which show the influence of J. Webber (q.v.), the official artist.
Examples: Nat. Hist. Mus.; Greenwich; Nat. Lib., Australia; Turnbull Lib., Wellington; B.P. Bishop Mus., Honolulu.

ELLISON, Thomas 1866 - c.1942
A painter of accomplished Continental townscapes and market scenes in the early years of the twentieth century. He used white heightening.

**ELMORE, Alfred, R.A.
1815 (Clonakilty, Co. Cork) - 1881 (London)**
A historical painter who moved to London, with his father, a retired army surgeon, at the age of twelve. There he made drawings from the antique at the B.M., entered the R.A. Schools in 1834 and first exhibited at the R.A. two years later. He travelled in France, Germany and Italy, returning to London in 1844. Pictures from this year, which he exhibited at the B.I. and the R.A., established him as a historical painter of the first rank and won his election as A.R.A. He became a full R.A. in 1857 and was made an Honorary R.H.A. in 1878.
Examples: B.M.; V.A.M.; Ashmolean; N.G., Scotland.
Bibliography: *A.J.,* April 1857; 1865; 1866; 1881. *Portfolio,* 1881.

**ELPHINSTONE, Major-General Sir Howard Craufurd, V.C.
1829 (Wattram, Livonia) - 1890 (at sea)**
A descendant of a Scottish family which had served with distinction in both the Russian and the British Navies, he passed out top of his batch at the R.M.A. Woolwich in 1847. He became a full lieutenant in the R.E. in 1851, full captain in 1862, full colonel in 1884 and major-general in 1887.
He attended reviews in Prussia in 1853 and served in the Ordnance Survey in Scotland until posted to the Crimea in the following year. He won his V.C. for his conduct before the Redan. During the latter part of the 1850s he worked on a number of reports and publications dealing with the engineers in the Crimea, and in 1859 he was appointed governor to the future Duke of Connaught. In that capacity, and later as Comptroller, he attended Woolwich again with the Prince, and toured Canada, India, the Mediterranean and elsewhere. He was ADC to the Queen from 1877 and commanded the engineers at Aldershot. His final post was commander of the Western District, but in 1890

EMES, John (1762-1808)
The Lake of Keswick. *Watercolour, 4in. x 6½in.*

he fell overboard off Ushant while on a month's leave. Throughout his career he was a keen landscape sketcher.

ELPHINSTONE, Hon. John
1706   - 1753
The eldest son of the 9th Lord Elphinstone was a topographer who worked in Edinburgh and also London in the 1730s. He was a notable engraver and mapmaker, and his drawing style is reminiscent of that of A. Devis (q.v.), with spindly figures. In the late 1730s he drew *Fifteen Views of the Most Remarkable Buildings of the City of Edinburgh,* which were issued in book form at the time, and later used as illustrations for Arnot's *History of Edinburgh,* 1779. His maps of Britain (1744) and Scotland (1745) were used by both sides during the Jacobite Rebellion.
Examples: Edinburgh City Coll.

ELPHINSTONE, Hon. Mountstuart
1779 (Cumbernauld) -
1859 (Limpsfield, Surrey)
The fourth son of the 11th Lord Elphinstone, he was educated in Scotland and London before going to India in 1796. There he continued to educate himself, travelled widely, escaped the massacre at Benares in 1798 and fought and drew in the Deccan campaign of 1803. From 1804 he was Resident in Nagpore, in 1808 Ambassador to Kabul and from 1810 Resident at Poona, once again escaping massacre in 1817. He was Governor of Bombay from 1819 to 1827, where a college was named after him, and in later life he was regarded as the great expert on Indian affairs. He travelled home by Greece and Italy, and much of his later life was devoted to writing. He steadfastly rejected public honours and appointments. His watercolours are competent enough, if a little tentative and old-fashioned.

Published: *History of India; The Rise of British Power in the East,* 1887.
Bibliography: Sir E. Colebrooke: *Life,* 1884; J. Mill: *History of India.*

ELTON, Samuel Averill
1827 (Newnham) - 1886 (London)
A landscape painter in oil and watercolour who exhibited between 1860 and 1884 and became Master of the Darlington School of Art.
His son **Edgar Averill ELTON (1859-1923)** succeeded him in the post in 1886, retiring soon after the First World War. He also painted landscapes.
Examples: V.A.M.

EMANUEL, Frank Lewis
1865 (London) - 1948 (St. John's Wood)
An etcher and illustrator who was educated at University College School and University College, London, and studied at Julian's and the Slade. He travelled widely, visiting South Africa and Ceylon as well as the Continent. He worked as a town planner for a while and taught art at the Central School of Art, Forest School, Claremont and Linden House School. He was also a special artist for the *Manchester Guardian* and art critic for the *Architectural Review.* His subjects were usually landscapes and coastal scenes, and his style derived from those of de Wint and W.R. Beverly (qq.v.). He sometimes used tinted paper.
Examples: V.A.M.; London Mus.
Bibliography: *Studio,* VIII, 1896; XVIII, 1900; XXX, 1904. *A.J.,* 1906.

EMERSON, Caroline Elizabeth Douglas
1843 (Great Yarmouth) -
This lady seems to have been the author of a number of watercolours of the Lake District and Scotland which were exhibited by 'C.E. Emerson' at the R.A. between 1866 and 1881.

EMERY, John
1777 (Sunderland) - 1822 (London)
A leading comedian of the day, whose acting was said to be like 'a bottle of old port and to possess a fine, rough and mellow flavour that forms an irresistible attraction'. He was also a painter in oil and watercolour, exhibiting at the R.A. from 1801 to 1817. Perhaps because his early life was spent at seaside theatres, he specialised in marine subjects and racehorses.
His son, the actor **Samuel Anderson EMERY (1817 London - 1881 London),** was also a draughtsman. He visited America and Australia.

EMES, John
1762 (Mackworth, Derbyshire) - 1808
An etcher, engraver and silversmith who was apprenticed to W. Woollett (q.v.) and entered the R.A. Schools in 1780. One of his earliest, and best-known engravings is *The Destruction of the Spanish Batteries before Gibraltar,* 1786, after Jefferys. There are prints by him in *Vitruvius Dorsettiensis,* 1816. He exhibited at the R.A. in 1790 and 1791 and made Hearne-like tinted drawings in the Lake District. Some of these were engraved for T. West: *Guide to the Lakes,* 1778. As a smith he was in partnership with Henry Chawner and specialised in tea and coffee services. His widow, Rebecca, continued the business.
Examples: B.M.; V.A.M.; Abbot Hall A.G., Kendal.

EMMS, John
1841 (Blofield, Norfolk) - 1912 (Lyndhurst)
The son of an artist and a brother-in-law of Sir W.B. Richmond, he began as an assistant to Lord Leighton (q.v.) in London and at Lyndhurst. He gradually developed into a landscape and animal painter in oil and occasionally watercolour, and he finally settled in Lyndhurst in the 1880s. Much of his produce was painted to pay off bills, and having done so he would take his family up to town to celebrate. His work can be pleasantly free, and his hounds are particularly well done.

EMSLIE, Alfred Edward, A.R.W.S.
1848   - 1917
A son of John Emslie (*vide infra*), he became a genre and portrait painter, exhibited in London from 1867 and was elected A.R.W.S. in 1888. He contributed to the *I.L.N.* and the *Graphic,* and his work there was admired by van Gogh. An exhibition of his work was held at the Fine Art Society in 1896. His masterpiece is the oil painting 'Dinner at Haddo House' in the N.P.G.
Bibliography: *A.J.,* 1900. *Studio,* XX, 1904; XXXII, 1904.

EMSLIE, John Phillipp
1839   - 1913 (London)
A son of the engraver, **John EMSLIE (1813-1875),** who also painted landscapes and architectural subjects, he followed the same profession and painted genre and topographical subjects, which he exhibited

from 1869. He lived in London.
Examples: Bishopsgate Inst.

ENFIELD, Anne, Mrs. William, née Needham - 1865
From 1825 the wife of William Enfield, Town Clerk of Nottingham from 1845 to 1870, she was a pupil and imitator of J.B. Pyne (q.v.). Several of her views of Nottingham were lithographed.

A relative was **Mary Pindlebury ENFIELD (1859-c.1945)** who exhibited miniatures at the R.A. from 1892. Another painting relative was **Russell DOWSON**, who visited Japan and Hong Kong, and exhibited French, Venetian and other landscapes at the R.A. and S.B.A. from 1886.
Examples: Castle Mus., Nottingham.

ENFIELD, Henry
1849 (Bramscote, Notts.) - p.1904
He entered the family firm of solicitors in Nottingham and was an amateur artist, painting landscapes in oil and watercolour. He exhibited at the R.A. and Suffolk Street from 1872 to at least 1904.

ENGLAND, J
A topographer working around London from 1790 to about 1800. The watercolours in the B.M. are of Clapham and Enfield.
Examples: B.M.; Brighton A.G.

ENGLEFIELD, Sir Henry Charles, Bt., F.R.S., F.S.A.   1752 - 1822 (London)
An antiquary, collector and patron, and a scientific writer, he succeeded his father in 1780 and was the last baronet. He was elected F.S.A. in 1779 and was President in 1811 and 1812. He was also a member of the Dilettanti and Linnaean Societies. He was a friend of Dr. Monro and a patron of J.S. Cotman, probably introducing him to his brother-in-law, Francis Cholmeley. Cotman dedicated his first series of etchings to Englefield in 1811. His own drawings are rather old-fashioned.
Published: *On the Determination of the Orbits of Planets*, 1793. *A Walk through Southampton*, 1801. *Observations on...the Demolition of London Bridge*, 1821. &c.
Examples: Brighton A.G.

ENGLEHEART, George
1752 (Kew) - 1839 (Blackheath)
A miniaturist who was a pupil of Reynolds and studied at the R.A. Schools. Occasionally he also painted rather dull topographical watercolours. He was Miniature Painter to George III.
Examples: V.A.M.; Salisbury Mus.

ENNISKILLEN, William Willoughby, 3rd Earl of, F.R.S.   1807 - 1886
A pupil of H. Bright (q.v.). Until his succession in 1840 he was Viscount Cole. He was a fellow of the R.G.S. and the Hon. Colonel of the 3rd Battalion, the Royal Irish Fusiliers.

His aunt, **Lady Frances COLE (d.1847)**, a daughter of the 1st Earl of Malmesbury and wife of Gen. Sir G.L. Cole, and her daughter **Florence Mary Georgiana COLE (1816/17-1888)** were both also taught by Bright.

ENOCK, Arthur Henry
1828/9 (Glamorganshire) - 1917 (?Newton Abbot)
A self-taught painter of landscapes and moorlands who began his career working for a Brazilian merchant in Birmingham. There he studied the Coxes, and during his holidays he sketched at Betws-y-Coed and around Snowdon. He exhibited at Birmingham from 1869 to 1910 as well as in London. In about 1890 he turned to art as a profession and moved to Devon, where he was known as the 'Artist of the Dart'. He painted in both oil and watercolour, the latter particularly later in life, and he was noted for his handling of mist and sunlight.
Examples: Exeter Mus.

EPPS –
see **TADEMA, L.A., and PRATT, A.J.E.**

ESPIN, Thomas
1767 (Holton, Lincolnshire) - 1822 (Louth)
The son of a farmer, he became an antiquarian, schoolmaster, occasional architect and artist. Most of his career was spent in Louth where he ran a 'Mathematical, Architectural, Nautical and Commercial Academy'. His architectural work was in the Gothic style. His drawings were used for such books as Howlett's *Views in the County of Lincoln*, 1805.
Examples: Lincs. Co. Record Office.
Published: *A Short History of Louth Church*, 1807. *A Description of the Mausoleum in Brocklesby Park*, 1812.
Bibliography: *Gentleman's Mag.*, 1822, ii. See R.W. Goulding: *Notes on Books and Pamphlets printed at Louth, 1801-50*, 1920.

ESSEX, Arthur Algernon, 6th Earl of
1803 - 1892 (Cassiobury)
The nephew and successor of 'Girtin's saviour', he was a very competent landscape painter in a splashy Leitch-like manner. The family seats were Hampton Court, Herefordshire and Cassiobury, Hertfordshire.

ESSEX, Richard Hamilton
1802 - 1855 (Bow)
An architectural and topographical draughtsman who was A.O.W.S. from 1823 until his resignation in 1837. Very occasionally he produced subject pieces, but he usually concentrated on English cathedrals and churches, or, in 1830 and 1831, Belgian cathedrals. He made a number of diagrams and drawings of the Temple Church for the Benchers and appears to have lived in London throughout his career.
Examples: V.A.M.

ESTALL, William Charles
1857 (London) - 1897 (Thakeham)
A painter of landscapes, moonlight and sheep,

he was brought up in Manchester and studied in London, France and Germany. He exhibited from 1874.
Examples: V.A.M.; Leeds City A.G.
Bibliography: *Studio*, XII, 1898.

ETTY, William, R.A.
1787 (York) - 1849 (York)
He began to draw on the floor of his father's bakery and, after serving an apprenticeship with a Hull printer, he moved to London in 1805 determined to become an artist. With the support of Opie and Fuseli he attended the R.A. Schools, and he boarded with Lawrence, who gave him some tuition. In 1811 he first exhibited at the B.I. and the R.A. and by about 1820 had won a measure of success. He visited Italy briefly in 1816 and again in 1822-3, spending eighteen months in Venice. He also visited Paris several times, and later Belgium. His life was entirely devoted to painting, and towards the end of his career he achieved financial success and his work briefly became a cult. He was elected A.R.A. and R.A. in 1824 and 1828. 'Finding God's most glorious work to be woman', he set himself to extol her naked virtues. His remaining works were sold at Christie's, 6-14 May 1850.
Examples: B.M.; V.A.M.; Cartwright Hall, Bradford; Leicestershire A.G.; City A.G., Manchester; York City A.G.
Bibliography: A. Gilchrist: *Life of W.E.*, 1855. W.C. Monkhouse: *Pictures by W.E.*, 1874. W. Gaunt: *E. and the Nude*, 1943. D. Farr: *W.E.*, 1958. B.J. Bailey: *W.E.'s Nudes*, 1974. *A.J.*, 1849; 1858; 1859; 1903. Soc. of Arts, Exhibition Cat., 1849. York City A.G., Exhibition Cat., 1949. *Country Life*, 11 November 1949. Arts Co., Exhibition Cat., 1955. *Connoisseur*, CLIII, 1963. RSA *Journal*, July 1990.

EVANS, Rev. Arthur Benoni
1781 (Compton Beauchamp) - 1854 (Market Bosworth)
A miscellaneous writer, a musician and an amateur artist, he was educated at Gloucester College School and St. John's College, Oxford. In 1805 he was appointed Professor of Classics and History at the Royal Military College, Great Marlow, which moved to Sandhurst in 1812. He resigned in 1822, and became curate of Burnham, where he ran a crammer until 1829, when he was appointed Headmaster of Market Bosworth Grammar School. His writings are very varied, and his drawings included works in pencil, pastel and brown wash. He was particularly praised for his cattle subjects.

EVANS, Bernard Walter, R.I.
1848 (Birmingham) - 1922 (London)
The son of the designer Walter Swift Evans, and a cousin of George Eliot, he was a pupil of Samuel Lines and then settled in London exhibiting at the R.A. from 1871 to 1886. He was elected R.I. in 1888 and was a member of the R.B.A. as well as a founder of the short-lived City of London Society of Artists. He specialised in English and Continental

EVANS, Bernard Walter (1848-1922)
'Barden Tower', the house of the shepherd Lord Wharfedale. *Watercolour, signed and inscribed on reverse, 18⅛in. x 27½in.*

landscapes and he had a very good sense of distance and atmosphere.
Examples: V.A.M.; Blackburn A.G.; Cartwright Hall, Bradford; Laing A.G., Newcastle.
Bibliography: *Studio*, Summer Special No., 1900.

EVANS, Edmund
1826 (Southwark) - 1905 (Ventnor, IoW)
A pioneer and master of colour printing, a wood engraver, illustrator and watercolourist. He was a fellow apprentice of Birket Foster with Landells, and became a notable producer of illustrated books. He lived in Bayswater and Wandsworth, and in 1864, when he married Foster's niece, he also took a house in Witley. His work as a printer was the making of Caldecott and Greenaway. In 1892 he retired from business and settled at Ventnor. As a painter he exhibited watercolours of Wales, Norway and elsewhere at Suffolk Street from 1857 to 1873.
An **E.W. EVANS**, with whom he has sometimes been confused, lived in Chelsea and Hackney between 1879 and 1882 when he was exhibiting Thames and Essex views at Suffolk Street.
Bibliography: M. Hardie: *English Coloured Books*, 1906. E. Evans: *The Reminiscences of E.E.*, 1976. *A.J.*, 1898. *British & Colonial Printer*, 31 March 1904; 7 Sept. 1905. *Publishers' Circular*, 14 Oct. 1905.

EVANS, Frederick James McNamara
A genre painter who exhibited from 1886 and at the R.A. from 1891. At times he had a strange apocalyptic vision. He lived in London from 1888 to 1894 and from 1914 to 1928, and, in the interim, at Penzance where he painted fisherfolk and their cottages in a manner that shows an admiration for W.

Langley (q.v.). He signed 'FRED.M.EVANS'.
Examples: Maidstone Mus.

EVANS, John
A painter who began by exhibiting English landscapes at Suffolk Street in 1849 and '50, returning in the 1870s with Welsh landscapes and views on Skye. He soon moved on to French and Italian subjects, and from 1880 concentrated on Venice. During the early period he was living in London, and during the later his address was in Blackheath.

EVANS, Marjorie, Mrs. A. Scott Elliot
c.1850 (?Aberdeen) - 1907 (?Aberdeen)
A flower, still life, landscape and occasional portrait painter who was based on Aberdeen, but also worked in Edinburgh and the South. She was elected R.I. in 1891, but resigned in 1902.

EVANS, Richard
1784 (Birmingham) - 1871 (Southampton)
He studied at the R.A. Schools in 1815 and began as a copyist of his friend Cox, continuing in Rome as a copyist of old masters. He was assistant to Lawrence for a time and exhibited portraits at the R.A. from 1816 to 1859.
Examples: B.M.
Bibliography: *A.J.*, March, 1872.

EVANS, Samuel Thomas George, R.W.S.
1829 (Eton) - 1904 (R.W.S., Pall Mall)
The son and successor of Evans of Eton, where their house is still called Evans's, he entered the R.A. Schools in 1849, exhibited from 1854, and produced Thames views reminiscent of those of T.M. Richardson, Yr. (q.v.). In the 1860s he

built himself a chalet and boathouse on Lake Hallstadt in the Tyrol. He was elected A.R.W.S. and R.W.S. in 1858 and 1897. He taught Princess Beatrice and Prince Leopold. He died of a heart attack while carrying pictures to the winter exhibition of the R.W.S.
In turn his son **William Sidney Valentine EVANS (1866-1949)** became a landscape painter.
Published: *A Primer for Beginners*, 1891; *Learning to Draw*, 1899.
Examples: B.M.; N.G., Ireland.
Bibliography: *A.J.*, 1905. Brewhouse Gall., Eton Coll., *Exhibition Cat.*, 1998.

EVANS, Wilfred
A painter of corners in and about Westminster Abbey, genre subjects and fishy or fruity still lifes. He moved from Clapton, to Hornsey to High Barnet during his exhibiting years at Suffolk Street, 1880 to 1890.

EVANS, William 1772 -
A draughtsman and engraver who studied at the R.A. Schools and was working for the Society of Dilettanti, Boydell and others by about 1800. He also took pencil and wash portraits. He contributed to Cadell's *Gallery of Contemporary Portraits*, 1822.

EVANS, William, of Eton, O.W.S.
1798 (Eton) - 1877 (Eton)
The son of **Samuel EVANS (1762-1837)**, drawing master at Eton, whom he succeeded in 1823, and the father of S.T.G. Evans (q.v.), who in turn succeeded him in the post thirty years later. He was educated at Eton and was a pupil of de Wint and W. Collins (qq.v.). He lived at Eton all his life and was housemaster at the College from 1839. He made regular visits to Scotland from 1831, on the first occasion accompanied by J.F. Lewis and G. Cattermole (qq.v.), and to Blair Atholl in particular from 1848. He visited Ireland in 1835 and '38, providing drawings of Galway and Connemara for the Halls' *Ireland, its Scenery and Character*, 1843, and he also painted in Wales. He may have visited Belgium in 1828, and he spent Christmas 1847-8 in Paris, but his only serious visit to the Continent was in 1867-8, when he overwintered on the Riviera. He was a noted Psychrolute. He was elected A.O.W.S. and O.W.S. in 1828 and 1830, and he acted as unofficial vice-president for Lewis, but the retirement of the latter in 1858 led to an irremediable breach between the old friends. Like his Bristol namesake (q.v.) he was a great one for working up the texture of his paintings with white or by scraping and scumbling in the studio. His sketches show much more freedom, but he was not strong on composition.
Examples: B.M.; V.A.M.; Haworth A.G., Accrington.
Bibliography: E. Gambier Parry: *Annals of an Eton House*, 1907. *A.J.*, 1878. *Connoisseur*, CXII, 1943. Brewhouse Gall., Eton Coll., *Exhibition Cat.*, 1998.

EVANS, William, of Bristol, A.O.W.S.
1809 (Bristol) - 1858 (London)

Evans seems to have spent most of his earlier life in Bristol, where he was a pupil of F. Danby (q.v.), and in Wales. His sister Helen probably became Danby's mistress. After 1845, when he was elected A.O.W.S., he stayed in London for some periods, although he still spent much time in Wales. He illustrated an edition of Scott in 1834. He made at least one Continental tour, from 1852 to 1854, to the Rhine and Italy, and he may also have been in the Lake District with J.B. Pyne (q.v.) in 1857 or 1858. He was a teacher both of drawing and of the guitar, but was not himself a prolific artist. In style he was a great technician, soaking, pumping, scraping and scratching his paper, and using its texture to aid his compositions. His drawings are gay and rich in colouring.

Examples: B.M.; Brighton A.G.; Bristol City A.G.; Newport A.G.

Bibliography: A.J., May, 1859. W&D, 1988, i; 1991, iii.

EVANS, William, of Eton (1798-1877)
Boats and a rider by the Thames. *Watercolour.*

EVERITT, Allen Edward
1824 (Birmingham) - 1882 (Edgbaston)

The son of an art dealer and grandson of D. Parkes (q.v.), Everitt took lessons from Cox. Until about the age of thirty he concentrated on drawing the old buildings of the Midlands. Between thirty and forty he made tours in Germany, Belgium and France gathering similar material. Later he painted interiors. He had a large practice as a drawing master and taught at the Birmingham Deaf and Dumb Institution. He was a member of the Royal Society of Artists of Birmingham and became its secretary.

Illustrated: Davidson: *History of the Holtes of Aston,* 1854. J.T. Bunce: *History of Old St. Martin's,* 1875.

Examples: City A.G., Birmingham; Birmingham Lib.; Grosvenor Mus., Chester; Gloucester City A.G.; Shrewsbury Lib.; Nat. Mus., Wales.

Bibliography: A.J., 1882. *Chronique des Arts,* 1882.

EWART, Vice-Admiral Charles Joseph Frederick   1816   - 1884

A professional sailor who accompanied the Lycian expedition of 1842 and served in the Mediterranean in 1854 and the Lebanon in 1861. He had retired by 1868. He was a competent draughtsman, working in a style based on that of E. Lear (q.v.).

EWBANK, John Wilson, R.S.A.
1799 (Gateshead) - 1847 (Edinburgh)

Intended for the Catholic Church, he ran away from Ushaw College and in 1813 apprenticed himself to T. Coulson in Newcastle. He moved to Edinburgh with his master and studied under A. Nasmyth (q.v.). He became a successful drawing master and in 1830 was a Foundation Member of the R.S.A. In 1838 he lost his membership, and during his last twelve years he became an alcoholic; his pictures

were painted in alehouses or in the cellar where he lived. These were slapdash efforts, painted on tin, and immediately sold to pay for his drinking. His best works were small pictures in oil or watercolour of rivers, coastal or marine subjects. From about 1829 he also painted large historical scenes.

Illustrated: J. Browne: *Picturesque Views of Edinburgh,* 1825.

Examples: B.M.; Haworth A.G., Accrington; N.G., Scotland.

Bibliography: A.J., 1848; 1851.

EYRE, Edward

A landscape and architectural painter who was working between about 1771 and 1792. He visited Bath each season from 1772 to 1776 and also painted in Derbyshire. His buildings are good, but his figures poor. His monogram can be confused with the initials of Edward Edwards (q.v.).

Examples: B.M.; V.A.M.; Victoria A.G., Bath; Brighton A.G.

EYRE, James
1807 (Ashbourne) - 1838 (Derby)

After training as a solicitor, he took up art and came to London where he studied under de Wint and Creswick (qq.v.), exhibiting at the B.I. and Suffolk Street. He established a class for drawing and design at the Derby Mechanics Institute. He painted a few landscapes in oil.

Examples: Derby A.G.

EVANS, William, of Bristol (1809-1858)
View of Snowdon. *Signed and dated 1843, watercolour, 9in. x 12½in.*

F

FAED, James
1821 (Barley Mill, Kirkcudbright) -
1911 (Edinburgh)
Brother of J. and T. Faed (q.v.), he exhibited
portrait miniatures, landscapes and genre
subjects in London and Edinburgh from 1855.
He was also a print maker, and a practical
handyman, making guns and building boats.
After his marriage to a tobacco heiress in 1852
he moved to London, but he returned to
Scotland three years later, buying country
estates as well as an Edinburgh property.
Examples: S.N.P.G.; Aberdeen A.G.; Edinburgh City
Coll.; Glasgow A.G.
Bibliography: M. McKerrow: *The Faeds*, 1982.

FAED, James, Yr.
1856 (Mid Calder) - 1920 (New Galloway)
The elder surviving son of J. Faed (q.v.), he was
a painter of portraits and moors, for the most
part in watercolour. He exhibited from the age
of twenty, despite having no extra-familial
training. He married a daughter of R. Herdman
(q.v.) and lived for many years in London, but
Galloway and its heather remained his principal
inspiration. In turn, it was a watercolour in his
studio, as well as the death of his own son, that
inspired Harry Lauder's 'Keep right on to the
end of the road'. He returned to the area shortly
after the First World War.
His younger brother **William Cotton FAED
(1858 Mid Calder - 1937 Jersey)** was also a
painter in oil and watercolour.
Examples: Town Hall, New Galloway.

FAED, John, R.S.A.
1819 (Barley Mill, Kircudbright) -
1902 (Kirkcudbright)
He began his career as a self-taught miniaturist,
achieving success after moving to Edinburgh in
1841. During the next ten years he turned from
miniatures to larger works in oil and watercolour,
specialising in genre scenes which were greatly
influenced by Wilkie. He was a regular exhibitor
at the R.S.A. and was elected A.R.S.A. in 1847
and R.S.A. in 1851. He moved to London in
1862, where he exhibited at the R.A. until 1880.
His style is akin to that of his brother Thomas,
and throughout his life he remained close to
Wilkie, especially in his wash drawing.
Examples: Cartwright Hall, Bradford; Glasgow
A.G.; Royal Shakespeare Theatre, Stratford.
Bibliography: M. McKerrow: *The Faeds*, 1982. *A.J.*,
1865; 1867-9; Oct. 1871; 1872; 1874. *Gallovidian
Mag.*, Spring 1902.

FAED, Thomas, R.A., A.R.S.A.
1826 (Barley Mill, Kirkcudbright) -
1900 (London)
The pupil of his brother, John Faed (q.v.), he

studied at the Edinburgh School of Design and
was elected A.R.S.A. in 1849. He moved to
London in 1852 and was elected A.R.A. and
R.A. in 1861 and 1864, retiring in 1893 because
of increasing blindness. He was a good
draughtsman, and his subjects were Scottish,
sentimental and pathetic. His remaining works
were sold at Christie's, 16 February 1901.
His son **John Francis FAED (1859-1904)**
was a marine painter.
Examples: B.M.; V.A.M.; Haworth A.G.,
Accrington; Brighton A.G.; Dundee A.G.; Exeter
Mus.; Glasgow A.G.; Paisley A.G.
Bibliography: M. McKerrow: *The Faeds*, 1982. *A.J.*,
1851-61; 1863-68; 1870-72; 1876; 1880; 1906.
Mag. of Art, 1878. N.G.S.: MS notes and
sketchbooks of T.F. Nat.Lib.S.: MSS letters of T.F.

FAGAN, Louis Alexander
1845 (Naples) - 1903 (Florence)
Diplomat, art critic and amateur artist. After
serving in Italy, Venezuela, Sweden and
France, he retired from the foreign service and
joined the staff of the B.M. where he became
Assistant Director of Prints. He produced a
number of books on old master and more
contemporary painters.
Published: *Reform Club: its founders and architect,*
1887. &c.

FAHEY, Edward Henry, R.I.
1844 (Brompton) - 1907 (Notting Hill)
The son of J. Fahey (q.v.), he studied architecture at South Kensington and the R.A.
Schools and was in Italy from 1866 to 1869.
On his return he re-entered the R.A. Schools to
study painting. He exhibited from 1863 and
was elected A.R.I. and R.I. in 1870 and 1876.
He painted landscapes, coastal and genre
scenes, and his work can be very pretty.
Examples: V.A.M.

FAHEY, James, R.I.
1804 (Paddington) - 1885 (London)
He began by training as an engraver under his
uncle, John Swaine, after which he turned to
watercolours and studied under G. Scharf
(q.v.) and in Paris. There he made anatomical
drawings for lithographs. He first exhibited in
1825 and was a founder of the N.W.S. He was
Secretary from 1838 to 1874, retiring because
of financial mismanagement. In 1856 he was
appointed drawing master at the Merchant
Taylors' School. Early in his career he painted
portraits, but by the mid-1830s he had turned
almost exclusively to landscapes.
Examples: B.M.

FAHEY, Patricia Emma –
see ALABASTER, P.E., Mrs.

FAIRBAIRN, Thomas, R.S.W.
1820 (Campsie, Stirling) - 1884 (Glasgow)
A pupil of Andrew Donaldson in Glasgow, he
lived in Hamilton, and exhibited landscapes at
Suffolk Street from 1865 to 1877. He also
made a series of drawings of old Glasgow,
1844-49. He was an unsuccessful candidate
for the N.W.S. in 1867. A friend of A. Fraser,
S. Bough and later W. Simpson (all q.v.), he
worked in oil paints and chalk as well as
watercolour. Despite creeping paralysis from
around 1871, he still managed to paint
impressively at the end of his life.
Published: *Relics of ancient architecture...in
Glasgow,* 1849.
Examples: Glasgow A.G.

FAIRHOLT, Frederick William, F.S.A.
1814 (London) - 1866 (London)
The son of a German immigrant, he won a
silver medal for drawing from the Society of
Arts when a boy. He worked for a scene
painter and then, at twenty-one, became
assistant to S. Sly, the wood-engraver. He later
worked for the Society of Antiquaries, of
which he was a Fellow, the British
Archaeological Association, the Numismatic
Society, and on the *A.J.* In 1856 he visited the
South of France and Rome with Lord
Londesborough, and on two later occasions he
went to Egypt with Londesborough's eldest
son. He left a number of books to the museum
in Shakespeare's House at Stratford.
Published: *Lord Mayors' Pageants,* 1841. *Costume
in England,* 1846. *The Home of Shakespeare,* 1847.
Tobacco, its History and Associations, 1859. *Gog
and Magog,* 1860. *Up the Nile,* 1862.
Illustrated: C. Roach Smith: *History of
Richborough.* C. Roach Smith: *Roman London.*
Examples: B.M.; V.A.M.
Bibliography: *A.J.*, June, 1866.

FAIRLIE, William Jordan
1825 (Carlisle) - 1875 (Carlisle)
A gingham manufacturer who was possibly a
pupil of M.E. Nutter (q.v.). He exhibited one
landscape at Carlisle in 1846, and also showed
at the R.A. between 1853 and 1865.

FAIRMAN, Frances C
1836 - 1923 (Chelsea)
A painter of canines, mostly in oil, she only
turned to art as a profession after a dog of a
land speculation in Florida. She painted for
Queens Victoria and Alexandra and rescued
animals in London. In about 1870 she made a
number of watercolours of Continental scenes.
They are sloppy and weak with no pencil
underdrawing.
Bibliography: *Evening News,* 24 Feb. 1910.

FAITHORNE, William, Yr.
1656 (London) - c.1710 (London)
The eldest son of the elder **William FAITHORNE (1616 London - 1691 London)**, the portrait draughtsman and engraver, of whom Thomas Flatman wrote: 'A Faithorne Sculpsit is a charm can save, From dull oblivion, and a gaping grave'. Among the subjects of the father's crayon portraits were F. Le Piper (q.v.), and the mezzotint engravers Prince Rupert and John Smith, and he published *The Art of Graving and Etching...*, 1662. In 1692 the son was the first drawing master appointed by Christ's Hospital, but he lost the post four years later. It is likely that he drew in pen and ink and sepia wash, as well as scraping engravings.

FALL, George   1848   - 1925 (York)
A York topographer who studied at the York School of Drawing and taught at Selby. In 1875 he married the daughter of an engraver. The Minster is his favourite subject, but he did draw elsewhere in Yorkshire, and he also produced portraits in oil.
Examples: York City A.G.
Bibliography: *Notes and Queries,* 10th series, XV.

FALLOWES, William
A Bridlington painter and decorator. He worked in oil, watercolour and brown wash between 1870 and 1900.
Examples: Bayle Gate Mus., Bridlington; Bridlington Lib.

FANE, Major-General Walter
1825   - 1885 (Fulbeck)
The son of a clergyman, he joined the Madras Army in 1849 and served in the Punjab prior to the Indian Mutiny. At the end of 1859 W. Simpson (q.v.) shared his digs in Calcutta, where he was a member of Lady Canning's (q.v.) sketching circle, and in about 1860 he raised a regiment of irregular cavalry to fight in China. They were present at the capture of Peking. He was promoted colonel and retired in 1879. His watercolours, which show Japanese as well as Indian and Chinese scenes, are very accomplished.
Examples: B.M.

FANSHAWE, Admiral Sir Edward Gennys
1814   - 1906
An artist who joined the Navy in 1828, served in the Mediterranean and was promoted commander in 1841. He painted in the East Indies in 1844, the Falklands, Pitcairn, Tahiti and Borabora in 1849, Panama in 1850, China in 1851 and in San Francisco. His ships are well drawn, and his landscapes brightly coloured, if a little crude. His second son was Admiral commanding Portsmouth.
Examples: Greenwich.

FARINGTON, Joseph, R.A.
1747 (Leigh, Lancashire) - 1821 (Didsbury, Lancashire)
A landscape painter who moved to London in 1763 and spent several years working under Richard Wilson. He was a member of the Society of Artists from 1768 to 1773 and entered the R.A. Schools in 1769. In the summer of 1773, he and his brother George went to Houghton to draw the pictures which were later mezzotinted by Earlom and published by Boydell. In the late 1770s he returned to the North of England, remaining until 1781, during which time he sketched in the Lake District. In 1781 he moved back to London and he lived there, at the political heart of the art world, for the rest of his life. He was elected A.R.A. and R.A. in 1783 and 1785, and in 1793 he began to keep his diary, which is one of the most important sources of knowledge of the arts of the period.

In his finished topographical drawings he first sketched his subject lightly in pencil, then added painstaking pen and black or brown ink outlines and finally a grey or brown wash, with occasional local colour such as blue. The whole effect is careful and self-controlled. His sketch books, however, show him in a much freer and more dashing vein.
Published: *Views of the Lakes,* 1789. *Views of Cities and Towns of England and Wales,* 1790.
Illustrated: W. Combe: *History of the River Thames,* 1794.
Examples: B.M.; V.A.M.; Ashmolean; Cartwright Hall, Bradford; Brighton A.G.; Ferens A.G., Hull; Fitzwilliam; Glasgow A.G.; Leeds City A.G.; Walker A.G., Liverpool; N.G., Scotland; Laing A.G., Newcastle; Wakefield A.G.; York A.G.
Bibliography: J. Grieg: *Farington's Diaries,* 1922-28; 1978-84. F. Rutter: *Wilson and F.,* 1923. *Walker's Quarterly,* October, 1921.

FARMER, Emily, R.I.
1826 (London) - 1905 (Porchester)
The pupil of her brother **Alexander FARMER (d.1869)**, she was a miniaturist who later turned to genre painting. She exhibited at the R.A. from 1847-50 with miniatures and the N.W.S. from 1847 to 1904 and she was elected to the N.W.S. in 1854. She is best known for her groups of children. They tend to be slightly manic, perhaps because of an excess of saccharine. She lived at Porchester House, Porchester for over fifty years.
Examples: V.A.M.

FARNBOROUGH, Amelia, Lady
1772   - 1837 (Bromley Hill, Kent)
The elder daughter of Sir Abraham Hume, the connoisseur, she married **Charles LONG (1761-1838)** in 1793. He was knighted in 1820 and created Baron Farnborough in 1826. Like her, he was a patron of the arts and an etcher and he helped Girtin (q.v.) to make his visit to Paris in 1801. Lady Farnborough was Girtin's favourite pupil, and, in the words of the

Somerset House Gazette, she had 'a talent for painting and drawing that might fairly rank with the professors of the living art'. She may also have been taught by J. Varley (q.v.), since she produced works which are very close to his in style. She also shows the influence of Dr. Monro (q.v.) in some of her pencil drawings. She lived at Bromley Hill Place, Kent, and many of her subjects are taken from the area. Her botanical watercolours are also of very high quality. Her sister was Lady Brownlow (q.v.), and M.E. Long (q.v.) was a niece.
Examples: B.M.; Bromley Lib.; Dundee City A.G.; Glasgow A.G.; Leeds City A.G.; N.G., Scotland.

FARQUHAR, Sir Robert Townsend, 6th Bt.
1841 (Golding) - 1924 (? Brighton)
An amateur landscape painter who lived at Grasmere and Brighton and exhibited in London from 1873. He was the fourth son of the 2nd baronet, succeeding in 1877. Previously he had served as a lieutenant in the Royal Artillery.

FARQUHARSON, David, A.R.A., A.R.S.A., R.S.W.   1840 (Blairgowrie) - 1907 (Birnam, Perthshire)
Landscape, cattle and snow painter in oil and watercolour, he was the son of a dyke-builder and was apprenticed to a painter-decorator. He exhibited at the R.S.A. from 1868 and was elected A.R.S.A. in 1882, and R.S.W. in 1885. He was elected A.R.A. in 1905. He was in London from 1886 to 1894, and had a studio near Land's End, but often revisited Scotland
Bibliography: *Studio,* XXXVIII, 1906.

FARRER, Thomas Charles
1839   - 1891
A landscape painter in oil and watercolour. He lived in London and specialised in views in the Thames Valley, although he also painted at Rochester and Cromer.
Bibliography: *A.J.,* 1871.

FARRIER, Robert
1796 (Chelsea) - 1879 (London)
After working for an engraver, he entered the R.A. Schools, supporting himself by taking portrait miniatures. He first exhibited at the R.A. in 1818. His later subjects, many of which were engraved for the *Annuals,* were often scenes of schoolboy life. His sister, Charlotte Farrier, frequently exhibited miniatures at the R.A.
Examples: V.A.M.

FAULKNER, John c.1830   - 1888
An Irish landscape and marine painter in oil and watercolour who entered the R.D.S. Schools in 1848 and first exhibited at the R.H.A. in 1852. He was elected A.R.H.A. and R.H.A. in 1861. In 1870 he was expelled from the Academy and left Dublin for America. Later he came to London, where he earned his living by painting watercolours for dealers. He

FAULKNER, John (c.1830-1888)
View of a riverside town, perhaps Lucan, with hills in the distance. *Watercolour heightened with bodycolour, signed and dated 1876, 17¾in. x 30½in.*

exhibited at the R.H.A. again from 1880 to 1887 and was living in Kenilworth in 1883.
Examples: Whitworth Inst., Manchester.

FAWKES, Francis Hawksworth
1797   - 1871
Eldest son of Walter Ramsden Fawkes of Farnley Hall, near Otley, Yorkshire, he drew wash caricatures, and was a friend and patron of Turner, as had been his father. It was he who witnessed and described Turner's methods of painting 'A First-Rate taking in Stores' in 1818. On his death in 1871, the estate and collection passed to his brother, the Rev. Ayscough Fawkes.

FAWKES, Colonel Lionel Grimston
1849   - 1931 (Culzean)
A nephew of F.H. Fawkes (q.v.) of Farnley, he was at Woolwich in 1868 and was commissioned in the artillery two years later. However, in 1876 he was admitted to the R.A. Schools on the recommendation of G. Richmond (q.v.). From 1878 to 1884 he was attached to the Governor's household in Barbados. He visited many other parts of the Caribbean, painting very competent and pleasing watercolours. He then served at Gibraltar and attended the Staff College. He was promoted major in 1886 and ten years later was appointed Professor of Military Topography at Woolwich. He was promoted colonel in 1899 and retired in 1903, later serving as a J.P. for Hampshire. He married Lady Constance Eleanor Kennedy (d.1941), daughter of the 2nd Marquis of Ailsa.

His work is free and colourful with little underdrawing, but some scratching out. He also drew for *Punch*.

FEARNSIDE, William
A painter of landscapes, cattle and rustic genre

scenes who exhibited at the R.A. from 1791 to 1801. He worked in water and bodycolour.
Examples: V.A.M.

FELIX, Major-General Orlando
1790   - 1860/1 (Geneva)
A painter of landscapes and figures who joined the Army in 1810. He was at Waterloo with the 95th. From 1826 he was on half-pay, and he travelled in Egypt and Nubia with Lord Prudhoe (later 4th Duke of Northumberland). This might make him a model for a figure in J.F. Lewis' great watercolour 'A Frankish Encampment in the Desert'. From 1841 he held a staff appointment as Deputy QMG for the East Indies. He was promoted to full colonel in 1851 and to major-general in 1858.

FENN, Charles
A drawing master who was in Birmingham in 1747. There he provided designs for enamellers, notably his neighbour John Taylor. He contributed plates to *The Ladies' Amusement*, 1758-62.

FENN, William Wilthieu
1836   - 1906 (Marylebone)
A painter of landscapes and coasts who lived in London and exhibited at the R.A. and other galleries from 1848. He painted in London, the southern counties, Wales, Nottinghamshire, Scotland, Jersey and no doubt elsewhere. The middle name, not surprisingly, is given as 'Wilthew' in the register of deaths.
Bibliography: *A.J.*, 1860; 1907. *Portfolio*, 1886.

FENNELL, John Greville
1810 (Irish Sea) - 1885 (Henley)
Angler and artist, he studied with H. Sass and with the Findens, where he was a close friend of 'Phiz' Browne (q.v.). Although some

sources give his birth date as 1807, when he entered the R.A. Schools in December 1827 he was aged seventeen. Most of his life was devoted to the theory and practice of fishing, which plays an equally large part in his painting. His work includes caricatures and pure landscapes. He was a friend of Dickens and Thackeray, and his epitaph reads: 'The fishers also shall mourn, and all they that cast angle in the brooks shall lament.' Isaiah XIX, 8.

FENNELL, Louisa 1847   - 1930
There are a number of watercolours in the Wakefield A.G. by this artist. She painted landscapes and buildings, and she exhibited at Suffolk Street between 1876 and 1882.
Published: *Twelve Sketches illustrating the life of St. Paul in Rome*, 1881.

FENTON, Fanny 1813/14 (London) -
A painter of Shakespearean subjects in watercolour who exhibited at Suffolk Street in 1859 and was still active in London two years later.

She may have been connected with **Enos FENTON** who lived in Smithfield and exhibited landscape compositions between 1832 and 1841.

FERGUSON, J
A painter of army uniforms, primarily of Scottish regiments. He was probably the illustrator of *Army Equipment*, 1865-6 and may well be identifiable with James Ferguson who painted landscapes in London, Edinburgh and Keswick and was an unsuccessful candidate for the N.W.S. in 1850. He was living in London until at least 1864, and exhibited at the R.A. from 1817 to 1868.

An earlier **James FERGUSON**, presumably a drawing master, published *The Art of Drawing in Perspective made Easy*, in 1775. He may have been the pen and ink miniaturist (1710-1776) who is represented in the V.A.M. and the N.G., Scot.

FERGUSON, John
An artist working in Preston in about 1830. Lithographs were published after his drawings by Day and Haghe.

FERGUSON, Samuel
1810 (Belfast) - 1886
An architectural draughtsman who also sketched from nature. He made a Continental tour, 1845-46, was a close friend of Sir F.W. Burton (q.v.), and an acquaintance of G. Petrie (q.v.).

FERGUSON, William J
A landscape painter who specialised in trees, buildings and views of the Italian Lakes. He was working between 1849 and 1886 and was an unsuccessful candidate for the N.W.S. in 1868 and 1869. On the latter occasion he went

unballoted because he had apparently lied about his age – neither truth nor lie was minuted. He lived in London, Keswick and Cheltenham. This may well relate him to one of the James Fergusons above.

FERNYHOUGH, William   - 1805
A Lichfield artist who may have been a pupil of Glover and was active at least in 1804.

There were a number of other painters of the name in the area including **Fanny FERNYHOUGH; John ROBERT FERNYHOUGH;** and **Thomas FERNYHOUGH.** There are examples of their work in Stafford Lib. A **William H. FERNYHOUGH** published twelve profile portraits of *Aborigines of New South Wales* in 1836.

FERREY, Benjamin, F.S.A.
1810 (Christchurch, Hants.) - 1880 (London)
An architect and draughtsman, he was drawing old buildings while still at school at Wimborne. He was apprenticed to the elder Pugin (q.v.) with whom he toured England and Normandy. Later he worked on the National Gallery with Wilkins, and then set up his own practice. He was one of the best employed and best liked architects of his day. A very full list of his building works is given in *The Builder,* XXXIX, 4 Sept. 1861.

Published: (with E.W. Brayley): *Antiquities of the Priory Church of Christchurch,* 1834; *Recollections of A.N.W. Pugin and his Father,* 1861.

FERRIER, George STRATTON-, R.I., R.S.W.   (Edinburgh) - 1912 (Edinburgh)
The son of **James FERRIER (c.1820-1883/4),** a good, rather Pre-Raphaelite, landscape painter in watercolour, who worked on a large scale and exhibited at the R.S.A. from 1843. He in turn exhibited Scottish views and scenes at the R.A. and the R.I. to which he was elected in 1898. He was also an engraver.

FICKLIN, Alfred
A landscape painter who lived in Kingston-on-Thames and Norbiton. He worked in the South-West and Ireland and also produced still lifes. He was perhaps a brother of **George FICKLIN,** who lived in South London and Falmouth and painted landscapes. Both were active from about 1865 to 1890.

FIDLER, Gideon Mathew
1857 (Tisbury) - 1942
A painter of rustic scenes and landscapes in oil and watercolour. He lived in Wiltshire and exhibited at the R.I. from about 1887.

FIDLER, J – see FIDLOR, J   H

FIDLOR, Isaac
A painter of landscape and shore scenes who was working in Devonshire in the 1820s. At his best he was a restrained follower of W.

FERGUSON, William J.
Midday in Glen Falloch, Loch Lomond. *Signed and dated 1885, watercolour, 19in. x 34in.*

Payne (q.v.), otherwise he worked rather in the manner of J. Varley (q.v.), with weak figures and cattle and stilted architectural drawing.
Examples: Exeter Mus.

FIDLOR, J   H
A topographer and architect who was active from 1797 to 1808 and who worked in Monmouthshire in the early style of S. Prout (q.v.). He is presumably to be identified with the J. Fidler who exhibited landscapes at the R.A. This last was the pupil of J. Yenn who prepared unexecuted designs for a temple near Monmouth, now in the Nat. Lib. Wales.
Examples: B.M.

FIELD, Edwin Wilkins
1804 (Leam, Warwickshire) - 1871 (the Thames)
A solicitor who in 1840 began the agitation for Chancery Law reform. Another measure with which he was associated was the Act of 1862 establishing artistic copyright. Early in his career he set up a drawing class at the Harp Alley School. In his free time he sketched in the Isle of Wight, and regularly on the Thames with Dodgson, George Fripp (qq.v.) and others. He was legal adviser to the O.W.S., by whom he was presented with a portfolio of original drawings in 1863. He was drowned in a boating accident.

FIELD, John
1771 (Molesey) - 1841 (Molesey)
A landscape, portrait, architectural and coastal painter who exhibited at the R.A. from 1800 to 1836. He worked in Kent, Buckinghamshire, Monmouthshire and Pembrokeshire as well as London. His work of this kind is predominantly in blues and greens with little drawing, and is rather flat.

However, his real importance was as a

silhouettist. He was trained by the great John Miers, and became his assistant and partner. In the reign of William IV he was Profile Painter to Their Majesties and H.R.H. the Princess Augusta, and on occasions he produced elaborate silhouette groups, sometimes with landscape backgrounds.
Examples: B.M.
Bibliography: E.N. Jackson: *Silhouette,* 1938.

FIELD, Walter, A.R.W.S.
1837 (Hampstead) - 1901 (Hampstead)
The son of E.W. Field (q.v.), he was educated at University College School, was a pupil of J.R. Herbert and of John Pye and studied at the R.A. Schools. He lived at Hampstead, exhibited landscapes, often on the Thames, genre subjects and portraits from 1856, and he was elected A.R.W.S. in 1880. He was a founder of the Hampstead Heath Preservation Society.
Examples: V.A.M.

FIELDER, Henry
A painter of Surrey and Sussex landscapes. He lived in Dorking and exhibited at Suffolk Street from 1872 to 1885.

An **R.W. FIELDER** exhibited a very modestly priced watercolour from a Dorking address in 1877.

FIELDING, Anthony Vandyke Copley, P.O.W.S.
1787 (Sowerby Bridge) - 1855 (Worthing)
The third son of N.T. Fielding (q.v.), who gave him his first lessons. The family moved to London a few months after his birth, and to the Lake District when he was fifteen. In 1807 he visited Liverpool to sell drawings, and in 1808 he toured Wales and visited London, where he settled the following year. He became a pupil of J. Varley (q.v.) and was one of the Monro

FIELDING, Anthony Vandyke Copley (1787-1855)
Minehead with distant view of Dunster. *Watercolour, 28in. x 20in.*

FIELDING, Anthony Vandyke Copley (1787-1855)
The head of Glencoe, 1823. *Watercolour, signed with initials, inscribed and dated 1823, 12in. x 16in.*

circle. In 1810 he made a tour of the Borders and was elected A.O.W.S. In 1811 he sketched in Wales, and the next year he made a short trip to Kent and was elected O.W.S. In 1813 he was in Durham and Yorkshire, in 1814 on the Thames, in 1815 in North Wales, and in 1816 he toured the Wye Valley. In the same year his elder daughter fell ill, and he spent as much time as possible with his family on the coast at Sandgate. During the 1820s he painted a large number of marine subjects. In 1829 he settled in Brighton, keeping a studio in London, and in about 1847 he made a final move to Worthing.

In 1813 he became Treasurer of the O.W.S. and in 1815, Secretary. He was President from 1831 until his death.

Fielding, it has been said, was a man of 'one sea, one moor, one down, one lake, one misty gleam' and this is largely true. Early in his career, as exemplified by his Wye drawings, his works are smaller, fresher and more appealing than later. He is not only limited in his subject matter, but in his mannerisms and his palette, which usually consists of blues, purples, yellows and browns. His mannerisms include the dragging of the brush to give an idea of distance and the effect of sunlight through mist, which cleverly disguises the lack of more original ideas. His stormy marine subjects catch the feeling of the British coasts,

FIELDING, Anthony Vandyke Copley (1787-1855)
Harlech Castle. *Signed, watercolour, 20½in. x 29in.*

but they too are repetitive in composition and palette. Copley Fielding's surviving daughter was Emma, who died in 1867.

Examples: B.M.; V.A.M.; Aberdeen A.G.; Blackburn A.G.; Grundy A.G., Blackpool; Brighton A.G.; Bury A.G.; Coventry Mus.; Derby A.G.; Doncaster A.G.; Dudley A.G.; Towner Gall., Eastbourne; Exeter Mus.; Glasgow A.G.; Gloucester City A.G.; Harrogate Mus.; Abbot Hall A.G., Kendal; Leeds City A.G.; City A.G., Manchester; Newport A.G.; Castle Mus., Nottingham; Sydney A.G.

Bibliography: *A.J.*, 1855. *Burlington Mag.*, XIX, 1911. *O.W.S. Club*, III, 1925. *Antique Collecting*, May 2000.
See Colour Plate

FIELDING, Edward
A son of N.S.L. Fielding (q.v.). He and his sister **Emily FIELDING** painted in the family manner, and he exhibited a watercolour of Langdale Pikes in 1859, when living in his late uncle Copley's house. He was notably eccentric.
Bibliography: *Antique Collecting*, May 2000.

FIELDING, Felix Ferdinand Frederick Raffael
c.1784 (Sowerby Bridge) - 1853 (London)
The second son of N.T. Fielding (q.v.), he painted views of Cumberland and elsewhere in oil and watercolour. With Copley he worked for a while in the Enrolment Office of the Court of Chancery before becoming a painter. He was living in the family home in London at various dates between 1808 and 1826, and in 1810-11 he was in Carlisle. In 1826 he exhibited for the last time, and in the following

year he was admitted to Gray's Inn, being called to the Bar in 1832. Any reference to his working as an assistant in the family studios thereafter is nonsense. Ten years later he married the Hon. Lady Heslerigg, daughter of Lord Wodehouse, and widow of Sir Thomas Maynard Heslerigg, and thereafter he lived at her town house in Upper Brook Street. He continued to paint as an amateur, and his style

owes much to Copley, although it is sometimes rather less definite. His usual signature is 'Frederick F. Fielding'.
Examples: Carlisle A.G.
Bibliography: See H.M.Cundall: *Birket Foster*, 1906. *Antique Collecting*, Oct. 1985. *Antique Collecting*, May 2000.

FIELDING, Mary Anne, Mrs., née Walton, O.W.S.
- 1835
The daughter and sister of artists and the wife of T.H.A. Fielding (q.v.) with whom she worked. She painted flowers and still lifes and was a Lady Member of the O.W.S. from 1820 to 1835. In the first year she was Miss Walton of Manchester, and she was elected a member, as Mrs T.H.Fielding, in the following year.
Bibliography: *Antique Collecting*, May 2000.

FIELDING, Nathan Theodore
1747 (Sowerby Bridge) - 1819
Landscape painter in oil and watercolour, he was the father and mentor of at least five painting sons. He worked in the North of England and in London, and he exhibited from 1775 to 1814. As well as the five sons there was one daughter, Cleobulina Amelia (born c.1790), who naturally preferred her second name. She was a noted beauty and married Henry Reveley.
Bibliography: *Antique Collecting*, May 2000.

FIELDING, Newton Limbird Smith
1799 (London) - 1856 (Paris)
The youngest son of N.T. Fielding (q.v.), he first exhibited at the Oil and Watercolour Society in 1815 and 1818. He ran the family

FIELDING, Edward
A road to a lake. *Signed, watercolour, 1855. 8in. x 10in.*

FIELDING, Newton Smith Limbird (1799-1856)
Barnyard Fowl. *Watercolour, 9½in. x 13in.*

engraving business in Paris from about 1827 to 1830 when the Revolution drove him back to England. At this time W. Callow (q.v.) was working under him. He worked with his brothers Thales and Theodore in England for a time and then returned to Paris where he remained until death. He had an extensive teaching practice, his pupils including members of the family of King Louis-Philippe. His best known works are studies of farmyards and small wild animals. They are executed with a pleasing mixture of accurate detail and impressionistic effects.

His wife, Eliza Josephine Berger, was French, and their six children included Frederick, Edward (q.v.) and Emily Fielding (q.v.).
Published: *Three Hundred Lessons, &c...,* 1852. *Lessons on Fortifications, &c.,* 1853. *A Dictionary of Colour, &c.,* 1854. *What to Sketch with, &c.,* 1856. *How to Sketch from Nature,* 1856 (2nd. ed.).
Examples: B.M.; V.A.M.
Bibliography: *Antique Collecting,* May 2000.

FIELDING, Thales Angelo Vernet, A.O.W.S.
1793 (Stamford, Lincs.) - 1837 (London)
Pupil and fourth son of N.T. Fielding (q.v.), he exhibited with the O.W.S. from 1810 and was elected Associate in 1829. He entered the R.A. Schools in 1814. Although he kept rooms in the family house in Newman Street from 1818 until the end of his life, he worked in the Paris business from about 1820 to 1827 and shared a house there with Delacroix, of whom he painted a portrait. He was for some years teacher of drawing at the R.M.A., Woolwich.

His landscapes are usually English or Welsh, and generally make a strong feature of a group of cattle. He also made figure studies of gypsies, fishermen and the like, and occasionally attempted classical or literary themes.

Examples: B.M.; V.A.M.; Gloucester City A.G.
Bibliography: J.L. Roget: *Journal of Eugène Delacroix,* 1893-5. *Gaz. des Beaux Arts,* II, 1912. *Antique Collecting,* May 2000.
See Colour Plate

FIELDING, Theodore Henry Adolphus
1781 (Sowerby Bridge) - 1851 (Croydon)
The eldest son of N.T. Fielding (q.v.), he was an engraver and landscape painter. He exhibited at the R.A. from 1799 and worked at the family studios in Newman Street until 1825 when he moved to Kentish Town. In 1827 he was appointed Professor of Drawing at the Military Academy, Addiscombe. From this time he lived in or around Croydon.

His engravings include plates after his brother Copley, Barker of Bath and Bonington. His watercolours are difficult to tell from those of his brother Thales. His pupils included W.

Callow and C. Bentley (qq.v.), and his brother-in-law was J. Walton (q.v.) with whom he collaborated on Lake District views.
Published: *A Picturesque Tour of the English Lakes,* 1821 (with J. Walton). *British Castles,* 1825. *Synopsis of Practical Perspective, &c.,* 1829. *On Painting in Oil and Water Colours,* 1830. *Index of Colours and Mixed Tints,* 1830. *On the theory of Painting,* 1836. *The Art of Engraving, &c.,* 1844. *The Knowledge and Restoration of Oil Painting,* 1847.
Examples: B.M.; V.A.M.; Towner A.G., Eastbourne; Leeds City A.G.
Bibliography: *Antique Collecting,* May 2000.

FILDES, Sir Samuel Luke, R.A.
1844 (Liverpool) - 1927 (London)
Illustrator, portrait and genre painter, he studied at Liverpool Mechanics Institute, the Warrington School of Art and South Kensington. He worked on various magazines including the *Graphic,* and he illustrated Dickens' *Edwin Drood.* In the 1870s he turned to genre painting in oil, and in the 1890s to portraits. He was elected A.R.A. and R.A. in 1879 and 1887 and knighted in 1906. His remaining works were sold at Christie's, 24 June 1927.

His wife, **Fanny, Lady FILDES, née Woods,** was also a painter.
Examples: V.A.M.; Glasgow A.G.
Bibliography: L.V. Fildes: *L.F., R.A., a Victorian Painter,* 1968. *A.J.,* 1877; 1895; 1897; 1898; 1900; 1901; 1902; 1909. *Art Annual,* 1895.

FILKIN, G   GRIFFIN
A Birmingham painter of coastal, genre and rural subjects who exhibited there between 1873 and 1882.

FINCH, Rev. and Hon. Daniel
1757   - 1840
The sixth son of the 3rd Earl of Aylesford, he was a pupil of J.B. Malchair (q.v.) at Oxford. He was rector of Cwm, Flintshire, and Harpsden, Oxfordshire, and became a Prebend

FINCH, Rev. and Hon. Daniel (1757-1840)
Margate Beach. *Inscribed and dated 1818 on original mount, pencil, pen and sepia ink and grey wash, 5¼in. x 11in.*

of Gloucester and Senior Fellow of All Souls. He drew caricatures as well as landscapes.

He should not be confused with his nephew, Hon. Daniel Finch, for whom, and for others of the family, *see* Aylesford, 4th Earl of.
Examples: B.M.; Fitzwilliam.
See Aylesford Family Tree

FINCH, General Hon. Edward
1756 - 1843
The brother of H. Finch, 4th Earl of Aylesford (q.v.) and of D. Finch (q.v.), he was educated at Westminster and Cambridge and in 1778 enlisted as a Cornet in the 2nd Light Dragoons. He served through the campaigns in Flanders, Denmark and Egypt among others, and in 1796 he was promoted major-general. In 1799 he was elected M.P. for Cambridge, holding the constituency for twenty years. He retired from active service in 1808 and was promoted full general in 1819. He was a keen sketcher, although only one drawing definitely by his hand has so far been identified outside the Packington collection.
See Aylesford Family Tree

FINCH, Francis Oliver, O.W.S.
1802 (London) - 1862 (London)
An orphan, he had little formal education and was largely brought up by his grandmother near Aylesbury. In 1814 or 1815 he was apprenticed to J. Varley (q.v.) for three years, remaining as a pupil for two further years. He exhibited at the R.A. from 1817. In 1820 he made one of only two journeys outside the southern counties, sailing to Edinburgh and touring the Highlands. Two years later, when only nineteen, he was elected A.O.W.S., becoming a full Member in 1827. Prior to this he had also studied at Sass's Life School and may have attended Fuseli's R.A. lectures. He was a great admirer of Fuseli, as of Blake (qq.v.), whom he had met through Varley, becoming one of the Shoreham disciples. Although he disliked teaching, he took pupils in order to raise the money to marry, which he did in 1837. He lived in London throughout his career and only once ventured abroad, in the summer of 1852 when he visited Paris. In 1857 he had a stroke which led to increasing paralysis and deafness. However he was still able to make pencil copies of his earlier works.

As well as a painter, he was a poet and a deeply religious man, being much involved with the Swedenborgian Church. As an artist he is best described as 'a poetic landscapist'. He shared the dislike of Cox (q.v.), with whom he is often bracketed, for mere portraits of places. In style the two were not alike, Finch working more in the quiet romantic vein of the younger Barret (q.v.).
Examples: B.M.; V.A.M.; Ashmolean; Brighton A.G.; Fitzwilliam.
Bibliography: E. Finch: *Memorials of F.O.F.*, 1865. See R. Lister: *Edward Calvert* (appendix), 1962. *A.J.*, 1862; 1893. *Connoisseur*, CIII, 1939.

FINCH, Francis Oliver (1802-1862)
Lake Scene, *Watercolour, 29¼in. x 39½in.*

FINDLAY, J
An architectural draughtsman who lived in London and exhibited studies of old buildings for thirty years from 1826.

FINN, Herbert John
1861 (London) -
A landscape painter in oil and watercolour, and an etcher, he studied at South Kensington, where he won a scholarship. He lived in London and worked there and at Folkestone.
Illustrated: E.J. Macdonald: *Castles of England and Wales*, 1925.
Examples: Maidstone Mus.; . Castle Mus., Nottingham.
Bibliography: *A.J.*, 1900-1903. *Evening Standard*, 8 June 1908. *The Times*, 22 Nov. 1912.

FINNEMORE, Joseph, R.I.
1860 (Birmingham) - 1939
A genre, figure and architectural painter in oil and watercolour, who studied at the Birmingham School of Art and in Antwerp. He then made a tour of the Near East and Southern Russia, returning to work in London for a while from 1884. Thereafter he worked for the *Graphic* and other magazines, and lived in Birmingham for the most part. He was elected R.I. in 1898 and retired in 1930.
Illustrated: G.A. Henty: *When London Burned*, 1894.

FINNIE, John
1829 (Aberdeen) - 1907 (Aberdeen)
A landscape painter, illustrator and mezzotinter who studied at Newcastle under W.B. Scott (q.v.). He lived in Edinburgh, Wolverhampton and Newcastle before moving

to London in 1853. Later he settled in Liverpool where he became President of the Academy and, until 1896, Head of the School of Art. His last move was to Llandudno. He was an unsuccessful candidate for the N.W.S. in 1869.
Examples: V.A.M.; Leeds City A.G.; Walker A.G., Liverpool.
Bibliography: *Studio*, VII, 1896; XXIV, 1902; XXVIII, 1903; XLII, 1908. *A.J.*, 1907.

FIRMINGER, Rev. Thomas Augustus Charles 1812 (London) - 1884
Educated at Pembroke College, Cambridge, Firminger lived in Edmonton for some years and visited Ireland, France and the Rhine. He was elected N.W.S. in 1834 but retired ten years later 'in consequence of his having entered the Church'. In 1846 he was appointed to the honorary curacy of Sittingbourne and to a practical chaplaincy to the Bishop of Calcutta. At first he was based on Ferozepore, later at Howrah, Chinsurah and Gowhatty. In 1854 he made an extensive Indian tour and in 1864-5 served with the Bhutan expedition. He retired in 1868. Despite the abandonment of the N.W.S. for the cloth, he continued to exhibit Indian views there, at the R.A. and the B.I. until 1871.
Published: *Manual of Gardening for India*, 1863.

FISCHER, John George Paul
1786 (Hanover) - 1875 (London)
The son of an engraver, he was the pupil of the court painter J.H. Ramberg. He came to England in 1810 and was commissioned to paint miniatures for members of the Royal Family and military uniforms for the Prince

Regent. He exhibited at the R.A. and elsewhere from 1817 to 1852 and occasionally painted landscapes as well as publishing a few prints. He may have visited India.
Examples: B.M.

FISHER, Alfred Thomas
1861 (Plymouth) -
A landscape painter who was the son of a Chaplain to Seamen and was educated at St. John's, Leatherhead. He lived in Cardiff and was Secretary of the South Wales Art Society from 1913 to 1924.

FISHER, Amy E
A painter of domestic scenes and town views who exhibited at the R.A., the R.I. and elsewhere from 1866 to 1890. She lived in London.
Examples: V.A.M.

FISHER, Major General Sir George Bulteel
1764 - 1834
A landscape and shipping painter who was a pupil of F. Towne (q.v.). He served in the Artillery in the Peninsula and in Canada and at the end of his life was Commandant at Woolwich. He exhibited at the R.A. from 1780 to 1808 and a number of engravings were made from his views from about 1790. Williams pointed out that his drawings are constructed 'in a series of a few superimposed vertical planes, like stage scenery'.
Examples: B.M.; V.A.M.; Leeds City A.G.; Laing A.G., Newcastle.

FISHER, J   H   Vignoles
- c.1920
A landscape painter who lived in London and later at Lewes and exhibited at the R.A., the R.I. and at Suffolk Street from 1884. Various exhibitions of his work were held at the Dowdeswell Galleries in the 1890s and 1900s.
Examples: Towner Gall., Eastbourne.

FISHER, John, Bishop of Salisbury
1748 (Hampton) - 1825 (London)
Educated at St. Paul's and Peterhouse, Cambridge, he became a Fellow of St. John's in 1774. He was private tutor to a number of distinguished pupils including Prince Edward, Duke of Kent, from 1780 to 1785, and he also gave drawing lessons to the Princess Elizabeth (q.v.). He was in Italy in 1785 and 1786 and was then appointed Canon of Windsor by the King, of whom he was a favourite. In 1803 he became Bishop of Exeter and in 1807 of Salisbury. In 1818 he paid an episcopal visitation to the Channel Islands. He was a distinguished connoisseur and patron, whose protégés included Constable although he should not be confused with his nephew and chaplain, Archdeacon John Fisher (1788 Brentford - 1832 Boulogne), who was Constable's close friend. The Bishop's own work shows poor drawing, but a good sense of composition and pleasing light washes of colour. He drew in Italy as well as in East Anglia and the West Country.
Examples: Ashmolean; Abbot Hall A.G., Kendal.
Bibliography: R.B. Beckett: *John Constable and the Fishers*, 1952.

FISHER, Jonathan
c.1740 (Dublin) - 1809
A Dublin draper who became a landscape painter. He appears to have been self taught, although he may have had some lessons when he visited England early in his career. He exhibited with the Society of Artists from their opening exhibition in 1765 until 1801. His pictures, which are rather stiff, were not popular, and in 1778 he was forced to take a position in the Stamp Office, where he remained until his death. The prints which were made after his drawings, however, were more successful. In 1770 he published six *Views of Killarney*, and in 1772 six *Views of Carlingford* were published in London. Other sets followed, including, in 1789, a folio volume *A Picturesque Tour of Killarney* which he dedicated to his friend and patron, John, Earl of Portarlington (q.v.). His major work was a *Scenery of Ireland*, 1796, with sixty plates aquatinted by himself. Four of his drawings were used in Grose's *Antiquities of Ireland*. After his death, his collection of old master paintings was auctioned at 12, Bishop Street, Dublin, and he left his drawings to H. Graham (q.v.).
Examples: B.M.; V.A.M.; Nat. Lib., Ireland; City A.G., Manchester.

FISHER, Joseph   1796   - 1890 (Oxford)
After serving an apprenticeship with the Oxford engraver F. Whessell, he spent some time in London before returning to Oxford in the early 1830s. He was the first Keeper of the University Galleries from 1844, and became a Freeman of the City. His work is topographical and includes copies of early works by Turner.
Examples: Fitzwilliam.

FISHER, Joshua Brewster
1859 (Liverpool) -
A landscape and figure painter who was the son of a painter-decorator. He studied at the Liverpool School of Art under J. Finnie (q.v.) and was President of the Liverpool Sketching Club in 1918.
Illustrated: J.M. Cobban: *The Tyrants of Kool Sim*, 1896.
Examples: Nat. Lib., Wales.

FISHER, Mark –
see FISHER, William Mark

FISHER, Richard Siddons
1864 - 1928
The son of **Richard FISHER**, manager of the Derby gas works and an amateur artist, who contributed drawings to the Anastatic Drawing Society and died at the age of ninety-six. The son worked as an accountant at the gas works and was a member of the Derby Sketching Club for many years.
Examples: Derby A.G.

FISHER, Simon
A topographer who worked in a Grimm-like manner and Herefordshire in the late 18th and early 19th centuries.

FISHER, Thomas, F.S.A.
1772 (Rochester) - 1836 (Stoke Newington)
A painter of landscapes and town scenes and an antiquarian draughtsman and engraver, he worked in the India Office. There a colleague, the antiquary H.H. Goodhall who had Bedfordshire connections, introduced him to that county. Other patrons there included the Rev. T.O. Marsh and the Duke of Bedford, and much of his subsequent career was devoted to the antiquities of the area. His first engraved works had been views near Rochester for J. Thorpe: *Custumale Ruffensis*, published in 1788 when the artist was only sixteen. At a more mature age he exhibited three water-colours at the R.A. between 1804 and 1807. His collections and remaining works were sold by Southgate & Son, 15 March and 30 May 1837.
Published: *Collections Historical, Genealogical and Topographical for Bedfordshire*, 1822-36. *Monumental Remains & Antiquities...Bedfordshire*, 1828.
Examples: B.M.; Cecil Higgins Mus., Bedford.
Bibliography: O.W.S. Club, LVII, 1982.

FISHER, William Mark, R.A., R.I.
1841 (Boston, U.S.A.) - 1923 (London)
Painter of landscapes and cattle, he studied in Boston and Paris and came to England in 1872. He was elected R.I. in 1881, A.R.A. in 1911 and R.A. in 1919, and he was also a Member of the N.E.A.C. He was strongly influenced by Corot, and his work in both oil and watercolour is full of light.
His daughter Millicent Margaret Fisher Prout was also an artist.
Examples: V.A.M.; Blackburn A.G.; Exeter Mus.; Leeds City A.G.; Ulster Mus.
Bibliography: V. Lines: *M.F. and Margaret Fisher Prout*, 1966. *Studio*, II, 1894. *A.J.*, 1896; 1900; 1905; 1908; 1910. *Burlington Mag.*, XII. *Connoisseur*, XXIX. R.W.S., Exhibition Cat., 1966. VAM, MSS, letters from M.F. to H.M. Cundall with biographical information.

FISK, William Henry
1827   - 1884 (Hampstead)
The son and pupil of the painter William Fisk (1796 Thorpe-le-Soken - 1872 Danbury), and a student at the R.A. Schools from 1842, he was appointed anatomical draughtsman to the Royal College of Surgeons and exhibited landscapes from 1846. He taught drawing and painting at University College, London for forty years, and is said to have made drawings of trees for the Queen. He was at Balmoral in

FISHER, William Mark (1841-1923)
Hatfield Heath. *Watercolour and pencil, signed and dated 1900, 10¾in. x 13¾in.*

1849, and several of his drawings appeared in an *I.L.N.* Supplement in September 1850. He painted in oil and a rather Pre-Raphaelite manner as well as producing landscape watercolours and drawings, and in 1869 he designed figures for the mosaics in the South Kensington Museum Grill Room.
Published: *The Forbes Camp*, 1855.
Examples: V.A.M.
Bibliography: *The Times*, 21 Nov. 1884.

FITCH, Walter Hood
1816/7   - 1892 (Richmond, Surrey)
He made botanical illustrations for the works of Sir W.J. Hooker (q.v.) from 1827, the majority after 1835, and he was active right up to the year of his death.
Illustrated: W.J. Hooker: *Icones Plantarum*, 1827-54. W.J. Hooker: *The Botanical Magazine*, 1827-65. J.E. Howard: *Illustrations of the Nueva Quinologia of Pavon*, 1859. J.L. Stewart: *The Forest Flora of N.W. and Central India*, 1874.
Examples: B.M.

FITTON, Hedley
1859 (Manchester) - 1929 (Haslemere)
An etcher and occasional watercolour painter of architectural subjects. He worked in France, Italy and Scotland as well as England, and he lived in Cheshire, London and Surrey.
Examples: City A.G., Manchester.

FITZGERALD, Frederick R
A painter of coastal and marine subjects who lived in Cheltenham. He visited Norway, and he exhibited in Birmingham in 1897.

FITZGERALD, Captain Lord Gerald
1821   - 1886
The second son of the 3rd Duke of Leinster, he served in the Scots Fusilier Guards. He was an active member of the Etching Club of Dublin, producing illustrations to the poems of Tom Hood (q.v.), and he was also a draughtsman and watercolour painter.

FITZGERALD, John Anster
1823 (Lambeth) - 1906 (London)
The painter of fairy subjects in oil and watercolour, many of them dealing with presumably opium influencd dreams. FitzGerald was the son of 'a small beer poet' – the opinion of William Cobbett – who died when the boy was about six, and it is not known where he got his training. He exhibited at the B.I. from 1845 and by the late 1860s he had become a regular contributor to the *I.L.N.* He was a member of the Maddox Street Sketching Club, and a fixture at the Savage, where he made himself a character as a stage Irishman. He had many artist friends and towards the end of his life was nominated for a Royal Academy pension. In the 1890s he also provided watercolours at £2 a time for the swindler Leigh Sampson (q.v.), who signed them with one or another alias before passing them off as his own at £12, if he could get it.
Examples: Cecil Higgins A.G., Bedford. Walker A.G., Liverpool.
Bibliography: J. Maas: *Victorian Painters*, 1969. B. Phillpotts: *Fairy Paintings*, 1978. J. Martineau (ed.): *Victorian Fairy Painting*, 1997. *A.J.*, 1859; 1860. *Country Life*, 4 April 2002.

FITZJAMES, Anna Maria
(Bath) -
A flower painter who took lessons from V. Bartholomew (q.v.) and was one of William Henry Hunt's (q.v.) few known pupils. She exhibited in London from 1852 to 1876 and became a highly successful teacher.

FITZPATRICK, Thomas
1860 (Cork) - 1912
A draughtsman and lithographer, he was apprenticed to a printing and publishing firm in Cork, after which he worked as a lithographer in Dublin and was cartoonist for the *Weekly Freeman* and the *Weekly National Press*. In 1905 he started the monthly *Leprechaun* in which his skill as a humorous cartoonist was amply demonstrated. As well as his illustrations, he painted in oil and watercolour.

FLACK, Thomas
1771 (Garboldisham) - 1844 (Arras)
A landscape painter in oil and watercolour who worked mainly on the Continent.
Examples: Mus. d'Arras.

FLEETWOOD, Sir Peter HESKETH, Bt.
1801   - 1866
A pupil of H. Bright (q.v.) who lived at Fleetwood, Lancs. He was an M.P. and was created a baronet in 1838.

FLEMING, John, of Greenock
1792 (Greenock) - 1845
A painter in oil and watercolour of landscapes and above all of lochs, of which he provided many among his illustrations for Swan's *Select Views of Glasgow* and its environs, 1828, *Views on the Clyde*, 1830, and *The Lakes of Scotland*, 1834. His favourite subjects were in Ayrshire and the Highlands.
A later **John FLEMING, II,** exhibited landscapes and animals in oil and watercolour and was living in Glasgow in 1880.
Examples: Glasgow A.G.; Greenock A.G.; Paisley A.G.

FLEMWELL, George Jackson
1865 (Mitcham) - 1928 (Lugano)
A painter of the Alps and their wildlife who was a pupil of W.P. Frith and studied in Antwerp before settling in Switzerland. He exhibited at the R.A. from 1892, and an exhibition of his work was held at the Baillie Gallery, London, in 1910.
Published: *Alpine Flowers and Gardens*, 1910. *The Flower Fields of Alpine Switzerland*, 1911. *Beautiful Switzerland*, 1913.

FLETCHER, Edward 1857   -1945
A marine painter who lived at Rochester and worked in the manner of W.L. Wyllie (q.v.) and C. Dixon (q.v.). He used the name 'John Hayes' on occasion.

FLINT, Sir William Russell (1880-1969)
'Sheltering from a Storm.' *Watercolour, signed, 27in. x 20in.*

**FLETCHER, William Teulon Blandford
1858   - 1936**
He studied at South Kensington from 1875 to 1879 and under Verlat in Antwerp until 1882. In France, where he painted during his summers, he came into contact with such artists as Stanhope Forbes and Bastien-Lepage, his friendship with Forbes continuing at Newlyn. In Cornwall, and later near Dorking, where he lived after his marriage, he painted and sketched village scenes as well as landscapes, seascapes and portraits. He exhibited at the R.A. from 1879.

With the exception of his very early and very late works, which are muted in tone, his colour is rich, and he shows the influence of F. Walker (q.v.) whom he much admired, and his watercolour style is sometimes reminiscent of that of L. Rivers (q.v.).
Examples: Ashmolean; Worcester City A.G.

**FLINT, Robert Purves, R.W.S., R.S.W.
1883 (Edinburgh) - 1947**
The son of a painter and designer, and younger brother of Sir W.R. Flint (q.v.), he was educated at Daniel Stewart's College, Edinburgh, and later lived at Whitstable, Kent. He was elected R.S.W. in 1918, A.R.W.S. in 1932 and R.W.S. in 1937, and held a one-man show at the Leicester Galleries in 1926. His subjects are often views in the South of France and North Africa.
Examples: Glasgow A.G.

**FLINT, Sir William Russell, R.A., P.R.W.S.,
R.S.W. 1880 (Edinburgh) - 1969 (London)**
The well-known watercolour painter was the son of an artist, **Francis Wighton FLINT**. He was educated in Edinburgh where he also worked for a lithographer before moving to London in 1900. He studied at Heatherley's, turning to pure watercolour, and produced many fine illustrations. During the First World War he was in the R.N.V.R. and the R.A.F., working on airships. He was elected A.R.A. and R.A. in 1924 and 1933 and P.R.W.S. three years later.

His early illustrative work, in the tradition of Dulac, Rackham and the young Heath Robinson, can be very beautiful. He also produced a number of landscapes whose merits are often overlooked in the contemplation of the banal and meretricious breastscapes which filled his later years. In the latter he could seldom bring himself to travel by any but the easiest route: three-quarter profiles are his trademark.
Published: *In Pursuit: An Autobiography,* 1969. &c.
Examples: B.M.; V.A.M.; Aberdeen A.G.; Blackburn A.G.; Darlington A.G.; Glasgow A.G.; Greenock A.G.; Harrogate Mus.; Leeds City A.G.; Leicestershire A.G.; Maidstone Mus.; Newport A.G.; Paisley A.G.
Bibliography: R. Lewis: *Sir W.R.F.,* 1980. *Studio,* 1914; 1928; 1943; R.A., Exhibition Cat., 1962.

FLOCKTON, Frederick S
A painter of birds' nests rather in the manner of W.H. Hunt (q.v.). He lived in Fulham and at Pangbourne and was active from 1854 to at least 1879. He also produced figure subjects.

**FLOWER, Charles Edwin
1871 (Merton) -**
An architectural and garden painter who studied at the R.C.A. and became an art master. He was much patronised by the Royal Family, worked as an illustrator and lived in south London and near Wallingford, Oxfordshire.
Illustrated: G.F. Edwards: *Old Time Paris,* 1908.
C.E. Pascoe: *No. 10, Downing Street,* 1908.
Examples: London Mus.

**FLOWER, John
1793 (Leicester) - 1861 (Leicester)**
A topographer who spent a year in London as a pupil of de Wint (q.v.). As well as working in his native county, he painted in Wales, Yorkshire, Lancashire, Derbyshire, the Isle of Man, Cheltenham, Kent, Middlesex and other parts of the British Isles. He worked in oil as well as watercolour, and his style is close to that of the master.

In turn, his daughter, **Elizabeth FLOWER,** painted in a manner similar to his.
Examples: B.M.; Leicestershire A.G.; Nat. Lib., Wales.

FLUDYER, Maria, Mrs. Warren
c.1796 - 1884

The elder daughter of the 2nd Fludyer baronet, who was M.P. for Aldborough, she married B.C. Warren in 1841. She was a pupil of P. de Wint (q.v.), as was her sister **Caroline Louisa FLUDYER (1798-1888),** who married Cobbett Derby of Horton, Bucks, in 1828.

FOLEY, Joseph B

A landscape and marine painter in oil and watercolour who exhibited at the B.I. and Suffolk Street from 1863 to 1877.

FOLINGSBY, George Frederick
1830 (Co. Wicklow) - 1891 (Melbourne, Australia)

A historical painter who, at the age of eighteen, left Ireland for Canada and later New York, where he was draughtsman to *Harper's Magazine* and studied drawing at the New York Academy. He then travelled through Europe, visiting Greece and Turkey, and from 1852 to 1854 studied in Munich. After six months in Paris he spent a further five years working in Munich. He visited Belfast in 1862, returned once more to Munich and settled in Australia in 1879. He was appointed Director of the National Gallery of Victoria in 1884.

Examples: Melbourne A.G.

FONNEREAU, Thomas George
1789 (Reading) - 1850 (Bushey)

A barrister, author and amateur artist who gave up his legal practice in 1834 to devote himself to writing. In about 1840 he visited Italy with C. Stanfield (q.v.) and later wrote *Memoirs of a Tour in Italy* which was privately printed, and was illustrated with fifteen of his landscape sketches. He built himself a villa at Bushey.

Published: *Diary of a Dutiful Son,* 1864.

FORBES, Elizabeth Adela Stanhope, Mrs., née Armstrong, A.R.W.S.
1859 (Ottawa) - 1912 (Newlyn)

After a London upbringing and studying at South Kensington, she returned to Canada. She spent some time at the Art Students' League in New York and then, in 1882, studied and painted in Munich and Brittany. In 1883 she came back to London, and, after a period in Holland, she settled at Newlyn, Cornwall. She married Stanhope Alexander Forbes, R.A. in 1889, and in 1898 she was elected A.R.W.S.

Published: *King Arthur's Wood,* 1904.

Examples: B.M.; V.A.M.

Bibliography: Mrs. L. Birch: *S.A. Forbes and E.F.,* 1906. C. Fox: *S.F. and the Newlyn School,* 1993. *A.J.,* 1889; 1896; 1904. *Studio,* IV, 1894; Special No., 1898; XVIII, 1900; XXIII, 1901.

FORBES, James, F.R.S., F.S.A.
1749 (London) - 1819 (Aix-la-Chapelle)

In 1765 he went to Bombay as a writer to the

FORD, F.J.
Rue de la Grande, Malo. *Watercolour with scratching out, heightened with bodycolour, signed and dated '46, 23½in. x 18in.*

East India Company, and in 1775 accompanied Colonel Keating on a Mahrattas expedition. He held posts in Goojerat and Dubhoy and returned to England in 1784. He married in 1788 and thereafter lived in London and at Stanmore. He and his family visited Switzerland and Germany, and France during the Peace of Amiens. They were detained in France until June 1804. In 1811 he took charge of his grandson, Charles de Montalembert, and after Waterloo they went to live in France with his daughter and son-in-law. Two years later they returned to England and in 1819 set out for Stuttgart, Forbes dying *en route.*

In India Forbes filled one hundred and fifty folio volumes with sketches and notes on the flora, manners, religions and archaeology of the country. He also produced views in France, mainly in brown ink and brown wash.

Published: *Letters from France,* 1806. *Oriental Memoirs,* 1813-15.

Bibliography: *Country Life,* 17 Sept. 1964.

FORD, F   J

A painter of coastal views and Continental town scenes. He exhibited from 1845 to 1860 and was an unsuccessful candidate for the N.W.S. in 1848. He lived in London and worked in Sussex, Guernsey, Normandy and Belgium.

A group of local views in the Brighton A.G. by **Frederick FORD,** one dated 1887, may perhaps be attributable to him or to a relative.

Examples: Bishopsgate Inst.

FORD, Henry Justice (1860-1941)
A study of a maiden and a medieval knight. *Watercolour,
signed and dated 1906, 12in. x 7in.*

FORD, Henry Justice
1860 (London) - 1941
An illustrator of children's books and an occasional painter of historical subjects. He was educated at Repton and Clare College, Cambridge. He then studied at the Slade and with Herkomer (q.v.) at Bushey, and became a friend of Burne-Jones (q.v.). His illustrations to Andrew Laing's books of fairy stories and similar publications won the approval of their intended market.
Illustrated: A. Laing: The Blue Fairy Book, 1889, &c.
Bibliography: *Studio*, Winter No., 1897; *A.J.*, 1900; 1901; 1905.

FORD, J
In the Beecroft A.G., Southend, there is a watercolour of the old pier with this signature, dated 1883.

FORD, Richard
1796 (London) - 1858 (Heavitree, Essex)
The son of Sir Richard Ford, M.P. and Lady Ford, an amateur artist, he was educated at Winchester and Trinity College, Oxford, and was called to the bar, but never practised. Between 1830 and 1834 he lived in the Alhambra and Seville, making long tours around the country and entertaining artist friends such as J.F. Lewis (q.v.). On his return

he built himself a house near Exeter and he concentrated on writing and criticism., but also took lessons from J. Gendall (q.v.). He spent the winter of 1839-40 in Rome.

His book, the *Handbook,* has become a classic. He was a collector and connoisseur as well as an amateur artist. His work shows the influence of Lewis, but his drawing is generally weak and his colours can be rather sickly.

His first wife, **Harriet FORD (1806-1837)**, the illegitimate daughter of the 5th Earl of Essex, was also a watercolourist in the Lewis manner.

Their son, **The Rt.Hon. Sir Francis Clare FORD (1828-1899)** was a distinguished ambassador to Madrid, Constantinople and Rome. Ruskin was a generous admirer of his watercolour landscapes, and he himself was a noted admirer of Effie Ruskin.
Published: *Handbook for Travellers in Spain,* 1845. *Gatherings from Spain,* 1846. *Apsley House and Walmer Castle,* 1853.
Examples: Newport A.G.
Bibliography: *A.J.,* Oct. 1858. *Burlington Mag.,* LXXX, May, 1942. Wildenstein, London, Exhibition Cat., 1974.

FORD, Major-General William Henry
c. 1770 - 1829
The originator of the chain of Martello Towers to defend the southern coasts of Britain and Ireland from Napoleonic invasion. He was a military engineer and a gunner, and he absorbed his Woolwich drawing lessons admirably. In May 1811 he was appointed commander of artillery and engineering for the Dover district, where he oversaw his own towers. Later he became Lieutenant-Governor of Woolwich. He was a fine and lively draughtsman, and was as happy with figures and animals as with buildings and shipping.
Examples: Canterbury Mus.

FORDE, Samuel 1805 (Cork) - 1828 (Cork)
He studied at the Cork Academy under J. Chalmers (q.v.), who also taught him scene painting. He tried mezzotint engraving, but abandoned it to become a drawing master at the Cork Mechanics' Institute and elsewhere. His pictures were ambitious and literary, including a distemper painting, 'The Vision of Tragedy', for which he made many sketches. He died of consumption at the age of twenty-three while engaged upon what he considered his most important painting, 'The Fall of the Rebel Angels'.
Examples: V.A.M.; Crawford A.G.,Cork.
Bibliography: *Dublin University Mag.,* Mar. 1945.

FORREST, Charles
c.1748 (Ireland) -
He entered the R.D.S. Schools in 1765, and exhibited miniatures and chalk portraits in Dublin until 1780. There is a watercolour of Dunbrody Abbey, County Wexford, by him in the R.I.A.

FORREST, Lt.Col. Charles Ramus
c.1750 - 1827 (Chatham)

An officer who served with the Buffs in India from 1802-14, transferring to the 34th Foot as a major. In 1822 he was in Canada, and from 1824-26 he was Permanent Assistant Quartermaster-General. He illustrated his book with good Daniell-like pencil and watercolour views.

Published: *A Picturesque Tour along the Rivers Ganges and Jumna*, 1824.

Examples: V.A.M.

FORREST, Thomas Theodosius
1728 (London) - 1784 (London)

The son of Ebenezer Forrest, the solicitor who wrote the account of Hogarth, Scott, Thornhill and company's *Five Days Peregrination down the Thames* in 1732. Theodosius studied under G. Lambert (q.v.) but adopted his father's profession, becoming solicitor to Covent Garden where one of his musical compositions was once performed. He was a member of the Beefsteak Club, and he exhibited at the R.A. from 1762 to 1781, after which date he suffered from the nervous illness which led to his suicide. In 1774 he accompanied T. Sandby (q.v.) on a tour of Yorkshire and Derbyshire.

Examples: B.M.; V.A.M.

Bibliography: *Gentleman's Mag.*, 1784, p.877. *W&D*, 1987, i.

FORREST, Thomas Theodosius (1728-1784)
Capriccio landscape. *Watercolour.*

FORRESTER, James
1729 (Ireland) - 1775

A landscape painter and engraver known as the 'Irish Sandby'. He studied in the George's Lane School, Dublin, from 1747 and in 1752 he received the School's drawing prize. Soon afterwards he went to live in Rome, occasionally sending pictures for exhibition in Dublin and London. He produced a number of carefully etched Italian scenes.

Examples: V.A.M.; Ulster Mus.

FORRESTER, Joseph James, Baron de, F.S.A. 1809 (Hull) - 1861 (River Douro)

A wine merchant in Hull and Portugal who exhibited watercolours at Hull in 1827, '28 and '29. He went to Oporto in 1831 to work in the family firm. Whilst there he compiled an elaborate map of the Douro which was published in 1848. He strove to raise the standards of the port trade and published many pamphlets on it.

FORSTER, Charles, Yr.
1824/5 - 1880 (Islington)

A painter of rustic genre scenes, Dickensian illustrations and fisherfolk who was active from his schooldays to the end of his life. He lived in Islington and Hackney, and he may have been the son of 'C.T. FORSTER, Sen.', who exhibited at Suffolk Street in 1846 and 1849. Equally, this last may be a misprint for the Charles Francis Forster of Hackney who died in 1850. The elder Forster also exhibited

portraits at the R.A. from 1828 to 1847, including one of Prout.

FORSTER, J

A topographer who made pen and wash or watercolour drawings of Edinburgh and the Lowlands from 1785 to 1790.

It is possible that this is the **John FORSTER** who was educated in Paris and active in Ireland from 1773 to 1780 and again in 1794.

Examples: N.G., Scotland.

FORSTER, Johann Georg 'George' Adam
1754 - 1794

The son of J.R. Forster the naturalist. The family was originally from Yorkshire, but had settled in Germany during the Civil Wars. He accompanied Captain Cook's second voyage, 1772-75, making large drawings of birds and animals. They are not very impressive.

Examples: Nat. Hist. Mus.

FORSTER, (Emma Judith) Mary, Mrs LOFTHOUSE
1853 (Bath) - 1885 (Lower Halliford)

Until her marriage she lived at Holt Manor, near Bradford on Avon, Wiltshire, the seat of her father T.B.W. Forster (q.v.). Father and daughter painted in Wales and France as well as locally. She also exhibited subjects from Yorkshire, Norfolk and Hampshire. She may also have visited Switzerland with him, and probably knew Scotland, her mother being a Galbraith from Macrahanish. From the age of

twenty she exhibited in the annual General Exhibitions at the Dudley Gallery, and she showed at the Royal Academy in 1876, 1878 and 1880. In early 1884 she was elected A.R.W.S., but her art was 'too delicate and refined to attract the attention which it deserved during the two years only in which her landscapes were accorded a place in the gallery. But they afforded fair ground for anticipation that had she lived longer they would have become a much more important feature in the annual gatherings' (Roget). In June 1884 she married Samuel Hill Smith Lofthouse (*b* 1841), a barrister, who had himself exhibited a winter landscape at the S.B.A. in 1874. For her final exhibits she used her married name. She died in childbirth during the summer exhibition of the R.W.S., at which her *Pembroke Castle* was attracting very favourable attention. A collection of 26 frames of her studies and sketches was hung in the Society's winter show that year by way of memorial.

Bibliography: *Times*, 5 May 1885.

FORSTER, Thomas Burton Watkin
1821 - 1887 (London)

The son and father of colonels, and father of (Emma Judith) Mary Forster (q.v.), he painted landscapes in Wiltshire, Scotland – his wife was from Machrahanish – Wales, France and Switzerland. He was educated at Winchester and Oriel College Oxford, exhibited from 1859 to 1886 and lived at Holt Manor, near Bradford on Avon.

FORTESCUE, Henrietta Anne, Hon. Mrs. (c.1765-1841)
A mountain landscape. *Pen and washes, signed and dated Nov 28th 1817, size unknown.*

FORTESCUE, Henrietta Anne, Hon. Mrs.
c.1765 - 1841
The daughter of Sir Richard Hoare, 1st Bt., and sister of Sir R.C. Hoare (q.v.), she was a landscape painter who married firstly Sir T.D. Acland, 9th Bt., and secondly, in 1795, Captain the Hon. Mathew Fortescue, R.N., brother of the first Earl Fortescue. Sir T.D. Acland (q.v.) was her son. She painted in Italy in 1817 and 1821, the Pyrenees in 1818, Scotland in 1823 and in the Lake District, Cornwall and other parts of Britain. She supplied F. Nicholson with Continental subjects to work up and turn into prints. Her work, although in no way original, would be a credit to many of the professionals of the period.
Examples: Coventry Mus.; Abbot Hall A.G., Kendal.

FOSBROOKE, Leonard
A landscape painter who lived at Ashby de la Zouch and exhibited in London from 1884.

FOSTER, John
c.1787 (Liverpool) - 1846 (Birkenhead)
The second son of his namesake, an influential Liverpool architect, he became a pupil of Jeffry and James Wyatt, and exhibited drawings at the R.A. from 1804. In 1809 he travelled on the Continent, and he was in Greece the following year with Haller and C.R. Cockerell (q.v.). He returned to England in 1816 and worked as a partner in the family firm until 1824. Until 1835 he was Architect and Surveyor to the Liverpool Corporation, designing many of the city's most important buildings.

His Greek and Turkish watercolours show an ability to handle both landscape and architectural detail. They are in clear brown or coloured washes, and they are often inscribed and initialled.
Examples: B.M.; Walker A.G., Liverpool.

FOSTER, Myles Birket, R.W.S.
1825 (North Shields) - 1899 (Weybridge)
The course of Foster's early career may have been influenced by his parents' knowledge of Bewick. When the family moved to London in 1830, he was given a Quaker education and apprenticed to the wood-engraver Ebenezer Landells. Until about 1850 he worked exclusively as an engraver and a black and white illustrator, making many designs for the *I.L.N.* Throughout the 1850s he was teaching himself to paint in watercolour and he turned to it seriously in about 1859. Thereafter he exhibited some four hundred works with the O.W.S., of which he was elected Associate and Member in 1860 and 1862. His house at Witley, Surrey, was partly decorated by the Pre-Raphaelites and became a centre for artists of many different types. He lived there until illness forced a move to Weybridge in 1893. He travelled widely on the Continent from his first visit to the Rhine in 1852, and he first visited Venice with F. Walker (q.v.) in 1868. He was commissioned to make a series of fifty Venetian views by Charles Seeley of Nottingham at a fee of £5,000.

Although he has been hugely faked, his genuine works are fairly easy to recognise. His early experience as a wood-engraver left its mark on his style. In finished watercolours he employs a stipple technique, especially on flesh, and his drawing is always minutely accurate. He generally worked on a comparatively small scale, but he is also one of the very few watercolourists to have made a complete success of a really large composition. To many tastes there is too much sentiment mixed with his pigments, but among artists his reputation has always been high.
Examples: B.M.; V.A.M.; Tate Gall.; Aberdeen A.G.; Haworth A.G., Accrington; Ashmolean;

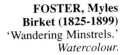
FOSTER, Myles Birket (1825-1899)
'Wandering Minstrels.'
Watercolour.

Blackburn A.G.; Grundy A.G., Blackpool; Brighton A.G.; Exeter Mus.; Glasgow A.G.; Greenwich; Hitchin Mus.; Huntington Lib., California; Inverness Lib.; City A.G., Manchester; Whitworth A.G., Manchester; N.G., Scotland; N.Lib., Wales; Laing A.G., Newcastle; Newport A.G.; Paisley A.G.; City of Sheffield Mus.; Ulster Mus.; Yale
Bibliography: H.M. Cundall: *B.F.*, 1906. J. Reynolds: *B.F.*, 1984. *A.J.*, 1863; May, 1871; Christmas No.,1890. *Portfolio*, 1891. *Studio*, 1902. O.W.S. Club, XI, 1933. F.T.Sabin, Exhibition Cat., 1999.

FOSTER, Walter H   W
A river and landscape painter in oil and occasionally watercolour who lived in Dalston and exhibited at the R.A. and the S.B.A. from 1861 to 1888. This may have been the year of his death.

His wife, **Kate E. FOSTER,** was also a watercolourist, exhibiting in the 1880s. **Frederick FOSTER,** who lived next door to them with his daughter, **Miss F.E. FOSTER,** was presumably a brother. He too had a fondness for rivers, exhibiting from 1867 to 1876. She showed birds' nests and hedgerows from 1871 to 1879. **Helen FOSTER,** who lived nearby and exhibited views of streams in 1879 and 1880, may also have been a relative.

FOSTER, William   - 1812
A portrait and figure painter in oil and watercolour who exhibited from 1772. His figures can be reminiscent of those of Cristall, and he drew actresses in pencil and watercolour.
Examples: B.M.

FOSTER, William, II
1853 (London) - 1924 (London)
The second son, and only painting child, of M.B. Foster (q.v.). The family moved to Witley in 1863, and it remained his home for thirty years. He was educated at Guildford Grammar School and studied at Heatherley's, exhibiting from 1871. He was a birdwatching and sketching companion of B. Hook, son of a neighbour J.C. Hook (qq.v.), and he was a wildlife artist of considerable ability as well as producing impressive landscapes in the manner of his father. He also produced still-lifes, genre subjects, and black and white and colour illustrations, mostly for bird books. Some of his children's illustrations, usually for Ernest Nister's books, are akin to those of H.B. Potter (q.v.). In 1894 he accompanied his father and stepmother to Weybridge, and only in 1904 did he escape into matrimony. Thereafter he lived in London.
Published: *Follies, Foibles and Fancies of Fish, Flesh and Fowl,* 1889. *Keeper Jacko,* 1904.
Illustrated: A.O. Hume & C.H.T. Marshall: *The Game Birds of India, Burmah and Ceylon,* 1879-81. C.A. Johns: *British Birds in their Haunts,* 1909, &c.
Bibliography: *Ibis*, 1924. *Ant. Dealer & Collectors' Guide,* Sept. 1993.

FOSTER, Myles Birket (1825-1899)
Lucerne. *Watercolour, signed with monogram.*

FOSTER, William Gilbert
1855 (Manchester) - 1906
The son of a portrait painter who taught him until 1876 when he first exhibited at the R.A., and moved to Leeds. He became a member of the R.B.A. in 1893. He painted in oil and watercolour and drew in charcoal, and his favourite subjects were farms and evenings.
Examples: Cartwright Hall, Bradford.
Bibliography: *Studio*, XXX, 1904. *A.J.*, 1906.

FOTHERGILL, George Algernon
1868 (Leamington) - 1945
A doctor and sporting artist, he studied medicine at Edinburgh University and art at Uppingham. He practised in Darlington, where he played a prominent part in sporting life and illustrated a number of books on sporting subjects. He worked in watercolour, pen and ink and pencil. Although he had given up medicine for art in 1906, he served as medical officer to the 1st Cavalry Brigade in the First World War. Thereafter he settled as an artist at Crammond Bridge, near Edinburgh. Walker's Gallery, London, held an exhibition of his work in 1938.
A **Charles W. FOTHERGILL** exhibited marine watercolour, signed with initials, from 1896 to 1900.
Published: *Fothergill's Sketch Books,* 1903. &c.
Examples: Darlington A.G.
Bibliography: *A.J.*, 1902.

FOURNIER, Daniel
c.1710   - ?1766
Perhaps a member of the Huguenot family which gave its name to the famous Spitalfields street, he was a silver chaser, butter and egg seller, 'mad geometer', writer on perspective, etcher, mezzotinter, surveyor, modeller in wax and drawing master. He also built a fiddle and taught himself to play it.
Published: *A Treatise of...Perspective,* 1761.

FOWLER, Daniel 1810   - 1894 (Canada)
A painter of landscapes, figure subjects and old buildings. He exhibited from 1836 to 1842, when living in London, and he painted in Germany, Italy and Switzerland as well as England and Wales. He also showed a still life of dead game.

FOWLER, Robert, R.W.S.
1853 (Anstruther) - 1926 (London)
He studied in London and then lived in Liverpool until 1904, when he returned to the metropolis. He exhibited from 1876 and was a member of the R.I. from 1891 to 1915 when he transferred to the R.W.S. His earlier work is in the neo-classical manner of A. Moore (q.v.), sometimes with an admixed Japanese influence. Later he painted landscapes in oil and watercolour and also posters.
Examples: Exeter Mus.
Bibliography: *Studio*, IX, 1897; Special No., 1898; Special No., 1900; XXXII, 1904.

FOWLES, Arthur Wellington
1815 (Ryde) - 1883
The son of an Isle of Wight grocer, he became a marine painter. Although he never exhibited, he was described by the *A.J.* as 'perhaps the most accurate of the portrait painters...but his faults of perspective, bad colouring, immobility, and inability to depict waves,

FOX, Henry Charles (1860-c.1913)
'Homewards.' *Watercolour heightened with bodycolour, signed and dated 1896, 13½in. x 20½in.*

rendered his pictures of yachts of little value'. His unchanciness did not end there, for he was accidentally shot by his young son.
Bibliography: *A.J.*, 1876.

FOX, Charles
1794 (Costessey, Norfolk) - 1849 (Leyton)
He was brought up in the gardens of Lord Stafford at Costessey Hall, Norfolk, whence he derived his lifelong interest in flowers. He took drawing lessons from C. Hodgson (q.v.) and trained as an engraver with William Edwards at Bungay, Suffolk. Afterwards he came to London and assisted John Burnet on plates after Wilkie. He also worked for the *Annuals*. He was a judge of the Horticultural Society and superintended the illustrations of *The Florist*. As well as making watercolours of plants, he took portraits of his friends.
Bibliography: *Gentleman's Mag.*, 1849, i.

FOX, Charles James
1822 (Leeds) - c.1904
A Sheffield and London painter of landscapes in oil and watercolour who exhibited from 1883.

FOX, Edward   1791
A London painter who exhibited landscapes in oil and watercolour at the R.A., the O.W.S. and elsewhere from 1813 to 1854. He moved to Brighton in 1829.
Examples: V.A.M.; Brighton A.G.

FOX, Henry Charles
1860   - c.1913
A painter of rustic scenes who exhibited at the R.A. and Suffolk Street from 1879 to 1913, and lived for a time at Kingston-on-Thames.

His backgrounds, although not his figures, are in the Birket Foster (q.v.) tradition. He generally uses white heightening.
Examples: Reading A.G.

FRANCIA, François Louis Thomas
1772 (Calais) - 1839 (Calais)
Francia came to England in 1795, when he first exhibited at the R.A. He was a fellow student with Girtin at Dr. Monro's, and in May 1799 he was Secretary and a co-founder of Girtin's sketching club 'The Brothers'. He worked as an assistant at J.C. Barrow's drawing school in Holborn and in 1805 he set up as a drawing master in Kensington. In 1810 he joined the A.A. and the next year became Secretary. He was also Painter in Watercolours to the Duchess of York. In 1816 he failed to gain election as A.R.A. and in 1817 he returned to Calais where he spent the rest of his life, and where he gave lessons to his most famous pupil R.P. Bonington (q.v.).

His early work is executed in deep dark tones, both of monochrome and colour washes, and shows the influence of Girtin (q.v.). Later his colours became thinner, tending more to yellow-browns and greys, and the works of this period can be similar to those of J.S. Cotman (q.v.). In the coastal scenes of his Calais years, which are among his best works, it is often difficult to tell which of the two, he or Bonington, influence the other more. They are often signed 'L.F.' on a floating spar or piece of timber.

His son, **Count Alexandre Thomas FRANCIA (1813 London - 1884 Brussels)** was his pupil and exhibited in Paris and London between 1841 and 1867. He was a marine painter and talented, although without his father's originality. He also produced landscapes, including a few Irish subjects.
Published: *Studies of Landscapes*, 1810. *Marine Studies*, 1822.
Examples: B.M.; V.A.M.; Aberdeen A.G.; Ashmolean; Brighton A.G.; Ferens A.G., Hull; Fitzwilliam; Greenwich; Leeds City A.G.; N.G., Ireland; Newport A.G.
Bibliography: (A.T.F.) *Journal des Beaux Arts*, Brussels, 1878; 1884.
See Colour Plate

FRANCIA, François Louis Thomas (1772-1839)
Dunkirk Beach. *Watercolour on blue paper, heightened with white, signed and dated 1829. 7¾in. x 11½in.*

FRANK, William Arthur, A.R.H.A.
1848 - 1908 (Dublin)
An Irish landscape painter, whose work can have a rather stark Buckley-like feel. He exhibited in London and Scotland as well as at the R.H.A., and he was in Liverpool in 1835.

He is not to be confused with **Walter Arnee FRANK (1808-1897)**, a competent painter of river landscapes.

FRANKLAND, Sir Robert (RUSSELL), 7th Bt. 1784 - 1849 (Thirkleby)
An amateur artist, and M.P. for Thirsk, Yorkshire, from 1815 to 1824. He lived at Thirkleby Park and took the additional name of Russell in 1837. His father, **Sir Thomas FRANKLAND (1750-1831)** was a pupil of J.B. Malchair (q.v.). His wife was a sister of the Hon. A.M. Murray (q.v.).

FRANKLIN, John
An Irish landscape and genre painter who entered the R.D.S. Schools in 1819, after which he worked in Dublin. He exhibited at the opening exhibition of the R.H.A. in 1826 and again in 1827 and 1828. He then moved to London, where he exhibited at Suffolk Street, the B.I. and the R.A. from 1830 to 1868, specialising in scenes from Venetian history.
Illustrated: Hall: *Ireland, its Scenery and Character,* 1841. W. Harrison Ainsworth: *Old St. Paul's.* Carleton: *Traits and Stories of the Irish Peasantry,* 1852.
Examples: B.M.; V.A.M.

FRANKS, Captain Frederick - 1844
A' painter of landscapes and architectural subjects. He served in the Navy and was promoted lieutenant in 1813 and captain in 1824.

FRASER, Alexander, R.S.A., R.S.W.
1828 (Linlithgow) - 1899 (Musselburgh)
The son of A.G. Fraser (q.v.), he studied at the Trustees' Academy, where, he claimed, he learned nothing, his true masters being Cox and Müller (qq.v.). He was elected A.R.S.A. and R.S.A. in 1858 and 1862, and R.S.W. in 1878. From 1847 to 1857 he spent the winters in London, and he also sketched in Wales. However his subjects were usually Scottish landscapes, often painted alongside his friend S. Bough (q.v.). He was partially disabled by rheumatism from 1885. As well as landscapes he painted still lifes and interiors. His work became progressively less detailed.
Published: *Scottish Landscape: The Works of Horatio MacCulloch,* 1872.
Examples: V.A.M.; N.G., Scotland; Newport A.G.
Bibliography: *A.J.,* 1873; 1904; 1906. *Portfolio,* 1887.

FRASER, Alexander George, A.R.S.A.
1785 (Edinburgh) - 1865 (Wood Green)
A fellow student at the Trustees' Academy, he became Wilkie's assistant. He exhibited his own work at the R.A. from 1810 to 1848 and in 1840 was one of the first A.R.S.A.s. His drawings are very much in the Wilkie mould of Scottish domestic and historic genre. He gave up painting in the early 1850s because of poor health.
Examples: B.M.; N.G., Scotland; Paisley A.G.
Bibliography: A.Cunningham: *Life of Sir David Wilkie,* 1843, *A.J.,* 1865. *Gentleman's Mag.,* 1865. *Portfolio,* 1887.

FRASER, Claud Lovat
1890 (London) - 1921 (Sandgate)
An illustrator and stage designer who was educated at Charterhouse and was a pupil of Sickert. He was gassed at Loos, and he later worked in the Records Office for two years. His greatest theatrical success was *The Beggar's Opera.* His watercolours include bird studies.
Examples: B.M.; V.A.M.

FRASER, James Baillie
1783 (Reelick, Inverness) - 1856 (Reelick)
A traveller, man of letters and landscape painter. Early in life he went to the West Indies and then to India where he was a pupil of G. Chinnery and W. Havell (qq.v.), exploring the Nepalese Himalayas in 1815. In 1821 he accompanied Dr. Jukes on his mission to Persia, and he tried to make his way to Bokhara in Persian dress but got only as far as Tabriz. In 1833-34 he was again on a long diplomatic mission to Persia, and in 1835 he was in charge of the arrangements for the visit of the Persian Princes to England. He published numerous works, and spent the latter part of his life improving his estate and serving as a deputy lieutenant for the county. He was distantly related to the Chambers family (see Appendix II).
Published: *Journal of a Tour through part of the Himala Mountains…,* 1820. *Views of Calcutta,* 1824-6. *Highland Smugglers,* 1832. &c.

FRASER, John Simpson, R.S.W.
1858 - 1927
A marine, landscape, still-life and figure painter in oil and watercolour who exhibited in London from 1879 and was a member of the R.B.A. He was a founder member of the R.S.W. in 1878. He lived in Edinburgh until about 1887, when he moved to Auchmithie, Forfarshire.
Examples: Greenwich; Hove Lib.

FRASER, Captain Thomas
1776 - 1823 (Bath)
The son of a Morpeth portrait painter, he served with the Madras Engineers from 1796 to 1819. He carried out surveys at Seringapatam in 1799 and, with J. Gantz (q.v.), in the districts of Bellary, Kurnod, Anantapur and Cuddapah in 1802. As well as plans and surveys, he made watercolours of ruins and waterfalls. On his return home he lived in Oxfordshire, where he was Sheriff in 1820, and he had a Scottish estate.
Examples: India Office Lib.

THE FRASER FAMILY OF HUNTINGDONSHIRE
See Fraser Family Tree
Dr. Robert Winchester Fraser, a retired army surgeon and the youngest son of the Laird of Findrack in Aberdeenshire, settled in Bedford in 1861. His family traced its origins back to a sister of Robert the Bruce, and his painting sons paid obeisance to their ancestry in a fervent and most convivial Jacobitism long after the cause had died elsewhere.

He had seven sons and at least two daughters. At least six of his sons became watercolour painters and in some cases cartoonists. The exception seems to have been Michie Forbes Anderson Fraser (b.1851), who was in the Consular service in Hong Kong and Shanghai and is not known to have been an artist, although according to a member of the family there was 'never a Fraser who did not draw'. In order of seniority the others were:
Francis Arthur Anderson FRASER (1846 Corfu - 1924 Walmer) entered the R.A. Schools in 1865. He became a cartoonist for *Fun* and painted watercolours and occasional works in oil. He signed the cartoons 'F.A.F.', and he exhibited from 1867 to 1883.
Robert Winchester FRASER (1848 Scotland - 1906 Gibraltar) lived in London and Staines before moving back to the Fens. He has often been conflated with his son **Robert James Winchester FRASER (1872 East Cotts, Beds. - 1930),** who signed 'Robert Winter'. The son is the best known, and perhaps the best, of the family. His clear, rather acidic and photographic watercolours of the Fens and the Ouse have great merit. His younger brother was **Francis George FRASER (1879-1940).**
Garden William FRASER (1856 Chatham - 1921 ?Huntingdon) generally signed 'W.F. Garden' to difference himself from the rest of the clan. He also seems to have used the name 'William Fraser-Gardener', although this may merely have been to confuse census-takers and debt-collectors. He was educated at Bedford School before working in an insurance office and studying at the R.S.A. Schools. He was living and painting at Hemingford Abbots by 1890, moved to Holywell in about 1898 and back again before 1920. His work is detailed and accurate and a little less harsh than that of his nephew.
George Gordon FRASER (1860 Scotland - 1895 California, nr. Hemingford Abbots) was a scholar at Bedford School, leaving in 1875-6 to become 'an artist at £6 per month'. He too painted cartoons for *Fun,* often on Irish themes, his wife being from Larne. He also made painstakingly accurate watercolours of the Fens. By 1894 he was living close to the family at Houghton. He died by falling through the ice while skating, and since the

FRASER, Robert James Winchester ('Winter') (1872-1930)
Pangbourne-on-Thames. *Watercolour heightened with white, signed and inscribed, 11in. x 17¼in.*

body was not found for eight weeks, there was much unpleasant speculation.

Arthur Anderson FRASER (1861 Bedford - 1904 Holywell) left Bedford School in 1880 and was a cartoonist as well as a most competent local landscape painter.

Gilbert Baird FRASER (1866 Bedford - 1947) lived at Holywell from at least 1906. He was generally impecunious,and he painted local scenes, postcards and illustrations in watercolour or crayon. He married a Hesletine who was a great-granddaughter of C. Dibdin (q.v.).

The two sisters, who may very well have painted, were: **Margaret S. FRASER (b.1852 Scotland)** and **Catherine B. FRASER (b.c.1862 Scotland)**.

Examples of the work of various members of the family can be found in the Darlington A.G.; the Cecil Higgins A.G., Bedford, and elsewhere.
Bibliography: *W&D*, 1989, i.

FREEBAIRN, Robert, A.O.W.S.
            1764 (London) - 1808 (London)
A pupil of Richard Wilson, after whose death in 1782 he entered the R.A. Schools but soon after went to study and work in Italy, returning in 1792. Although chiefly an oil painter, he was one of the first group of Associates elected to the O.W.S. in December 1805. In his two years he only exhibited eight drawings, all of Italian subjects. His son Alfred Robert Freebairn (b.1795) was an engraver.
Examples: Lancaster Mus.

FREEBORN, William
An artist who painted London views in about 1850.

FREEMAN, William Philip Barnes
            1813 (Norwich) - 1897 (Norwich)
The son of William Freeman, Secretary of the Norwich Society and Crome's companion in Paris, he was a pupil of J.S. Cotman and J.B. Ladbroke and was a member of the Norwich Amateur Club. He exhibited in London in 1860 and 1862 and was three times an unsuccessful candidate for the N.W.S. between 1862 and 1865.
Examples: Castle Mus., Norwich; Gt. Yarmouth Lib.
Bibliography: J. Walpole: *Art and Artists of the Norwich School*, 1997.

FRENCH, William Percy
            1854 (Cloonyquin) - 1920
An engineer and composer and arranger of folk songs such as 'Slattery's Mounted Foot', he was educated at Trinity College, Dublin. He painted landscapes using a wet technique and specialised in mists and moors. He also produced humorous drawings.
Examples: County Mus., Armagh; Ulster Mus.
Bibliography: *The Tatler*, 17 Jul. 1901.
See Colour Plate

FRIER, Harry   c.1849 - 1919
A Scottish landscape painter who studied in Paris and lived in Somerset.

He was related to **Jessie and Robert FRIER**, who painted in Edinburgh and a Pre-Raphaelite manner from about 1853 to 1912. Their sister was **Jean Jamieson FRIER**, active from 1869 to 1883.

FRIPP, Alfred Downing, R.W.S.
            1822 (Bristol) - 1895 (Hampstead)

The brother of G.A. Fripp (q.v.), and a grandson of N. Pocock (q.v.), he came to London in 1840 and studied at the B.M. and the R.A. Schools. He exhibited with the O.W.S. from 1842 and was elected A.O.W.S. and O.W.S. in 1844 and 1846. He was Secretary from 1870 until his death. He went to Rome in 1850, and for the next four years Italian landscapes and peasants are prominent among his subjects. Before and afterwards, despite another Italian visit in 1859, English, Irish and Welsh views form the major part of his work.
Examples: V.A.M.; City A.G., Bristol; Sydney A.G.
Bibliography: C.E.M. Roberts: *A.F.*, 1932. *Mag. of Art*, 1895. *Walker's Quarterly*, XXV, XXVI, 1927-8.

FRIPP, Charles Edwin, A.R.W.S.
            1854 (London) - 1906 (Montreal)
A son of G.A. Fripp (q.v.) he studied at Nuremberg and Munich. From 1878 to 1900 he was a war correspondent for the *Graphic*, his extensive travels including a visit to Japan. He was elected A.R.W.S. in 1891. Presumably the C.L. Fripp noted by the *A.J.* as an exhibitor at the B.I. in 1873 was one of his eleven siblings.
Illustrated: B. Field: *Fairy Tales*, 1898.
Examples: V.A.M.

FRIPP, George Arthur, R.W.S.
            1813 (Bristol) - 1896 (London)
A grandson of N. Pocock (q.v.), he was taught to paint in oil and watercolour by J.B. Pyne and S. Jackson (qq.v.). He began his career as a portrait painter in Bristol. He visited Italy in 1834 with W.J. Müller (q.v.). He began to exhibit with the O.W.S. in 1837 and moved to

FRIPP, George Arthur (1813-1896)
Old British Camp in Bulstrode Park. *Watercolour, exhibited OWS 1860.*

London in the following year. In 1841 he was elected A.O.W.S. and in 1845 O.W.S., serving as Secretary from 1848 to 1854. In 1864 he stayed at Balmoral drawing local views for the Queen. His style is varied, in his early landscapes showing an affinity to Cox (q.v.), and later a rather old-fashioned effect of greens and yellows over careful pencil drawing.
Examples: B.M.; V.A.M.; Aberdeen A.G.; Ashmolean; Blackburn A.G.: Coventry A.G.; Leeds City A.G.; City A.G., Manchester; N.G. Scotland; Newport A.G.; Richmond Lib.; Beecroft A.G., Southend; Ulster Mus.
Bibliography: H.S. Thompson: *G.A.F. and A.D. Fripp*, 1928. *A.J.*, Feb., 1877. *Walker's Quarterly*, XXV, XXVI, 1928.

FROHAWK, Frederick William
1861 (Brisley Hall, Norfolk) -
1946 (Sutton, Surrey)
The son of a gentleman farmer at East Dereham, he was brought up there, Great Yarmouth and Ipswich. The family later settled at Upper Norwood. His interest in drawing and natural history appeared early, and he became 'one of the greatest names in British butterflies.' The New Forest was a favourite area; his youngest daughter Valezina (Lady Bolingbroke) was named after the New Forest version of the Silver-washed Fritillary, and there is now a 'Frohawk Ride' in the Forest. He drew for *The Field* – of which he became natural history editor – *The Entomologist* and other scientific periodicals. His friend and fellow butterfly collector Lord Rothschild bought the original watercolours

for his first book and left them to the nation with his collection.
Published: *Natural History of British Butterflies*, 1924. T*he Complete Book of British Butterflies*, 1934. *Varieties of British Butterflies*, 1938.
Examples: Nat. Hist. Mus.
Bibliography: M.A. Salmon: *The Aurelian Legacy*, 2000.

FROST, George
1734 (Ipswich) - 1821 (Ipswich)
An admirer of Gainsborough and a friend of Constable, Frost was an amateur artist who, confusingly, taught other amateurs. He worked first in his father's building business and then in the office of the Blue Coach at Ipswich. His subjects are taken from Ipswich and the neighbourhood, and the black chalk and grey wash drawings which form the majority of his work can be very close to Gainsborough. He also made watercolours of boats and buildings on the Orwell, and figure studies. A characteristic touch is his use of a purplish red.
Examples: B.M.; Glasgow A.G.
Bibliography: F. Brown: *Frost's Drawings of Ipswich*, 1895.

FROST, William Edward, R.A.
1810 (Wandsworth) - 1877 (London)
He studied at Sass's drawing school on the advice of W. Etty (q.v.), the B.M. and the R.A. Schools, and he began his career as a portrait painter. He was elected A.R.A. in 1845, R.A. in 1870 and retired in 1876. By the 1840s his naked nymphs had become so popular that he gave up portrait painting to give them his

undivided attention. His subjects are usually taken from Milton, Spenser and the ancients. His ladies and their attendants are all the same, with long sensuous outlines, glowing pink complexions and discreetly placed draperies.
Examples: B.M.; Ashmolean; Fitzwilliam.
Bibliography: *A.J.*, 1849; 1856; Jan. 1857; 1858; 1866;1877. *I.L.N.*, 1871. *Athenaeum*, 1877. *The Times*, 8 June 1877.

FROUDE, Rev. Robert Hurrell
1779 - 1859
Educated at Oriel College, Oxford, he became Rector of Dartington and Denbury, Devonshire, and Archdeacon of Totnes. He sketched in the West Country and in France. His subjects are village streets, ruins and landscapes, his washes of colour or monochrome soft and gentle, and his pen outlines economical. He was the father of J.A. Froude, the historian, and of Richard Hurrell Froude, the friend of J.H. Newman.
According to Farington his sketches, 'as far as outlines go, are very like the drawings of an Artist'.
Examples: Cathedral Lib., Exeter.

FRY, William Arthur 1865 (Otley) -
A landscape and marine painter who lived in Hollywood, Co. Down. He also painted portraits and genre pictures.

FRYER, Edward Langley
A painter of Venetian scenes and English landscapes. He lived in London, was active from about 1834, and was presumably encouraged by the reception of the three works

FUSELI, John Henry (1741-1825)
The Power of Fancy in Dreams. *Grey, blue and pink washes, heightened with white and touches of red ink, 14¼in. x 10¼in.*

which he exhibited in 1866 to apply for membership of the N.W.S. in the following year. He was turned down.

FUGE, James, N.W.S   - 1838 (London)
A landscape painter who exhibited from 1832. He appears to have been a member of the N.W.S. for a few months in 1838.

FULLEYLOVE, John, R.I.
1847 (Leicester) - 1908 (London)
A painter of towns, landscapes and genre subjects, he was apprenticed to an architect. He travelled widely in Europe and the Near East, illustrating books on the Holy Land, Greece, Oxford and elsewhere. He exhibited in London from 1871, was a member of the R.W.S. for a short time and was elected A.R.I. and·R.I. in 1878 and 1879. He was a friend of T. Collier (q.v.), whose influence can occasionally be seen in his work. Although his drawing and colour are good, the overall effect can sometimes be a little messy.

Various exhibitions of his work were held at the Fine Art Society, including 'Greek Views' in 1896 and 'Views of the Holy Land' in 1902.
Examples: B.M.; V.A.M.; Ashmolean; Brighton A.G.; Coventry Mus.; Fitzwilliam; Greenwich; Leicestershire A.G.; Maidstone Mus.; Newport A.G.; Stalybridge A.G.
Bibliography: *Studio*, VII, 1896; XXV, 1899; Summer No., 1900. *A.J.*, 1908.

FULLWOOD, John
1854 (Birmingham) - 1931
A landscape painter and etcher who was educated in Birmingham and studied in Paris. He was a member of the R.B.A. and exhibited from 1874. He was living at Twickenham in 1927, and he may have been the brother of **Albert Henry FULLWOOD (b.1864)**, a Birmingham landscape painter who was working from 1881 to at least 1904 and living in London in the latter year. Thereafter he went to Australia.
Published: *Remnants of Old Wolverhampton*, 1880. *Fairlight Glen*, 1892.
Bibliography: *A.J.*, 1886; 1893; 1895; 1896; 1902.

FULTON, David, R.S.W.
1848 (Glasgow) - 1930 (Glasgow)
A painter of interiors, landscapes and angling subjects who studied at the Glasgow School of Art and exhibited in London, Venice, Prague and St. Louis as well as in Scotland. He was elected R.S.W. in 1891.
Examples: Paisley A.G.

FUSELI (FÜSSLI), John Henry, R.A.
1741 (Zürich) - 1825 (Putney)
Fuseli came of a distinguished and artistic Swiss family, and in his early years he showed more of a leaning towards literature than painting. His friendship with the physiognomist, J.C. Lavater, had a great influence on his later style. In 1761 they were both ordained, but two years later they left Zürich for Berlin as a result of a political disturbance. Early in 1764 Fuseli moved to England, where he was much encouraged by Reynolds, who inspired him to paint in oil. In 1769 he went to Rome, and he remained in Italy for eight years, studying the old masters and working under Raphael Mengs. In Rome he was the centre of a circle which included A. Runciman (q.v.) and J. Brown (q.v.). In 1788 he left Rome and in the following year returned to England by way of Switzerland. He was elected A.R.A. and R.A. in 1788 and 1790. In 1790 he was appointed Professor of Painting at the R.A., and he held the post virtually until his death. His lectures had a wide influence on the younger generation of artists.

Fuseli was a figure draughtsman who occasionally added coloured washes to his drawings. His work is related stylistically to the wash drawings of Romney, and he is of the school of illustration which includes Stothard and Westall. He, however, takes the conventions of this school to an extreme, and his drawings are decidedly individual in a theatrical manner. It seems probable that Blake's pen work was more strongly influenced by that of Fuseli than the other way around. Fuseli's inspiration is mainly drawn from history, romance and literature – he contributed nine subjects to Boydell's *Shakespeare*. His women, in particular, are stately and stylised with fantastic headdress and coiffures.

He was ambidextrous.
Published: *Lectures on Painting*, 1801.
Examples: B.M.; V.A.M.; Ashmolean; Fitzwilliam; NG., Scotland; Ulster Mus.
Bibliography: J. Knowles: *Life and writings of H.F.*, 1831. P. Ganz: *The drawings of H.F.*, 1949. N. Powell: *The drawings of H.F.*, 1951. F. Antal: *F. studies*, 1956. P. Tomory: *The Life and Art of H.F.*, 1972. *A.J.*, May, 1859. Nov.1861. Tate Gal., Exhibition Cat., 1975.

FUSSELL, Joseph   1818 (Birmingham) -
1912 (Point Loma, Canada)
A landscape painter who studied at the R.A. Schools from 1838 and afterwards worked for a time as an engraver. He lived for most of his life in Nottingham, where he taught at the School of Art, of which his brother **Frederick Ralph FUSSELL** was Headmaster. In 1903 he emigrated to Canada to live with one of his sons. He also painted still lifes.

His daughter **Alice FUSSELL (b.c.1850)** gave drawing lessons and later became an art mistress at the Nottingham High School for girls. She exhibited locally.
Examples: Castle Mus., Nottingham

G

GADSBY, William Hippon
1844 (Derby) - 1924 (London)
The son of a Derby solicitor, in whose office he worked for two years. He was determined to study art and trained at Heatherley's and for five years at the R.A. Schools, where Millais (q.v.) took an interest in him. He visited the Continent, and studied in Rome and Venice in 1870. In 1896 he worked on a commission to copy a portrait of Queen Victoria at Buckingham Palace. He exhibited at the R.A. and on his death was the oldest member of the R.B.A. He painted in oil and watercolour and was best known for his sentimental portraits of children. In 1922 he contributed a watercolour of a child's head to the Queen's Dolls' House. He also painted still life and figure subjects, and he rarely signed his work.
Examples: Derby A.G.

GAGE, Sir Thomas, Bt.
c.1780 - 1820
An amateur marine and landscape artist who was a patron of J. Bourne (q.v.). He succeeded to the title in 1798, and in 1809 he married a daughter of the Earl of Kenmare. He sketched in many parts of England and the Pale. In about 1725 the greengage had been named in honour of one of his forebears.

GAINSBOROUGH, Thomas, R.A.
1727 (Sudbury, Suffolk) - 1788 (London)
'At ten years old Gainsborough had made some progress in sketching, and at twelve was a confirmed painter' (Cunningham). At fourteen he was sent to London and became a pupil of Gravelot, the engraver. He then attended the St. Martin's Lane Academy and spent three years as a pupil of Francis Hayman. He tried to establish himself in London, but returned to Sudbury in 1745. He married and settled in Ipswich, where he built up a successful practice. In 1760 he moved to Bath, where his portraits were highly fashionable. He was a founder member of the R.A. in 1768, and he made a final move to London in 1774. He quarrelled with the Academy twice and exhibited nothing with them from 1769 to 1772 and from 1784 to his death. He became a favourite painter at Court as well as in society.

He worked in a variety of media including pencil, black and white chalk, monochrome and occasionally water or bodycolour. Usually his drawings are the result of a mixture of several techniques. His Suffolk drawings show more naturalism than those of the Bath or London periods, which became more Italianate and composed as his style found favour among amateurs. Although he used watercolour, he cannot be classed as a true

GAINSBOROUGH, Thomas (1727-1788)
A wooded path with traveller. *Coloured chalks and watercolour on green paper, varnished, 9¾in. x 11½in.*

watercolourist, and his importance in this field lies mainly in the stylistic influence which he exerted on artists such as G. Frost (q.v.) and Dr. Monro (q.v.), and indirectly on many more.
Examples: B.M.; V.A.M.; Ashmolean; Cartwright Hall, Bradford; Fitzwilliam; Leeds City A.G.; City A.G., Manchester; N.G., Scotland; Wakefield A.G.
Bibliography: P. Thicknesse: *A Sketch of the Life and paintings of T.G.*, 1788. Lord R. Leveson Gower: *The Drawings of T.G.*, 1907. W.T. Whitley: *T.G.*, 1915. Sir C.J. Holmes: *Constable, G., and Lucas*, 1921. M. Woodall: *G's Landscape Drawings*, 1939. M. Woodall: *T.G.*, 1949. O. Millar: *T.G.*, 1949. B. Taylor: *G.*, 1951. E.K. Waterhouse: *G.*, 1958. J. Hayes: *The Drawings of T.G.*, 1970. J. Hayes: *G.*, 1975. J. Lindsay: *T.G., His Life and Art*, 1981. M. Cormack: *The Paintings of T.G.*, 1992. *Country Life*, 29 Feb. 1936. Victoria A.G., Bath, Exhibition Cat., 1951. Arts Council, Exhibition Cats., 1953; 1960. *Connoisseur*, CLXI, 1966. Tate Gall.: Exhibition Cat., 1980; 2002.
See Colour Plate

GALE, Benjamin
1741 (Aislaby, Yorkshire) - 1832 (Bridlington)
He worked as a portrait painter and landscapist in the Hull area from about 1775 until 1803. In 1800 he became a friend of the young J.C. Ibbetson (q.v.), whom he helped to some of his first commissions. In 1803 he became resident drawing master at Scawby Hall, Lincolnshire, the home of the Nelthorpe family, and he also worked for other patrons in the area, including J. Uppleby (q.v.) and Sir Charles Anderson of Lea. He was still exhibiting at Hull in 1829.
Illustrated: Tickell, *History of Hull*, 1796 (?).

Examples: Wilberforce House, Hull.
Bibliography: R.M. *Clay: Life of J.C. Ibbetson*, 1948.

GALE, George
An artist who painted Venetian views about 1832.

An **R.L. GALE** was an unsuccessful candidate for the O.W.S. and N.W.S. in 1841. He exhibited at Suffolk Street and the R.A. between 1832 and 1841, showing Italian, German, Swiss and Irish subjects.

GALE, Roger, F.S.A.
1672 - 1744 (Scruton, Yorks.)
The eldest son of Thomas Gale, Dean of York, and a kinsman of Samuel Pepys, Gale was an antiquary and a friend and correspondent of both F. Place and Sir J. Clerk (qq.v.). He was also a friend of W. Stukeley (q.v), who married his sister and toured with him.

His brother **Samuel GALE, F.S.A. (1682 London - 1754 Hampstead)** and their cousin, **Rev. Miles GALE (1647 Farnley Hall, Yorks. - 1721 Keighley)** shared his tastes. All three produced papers, treatises or books, and it would be most surprising if no drawings by them survived. Miles Gale was a close friend of H. Gyles (q.v.).

GALE, William 1823 - 1909
A figure and genre painter in oil and watercolour, who lived in London and studied at the R.A. Schools from 1841. He was in Italy in 1851, Syria 1862, Palestine 1867 and Algeria 1876-7. Occasionally he essayed modern political or polemical subjects and, un-

GARDNER, William Biscombe (1847-1919)
Looking up the creek from Tomlin's Wharf, Old Leigh, Essex. *Watercolour, signed and inscribed in pencil on reverse, 7¾in. x 13¾in.*

surprisingly, also Oriental themes.
Bibliography: *A.J.,* 1859; 1869.

GALTON, Ada Mary
A landscape painter who lived in London and first exhibited in 1899.

GALTON, J
An artist who sketched in Yorkshire, Devon and Provence between 1839 and 1852.

GAMBLE, Rev. John
c.1763 **- 1811 (London)**
A writer on telegraphy and a draughtsman. He was educated at Pembroke College, Cambridge, taking his B.A. in 1784 and there-after becoming a Fellow. He was also chaplain to the Duke of York and Chaplain-General to the Forces. He held the livings of Alphamstone and Bradwell-juxta-Mare, Essex. His writings, with illustrations, made 'some stir in the scientific world'. He also drew landscapes.
Published: *Observations on Telegraphic Experiments, &c.,* 1795. *Essay on the different Modes of Communication by Signals,* 1797.

GAMLEY, Andrew Archer, R.S.W.
1869 (Johnshaven) - 1949
A painter of coasts and harbours, landscapes and figures, as well as portraits, for the most part in watercolour. He studied at the R.S.A. Schools and lived in Edinburgh before moving to Pittenweem, Fife, and, in the 1930s, to Gullane, East Lothian. He also visited Spain. He was elected R.S.W. in 1924. His effects of light on water show, in McEwan's words 'a delicate, almost indeterminate approach'.

GANDON, James, R.H.A., F.S.A.
1743 (London) 1823 - (Lucan, Co. Dublin)
An architect and artist, he studied at Shipley's

Academy in St. Martin's Lane, under Sir William Chambers until 1765, and at the R.A. Schools from 1769. He exhibited drawings at the Free Society and Society of Arts from 1762 and the R.A. from 1774 to 1780. He went to Dublin in 1781 to build the new docks and Custom House. He designed a number of other important buildings in Dublin, including the Four Courts. In 1808 he retired to his estate near Lucan, where he concentrated on improvements.
Bibliography: T. Mulvany (ed.): *The Life of J.G.,* 1846, 1969. M. Craig: *Dublin 1660-1860,* 1952; 1992. E. McParland: *J.G., Vitruvius Hibernicus,* 1985. *Gentleman's Mag.,* 1824, i. *Literary Gaz.,* Mar. 1824. *Country Life,* 22 Oct. 1948. *Journal of the Warburg Inst.,* 1954. *Journal of the R.S.A.,* Irl., CII, 1972.

GANDY, Joseph Michael, A.R.A.
1771 (London) - 1843
Like his brothers, J.P. Gandy-Deering and Michael Gandy, he was principally an architect, and was a pupil of James Wyatt. He studied at the R.A. Schools, and travelled on the Continent from 1793 to 1799. He was elected A.R.A. in 1803. In 1811 he returned to London from a spell in Liverpool to work for Sir John Soane as he had previously, making numerous drawings for which Soane got the credit. He seems to have died insane.
His drawings show a strong architectural bias and a preference for neo-classicism. In his larger and more elaborate works he employs a strange blend of architecture and mysticism. His son Thomas became a portrait painter.
Published: *Designs for Cottages...,* 1805. *The Rural Architect...,* 1805.
Examples: B.M.; V.A.M.; R.I.B.A.; Soane Mus.
Bibliography: *A.J.,* 1899. Architectural Ass., Exhibition Cat., 1982.

GANTZ, John **1772** **- 1853 (Madras)**
A draughtsman and surveyor of Austrian extraction who worked for the East India Company from about 1800 to 1803. He set up as an architect and lithographer in Madras.
His eldest son **Justinian GANTZ (1802-1862)** was a partner in the business as well as painting miniatures and visiting Burma as a Company Surveyor. His work is less classical and lighter in feeling than that of his father. In 1856 he published *A Manual of Instruc-tion...Architectural Drawing.*
Published: *The Indian Microcosm,* 1827.
Examples: B.M.; India Office Lib.
Bibliography: *Antique Collector,* XXXI, March 1960; *Country Life,* 17 Dec. 1970.

GARBUT, Joseph, 'Putty'
c.1820 (South Shields) - c.1900
A house painter who lived in South Shields and also painted landscapes and genre subjects in oil and watercolour. He was active as an artist from about 1870. His first name may in fact have been James.

GARDEN, W.F. – *see* **FRASER FAMILY**

GARDINER, Mary
An amateur landscape painter in oil, watercolour and the manner of Devis. Many of her subjects – some direct copies of Devis – are from Wales, and she was active from about 1759 to 1783. She exhibited at the S.A. from 1762 to 1770 and at the R.A. in 1783.

GARDINER, General Sir Robert William
1781 **- 1864 (Claremont)**
He entered the R.M.A., Woolwich, in 1795 and in 1797 left for Gibraltar as a second lieutenant in the Royal Artillery. He served at the capture of Minorca, and in 1805 in Germany. He was then posted to Sicily, returning via Gibraltar in December 1807. He was with Wellington in Portugal, served on the Walcheren expedition, and thereafter fought through the Peninsular Campaign. He was made K.C.B. in 1814 and fought at Waterloo. He was appointed principal equerry to Prince Leopold on his marriage to Princess Charlotte, and was Governor of Gibraltar from 1848 to 1855. In 1854 he was promoted general.
He was an amateur artist, working generally in light washes, and he wrote several military treatises.

GARDINER, William Nelson
1766 (Dublin) - 1814 (London)
Principally an engraver and bookseller, he showed an early interest in drawing, and was sent to the R.D.S. Schools for three years from 1781. After this he moved to London studying at the R.A. Schools from 1788, but, growing tired of his profession as an engraver, returned to Dublin and squandered all his money. He then came back to England, and tried un-successfully for a Cambridge fellowship. For a

time he was employed by Edward Harding (q.v.), for whom he had previously worked as an engraver, to copy oil paintings in watercolour. He exhibited genre subjects at the R.A. between 1787 and 1793. In 1801 he opened a book shop in Pall Mall, but, although to begin with his eccentricities attracted customers, he deteriorated in manner and appearance and business slackened. He became ill and finally committed suicide. His chequered career also included periods as a silhouette painter, an actor and scene painter, and a portraitist.

Examples: B.M.; N.P.G.

GARDNER, William Biscombe
1847 - 1919 (Tunbridge Wells)

He was primarily an engraver, making prints after Alma Tadema and Leighton as illustrations for the *Graphic* and the *I.L.N.* He also painted landscapes in oil and watercolour and exhibited at the R.A. from 1874. He lived in London from 1880 to 1882 and from 1897 to 1905, Surrey from 1883 to 1896 and Tunbridge Wells from 1906.

Examples: V.A.M.; Margate Mus.
See Colour Plate

GARDNOR, Rev. John
1729 - 1808 (Battersea)

A drawing master who kept a school in Kensington Square and exhibited with the Free Society from 1763 to 1767. He entered the Church and became Vicar of Battersea in 1778, officiating at Blake's wedding in 1782, and remaining there until his death. He exhibited landscapes at the R.A. from 1782 to 1796.

In 1787 he toured France, Switzerland and the Rhine with his nephew **Richard GARDNOR,** who was also a drawing master, and who exhibited between 1766 and 1793.

Published: *Views Taken on and near the River Rhine...,* 1788.

Illustrated: D. Williams: *History of Monmouthshire,* 1796.

GARLAND, Robert
1808 - 1863 (Hammersmith)

A London architect and topographer who studied at the R.A. Schools from 1827. He supplied pencil and sepia wash drawings for Wood: *Views in London, Westminster, &c.,* 1837. With his partner Henry Christopher he designed houses in Eccleston Square, Westminster, and the west tower of All Saints, Upper Norwood.

Illustrated: Winkles: *Cathedral Churches of England and Wales, 1836-42.*

Examples: Cooper Union Mus., New York.

GARLAND, William
1815/16 - 1882 (Winchester)

A painter of landscapes and rustic genre subjects who lived in Winchester and exhibited watercolours and oil paintings at Suffolk Street and the R.A. between 1857 and 1875.

GASTINEAU, Henry (1791-1876)
A view of Edinburgh. *Watercolour, 22⅞in. x 35in.*

GARRARD, George, A.R.A.
1760 - 1826 (Brompton)

A sculptor and animal painter in oil and watercolour. He studied under S. Gilpin (q.v.) and at the R.A. Schools. He exhibited from 1781 to 1826 and was elected A.R.A. in 1802. He married Gilpin's daughter, and their son **Charles GARRARD (b.1798)** sculpted portrait busts.

Published: *A description of the different varieties of oxen common to the British Isles,* 1800.

Examples: B.M.
Bibliography: *A.J.,* 1899.

GARTSIDE, Mary

The author of a fascinating *Essay on Light & Shade, on Colours, on Composition in General,* 1805, which uses a Cozens blot technique for flower painting. However, the theory and practice also looks forward to Turner and the scientific experiments of George Field. In 1806 she stood for election to the O.W.S.

GARVEY, Edmund, R.A.
(Ireland) - 1813 (?London)

An Irish landscape painter in oil and watercolour. He visited Italy and Switzerland and then settled in Bath. He exhibited with the Free Society from 1767 and at the R.A. from 1769. He was one of the first A.R.A.s in 1770, and was elected R.A. in 1783. In 1778 he moved to London.

His favourite subjects are foreign views and country seats. His pictures are rather monotonous, he being, according to Pasquin, 'a Royal Academician whose qualifications are, if possible, more doubtful than any of his compeers'.

GASTINEAU, Henry, O.W.S.
1791 - 1876 (Camberwell)

After an apprenticeship with an engraver, he entered the R.A. Schools. He exhibited at the R.A. from 1812 and with the Oil and Water-colour Society between 1818 and 1820. He was elected A.O.W.S. and O.W.S. in 1821 and 1823. He travelled widely in the British Isles, and in Switzerland and Italy from 1829. He built himself a house in Camberwell in 1827, and lived there for the remainder of his life. He had a very wide practice as a drawing master.

He was an extremely prolific artist and exhibited regularly for fifty-eight years. He loved painting the wild scenery of the coast of Devon and Cornwall, Wales, Yorkshire and particularly Scotland and Antrim. Although contemporary with innovators such as Cox, his own style remains rooted in the 1820s; at their best his works can be marvellous examples of this period. He occasionally practised lithography. His remaining works were sold at Christie's, 19 May 1876.

John GASTINEAU, who exhibited in 1826, was a son.

Published: *Wales Illustrated,* 1829.

Examples: B.M.; V.A.M.; Birmingham City A.G.; Blackburn A.G.; Cartwright Hall, Bradford; Brighton A.G.; Cardiff A.G.; Fitzwilliam; Greenwich; N.G., Ireland; City A.G., Manchester; Newport A.G.; Ulster Mus.; Nat. Mus. Wales; York A.G.

Bibliography: *A.J.,* 1876. *The Builder,* 1876. *The Year's Art,* 1885. *Country Life,* 14 Oct 1976. O.W.S. Club, LII, 1977.

GASTINEAU, Maria
1824 - 1890 (Llantysilio)

A daughter of H. Gastineau (q.v.), she exhibited landscapes between 1855 and 1889 and was a

GEAR, Joseph (1769-1853)
Elephant and Castle. *Watercolour from an album of variously sized drawing of pub signs.*

member of the Society of Female Artists.

Her sister **Annie Jane GASTINEAU, Mrs. Hills,** no doubt also painted, but not professionally, as Mr. Hills was a millionaire steel tube manufacturer.

GAUCI, Paul
The son and brother of lithographers working in London, he too produced lithographs as well as landscapes in oil and watercolour, some of Near Eastern, Indian or Jamaican subjects. He exhibited at the R.A. and elsewhere from 1834 to 1863 and in 1866 began publication of a *Practice Drawing Book*.
Examples: V.A.M.

GAY, Susan Elizabeth
(Oswestry, Shropshire) -
A figure painter and illustrator who was a daughter of **William GAY,** a Post Office official and amateur artist. She received little instruction since the family was constantly moving about England and Scotland. She was also a writer and a spiritualist. She lived in Falmouth and wrote on its history, although when she exhibited at the R.A. in 1874 and

1876 she gave a Croydon address.
Published: *Harry's Big Boots*, 1873. *Old Falmouth*, 1903. &c.

GEAR, Joseph
1769 (Gosport) - 1853 (Cambridge, Mass.)
The son of a cloth merchant, Gear was brought up in Gosport, and as early as 1780 he seems to have been drawing in watercolour. He produced charming small studies of trades, pub names and emblems. By 1810 he had established himself as a portrait and marine painter in London, and at about that date he was appointed Marine Painter to the Duke of Sussex. He also styled himself 'Painter to His Majesty'. He exhibited at the R.A. from 1811 to 1820, but moved to America in 1824. He was in New York from 1826 and living in Boston from about 1829, when he exhibited a religious oil painting at the Boston Athenaeum. There he listed himself as 'artist and musician', but in time music seems to have taken over from painting.

His son **Joseph (or John) William GEAR, Yr.,** who was born about 1800 and active until 1860, does not seem to have accompanied him to America. He painted watercolour portraits,

sometimes of actors.
Examples: Peabody Mus., Salem.
Bibliography: *W&D*, 1990, i.

GEDDES, Andrew, A.R.A.
1783 (Edinburgh) - 1844 (London)
A painter and etcher who was educated at Edinburgh High School and University. In 1806 he went to the R.A. Schools and in 1810 set up as a portrait painter in Edinburgh. In 1814 he went to Paris. Later he settled in London, and in 1827 married the daughter of Nathaniel Plymer, a miniaturist. They travelled on the Continent, mainly in Italy, in 1830-1. In 1832 he was elected A.R.A., and in 1839 he visited Holland.

His etchings are more skilful than his paintings. The latter, in oil and occasionally watercolour, include landscapes and copies from old masters as well as portraits. His studio sale was held by Christie's, 8-12 April 1845.
Examples: B.M.; N.G., Scotland.
Bibliography: Mrs. Geddes: *Memoir of the late A.G.*, 1844. D. Laing: *Etchings by Wilkie and G.*, 1875. C. Dodgson: *The etchings of...A.G.*, 1936. *Art Union*, 1844. *The English Illustrated Mag.*, 1884. *Portfolio*, 1887.

GEDDES, Ewan, R.S.W.
1866 (Blairgowrie) - 1935 (Blairgowrie)
An Edinburgh landscape painter whose work was very popular in the U.S.A. He exhibited in Edinburgh from 1884 and London from 1891 and was elected R.S.W. in 1902.

His father **William GEDDES (1841-1884),** who also was born and died in Blairgowrie, painted landscapes in oil and watercolour.
Bibliography: *Studio*, XXVIII, 1903; LXIII, 1915; LXVII, 1916.

GEE, David
1793 (Coventry) - 1872 (Coventry)
An oil painter who worked at Coventry from 1815 to 1868. He painted marine and terrine battle subjects, landscapes, town views, portraits and Lady Godiva. His obituary states that he made watercolour copies of all his paintings. His style is rather naïve but charming. He seems to have been an associate of E. Rudge (q.v.). His name is sometimes given as 'Jee', but Gee seems to be correct.
Examples: Coventry A.G. (with his own list of works).

GEIKIE, Walter, R.S.A.
1795 (Edinburgh) - 1837 (Edinburgh)
An illustrator and landscape painter who studied at the Trustees' Academy. He was elected A.R.S.A. and R.S.A. in 1831 and 1834. Towards the end of his life he became a deaf-mute. His figures are good and his subjects anticipate those of E. Nicol (q.v.).
Published: *A Collection of Original Drawings of Edinburgh and Environs*, 1830. With Sir T.D. Lauder: *Etchings Illustrative of Scottish Character and Scenery*, 1841.
Examples: B.M.; N.G., Scotland. Edinburgh City Coll.

GELDART, Joseph
1808 - 1882 (Altrincham)
A friend and sketching companion of J.J. Cotman (q.v.). He abandoned a legal career for painting, and, from the late 1830s, spent much time in Italy studying Venetian colouring.
Examples: B.M.
Bibliography: J. Walpole: *Art and Artists of the Norwich School*, 1997.

GELL, Sir William, F.R.S., F.S.A.
1777 - 1836 (Naples)
A classical archaeologist, he was educated at Jesus College, Cambridge, graduating in 1798 and becoming a Fellow of Emmanuel College. He attended the R.A. Schools and, although he did not exhibit thereafter, he made many sketches of archaeological sites and discoveries, some of which he used to illustrate his books. He visited the Troad in 1801 and was knighted on his return from the Ionian Islands in 1803. He travelled to the Morea in 1804 and Ithaca in 1806. In 1814 he accompanied Princess Caroline to Italy. He returned to Italy in 1820, and lived there for the rest of his life.

The drawings, nearly eight hundred in number, which he made on his travels through Spain, Italy, Syria, Dalmatia, the Ionian Islands, Greece and European Turkey, were left on his death to his friend Kepple Craven, by whom they were bequeathed to the B.M.
Published: *Topography of Troy*, 1804. *Geography and Antiquities of Ithaca*, 1807. *Itinerary of Greece*, 1810. *Itinerary of the Morea*, 1817. *Narrative of a Journey in the Morea*, 1823. *Pompeiana*, 1817-19, 1832. *Topography of Rome*, 1834.
Examples: B.M.; Barrow-in-Furness Mus.; N.G., Scotland.

GENDALL, John
1790 (Exe Island, Exeter) - 1865 (Exeter)
Showing early aptitude, he was sent to Sir John Soane in London, from whom he received his first commission and an introduction to Ackermann. He worked for Ackermann for several years, during which time he was sent to sketch in Normandy. He was also sent about Britain to make topographical drawings, and the views he made of Edinburgh, Richmond, Kew and elsewhere were aquatinted by R. Sutherland. He exhibited at the R.A. from 1846 to 1863. In about 1830 he retired to Exeter, where he painted Devonshire views, and taught at Cole's School in the Cathedral Close.

Despite occasional weaknesses of colour, his work has an affinity to that of Turner, who was his admirer. The overall effect can be rather messy. He painted in oil, water and bodycolour.
Published: with A. Pugin: *Picturesque Views on the Seine*, 1821. with R. Westall and G. Shepherd: *Country Seats*, 1823-28.
Examples: B.M.; V.A.M.; Exeter Mus.
Bibliography: G. Pycroft: *Art in Devonshire*, 1883.

GENT, George William
1786 - ?1861
The son of Major-General William Gent, he was an amateur topographer and landscape painter. He inherited Moyns Hall, Essex, where his family had been seated since the fourteenth century, and which he papered with his drawings. He exhibited at the R.A. from 1804 to 1822. His wash drawings show neat pencil work but shaky perspective.
Examples: B.M.; V.A.M.

GENT, Susan S , Mrs. c.1813 -
One of the four daughters of W. Daniell (q.v.), she painted miniatures and watercolour portraits, and also genre subjects. She exhibited from 1826 to 1845, as Miss S.S. Daniell until her marriage in 1831/2.

GEORGE IV, H.M. King
1762 (St. James's Palace) - 1830 (Windsor Castle)
A weak but amusing draughtsman, whose speciality was designing costumes and uniforms.
Examples: B.M.

GEORGE, Sir Ernest, R.A.
1839 (London) - 1922 (London)
An architect who was educated at Brighton and Reading and entered the R.A. Schools in 1858. From 1861 he practised on his own. In 1908 he became P.R.I.B.A. and he was knighted in 1911. He was elected A.R.A. and R.A. in 1910 and 1917.

His watercolours were mostly the fruits of holiday tours, sometimes in Northern France, as in 1875 and 1884.
Examples: V.A.M.; Doncaster A.G.; Leeds City A.G.; Maidstone Mus.; Ulster Mus.
Bibliography: *Portfolio*, 1874-77; 1881; 1882; 1887. *Studio*, I, 1893; VII, 1896. *A.J.*, 1910.

GEORGE, Lieutenant-Colonel James
1782 (Lewisham) - 1828 (Shajahanpur)
The son of a clergyman he went to India as a cadet in 1799. In 1806, the year of his first known sketch, he took part in the taking of Gohad. He travelled widely in India and was acquainted with Chinnery (q.v.) and his circle. In 1811 he was on the staff of Lord Minto for the Java campaign. He returned to India in 1812 and served in East Bengal for the next eleven years. He visited London, where he married, in 1826. Minto described him as an excellent draughtsman, and he was right.
Examples: B.M.; India Off. Lib.

GEORGE, John Reed
1832 (Tynemouth) - 1890 (Tynemouth)
A house painter and decorator who produced landscapes and coastal subjects in his spare time.

His son, **Charles GEORGE (1872-1937)**, became a painter and art master as well as continuing in the family business.

GERARD, Ebenezar
An amateur caricaturist working between 1800 and 1817.
Examples: B.M.

GERE, Charles March, R.A., R.W.S.
1869 (Gloucester) - 1957 (Gloucester)
A landscape and decorative painter who lived in Leamington, studied and then taught at the Birmingham School of Art for many years. He also worked with Morris's Kelmscott Press as an illustrator, and exhibited from 1890. His subjects are often found in Italy and the Cotswolds. He exhibited at the R.A., R.W.S. and elsewhere and was elected A.R.A. and R.A. in 1934 and 1939.
Examples: Cartwright Hall, Bradford.
Bibliography: *Studio*, XLII, 1908; LV, 1912; LVII, 1913; LIX, 1913; LX, 1914; LXVI, 1916. *Connoisseur*, XXXIX. Wheatstone Hall, Gloucester, Exhibition Cat., 1963.
See Colour Plate

GESSNER, Johann Conrad
1764 (Zürich) - 1826 (Zürich)
A horse and military artist who studied at Dresden and worked in Italy and Switzerland before coming to England in 1796. He exhibited at the R.A. from 1799 to 1804 when he returned to Zürich.
Examples: V.A.M.

GETHIN, Percy Francis
1874 (Holywell, Co. Sligo) - 1916 (the Somme)
Descended from a family of Cork baronets, he studied in Paris and became a teacher in London and Liverpool.
Illustrated: W.M. Crowdy: *Burgundy and Morvan*, 1925.
Examples: B.M.; Cartwright Hall, Bradford.

GIANTS, Master of the –
see JEFFERYS, James

GIBB, Robert, R.S.A
1801 (Dundee) - 1837 (Edinburgh)
A landscape painter in oil and watercolour who was a foundation member of the R.S.A. He was one of the first Scottish painters to work on the spot.
Examples: N.G., Scotland.

GIBB, Robert, II, R.S.A.
1845 (Laurieston, near Falkirk) - 1932 (Edinburgh)
Trained as a lithographer, he became a military painter and was King's Limner for Scotland from 1908 to 1932. He studied at the R.S.A. and exhibited there from 1867. He was elected A.R.S.A. and R.S.A. in 1878 and 1882. He was Keeper of the N.G., Scotland from 1895 to 1907 and is most remembered for his oil painting 'The Thin Red Line'.
Bibliography: *A.J.*, 1897. *Studio*, LXV, 1915.

GIBB, William
1839 (Laurieston, near Falkirk) - 1929 (London)
The brother of R. Gibb, II (q.v.), he was a painter in various media, a lithographer, designer and book illustrator. He was working in London for some years before his death.
Illustrated: A.C. Lamb: *Dundee, its Quaint and Historic Buildings*, 1895. &c.

GIBBONS, F
There is a view of Cirencester in the V.A.M. signed and dated 1880 by this artist. If perhaps he was a member of the family of baronets, then Captain Frederick Gibbons (b. 1832), who lived at Sunninghill, Berks, would be a candidate.

GIBBS, Albert and Arthur
Brothers from Coventry who moved to York in about 1897 as valets to Archbishop Maclagan and vergers in the Minster. They exhibited topographical subjects at York in 1900.

GIBBS, James, of Bath
c.1792 - 1841
An artist painting Welsh views in 1835. He may have been working in Bath from 1819. A James Gibbs, perhaps the same, exhibited views of Battersea Railway Bridge and Cape Finisterre at the R.A. in 1840 and 1841, from a London address.
Examples: Leeds City A.G.

GIBERNE, Edgar
A genre, landscape and sporting painter in oil and watercolour who was active from 1872 to 1888. He lived at Epsom and in Kensington, and he painted in Devon and Cornwall. He used white heightening.

GIBSON, Edward
1787 - 1859 (Hornsea)
The son of a naval shipbuilder, he combined shipbuilding and marine painting. His earliest known watercolour is a three-position view of a corvette, dated 1805. He was Sheriff of Hull in 1824 and Mayor in 1834 and 1835. He was principal judge at the Hull Art Exhibition of 1829.
Examples: Ferens A.G., Hull; Trinity House, Hull.
Bibliography: V. Galloway: *Hull Art Directory*, 1951.

GIBSON, Francis
1753 (Whitby) - 1805 (Whitby)
A writer and occasional painter of landscapes and no doubt marine subjects. As a seaman he voyaged to North America, and as master mariner in a ship of his father's to the Baltic. In 1787, through the patronage of Lord Mulgrave (*see under* Phipps, A.) he was appointed collector of customs at Whitby.
Published: *Sailing Directions for the Baltic*, 1791; *Streanshall Abbey* (a play), 1800; *Memoirs of the Bastille*, 1802; *Poetical Remains*, 1807.

GIBSON, John Stafford
1837 (Kilmurry) - 1919
A Corkman with strong Spanish connections; he spent much time there and travelling elsewhere on the Continent. He was an amateur landscape painter, his work, according to Crookshank and Glin, 'varying from delicacy to abstract with extraordinary verve'. He was a friend of J. Brennan (q.v.), and left his life's work to the Crawford A.G., Cork.

GIBSON, Joseph Vincent
A genre painter in oil and watercolour who worked in London and Manchester and who exhibited at the R.A. from 1861 to 1888, and elsewhere.
Bibliography: A.J., 1861.

GIBSON, Patrick, R.S.A.
1782 (Edinburgh) - 1829 (Dollar)
After a classical education, he studied art under A. Nasmyth (q.v.) and at the Trustees' Academy. He was living in Lambeth from 1805 to 1808, and he exhibited at the R.A. He returned to Edinburgh, and in about 1811 visited the Faroes. In 1826 he was a Foundation Member of the R.S.A. He was drawing master at the Dollar Academy from 1824 to 1829.
His topographical views of London and Scotland are delicate with low and limited colour and neat pen or pencil outline.
Published: *View of the Arts in Great Britain* (Edinburgh Annual Register, 1816).
Illustrated: *Select Views of Edinburgh with Historical and Explanatory Notes*, 1817.
Examples: B.M.; N.G., Scotland.

GIBSON, Richard
1615 (Cumberland) - 1690 (London)
A dwarf and miniaturist. He was a page at Mortlake before taking lessons from Francis Clein, the manager of the tapestry works. Thereafter he became a page to Charles I and Queen Henrietta Maria, and he had considerable success as a portrait painter and a copyist. After the Restoration he taught the future Queens Mary and Anne at Richmond Palace, and he accompanied Mary to Holland in 1677. He was a keen archer.
One of his daughters, **Susan Penelope GIBSON (1652-1700)** was also a miniaturist. She married one Rose, a jeweller.

GIBSON, Thomas
1810 (North Shields, Northumberland) - 1843 (London)
A landscape and portrait painter in oil and watercolour who practised in Newcastle and Carlisle. He exhibited locally and in 1841 at Suffolk Street. In 1843 he moved to London.

GIBSON, William Sidney
1814 (Fulham) - 1871 (London)
After working on a Carlisle newspaper, Gibson was called to the bar in 1843, and appointed Registrar of the Newcastle Court of Bankruptcy. After the Bankruptcy Act of 1869 had abolished the Court, he was retired on a pension and devoted himself to antiquarian watercolours, which included coastal scenes and landscapes.
Published: *History of Tynemouth. Northumbrian Castles, Churches and Antiquities. Descriptive and Historical Guide to Tynemouth.* &c.
Examples: Laing A.G., Newcastle.

GIBSONE, George
1762 (Deptford) - 1846 (Low Fell)
The son of an architect, rather than a baronet as stated in the first edition of this dictionary, he was an amateur conchologist and a painter of plants and specimens. He travelled in Italy and worked with his father in London and elsewhere before marrying in 1796 and moving to Newcastle with his family. There he and his father designed and ran an iron and lead works until it collapsed in 1803. He then helped his brother in a colour works and his wife, as drawing master, in a school for upper class girls. The latter enterprise was a success and in 1831 they retired to a house of his designing at Low Fell near Gateshead. He was a keen gardener. His watercolours, over 7,000 of them of sea shells, were bought by public subscription and presented to the Newcastle Central Library in 1890.

GIFFARD, Frances, Mrs. Throckmorton
c.1770 -
A member of a Staffordshire family which traced its descent from the pre-Conquest Norman Count of Longueville, she was the daughter of Thomas Giffard of Chillington by his third wife, Frances Stonor. She painted Devonshire, and no doubt local views, rather in the manner of J. Swete (q.v.), during the 1790s. She married William Throckmorton (1762-1819), her step-cousin, and a grandson of the 4th Throckmorton baronet in 1798. Their son succeeded as 8th baronet.

GIFFORD, Augustus Edward
The Headmaster of Coventry School of Art in about 1850, he produced local views.
He was perhaps related to **E.A. GIFFORD**, who painted landscapes and figures between 1837 and 1876. He was an architect by profession, and lived in London and Bath.
Examples: Coventry A.G.

GILBERT, Annie Laurie
c.1848 (Nottingham) - 1941 (Nottingham)
The daughter of **Isaac Charles GILBERT (c.1816-1890)**, a Nottingham architect and occasional landscapist. She painted topographical views in and around Nottingham, which she annotated, as well as landscapes in other parts of England, and in Wales.

GILBERT, Ellen ?1830 - 1903 (Surrey)
A painter of genre subjects who lived in

Blackheath and exhibited from 1863 to 1893 and in 1903. The **F. GILBERT** of Blackheath who was an unsuccessful candidate for the N.W.S. in 1862 was presumably Frederick Gilbert the illustrator and a relation, and they were probably both related to Sir John Gilbert (q.v.).

In the Ashmolean there is a crude caricature dated 1851 and signed **Henry GILBERT.**

GILBERT, Sir John, R.A., P.R.W.S.
1817 (Blackheath) - 1897 (Blackheath)
The historical painter. After two years as an estate agent's clerk, he took a few lessons in colour from G. Lance (q.v.), and taught himself to engrave, etch and model as well as paint in oil and watercolour. He exhibited at Suffolk Street for the first time in 1836 and at the R.A. in 1838. His chief work in the early part of his career was black and white book illustration, culminating in Staunton's edition of Shakespeare, 1856-60. He was the main artist of the *I.L.N.* from its foundation in 1842. He was elected A.O.W.S. and O.W.S. in 1852 and 1854 and became President in 1871 when he was also knighted. He was elected A.R.A. and R.A. in 1872 and 1876. From 1885 he sold no pictures, but kept them for the nation.

His work is monumental in style and execution, and always worthy, if sometimes dull to a modern eye. His favourite colours are reds and deep black shadows.
Examples: B.M.; V.A.M.; Haworth A.G., Accrington; Ashmolean; Towneley Hall, Burnley; Harrogate Mus.; Manor House, Lewisham; City A.G., Manchester; Newport A.G.; N.G., Scotland; Ulster Mus.
Bibliography: *A.J.*, August 1857; 1908. O.W.S. Club X, 1932. *Country Life*, 25 Aug. 1966.

GILBERT, Josiah
1814 (Rotherham) - 1892 (London)
The son of the Rev. Joseph Gilbert, who moved to Nottingham in 1825 to take up an appointment. Josiah studied at the R.A. Schools and Sass's School and became a portrait painter in watercolour and pastel. He remained in London for the rest of his life and exhibited at the R.A. and elsewhere between 1837 and 1865.
Examples: Castle Mus., Nottingham.
Bibliography: *The Year's Art*, 1893.

GILDER, Henry 1750 - p.1791
An artist who exhibited views at the R.A. from 1773 to 1778. He lived with T. Sandby (q.v.) at Windsor, and was probably his architectural assistant and servant. By 1785, however, he was earning 5s. *per diem* as a drawing master at the Tower, to Sandby's 3s.6d. Gilder worked at the Tower from at least 1779 to 1791.
Examples: V.A.M.

GILES, James, R.S.A.
1801 (Glasgow) - 1870 (Aberdeen)
The son of P. Giles (q.v.) from whom he learnt drawing. By the age of thirteen he was

GILBERT, Sir John (1817-1897)
The Herald. *Watercolour, 12¼in. x 18¼in.*

painting the lids of wooden snuff boxes, and by nineteen he was a drawing master himself. In 1823 he went to London to complete his studies and in the following year moved on to France and Italy, returning to Aberdeen in 1826. During his Continental tour he made over one thousand sketches, as well as forty copies of Old Masters. His first important patrons were Gordon of Fyvie and the 4th Earl of Aberdeen. In 1827 he was a co-founder with Archibald Simpson of the Aberdeen Artists' Society, and in 1829 was elected to the re-formed R.S.A.

Giles is best known for his watercolours of Aberdeenshire Castles, most notably the Haddo House Collection. However, he was a man of wide and varied talents, both as a painter and as a landscape gardener, advising Prince Albert on the layout of Balmoral. His pen drawings and panoramas are careful, but a little dull; his full watercolours show great beauty of colour and composition. They are usually traditional in conception. He did not have the middle name 'William' which has

often been given to him.
Examples: B.M.; Haddo House, Aberdeen; Aberdeen A.G.; N.G., Scotland.
Bibliography: *Connoisseur*, CLXII, 1966. *Country Life*, 1 Oct. 1970; 10 Jan. 1991. *Scotland's Magazine*, n.s. LXLIII, 1970.

GILES, Peter
The father of J. Giles (q.v), he worked as a pattern designer and drawing master in Aberdeen, and pioneered a scheme for hiring out his pictures. He is said to have died early in his son's childhood. However in about 1810 a drawing master and portrait painter named Peter Giles moved from Glasgow to Belfast where he worked until about 1825.

GILES, Robert Humphrey
1802 - 1881 (London)
A portrait and figure painter who worked and exhibited from 1826 to 1876 from London and Gravesend, where he was headmaster of St. George's C. of E. School until 1830. He considered standing for the N.W.S. in 1855.

GILFILLAN, John Alexander
1793 (Jersey) - 1863 (Melbourne)

A landscape painter who served as a naval lieutenant, studied at Edinburgh, and was Professor of Painting at the Andersonian University, Glasgow, from about 1830 to 1840. He emigrated to New Zealand, but his farm failed and he moved on to Australia where he worked in the Melbourne Post Office.
Examples: B.M.; V.A.M.; Glasgow A.G.

GILL, Edmund Marriner, 'Waterfall'
1820 (Clerkenwell) -
1894 (Hackbridge, Carshalton)

He started his career as a portraitist like his father Edmund Ward Gill (1794 Aylsham - 1854 London), but in 1841, under the influence of Cox, he turned to landscapes and sketched in Wales. In 1843 he went to the R.A. Schools. For much of his career he lived in Ludlow and Hereford. He exhibited at the R.A. from 1842 to 1886, and should not be confused with **Edward GILL** who was active from 1835 to 1865 and who also painted waterfalls.

E.W. Gill had two other sons, **William Ward GILL (1823-1894),** a modeller, watercolour and oil painter, and **George Reynolds GILL (1827-1904),** who became Master of the Truro School of Art. There were also two daughters, who may well have painted: **Mary Anne GILL (b.1826),** and **Margaret GILL (b.1828).**
Examples: V.A.M.; Victoria A.G., Bath; Brighton A.G.; Hereford Lib.
Bibliography: *A.J.,* 1874.

GILL, Edwyn

In the Gilbey sale of 1940 at Christie's there were two angling caricatures by this artist dated 1812.

GILLETT, William J

A modest watercolourist who lived in London and was active from about 1878 to 1885. He exhibited views of Venice and of the Wey, near Guildford.

GILLIES, Margaret, R.W.S.
1803 (London) - 1887 (Westerham, Kent)

At three years she visited Lisbon where her mother died. She was adopted by her uncle, Lord Gillies, an Edinburgh judge, who introduced her to Scottish literary society. At about eighteen she and her elder sister came to London to make a career as artists, and she took lessons from G. Cruikshank (q.v.) and set up as a miniaturist. Gradually she moved to subject painting and to watercolours. In 1851 she went to Paris to study with the Scheffers, and thereafter made frequent Continental journeys, visiting many parts of France and Italy. She also painted Scottish and Irish peasants. Her works were often engraved. She became a Lady Member of the O.W.S. in 1852, having failed as candidate for the N.W.S. in the previous year.

Her younger sister Mary (d.1870), who

GILLRAY, James (1757-1815)
Cymon and Iphigenia. *Pen and brown ink and watercolour, 9½in. x 8¼in.*

lived with her for most of her life, became an authoress.
Examples: B.M.; V.A.M.
Bibliography: Mary Howitt: *Autobiography,* 1889, II. *Art Union,* 1839. *The Times,* 26 July 1887.

GILLRAY, James
1757 (Chelsea) - 1815 (London)

The caricaturist. He was the son of a Chelsea Pensioner and was apprenticed to a letter engraver. He ran away to join a company of strolling players before entering the R.A. Schools and studying engraving under W.W. Ryland and Bartolozzi. His political works date from 1780 and the majority were published by Mrs Humphrey with whom he lived. His last print was engraved in 1811 when he went mad.

His watercolours are very rare, since most of his work was drawn directly on to the plates. Some of his more serious figure drawings, especially those made for a series of military subjects painted in conjunction with P.J. de Loutherbourg (q.v.), have been attributed to the latter.
Published: *The Caricatures of G.,* 1818. *The Genuine Works of Mr J.G.,* 1830.
Examples: B.M.; V.A.M.; Ashmolean. Greenwich.
Bibliography: T. Wright: *The Caricatures of J.G.,* 1851. T. Wright: *The Works of J.G.,* 1873. D. Hill:

Mr. G. the Caricaturist, 1965. D. Hill: *Fashionable Contrasts: Caricatures by J.G.,* 1966. *Country Life,* 5 Dec. 1952; 12 Jan. 1967. *Scotland's Mag.,* Dec. 1957. Tate Gall.: Exhibition Cat., 2001.

GILMAN, Harold John Wilde
1876 (Road, Somerset) - 1919 (London)

A painter of landscapes, interiors and portraits in oil and occasionally watercolour, he studied at Hastings Art School and became a member of the Camden Town and London Groups.
Examples: City A.G., Manchester.
Bibliography: W. Lewis and L.F. Fergusson: *H.G.,* 1919. Arts Council: Exhibition Cat., 1981.

GILPIN, Captain John Bernard
1701 (Scaleby Castle) -
1776 (Scaleby Castle)

An amateur artist who lived at Irthington, Cumberland, and was the father of W. Gilpin (q.v.) and S. Gilpin (q.v.), and the first patron of J. 'W'. Smith (q.v.). After the '45, when he had to leave home, he worked for a time in Plymouth. He has a rather chunky, grey wash landscape style, sometimes with touches of watercolour. On occasions he copied P. Sandby (q.v.).

His father, **William GILPIN (1657-1724)** was also an amateur.
Bibliography: O.W.S. Club, XXIX.

GILPIN, Sawrey, R.A.
1733 (Carlisle) - 1807 (Brompton)

The seventh child of Captain J.B. Gilpin (q.v.), from whom he received instruction. At the age of fourteen his father sent him to work under S. Scott (q.v.) in London, with whom he remained for ten years. However, his talent was almost exclusively for animal painting, and his independent career began with a commission from the Duke of Cumberland to draw in his stud at Windsor and Newmarket. After this he lived in Knightsbridge until the death of his wife, when he spent some time in Bedfordshire with Samuel Whitbread. During his last years he lived with his daughters in Brompton. He exhibited with the Incorporated Society from 1762, becoming President in 1774. He was elected A.R.A. in 1795 and R.A. in 1797.

His drawing of animals, especially of horses, is of very high quality, but for his landscape backgrounds he often relied upon other artists such as G. Barret (q.v.) for whom he provided animals in return. Many of his drawings were intended as illustrations for the books of his brother, W. Gilpin (q.v.).

Examples: B.M.; V.A.M.; Fitzwilliam; Leeds City A.G.; Leicestershire A.G.; Newport A.G.; Ulster Mus.; York A.G.

Bibliography: O.W.S. Club, XXIX.

GILPIN, Rev. William
1724 (Scaleby Castle, nr. Carlisle) - 1804 (Boldre, Hampshire)

The elder brother of S. Gilpin (q.v.), he was educated at Carlisle, St. Bees and Queens College, Oxford, before being ordained in 1746. He published his first book in 1753 in order to pay off his Oxford debts. He was a curate at Irthington, Cumberland, and in London, and then took over a boys' school at Cheam, Surrey, which he ran for some thirty years. He made sketching tours of East Anglia in 1769 and 1773, the Wye and South Wales in 1770 and 1782, the South East Coast in 1774 and the Lake District and Highlands in 1776. In 1777 he was made vicar of Boldre in the New Forest, where he remained as a progressive parish priest until his death. He was the high priest of the 'picturesque', and was the inspiration for Combe and Rowlandson's *Doctor Syntax*.

His drawings are executed with the brush, in indian ink, sometimes on a yellow foundation rather in the manner of A. Cozens (q.v.) and often over a pencil outline. He used a reed pen to strengthen his outlines and compositions. His penwork and his inscriptions, once seen, are quite unmistakable. His subjects are generally imaginary and were often done to illustrate his theories of the picturesque. As he himself said, they are meant 'rather to explain the country than to give an exact portrait of it'.

Two sales of his drawings were held at Christie's, 6 May 1802 and 6 June 1804, and the proceeds were used to endow the village school at Boldre. A loan exhibition of his work was held at Kenwood in 1959.

GILPIN, Sawrey, R.A. (1733 -1807)
A Riderless Horse. *Bears signature and date 1797, sepia ink and grey and sepia washes, 12¼in. x 17¼in.*

Published: *Essays on Prints*, 1768. *Observations on the River Wye…*, 1782. *Observations on the Lakes of Cumberland and Westmorland*, 1786. *Picturesque Remarks on the Western Parts of England and the Isle of Wight*, 1798. *Observations on the Coasts of Hampshire, Sussex and Kent…*, 1804. *Two Essays…on the Author's mode of executing Rough Sketches*, 1804. *Observations on…Cambridge…*, 1809. &c.

Examples: B.M.; V.A.M.; Fitzwilliam; Leeds City A.G.; Leicestershire A.G.; Newport A.G.; Portsmouth City Mus.; Ulster Mus.

Bibliography: W.D. Templeman: *The Life and Work of W.G.*, 1939. C.P. Barbier: *W.G., his Drawings, Theory and Teaching of the Picturesque*, 1963. O.W.S. Club, XXIX.

GILPIN, William Sawrey, P.O.W.S.
1762 - 1843 (Yorkshire)

The son of S. Gilpin (q.v.) and nephew of W. Gilpin (q.v.), he became a drawing master and

GILPIN, Rev. William (1724-1804)
River Gorge.

GILPIN, William Sawrey (1762-1843)
Landscape with farm buildings and a timber stack. *Grey wash over pencil, 8in. x 13¼in.*

the first President of the O.W.S. in 1805. He is said to have resigned the Presidency in the following year because he felt outdone by the other exhibitors. This seems unlikely, since his work is at least as competent as that of Holworthy or Nattes, for instance. He accepted the post of drawing master at the R.M.C. Great Marlow at that point, and this necessary absence from London provides a more reasonable explanation of his resignation. He later moved to Sandhurst, and continued to exhibit with the Society until 1815, after which date he gave up drawing and became a landscape gardener, working in England and Ireland. He had already visited Ireland and sketched there, and also exhibited views on the Thames and in the Southern Counties.

His earliest landscape drawings are influenced by those of his artistic family, and have an affinity with those of N. Pocock (q.v.), or even his fellow landscape gardener, H. Repton (q.v.). Later, he seems to show the influence of Girtin (q.v.). His favourite and most characteristic colour is a greenish-grey, often laid over careful pencil drawing. Due to the variations of style throughout his life, it is possible that drawings attributed to more important artists are in fact by him.
Published: *Practical Hints upon Landscape Gardening…,* 1832.
Examples: B.M.; Fitzwilliam.
Bibliography: O.W.S. Club, XXIX.

GIRLING, Edmund
    1796 (Yarmouth) - 1871 (London)
An etcher and landscape painter who was a fellow clerk with Frederick Crome at Gurney's Bank. He was a good draughtsman and engraved after Rembrandt, J. Crome (q.v.) and others.
Examples: B.M.

GIRLING, Richard
    1799 (Yarmouth) - 1863 (London)
The brother of E. Girling (q.v.), he also etched after Crome and was a draughtsman.

GIRTIN, Thomas
    1775 (Southwark) - 1802 (London)
The elder son of a Southwark brush maker, who died when Girtin was three. His mother

later married Mr. Vaughan, a pattern designer, who encouraged his artistic leanings. His first lessons were from a Mr. Fisher in Aldersgate Street, after which he was apprenticed to E. Dayes (q.v.). There is evidence that they quarrelled but the story that Dayes had him imprisoned is apocryphal. He was supposed to have been extracted from both gaol and apprenticeship by the 5th Earl of Essex. He attended the evening drawing classes of Dr. Monro (q.v.) and J. Henderson (q.v.), where he became a close friend of Turner. Together they copied drawings by J.R. Cozens, Hearne, Malton, Morland, Wilson (qq.v), Canaletto, Piranesi and Ricci. He may have gone to Scotland with J. Moore (q.v.) in 1792, and in 1794 he visited Peterborough, Lincoln, Warwick and Lichfield with him. In this year he first exhibited at the R.A. with a view of Ely Cathedral based on a sketch by Moore. They visited the Cinque Ports in 1795.

In 1796 he toured the North of England and the borders and in 1798 he was again in the North, staying at Harewood. Some of the sketches from these tours were worked up for J. Walker's *Itinerant*. In 1799 he and Francia founded the sketching club known as 'The Brothers', of which R. Ker Porter (q.v.) was Treasurer. In 1800 he married the daughter of the goldsmith Phineas Borrett, and they moved to St. George's Row, Hyde Park, where P. Sandby was a neighbour. In this year he seems to have made a further visit to the North. He was also working on a panorama of London from a spot at the south end of Blackfriars

GIRTIN, Thomas (1775-1802)
Bamborough Castle, Northumberland. *Watercolour over slight pencil outlines, signed and dated 1797, laid down on original mount, inscribed on reverse, 16½in. x 21½in.*

GIRTIN, Thomas (1775-1802)
The village of Jedburgh, Roxburgh. *Signed and dated 1800, 11⅞in. x 20⅛in.*

Bridge. His patrons included Lords Essex, Hardwicke and Mulgrave, Sir G.H. Beaumont (q.v.) and the Hon. Spencer Cowper. From 1800 his health was failing and he was in Paris on doctor's orders from November 1801 to May 1802. He died in his studio in the Strand in the following November.

The influence of Dayes appears more strongly in the early work of Turner than in that of Girtin, who was his pupil. At this stage Girtin instigated the development from the tinted drawing to the pure watercolour, and Turner quickly followed. He discarded the careful outlining and grey wash base of his predecessors. His buildings and landscapes show nothing of the 'neat precision of Malton and his school'; rather his use of a full brush, freely handled, rougher and more absorbent cartridge paper and his concentration on atmosphere, altered the artistic climate of the time. He suggests rather than paints details by the use of shorthand dots and whirls, and his effects are gained by broad massing of form and light. His composition shows great daring in its simplicity and the abandonment of the Claudean framework. What eighteenth century topographer would have imagined that an empty Rue St. Denis could be so much more effective than one cluttered with figures?

The original effect of his colours can rarely be judged nowadays, since his work has suffered particularly from fading. He seems to have used a preponderance of mellow browns, yellows, greens and purples. His drawings sometimes show a central fold line which is a characteristic of his cartridge paper (see Mallalieu: *Understanding Watercolours*, 1985, p.40).

His influence is seen directly in his pupils and immediate followers such as Lady Farnborough, the Duchess of Sutherland, W. Pearson, F.J. Manskirsch and T. Worthington

(qq.v.), as well as in the work of more gifted contemporaries such as Francia, Cotman and even Cox (qq.v.).
Examples: B.M.; V.A.M.; Aberdeen A.G.; Ashmolean; Birmingham City A.G.; Blackburn A.G.; Brighton A.G.; Bowes Mus., Durham; Ferens A.G., Hull; Fitzwilliam; Glasgow A.G.; N.G., Ireland; Leeds City A.G.; Leicestershire A.G.; Usher A.G., Lincoln; City A.G., Manchester; N.G., Scotland; Laing A.G., Newcastle; Newport A.G.
Bibliography: R.L. Binyon: *T.G.*, 1900. R.L. Binyon: *English Watercolours from the work of Turner, Girtin...* 1939. R. Davies: *T.G.'s Watercolours*, 1924. J. Mayne: *T.G.*, 1949. T. Girtin and D. Loshak: *The Art of T.G.*, 1954. O.W.S. Club, XI, 1933. Walpole Soc. XXXVII, 1938. *W&D*, 1987, iv. Tate Gall.: Exhibition Cat., 2002.
See Colour Plate

GISBORNE, Rev. Thomas
1758 (Yoxall, Staffordshire) - 1846 (Yoxall)
An amateur artist, he was educated at Harrow and St. John's College, Cambridge, and was a friend of Wright of Derby (q.v.) who painted his portrait in 1777, and with whom he sketched. He was curate of Barton-under-Needwood, Staffordshire, from 1783, and became a Canon of Durham. In 1792 he met W. Gilpin (q.v) and in the following year visited the Lake District with Wright. He also knew J. 'W'. Smith (q.v.), from whom he learnt several techniques. He was an author and poet, and an amateur botanist. In 1990 Messrs Abbott & Holder had a view in Ceylon, c. 1830, inscribed either by or to him.
Published: *Walks in a Forest*, 1794.
Examples: Derby A.G.
Bibliography: *Burlington Mag.*, CVII, Feb. 1965.

GLASGOW, Edwin
1874 (Liverpool) - 1955 (Charlbury)
An amateur artist who was educated at

Wadham College, Oxford, and became an Inspector for the Board of Education, working on Tyneside and later in Northumberland. He exhibited local landscapes and buildings at the R.A., the R.I. and elsewhere, painting in both watercolour and oil. Later in life he became Keeper of the N.G. He was living in Birmingham in 1927.
Published: *Sketches of Magdalen College*, 1901. *Sketches of Wadham College*, 1901. *The Painter's Eye*, 1936.

GLASS, John Hamilton
A prolific landscape, coastal and river painter in watercolour and sometimes oil. He lived in Musselburgh and Pencaitland, where he was active between 1890 and 1925. He painted on the East coast of Scotland and Iona, and also in Holland. He often collaborated with his wife **Elizabeth GLASS**, signing her work, which helps to explain the size of his output. His colours tend to greys and browns, and his figures to dumpiness.

GLASS, John James, A.R.S.A.
1820 (Edinburgh) - 1885 (Edinburgh)
A painter of portraits, horses and landscapes, mostly in oil but sometimes watercolour, he was elected A.R.S.A. in 1849. He exhibited at the R.A. in 1847 and 1859.

GLEN, James 1795/6   - 1865 (Inverness)
A landscape and figure painter who studied at Sass's and entered the R.A. Schools in 1828. After some years in Glasgow, he moved to Inverness in 1845, where he became a most influential figure in cultural circles. He taught at the Inverness Royal Academy until 1851, when he returned briefly to Glasgow, and then again from 1852. His watercolour Highland landscapes are rather like brown versions of those of W.L. Leitch (q.v.).

GLENDENING, Alfred Augustus
1861 (Greenwich) - 1907 (Southend)
The son of the oil painter Alfred Glendening of Greenwich (d.c. 1910), he painted genre subjects in oil and watercolour and exhibited from 1881. He was a member of the R.B.A. and latterly worked as a scene painter. He visited New York in 1901.

GLENNIE, Arthur, R.W.S.
1803 (Dulwich Grove, Surrey) - 1890 (Rome)
Taught by S. Prout (q.v.) at school at Dulwich Grove, he was later advised by W. Havell (q.v.) but only turned professional artist when ill-health prevented a mercantile career. He had already visited Rome when he was elected A.O.W.S. in 1837, but for the next eighteen years he lived either in Kent or London, with about two years as a drawing master in Sidmouth, probably from 1840. In 1855 he took up permanent residence in Rome and thereafter his exhibited subjects are almost all

GLENDENING, Alfred Augustus (1861-1907)
Flower sellers on the Embankment. *Watercolour heightened with bodycolour, signed with monogram, dated 1899, 23¾in. x 35¼in.*

Italian. He was elected O.W.S. in 1858, and in 1865 he married Anne Sophia Parker, daughter of the Chaplain to the Forces. They travelled much in Italy and Istria and visited the Baltic at least once, probably in 1862 or 1863, and possibly again in 1881. Glennie tried to work up his drawings as much as possible on the spot and kept to pure watercolour rather than achieving his effects with bodycolour.
Examples: V.A.M.

GLENNIE, George F ?1841 (London) -
A landscape painter who lived in London and Kent and exhibited from 1861 to 1882. His views are mainly in the Southern counties or France. He was the son of A. Glennie (q.v.).

GLINDONI, Henry Gillard, A.R.W.S.
1852 (Kennington) - 1913 (London)
A genre and Cardinal painter who exhibited from 1872 and was elected A.R.W.S. in 1883. He had studied at the Working Man's College, and began by colouring photographs. He lived at Chadwell Heath, Essex.
Examples: Barking Lib.; Sunderland A.G.
Bibliography: *The Essex Review*, date unknown.

GLOAG, Isobel Lilian
1865 (London) - 1917 (London)
Of Scottish parentage, she studied at St. John's Wood Art School, the Slade, Mr. Ridley's studio, South Kensington and Paris. She exhibited at the R.A., R.I., R.B.A. and elsewhere from 1889. She painted in both oil and watercolour, and produced legendary and romantic subjects, portraits, flower pieces, book illustrations, posters and designs for stained glass. She also contributed to *The Graphic*.
Examples: B.M.; V.A.M.
Bibliography: *Mag. of Art*, 1902. *Studio*, LXV, 1915; LXVI, 1916; LXVII, 1916.

GLOVER, John, O.W.S.
1767 (Houghton-on-the-Hill, Leicestershire) - 1849 (Launceston, Tasmania)
The son of a small farmer, Glover was largely self taught, although he had seven lessons from W. Payne (q.v.) and one from J. 'W.' Smith (q.v.). He had two club feet, but worked in the fields as a youth and was extremely agile and active throughout his life. He had a great love of birds, animals and nature in general. In 1786 he was appointed writing master at a school in Appleby, and in 1794 he set up as a drawing teacher in Lichfield. He began to exhibit at the R.A. in 1795. He was a founder member of the O.W.S. and as a result of the success of the first exhibition in 1805, he moved to London. He was a prime instigator of the change to the Oil and Watercolour Society in 1813 and became President two years later. However, he resigned at the end of 1817 in order to try for the R.A. Being unsuccessful, he held a series of one-man exhibitions from 1820 and in 1824 was one of the founders of the S.B.A. Before 1820 he had bought himself a house on Ullswater to which he had intended to retire, but, reversing more recent practice, he sold it to buy a Claude. In 1831 he went to Tasmania with his family and remained there, sending pictures of local scenery to London for exhibition, until his death.

The influence of Payne is not evident so much in Glover's style as in his adoption of an easily recognisable formula. His method of work was always the same, beginning with a ground base of indigo, indian red and indian ink. He damped the paper for the soft effects, and used a few basic local colours. His hallmark is an individual use of the split-brush technique. Other artists, including 'Grecian' Williams, had experimented in a similar manner, but Glover made it the prime feature of his foliage drawing. This has become more prominent with fading – Glover's skies have almost entirely disappeared and his local colour has often turned to a rather sulphurous yellow.

His composition is largely based on Claude. His subjects are mainly landscapes, particularly of the Lake District, Wales and Dovedale. He also painted sea-pieces and life-size cattle pictures, and made many pencil sketches. His pupils included E. Price, J. Holworthy, H.C. Allport and H. Salt (qq.v) and his style was also widely imitated by professionals and amateurs.
Examples: B.M.; V.A.M.; Aberdeen A.G.; Ashmolean; Cartwright Hall, Bradford; Brighton A.G.; Grosvenor Mus., Chester; Fitzwilliam; Leeds City A.G.; Leicestershire A.G.; Manchester City A.G.; Newport A.G.
Bibliography: *A.J.*, 1850. *Walker's Quarterly*, XV, 1924. O.W.S. Club, LVII, 1982.

GLOVER, John, Yr.
A son of J. Glover (q.v.), he exhibited at the R.A. from 1808 to 1829 and emigrated to Tasmania with his family in 1831.

GLOVER, William
A son of J. Glover (q.v.), who was probably teaching drawing in Birmingham in 1808 with H.C. Allport (q.v.). He exhibited with the Oil and Watercolour Society and in 1822 was giving lessons in both media at half a guinea an hour. In 1831 he emigrated to Tasmania with his family. His style is close to his father's, and his drawings can be very charming.
Examples: V.A.M.

GLOVER, William, R.S.W.
1848 - 1916
A painter of Highland scenes in watercolour and oil, he was manager of the Theatre Royal, Glasgow at the end of the century. He was a scene painter and also produced rather weak coastal subjects. Towards the end of his life he lived in Cumbernauld.

GOBLE, Warwick 1862 - 1943
An illustrator in black and white and watercolour, he was educated at the City of London School and then joined the *Pall Mall Gazette* and later the *Westminster Gazette*. He also worked extensively for the colour-plate publishers such as Messrs. Black and Macmillan.

272

GLOVER, John (1767-1849)
Scene in the Appenines to illustrate 'The Mysteries of Udolpho' by Mrs. Radcliffe. *Watercolour, 5in. x 6⁵⁄₁₆in.*

In 1919 he made a tour to record the battle-fields of the Western Front. He was strongly influenced by Chinese and Japanese painting, especially in his use of colour washes.
Illustrated: A. van Milligen: *Constantinople*, 1905. C. Kingsley: *The Water Babies*, 1909. G. James: *The Green Willow and other Japanese Fairy Tales*, 1910. &c.

GODBOLD, Samuel Berry
1820/1(London) - 1884 (Bedlam)
The son of a clergyman, he became a painter of miniature and other portraits, landscapes and genre subjects. He entered the R.A. Schools in 1841, lived in Dublin and London and exhibited from 1842 to 1875. From about 1861 there are a number of Irish views and figure subjects.

GODDARD, George Bouverie
1832 (Salisbury) - 1886 (London)
A self-taught animal painter in oil and watercolour who was hailed as a genius at the age of ten. In 1849 he came to London and spent two years sketching at the Zoological Gardens, meanwhile drawing sporting subjects on wood for periodicals such as *Punch*. He returned to Salisbury, where he took commissions, and finally settled in London in 1857. He exhibited at the R.A. from 1856.
Bibliography: *A.J.,* 1886. *The Times,* 18 and 29 March 1886.

GODDARD, J   (Bedloe)
A landscape painter from Christchurch, Hants., he was active from at least 1875 to 1894.

GODET, Julius
A landscape painter who was living in London

and exhibiting between 1844 and 1884. He painted in Cornwall, the Isle of Wight, Sussex, Derbyshire and North Wales, as well as on Hampstead Heath.

GODFREY, Richard Bernard
1728 (London) - p.1795
An antiquarian topographer, who entered the R.A. Schools in 1769. In later life he must have fitted into the antiquarian set very well. He was principally an engraver, but also helped F. Grose (q.v.) to edit his *Antiquarian Repertory,* 1753.

GODWARD, John William
1861 (Battersea) - 1922 (Fulham)
The painter of classical genre subjects, generally featuring pretty girls. Despite their often languid poses, these often have more allure than their sisters by Alma-Tadema. Occasionally he worked in watercolour. He visited the south of Italy in 1905 and lived in Rome for eleven years from 1911, returning to England in the summer of 1921. A lonely and reclusive man, who never married, he committed suicide on 13 December 1922.
Bibliography: V. Swanson: *J.W.G. – The Eclipse of Classicism,* 1998.

GOFF, Frederick Edward Joseph
1855 (London) - 1931 (London)
A painter of rather lurid London views. He worked on a small scale using a magnifying glass, and he exhibited from 1890. He also

GODWARD, John William (1861-1922)
A Song without Words. *Watercolour and pencil, 11⅛in. x 8⅞in.*

GOFF, Frederick Edward Joseph (1855-1931)
Winchester Cathedral. *Watercolour over traces of pencil, heightened with white, signed and inscribed, 10in. x 17¾in.*

painted Thames views and landscapes in Kent. He lived in Clapham and, at the end of his life, Tooting.
Examples: B.M.

GOFF, Colonel Robert Charles
1837 (Dublin) -
1922 (La Tour de Peitz, Vevey)
An Irishman who was commissioned in 1855 and served in the Crimea, Ceylon, Malta and China. He retired in 1878 and lived in Hove before settling in Florence and Switzerland, and he travelled widely. He sketched and etched in England, Scotland and France as he had throughout his career.
A memorial exhibition was held at the Fine Art Society in 1923.
Illustrated: C. Goff: *Florence and some Tuscan Villas,* 1905. C. Goff: *Assisi of St. Francis,* 1908.
Examples: V.A.M.; Hove Lib.
Bibliography: *Studio,* III, 1894; XLVI, 1909. Rembrandt Gall, London, Exhibition Cat., 1896. *Mag. of Art,* 1904. Walker's Gall., London, Exhibition Cat., 1934.

GOGIN, Charles
1844 (London) - 1931 (Redhill)
A Newlyn painter of portraits and genre. He studied under J.P. Laurens and occasionally exhibited works in oil, watercolour and gesso. He also made a number of illustrations.
Published: *Things are waking up at Mudham,* 1929.
Examples: Cartwright Hall, Bradford; Glasgow A.G.; Hove Lib.

GOLDICUTT, John
1793 (London) - 1842 (London)
An architect and draughtsman, he was a pupil of Henry Hakewill and entered the R.A. Schools in 1812. In 1815 he went to study in Paris and later spent some time in Italy. In 1819 he returned and worked as an architect, both with Hakewill and independently. He worked in a strictly classical manner, reminiscent of C.R. Cockerell (q.v.), and his drawings are highly finished and show a love of strong colour.
Published: *Antiquities of Sicily,* 1819. *Specimens of Ancient Decoration from Pompeii,* 1825. *Heriot's Hospital, Edinburgh,* 1826. *Ancient Wells and Reservoirs,* 1836.
Examples: V.A.M.; R.I.B.A.
Bibliography: *Architectural Review,* XXXI, 1912.

GOLDSMITH, Georgina S
A landscape painter who lived in Penge and exhibited views of Surrey, Sussex and Jersey at the S.B.A. in 1869 and 1870.

GOLDSMITH, Walter H
A landscape painter who lived at Maidenhead and worked on the Thames. He exhibited from 1880.
Examples: Maidenhead Lib.; Reading A.G.

GOMPERTZ
A family of watercolourists, and perhaps architects, who lived in Lambeth and were active in the 1830s and 1840s. **George GOMPERTZ (b.1821)** entered the R.A. Schools in 1840, followed in 1843 by **James Edward GOMPERTZ** apparently born in the same year. **Francis T. GOMPERTZ (b.1830/1)** was admitted to the architecture school in 1853. Others of the name who painted figures and architectural subjects were **E., M., and S. GOMPERTZ.** Some of them at least are likely to have been the children, or wives and children, of the philanthropic Benjamin and Lewis Gompertz who lived in Kennington.

GONNE, Mrs. Anne
1816 (Devonshire) -
A flower painter who in 1840 married the Irish engraver Henry Gonne. She exhibited frequently at the R.H.A. and was a drawing teacher. She also modelled wax flowers, examples of which were in the Dublin exhibition of 1853.

GOOCH, James
A painter from Norfolk who produced landscapes, animals and rusticities. He exhibited in Norwich from 1812 and at Suffolk Street from 1819 to 1837. After about 1824 he was painting portraits and views around Twickenham, where he had settled, and he was still active in the mid-1840s.
Matilda GOOCH, who exhibited modest views, rural subjects and still lifes of flowers and dead birds from 1857 may have been his daughter. She lived at Twickenham until 1874 when she moved to South Kensington, and she was active until at least 1877.

GOOCH, John   1752   - 1823
A topographer who painted a view of Oxford in 1777 which was etched in the following year. He is not to be confused with James Gooch *(vide supra).*

GOOD, Clements 1810   - 1896
The Danish Consul in Hull. He made a number of local views and also painted shipping subjects.

GOOD, Thomas Sword, H.R.S.A.
1789 (Berwick-upon-Tweed) -
1872 (Berwick-upon-Tweed)
He began as a house painter, taking portraits on the side. He moved on to genre painting and to London in 1822, exhibiting there between 1820 and 1834, at which date he gave up painting and returned to Berwick. His paintings, in oil and watercolour, are rather in the manner of Wilkie. His favourite subjects were rustics and fishermen.
Bibliography: *A.J.,* 1852; 1901. *Country Life,* 23 Jan. 1948.

GOODALL, Edward Angelo, R.W.S.
1819 (London) - 1908 (London)
The eldest son of Edward Goodall (1795-1870), the engraver. He accompanied the Schomburg Guiana Boundary Exhibition in 1841 and was in the Crimea for the *I.L.N.* in 1854. He also travelled in Spain, Portugal, Morocco and Italy. He exhibited from 1841 and was elected A.R.W.S. and R.W.S. in 1858 and 1864.
His work is neat and restrained. His death certificate gives his names as here, although some authorities have rechristened him 'Alfred'.
Examples: B.M.; V.A.M.; Ashmolean; Greenwich; N.G., Ireland; City A.G., Manchester; Sydney Mus.
Bibliography: *A.J.,* 1859; 1908.
See Colour Plate

GOODALL, Frederick, R.A.
1822 (London) - 1904 (London)

The second son of Edward Goodall, in whose studio he was placed to learn engraving at the age of thirteen. Frederick and his brother Edward Angelo (q.v.) were encouraged to paint by such artists as Ruskin, Roberts and Turner, who were frequent visitors to the house. He drew from casts and made sketching exhibitions along the Thames and to the Zoological Gardens. In 1837 he won a silver medal of the Society of Arts and he visited Normandy in 1838, 1839 and 1840, Brittany in 1841, 1842 and 1845, and Ireland with F.W. Topham and G. Fripp (qq.v.). He exhibited at the R.A. from the age of sixteen and was elected A.R.A. in 1852 and R.A. in 1863. In 1858-9 he spent eight months in Egypt, where he shared a house in Cairo with C. Haag (q.v.) with whom he toured the countryside. In 1870 he returned to Cairo with Edward Angelo. On his return Norman Shaw built him an exotic house in Harrow Weald, which he surrounded with weird shrubs and filled with Egyptian sheep.

His sons, **Frederick Trevelyan GOODALL (1848-1871)** and **Herbert Howard GOODALL (1850-1874)**, both exhibited at the R.A. Frederick Trevelyan, of whose work there are examples at the V.A.M. and the Paisley A.G., died at Capri, accidentally shot by his brother, and Herbert Howard at Cairo.

A second **Herbert GOODALL** exhibited during the 1890s and died in 1907.

Published: *Reminiscences of F.G.*, 1902.

Examples: B.M.; V.A.M.; City A.G., Manchester; Sydney A.G.

Bibliography: *A.J.*, 1850; 1855; 1862; 1895; 1904. (F.T. Goodall), *A.J.*, 1871. (H.H. Goodall), *A.J.*, 1874.

GOODALL, Walter, R.W.S.
1830 (London) - 1889 (Clapham, near Bedford)

The youngest son of Edward Goodall, he was trained at the Government School of Design at Somerset House and the R.A. Schools, from 1847 and attended the 'Clipstone Street Academy' (later the Langham Sketching Society). He was elected A.O.W.S. in 1853 and O.W.S. in 1861, and he confined himself entirely to watercolours. He spent the winter of 1868-9 in Rome, and also visited Venice. In about 1875 he became partially paralysed, and eventually totally helpless. His works are generally small figure subjects, often of rather idealised peasants. He also specialised in Venetian boats. Apart from Italy he visited Holland, Brittany and the Pyrenees. From 1865 to 1872 he lived off Oxford Street; he then moved to Bedfordshire.

Published: *W.G.'s Rustic Sketches*, 1855-7.

GOODEN, James Chisholm – see
CHISHOLM, James Chisholm GOODEN

GOODWIN, Albert, R.W.S.
1845 (Maidstone) - 1932 (London)

The son of a builder, and a brother of H. Goodwin (q.v.), he was a pupil of A. Hughes

GOODALL, Edward Angelo (1819-1908)
Aqueduct at Segovia. *Watercolour.*

(q.v.) and F.M. Brown (q.v.). In 1872 he went to Italy with Ruskin and A. Severn (q.v.). From this time he travelled widely, sometimes with his brother, visiting India, Egypt and the South Seas, as well as many parts of Britain and Europe. He was elected A.R.W.S. and R.W.S. in 1871 and 1881 and held one-man shows at Leggatt Bros. in 1912, Vicars Gallery in 1925 and Birmingham Art Gallery in 1926. He lived for much of his life at Arundel. His diary for the years 1883 to 1927 was printed privately in 1934.

His style is highly idiosyncratic and at its best very impressive. It can be described as a reversal of the usual processes, with the drawing coming last.

His youngest brother **Frank GOODWIN (1848-c.1873)** was also an artist. An elder brother, Charles, made frames and mounts for the family.

Examples: B.M.; Aberdeen A.G.; Ashmolean; Blackburn A.G.; Cardiff A.G.; Fitzwilliam; Leeds City A.G.; Maidstone Mus.; City A.G., Manchester; Melbourne A.G.; Newport A.G.; Paisley A.G.; Wakefield A.G.; Ulster Mus.

Bibliography: *Portfolio*, 1870; 1886. *Studio*, XXXI, 1904; XXXXV, 1905; XLIX, 1910. Birmingham City A.G., Exhibition Cat. 1926. Laing A.G., Newcastle, Exhibition Cat., 1968. O.W.S. Club, LIV, 1979. C. Beetles, London, Exhibition Cat., 1996.

GOODWIN, Albert (1845-1932)
Beachy Head – a windy day. *Watercolour over pencil, heightened with white, signed, inscribed and dated* Beachey Head 1914, *10in. x 14¾in.*

GOODWIN, Edward

A painter of landscapes and church interiors who lived in Manchester and Liverpool. He exhibited at the R.A. and the O.W.S. from 1801 to 1815 and was a founder of the Liverpool Academy in 1810. He painted in Wales, Scotland and the North of England. His landscapes are good but his drawing of cattle is poor. His interiors are in the manner of A. Pugin (q.v.) and are dramatically lit. He was probably the E. Goodwin active in 1835.

Examples: B.M.; V.A.M.; Ashmolean; Derby A.G.; Maidstone Mus.; City A.G., Manchester; Ulster Mus.

GOODWIN, Francis
1784 (King's Lynn) - 1835

An architect and engineer who was a pupil of J. Coxedge, a Kensington architect, and who first exhibited at the R.A. in 1806. His plans for the new House of Commons were printed in 1833. He had a considerable practice in the North of England and visited Ireland in 1834. He died of apoplexy brought on by preparing for the competition for the Houses of Parliament. His work is architectural in the main, but includes views as well as designs.

Published: Domestic Architecture…, 18334.

Examples: Soane Mus.

Bibliography: Architectural Mag., ii, 1835. Gentleman's Mag., 1835, ii. Architectural History, I, 1958; XXVIII, 1985.

GOODWIN, Harry (Henry Richard)
1841 (Tonbridge) - 1925 (Hastings)

An elder brother of Albert, with whom he visited the Italian Lakes and Lucerne in 1887. He was also in Italy in 1892 and 1920. He exhibited from 1867 and worked in a manner which is close to that of his brother. He has an excellent feeling for distance.

Illustrated: W.A. Knight: Through the Wordsworth Country, 1887.

Examples: Ashmolean; Maidstone Mus.; City A.G., Manchester.

GOODWIN, Sidney (or Sydney) Paul
1867 (Southampton) - 1944

The son of William Sydney GOODWIN (1833-1916), the eldest of A. Goodwin's brothers, who was an artist and an engineer working for the R.E. Ordnance Office in Southampton, France, Belgium, Mount Sinai and London. He left paintings to the Southampton A.G.

Sidney Goodwin painted landscapes and marine subjects. He was in Canada in the late 1880s, and seems to have visited Australia. At times he is very like Uncle Albert. In about 1912 he settled in Dublin, where he exhibited at the R.H.A. until 1922.

A brother, Charles Albert GOODWIN, was a competent watercolourist and remained in Southampton all his life.

Examples: Maidstone A.G.; Portsmouth City Mus.

GOODWIN, W Katherine, 'Kate', née Malleson

Landscape painter and wife of H. Goodwin (q.v.). She exhibited at the R.A. and elsewhere from 1870, and they lived in Brighton, Croydon and Torquay. Before marriage she signed 'K. Malleson'.

Examples: City A.G., Manchester.

GORDON, Caroline Emilia Mary, Hon. Mrs 1830 - 1909

A daughter of Sir John Herschel, Bt., she married the second son of the Prime Minister Earl of Aberdeen in 1852. She was a Woman of the Bedchamber from 1855, and the Queen described her as 'drawing and playing so well'. She painted and drew Scottish houses and landscapes.

GORDON, Lady Catherine Susan –
see CHESHAM, Lady

GORDON, Julia Isabella Lavinia, Lady, née Bennet
1772 (Beckenham) - 1867 (London)

A pupil of Kennion, Turner in 1797, Girtin and Cox, she married General Sir James Wiloughby GORDON, 1st Bt. (1773 - 1851 Chelsea), himself a sketcher, in 1805. He was military secretary to the Duke of York and later quartermaster-general in the Peninsula and at the Horse Guards, and was created a baronet in 1818. They lived at Beckenham near Lady Farnborough (q.v.), in Chelsea and at Northcourt, Isle of Wight, where Turner stayed with them in 1827. She was sister-in-law of Sir John Swinburne of Capheaton, brother of E. Swinburne (q.v.).

Her work is often in direct colour and has been confused with that of her daughter, Julia Emily GORDON (1810-1896), another very talented amateur, who worked on the island, in various parts of England, on the Rhine and in Provence. She used a number of media, but from the 1830s preferred elaborate monochrome drawings on blue paper. She was also a fine draughtswoman and many of her coloured and monochrome works are over a careful pen outline. She published a volume of etchings in 1847. The Tate has a Wilkie watercolour of her, and her father refused the artist permission to seek her hand.

An exhibition of the work of both ladies was held at the Brook Street Galleries, London, in 1939.

Bibliography: Country Life, 8 July 1939. Burlington Mag., XCIX, 1957.

GORDON, Pryse Lockhart
1762 (Ardersier, Inverness) - 1834 (Brussels)

A memorialist and occasional caricaturist. He served in the Marines and the Army in Britain, Italy and Minorca. He lived in Sicily with Lord Montgomery from 1811 to 1813 and thereafter in Brussels. In the B.M. is a drawing by him in the manner of G.M. Woodward (q.v.), but with thinner people.

Published: A Companion to Italy, 1823. A Companion for the Visitor at Brussels, 1828. Personal Memoirs, 1830. Holland and Belgium, 1834.

GORDON, Rachel Emily, Lady HAMILTON c.1834 - 1889

A talented landscape painter who was the wife of Sir Arthur Hamilton-Gordon, later created Lord Stanmore, the youngest son of the Premier Earl of Aberdeen. He was Lieutenant-Governor of New Brunswick from 1861 to 1866, Governor of Trinidad from 1866 to 1870, Fiji from 1875 to 1880 and Ceylon from 1883 to 1890. She was the eldest daughter of Sir J.G. Shaw Lefevre, married in 1865, and signed her work variously R.S.L., R.H.G. or Lady Gordon. Her drawings are very professional and she may well have been a pupil of W. Page, W. Collingwood Smith and P. de Wint (qq.v.).

Other members of her family who show more or less talent include her sisters, Mary Jane Georgina, Lady RYAN; Madeleine Shaw LEFEVRE; and Emily Shaw LEFEVRE; and cousins or nieces Caroline, Lady GORDON; Kathleen Isabella GORDON; Emily Octavia Shaw LEFEVRE; and Mary Emma Shaw LEFEVRE.

GORDON, General Sir Thomas Edward
1832 - 1914

Author, linguist, geographer, surveyor and draughtsman, he joined the army in 1849 and served through the Indian Mutiny, 1857-9, and the 1879-80 Afghan War. Between 1873 and 1875 he was second-in-command on the Forsyth mission to Yakub Beg of Kashgar in Chinese Turkestan. This enabled him to explore the Tien Shan plateau and the Pamirs. He was Oriental and Military Secretary at Tehran between 1889 and 1893, was promoted general in 1894 and made K.C.B. in 1900. He illustrated his journals and publications with very good panoramic and atmospheric water-colours.

Published: The Roof of the World, 1876. A Varied Life, 1906.

GORDON, Rev. William - 1853

An amateur landscape painter who was vicar of Mundesley on the Norfolk coast. He was closely connected with the second generation of Norwich artists.

Another William GORDON, with his son G. GORDON, was an architect, surveyor and speculative builder in Hammersmith during the first half of the nineteenth century. A folio of their drawings dating from 1820 to 1838 passed through Sotheby's, 25-6 April 1990.

GORE, Charles
1729 (Horkestowe, Yorkshire) - 1807 (Weimar)

A Yorkshire landowner, Gore was primarily a marine artist, and for a time worked at

Southampton. In 1773 his wife's ill-health forced them abroad, and he went to Lisbon and on to Italy by sea. He visited Rome, Naples, Leghorn, Florence, Corsica, Nice, Marseilles and other Mediterranean towns, and in 1777 spent April and May in Sicily with R.P. Knight (q.v.) and Philipp Hackert. His drawings on this visit were later worked up by J.R. Cozens (q.v.). Gore had returned to England by 1781, when he sketched in Sussex and became a member of the Dilettanti Society. Later, he went back to Florence, and from 1791 until his death was a member of the Ducal Court at Weimar and a friend of Goethe.

As well as his marine drawings, his studies of archaeological remains in Sicily are both extremely accurate and full of dramatic impact. His Sussex landscapes owe a little to P. Sandby (q.v.), and show a liking for yellowish greens, greys and pinks. Sometimes his monochrome marine drawings are reminiscent of those of W. Marlow (q.v.).

His daughter **Eliza M. GORE (1754-1802)** was a competent imitator of Cozens, and it is likely that her sister **Hannah Anne, Countess COWPER,** who married in Florence in 1775 and died there in 1826, also painted. Both are seen, Eliza with *porte-crayon* in hand, in Zoffany's 'Earl Cowper and the Gore Family', now at Yale.
Examples: B.M.; Ashmolean; Gloucester City A.G.; Greenwich; Leeds City A.G. Goethe Mus., Weimar.
Bibliography: Walpole Society, XXIII, 1935 (Introduction).

GORE, Spencer Frederick
1878 (Surrey) - 1914 (Richmond)
A post-Impressionist landscape painter who studied at the Slade. He was a member of the London Group and was much influenced by Sickert and Lucien Pissaro.
Examples: Cartwright Hall, Bradford.

GOSLING, William W
1824 - 1883 (Wargrave)
A landscape painter in oil and watercolour who lived at Wargrave. He exhibited from 1849 and was a member of the R.B.A. but was an unsuccessful candidate for the O.W.S. in 1866 and N.W.S. in 1869 and 1870. At his best he can be close to T. Collier (q.v.), but his work is varied.
Bibliography: *A.J.,* 1873.

GOSSELIN, Colonel Joshua
1739 (Guernsey) - 1813 (Bengeo Hall, Hertfordshire)
A topographer and landscape painter from an old Channel Islands family, who lived and worked in the Channel Islands, where he was a Colonel of the Second Regiment of Militia and was sworn Greffier in 1768, and in Hertfordshire. He also worked in Wales, and his drawings are more polished than those of M. Griffith (q.v.), with thin Sandby-like figures. His panoramas can be very impressive.

The landscape at Hertford Mus., which is looser and rather splashy, may possibly be by his son, **Joshua GOSSELIN, Yr. (1763-1789).**
See Colour Plate

GOTCH, Thomas Cooper, R.I.
1854 (Kettering) - 1931 (Newlyn)
A portrait, landscape and genre painter, he studied at Heatherley's, Antwerp, the Slade and Paris. He first visited Newlyn, Cornwall, in 1879, but lived in London until 1887, with a year in Australia in 1883. He was a founder of the Royal British Colonial Society of Artists, and, with Stanhope Forbes and W. Langley (q.v.), of the 'Newlyn School'. He was elected R.I. in 1912, and a retrospective exhibition of his work was held at the Laing A.G., Newcastle, in 1910.

After a visit to Italy in 1891, his painting, in oil and watercolour, became more allegorical than *plein-air.*
Illustrated: A. Le Braz: *The Land of Pardons,* 1906.
A.G. Bradley: *Round about Wiltshire,* 1907.
Examples: B.M.; A. East A.G., Kettering.
Bibliography: *Portfolio,* 1888. *A.J.,* 1889; 1902; 1903; 1905. *Studio,* XIII, 1898; Summer No., 1898; XXVI, 1902; XLII, 1908.

GOULD, Elizabeth, Mrs., née Coxon
1804 (Ramsgate) - 1841
The daughter of a sea captain, she came to London to take a post as a governess and in 1829 married John Gould. Together with E. Lear (q.v.) she produced finished watercolours as guides for the illustrations of Gould's ornithological publications, including *A Century of Birds from the Himalayan Mountains* and the *Birds of Europe.* In 1838 she and her husband sailed to Australia to work on the *Birds of Australia,* returning in 1840. He often took the credit for her work and, indeed, for that of the young Lear.
Bibliography: *Country Life,* 25 June 1964.

GOULD, Sir Francis Carruthers
1844 (Barnstaple) - 1925 (Porlock)
The son of an architect, he worked as a bank clerk and stockbroker before becoming the first newspaper cartoonist. He drew for *Punch,* the *Westminster Gazette* and the *Pall Mall Gazette,* and illustrated books of political lampoons by Sir Wilfred Lawson and others. The majority of his work is naturally in pen and ink.

His son **Alec Carruthers GOULD (1870-1948)** was an accomplished landscape painter in oil and watercolour and lived at Porlock. They were both members of the R.B.A.
Examples: B.M.; Towner Gall., Eastbourne.
Bibliography: *Studio,* XXIII, 1901; XXXVIII, 1906. *Mag. of Art,* 1903. *Country Life,* 10 Jan. 1925.

GOULDSMITH, Edmund
1852 - 1932
A painter of coasts and marine subjects in oil

and watercolour. He lived in London, Bath and Bristol, and studied at the Bristol and R.A. Schools. He exhibited from 1877, and travelled in the Antipodes.

GOULDSMITH, Harriet, Mrs. Arnold
1787 - 1863
She began to exhibit at the R.A. in 1809 and from 1813 to 1820 was a Lady Member of the Oil and Watercolour Society. She was an Honorary Member of the S.B.A. from 1824 to 1843 and continued to patronise the R.A. until 1854. She was primarily an oil painter, and was a landscapist, producing both compositions and topographical views in or near London. In 1819 she published four etched views of Charlemont and in 1824 *Four Views of Celebrated Places,* lithographed by C. Hullmandel. Early in life she was friendly with J. Linnell (q.v.), and comparatively late in life, in 1839, she married Captain Arnold, R.N.

GOUPY, Joseph
1689 (Nevers) - 1763 (London)
A drawing master and scene painter who worked in London from 1724 or earlier. He painted miniatures, figure subjects, caricatures, landscapes, copies of old masters and wash illustrations.
Examples: N.G., Scotland.
Bibliography: Walpole Society, XXII, 1934.

GOUPY, Louis
c.1670 (France) - 1747 (London)
An artist who subscribed to Kneller's Academy in 1711, accompanied Lord Burlington to Italy in 1719, and studied with L. Chéron (q.v.) on his return to London in the following year. He was a portrait painter in various media, and latterly had a fashionable practice as a drawing master in watercolour and crayon.

GOW, Andrew Carrick, R.A., R.I.
1848 (London) - 1920 (Burlington House)
The son of James Gow, a genre painter, he studied at Heatherley's and painted portraits, historical, military and genre subjects and town views. He exhibited from 1866, was elected A.R.A. and R.A. in 1880 and 1890 and was Keeper from 1911. He was elected A.N.W.S. and N.W.S. in 1868 and 1870. His style is free but accurate in drawing, and his colouring mellow.
Examples: V.A.M.; Fitzwilliam.

GOW, James Forbes Mackintosh
A prolific watercolourist from Edinburgh who was active at least between 1861 and 1898. He liked the coast of North-East Scotland, and in the 1890s he moved to Knocke-sur-Mer in Belgium. He also produced portraits, figures, landscapes and animal subjects.

GOW, Mary Louisa, Mrs. Hall, R.I.
1851 (Truro) - 1929 (London)
A member of the family of artists and sister of

GRACE, Alfred Fitzwalter (1844-1903)
Cattle watering by a stream. *Watercolour, signed and dated 1873, 16in. x 29in.*

A.C. Gow (q.v.), she studied at the Queen's Square School of Art and at Heatherley's. She exhibited from about 1869 and was elected N.W.S. in 1875, resigning in 1903; and she married S.P. Hall (q.v.). She specialised in genre and figure subjects.
Examples: V.A.M.; City A.G., Manchester.
Bibliography: *Studio*, LI, 1911; LXIII, 1915.

GOWANS, George Russell, R.S.W.
        1843 (Aberdeen) - 1924 (Aberdeen)
A painter of town views and Aberdeenshire landscapes in watercolour, oil, pen and ink and pastel. He studied in Aberdeen, London and Paris and exhibited in London from 1877. He was elected R.S.W. in 1893. A favourite sketching ground was Glen Gairn, upper Deeside. His watercolours are strong in sky and moor, and according to McEwan 'are more concerned with mood than detail'.
Examples: Aberdeen A.G.

GOWLAND, John
A Dundee whaling seaman and amateur artist, working in the first half of the nineteenth century. He mainly painted sailing ships.
Examples: Dundee City A.G.

GRACE, Alfred Fitzwalter
        1844 (Dulwich) - 1903 (Steyning)
A painter of Sussex landscapes and portraits who studied at Heatherley's and the R.A. Schools. He won the Turner medal, and he exhibited from 1863. He was a friend of Whistler and lived at Steyning.
Published: *A Course of Landscape Painting in Oils*, 1881.
Examples: V.A.M.
Bibliography: *A.J.*, 1904.

GRACE, Harriette Edith
        1860   - 1932
An artist who lived in Brighton and exhibited genre subjects at the R.A. and Suffolk Street from 1877.
Examples: Hove Lib.

GRACE, James Edward
        1851   - 1908 (Bedford Park)
A book illustrator and landscape painter who studied at the Liverpool Institute and at South Kensington. He exhibited at the R.A. and elsewhere from 1871 to 1907 and was elected S.B.A. in 1879. His wife also painted landscapes.
Illustrated: Marquis of Granby: *The Trout*, 1899.
Examples: City A.G., Manchester; Montreal A.G.; Sydney A.G.; Wakefield A.G.

GRAHAM, Alexander   1858   -
An architect and painter of architecture, usually abroad, who exhibited from 1875.
Examples: V.A.M.

GRAHAM, George, R.I., R.S.W
        1881 (Leeds) - 1949
A landscape painter who studied architecture before going to the Leeds School of Art and studying further under Brangwyn, Swann and Nicholson in London. He was elected R.I. in 1922 and R.S.W. in 1927 and was a music lover. He worked in both oil and watercolour.

GRAHAM, Henry
An Irish-born landscape painter. He entered the R.D.S. Schools in 1768 and studied under Jonathan Fisher (q.v.), with whom he lived and worked as assistant for many years. He exhibited with the Dublin Society of Artists in 1777 and 1780. Fisher, on his death in 1809, left him his painting materials and his sketches and drawings.

GRAHAM, Lord Montagu William
        1807   - 1878
A pupil of de Wint, he was son of the 3rd Duke of Montrose. He painted landscapes, cattle and shipping studies, sometimes on tinted paper. After service in the Coldstream Guards he was M.P. for Grantham and Hereford.

GRAHAM, Peter, R.A., H.R.S.A.
        1836 (Edinburgh) - 1921 (St. Andrews)
A painter of Scottish landscapes in oil and occasionally watercolour, he was a pupil of R.S. Lauder at the Trustees' Academy. He was elected A.R.S.A. in 1860, later resigning, being made H.R.S.A., A.R.A. in 1877 and R.A. in 1881. He was particularly good at painting mist.
Examples: Worcester City A.G.
Examples: *Portfolio*, 1887. *A.J.*, Christmas 1899. N.G. Scot., Exhibition Cat., 1983.

GRAHAM, Robert Brown
A landscape and marine painter from Edinburgh who was active at least between 1858 and 1878. He enjoyed castles and churches as well as shipping.

GRAHAM, Major-General William Henry
        1837   - 1888
Commissioned in the Royal Artillery in 1856, he was promoted lieutenant-colonel in 1883 and major-general on his retirement in 1886. He served in Egypt in 1882 and in India. His

landscapes are in pencil or pen and watercolour.

GRANT, Charles 1799 -
A portrait painter who entered the R.A. Schools in 1824 and worked in London from 1825 to 1839. After that date he probably went to India, where he published books of portraits until 1845.
Examples: B.M.

GRANT, Colesworthy
1813 - 1880
An artist and journalist who went to India in 1832. In 1849 he was appointed Drawing Master at the Engineering College at Howrah and later at the Presidency College, Sibpur. In 1846 he had visited Rangoon and in 1855 he was official artist to the embassy to the King of Ava. During the Mutiny he was the Correspondent for the *Durham Advertiser* and in 1857 he settled in Malnath. He drew portraits and topographical views.
Published: *An Anglo-Indian Domestic Sketch*, 1849. *Rough Pencillings of a Rough Trip to Rangoon*, 1853. *Rural Life in Bengal*, 1860. *To the Children of Calcutta. On Cruelty*, 1872.
Examples: India Office Lib.
Bibliography: P.C. Mittra: *Life of C.G.*, 1881.

GRANT, Mary Isabella
A landscape painter who lived at Cullompton, Devon, and exhibited at the R.I. and Suffolk Street from 1870.
Examples: V.A.M.

GRANT, 'Miss'
There is a watercolour figure drawing in the N.G., Scotland which is inscribed 'By "Miss Grant", a Drawing Mistress in Edinburgh, who later turned out to be a man'. It dates from the late eighteenth or early nineteenth century.

GRAPES, Elizabeth, Mrs., née Crump
c.1860 - c.1932 (Australia)
A Hull artist who painted landscapes in oil and watercolour. She emigrated to Australia late in life.
Her sister, **Harriet, Mrs. ELLERKER**, painted a number of copies.

GRATTAN, George
1787 (Dublin) - 1819 (Cullenswood)
He studied at the R.D.S. Schools, where he gained prizes in 1797 and later years. He was painting miniatures at this time, and in 1801 he sent portraits and landscapes to an exhibition in Parliament House. He was brought to the attention of the Earl of Hardwicke, for whom he made portraits and views in crayon. From 1804 he was working in Dublin, and he exhibited until 1813, occasionally visiting London to show at the R.A.
His early works were mainly landscapes in crayon and watercolour, but he later turned to historical and subject pictures in oil. A

GRAHAM, Lord Montagu William (1807-1878)
Figures with Horse and Cart in a Landscape. *Pencil and watercolour, 6¾in. x 10½in.*

memorial exhibition was held at 15 Dame Street, Dublin.
His younger brother **William GRATTAN (c.1792-c.1821)** was a landscape and figure painter who was trained at the R.D.S. Schools. He was active from 1801 to 1821 and exhibited in Dublin between 1809 and 1815. In 1818 he produced a pamphlet entitled *Patronage Analysed*.
Examples: V.A.M.

GRAVATT, Colonel William, F.R.S.
c.1771 - 1851 (Edmonton)
An engineer who was probably a pupil of P. Sandby (q.v.) at Woolwich. He was commissioned in 1791 and served in the West Indies. He was promoted captain in 1799 and full colonel in 1821. He worked in water and bodycolour and his penwork is sometimes untidy. His son and namesake was a distinguished mathematician and civil engineer.
Examples: B.M.

GRAVELOT, Hubert François
1699 (Paris) - 1773 (Paris)
The French draughtsman and book illustrator. His surname was properly Bourguignon, and he was the younger brother of the geographer J.B. Bourguignon d'Anville. He accompanied an abortive embassy to Italy, which got no further than Lyons, and he visited San Domingo before studying painting under Restout and Boucher at the age of thirty. In 1732 he moved to London, staying until 1745. He was in London again for a short period before 1755. He produced lovely pen and wash drawings for Gay's *Fables* (Vol. II) and Richardson's *Pamela*, and he taught

Gainsborough among others. He illustrated a number of other publications and also produced some topographical prints.
Published: *Treatise on Perspective*, n.d.
Examples: B.M.

GRAVES, Frederick Percy
A painter who lived in North London and worked in North Wales. He exhibited between 1858 and 1872, and produced figure subjects as well as landscapes.

GRAY, Catherine Esther, Mrs., née Geddes
1796 (Alderbury, nr. Salisbury) - 1882 (London)
The younger sister of M.S. Carpenter (q.v.), she married John Westcott Gray of Salisbury. She painted miniatures, larger watercolour portraits and landscapes.
She had three sons, W.J. Gray (q.v.), **Alfred GRAY (b.1820)**, and **Henry GRAY (1823 Salisbury - 1898 London)**, the last two being primarily miniaturists.
Bibliography: D.C. Whitton: *The Grays of Salisbury*, 1975.

GRAY, George
A painter of Highland landscapes, especially in the Trossachs, who came from Kirkaldy and was active at least between 1866 and 1910. Later he moved to Edinburgh and then to Musselburgh. He painted in oil as well as watercolour, but his colour is more impressive in the latter.
His wife **Jessie GRAY, née Dixon,** was also a painter of portraits, figures and rusticities in oil and watercolour, exhibiting at the R.S.A. and elsewhere between 1881 and 1892.

GRAY, Paul Mary
1842 (Dublin) - 1866 (Brighton)

An illustrator who was educated in a convent but returned to Dublin determined to become an artist. He worked as a drawing master at Tullabeg School and for Dillon the print seller, exhibiting genre and figure subjects at the R.H.A. from 1861 to 1863, in which year he moved to London. He produced illustrations for Kingsley's *Hereward*, after which he worked on *London Society, The Sunday Magazine, Fun, Punch* and other periodicals. Three of his watercolours were exhibited at the S.B.A. in 1867.

GRAY, William Henry
1818 - 1876

A sculptor, landscape and portrait painter of Ventnor, Isle of Wight, and London. He exhibited from 1835, and attended the R.A. Schools from 1839 to 1844 when he won a silver medal.

His son, who signed **'W. Hal GRAY'** (b.1852), was also a landscape painter.

GRAY, William John, of Salisbury
1817 (Salisbury) - 1895

A painter of intimate and pretty architectural watercolours between 1833 and 1840. They are not technically of a very high quality. He was the eldest son of C.E. Gray (q.v.) and a nephew of M.S. Carpenter (q.v.).
Examples: B.M.

GREEN, Amos
1735 (Halesowen, Birmingham) - 1807 (York)

He was apprenticed to Baskerville, a Birmingham printer, for whom he decorated trays and boxes. As an artist, he began by copying Dutch still lifes and later turned to landscape painting, primarily in watercolour. For a time he lived with the family of his friend Anthony Deane at Bergholt, Suffolk, and at Bath. He exhibited with the Incorporated Society in 1760, 1763 and 1765. He married Harriet Lister (q.v. as Green, Harriet) in 1796 and they made many sketching tours, often in the Lake District. His landscapes are generally of woods, waterfalls and lakes, in browns, greens and yellows. The effect is usually a little woolly.

His brothers **Benjamin I GREEN (c.1736-c.1800)** and **John GREEN** were engravers and drawing masters, Benjamin at Christ's Hospital and John at Oxford. Benjamin taught J.C. Smith (q.v.).
Illustrated: Miller: *History and Antiquities of Doncaster*, 1804.
Examples: B.M.; V.A.M.; Cartwright Hall, Bradford.
Bibliography: H. Green: *Memoir of A.G., Esq.*

GREEN, Benjamin Richard, N.W.S.
1808 (London) - 1876 (London)

The son of James Green (q.v.) and Mary Byrne (q.v. under Byrne, A.F.), he studied at the R.A. Schools from 1826 and was elected N.W.S. in 1834. He exhibited at the R.A., Suffolk Street and elsewhere from 1832, and was a drawing master and lecturer, and for many years Secretary to the Artists' Annuity Fund. In 1829 he published a numismatic atlas of ancient history. He spent some months in Inverness in 1840. He painted figure and architectural subjects, portraits, landscapes and interiors, predominantly in watercolour.

He should not be confused with the **Benjamin GREEN II (1813-1858),** who was an architectural draughtsman in Newcastle, or with their namesake noticed above.
Published: *A Guide to Pictorial Perspective*, 1851.
Examples: B.M.; V.A.M.; Coventry Mus.; Ulster Mus.
Bibliography: *A.J.*, 1877.

GREEN, Charles, R.I.
1840 - 1898 (Hampstead)

An illustrator who also painted genre subjects in oil and watercolour. He exhibited from 1862 and was elected A.N.W.S. and N.W.S. in 1864 and 1867. He drew for papers such as *Once a Week* and the *Graphic* as well as producing charming book illustrations such as the well-known drawings for *Robin Hood*. He was the brother of H.T. Green (q.v.).
Examples: B.M.; V.A.M.; Cardiff A.G.; Harrogate Mus.; Leicestershire A.G.; Maidstone Mus.
Bibliography: *A.J.*, 1873; 1908. *Studio*, XXXII, 1904.

GREEN, David Gould, R.I.
1854 - 1917 (London)

The brother of N.E. Green (q.v.), he exhibited landscapes from 1873 and was elected R.I. in 1897. He lived in London. The works of the brothers are similar in style.
Published: *Marine Painting in Watercolours*.
Examples: Maidstone Mus.

GREEN, Harriet, Mrs., née Lister

Possibly a relation of T. Lister of Mallam-Waterhouse, Craven, Yorkshire, the friend of Devis. She became a pupil of A. Green (q.v.) and married him in 1796. They made many tours of the Lake District, Scotland and Wales, and their drawings, when unsigned, are very difficult to tell apart. She was particularly fond of mountain scenery and soft light.

GREEN, Henry Towneley, R.I.
1836 - 1899 (London)

The brother of C. Green (q.v.), he started in banking, but soon turned to art. He exhibited from 1855 at the R.A., N.W.S. and elsewhere, and was elected A.N.W.S. and N.W.S. in 1875 and 1879. He worked as an illustrator both in black and white and full watercolour.

His remaining works were sold at Christie's, 13 January 1900.
Examples: V.A.M.

GREEN, J

A painter of birds and fish in the eighteenth century. He may be Amos Green's brother (*see* under A. Green) or possibly **'Johnny GREEN,'** the London dealer and draughtsman who was active between 1749 and 1763. His drawings are heightened with bodycolour.

GREEN, James
1771 (Leytonstone, Essex) - 1834 (Bath)

A portrait painter who was apprenticed to Thomas Martyn, a natural history draughtsman of Great Marlborough Street. He studied at the R.A. Schools and first exhibited at the R.A. in 1792. He was a member and Treasurer of the A.A. In 1805 he married Mary (1776-1845), daughter of William Byrne, the engraver, herself a miniaturist and a member of the A.A. They were the parents of B.R. Green (q.v.). Many of his portraits were engraved. They show careful draughtsmanship although no great flair. He occasionally painted literary, classical and genre scenes in oil and watercolour.
Published: *Poetical Sketches of Scarborough*, 1813.
Examples: B.M.
Bibliography: *Arnold's Mag. of Fine Arts*, May, 1834.

GREEN, Joshua

Painter of Lake District views and landscapes who exhibited in London from 1852 to 1868.
Examples: V.A.M.

GREEN, Nathaniel Everett
1823 - 1899 (St. Albans)

An astronomer and landscape painter who was admitted to the R.A. Schools at the end of 1844 and exhibited from 1854. He was an unsuccessful candidate for the N.W.S. in 1852 and 1858 when living in North London. He painted in Ireland and Madeira, and a great deal in Scotland, contributing illustrations to Queen Victoria's *More Leaves from the Journal of Life in the Highlands*, 1884. His work is pleasant, if lacking in detail, and he is fond of greens.

He was presumably related to the formidable Mary Anne Everett Green, and her husband **George Pycock Everett GREEN (1818-1893)** who painted portraits and landscapes in Wales, and was a musician. They lived at Cottingham, near Hull.
Published: *Hints of Sketching from Nature*, 1871. *Foliage Exercises for the Brush*, 1888. *A Guide to Landscape Animal Drawing*, 1888. *A Guide to Landscape Figure Drawing*, 1891.
Examples: Beecroft A.G., Southend.

GREEN, William
1760 (Manchester) - 1823 (Ambleside)

After briefly assisting a surveyor in North Lancashire and Manchester and studying engraving in London, he went to the Lake District, which provided him with a home and subjects for the rest of his life. His views are generally very much the same, with dejected-looking cows in the foreground and mountains across a lake. The weather for him is always bad, with thick clouds hanging over the lake. Sometimes, though, there is a dramatic flash of steely light, as if between showers. The colours are suitable greys, browns and dull greens.

He published sets of prints in 1808, 1809, 1810 and 1814.

Published: *The Tourists' New Guide...*, 1822.

Examples: B.M.; V.A.M.; Abbot Hall A.G., Kendal; Leeds City A.G.; Wakefield City A.G.

Bibliography: Lancs. & Cheshire Antiquarian Soc., XIV, 1897.

GREENAWAY, Kate, R.I.
1846 (London) - 1901 (London)

The daughter of a wood-engraver, and a cousin of R. Dadd (q.v.), she studied at the Islington School of Art, Heatherley's and the Slade. She first exhibited in 1868 and provided illustrations for the *I.L.N., Little Folks* and other papers. In 1877 she began her profitable association with Edmund Evans (q.v.), the printer and publisher, producing a long series of children's books and, from 1883 to 1897, the famous *Almanacks*. In 1889 she was elected R.I.

Ruskin, a great admirer, thought of her work as 'A Dance of Life'. With their sweetness, apparent naïvety and simplicity of technique, her drawings created a happy world which had never existed, but which nevertheless has become part of our cultural heritage. Their strength is in perfect drawing and in the muted washes of colour, which reinterpret the methods, as well as the modes, of the late eighteenth century. At the end of her career she attempted to go beyond the perfection of her 'petit maître' art, and to paint portraits in oil.

Examples: B.M.; V.A.M.; Ashmolean; City A.G., Manchester; Lady Lever A.G., Port Sunlight; Ulster Mus.

Bibliography: M.H. Spielmann: *K.G.*, 1905. H.M. Cundall: *K.G. Pictures from Originals Presented by Her to John Ruskin...*, 1921. A.C. Moore: *A Century of K.G.*, 1946. R.H. Viguers: *The K.G. Treasury*, 1967. R. Engen: *K.G.*, 1976. *Mag. of Art*, 1902. *A.J.*, 1902. *Gaz. des Beaux Arts*, 1910.

GREENBANK, Arthur

A figure and genre painter working in the 1880s and 1890s. He exhibited from a London address.

GREENE, Mary Charlotte
c.1860 - 1951 (Harston)

She was for several years President of the Cambridge Drawing Society, and exhibited at the R.A. She ran the Harston School and took an active part in village life, and she was a keen horticulturist. One of her one act plays, 'An Afternoon with Blake', was broadcast in 1940. She also published reminiscences and poems, and painted up to her death. Her work is sketchy, and she uses bodycolour.

Examples: Fitzwilliam.

GREEN, William (1760-1823)
Grasmere from Loughrigg Side. *Signed, inscribed and dated 1811 on the reverse, pencil and watercolour, 13¾in. x 19¼in.*

GREENLEES, Robert M   R.S.W.
1820 - 1904

A landscape and domestic painter who was head of the Glasgow School of Art. He was a founder member of the R.S.W. in 1878, as was his daughter G.M. Wylie (q.v.). She both studied and taught at Glasgow, and father and daughter resigned from the School in 1881 over the lack of life classes for lady students.

GREENWOOD, Colin H

A landscape painter who lived in London and exhibited between 1869 and 1881. He painted in North Wales, Lancashire, Scotland and the Southern counties.

An **F. GREENWOOD** was painting competent landscapes in the 1840s.

GREENWOOD, John, F.S.A.
1727 (Boston, Massachusetts) - 1792 (Margate, Kent)

In 1742 he was apprenticed to Thomas Johnston, a jobbing artist, and began to paint portraits. In 1752 he went to Surinam, where he lived for over five years, taking portraits and sketching flora and fauna. In 1758 he went to Holland to learn mezzotinting and for some time dealt in pictures in Amsterdam. In 1763 he visited Paris, and London, where he settled the following year. He joined the Incorporated

GREENAWAY, Kate (1846-1901)
Six Girls carrying Baskets of Flowers. *Signed with monogram, watercolour, 6in. x 13¾in.*

GRESLEY, Frank (1855-1946)
A Cottage Garden. *Signed, watercolour, 15⅜in. x 22⅜in.*

Society in 1765. In the 1770s he made a number of Continental journeys to buy pictures and he set himself up as an auctioneer in the Haymarket and Leicester Square.
Examples: B.M.

GREGAN, John Edgar
1813 (Dumfries) - 1865 (Manchester)
He studied architecture under Walter Newall and later at Manchester under Thomas Witlam Atkinson, and he practised in Manchester from 1840. He was an enthusiast for art education, and was a supporter of the local art school.

GREGORY, Charles
1810   - 1896
An Isle of Wight ship and yacht portraitist, who also painted more general shipping subjects, occasional landscapes, and even fruity still lifes. He lived at Cowes, and painted for many members of the Royal Yacht Squadron. He was the father of G. Gregory (q.v.).

GREGORY, Charles, R.W.S.
1849 (Surrey) - 1920 (Milford)
A genre and history painter who exhibited from 1873. He was elected A.R.W.S. and R.W.S. in 1882 and 1883, and exhibitions of his work were held in London, Liverpool and Melbourne. He lived at Milford, Surrey.
Examples: Bristol City A.G.
Bibliography: *A.J.,* 1882. *Portfolio,* 1887.

GREGORY, Edward John, R.A., P.R.I.
1850 (Southampton) - 1909 (Great Marlow)
An illustrator, portrait and genre painter in oil

and watercolour, he worked for P. & O. for a time before 1869, when he moved to London on Herkomer's advice. He studied at South Kensington and the R.A. Schools and from 1871 to 1875 worked on the decorations of the V.A.M. He also provided illustrations for the *Graphic.* He was elected A.R.A. and R.A. in 1879 and 1898. In 1882 he visited Italy.
Examples: B.M.; Ashmolean; City A.G., Manchester.
Bibliography: *Gaz. des Beaux Arts,* 1878; 1879. *Portfolio,* 1878; 1883. *A.J.,* 1895; 1897; 1905; 1908; 1909. *Studio,* XXXII, 1904; XLIII, 1908; XLVIII, 1910. *Mag. of Art,* VII, 1884. Maas Gall., London, Exhibition Cat., 1970.

GREGORY, George
1849 (Newport, Isle of Wight) -
1938 (Newport)
A marine painter in oil and watercolour, he was the son of the earlier C. Gregory (q.v.). At the age of seven George's eyesight was damaged in a fire, which made sustained painting difficult.

As well as the shipping about the island, which he painted with love and accuracy, he produced occasional Continental landscapes. Most of his life was spent in East Cowes.

GREGORY, Mary Florence
A landscape painter who exhibited from 1870 to 1874 and lived in St. John's Wood. She worked in the Cotswolds, on the Thames and the South Coast, and she also painted exotic birds.

GREIG, George M   c.1820 (Edinburgh) -
1867 (Edinburgh)
A painter of old Edinburgh interiors. He was a

good draughtsman and exhibited at the R.A. in 1865. He also painted children and seasides.

GREIG, John
A landscape painter and lithographer who was working between 1807 and 1824. He produced a series of prints of Yorkshire antiquities from his own drawings, and contributed to Britton's *Beauties.*
Illustrated: D. Hughson: *Promenades across London,* 1817. J. Hakewill: *Views of London.* F.W.L. Stockdale: *Tours in Cornwall,* 1824.

GRESLEY, Frank
1855 (Derby) - 1946 (Derby)
The son of J.S. Gresley (q.v.), he lived at Chellaston, near Derby, and painted landscapes, particularly on the Trent around Barrow and Ingleby. For his sons, see the following notice.

GRESLEY, James Stephen
1829 (Derby) - 1908
The first of a family of Derby artists and drawing masters, he lived in Derby and then at Bolton Abbey, Yorkshire. He painted landscapes in oil and watercolour and exhibited in London from 1866 to 1883. He illustrated S.T. Hall: *Days in Derbyshire,* 1863.
Cuthbert GRESLEY (1876-1963), who worked for the Porcelain Company, and **Harold GRESLEY (1892-1967),** who taught art at Repton School, were his grandsons, sons of F. Gresley (*vide supra*).
Examples of the family's work can be seen at the Derby A.G.

GRESSE, John Alexander
1741 (London) - 1794 (London)
The son of a Genevese with property in London, 'Fat Jack Grease' began as an engraver under Gerard Scotin and Major. He later worked as an assistant to Cipriani (q.v.), while taking lessons from Zuccarelli (q.v.). Turning to drawing he worked for Boydell. He became a fashionable drawing master, in 1773 being the first recorded at Harrow School, and from 1777 he taught the Princesses. R. Hills (q.v.) was also his pupil.

His style is typical of the neat eighteenth century tinted manner with the colours laid on a basis of grey wash. He also produced miniatures and large gouache landscapes in the tradition of F. Zuccarelli (q.v.).

Gresse Street, W.I. was the property of his family.
Examples: B.M.; V.A.M.

GREVILLE, Hon. Charles Francis
1749   - 1809
The second son of the 1st Earl of Warwick, Greville was a patron and sketching companion of P. Sandby (q.v.). He learnt aquatint engraving – or at least purchased the secret of the process – from Le Prince and in turn taught Sandby.
Examples: B.M.

GREVILLE, Hon. Robert Fulke
1751 - 1824

Groom of the bed chamber to George III. Like his brother the Earl of Warwick (q.v.), he was an amateur watercolourist and a patron of J. 'W'. Smith (q.v.). In 1792 he made a tour of Wales with Smith and J.C. Ibbetson (q.v.). In 1797 he married Louisa, Countess of Mansfield.
Bibliography: R.M. Clay: *Life of J.C. Ibbetson,* 1948.

GREY, Jane Willis, Mrs.

A modest painter of contemporary genre subjects, she exhibited between 1882 and 1896. She lived in London and later at Hayward's Heath.

GREY, Ralph William
c.1746 - 1812

The son of Ralph Grey of Backworth, Northumberland, he was a pupil of A. Cozens (q.v.) at Eton and went on to Trinity, Cambridge. He was later High Sheriff of his county. He was an enthusiastic amateur.

GRIBBLE, Bernard Finegan
1873 (London) - 1962

A marine and portrait painter in oil and watercolour. He was the son of Herbert Gribble, the architect of the Brompton Oratory, and after an education in Bruges he was trained as an architect. However he turned to painting and acted as an artist-correspondent during the Hispano-American War of 1898. He exhibited at the R.A. from 1891 to 1904, as well as at the R.I. and R.H.A., and in Paris in 1907. He lived in London and at Parkstone, Dorset.
Bibliography: *The Artist,* XXVII, 1900.

GRIERSON, Charles MacIver
1864 (Queenstown, Co. Cork) - 1939

A painter of literary and genre subjects in watercolour, pastel and black and white. He was educated in Plymouth, lived in London and was elected R.I. in 1892, but later retired. He had settled in Sligo by 1900.

GRIEVE, Thomas
1799 (London) - 1882 (London)

The son of John Henderson Grieve (1770-1845) and a member of a family of scene painters at Covent Garden. He became principal painter there in 1839 and later moved to Drury Lane. He worked on a number of highly successful panoramas, at first with W. Telbin (q.v.) and J. Absolon (q.v.), and later with his son **Thomas Walford GRIEVE.** 'Grieve & Son' became a hallmark of quality. He occasionally exhibited landscapes at the R.A.
Examples: V.A.M.

GRIEVE, William
1800 (London) - 1844 (London)

The younger brother of T. Grieve (q.v.), he was first employed as a scene painter at Covent Garden Theatre, later moving to Drury Lane and

GRESSE, John Alexander (1741-1794)
Nr. Framlingham. *Pencil, pen and black ink and watercolour, signed and dated 1781, 10in. x 14in.*

the Royal Opera House. The quality of his work was such that he was once given a curtain call.

He painted small landscapes in oil and watercolour.

GRIFFITH, Kate

A still-life painter who exhibited dead and live birds, fruit and flowers from a Hampshire rectory at Suffolk Street and the R.A. between 1879 and 1885. She was the daughter of the Rev. Charles Highman Griffith who was curate of Stratfield Turgiss from 1858 to 1862 and rector thereafter.

GRIFFITH, Moses
1747 (Trygrainhouse, Caernarvonshire) - 1819

Of poor parents, Griffith was self taught as an

GRIFFITH, Moses (1747-1819)
Chester Castle. *Signed and dated 1781 on mount, pen and ink and watercolour, 9in. x 12¾in.*

artist, and from 1769 was employed by Thomas Pennant (1726-1798) as a drawing manservant. He accompanied his master to Scotland in 1769, Cumberland and Yorkshire in 1773, the Isle of Man in 1774, the Midlands in 1776, Yorkshire and Derbyshire in 1777, Staffordshire in about 1780, the Severn Valley in 1783 and Cornwall in 1787. He continued to work for Pennant's son between 1805 and 1813, and may have set himself up as an engraver near Holyhead. 'He was a real primitive, a sort of untaught rustic Sandby' (Williams), producing antiquarian and topographical drawings in the tinted manner.

Several hundred of his drawings were included in the sale of Pennant's Collection at Christie's, 4 July 1938.

Examples: B.M.; V.A.M.; Brighton A.G.; Grosvenor Mus., Chester; Coventry Mus.; Hawarden Co. Record Office, Flintshire; Manx Mus.; Newport A.G.; Staffordshire County Mus.; York A.G.; Nat. Lib. Wales.

Bibliography: T. Pennant: *The Life of Thomas Pennant*, 1793. *Country Life*, 2 July 1938. *Walker's Monthly*, August and September, 1938.

GRIFFITHS, John
1837 (Wales) - 1918 (Norton, Sherbourne)
After studying at the National Art Training School and working on the decoration of the South Kensington Museums, he was appointed first Principal of the Bombay School of Art. He made many studies of Indians, and he exhibited Indian subjects in oil and watercolour at the R.A. from 1869 to 1904.
Examples: V.A.M.

GRIGNION, Charles, Yr.
1752 (London) - 1804 (Leghorn)
The son of the engraver Charles Grignion (1716-1810) he became a portrait and history painter and occasional draughtsman. He studied under Cipriani and at the R.A. Schools from 1769, winning a gold medal in 1776. He went to Rome in 1782 on the R.A. travelling scholarship, and remained in Italy for the rest of his life. He is said to have painted landscapes and Downman-like portraits. His oil paintings show the influence of A. Kauffmann (q.v.).

GRIGGS, Frederick Landseer Maur, R.A.
**1876 (Hitchin, Hertfordshire) -
1938 (Chipping Campden)**
A book illustrator and topographer with a love of medieval architecture. From 1912 he turned increasingly to aquatinting. He was elected A.R.A. and R.A. in 1922 and 1931, and lived at Chipping Campden.
Illustrated: M.P. Milne-House: *Stray Leaves from a Border Garden*, 1901. P.B. Shelley: *The Sensitive Plant*, 1902. E.V. Lucas: *Highways and Byways in Sussex*, 1904. W.F. Rawnsley: *Highways and Byways in Lincolnshire*, 1914. &c.
Examples: B.M.; Hitchin Mus.; Cas. Mus., Nottingham.

GRIMM, Samuel Hieronymus (1733-1794)
Peasants with sheep among ruins. *Watercolour, signed and dated 1770, 7¾in. x 9½in.*

GRIMM, Samuel Hieronymus
**1733 (Bergdorf, Switzerland) -
1794 (London)**
He began as a poet and oil painter in Switzerland, where he was a pupil of J.L. Aberli, occasionally producing watercolour views. In 1765 he moved to Paris, and stayed in France until the beginning of 1768, when he crossed the Channel and made his home in England. In 1766 he had made a sketching tour of Normandy with Philipp Hackert and Nicholas Perignon. In 1768 he contributed to the first exhibition at the R.A., and he later exhibited with the S.A. and the Free Society. In 1776 Gilbert White employed him at Selborne to make drawings for the great *Natural History*. In 1777 he toured Wales with the antiquary Henry Penruddocke Wyndham; later he worked for Cornelius Heathcote Rodes of Barlborough Hall, Derbyshire, Sir William Burrell in Sussex, the Rev. Sir Richard Kaye in Sussex, the Farne Islands and elsewhere, and Richard Gough. He was also well known for caricature drawings, and illustrations to Shakespeare.

Of his methods for topographical work, Gilbert White wrote: 'He first of all sketches his scapes with a lead-pencil; then he pens them all over, as he calls it, with Indian ink, rubbing out the superfluous pencil-strokes; then he gives a charming shading with a brush dipped in Indian ink; and last he throws a light tinge of watercolours over the whole'.
Examples: B.M.; V.A.M.; Ashmolean; Birmingham City A.G.; Brighton A.G.; Canterbury Cathedral Lib.; Derby A.G.; Fitzwilliam; Guildhall; Leeds City A.G.; Usher A.G., Lincoln; N.G., Scotland; Newport A.G.; Taunton Cas.; Ulster Mus.; Weymouth Lib.; Nat. Lib. Wales.
Bibliography: R.M. Clay: *S.H.G.*, 1941.
See Colour Plate

GRIMSHAW, John Atkinson
1836 (Leeds) - 1893 (Leeds)
The painter of moonlit docks and autumn lanes. He was the son of a policeman and worked as a clerk on the G.N.R., teaching himself to paint. In 1858 he married a cousin of T.S. Cooper (q.v.), and became a professional artist. From 1870 he lived at Knostrop Hall, near Leeds, which appears in many of his works. He also lived and worked in Scarborough and Chelsea.

His early work is very much in the Pre-Raphaelite manner, and his rare, jewel-like watercolours usually date from this period. He signed 'J.A. Grimshaw' until about 1867, and he used bodycolour lavishly.
Examples: Leeds City A.G.
Bibliography: G.R. Phillips: *The Biography of A.G.*, 1972. A. Robertson: *A.G.*, 1988. Richard Green Gall., London, Exhibition Cat., 1990.

GRIMSTON, Lady Katherine
c.1810 - 1874
A landscape painter, she was the daughter of the 1st Earl of Verulam and married J. Foster-Barham, M.P. in 1834, and the 4th Earl of Clarendon in 1839.

GRINDLAY, Captain Robert Melville
1786 - 1877
Soldier, artist and founder of the eponymous bank. He went to India as a cadet in 1803 and remained there until 1820. At one time he was ADC to the Governor of Bombay and at another secretary to the committee of embarkation there. He travelled extensively in Western and Central India filling many sketchbooks with accomplished drawings. On his return to England he interested first Ackermann (1826) and then Smith Elder (1830) in a scheme for their publication in aquatint, together with work by other artists such as W. Westall (q.v.). He exhibited an Indian view at the S.B.A. in 1828. Thereafter his business energies were devoted to the bank.

GRISET, Ernest Henry
1844 (France) - 1907
An animal painter and humorist, he settled in London in the 1860s. He worked for the Dalziels and for *Punch* and *Fun*. His style relies on heavy outlines and thin pale colours.
Examples: B.M.; V.A.M.
Bibliography: *A.J.*, XIV, 1898. *Country Life,* 6 Jan. 1977.

GROGAN, Nathaniel
c.1740 (Cork) - 1807
A landscape and humorous painter. He worked under his father, a wood-turner, but his preference for drawing angered the father, and he was obliged to leave home. He joined the Army, and served through the American War and in the West Indies. On returning to Cork he gave drawing lessons, painted landscapes and caricatures of country life, did some house decorating and produced a number of large aquatints. He exhibited with the Free Society in 1782, and may have stayed briefly in London.

Eighteen of his pictures, including a self-portrait, were in the Cork Exhibition of 1852.

Two sons, **Nathaniel GROGAN, Yr and Joseph GROGAN (b.c.1775),** imitated his style; Nathaniel, who worked in Cork, also made copies of his father's pictures. Joseph, of whose work there is an example in the Cork A.G., left Cork for London after 1810.
Examples: B.M.

GROOM, Alfred H
A Londoner who exhibited modestly priced landscapes at Suffolk Street from 1858 to 1870. He worked in Lancashire, North Wales and the Southern counties.

An **Edward GROOM,** also of London, exhibited three genre subjects in 1859 and 1860.

GROSE, Captain Francis (1731-1791)
A South East View of the Inside of the Ruins of Caister Hall, Norfolk, 1775. *Signed, inscribed and dated 1775, pen and black ink and watercolour, 12⅝in. x 20¼in.*

GROOM, Rev. Robert Hindes
1810 (Framlingham) - 1889 (Monk Soham)
The rector of Monk Soham and Archdeacon of Suffolk. He was educated at Norwich and Caius, Cambridge, and he took lessons from H. Bright (q.v.). He travelled in Germany in 1835 and was curate (and once Mayor) of Corfe Castle before succeeding his father at Monk Soham in 1845. He was editor of *The Christian Advocate and Review* from 1861 to 1866 and had many intellectual friends including the poet Edward Fitzgerald.

GROOMBRIDGE, William
1748 (?Goudhurst, Kent) - 1811 (Baltimore)
A painter of miniatures, and small landscapes in both oil and watercolour. He was a pupil of the elder James Lambert (q.v.) and exhibited at the R.A. from 1770 to 1790. He moved from Kent to London around 1776, and perhaps back to Canterbury in 1786. He published a volume of sonnets in 1789, and after periods in Paris, a debtors' prison and perhaps Jamaica, settled in the United States around 1794. There his wife **Catherine Groombridge** (?1760, ?Jamaica - 1837, Jamaica), an amateur watercolourist, ran schools for girls, which appear to have kept them both. Despite his industry – over 123 paintings and drawings are recorded although few have survived with the attribution – he was not successful in the New World. He was one of the founders of the Philadelphia Columbianum, or 'American Academy', in 1795, seems to have worked for a time in New York, and moved to Baltimore in 1804.

He acquired an uncomfortable champion in Eliza Anderson, the vitriolic publisher and editor of the Baltimore *Observer.* Writing as 'Beatrice Ironsides' and comparing him favourably with his fellow English immigrant Francis Guy, she claimed that 'to produce paintings really fine, he needs only to meet with persons sufficiently generous and discerning, to indemnify him for the time and expence the necessary studies would cost him.' Double-edged, indeed.
Examples: Baltimore Mus. of Art; Maryland Hist. Soc.; Pennsylvania Hist. Soc.
Bibliography: J.H. Pleasants: *Four Late Eighteenth Century Anglo-American Landscape Painters,* 1943.

GROOME, William H   C
A landscape and genre painter working from about 1880 until after 1901. He lived in West London and painted in Wales, Sussex and Somerset. He was also an illustrator.

GROSE, Daniel Charles
c.1760 (London) - 1838 (Carrick-on-Shannon)
A topographical draughtsman, and nephew of F. Grose (q.v.), after whose death he completed the drawings for the *Antiquities of Ireland.* He was in the Invalid Artillery, and he wrote legends in verse and prose. His drawings were used to illustrate the *Irish Penny Journal* in 1841.

A painting relative was **Lt. Arthur GROSE.**

GROSE, Captain Francis, F.S.A.
1731 (Greenford, Middlesex) - 1791 (Dublin)
A topographical draughtsman, he was the son of a Swiss jeweller living at Richmond, Surrey. He studied at Shipley's Drawing School, and lived at Wandsworth. From 1755 to 1763 he was Richmond Herald, and was

thereafter Adjutant to the Hampshire and the Surrey Militias. He exhibited architectural views with the Incorporated Society, of which he was a member, in 1767 and 1768, and at the R.A. from 1769 to 1777. He made frequent sketching tours, often with other amateurs, such as J. Nixon (q.v.) or Thomas Pennant and M. Griffith (q.v.) with whom he visited the Isle of Man in 1774. In 1789 he toured Scotland, and he died of an apoplectic fit at Horace Hone's house in Dublin, in the middle of an Irish tour.

His drawing is very weak and conventional, but generally it has charm and pretty colouring. Some works attributed to him may in fact be by his servant, T. Cocking (q.v.). He also produced landscapes entirely in bodycolour.

Published: *Antiquities of England and Wales*, 1773-87. *The Antiquarian Repertory*, 1775. *A Treatise on Ancient Armour and Weapons*, 1786. *Military Antiquities*, 1786-88. *Antiquities of Scotland*, 1789-91. *Antiquities of Ireland*, 1791-95.
Illustrated: J.H. Grose: *Voyage to the East Indies*, 1776. Rev. W. Darrell: *History of Dover Castle*, 1786.
Examples: B.M.; Ashmolean; Brighton A.G.; N.G., Scotland; Portsmouth City Mus.; Ulster Mus.

GROSE, Millicent S
A painter of landscapes and flowers who exhibited at Suffolk Street, and once at the R.A., between 1879 and 1885. In the first year she was living in London; thereafter she gave either the address of her brother, the Rev. Thomas Hodge Grose, at Queen's College Oxford, or Pont Aven in Brittany. In the last year she showed a Cornish subject, having visited St. Ives. She was a member of the Society of Female Artists, and was active at least until 1890.

GROVES, John Thomas
c.1761 (London) - 1811 (London)
An architect who exhibited views of Westminster Abbey at the R.A. in 1778 and 1780. He lived in Italy from 1780 to 1790 and exhibited Italian views on his return. He was Clerk of the Works at St. James's, Whitehall and Westminster from 1794, and architect to the G.P.O. from 1807. He had a wide practice and built the Baths at Tunbridge Wells and the Nelson monument on Portsdown Hill.

GRUBB, William Mortimer
A landscape and domestic painter who taught art at Dundee High School in the 1880s and exhibited from 1890 to 1895.
Published: with A.G. Grubb: *The First Grade Freehand Drawing Book*, 1879.
Examples: Dundee City A.G.

GRUNDY, Sir Cuthbert Cartwright
1846 - 1946
A philanthropist and landscape painter, who was descended from Captain Cook. He was president or vice-president of many art societies, and with his brother donated the Grundy Art Gallery, Blackpool. He was knighted in 1919. The brother, **J.C. GRUNDY (d.1915)** was also a landscape painter and lived in Blackpool.

GRUNDY, Edwin Landseer
1837 - 1898
A Liverpool art critic. He spent a part of his early life at sea, and during the Crimean War took watercolour views of the harbours.

GRUNDY, Robert Hindmarsh
1816 - 1865
A friend and sketching companion of D. Cox (q.v.). He lived in Liverpool and was one of the founders of the Print-Sellers Association.
Examples: V.A.M.

GUEST, Thomas Douglas
1781 -
A portrait, mythological and historical painter who studied at the R.A. Schools, winning a gold medal in 1805, and who exhibited from 1803 to 1839.
Published: *An Inquiry into the Causes of the Decline of Historical Painting*, 1829.
Examples: B.M.

GUILD, James Horsburgh
An Edinburgh landscape and figure painter who was a very occasional exhibitor at the R.S.A. and elsewhere between 1885 and 1932.

GUINNESS, Elizabeth Smyth
1850 - ?1934
A member of the brewing family. She was a painter of figures, flowers and historical genre subjects who lived in London and was active at least until 1900. She studied at Heatherley's and entered the R.A. Schools in 1872.

GUINNESS, Mary Jane Grattan, Mrs. Pitcairn
One of the daughters of Arthur Guinness of Beaumont (1763-1855), she married David Pitcairn, of Torquay, in 1845. She painted views in Ireland, Devonshire and Scotland before and after her marriage. She was active at least from 1842 to 1851, and drew neatly in pencil and coloured washes, sometimes on brown paper.

In 1881 **Constance PITCAIRN (b.1853)**, perhaps her daughter, entered the R.A. Schools.

GULICH, John Percival, R.I.
1865 (Wimbledon) - 1898
A black and white illustrator, etcher and caricaturist who was the son of a City merchant and was educated at Charterhouse. He attended evening classes at Heatherley's, and drew for the *Graphic*. He was elected R.I. in 1897 and died of typhoid.

GUNN, Harriet –
see under **TURNER, Dawson**

GUNSON, J   H
A landscape painter who sketched in North Wales in 1800. He would seem to have been a pupil of J. Baynes (q.v.) who no doubt worked up some of his sketches.

GUTHRIE, Sir James, P.R.S.A., R.H.A., R.S.W.
1859 (Greenock) - 1930 (Row, Dumbartonshire)
A lawyer who turned to painting in 1877 and studied in London and Paris. He was the leader of the Glasgow School. He was elected A.R.S.A. and R.S.A. in 1888 and 1892 and was President from 1902, when he was knighted, until 1919.
Examples: Glasgow A.G.; N.G., Scotland.
Bibliography: Sir J.L. Caw: *Sir J.G.*, 1932. *A.J.*, 1894; 1903; 1909; 1911. *Studio*, LIV, 1912. *Connoisseur*, LXXXVI, 1930. Fine Art Soc.: Exhibition Cat., 1982.

GYFFORD, Edward
1772 - 1856 (Fulham)
A pupil of the architect James Lewis, he entered the R.A. Schools in 1789. He practised as an architect to some extent, his one identifiable work being Bellevue House, Walthamstow, but is best known for his pen, brown ink and wash drawings of the London Thames. He contributed an illustration to Hughson's *London*, 1809.

His son, **Edward A. GYFFORD (or GIFFORD)**, won the R.A. Schools gold medal for architecture in 1837, but turned to painting. He exhibited genre subjects at the R.A. from 1833 to 1870.
Published: *Designs for Elegant Cottages and Small Villas*, 1806.
Examples: B.M.; V.A.M.; R.I.B.A.

GYLES, Henry c.1640 (York) - 1709 (York)
The stained glass painter. He may be said to have revived the art after the ravages of the iconoclasts of the Reformation and Civil War. He worked at Oxford and Cambridge as well as in York and Yorkshire. He was a close friend of F. Place (q.v.), who engraved his portrait in mezzotint, and it is likely that he made drawings in the manner of Place as well as producing enamel and chalk portraits. His declining years were marred by ill-health, discontent and domestic 'dissensions'.

HAAG, Carl, R.W.S.
1820 (Erlangen, Bavaria) - 1915 (Oberwesel)
Haag began his career as a miniaturist and book illustrator in Munich, but in 1846 he left Bavaria with the intention of going to Paris. At the end of a five month stay in Brussels he decided to study English watercolour painting instead, and first visited this country in the spring of 1847. After spending the winter in Rome he returned to London the following year, and it was at this point that he studied in the R.A. Schools. In December 1848 he nearly lost his right hand in an accidental explosion, but it was saved by Sir P. Hewett (q.v.), who became a friend and patron. In 1850 he was elected A.O.W.S., and he became a Member in 1853. He continued to travel widely, returning to Nuremburg in the winter of 1851, visiting Rome and the Tyrol in 1852 and 1853, Dalmatia, Montenegro and Venice in 1854 to 1855, Rome in 1856, Munich in 1857-58, and the Near East with F. Goodall (q.v.) from the autumn of 1858 to 1860. He revisited Egypt in 1873 and Jerusalem in 1890 or 1891. For a while from 1860 to 1903 he maintained studios both at Oberwesel and in Hampstead.

He was always able to attract Royal and aristocratic patrons, and spent the autumn of 1853 at Balmoral and that winter at Windsor.

His style developed from the tight precision of the miniaturist to the greater diffuseness of handling associated with his friend Goodall. His colours in this later period are often so muted that the works are almost in monochrome.

Examples: B.M.; V.A.M.; Blackburn A.G.; Leeds City A.G.; Ulster Mus.

Bibliography: *Portfolio,* 1878; 1882; 1885. *A.J.,* 1883. *Mag. of Art,* 1889. Sotheby's: Sale Cat:, 29 Apr. 1982. Dreweatt Neate: Sale Cat. 6 June, 2000.

HACCOU, Johannes Cornelis
1798 (Middleburg) - 1839 (London)
A marine and moonlight painter in oil and watercolour who was a pupil of J.H. Koekkoek and travelled in Switzerland, France and Germany before settling in London.

Examples: Preston Manor, Brighton.

HACKER, Arthur, R.A., R.I.
1858 (London) -1919 (London)
A portraitist and painter of historical genre, he studied at the R.A. Schools from 1876 and in Paris, and exhibited from 1878. He travelled in North Africa, Spain and Italy. He was elected A.R.A. and R.A. in 1894 and 1910, and R.I. in 1918.

Examples: Greenwich.

Bibliography: *Studio,* XXIX, 1903; XXXII, 1904; XXXVIII, 1906; XLI, 1907; XLIII, 1908; XLIV,

HAAG, Carl (1820-1915)
'A Shepherd of Jerusalem.' *Watercolour, signed and inscribed, 14⅛in. x 9⅞in.*

1908; XLVI, 1909; LXVIII, 1916. *Connoisseur,* XXVIII; XXXVI.

HACKERT, Johann Gottlieb
1744 (Prenzlau) - 1793 (Bath)
A landscape painter who was the son and brother of artists and studied under Le Sueur in Berlin. He visited Italy before coming to England in about 1770.

Examples: Coventry A.G.

HACKSTOUN, William
1855 (Balbreakie, Fife) - 1921 (London)
A landscape and topographical artist who

trained as an architect in Glasgow. His watercolours attracted Ruskin's attention, and in 1876 he began studying under him. He worked largely in Perthshire and Edinburgh and also painted in Kent. In 1896 he was living in London and in 1916 in Glasgow.

Examples: Glasgow A.G.; N.G., Scotland.

HADDON, Arthur Lumley
A landscape painter who lived in London and St. Leonards. He was active at least between 1866 and 1893 and his subjects are often in the Home Counties.

He was a distant cousin of **Arthur Trevor**

HADDON (1864-1941), a pupil at the Slade and under Herkomer (q.v.), who painted landscapes and genre subjects in oil and watercolour. He also studied in Madrid and travelled in the Americas. He lived in London, Cambridge and, for a while, in Rome.

HADEN, Sir Francis Seymour
1818 (London) -
1910 (Woodcote Manor, near Alresford)
A surgeon who took up etching and painting as a hobby. He studied medicine in London and France and was made F.R.C.S. in 1857. He was a founder member of the R.P.E. in 1880 and was knighted in 1894. His wife was Whistler's half-sister. He was an ardent campaigner against cremation.
Examples: B.M.; V.A.M.

HADLEY, J
A landscape painter, probably amateur, who was working in the southern counties from about 1730 to 1758.
Examples: V.A.M.
Bibliography: *Magazine of Art*, II, 1904.

HADLEY, W   H
A landscape painter in watercolour and oil. He lived in Liverpool and exhibited in London during the 1870s.

HAFFIELD, Cooper   - 1821
An amateur draughtsman and painter who worked as a clerk in his father's auditing office in Dublin. He had a keen interest in natural history.

HAGARTY, Mary S
c.1860 (Canada)   - 1938
A painter of farms and landscapes who was active from 1882 and exhibited in London from 1885. She lived in Liverpool, Egremont, Seacombe and finally London again from 1896. She was noted for her plough horses and her shimmering light.

HAGARTY, Parker
1859 (Canada) - 1934
The brother of M.S. Hagarty (q.v.), he was a landscape and figure painter in oil and watercolour. He lived in Liverpool and Cardiff.

HAGHE, Louis, P.R.I.
1806 (Tournai, Belgium) - 1885 (London)
A sound lithographer and rather indifferent watercolourist, Haghe studied printing at Tournai under the Chevalier de la Barrière and J.P. de Jonghe, and then, moving to London in 1823, formed a partnership with William Day the publisher. His most important lithographic work was David Robert's *Holy Land*. In 1852, however, he gave up printing and resigned from the firm. He became a member of the N.W.S. in 1835 and was its President from 1873 to 1884. He travelled much on the Continent, especially in Belgium, Germany and Northern France, and in 1853 was in Rome with Roberts. His work is much in the manner of Cattermole, but where Cattermole is happy to sketch, and hint at details, Haghe is infinitely conscientious, and this can give his work a less lively effect. Owing to a deformed right hand, he painted entirely with the left.
His brother **Charles HAGHE (d.1888)** was also a lithographer and worked with him.
Published: *Travels through Sicily*, 1827. *Sketches in Belgium and Germany*, 1840.
Examples: B.M.; V.A.M.; Bethnal Green Mus.; Blackburn A.G.; Glasgow A.G.; Abbot Hall A.G.; Kendal; Leicestershire A.G.; City A.G., Manchester; Newport A.G.; Sydney A.G.; Ulster Mus.
Bibliography: *A.J.*, Jan. 1859.

HAGREEN, Henry Browne
c.1831   - 1912 (Putney)
An architectural draughtsman who taught at the National Art Training Schools for forty-six years, and who exhibited at the R.A. between 1883 and 1885.
Examples: V.A.M.
Bibliography: *Daily Telegraph*, 10 Dec. 1912.

HAGUE, Joshua Anderson, R.I.
1850 (Manchester) - 1916 (Deganwy)
A landscape painter who lived in Stockport, exhibited from 1873 and was elected R.I. in 1889.
An exhibition of his work was held at the Dowdeswell Gallery, London, in 1891.

HAIG, Axel Herman, né Hägg
1835 (Katthamra, Gotland) -
1921 (Haslemere)
An architectural draughtsman and etcher, he studied naval architecture at Carlskrona and worked for a shipbuilder in Glasgow before moving to London and ecclesiastical work. He painted churches in many parts of Britain and the Continent as well as making designs for interiors. For the last thirty years of his life he concentrated on etching. He revisited Sweden each year.
Bibliography: E.A. Armstrong: *A.H.H. and his Work*, 1905. J.M. Crook and C. Lennox-Boyd, *A.H.H.*, 1984. *A.J.*, 1892. *American Art News*, 1921.

HAILEY, George
A painter who was working in London in 1851 and 1866. He used white heightening and painted town views.

HAINES, George –
see under **PAYNE, William**

HAINES, William
1778 (Bedhampton, Hampshire) -
1848 (East Brixton)
A painter of miniatures and watercolour portraits who was educated at Midhurst Grammar School and studied under the engraver Thaw. He visited the Cape in about 1800, returning to England some five years later by way of Philadelphia. He exhibited from 1808 to 1840 when he retired on an inheritance.

HAINES, William Henry
1812 (London) - 1884 (London)
A painter and copyist in oil and watercolour, who worked as a picture restorer until 1856. Thereafter he turned to painting full time. He had a few lessons from A. Stewart, a miniaturist. He painted landscapes, London scenes and genre subjects as well as copies of Guardi and Canaletto. He sometimes used the name 'William Henry'.
Examples: V.A.M.

HAIR, Thomas Henry
1810 (Scotswood, nr. Newcastle) - 1882
A painter of landscapes and street scenes in the North-East in watercolour and oil. In 1839 he published a series of etchings of coal mines from his own watercolours, and he was working at least as late as 1875.
Examples: B.M.; Newcastle Univ.

HAITÉ, George Charles, R.I.
1855 (Bexley Heath) - 1924 (London)
The son of a designer, he was largely self taught as a landscapist and illustrator. He designed the cover of the *Strand Magazine* and was first President of the London Sketch Club. He exhibited from 1883 and was elected R.I. in 1901. As well as producing English landscapes, he painted in Spain and Morocco.
An exhibition of his work was held at the Modern Gallery, London, in 1907.
Examples: B.M.; Cartwright Hall, Bradford; Cardiff A.G.; Leeds City A.G.; City A.G., Manchester.
Bibliography: *Studio*, XXV, 1902; XXX, 1904.

HAKEWILL, James
1781 (London) - 1843 (London)
Son of **John HAKEWILL (1742 London - 1791 London)** a painter and decorator who had studied at the R.A. Schools and under S. Wale (q.v.), James was trained both as an architect and a painter, entering the R.A. Schools in 1807 (when his age is given as twenty-five, making his birth date 1781, not 1778 as previously recorded) and exhibiting designs at the R.A. In 1816 and 1817 he was in Italy and in 1820 and 1821 in Jamaica. As an architect he worked at High Legh and Tatton in Cheshire. In 1807 he married Maria Catherine Browne (d.1842), who exhibited portraits at the R.A. Their sons Arthur William (1808-1856), Henry James (1813-1834), and Frederick Charles (?b.1811) were respectively an architect, a sculptor and a portraitist.
He made drawings for his own publications, some of which were worked up by Turner, and others.
His brothers **Henry HAKEWILL (1771-1830)** and **George HAKEWILL (1788-1836)** were also artists and architects, although the latter gave up both professions for the army.
Published: *Views in the Neighbourhood of Windsor, &c.*, 1813. *A Picturesque Tour of Italy. A Picturesque Tour in the Island of Jamaica. Plans, sections and elevations of the Abattoirs in Paris*, 1828. &c.

Bibliography: T. Cabberley and L. Herrmann: *Twilight of the Grand Tour, a Cat. of the drawings of J.H. in the British School at Rome*, 1992. *Gentleman's Mag.*, 1843, ii. *Civil Engineer and Architects' Journal*, VI, 1843. *Art History*, V, 1982.

HALE, William Matthew, R.W.S.
1837 (Bristol) - 1929
A landscape and marine painter who was a pupil of J.D. Harding and W. Collingwood Smith (qq.v.). He was elected O.W.S. in 1871 and painted in England, Scotland, Norway and Spain.
Examples: Bristol City A.G.; Cardiff; Dundee City A.G.; Paisley A.G.
Bibliography: W.M. Hale: *The Family of Hale*, 1936.

HALFNIGHT, Richard William
1855 (Sunderland) - 1925 (London)
A Sunderland artist who painted local scenes and Thames views in oil and watercolour. He exhibited at the R.A. from 1884 to 1889 when he was working with H.J.Y. King (q.v.) in London, and later he lived in Newcastle.

HALFPENNY, Joseph
1748 (Bishopsthorpe, Yorkshire) - 1811 (York)
An architectural draughtsman who was apprenticed to a housepainter and later practised in York. He became a drawing master and acted as Clerk of the Works during the restoration of York Minster, making many drawings of the Gothic ornaments. He also made a number of topographical drawings of churches and monuments in Yorkshire.
Published: *Gothic Ornaments in the Cathedral Church of York*, 1795-1800. *Fragmenta Vetusta*, 1807.
Examples: B.M.; V.A.M.; York A.G.

HALFPENNY, J.S. – *see* ALPENNY, J.S.

HALL, Ann Ashley
A painter of Venetian and coastal scenes who lived at Bilston, Staffordshire, and exhibited in Birmingham and at the Society of Female Artists in 1873.

HALL, George Lothian
1825 - 1888 (Wales)
The son of John Hall of Liverpool and Kircudbrightshire, he was educated at Rugby and B.N.C., Oxford. He was in Brazil from 1848 to 1854 and visited Ireland in 1856. Thereafter he lived in London and took up painting, exhibiting landscapes and coastal scenes until 1878. In 1880 he retired to Wales.
Examples: B.M.; V.A.M.; Shipley A.G.; Gateshead; Maidstone Mus.; Melbourne A.G.

HALL, Jessie 1846 - 1915 (Norwich)
A genre painter who lived in Croydon. She was active at least from the 1890s and was a member of the Female Artists.

HALL, John George 1835 - 1921
A City Councillor, painter and decorator at Hull. His watercolours of local scenes are of distinctly higher quality than his oil paintings.
Published: *Notices of Lincolnshire*, 1890. *A History of South Cave*, 1892.
Examples: Library; Guildhall; Wilberforce House, Hull.

HALL, Sydney Prior
1842 (Newmarket) - 1922 (London)
The son and pupil of Harry Hall, a sporting artist, he was educated at Merchant Taylors' School and Pembroke College, Oxford. He also studied with A. Hughes (q.v.) and at the R.A. Schools from 1868. He provided illustrations for the *Graphic*, covering the Prince of Wales' Indian tour and the Franco-Prussian War, and for a number of books, and he also painted portraits and Royal or military occasions in oil and watercolour. His second wife was M.L. Gow (q.v.).
Examples: India Off. Lib. Osborne Ho., I o W.
Bibliography: *A.J.*, 1905.

HALL, William Henry
1812 - 1880
A Birmingham landscape painter in oil and watercolour who was a friend and biographer of D. Cox (q.v.). He was a prolific worker, painting particularly in North Wales and the Lake District. At times he had a London base, and he exhibited in London and Birmingham, although for a few years it is difficult to disentangle him from his son **William Henry HALL, Yr.**, who painted similar subjects and was active from 1874 to 1926.

HALLEWELL, Colonel Edmund Gilling
1822 - 1869
A painter of town views who was commissioned in 1839, served in Canada, Malta and the Crimea, where he was a friend and subject of the photographer Roger Fenton. He was promoted colonel in 1860 and retired from active service in 1864. He was Commandant of Sandhurst in 1869. His home was in Stroud, and he was an unsuccessful candidate for the N.W.S. in 1850 when a captain in the XXth Regiment. He exhibited at the R.A. in 1865. For some reason the V.A.M. catalogue (1927) and Graves give his Christian name as 'Benjamin'.
Examples: V.A.M.
Bibliography: *The Photographic Collector*, date unknown.

HALSWELLE, Keeley, A.R.S.A., R.I.
1832 (Richmond, Surrey) - 1891 (Paris)
Illustrator and landscape painter. His career began with drawings for the *I.L.N.* and continued with book illustrations. He exhibited at the R.S.A. from 1856 and was elected A.R.S.A. in 1865, and R.I. in 1882. From 1869 he spent some years in Italy. At the end of his life he lived near Petersfield and was the

moving spirit of the Primrose League. His work for much of his career was either literary illustration or life drawing. Later he turned to landscapes in the splashy style of the time.
Published: *The Princess Florella and the Knight of the Silver Shield*, 1860. *Six years in a Houseboat*.
Examples: N.G., Ireland; N.G., Scotland.
Bibliography: *A.J.*, 1879; 1884; 1891; 1893. *Portfolio*, 1884. *Mag. of Art*, IV.

HAMERTON, Robert Jacob
1811 (London) -
An Irish book illustrator who taught drawing at the age of fourteen at a school in Longford. He moved to London where he worked as a lithographer for Hullmandel, and exhibited portraits and figure studies in oil and watercolour between 1831 and 1858 at the R.A., the B.I., and the S.B.A., of which he was a member. He worked for *Punch* until 1848, using the name 'Shallaballa' and signing himself with a rebus. Later in his career he was mainly involved in lithography, until in 1891 'the drawings on the huge stones became too much for my old back'.
Illustrated: G. à Beckett: *Comic Blackstone*. J. Forster: *Life of Goldsmith*, 1848.
Examples: B.M.

HAMILTON, Lady Anne
1766 - 1846
The eldest daughter of the 9th Duke of Hamilton, she painted topographical subjects, contributing a view of a Lancashire house to Britton's *Beauties*, 1807. She did not marry. For her sister-in-law Susan, Duchess of Hamilton, *vide infra*.

HAMILTON, Andrew
1815 - 1875 (Cricklewood)
A painter of coastal watercolours who exhibited between 1859 and 1875. He lived in Islington and Cricklewood and painted in South Wales, on the Isle of Wight and at Margate.

HAMILTON, Caroline, Mrs., née Tighe
1777 (Rossana, Co.Wicklow) - 1861
A daughter of William Tighe of Rossana, she was a cousin of one of 'the two ladies of Llangollen', and married Charles Hamilton of Hamwood in 1801. She visited Italy with her mother and sister and on her return to Ireland had lessons from J.I. Spilsbury (q.v.). Later she employed M. Spilsbury, Mrs. Taylor (q.v.), in Dublin. She also studied Hogarth and Le Brun in printed form. Her drawings of domestic and political life in England as well as Ireland are usually in grey and yellowish washes, with strong chiaroscuro, and firm, simple outlines, although sometimes she is more tentative. In 1994 her drawings were all in private hands.

Her sister, **Elizabeth TIGHE**, married the Rev. Thomas Kelly of Kellyville, Queen's County, and was a less talented amateur artist.
Bibliography: Mrs G.H. Bell: *The Hamwood Papers*, 1930.

HAMILTON, Dacre Mervyn
1837 - 1899
A talented amateur painter of landscapes and old buildings, he lived at Cornacassa, Co. Monaghan. He visited France, where he painted in a manner which may owe something to W. Page (q.v.), and he exhibited with the Irish Fine Art Society, a precursor of the Watercolour Society. His daughter was Lady Bangor (q.v.).

HAMILTON, Gustavus
1739 - 1775
The Irish miniaturist and painter of floral watercolours as well as pastel portraits. He studied at the R.D.S. Schools and was apprenticed to S. Dixon (q.v.).

HAMILTON, Hugh Douglas
1740 (Dublin) - 1808 (Dublin)
The portrait painter in pastel and oil, he also occasionally worked in watercolour. He was taught by J. Mannin (q.v.) and at the R.D.S. Schools from 1750 to 1756, and he moved to London after early success in Dublin. He won a Premium at the S.A. in 1765, and he had many eminent sitters. In 1778 he went to Rome, where he concentrated on pastels and oil painting, and he returned to Dublin in 1792.

HAMILTON, James Whitelaw, R.S.A., R.S.W. 1860 (Glasgow) - 1932 (Helensburgh)
A landscape and marine painter in oil and watercolour who was educated in Glasgow and at Helensburgh where he later lived. He was more widely appreciated on the Continent and in America than at home and studied in Paris. He was a member of the 'Munich Secession'. He was elected A.R.S.A. and R.S.A. in 1911 and 1922.
Bibliography: *Studio*, XXIV, 1902; XXXVII, 1906; XLII, 1908; LXII, 1914; LXVI, 1916; LXVIII, 1916; LXXXIII, 1922.

HAMILTON, John
c.1750 (Dublin) - (London)
An Irish amateur draughtsman and etcher who moved to England while young. He exhibited landscapes with the Incorporated Society from 1767 to 1777, being elected a Fellow in 1772, and later Vice-President. He was a close friend of F. Grose (q.v.) and etched most of the plates for his *Ancient Armour and Weapons*, 1786.
Examples: B.M.

HAMILTON, John Guy - 1838 (Inverness)
A drawing master at the Inverness Royal Academy who, despite the disadvantage of having neither fingers nor toes, produced landscapes and portraits in various media. In 1825 he published what was intended to be the first part of a series of lithographs, *Picturesque Delineations of the Highlands*. Hamilton was described as 'a very intellectual man with great charm of manner, and a great favourite with his pupils'. His remaining works were put to auction after the death of his widow in 1843.

HAMILTON, Susan Euphemia, Duchess of
1786 (Switzerland) - 1859
The younger daughter and heiress of William Beckford of Fonthill, she was 'one of the handsomest women of her time' and married the Marquess of Douglas in 1810. He became 10th Duke of Hamilton nine years later, considered himself rightful King of Scotland, and died in 1852. They lived at Hamilton Palace and Brodick Castle, Arran, where they amassed great collections. During her childhood she had come under the influence of A. Cozens (q.v.), but her landscape watercolours seem unadventurous, using a quiet palette on a grey ground.

HAMILTON, Thomas, R.S.A.
1784 (Edinburgh) - 1858 (Edinburgh)
An architect and, according to 'Grecian' Williams, 'a careful and correct draughtsman'. Most of his buildings are in Edinburgh and the Lowlands. He was a founder member of the R.S.A. and was F.R.I.B.A.
His son and pupil, **Peter HAMILTON (d.1861)** was a drawing master at the Birmingham School, but rejoined his father's practice towards the end of his life.
Examples: R.I.B.A.
Bibliography: *Gentleman's Mag.*, 1858, i. *The Builder*, XVI, 1858; XVII 1859. *Book of the Old Edinburgh Club*, XII, 1923. *R.I.A.S. Quarterly*, 20, 1926. Sc. Georgian Soc., 1984.

HAMILTON, Lieutenant Thomas Richard
1758 - 1839 (Hesket Newmarket)
A painter of landscape and plants who painted during an army career and thereafter. He was a pupil of P. Sandby (q.v.) and lived in Cumberland.

HAMILTON, William, R.A.
1751 (Chelsea) - 1801 (London)
His father was an assistant to Robert Adam, who sent William to Rome, where he studied under Zucchi. He returned in 1769 and entered the R.A. Schools. He began to exhibit at the R.A. in 1774. In 1784 he was elected A.R.A., and in 1789 R.A. Until 1789 he concentrated on portraits and afterwards turned to biblical, historical, Shakespearian and poetical subjects. He painted a number of large pictures of this nature for places such as Fonthill Abbey, but was more successful with his small watercolour illustrations of poets including Gray, Milton and Thomson. He worked in a number of different styles but was mostly influenced by Cipriani and Kauffmann. His colour can be rather harsh.
His sister and pupil, **Maria, Lady BELL,** also studied with Reynolds and produced paintings and sculptures. She married Sir Thomas Bell, Sheriff of London, and died in 1825.
Examples: B.M.; V.A.M.; Cecil Higgins A.G., Bedford; Fitzwilliam; Leicestershire A.G.

HAMMERSLEY, James Astbury
1815 (Burslem, Staffordshire) - 1869 (Manchester)
He studied under J.B. Pyne (q.v.). From 1849 until 1862 he was Headmaster of the Manchester School of Design, and he was President of the Manchester Academy of Fine Arts from its foundation in 1857 until 1861. In about 1848 he was commissioned by Prince Albert to paint Rosenau Castle, and also produced other German views in watercolour.
Illustrated: G.R. Dartnell: *The Shipwreck of the...'Premier'*, 1845.

HAMMOND, Colonel
A recorder of landscapes and country houses in southern England who was active around 1800. His style is reminiscent of that of C.F. Annesley (q.v.). He would appear to have been **Francis Thomas HAMMOND,** who joined the army in 1780, and was promoted full colonel in 1802. Eventually he rose to general, and was Lieutenant-Governor of Edinburgh Castle from 1831 to his death in 1850.

HAMMOND, Gertrude Ellen Demain, Mrs. McMurdie, R.I.
1862 (Lambeth) - 1952
An historical and genre painter who exhibited from 1886 and was elected R.I. in 1896. She illustrated Shakespearian and similar editions.
Her sister **Christiana 'Christine' Mary Demain HAMMOND (1860/1 - 1900 Fulham)** painted similar subjects.
Examples: Shipley A.G.; Gateshead; Sydney A.G.

HANBURY, Blanche
A painter of flowers and parklands. She lived in London and exhibited from 1876 to 1887.

HANCOCK, Albany
1806 (Newcastle) - 1873 (Newcastle)
A lawyer until 1832, his passion was for conchology and natural history. He was a prolific artist, painting shells, flowers, fruit and fish, and he was also a modeller. Alone or in collaboration he published some seventy-four scientific works, a number of which he illustrated.

HANCOCK, Charles
1802 (Marlborough) - 1877 (? Medmenham)
The son of a cabinet maker, he became a pupil of J. Stark (q.v.) in London and Norwich. In 1821 he moved to London with a number of his eleven siblings, and they attempted to manufacture a rubber solution to waterproof ships' bottoms. This ended badly, as did later schemes with guttapercha and insulation for underwater cables. Between bankruptcies he relied on painting and illustrating sporting and genre subjects, celebrities and murderers in oil and watercolour, and selling the resultant prints. He was also helped by his wife, a daughter of the vicar of Medmenham. His draughtsmanship is said to have been weak, as was his sight in later years. Another of his

inventions was scentless colours, which he advertised in 1826.

HAND, Thomas   - 1804 (London)
A friend and follower of G. Morland (q.v.). His work is sub-Morland, and his drawing a little like that of P. La Cave (q.v.). He exhibited from 1790.

A **Francis HAND** was working in Brighton at much the same time. He may have been a draughtsman employed by Henry Holland on the Pavilion around 1785.

HANHART, Michael
A painter of landscapes and rustic genre subjects in oil and watercolour. He exhibited from 1870 to 1900. In the 1870s he shared a Hampstead address with **Henry A. HANHART,** who exhibited farm scenes, and he also used an address in Somerset.

HANKEY, William LEE-
1869 (Chester) - 1952 (London)
One of the best of the English Impressionists, he was primarily an oil painter. However, he was a member of the R.I. from 1898 to 1906 and again between 1918 and 1924. He painted both landscapes and genre subjects, and illustrated editions of Goldsmith's *The Deserted Village* and Walton's *Compleat Angler.*
Published: *An Old Garden. At the Well.*
Examples: V.A.M.; Brighton A.G.; Grosvenor Mus., Chester; Dundee City A.G.; Glasgow A.G.; City A.G., Manchester; Newport A.G.; Ulster Mus.

HANN, Walter
A scene painter who lived in London and exhibited between 1859 and 1904. He produced architectural subjects and landscapes including views of Rochester, Pevensey and in Derbyshire, and he also exhibited stage designs.

HANNAFORD, Charles E
1865 (Islington) - 1955
A landscape and marine painter who studied in London and Paris. At the age of seventeen he was articled to Henry Alty, Borough Engineer of Plymouth, and his work brought him to the notice of W. Cook (q.v.). In 1888 he was elected to the Institute of Civil Engineers, after which he turned to architecture, practising in South Wales. He made frequent sketching tours of Devon and Cornwall, and in 1897 he gave up his career and settled in Plymouth. In 1899 he studied with Stanhope Forbes. He held one-man exhibitions at the Walker Gallery in 1910 and 1912 and was much patronised by the Royal Family. A miniature painting by him is in the Queen's Doll's House. Later he lived in London and Norfolk, and he signed with the surname only.
Examples: Exeter Mus.

HANNAN, William
(Scotland) - 1775 (West Wycombe)
A draughtsman and decorator who worked for Sir Francis Dashwood at West Wycombe. His views of the house and grounds were published between 1754 and 1757. He was active from at least 1751, exhibiting views of the Lake District and Cumberland at the Incorporated Society from 1769 to 1772.
Examples: B.M.

HARCOURT, Lady Catherine Julia VERNON- 1811   - 1877 (Uckfield, Sussex)
The eldest daughter and co-heiress of the 3rd Earl of Liverpool, and niece of the Premier 2nd Earl, she was a Lady of the Bedchamber to Queen Victoria's mother the Duchess of Kent. With her sisters, the Ladies Selina and Louisa Jenkinson (qq.v) she was one of the Queen's oldest friends. In 1837 she married one of the Duchess's equerries, **Colonel Francis Venables VERNON-HARCOURT (1801-1880),** the 9th son of the Archbishop of York. Having served in the Coldstream Guards from 1817 to 1846 he was a deputy-lieutenant and M.P. for the Isle of Wight, where he painted watercolours, although much of his work was in oil paint.

From 1838 to 1840 they were in Canada with the regiment, but thereafter they lived at St Clare on the Isle of Wight, where the Queen visited them in 1843. In 1851 she inherited her childhood home, Buxted Park, Sussex, on the death of her father. Lady Catherine visited the Rhine and Switzerland with her sisters in 1829, accompanied the Duchess and Princess Victoria to North Wales in 1833, and painted at the Harcourt seat Nuneham Park, as well as in Canada. There are a number of her watercolours in the Royal collection.

HARCOURT, George Simon, 2nd Earl, F.R.S.   1736   - 1809
M.P. for St. Albans from 1761 to 1768 and Master of the Horse to Queen Charlotte from 1790, he was a pupil, friend and patron of P. Sandby (q.v.), some of whose drawings he etched. He succeeded to the title in 1777, having been Viscount Newnham. From his correspondence it appears that he had already taken lessons from A. Cozens (q.v.), R. Dalton (q.v.) and the pastellist Knapton. He made a Grand Tour in 1775-76. His sister was Lady E. Lee (q.v.).
Published: *Ruins of Stanton Harcourt,* 1763. *An account of the Church…at Stanton Harcourt,* 1808.
Bibliography: *Gentleman's Mag.,* LXXIX, i.

HARCOURT, Mary, Countess of
1749   - 1833
The daughter of the Rev. W. Danby of Swinton, Yorks. sometime rector of Farnley, she married firstly Thomas Lockhart and secondly, in 1778, General William Harcourt, later Field Marshal and 3rd Earl Harcourt (1743-1830). She was a pupil of A. Cozens (q.v.) and her drawings were praised by Horace Walpole. She and Lord Harcourt were close friends of the Royal Family, and she accompanied Princess Caroline, wife of George IV, on her wedding journey to England. She exhibited at the B.I. For the Harcourts' activities in art politics, see Farington's *Diary,* 1978-84.
Examples: Leeds City A.G.

HARDCASTLE, Charlotte
A painter of flowers and dead birds who lived in London and was active at least from 1852 to 1866.

HARDEN, John
1772 (Borrisoleigh, Co. Tipperary) - 1847 (Miller Bridge, Ambleside)
An amateur landscapist and painter of conversation pieces, who, according to Hartley Coleridge, 'had he not been too happy to wish for greatness would himself have been a great painter'. He paid his first visit to England and Wales in 1795 and two years later toured South-West Ireland with G. Holmes (q.v.). In 1798 he visited the Lake District for the first time, with D.B. Murphy (q.v.) and in 1799 the South of England and the Isle of Wight with William Cuming, P.R.H.A. In 1801 he was again in England, and met his future second wife on the return boat from Holyhead. In 1802 he went to Edinburgh to marry her, and in the following year they revisited the Lakes, where they settled in 1804. At Brathay Hall and later at other nearby houses they were at the centre of an artistic and literary circle and were visited by such men as Constable, Farington and W. Havell (qq.v.). Harden revisited Ireland at intervals throughout his life, and from 1809 to 1811 he was in Edinburgh assisting his father-in-law, the proprietor of the *Caledonian Mercury.* In 1829 he and his family made a Grand Tour of the Low Countries, Germany, Switzerland, Italy and France, returning by way of Ireland. The last few years of Harden's life were spent living with his children in Edinburgh and the Lakes. He revisited Ireland for the last time in 1844.

Harden was a very good amateur indeed and, although apparently self taught, he knew how to learn from his professional friends. His earliest known works date from 1797, although it is possible that earlier drawings have been given to other amateurs working in Ireland, such as J. Nixon (q.v.). His work is often on a small scale and he drew in pencil, pen and ink, pen and wash, and full watercolour, sometimes using white heightening and buff or grey paper. His figure drawing is surprisingly good and his sketches from nature have spontaneity, freshness and strong colouring. He often painted into the light, rather in the manner of Wright of Derby (q.v.).

His family, especially his daughter **Jessie, Mrs. CLAY (1814-1908),** were all keen sketchers.

A loan exhibition of a hundred of his drawings was held at the N.G., Scotland in the

HARDING, James Duffield (1797-1863)
Ightham Mote. *Watercolour signed, 17in. x 23in.*

summer of 1939. Another exhibition was held at South London A.G., in January 1952.
Examples: B.M.; Armitt Lib., Ambleside; Burton-on-Trent Gall.; Tullie Ho. Mus., Carlisle; R.I.A.; Abbot Hall A.G., Kendal; N.G., Scotland; Nat. Lib., Scotland.
Bibliography: D. Foskett: *J.H. of Brathay Hall,* 1974. Cork Historical and Archaeological Society, LVIII, 1953; LX, 1955.

HARDIE, Charles Martin, R.S.A.
1858 (East Linton) - 1916 (Edinburgh)
Although almost entirely an oil painter, in his early days he produced a number of landscapes in watercolour. He studied at the R.S.A. Schools, and he was elected A.R.S.A. in 1886 and R.S.A. in 1895.
His nephew was **Martin HARDIE, R.I., Hon. R.W.S., R.S.W. (1875-1952),** the writer on watercolours.
Illustrated: D.M. Moir: *The Life of Mansie Wauch,* 1911.

HARDING, Edward
1755 (Stafford) - 1840 (London)
The brother of S. Harding (q.v.) with whom he went into partnership after an apprenticeship to a barber. He was a sound copyist and also produced original portraits. In 1803 he was appointed Librarian to Queen Charlotte, with whom he was a favourite, and in 1818 to the Duke of Cumberland, later King of Hanover.
One of his nephews, a son of Sylvester, was **Edward HARDING, Yr. (c.1776-1796)** who became an engraver.

HARDING, Edward J
1804 (Cork) - 1870
A portrait painter in oil, watercolour and pen and ink who worked in Cork. He was highly thought of as a miniaturist. Pictures by him were in the Cork Exhibition of 1852.

HARDING, George Perfect
1781   - 1853 (Lambeth)
A son of S. Harding (q.v.), he was a miniaturist and portrait copyist. He exhibited at the R.A. from 1802 to 1840. He published a series of portraits of the Deans of Westminster, 1822-1823, and later worked on a similar series of the Princes of Wales. Between 1840 and 1843 he was involved in the Granger Society, which intended to publish hitherto unengraved historical portraits, and after the Society's collapse published fifteen of them on his own account. He was F.S.A from 1839 to 1847, when he resigned.
Illustrated: T. Moule: *Ancient Oil Paintings and Sepulchral Brasses in the Abbey Church of St. Peter, Westminster,* 1825. J.H. Jesse: *Memoirs of the Court of England during the Reign of the Stuarts,* 1840.
Examples: B.M.; Victoria A.G., Bath; City A.G., Manchester; Newport A.G.

HARDING, James Duffield, O.W.S.
1797 (Deptford) - 1863 (Barnes, Surrey)
He received a good artistic education from his father J. Harding (q.v.), who sent him to Prout for further lessons and apprenticed him to Charles Pye, the engraver. However, disliking engraving, he left after one year and from the age of thirteen exhibited landscapes at the R.A. He was elected

A.O.W.S. in 1820 and a full Member in 1821. He first visited Italy in 1824 and was there again in 1831, 1834 and 1845. He also visited Gibraltar, the Rhine in 1834 and 1837, and Normandy in 1842. He was throughout his life an ardent teacher and a most popular drawing master, J. Ruskin (q.v.) being a pupil.
His pencil and wash drawings are intended for copying and also for the production of lithographs with which he was most at home. He worked for Hullmandel and other publishers, making prints from drawings by Lewis, Bonington, Roberts and Stanfield, as well as from his own works. Harding's pure watercolours tend to show the faults of works produced for engravers. The effects and contrasts are overplayed; there is too much fussy detail and a weakness of composition. Perhaps because of his early difficulty in drawing trees, he was determined to master the technique, and did so so successfully that Ruskin called him 'after Turner, unquestionably the greatest master of foliage in Europe'.
His remaining works were sold at Christie's, 19-20 May 1864.
Published: *Lithographic Drawing Book,* 1832. *Elementary Art, or the Use of the Lead Pencil,* 1834. *Principles and Practice of Art,* 1845. *Lessons on Trees,* 1852. &c.
Examples: B.M.; V.A.M.; Ashmolean; Cartwright Hall, Bradford; Brighton A.G.; Fitzwilliam; Glasgow A.G.; Leeds City A.G.; City A.G., Manchester; Laing A.G., Newcastle; Newport A.G.; Nottingham Univ.; Ulster Mus.
Bibliography: *A.J.,* 1850; Sept. 1856; Feb. 1864. *Portfolio,* 1880. O.W.S. Club XXXVIII, 1963.

HARDING, John c.1777   - 1846
An engraver and drawing master in Deptford, he was a pupil of Sandby and an imitator of Morland (qq.v.). He exhibited at the R.A. between 1800 and 1807, and was the father of J.D. Harding (q.v.).
Examples: B.M.

HARDING, Mary Elizabeth
1861   - 1916 (Birmingham)
A flower, figure and landscape painter who lived in London and visited Italy. She won the Queen's Gold Medal at the Female School of Art in 1881, and exhibited from 1880 until the year of her death.

HARDING, Patty, Mrs., née ROLLS
A pupil of W. Callow (q.v.) and W. Collingwood Smith (q.v.), she married Rev. J.T. Harding, vicar of Rochfield, Monmouth. In Britain she sketched on the Wye, the Thames and the Welsh and Cornish coasts. She also visited Italy and Norway, and she exhibited with the Society of Female Artists.

HARDING, Sylvester
1751 (Newcastle-under-Lyme) -
1809 (London)
At the age of fourteen he ran away from his

uncle's house in London and joined a company of actors. In 1775 he returned to London, entering the R.A. Schools and first exhibiting miniatures at the R.A. the next year. The register of the schools for November 1776 states, presumably on his own authority, that he was '25 5th Augst last', but the *D.N.B.* gives his date of birth as 25 July 1745. From 1786 to about 1797 he and his brother Edward ran a publishing business in Fleet Street and Pall Mall, and issued many prints after his drawings by Bartolozzi, Delatre, Gardiner and others. Thereafter they carried on separately. Like his son G.P. Harding (q.v.), he is best known for his copies of portraits and old masters.

Examples: B.M.; Victoria A.G., Bath; Fitzwilliam.

HARDING, W

An illustrator who worked between 1787 and 1792. The B.M. has drawings for Sterne's *Sentimental Journey* and Thomas Hull's *Sir William Harrington*. They are large and circular with good figures, poor perspective and light washes of colour.

Examples: B.M.

HARDINGE OF LAHORE, Henry, Field Marshal, 1st Viscount
1785 (Wrotham, Kent) - 1856 (South Park, Tunbridge Wells)

An amateur artist who succeeded the Duke of Wellington as General Commanding in Chief of the forces in 1851. He was commissioned as an ensign in 1798, was at the R.M.C., High Wycombe in 1805 and 1806, and served throughout the Peninsular Campaign from 1807, much of it on the staff of the Portuguese Army. He was British military commissioner at Blücher's headquarters in 1815 and lost his left hand when sketching at Quartre Bras. He was an M.P. from 1820 to 1844 and served two terms each as Secretary of War and Irish Secretary in Wellington and Peel's administrations. In 1844 he was appointed Governor General of India, and he travelled out by way of Egypt. He was created Viscount in 1846 as a result of his successes in the Sikh War and retired from India at the beginning of 1848. As Commander-in-Chief he was blamed for the lack of preparedness at the outbreak of the Crimean War.

He drew landscapes in India, France, Belgium, Switzerland, Italy, Spain and Germany as well as in England, Wales and Scotland. An exhibition of his work was held at 23 Park Lane, 23-24 June 1892.

Charles Stuart HARDINGE, the 2nd Viscount (1822 London - 1894 Penshurst), who was educated at Eton and Christ Church and became Under Secretary for War, was also an able landscape painter. He served and painted in the Crimea.

HARDWICK, John Jessop, A.R.W.S.
1831 (Beverley, Yorkshire) - 1917 (Thames Ditton)

Apprenticed to Henry Vizetelly, the engraver and

HARDY, Dudley (1867-1922)
'Return of the Boats, Estaples.' *Watercolour, signed, 13½in. x 19¾in.*

founder of *I.L.N.*, he joined its staff in 1858 as an illustrator, only continuing to work in full colour as a sideline. He exhibited fruit and flower subjects in the manner of Hunt at the R.A. from 1861 to 1915 and also produced landscape drawings. He was elected A.R.W.S. in 1882.

Examples: Reading A.G.

Bibliography: *Studio*, LXX, 1917.

HARDWICK, Philip, R.A., F.S.A.
1792 (London) - 1870 (Wimbledon)

The son of the architect Thomas Hardwick (1752-1829), he was educated at Dr. Barrow's School, Soho, and trained at the R.A. Schools and in his father's office. He exhibited architectural drawings at the R.A. from 1807 to 1814. In 1815 he went to Paris, and he was in Italy in 1818 and 1819. After his return he set up as an independent architect and exhibited Italian views at the R.A. as well as architectural designs. He was elected A.R.A. in 1840 and R.A. the following year. His most important buildings included Euston and Victoria stations and the City Club. His son Philip Charles (1822-1892) succeeded to his business.

Examples: Ulster Mus.

Bibliography: H. Hobhouse in *Seven Victorian Architects* (ed. J. Fawcett), 1976. *Builder*, XXIX, 1871. Inst of Civil Engineers, Minutes, XXXIII, 1871-2.

HARDWICK, William Noble, N.W.S.
1805 - 1865

A landscape painter who was a pupil of J.M.W.

Turner. He was a member of the N.W.S. in 1834 and settled in Bath in 1838. He exhibited from 1829 and worked in the West Country and on the Continent.

Examples: B.M.; V.A.M.; Bath Lib.; Victoria A.G., Bath; City A.G., Manchester; Nat. Mus. Wales.

HARDY, David

A painter of genre subjects in oil and watercolour. He lived in Bath and exhibited from 1855 to 1870.

HARDY, Dudley, R.I.
1867 (Sheffield) - 1922 (London)

The son and pupil of T.B. Hardy (q.v.), he also studied in Düsseldorf, Antwerp and Paris. He exhibited at the R.A. from 1884, and was elected R.I. in 1897. Although best known as an illustrator and cartoonist, he also produced fashion drawings, theatre posters, landscapes, seascapes, biblical and genre subjects and North African and Oriental views in the manner of N.H. Leaver (q.v.).

An exhibition of views taken in Northern France was held at the Continental Gallery, London, in 1902.

Illustrated: Werner: *The Humour of Holland*, 1894. B. Harte: *The Bell Ringer of Angels*, 1897. R. Strong: *Sensations of Paris*, 1912.

Examples: Leeds City A.G.; Leicestershire A.G.; Newport A.G.

Bibliography: A.E. Johnson: *D.H.*, 1909. P.V. Bradshaw: *The Art of the Illustrator*, 1918. *Studio*, VIII, 1896; XXX, 1904; XLVIII, 1910; LVIII, 1913; LXIX, 1917. *A.J.*, 1897.

HARDY, James (1801-1879)
A young boy standing on a beach holding a gun and a dead bird.
Watercolour, signed, 17¾in. x 12¼in.

N.W.S. in 1874 and 1877 and studio sales of his work were held by Christie's, 9 March 1878 and 4 April 1889.
Examples: V.A.M.; Williamson A.G., Birkenhead; Brighton A.G.
Bibliography: *Country Life*, Sept. 1963.

HARDY, Thomas Bush
1842 (Sheffield) - 1897 (London)
A marine painter who went to America in youth and fought for the Union in the Civil War. On returning to Europe he spent some time in France and Holland before exhibiting for the first time in London in 1871. He was an unsuccessful candidate for the N.W.S. on several occasions in the 1870s, but was elected to the R.B.A. in 1884.

His best work is usually on a small scale, sketches of Venice, the Broads or Dutch beaches. Once he had found his well-known formula of sickly yellow-green seas heightened with a knife, and brown knotted ships and rigging, his finished pieces became facile and repetitive.

Three of his eight children, Dudley (q.v.), **Florence HARDY**, an illustrator and miniaturist, and **Frank HARDY**, a sporting artist, followed his profession.
Examples: B.M.; V.A.M.; Haworth A.G., Accrington; Cartwright Hall, Bradford; Brighton A.G.; Dundee City A.G.; Towner Gall., Eastbourne; Greenwich; Gray A.G., Hartlepool; Leeds City A.G.; Leicestershire A.G.; City A.G., Manchester; Newport A.G.; Nottingham Univ.; Portsmouth City Mus.; Sydney A.G.
Bibliography: *Studio*, 1919.

HARDY, Frederick Daniel
1826 (Windsor) - 1911 (Cranbrook, Kent)
A genre painter who began as a musician and was a pupil of T. Webster (q.v.). He lived at Cranbrook from about 1854 as a member of the 'Colony' and was noted for his luminous colours.
Bibliography: *A.J.*, 1875. *Mag. of Art*, 1889. Wolverhampton A.G., Exhibition Cat., 1977. *Country Life*, 24 March 1977.

HARDY, James
1801 (Hounslow) - 1879 (Bath)
A painter of landscapes and old buildings in oil and watercolour who worked in London and, from about 1845, in Bath. His daughter, a still-life painter, married H. Hobson, Yr. (q.v.). His three sons, David Hardy, Heywood Hardy (1842-1933) and J. Hardy, Yr. (q.v.), all became painters.
Examples: Victoria A.G., Bath; Blackburn A.G.

HARDY, James Yr., R.I.
1832 (Brighton) - 1889 (Virginia Water)
A son of J. Hardy (q.v.), he worked in Bristol painting moors and sporting scenes in oil and watercolour. He was elected A.N.W.S. and

HARDY, James Yr. (1832-1889)
'The Day's Bag.' *Pencil and coloured washes, signed and dated '69, 9⅞in. x 14⅛in.*

HARDY, Thomas Bush (1842-1897)
'The Hay Barge.' *Watercolour, signed and dated 1890, 16½in. x 26½in.*

HARDY, W   J
A painter of views on the Clyde and the Yorkshire coast who lived in Brook Green and was active in the 1850s.

HARDY, William Wells
A London flower painter and drawing master who exhibited from 1818 to 1856. He also painted landscapes, often in Surrey.

HARE, Augustus John Cuthbert
1834 (Rome) - 1903 (St. Leonards)
Author of guide books and biographies, illustrator and topographer, he was a kinsman of Sir J. Dean Paul (q.v.) and the Chambers family and was educated at Harrow, privately, and at University College, Oxford. He spent a year in Italy from 1857 to 1858 and wrote his first guide book on his return. He was abroad again for most of the time between 1863 and 1870. Thereafter he lived in St. Leonards, visited country houses and won a reputation as a writer of ghost stories.

His watercolours are often attractive and very competent, and are usually in a free and wet manner.
Published: *Berks, Bucks and Oxfordshire,* 1860. *Handbook to Durham,* 1863. *Walks in Rome,* 1871. *Cities of Northern and Central Italy,* 1876. *Memorials of a Quiet Life,* 1876. *Walks in London,* 1878. *The Story of My Life,* 1896-1900. &c.
Examples: Dundee City A.G.; Leeds City A.G.

HARE, St. George, R.I.
1857 (Limerick) - 1933 (London)
A painter of historical genre subjects, portraits, and above all, of nudes. He studied with N.A. Brophy before going to South Kensington in 1875. His first notable nudes date from 1890, and he was elected R.I. two years later. He also painted in oil and pastel.
Bibliography: *Studio,* XXII, 1901; XXXV, 1905; XXXVIII, 1906; XLIV, 1908; LXVI, 1916. *A.J.,* 1908.

HARFORD, John Scandrett
1785   - 1866
A writer, collector, banker and improving landlord, Harford inherited property near Bristol and in Wales. He made something of a grand tour from 1815 to 1817 during which he bought many old masters. He also visited Italy in 1846 and 1852. He was a deputy-lieutenant

HARDY, Thomas Bush (1842-1897)
The Lagoon, Venice. *Watercolour, signed, 9¾in. x 13¾in.*

HARGITT, Edward (1835 -1895)
On the Spanish Frontier, Pyrenees. *1858. 9½in. x 13¾in.*

for Gloucestershire and Cardiganshire and twice stood for Parliament at Cardigan. He went blind in 1862.
Published: *Life of Michael Angelo Buonarotti*, 1857. *Illustrations of the Genius of M.A. Buonarotti*, 1857.

HARFORD, W
A Londoner who exhibited landscapes and coastal scenes between 1874 and 1878. He worked in Northumberland, the Channel Islands and the Bristol area.
There was also a painting **Alfred HARFORD** in Bristol in the 1880s.

HARGITT, Edward, R.I.
1835 (Edinburgh) - 1895 (London)
A Highland landscape painter, he was a pupil of H. MacCulloch (q.v.). He was elected A.N.W.S. and N.W.S. in 1867 and 1871, by which dates he had moved to London. He visited Ireland, was a keen ornithologist and a good painter of cattle.
His brother, **George F. HARGITT** occasionally painted landscape watercolours.
Examples: V.A.M.; Glasgow A.G.; City A.G., Manchester; Paisley A.G.; Sydney A.G.

HARLE
A drawing master in Durham in about 1803 who gave G.F. Robson (q.v.) his first lessons.

HARLEY, George
1791   - 1871 (London)
A drawing master who worked in many parts of the country and exhibited in London from 1817 to 1865. He painted landscapes and topographical subjects.
Published: *Lessons in Landscape*, 1820-2.

Rudiments of Landscape, 1833. *Guide to Pencil and Chalk Drawing from Landscape*, 1848.
Examples: B.M.; V.A.M.; Newport A.G.
Bibliography: *Studio*, XLIX, 1910.

HARLING, William Owen
1813   - 1879 (Brighton)
A portrait and genre painter who lived in Chester and London, entered the R.A. Schools in 1837 and exhibited in London from 1849 to 1878. In the latter year he showed Italian views.
Bibliography: *A.J.*, 1876.

HARLOW, George Henry
1787 (London) - 1819 (London)
The son of a china merchant, Harlow was educated at Dr. Barrow's, Mr. Roy's in Burlington Street, and at Westminster. He was a pupil of H. de Cort (q.v.) and Samuel Drummond, A.R.A. (q.v.), before spending a year with Sir T. Lawrence (q.v.). He combined a wild social life with hard work and, despite a dislike of the R.A., exhibited there from 1804. He went to Italy in 1818 to study old masters and made a stir both as an artist and as a social lion. He died within a month of his return to England.
Harlow is best known for his portraits in the manner of Lawrence, with an emphasis on eyes and red lips. They are often of actors and were said to be very good likenesses. His history and literary subjects are generally less successful, showing poor composition and draughtsmanship.
His remaining works were sold at Foster's, London, 21 June 1819 and 3 June 1820.
Examples: B.M.; V.A.M.; Ashmolean.
Bibliography: *Annals of the Fine Arts*, IV, xii, 1820.

HARPER, Edward 1813   - c.1880
A barrister who lived in Brighton and York and was a collector and amateur watercolourist. He was a pupil of H. Bright (q.v.), as was his wife. He was working from 1836 to 1879 and should not be confused with **Edward Samuel HARPER (1854-1941)**, a Birmingham man, nor he in turn with the two **Edward Steel HARPERS (1854-c.1920)** and **(1878-1951)**.
Examples: Hove Lib.; Nat. Mus., Wales; York A.G.

HARPER, Henry Andrew
1835 (Blunham, Bedfordshire) -
1900 (Westerham Hill, Kent)
An author and painter of the Holy Land who exhibited from 1858. He accompanied the Earl of Dudley to the Near East, and Agnew held an exhibition of Palestine, Egypt and Nubia in 1872. This did not, however, impress the N.W.S. who rejected his candidacy two years later. Various exhibitions of his work were also held at the Fine Art Society.
Examples: Bridport A.G.; Wallace Coll.

HARPER, John
1809 (nr. Blackburn, Lancashire) -
1842 (Naples)
An architect and brother of E. Harper (q.v.), he studied under Benjamin and Philip Wyatt, helping them with plans for Apsley and York Houses. He practised at York. He had many artist friends including Etty, Roberts and Stanfield (q.v.). He died of malaria during a tour of Italy to study art.
He was a prolific sketcher of landscape and architecture, and was praised by Etty for his 'elegant execution and correct detail'.
Examples: B.M.; Brighton A.G.; Ferens A.G., Hull. Laing A.G., Newcastle; York A.G.

HARPER, Thomas
1820 (nr. Gateshead) - ? 1891
A marine and landscape painter who lived in Newcastle, where he was taught by the elder T.M. Richardson (q.v.). He was an unsuccessful candidate for the N.W.S. in 1850 and exhibited in 1875. His subjects are mostly, but not exclusively, Northern. He was a drawing master.
Examples: Shipley A.G., Gateshead; Laing A.G., Newcastle.

HARPUR, John - *see* **HARPER, John**

HARRADEN, Richard
1756 (London) - 1838 (Cambridge)
An engraver and topographical artist, he worked in Paris for some years before 1789. He then returned to London and, in 1798, he moved to Cambridge. He is best known for his various prints of Cambridge. He was the father of R.B. Harraden (q.v.). His views in the Lake District and Wales can be reminiscent of the work of F. Nicholson (q.v.).
Published: *Six Large Views of Cambridge*, 179-78. *Costume of the Various Orders in the University of*

Cambridge, 1803. With R.B. Harraden: *Cantabrigia Depicta*, 1811.
Examples: B.M.

HARRADEN, Richard Bankes
1778 (?Paris) - 1862 (Cambridge)

The son of R. Harraden (q.v.), he worked in conjunction with his father at Cambridge. He was a member of the S.B.A. from 1824 to 1849. With his father he made a number of prints after Girtin's Parisian views.

Published: With R. Harraden: *Cantabrigia Depicta*, 1811. *Illustrations of the University of Cambridge*, 1830.

Illustrated: Gosham: *The Antiquarian Itinerary*, 1818.

HARRINGTON, Charles
1865 (Brighton) - 1943 (Southwick, Sussex)

A self-taught Sussex landscape painter who was a late exponent of the Cox-Collier tradition. He was educated in Brighton and lived in Lewes. He was killed in an air raid. From 1910 to 1920 he had worked as a furniture salesman. In 1954 Walker's Gallery, London, held an exhibition of his work.

Examples: V.A.M.; Aberdeen A.G.; Darlington A.G.; Fitzwilliam; Towner Gall., Eastbourne; Gloucester City A.G.; Hove Lib.; Newport A.G.; Rochdale A.G.; Sargent Gall., Wanganui, N.Z.

HARRINGTON, Jane, Countess of, née Fleming
- 1824

The wife of the 3rd Earl, whom she married in 1779, she was a daughter of Sir John Fleming, Bt., of Brompton Park. The B.M. has a drawing of a romantic river landscape by her. It is a little in the manner of 'Grecian' Williams (q.v.), but there is chalk on top and the figures are out of proportion.

Her granddaughter-in-law, **Elizabeth STILL, Countess of HARRINGTON** (c.1819-1912), was also a painter. She was the daughter of Robert Lucas de Pearsall of Schloss Wartensee, Switzerland, and she married the future 7th Earl in Paris and 1839.

HARRIOTT, William Henry
c.1790 - 1839 (London)

A War Office clerk who spent several months each year sketching on the Continent. He exhibited from 1811 to 1837 and worked in a number of styles from that of Devis to those of Francia, Cotman and Gothic Prout. This was not a one-way traffic, however, since Cotman, who was a friend, took tracings of many of his compositions and later worked them up for exhibition.

Examples: B.M.; Bridport A.G.
Bibliography: *Portfolio*, 1897.

HARRIS, Daniel c.1761 - 1840

Architect, builder, draughtsman and Keeper of the Oxford County Gaol, which he built largely using the labour of the future inmates. He also supervised the building of the

HARRINGTON, Charles (1865-1943)
'The Hidden Brook.' *Watercolour, signed, 14⅛in. x 25⅛in.*

Abingdon Bridewell and a number of Thames locks using convict labour. He exhibited at the R.A. in 1799 and produced several Oxford drawings in the 1780s and 1790s, including illustrations for the *Oxford Almanack*. He was still working as an architect in 1820.

He was a competent if traditional artist. His figures are elongated and romanticised, his detail unfussy, and there is not too much ruler-work on the architecture. Greys and blues predominate.

Examples: V.A.M.; Ashmolean. Public Record Office.

HARRIS, Henry Hotham
1805 (Birmingham) - 1865

He studied art under W. Rider (q.v.) in Leamington, and his early work attracted the attention of the Duchess of St. Albans. He studied for a time in London, where he exhibited from 1826.

He was one of the founders of the Birmingham Society of Artists, and acted as Secretary from 1852 to 1859.

Examples: City A.G., Birmingham,

HARRIS, James
1810 (Exeter) - 1887 (Reynoldston, Glam.)

A marine painter working in Swansea between 1846 and 1876. He was a son of John Harris, a painter as well as a carver and gilder. In the late 1820s the family moved to Swansea, where Harris met G. Chambers and C. Jones (qq.v.). He was probably a sailor for a while, and later he and his mother ran an artists' materials business. He exhibited twice at the R.A., and he retired from business in 1882.

HARRIS, Sir James Charles
1831 (Genoa) - 1904

Vice-consul at Nice from 1881, then Consul-General to the Principality of Monaco, he was knighted by the Queen when she visited Nice in 1896. He was a landscape painter, naturally concentrating on Riviera views. He was turned down by the N.W.S. in 1869 and the O.W.S. in 1876, but elected Hon. R.I. in 1888, having exhibited in London from 1878.

HARRIS, John
1767 (London) - 1832 (London)

The second son of M. Harris (q.v.), he was brought up at Deptford, which gave him a taste for marine subjects. He was articled to the entomologist Thomas Martyn, whose 'Academy for Illustrating and Painting Natural History' was in Great Marlborough Street. Until about 1789 he also worked for James Edwards, the bookseller in Pall Mall, colouring prints and books. He exhibited landscapes and topographical subjects in watercolour at the Royal Academy from 1797 to 1815. In collaboration with his son, **John HARRIS, Yr.** (1791 - 1873), he published illuminated versions of early statutes and Magna Carta in 1816, and they lithographed a number of portraits of prominent masons in 1825. According to a memoir by the son, tipped in a Bible now at the Houghton Library, Harvard, 'as an Artist in the painting of Subjects of Natural History Viz Insects, Shells &c &c He was I Believe, without a rival,' but it is for the illustrating and ornamenting of books that he is best remembered. This Bible, with over 700 original watercolour

HARRISON, Charles Harmony (1842-1902)
Cows grazing at the end of an estuary. *Watercolour, signed and dated 1876, 21¼in. x 34¼in.*

illustrations, is perhaps his magnum opus.

The son continued to produce prints, including the 1833 lithograph of *The Raising of the Block of Granite which forms the pediment of the Porch for New Bridewell in Tothill Fields.*
Examples: B.M.; Exeter Mus.; Bridewell Lib., Houghton Lib., Harvard. Southern Methodist University, Dallas, Texas.
Bibliography: *The Book Collector*, 42, 1993. J.H. Yr.: *T.L.S.*, Jan. 23, 1919. *Bull. of the John Rylands Lib.*, 52, 1969.

HARRIS, Moses
1731 (London) - c.1785
An entomologist and botanical artist who drew for private patrons, as well as for his book on butterflies and moths. Although the arrangement of the drawings for his plates is rather stilted and naïve, his drawing and colouring is of high quality. He was Secretary of the second Aurelian ('Chrysalis') Society. He was the father of the elder John Harris (q.v.)
Published: *The Aurelian*, 1766. *An Essay preceding a supplement to the Aurelian...*, 1767. *Natural System of Colours*, 1811.
Examples: B.M.

HARRIS, R P
An artist who between 1868 and 1892 sketched in Skye, Corsica, Italy, the Tyrol, the Pyrenees, on the Rhine and the Riviera and at Reigate.

HARRIS, William Edward
1860 (Shropshire) - c.1930
A Birmingham landscape and coastal painter who exhibited there and in London from 1879 to 1900. He painted in Wales, Devon and the Pool of London.
Examples: Birmingham City A.G.

HARRIS, Major Sir William Cornwallis
1807 (Wittersham, Kent) - 1848 (Poona)
A big game hunter who was commissioned into the Bombay Engineers at the age of sixteen. He travelled in Southern Africa from 1836, and was knighted after his expedition to Ethiopia. He illustrated his publications, especially with watercolours of game.
Published: *Portraits of the Game and Wild Animals of Southern Africa*, 1840. *The Highlands of Aethiopia*, 1844.
Bibliography: *Country Life*, 27 August 1987.

HARRISON, Charles Harmony
1842 (Yarmouth, Norfolk) - 1902
A Norfolk artist who was apprenticed to a signwriter and, in 1859, enlisted in the Yarmouth Volunteers. He later joined the Rifle Volunteers, painting in his spare time. His early works were in oil but, on being presented with a box of watercolours in 1870, he turned exclusively to this medium, and soon afterwards made painting his profession, being helped by the commissions he received through Lady Crossley, of Somerleyton. In 1878 he moved to London, where he ran into financial difficulty, and he returned to Norfolk in 1880, making a tour of the Broads with S. Batchelder (q.v.). He exhibited in East Anglia and at the R.I.

He drew his inspiration from the Norfolk landscape, which he loved, and from the great Norwich artists on whom he based his style, and his pictures attained considerable local popularity. Towards the end of his life rheumatism, combined with the increasing financial necessity to sell pictures, lowered the standard of his work.
Examples: Great Yarmouth Lib.
Bibliography: A.H. Patterson and C.H. Smith: *C.H.H.*, 1903. *Country Life*, CLVII, March, 1975.

HARRISON, George Henry, A.O.W.S.
1816 (Liverpool) - 1846 (Paris)
The son of a failed merchant and landowner and of Mary Harrison (q.v.), he came to London when about fourteen and studied anatomy at the Hunterian School. He was advised and encouraged by Constable, and he began to exhibit at the R.A. in 1840 and was elected A.O.W.S. in 1845. He taught both in London and in Paris, where he lived during his last years, mainly through open air sketching classes. His style and subject matter are those of Boys and Bonington (qq.v.) in their Watteauesque moments.
Examples: V.A.M.; Williamson A.G., Birkenhead.
Bibliography: *Art Union*, 1847. *American Art Rev.*, II, 1881.

HARRISON, Harriet
A sister of G.H. Harrison (q.v.), she was a flower painter like her mother and sister. She was an Hon. Member of the Society of Female Artists.

HARRISON, James
Possibly another son of Mary Harrison (q.v.), he exhibited landscapes and architectural subjects at the R.A. from 1827 to 1846. He lived in London until 1881.
Examples: V.A.M.; Bristol City A.G.

HARRISON, Dr. John 1810 - 1896
Doctor to W.J. Müller (q.v.) with whom he often sketched from 1837 in Leigh Woods, Coombe Valley, on the banks of the Frome, Chew and Avon, and at other places in the neighbourhood of Bristol. He attended Müller in his last illness and contributed a memoir of him to *Solly's Life*, 1875.
Examples: Bristol City A.G.

HARRISON, Maria, O.W.S
1822/3 (Liverpool) -
A sister of G.H. Harrison (q.v.), she studied under her mother and in Paris, and became a drawing mistress and flower painter. In February 1847 she was elected a Lady Member of the O.W.S., filling the place of her late brother.

HARRISON, Mary P Mrs., née Rossiter, N.W.S.
1787 (Liverpool) - 1875 (Hampstead)
The daughter of a Stockport hatmaker, she was known as the 'Rose and Primrose painter'. She began painting regularly in France on her honeymoon in 1814, and was the first English lady to be given permission to copy in the Louvre. In about 1830 her husband's business and health collapsed, and they moved from Liverpool to London. She turned to art to support her family, and in 1834 was a founder of the N.W.S., with whom she exhibited flowers, fruit and birds' nests for some forty years, gradually progressing from cut to growing flowers.

Several of her twelve children are separately noticed. Another son, Robert Harrison (1820 - 1897), was Librarian of the London Library.
Examples: *A.J.*, 1876.

HARRISON, William Frederick
1814 (Amiens) -
1880 (Goodwick, nr. Fishguard)
The eldest son of Mary Harrison (q.v.) and brother of G.H. Harrison (q.v.), he showed an early aptitude for painting, although he was never a full-time professional. He worked at the Bank of England for more than forty years, and also exhibited marine subjects at the R.A., the Dudley Gallery and elsewhere.

HART, E   M   M
A landscape painter working in Kent in the 1830s.

HART, Colonel Horatio Holt
1850   - 1915
As the son of the proprietor of Hart's Army List and the younger brother of a V.C., his career was foreordained, and he served in the Royal Engineers. He was commissioned in 1870 and made full colonel in 1899, retiring in 1904. Much of his service was in India, where he saw action in the 1890s, being mentioned in despatches, and he drew landscapes there and elsewhere throughout his career.

HART, James Turpin
1835 (Nottingham) - 1899 (Nottingham)
The son of a cordwainer and lacemaker, he studied at the Nottingham School of Design and at the R.A. Schools from 1859 to 1867, where he was awarded a silver medal and a life studentship. Afterwards he returned to Nottingham, where he built up a portrait practice and taught at the School of Art. He also had a large number of private pupils. He painted many landscapes of rustic scenery in watercolour. A brother was Samuel Hart the musician.
Examples: Castle Mus., Nottingham.

HART, Joseph Laurence
1855   - 1907 (Morfa Nevin, Caernarvon)
A Birmingham landscape painter who worked in Worcestershire and the Isle of Man from 1870 to 1890. He then became a hermit at Morfa Nevin. A book of his poems was published in 1912.

HART, Solomon Alexander, R.A.
1806 (Plymouth) - 1881 (London)
The son of a goldsmith, he was apprenticed to Samuel Warren the engraver and entered the R.A. Schools in 1823. He exhibited from 1826, and was elected A.R.A. and R.A. in 1835 and 1840. He visited Italy in 1841 and 1842 and was Professor of Painting at the R.A. from 1854 to 1863. He painted landscapes, portraits and historical scenes in oil and watercolour.

HART, Joseph Laurence (1855-1907)
'The path through the meadow'. *Watercolour, signed, size unknown.*

Examples: B.M.; V.A.M.
Bibliography: A. Brodie: *Reminiscences of S.A.H.*, 1882. G. Pycroft: *Art in Devonshire*, 1883. *A.J.*, 1881. *Studio*, Spring No., 1916.

HART, Thomas, F.S.A.   - 1886
A coastal painter who lived in Plymouth and Falmouth. He stood unsuccessfully for the N.W.S. in 1862, 1863 and 1864, and exhibited in London from the following year to 1880. He is at his best with wide views of the Cornish coasts and estuaries, but is weak when he includes ships or figures. He was elected F.S.A. in 1856 and served on the council in 1861 and 1862.
There is a watercolour by **Percival HART** in the Newport A.G. He painted in Cornwall and the London docks in the 1890s.
Examples: B.M.; V.A.M.

HART, Thomas Gray
1797 (Fareham, Hampshire) - 1881
An amateur landscape and coastal painter who settled in Southampton in 1825. He was also strongly interested in music and cricket.

HART, William Matthew
1830 (Paisley) - 1908 (United States)
The son of a watercolourist, he was the illustrator of John Gould's last volumes of birds. He worked for Gould from 1851, and especially from 1872, even though he had emigrated to New York in 1853. He liked detail and bright colour, but was not always accurate.
Bibliography: Christie's, Sale Cat., 4 Oct. 1994.

HARTLAND, Henry Albert
1840 (Mallow, Co. Cork) - 1893 (Liverpool)
The son of a landscape gardener, he was

trained in the Cork School of Art. He made drawings for a bookseller, and was a scene painter at the Cork Theatre and the Theatre Royal, Dublin. He first exhibited at the R.H.A. in 1865, and sent landscapes to the Society of Artists in 1868 and the R.A. in 1869. In 1870 he toured Ireland and Wales, and settled in Liverpool, where his landscapes met with considerable success, and where he remained, except for a period in London from 1887 to 1890, a brief stay in Huddersfield and occasional visits to Ireland, for the rest of his life. He was elected to the Liverpool Academy.
Examples: V.A.M.; Williamson A.G., Birkenhead; Blackburn A.G.; Cork A.G.; Greenwich; Walker A.G., Liverpool; Reading A.G.; Ulster Mus.

HARTLEY, Mary c.1740   -
A daughter of the philosopher and physician David Hartley (1705-1757), for whom Hartley Coleridge was named, she was an enthusiastic correspondent of W. Gilpin (q.v.) in the 1780s. She became a most competent amateur watercolourist in his manner. She also drew portraits and architectural subjects and produced a number of prints.

HARTLEY, Thomas
A London painter of portraits, landscapes, topographical and genre subjects in oil and watercolour who was active for some forty years from 1820. He shared the fashionable taste for Italian peasant girls.

HARTRICK, Archibald Standish, R.W.S.
1864 (Bangalore) - 1950 (London)
An illustrator and genre painter who was educated at Fettes and Edinburgh University, and studied at the Slade and in Paris. He was himself a successful teacher and a prolific

magazine illustrator, and he also produced lithographs. He was a fine draughtsman, and he was elected A.R.W.S. and R.W.S. in 1910 and 1920. He married his stepsister Lily Blatherwick (q.v.) in 1896 and moved from London to Gloucestershire.
Published: A *Painter's Pilgrimage through 50 years*, 1939.
Examples: B.M.; V.A.M.; Brighton A.G.; Glasgow A.G.
Bibliography: *Studio*, Special Nos., 1898; 1900; XLIV, 1908; LXI, 1914; LXVII, 1916; Special Nos., 1917; 1919. *Apollo*, XXIV, 1936. O.W.S. Club, XXX.

HARTSHORNE, Rev. Charles Henry
1802   - 1865
An antiquarian author and topographical artist, he was educated at Shrewsbury and St. John's College, Cambridge. He took his B.A. in 1827 and was ordained in the same year. From 1850 until his death he was rector of Holdenby, Northamptonshire, and he was also Domestic Chaplain to the Duke of Bedford and Rural Dean of East Haddon. Among his publications was *A Guide to Alnwick Castle*, 1865, illustrated by P.H. Delamotte (q.v.). He is said to have been 'a very fine watercolour artist. He painted hundreds of sketches of churches and castles'.

HARVEY, Sir George, P.R.S.A.
1806 (St. Ninian's, Perthshire) -
1876 (Edinburgh)
Apprenticed to a Stirling bookseller, Harvey entered the Trustees' Academy in about 1824. He was one of the first A.R.S.A.s in 1826 and became R.S.A. in 1829. He was elected P.R.S.A. in 1864 and knighted in 1867. He painted both figure subjects, notably Covenanting pictures, and landscapes in oil and watercolour.
Published: *Notes on the Early History of the R.S.A.*, 1870.
Illustrated: J. Brown: *Rab and his Friends*, 1876.
Examples: B.M.; N.G., Scotland.
Bibliography: A.L. Simpson: *H's Celebrated Paintings*, 1870. *Recollections of Sir G.H.*, 1880. *A.J.*, 1850; 1858; 1876; 1904. *Portfolio*, 1887.

HARVEY, Lieutenant Henry Wise
c.1798   - 1861
A member of a distinguished naval family, he signed on in 1811, became a midshipman in 1814 and a lieutenant in 1819. Between 1815 and '19 he was on H.M.S. *Antelope*, his uncle's ship, but did not serve at sea thereafter, and went on half-pay in 1854. He used his leisure well, producing impressive marine watercolours.

HARVEY, Robert 1848   - c.1920
A ship's purser who was an accomplished amateur landscape painter. He was living in Glasgow when he exhibited at the Royal Institution in that city, and he painted all around Scotland. His profession took him to many parts of the world including North America, the Caribbean, Australia and China. He also painted in Switzerland, Norway and England. He signed 'R.Harvey, Jnr'.

HARVEY, William
1796 (Newcastle-upon-Tyne) -
1866 (Richmond)
Apprenticed to T. Bewick (q.v.), he went to London in 1817 and became a pupil of B.R. Haydon (q.v.) and studied at the R.A. Schools from 1821. He worked first as a wood-engraver and then as a designer. His style is florid and becomes mannered. His original works in oil and watercolour, which were sometimes engraved by others, are rare and generally on a small scale.
A **Captain William HARVEY** served and drew in the Crimea, and also painted marine subjects.
Illustrated: *Northcote: Fables*, 1828-1833. Lane: *1001 Nights*, 1838-1840. &c.
Examples: B.M.; Fitzwilliam.
Bibliography: *A.J.*, 1866. *Burlington Mag.*, II, 1903.

HARVEY, William Henry, F.R.S.
1811 (Limerick) - 1866 (Dublin)
A Quaker, doctor, colonial Treasurer and naturalist. He was educated in Ireland and spent some years in South Africa up to 1841. In Dublin he was Professor of Botany to the R.D.S. from 1848 and at Trinity from 1856. He travelled around the world between 1853 and 1856. His various botanical publications were illustrated with plates drawn and lithographed by himself.

HASELER, Henry
A topographical and landscape painter who exhibited from 1814 to 1817 and published a series of views of Sidmouth in 1825. He was in Devon in 1817. His work is pretty but weak and can have a feeling of Girtin about it.
Published: Sidmouth Scenery.
Examples: V.A.M.; Exeter Mus.

HASLEHURST, Ernest William, R.I.
1866 (Walthamstow, Essex) - 1949 (London)
A landscape painter and illustrator who was educated in Hastings, at Felstead and at University College, London. He lived in South London, and painted in England and Holland. He was elected R.B.A. in 1911 and R.I. in 1924.
Examples: V.A.M.

HASLEM, John
1808 (Carrington, Cheshire) - 1884 (Derby)
At the age of fourteen he entered the Derby Porcelain Works. In 1835 he moved to London, returning to Derby in 1851, after which date his output was small. He exhibited watercolour portraits at the R.A., R.B.A. and elsewhere, and painted enamel portraits for the Royal Family. He also painted in oil.

Published: *Old Derby China Factory; the Workmen and their Productions*, 1876. *Catalogue of China...the property of Mr. John Haslem of Derby*, 1879.
Examples: Derby A.G.

HASSALL, John, R.I.
1868 (Walmer) - 1948
The poster designer and illustrator. He was educated in Devon and at Heidelberg before farming in Manitoba. In 1891 he turned to art, studying in Antwerp and Paris, and by 1895 his career was set. He adapted the flat tones and thick outlines of the fashionable Japanese prints to form his own popular and successful style. As well as working for magazines, he was an effective illustrator of adventure stories for boys. He was elected R.I. in 1901. A centenary exhibition was held at Leighton House, London, in April 1968.
Examples: V.A.M.
Bibliography: A.E. Johnson: *J.H.*, c.1920. *Mag. of Art*, March 1899. *Studio*, Winter No. 1900-01; XXXVI, 1906.

HASSAM, Alfred
A painter and designer who was working in the middle of the nineteenth century. He produced portraits and visited the Near East. He also wrote *Arabic Self-Taught*, 1897.

HASSELL, Edward   - 1852 (Lancaster)
The son of J. Hassell (q.v.), he was a member of the R.B.A. from 1841 and became its Secretary. He also exhibited at the R.A. and the B.I. As well as for his landscapes and topographical views, he was noted for his Gothic interiors.
Examples: B.M.; V.A.M.; Guildford Mus.; N.G., Ireland; Lambeth Lib.; Merton Lib.; Wandsworth Lib.

HASSELL, John 1767   - 1825
An engraver and drawing master, he was also a prolific author. He produced a biography of his friend George Morland (q.v.), as well as treatises on watercolour painting and a series of elaborate guide books illustrated by aquatints from his own drawings. He exhibited at the R.A. from 1789.
Published: *Tour of the Isle of Wight*, 1790. *Picturesque Guide to Bath*, 1793. *Life of George Morland*, 1806. *Speculum: or the art of Drawing in Watercolours*, 1808. *Aqua Pictura*, 1813. *Picturesque Rides and Walks*, 1817. *The Tour of the Grand Junction Canal*, 1819. *The Camera: or the Art of Drawing in Watercolours*, 1823. *Excursions of Pleasure and Sports on the Thames*, 1823.
Examples: B.M.; Guildford Mus.; Lambeth Lib.; City A.G., Manchester; Merton Lib.

HASTIE, Grace H 1855   - 1930
A landscape, fruit and flower painter who exhibited from 1874 and was a member of the Society of Female Artists. She visited the Channel Islands. Her flower studies are

generally more impressive than her land-scapes.
Examples: B.M.

HASTINGS, Edmund
1781 (Alnwick) - 1861 (Durham)
A portrait and landscape painter who entered the R.A. Schools in 1802 and worked in Durham from 1804 to 1861. He exhibited at the R.A. from 1804 to 1827, and his landscape work can be in the manner of J.S. Cotman (q.v.). Although catalogues differ, Edmund seems to be the correct name.

HASTINGS, Captain Thomas
c.1779 -
An amateur etcher and artist who was the elder brother of E. Hastings (q.v.) and became Collector of Customs at Liverpool, where he was an Associate of the Academy. He was active between 1804 and 1835.
Published: *Vestiges of Antiquity, or a Series of Etchings of Canterbury,* 1813. *Etchings from the Works of Richard Wilson,* 1825. *The British Archer, or Tracts on Archery,* 1831.
Illustrated: Woolnoth: *Canterbury Cathedral,* 1816.

HATHERELL, William, R.I.
1855 (Westbury-on-Trim) - 1928 (London)
A painter of biblical subjects who lived in London and was elected R.I. in 1888. He worked in the City before going to the R.A. Schools in 1878 on the recommendation of E.J. Poynter (q.v.). He became well known as a *Graphic* and book illustrator.
Illustrated: E.J. Bradley: *Annals of Westminster Abbey,* 1895. E.R. Pennell: *Tantallon Castle,* 1895. S.L. Clemens (Mark Twain): *The Prince and the Pauper,* 1923.
Bibliography: P.V. Bradshaw: *The Art of the Illustrator,* 1918. *A.J.,* 1885. *Studio,* LVII, 1913; Special Spring No., 1916.

HATTON, Brian
1887 (Hereford) - 1916 (Oghratina, Egypt)
A child prodigy who by the age of twelve had attracted the attention of Princess Louise (q.v.) and G.F. Watts. He was put through a well-planned course of training, including one year at Oxford and a period at George Harcourt's painting school in Arbroath. He learnt modelling under Professor Lanteri. From 1908 to 1909 he was in Egypt and, in 1910, spent a short time at the Académie Julian in Paris. In 1912 he set himself up in London and began to receive important commissions. However, he joined up on the outbreak of war and was killed in 1916. He was concerned mainly with country figures and horses, and he also executed some portraits in oil.
Examples: B.M.; Brian Hatton Gall., Churchill Mus., Hereford.
Bibliography: C. Davies: *B.H.,* 1978. Hereford Mus.: Exhibition Cat., 1925. *Walker's Quarterly,* 1926. O.W.S. Club, XLVIII, 1973.

HAVELL, William (1782-1857)
Netting salmon. *Watercolour.*

HATTON, Richard George
1865 (Birmingham) - 1926 (Newcastle-upon-Tyne)
A painter of landscapes, portraits and genre subjects in oil and watercolour, he studied at the Birmingham School of Art. In 1890 he became assistant art master at Armstrong College, Newcastle, and, in 1895, Headmaster. In 1912 he was appointed Director of the King Edward VII School of Art and in 1917 Professor of Fine Art. The Hatton Gallery at Newcastle University was named after him.
Published: *Perspective for Art Students,* 1901. *Figure Drawing,* 1905. *The Craftsman's Plant-Book,* 1909. *Principles of Decoration,* 1925.

HAUGH, George 1755 - 1827 (York)
A landscape and portrait painter and a drawing master at York. He and his wife Ann ran a school for twelve young ladies at Hall Cross Hill from 1797. He was an excellent teacher, with a great love of sketching from nature. Among the pupils at the school were M.E. Best (q.v.) and her sister Rosamond. The novelist Barbara Hoole had taught there, and her second husband, T.C. Hofland (q.v.), was one of Haugh's closest friends.
Bibliography: See C. Davidson: *The World of Mary Ellen Best,* 1985.

HAUGHTON, Moses, Yr.
1772 (Wednesbury) - 1849
The nephew of **Moses HAUGHTON (1734 Wednesbury - 1804 Nr. Birmingham),** an enamel and still-life painter, he was a pupil of G. Stubbs (q.v.), and later studied at the R.A.

Schools. He was a friend of Fuseli (q.v.) and is best known as a miniaturist and engraver. He exhibited at the R.A. from 1808 to 1848.

He has sometimes been confused with his cousin, **Matthew HAUGHTON,** son of the elder Moses. Matthew was an engraver and an occasional watercolour painter and caricaturist. He was a lifelong friend of G. Shepheard (q.v.) with whom he enjoyed sparring.
Examples: B.M.

HAVELL, William
1782 (Reading) - 1857 (London)
A landscape painter who, despite his large artistic family, was almost entirely self taught. He made his first sketching tours to Wales and the Wye Valley in 1802 and 1803, meeting the Varleys and Cristall (qq.v.), who became his close friends. In 1805 he was a founder member of the O.W.S. with them. In 1807 he went to the Lake District and lived at Ambleside for more than a year. In 1812 and 1813 he visited Hastings and, between 1813 and 1816, he worked on a large number of small sepia landscapes for various annuals, such as Peacock's *Polite Repository.* In 1816 he sailed for China as artist to Lord Amherst's Embassy, visiting Madeira, Rio de Janeiro, the Cape and Java. It is not certain whether he accompanied Amherst to Peking or remained with the ships. It is also uncertain at which point he left the Embassy, and whether he was on board H.M.S. *Alceste* when she was wrecked. However, he next went to Calcutta and stayed in India for eight years, working as

a watercolour portrait painter. He returned to England in 1827, but, in the following year, went to Italy where he remained, staying with his friend T. Uwins (q.v.) until the spring of 1829. Although he had rejoined the O.W.S. on his first return to England, he finally retired on his second, and thereafter he tried to establish himself as an oil painter.

Havell's best landscapes are of his native Reading and the Thames Valley. They begin much in the manner of Girtin (q.v.) and later can come very close to De Wint (q.v.), especially in the massed forms of the trees. During his Italian stay, he broadened his subject matter to include such themes as peasants bringing in the grape harvest – subjects more usually associated with Uwins.

Examples: V.A.M.; Brighton A.G.; Newport A.G.; Nottingham Univ.; Reading A.G.; Richmond Lib.; Warrington A.G.

Bibliography: O.W.S. Club, XXVI, 1948. *Connoisseur*, Dec. 1949. Reading Mus. Cats., 1970; 1973.

See Havell Family Tree

See Colour Plate

HAVELL FAMILY

The Havells were primarily printmakers, but several of them were also drawing masters and occasional watercolour painters. They included **Charles Richard HAVELL (1827-1892)**; **Edmund HAVELL (1785-1864)**, younger brother of W. Havell (q.v.); and **Edmund HAVELL, Yr. (1819-1894)**.

See Family Tree

HAVERS, Alice Mary, Mrs. Morgan
1850 (Norfolk) - 1890 (London)

Daughter of the manager of the Falkland Islands, she was brought up there and in Montevideo. In 1872 she married Frederick Morgan, an artist, but continued to use her maiden name. She exhibited at the S.B.A. and, from 1873, at the R.A. In 1888-1889 she was in Paris.

She was an illustrator and painter of biblical and genre subjects.

Bibliography: *Portfolio*, 1890. *Art Chronicle*, XX.

HAWES, Captain Arthur Briscoe
1832 - 1897

The youngest son of Sir Benjamin Hawes, K.C.B., M.P., Permanent Under-Secretary for War. He was educated at Westminster from 1846 to 1849, in which year he was commissioned as a cadet in the Bengal Native Infantry. He retired as a captain in 1858. He produced Indian views in pen and wash.

Published: *Rifle Ammunition*, 1859.

Examples: India Office Lib.

HAWKER, J

A landscape painter who exhibited at the R.A. from 1804 to 1809 and contributed to Britton's *Beauties*, 1812.

A **George HAWKER** was painting in Corfu

HAYES, Claude (1852-1922)
'The Boat House, Guildford.' *Watercolour, signed, 6½in. x 9¾in.*

in 1835; and **Joseph HAWKER** exhibited a landscape at the S.B.A. in 1833.

HAWKINS, George Yr.
1809 - 1852 (Camden Town)

An architectural draughtsman and lithographer. He worked for Messrs. Day, and often coloured architects' designs for exhibition at the R.A. His own work is said to be particularly 'correct and delicate'.

His father was presumably the **George HAWKINS (b.c.1778)** who entered the R.A.Schools in 1800.

HAWKSWORTH, William Thomas Martin, R.I. 1853 - 1935 (Herne Bay)

A landscape and marine painter who was educated at King's School, Canterbury, apprenticed to E.W. Pugin the architect, and also became a pupil of Henry Tonks. He worked on the Sussex coast with E.L. Badham (q.v.), and in the West Country, Norfolk and Holland. He was elected R.I. in 1934, and Walker's Gallery, London, showed his work in 1937.

Examples: B.M.; V.A.M.; Glasgow A.G.

Bibliography: *Studio*, Special No., 1919.

HAY, Charles William

The son of a Newcastle schoolmaster, he may have taken lessons from T.M. Richardson (q.v.). He was working as a watercolourist in Newcastle during the 1840s.

Examples: Laing A.G., Newcastle.

HAY, George, R.S.A., R.S.W.
1831 (Edinburgh) - 1912 (Edinburgh)

Painter of figures and costume subjects in oil

and watercolour. He was elected R.S.A. in 1876 and was a founder member of the R.S.W. two years later.

Bibliography: *A.J.*, 1898.

HAY, James Hamilton
1874 (Liverpool) - 1916

The son of a Scottish architect, he himself trained as an architect before studying painting with J. Finnie (q.v.). He painted at St. Ives with Julius Olsson, R.A., and exhibited at the N.E.A.C. and elsewhere. He painted in oil and watercolour, and was an etcher.

Bibliography: *A.J.*, 1905. *Studio*, XXXVII, 1906; LXIII, 1915; LXIV, 1915; LXVI, 1916.

HAY, Thomas Marjoribanks, R.S.W.
1862 (Edinburgh) - 1921 (Edinburgh)

Landscape painter in oil and watercolour, he studied at Edinburgh and exhibited in London from 1885. He designed stained glass early in his career. He was elected R.S.W. in 1895.

Examples: Dundee City A.G.; City A.G., Manchester; N.G., Scotland.

Bibliography: *Studio*, Special No., 1909.

HAY, William

A portrait and miniature painter who also produced landscapes and occasional marine subjects rather in the manner of S. Atkins (q.v.), who exhibited at the R.A. from 1776 to 1797. For the most part he lived in London, but he was in Portsmouth in 1777 and in Bath in 1790.

HAYDON, Benjamin Robert
1786 (Plymouth) - 1846 (London)

The son of a Plymouth bookseller, and

schoolfriend of Prout (q.v.), Haydon is best known as an heroically unsuccessful historical painter in oil. He occasionally made very effective coloured wash drawings as preparatory sketches and memoranda.

His style is neo-classical in the manner of West or a narrower Fuseli (qq.v.). His many pupils included W. Bewick, Sir C. Eastlake, W. Harvey, G. Lance, C., E. and T. Landseer (qq.v.).

Examples: B.M.; Ashmolean; City A.G., Manchester.

Bibliography: T. Taylor: *Life of H.*, 1853. F.W. Haydon: *B.R.H., his Correspondence and Table Talk*, 1876. E. George: *The Life and Death of B.R.H.*, 1948; 1967. C. Olney: *B.R.H. Historical Painter*, 1952. *Art Union*, 1846. *A.J.*, Sept. 1853; June 1856.

HAYES, Claude, R.I.   1852 (Dublin) - 1922 (Brockenhurst, Hampshire)

His father, Edwin Hayes (q.v.), being determined to turn him into a businessman, Hayes ran away to sea. In 1867-1868 he served with the Abyssinian Expedition and then went to the U.S.A. for a year. On his return he became a student at the R.A. Schools, and later studied at Antwerp. He was elected R.I. in 1886.

He belongs to a group of landscape artists, including his brother-in-law W.C. Estall (q.v.), J. Aumonier (q.v.) and E.M. Wimperis (q.v.), whose artistic descent is from Cox and Collier (qq.v.). Like Collier, Hayes was particularly fond of wide stretches of moorland dominated by the sky. He was a very rapid worker but this, combined with ill-health and loss of money towards the end of his career, led to slipshod productions.

Examples: V.A.M.; Brighton A.G.; Towner Gall., Eastbourne; Leeds City A.G.; Newport A.G.; Ulster Mus.; Wakefield A.G.

Bibliography: *Studio*, XXXIII, 1905; Special No., 1909; LXVII, 1916. *Walker's Quarterly*, VII. *W&D*, 1992, ii.

HAYES, Edward, R.H.A.   1797 (Co. Tipperary) - 1864 (Bath)

A portrait painter in watercolour and miniature who studied under J.S. Alpenny (q.v.), and at the R.D.S. Schools. He practised as a miniaturist and taught drawing at Clonmel, Kilkenny and Waterford, before returning to Dublin in 1831 to build up a practice and exhibit at the R.H.A. until 1863. He was elected A.R.H.A. and R.H.A. in 1856 and 1861.

As well as portraits, he painted occasional landscapes in oil and watercolour.

He was the father of M.A. Hayes (q.v.).

Examples: N.G., Ireland.

HAYES, Edwin, R.H.A., R.I.   1820 (Bristol) - 1904 (London)

A marine painter who moved to Dublin at an early age and studied at the R.D.S. Schools. His love of the sea drove him to serve on the

HAYES, Edwin, (1820-1904)
Vessel entering Ostend Harbour. *Watercolour, signed and inscribed on the reverse, 15¼in. x 27¼in.*

crew of a ship bound for America, and on his return he worked for ten years in Dublin, exhibiting at the R.H.A. from 1842. He moved to London in 1852 where he painted scenery at the Adelphi and elsewhere, and exhibited at the B.I., R.A., S.B.A. and the N.W.S., of which he was elected Associate and Member in 1860 and 1863. He continued to exhibit at the R.H.A., and was elected Associate in 1853 and Member in 1871. He visited France, Spain and Italy, but the majority of his subjects were taken from the South coast of England. He has an accurate eye for detail, and is traditional in manner.

He was the father of C. Hayes (q.v.).

Examples: V.A.M.; Bowes Mus., Durham; Cardiff A.G.; Greenwich; Leeds City A.G.; Leicestershire A.G.

Bibliography: VAM: MSS letters to H.M.Cundall. *Studio*, Special no., 1919.

HAYES, Frederick William
1848 (New Ferry, Cheshire) - 1918 (London)

A landscape painter, he was the son of a glassmaker and trained as an architect in Ipswich. However, he then studied painting in Liverpool and, in 1870, moved to London as a pupil of H. Dawson (q.v.). He returned to Liverpool after eighteen months, and was a founder of the local Watercolour Society. He was also a musician, a songwriter and an historical and economic author, illustrating his own books. From 1872 he exhibited at the R.A., and from 1880 he lived in London.

Examples: B.M.; V.A.M.; Glasgow A.G.; Newport A.G.

Bibliography: C.R. Grundy: *F.W.H.*, 1922.

HAYES, George
c. 1823   - 1895 (Gorphwysfa Gyffin)

A Manchester painter in oil and watercolour

who exhibited from 1851 to 1875. He began by painting historical genre subjects and later turned to landscapes in the Cox tradition.

HAYES, John – *see* FLETCHER, Edward

HAYES, Michael Angelo, R.H.A., A.N.W.S.   1820 (Waterford) - 1877 (Dublin)

Best known for his racing and military subjects, he was the son and pupil of Edward Hayes (q.v.). He first exhibited at the R.H.A. in 1837, and in 1842 was appointed Military Painter-in-Ordinary to the Lord Lieutenant. He came to London and exhibited at the R.A. in 1848, in which year he was elected A.N.W.S. On returning to Dublin he became A.R.H.A. and R.H.A. in 1853 and 1854. He was elected Secretary in 1856 and served through a difficult time of schism, being expelled the following year. He was reinstated in 1861 and retired in 1870. He also served as Dublin City Marshal.

His work, in oil and watercolour, includes miniatures, portraits, landscapes and ceremonial pictures.

Published: *The Delineation of Animals in rapid Motion*, 1876.

Illustrated: A.G. Stark: *The South of Ireland*, 1850.

Examples: B.M.; N.G.I.

Bibliography: *A.J.*, 1878. Nat. Army Mus.: *The Costume of the 46th Reg. by M.A.H.*, 1972.

HAYES, William

An ornithological artist working in the second half of the eighteenth century, mainly in the Menagerie at Osterley. In 1794 he was living at Southall, Middlesex, in poor circumstances, having ten surviving children of twenty-one, of whom seven helped with his work.

The plates in his books are etched and carefully coloured by hand, with the subjects

HEAPHY, Thomas (1775 -1835)
A girl contemplating the decline of day. *Watercolour, signed and indistinctly dated, 6⅝in. x 9¾in.*

sometimes chosen rather for the effects of brilliant plumage than scientific interest.
Published: *A Natural History of British Birds &c..,* 1775. *Portraits of Rare and Curious Birds, from the Menagery of Osterly Park,* 1794.
Examples: Ashmolean.

HAYGARTH, Miss
An artist who was working in Italy in 1837. Rather earlier **William HAYGARTH,** active between 1810 and 1816, had produced wash figure studies in Rome.

HAYLLAR, James
        1829 (Chichester) - 1920 (Bournemouth)
An architectural and genre painter who entered the R.A. Schools in 1849. He lived in Surrey until 1898 and thereafter at Bournemouth, and he was active from about 1850 until 1902, when he retired. His daughters Jessica and Kate Mary were prolific oil painters.
Bibliography: *Connoisseur,* Apr.May, 1974.

HAYNES, John
A draughtsman and engraver from York who was active between 1730 and 1750. His engravings appear in Gent's *History of Kingston-upon-Hull,* 1735, and Drake's *Eboracum,* 1736. In the latter one print is credited to P. Monamy (q.v.). However, at least one example bears the handwritten subscription: 'This man Robb'd me. J.Haynes Delint'.
Examples: Burghley House.

HAYNES, Joseph
        1760/1 (Shrewsbury) - 1829 (Chester)
A landscape painter and engraver who was a

pupil of J.H. Mortimer (q.v.) and studied at the R.A. Schools from 1779. At one point he visited Jamaica, but returned to Shrewsbury and then settled as a drawing master in Chester.

HAYWARD, Arthur
        1857 (London) - 1937 (Eggleston)
A cabinet maker at Darlington, whither he moved in 1874, he was also a keen amateur landscape painter.

HAYWARD, John Samuel
        1778   - 1822
The son of a floor cloth manufacturer to whose business he succeeded, he was a friend of J. Cristall (q.v.), from the calico printing works at Old Ford. He helped Cristall to paint a panorama of Constantinople when he first arrived in London, and later worked on panoramas with James de Maria. Although an amateur he was a good watercolourist, exhibiting both figures and landscapes at the R.A. from 1798 to 1816, and acting as Secretary of the Sketching Society 'The Brothers' to which he was elected in 1803. His style after 1800 was closely modelled on that of Cristall in his looser manner, and was influenced by Cotman (q.v.). Previously it had been more old-fashioned, possibly based on that of Grimm (q.v.). He met Girtin (q.v.) in North Wales with Sir G. Beaumont (q.v.) in 1800, and again in Paris the following year. In 1802 he visited Italy, and in 1803 he made a tour of Liverpool, the Lakes, Loch Lomond and Edinburgh. In 1804 he went to Paris from Southampton, returning by way of the Isle of

Wight, which he had previously visited in 1799. In August 1805 he went to Dublin and Leixlip, returning to Liverpool, and in 1807 he was in the West Country and Cornwall where he went down a tin mine. In 1810 he revisited North Wales, and in 1811 he was at Stonehouse. He was in France and Italy again in 1816. He also produced Indian subjects, presumably worked up from the sketches of others.
    There were sales of his collection and library at Christie's, 27 June 1822 and 26-28 February 1823, on the last day of which his own remaining works were sold.
Examples: B.M.
Bibliography: see V.A.M. MSS: P.S. Munn: Letter to J.H., 1803. J.H. Barnes: *The Artistic Life of J.S.H.,* 1922.

HEAD, Major Charles Franklin
        - 1850
Commissioned in 1811, he was promoted captain in 1825 and major in 1833, retiring six years later. He served with the Queen's Royal Regiment in Egypt where he produced good brown wash drawings in the Roberts manner. His *Eastern Scenery* had a serious purpose. It was to 'shew the advantage and practicality of steam navigation from England to India'.
Published:*Eastern Scenery and Ruins &c.,* 1833. *Defence of British India from Russian invasion,* 1839.

HEAD, Guy1753 (Carlisle) - 1800 (London)
A pupil of J.B. Gilpin (q.v.), he studied at the R.A. Schools and first exhibited at the R.A. in 1779. He went to Italy in about 1782 and based himself on Rome, working as a copyist. In 1798 he returned to England with a large collection of drawings and copies, but died before he could put them on exhibition. He was a friend and protégé of Lord Nelson.

HEADLEY, Lorenzo Headley
        1860 (Harborne) -
A landscape and flower painter who was educated and lived in Birmingham and at Stoke Prior, Shropshire. He exhibited in Birmingham and London from 1888, and he visited the Channel Islands.

HEALD, H   Benjamin
        1819 (Nottingham) - 1888 (Nottingham)
A Nottingham lace designer and watercolour painter. Later in life he was connected with Heald and Naylor, Nottingham engravers.
Examples: Castle Mus., Nottingham; Mechanics Institute, Nottingham.

HEAPHY, Thomas
        1775 (London) - 1835 (London)
A descendant of Huguenot silkweavers and noble bastards, he was apprenticed to a dyer but soon transferred to R.M. Meadows the engraver. He spent his evenings at an art school in Finsbury, run by one Simpson. His

earliest exhibited works are portraits, but, to earn more money, he also copied popular prints. At the end of his apprenticeship he became a student at the R.A., but did not take kindly to academic teaching. In 1803 he was appointed portrait painter to the Princess of Wales and in 1806 elected A.O.W.S. He resigned from the Society in 1812. By this time he had largely turned from portraits to subject paintings, and it was with these that he attained his greatest popularity. However, he went to Spain in order to take portraits of the chief officers in the British Army during the Peninsular War. The chalk studies for these are strong and well characterised. Later, he almost abandoned painting for some years and became a property speculator in St. John's Wood. He was among the founders of the S.B.A. and its first President in 1823. He was in Italy in 1831 and 1832.

His early genre scenes were praised for their high finish and the brilliancy and harmony of their colour. On his return to painting he discovered that he had lost much of his former facility.

For his daughters, see Murray, Elizabeth, and Musgrave, Mary Anne.

Examples: B.M.; V.A.M.; Ashmolean; N.G., Scotland.

Bibliography: W.T. Whittley: *T.H.*, 1933. *Antique Collector*, April 1958.

HEAPHY, Thomas, 'Frank'
1813 (London) - 1873 (London)

The son of T. Heaphy, he was a portraitist who also painted genre scenes in oil. His portraits can be very close to those of G. Richmond (q.v.). He spent many years trying to establish the traditional likeness of Christ. He was in Italy with his father in 1831 and 1832, and first exhibited at the R.A. in 1831. He entered the Schools on their return to London. His searches, as well as commissions, led to much Continental travel, his last visit to Rome being in 1860. His middle name of 'Frank' was adopted to distinguish his work from that of his father, but was abandoned before 1850.

His brother, **Charles HEAPHY (1821-1881)**, entered the R.A. schools in 1837, and for much of his career worked as a draughts-man, surveyor and administrator in New Zealand. One of the brothers had a daughter, **Theodosia HEAPHY**, who exhibited figure subjects during the 1880s.

Examples: B.M.

Bibliography: *A.J.*, Oct. 1873. *Athenaeum*, 16 Aug. 1873. O.W.S. Club, XXVI, 1948.

HEARNE, Thomas, F.S.A.
1744 (Brinkworth, nr. Malmesbury) - 1817 (London)

A topographical artist who was apprenticed to W. Woollett (q.v.), the engraver. In 1771 he went to the Leeward Islands with the Governor-General Sir Ralph Payne, and stayed there for three and a half years. He

HEARNE, Thomas (1744-1817)
A scene near Keswick. *Brown wash, 7¼in. x 10½in.*

occasionally made drawings of West Indian subjects after his return, but his Continental scenes appear to be after sketches by other people. His most important work was in conjunction with the engraver William Byrne, with whom he produced *The Antiquities of Great Britain* between 1777 and 1781, and many of the plates for *Britannia Depicta* between 1806 and 1818.

His early works show the influence of P. Sandby (q.v.) and, in his turn, through Dr. Monro (q.v.), who owned many of his drawings, he influenced the early style of Girtin and Turner (qq.v.). He is one of the most successful, and can be one of the most charming, of the eighteenth century topographers. His drawings are frequently in grey wash, and when he uses colour it is never very strong. Often it is merely a warm base of orange or pale coffee. He is very good at suggesting the texture of his surfaces with slight touches. Although he used pencil for his basic outline and occasionally drew in pencil only, in his finished works he goes over these outlines with the brush.

Published: *The Works of T.H.*, 1810.

Examples: B.M.; V.A.M.; Aberdeen A.G.; Ashmolean; Cecil Higgins A.G., Bedford; Coventry A.G.; Bowes Mus., Durham; Fitzwilliam; Greenwich; Leeds City A.G.; Leicestershire A.G.; City A.G., Manchester; Newport A.G.; N.G., Scotland; Ulster Mus.

Bibliography: D. Morris: *H.and his Landscape*, 1989. *A.J.*, 1907.

HEARSEY, Major Hyder Young
1782 (India) - 1840 (Kareli)

A topographer who accompanied Webb to the

source of the Ganges in 1808 and Moorcroft to Tibet in 1812. His work is accurate but rather crude and flat in execution. His career in various armies, including two periods when he was virtually an independent raja, was a most romantic one. He was a son-in-law of the Emperor Akbar Shah.

Examples: India Office Lib.

Bibliography: H.W. Pearse: *The Hearseys: five generations of an Anglo-Indian family,* 1905.

HEATH, Charles 1783/4 - 1848 (London)

An engraver and illustrator, he was the illegitimate son and the pupil of the engraver James Heath. He entered the R.A. Schools in March 1805, when he is stated to have been aged twenty-one, and for a time he was a member of the S.B.A. Later he was best known as the promoter of the *Annuals*. His own work is colourful and in the manner of R. Corbould (q.v.), who was his cousin. King Louis Philippe was an admirer and allowed him to draw at Fontainebleau.

There are examples of the work of **James HEATH (1757-1834),** who was an occasional watercolourist, in Newport A.G.

Examples: B.M.; Castle Mus., Nottingham.

HEATH, William, 'Paul Pry'
1795 (Northumbria) - 1840 (Hampstead)

A portrait, genre and military painter and an engraver. He produced the first caricature magazine in Europe, *The Glasgow Looking Glass*, 1825-6 and provided illustrations for Jenks' *The Military Achievements of Great Britain and her Allies,* and E. Orme's *Historical, Military and Naval Anecdotes.* His

HEMY, Bernard Benedict (c.1855-1913)
Shipping off Sunderland. *Signed, pencil and watercolour, 23in. x 37in.*

work is in the tradition of R. Westall (q.v.), and his figures are drawn with a splendid exaggeration of emotion. He may have seen military service in his early years. After 1834 he gave up caricatures for topography.
Published: *Life of a Soldier*, 1823. *Rustic sketches*, 1824. *Marine studies*, 1824. *A collection of Prints after Paul Potter*.
Illustrated: Sir John Bowring: *Minor Morals*, 1834. &c.
Examples: B.M.; V.A.M.; N.G., Scotland.
Bibliography: *Studio*, Special Spring No., 1916.

HEATHCOTE, Lady Elizabeth Keith, née Lindsay c.1787   - 1825
The elder daughter of the 23rd Earl of Crawford, in 1815 she married R.E. Heathcote, M.P., of Appledale and Longton Halls, Staffordshire. They had one daughter who became a holiday friend of Princess Victoria at Ramsgate in 1822, and Lady Elizabeth sketched the girls at play. She is said to have been a pupil of Gainsborough and was related to Lady Waterford (q.v.), but the charming Ramsgate drawings bring A. Buck (q.v.) to mind.
Bibliography: *The Lady's Realm*, 1897, vol.II, no.8.

**HEATHCOTE, John Moyer
1800   - 1892**
A great-grandson of the 2nd Heathcote Bt., he was educated at Eton and St. John's College, Cambridge, and lived at Connington Castle. He was a patron and pupil of de Wint (q.v.), whose manner he weakly imitated.
His sons **John Moyer HEATHCOTE, Yr.** (1834-1912), the tennis champion, and **Charles Gilbert HEATHCOTE (1841, Conington - 1913)** worked in the same manner. There is an example of the last in the

Brighton A.G. The elder J.M. Heathcote's brothers married sisters of Admiral Sotheby (q.v.), and the family was connected by marriage to Thomas Wright (q.v.) and Cuthbert Bradley (q.v.).
The Evelyn Heathcote who had a show of illustrations to Shelley's *Songs* at the Fine Art Society in 1891 would seem to be a very remote kinsman, the **Rev. Evelyn Dawsonne HEATHCOTE (1844-1908)**, vicar of Sparsholt, Hants.
Examples: B.M.

HEATHER, F   T
A still-life painter working in the 1870s.

HEATON, Edward
A portrait painter working in the 1820s and '30s. He also copied old masters in watercolour.
Examples: V.A.M.

**HEDLEY, Johnson
c.1850 (Gilling, N. Yorks.) - 1914 (Sunderland)**
A confectioner who painted landscapes and genre subjects in oil and watercolour. He joined his brother, R. Hedley (q.v.) on Tyneside in 1880 and exhibited locally.
Examples: Sunderland A.G.

**HEDLEY, Ralph
1848 (Gilling, N. Yorks) - 1913 (Newcastle)**
A genre, landscape and portrait painter in oil and watercolour, he was apprenticed to a wood carver and studied under W.B. Scott (q.v.) and W.C. Way (q.v.). As well as being a successful portrayer of local life he set up a wood and stone carving business.
Examples: Laing A.G., Newcastle.

HEITLAND, Ivy   1875   - 1895
A designer who was the daughter and pupil of H.E. Heitland, an artist. She painted from the age of six and later took lessons from Sir J.D. Linton (q.v.). She painted landscapes and illustrations.
Examples: V.A.M.

HEMING, Matilda – *see* **LOWRY, Matilda**

**HEMSLEY, William
1819 (London) - 1906**
An architect who became a self-taught genre and view painter. He visited Germany and Holland, exhibited from 1848, and became Vice-President of the R.B.A. He was perhaps a son and grandson of the architects Henry Hemsley (c.1764-1808), and Henry Hemsley, yr. (c.1792-1825).
Examples: Ashmolean.
Bibliography: *A.J.*, 1853; 1866.

**HEMY, Bernard Benedict
c.1855 (Newcastle) - 1913 (South Shields)**
The younger brother of C.N. and T.M.M. Hemy (q.v.), he lived at North Shields until 1898 and thereafter at South Shields. He was primarily a marine painter.
Examples: Bootle; Gray A.G., Hartlepool.

**HEMY, Charles Napier, R.A., R.W.S.
1841 (Newcastle) - 1917 (Falmouth)**
The eldest son of a composer, he studied under W.B. Scott (q.v.). In 1852 the family moved to Australia where he worked briefly as a gold miner. On his return to England in the mid-1850s he entered the Ushaw College, Co. Durham, intending to become a priest. After a period working as an apprentice on a collier, he did in fact become a monk, serving for three years in monasteries in Newcastle and Lyons. He left before final vows and took up painting professionally, studying in Antwerp. In 1870 he settled in London, moving to Falmouth some twelve years later. He was elected A.R.W.S. and R.W.S. in 1890 and 1897, A.R.A. and R.A. in 1898 and 1910.
He put all his practical experience into his marine painting, and while his style became broader and more impressionist in the latter part of his career, he never lost his accuracy of detail or his feeling for the wind and sea.
Examples: B.M.; Grundy A.G., Blackpool; Dudley A.G.; Greenwich; City A.G., Manchester; Laing A.G., Newcastle.
Bibliography: *A.J.*, 1881; 1901; 1905; 1907. *Studio*, LXXII, 1918; Special No., 1919.

**HEMY, Thomas Marie Madawaska
1852 (at sea) -
1937 (St. Helens, Isle of Wight)**
The younger brother of C.N. Hemy (q.v.), he was born aboard the *Marie Madawaska* off the Brazilian coast on the way to Australia. On his parents' return to England he was educated at Newcastle and spent much of his youth at sea.

HEMY, Charles Napier, R.A., R.W.S. (1841-1917)
A Spanking Breeze, Falmouth. *Watercolour and bodycolour, signed with initials, dated 1914, 18in. x 26½in.*

At the age of twenty-one he attended the Newcastle Art School under W. Cosens Way (q.v.), and then studied in Antwerp for two years. He worked as a marine painter in Sunderland, later moving to London.
Published: *Deep Sea Days,* 1926.
Bibliography: *The Graphic, Pictures of the Year,* 1914.

HENDERSON, Charles Cooper
1803 (Chertsey) -
1877 (Lower Halliford-on-Thames)
The second son of J. Henderson (q.v.) and a pupil of S. Prout, he was educated at Winchester, and he read for the Bar, but never practised as a lawyer, becoming a prolific sporting and coaching painter. He visited Italy in his youth and etched some landscapes.

He was a skilful painter of horses, and his drawing is generally good. His colours are usually rather thin.
Examples: B.M.; V.A.M.
Bibliography: C. Lane: *C.H. and the Open Road,* 1984. *Country Life,* July, 1972.

HENDERSON, Georgina Jane, Mrs., née Keate 1770 - 1850 (London)
The daughter of G. Keate (q.v.), she exhibited at the S.A. in 1791. She painted a posthumous portrait of Prince Lee Boo for her father's book on the Pellew Islands. She married John Henderson (q.v.) in 1796.

HENDERSON, John 1764 - 1843
A neighbour of Dr. Monro (q.v.) in Adelphi Terrace, he also allowed young artists, including Girtin and Turner (qq.v.), to copy old masters at his house. Later he collected works by de Wint, Cattermole (qq.v.) and others and his collection was left to the nation. He was himself an amateur draughtsman, often working in grey or blue monochrome and the usual 'Monro school' format. His wife was G.J. Henderson (q.v.).

Their elder son, **John HENDERSON, Yr. (1797-1878),** was also a notable collector, patron and amateur artist, and the second son was C.C. Henderson (q.v.).
Examples: B.M.; Fitzwilliam.

HENDERSON, Joseph, R.S.W.
1832 (Stanley, Perthshire) -
1908 (Ballantrae, Ayrshire)
A landscape, portrait, genre and coastal painter who studied at the Trustees' Academy from 1849 to 1853. He then settled in Glasgow, where he was influenced by McTaggart (q.v.). He exhibited in London from 1871 to 1892. His work was mainly in oil, but he was a founder of the R.S.W.

His son, **Joseph Morris HENDERSON (1863-1936),** painted coasts and seascapes.
Bibliography: P. Bate: *The Art of J.H.,* 1908. *A.J.,* 1898.

HENNING, Archibald Samuel
c.1803 (Edinburgh) - 1864
The son, and brother of sculptors, he became painter of literary subjects and portraits who was active from 1825. In 1841 he joined his brother-in-law J.K. Meadows (q.v.) on *Punch,* designing the first cover and drawing the first political cartoons. He left after a year, to work for several short-lived magazines and to illustrate 'natural history' books. Confusingly, he appears to have had a sculpting brother also called Samuel, who died of cholera in 1832.
Illustrated: A.Smith: *The Natural History of the Gent,* 1847; *The Natural History of the Ballet Girl,* 1847; *The Natural History of 'Stuck Up' People,* 1847. Comte Chicard: *The Natural history of the Bal Masqué,* 1849.
Examples: B.M.

HENRY, George, R.A., R.S.A., R.S.W.
1858 (Irvine, Ayrshire) - 1943 (London)
Together with James Guthrie (q.v.) and E.A. Hornel he was a founder of the Glasgow School. He studied at the Glasgow School of Art and later worked with Crawhall, Walton and Guthrie at Brig o' Turk, Roseneath and

HENDERSON, Charles Cooper (1803-1877)
A French coaching scene. *Watercolour, signed with a monogram, 13in. x 19½in.*

HERBERT, Alfred (c.1820-1861)
A collier and a Boulogne fishing boat off Folkestone. *Watercolour, signed, 15¼in. x 26¼in.*

Eyemouth. He shared a studio with Hornel and they visited Japan in 1892. He was elected A.R.S.A. and R.S.A. in 1892 and 1902, and A.R.A. and R.A. in 1907 and 1920.
Examples: Glasgow A.G.
Bibliography: P. Bate: *The Work of G.H.,* 1904. *Studio,* XXIV, 1902; XXXI, 1904; LXVIII, 1910; LXXXIII, 1922. *A.J.,* 1904 1907; 1909. *Scottish Art Review,* n.s. VIII, 1960. Scottish Arts Council, Exhibition Cat., 1978.

HENRY, James Levin
1855 (London) - 1929
A London landscape painter who was educated at University College School and exhibited at the R.A., R.I. and elsewhere from 1877. In 1911 he was painting Swiss views in a wet style.
Bibliography: *Studio,* Special No., 1898; LXIV, 1908. *Athenaeum,* 1920, i.

HENRY, William –
see **HAINES, William Henry**

HENSHALL, John Henry, R.W.S.
1856 (Manchester) - 1928 (Bosham)
A genre and history painter in watercolour and oil. He studied at South Kensington and the R.A. Schools and exhibited from 1879, winning several international medals. He was elected A.R.W.S. in 1883 and R.W.S. in 1897. He lived in Pinner and Bosham, Sussex. His work is often in a very large scale.
Examples: V.A.M.; Cardiff.
Bibliography: *A.J.,* 1894; 1895; 1897.

HENSHAW, Frederick Henry
1807 (Birmingham) - 1891
He was articled to J.V. Barber (q.v.) at the age of fourteen. In 1826 he became a member of the Birmingham Society of Artists and in the same year he went to London and studied the works of the major English landscape painters,

especially Turner. In 1837 he visited the Continent, where he remained for three years, sketching in France, Germany, Switzerland and Italy. In 1841 he returned to Birmingham, where he remained for the rest of his life, making annual sketching tours.

He painted mainly landscapes, with occasional portraits and genre scenes, in oil and watercolour; he exhibited in London and Birmingham from 1829 to 1864.

A loan exhibition of his works was held at Birmingham City A.G. in 1886.
Examples: Birmingham City A.G.
Bibliography: *Portfolio,* 1891. *Art Chron.,* 1891.

HENTON, George Moore
1861 (Leicester) - 1924
A Leicester painter who worked at Eton and in Scotland as well as in his own county. He exhibited church interiors and landscapes at the R.I. from 1884.
Examples: Leicestershire A.G.

HERALD, James Watterson
1859 (Forfar) - 1914 (Arbroath)
The son of a shoemaker, he was educated at Forfar Academy and studied at the art class of the Dundee High School. He was apprenticed to a decorator and worked in a textile mill before becoming an artist. As a landscape, figure and, above all, harbour painter, he was strongly influenced by A. Melville (q.v.), and he also studied at Edinburgh and under Herkomer (q.v.) from 1891. He lived in Croydon and London until 1901, when he returned north to Arbroath, where he eventually died of cirrhosis of the liver. His style is close to Melville and the Glasgow School, as is his preoccupation with light and form. Some of his best works are impressions of the harbour and fishing boats at Arbroath.
Examples: B.M.; V.A.M.; Dundee City A.G.; Glasgow A.G.; Greenock A.G.; Paisley A.G.

HERBERT, Alfred
c.1820 (Southend) - 1861 (Southend)
The son of a Thames waterman, who apprenticed him to a boat builder. He exhibited coastal and fishing scenes and Thames views at the S.B.A. from 1844 and the R.A. from 1847 to 1860.

His style is unoriginal, and he won little popularity during his lifetime.
Examples: V.A.M.; Blackburn A.G.; Grundy A.G., Blackpool; Beecroft A.G., Southend.
Bibliography: *A.J.,* 1861.

HERBERT, Arthur John
1834 - 1856 (Mauriac, Auvergne)
The son and pupil of J.R. Herbert (q.v.), he also studied at the R.A. Schools. He exhibited historical genre subjects at the R.A. in 1855 and 1856, but died of fever before he could make his name.
Examples: V.A.M.
Bibliography: *A.J.,* 1882.

HERBERT, James Dowling
1762/3 (Dublin) - 1837 (Jersey)
An actor and portrait painter, his original surname was Dowling, and Herbert was adopted first for the stage and then permanently. He was at the R.D.S. Schools from 1779 and then studied with R. Home (q.v.). He painted in various media including watercolours, and sought subjects in Dublin, Cork, Bath and London. He also wrote as well as painting stage scenery. His small pencil and watercolour portraits are usually full-length with overlong limbs.

HERBERT, John Rogers, R.A., H.R.I.
1810 (Maldon, Essex) - 1890 (Kilburn)
He studied at the R.A. Schools from 1826 and became one of the first masters at the Government School of Design at Somerset House. He exhibited from 1830 to 1889 and was elected A.R.A. and R.A. in 1841 and 1846, retiring in 1886. He was also an Hon. R.I. He began as a portrait and romantic painter, later producing Italian views and still later after conversion to Roman Catholicism religious subjects.

His son **Cyril Wiseman Rogers HERBERT (1847-1882)** travelled and drew in Iraq and was appointed curator of the Antique School at the R.A. just before his death. Two others sons, A.J. Herbert (q.v.) and Wilfred Vincent Herbert were also oil painters.
Examples: B.M.; V.A.M.
Bibliography: *A.J.,* 1865. *Studio,* Special Spring No., 1916.

HERBERT, Mary, Mrs., née Balfour
1817 (Whittinghame, E. Lothian) - 1893
As the wife of H.A. Herbert of Muckross House, Killarney from 1837, she continued the Herbert traditions of recording and creating picturèsque buildings, and painting and collecting watercolours. According to

Crookshank and Glin, her landscapes 'began as rather fussy studies, are simplified with experience till her late work depicts with real talent the hazy blues and greens of Killarney's unmatchable landscape and lakes'. The Queen, who visited Muckross in 1861, was an admirer.

HERBERT, Sydney
1854 (Worcestershire) - 1914
A landscape and figurative painter in oil and watercolour, he taught at the Cheltenham Ladies' College. He painted in North Wales.

T. HERBERT, who lived in West Malvern, exhibited modest watercolours of British views at Suffolk Street from 1868 to 1870.
Bibliography: *Notes & Queries,* II Series IX, 1914.

HERDMAN, Robert, R.S.A., R.S.W.
1829 (Rattray, Perthshire) - 1888 (Edinburgh)
The youngest son of the minister of Rattray, he went to St. Andrews University, sometimes giving drawing lessons in the vacations. In 1847 he entered the Trustees' Academy, where he gained awards for both drawing and painting. During 1855 and 1856 he spent nearly a year in Italy, which he revisited in 1868 and 1869. He first exhibited at the R.S.A. in 1850 and the R.A. in 1861. He was elected A.R.S.A. and R.S.A. in 1858 and 1863.

He had a flourishing practice as a portrait painter, as well as painting literary and historical subjects. His landscapes and flower paintings are for the most part in watercolour. He made a large collection of artists' portraits which is now in Aberdeen A.G.

He was the father of **Robert Duddingstone HERDMAN, A.R.S.A. (1863-1922),** a portrait and genre painter. Another son, George Walker Herdman, married the only surviving daughter of J. Giles (q.v.).
Illustrated: T. Roscoe: *Legends of Venice,* 1841.
Bibliography: *A.J.,* 1873. *Studio,* Special No., 1907; XLI, 1907.

HERDMAN, William Gawin
1805 (Liverpool) - 1882 (Liverpool)
An art master at Liverpool, he exhibited at the R.A. and Suffolk Street from 1834 to 1861. He was an active member of the Liverpool Academy until about 1857, when he broke with them in protest against Pre-Raphaelitism, and founded his own Academy.

His works are primarily of local topography and sometimes show a not unpleasing naïvety in the handling.

His sons **William HERDMAN, W. Patrick HERDMAN** and **J. Innes HERDMAN** all became artists. There was also **Stanley HERDMAN,** who seems to have been a relative.
Published: *Views of Fleetwood-on-Wye,* 1838. *Studies from the Folio of W.H.,* 1838.
Examples: Birkenhead A.G.; Bootle; Liverpool Lib.; Stalybridge A.G.
Bibliography: Trans. Lancs. & Chesh. Hist. Soc. LXIII, 1912.

HERKOMER, Sir Hubert von (1849-1914)
Self portrait. *Watercolour, signed with monogram and inscribed 'Property of my wife, Maggie B. Herkomer',* 9in. tondo.

HERING, George Edwards
1805 (London) - 1879 (London)
The son of a London bookbinder of noble German extraction, he was sent to study in Munich in 1829, after working for some time in a bank. Subsequently he spent two years in Venice and travelled throughout Italy and to Turkey, before returning to Rome. He then journeyed through Hungary and Transylvania. After seven years abroad he settled in London, returning to Italy to sketch. In 1858 he was in Northern Italy with F.J. Wyburd (q.v.). He exhibited at the R.A. from 1836. He specialised in paintings of Danube scenery and very occasionally took English and Scottish views.

His wife exhibited at the R.A. in 1853 and 1858.
Published: *Sketches on the Danube, in Hungary and Transylvania...,* 1838. *The Mountains and Lakes in Switzerland, the Tyrol, and Italy,* 1847.
Examples: V.A.M.
Bibliography: *A.J.,* 1861; 1880.

HERIOT, George
1766 (Haddington, East Lothian) - 1844
Educated at Edinburgh High School and University, he was a cadet at Woolwich while P. Sandby (q.v.) was drawing master there. Later he became a civil servant, and from 1799 to 1816 he was deputy Postmaster General of Canada. He travelled through much of Quebec and Ontario. After his return to England in 1816 he travelled fairly widely on the Continent, visiting Salzburg, Spain, France and the Channel Islands.

His early drawings can be very Sandby-like and are characterised by neat penwork, but later his handling is less sure.
Published: *Travels through the Canadas,* 1807. *A Picturesque Tour,* 1824.
Examples: B.M.; Ashmolean; Williamson A.G., Birkenhead; Coventry A.G.; Glasgow A.G.; Newport A.G.
Bibliography: J.C.A. Heriot: *Americana,* V, 1910.

HERKLOTS, Rev. Gerard Andreas
1834 - 1915 (Hampstead)
An amateur landscape painter who was educated at Exeter College, Oxford, and ordained in 1858. He was curate at St. John's Hampstead before being appointed to the comfortable living of St. Saviour's, South Hampstead in 1872. There he remained until retirement in 1913. However, on 13 November 1891 he took a sabbatical and sailed from London on 'a 6 months Tour round the World'. He visited Sicily, Suez, Ceylon, Calcutta and Northern India, Australia, New Zealand, Japan, Canada and the United States. He sketched assiduously, but this did not affect his exhibited subjects at Suffolk Street which were Scottish and Cornish in 1878 and 1893.

HERKOMER, Sir Hubert von, R.A., R.W.S.
1849 (Waal, Bavaria) - 1914 (Budleigh Salterton)
The son of a German wood-engraver who settled at Southampton in 1857. He studied at South Kensington from 1866 and began

working for the *Graphic* three years later. He was the founder of Bushey School of Art and its Director from 1883 to 1904. From 1885 to 1894 he was also Slade Professor. He was a member of the R.I. from 1873 to 1890 when he moved to the R.W.S. He was elected A.R.A. and R.A. in 1879 and 1890. In 1899 he was ennobled by the Kaiser and added 'von' to his name, and in 1904 he was knighted.

His works include figure, genre and historical subjects, large group portraits and theatre designs. He also composed operas.
Published: *Autobiography*, 1890. *My School and my Gospel*, 1908.
Examples: B.M.; Leeds City A.G.; City A.G., Manchester; Ulster Mus.
Bibliography: W.L. Courtney: *Professor H.H.*, 1892. A.L. Baldry: *H.v.H.*, 1901. L. Pietsch, *H.*, 1901. J.S. Mills: *Life and Letters of Sir H.H.*, 1923. G. Longman: *The Beginning of the Herkomer Art School*, 1973. G. Longman: *H. as a Painter in Enamels*, 1988. *A.J.*, 1870; 1880. *Studio*, XXIX, 1903; L, 1910; LVI, 1912. *Country Life*, 25 Jan., 1 Feb. 1973; 5 Feb. 1982. Watford A.G., Exhibition Cat., Feb. 1982.

HERNE, Charles Edward
1848 (New South Wales) - 1894
A marine painter who taught members of the Royal Family including the Princess Royal and the daughters of the Prince of Wales. He exhibited in London from 1884 and also painted Venetian subjects. His name is sometimes given without the final 'e', but this is unlikely to be correct, since his signature usually has it, and the Fine Art Society used it for his memorial show.

HERRIES, Herbert Crompton
c.1815   - 1870
A landscape painter who lived in Pimlico and was active at least between 1865 and 1870. He may also have exhibited an Egyptian view in 1855. He was the son of Sir W. Herries and was called to the Bar in 1840.

HERRIES, Major William Robert
c.1818   - 1845 (Moodkee, India)
The second son of the Rt. Hon. J.C. Herries, he joined the 43rd Light Infantry as an ensign in 1835. With Sir R.G.A. Levinge (q.v.) he served in Canada, and at times their styles are similar. In 1837 the regiment was at Montreal during the Papineau rebellion. In 1841 they were posted to the Cape, and Herries was killed at the battle of Moodkee against the Sikhs in the Punjab. He was a talented amateur and recorded the lighter side of regimental life.

HERRING, E   L
A very awful artist who painted coastal scenes and landscapes in the 1880s.

HERRING, John Frederick
1795 (Blackfriars) - 1865 (Tunbridge Wells)
The son of an American fringemaker in London, he was in Doncaster in 1814 when the Duke of Hamilton's 'William' won the St. Leger. This is said to have inspired him to take up animal and coach painting. For a while he was also a coach driver working on the 'Nelson' from Wakefield to Halifax, Doncaster and Lincoln and the 'Highflyer' from London to York. He retired to Doncaster and, after working briefly with A. Cooper (q.v.), made a good living from horse portraiture. In 1830 he moved to Newmarket and later to London and Tunbridge Wells. He was a member of the S.B.A. from 1841.

His drawings of horses and farmyards are usually in muted colours with thick brown ink outlines and shading.
Examples: B.M.; Williamson A.G., Birkenhead; Fitzwilliam; Newport A.G.
Bibliography: Anon: *J.F.H.*, 1870. O. Beckett: *J.F.H. and Sons*, 1981. *A.J.*, Nov., 1865. *Connoisseur*, May, 1965. *Country Life*, April, 1965; *Annual*, 1970.

HERRING, John Frederick, Yr.
?1815 (Doncaster) - 1907 (Cambridge)
The eldest son of J.F. Herring, his work is very close to that of his father. He specialised in farmyard scenes using the same quiet colours and brown ink, often heightened with white. His drawing is more crude than his father's and he used an oval signature to distinguish his work. He exhibited at the R.A. from 1863 to 1873.

His brothers Charles (d.1856) and Benjamin (d.1871) were also painters.
Bibliography: O. Beckett: *J.F.H. and Sons*, 1981. *A.J.*, 1907.

HEWERDINE, Matthew Bede
c.1871 (Hull) - 1909
An artist, cartoonist and book illustrator living in Hull and later Oxford.
Illustrated: Lady Glover: *Lest we forget them*, 1900. C. Reade: *The Cloister and the Hearth*, 1904.

HEWETT, Sir Prescott Gardiner, 1st Bt., F.R.S., Hon. R.W.S.
1812 (Doncaster) - 1891
An eminent surgeon and patron, and an accomplished amateur watercolourist, he was one of the first Honorary Members of the O.W.S. in 1873. He was the surgeon who saved the young Carl Haag's hand, and he later introduced him to his first patron, Lord Penrhyn. He had himself studied painting, as well as surgery, in Paris. He became P.R.C.S. in 1876 and was created a baronet in 1883. On his retirement to Horsham in 1883 he devoted himself to painting.
Examples: V.A.M.

HEWETT, Sarah F
A Leamington painter of rustic genre subjects. She was an unsuccessful candidate for the N.W.S. in 1851 and exhibited in London, Birmingham and Glasgow from 1851 to 1885. In 1878 she was living in Kent. Her work was in the tradition of F.W. Topham (q.v.) or P.F. Poole (q.v.).
Published: *The Peasant Speech of Devon*, 1892. *Nummits and Crummits*, 1900.
Examples: Leamington A.G.
Bibliography: *A.J.*, 1859.

HEWITT, H
A landscape painter from Bristol who was active between about 1845 and 1870. He painted locally and in Wales.

HEWITT, Mrs. – *see* PEEL, Florence

HEWLETT, James
1789   - 1836 (Isleworth)
A flower painter, practising mainly in Bath, whose works are in the ornate Dutch tradition, with accurate botanical drawing. He occasionally painted gipsy and similar themes, and he exhibited at the R.A. and elsewhere.

Another **James HEWLETT**, possibly father to the above, was working in a similar manner in Bath at an earlier date. He died in London in 1829. The sister of one married B. Barker (q.v.).
Examples: V.A.M.

HIBBARD, Rowland
1777 (Adwick-on-Dearne) - 1844 (Sheffield)
An amateur painter of South Yorkshire churches and other landmarks. His work is usually on a small scale and derives from F. Nicholson (q.v.). He was at Oxford between 1795 and 1801, and generally seems to have led a gentlemanly life at Lamb Hill, Handsworth.
Examples: B.M.; Doncaster, A.G.; Graves A.G., Sheffield; York City A.G.
Bibliography: *Antique Finder*, Oct. 1981.

HIBBART or HIBBERT, William
An etcher and occasional draughtsman who was working in Bath from about 1760 to 1800. His trade card was engraved by Bartolozzi.

HICKEY, Thomas
1741 (Dublin) - 1824 (Madras)
After attending the Dublin Academy, he spent some years studying in Rome, returning to Dublin in 1767. He went to London in 1771 where he entered the R.A. Schools, exhibited at the R.A., and practised as a portrait painter. He worked for a while in Bath, and set out for India in 1780, pausing for some time in Lisbon. He was in India from 1784 to 1792, and there he may have been the author of *The History of Painting and Sculpture from the Earliest Accounts*, 1788. After returning to London, in 1792 he accompanied Lord Macartney's embassy to China as official portrait painter. After a last visit to Dublin in 1796, he returned to Madras in 1798, leaving again only for brief visits to Calcutta in 1807 and 1812.

While in India he made a large series of

striking pencil, chalk and wash portraits of soldiers and East India Company officials. He is often said to have produced nothing on the Macartney embassy; this seems unlikely.

His brother John Hickey (1751-1795) also studied at the R.A. Schools and was a sculptor.
Examples: B.M.; Stratfield Saye; N.G., Ireland.
Bibliography: *Memoirs of William Hickey*, 1923-1925. Sir H.E.A. Cotton: *T.H., Portrait Painter*, 1924. *Madras Government Gaz.*, 17 June 1824.

HICKIN, George Arthur
1821 - 1885 (Leicester)
A still-life and farmyard painter in oil and watercolour who lived in Greenwich and Birmingham. He exhibited in London, Brighton and Birmingham from 1839 to 1881.
Examples: V.A.M.

HICKS, George Elgar
1824 (Lymington, Hampshire) - 1914 (London)
A genre and portrait painter in oil and watercolour who had lessons from a marine painter when very young, but was trained as a doctor. He then studied at the Bloomsbury School of Art and the R.A. Schools and exhibited from 1848. His pictures are often of contemporary life and he used mixed media.
Examples: Ulster Mus.
Bibliography: *A.J.*, April, 1872. Geffrye Mus., London, Exhibition Cat., 1982-3.

HICKS, Lillburne, N.W.S.
1814/15 - 1861 (Kensington)
A genre painter who lived in Sloane Square and exhibited from 1830. He entered the R.A. Schools two years later and was elected N.W.S. in 1836.
Bibliography: *Studio*, XXVIII, 1906.

HIGHMORE, Anthony 1719 (London) -
1799 (Wincheap, Canterbury)
The only son of the artist Joseph Highmore (c.1692 London - 1780 Canterbury). He lived the greater part of his life in Canterbury, where he studied theology. He drew five views of Hampton Court, which were engraved by J. Tinney.
Bibliography: *Gentleman's Mag.*, 1799.

HIGNETT, George
A landscape painter in oil and watercolour who lived and exhibited in Birmingham from 1879 to 1887.

HILES, Frederick John, 'Bartram'
1872 (Bristol) - 1927 (Clifton)
He lost both arms in a road accident during his childhood, and learnt to write and draw holding the pencil and brushes in his mouth. He studied at the Bristol School of Art and won a Scholarship to South Kensington. He exhibited at the R.B.A. in 1893, and later at the R.I. and R.A. His subjects are generally landscapes and shipping subjects around Bristol.

HILLS, Robert (1769-1844)
Cattle on a country lane. *Watercolour.*

HILL, Arthur c.1829 (Nottingham) -
A painter of genre and Alma-Tademical figure subjects in oil and watercolour. He exhibited at the R.A. and Suffolk Street between 1858 and 1893.

An **Arthur HILL, A.R.I.B.A.,** published a number of illustrated works on Irish architecture in the 1870s.

HILL, David Octavius, R.S.A.
1802 (Perth) - 1870 (Edinburgh)
A landscape painter and photographer, he studied in Edinburgh. He was one of the first A.R.S.As. in 1826 and, after a contretemps, was elected R.S.A. in 1829. He was Secretary from 1830 to 1869. He illustrated a number of Scott's works and Burns subjects. From about 1843 he largely concentrated on photography.
Published: *Sketches of Scenery in Perthshire*, 1821.
Examples: Williamson A.G., Birkenhead; N.G., Scotland.
Bibliography: D. Bruce: *Sun Pictures*, 1973. *A.J.*, 1850; 1869; 1870.

HILL, James Stevens, R.I.
1854 - 1921
A landscape painter in oil and watercolour who studied at the R.A. Schools. He lived in Hampstead and worked for the most part in the Southern counties. He also painted floral still lifes.
Bibliography: *Studio*, 1898; LXVI, 1915. *A.J.*, 1905.

HILL, Thomas 'Jockey'
(Warwickshire) - c.1827 (London)
He moved from Derby to London before 1800, and there took a post as a dealer in government stores. He painted in subdued washes and some of his works were engraved. His nickname was due to his love of riding, and he was also a horse-dealer and ceramic painter. He died at an advanced age.

He may be identifiable with Thomas Hill who exhibited views of Derbyshire at the R.A. in around 1820.
Examples: Derby A.G.

HILLS, Robert, O.W.S.
1769 (Islington) - 1844 (London)
A founder member of the O.W.S., Hills was best known for his paintings of animals, and in this field he was largely self-taught, working from nature. He was the Society's first Secretary and later served as Treasurer, although he retired during the period of the Oil and Watercolour Society, from 1813 to 1820. In 1815 he made his only foreign journey, visiting Waterloo a month after the Battle, and touring in Holland and Flanders. He also made many tours in Britain, staying with such patrons as Fawkes of Farnley Hall, Yorkshire.

He had entered the R.A. Schools in 1788, and his earliest watercolours are executed in a limited range of low washes and outlined in a rather eighteenth century manner. They have a simplicity which is lacking in his work from about 1810 onwards. By this date he is working very much more in the manner of his friends Barret, Cristall and Robson with whom he often actually collaborated. He employs an almost pointillist technique which at its best is very effective but can become rather muzzy

HINE, Harry T. (1845-1941)
'Spring-time in Old Amersham.'

and mechanical. His snow scenes are experimental in that he would leave large areas of his off-white paper totally bare to represent a snowladen sky, and would vigorously scrape out snowflakes. This can be very impressive, but again can decline into a mere formula. Throughout his life he made small and free sketches. A development of this practice was to make elaborately finished miniatures from which he would work up his compositions. These he called his 'models' and they sometimes have a greater charm than his finished versions, which can appear overworked.

His sketches often bear shorthand notes both recto and verso. Many are also stamped with the initials 'J.G.' in a horizontal oval and come from the sale of his Trustee, John Garle, F.S.A., at Christie's, 27 April 1874.
Examples: B.M.; V.A.M.; Ashmolean; Blackburn A.G.; Brighton A.G.; Fitzwilliam; Leeds City A.G.; Newport A.G.; Ulster Mus.; Warrington A.G.
Bibliography: *Walker's Quarterly*, III, 1923. *Burlington Mag.*, LXXXVI, Feb. 1945. O.W.S. Club, XXV, 1947. *Connoisseur*, CL, 1962. *Country Life*, 25 July 1968.

HILTON, William, R.A.
1786 (Lincoln) - 1839
The son of his namesake (c.1750 Newark - 1822), a portrait painter, he studied under J.R. Smith (q.v.) from 1800, with P. de Wint (q.v.) as a fellow pupil. They made sketching tours together, and in 1828 de Wint married his sister. He entered the R.A. Schools in 1806 and was elected A.R.A. and R.A. in 1813 and 1819. He was keeper from 1827. In 1818 he was in Rome with Thomas Phillips, R.A. He painted landscapes and battle scenes, but was largely ignored by the patrons and never met

with great success.
Examples: B.M.; Fitzwilliam; Newport A.G.; N.G., Scotland.
Bibliography: *A.J.*, 1855; Sept. 1885; 1899.

HINDE, Mrs. B   L
A fruit and flower painter who exhibited with the Society of Female Artists in 1875.

HINDLEY, J
A competent topographer in the tighter manner of T. Sandby (q.v.). He was active from about 1760 to 1820.

HINE, Harry T   R.I.
1845 (London) - 1941 (Botesdale, Suffolk)
A son of H.G. Hine (q.v.) and husband of V. Hine (q.v.), he was educated at the North London Collegiate and Philological School. He served for a while as a mate in the Merchant Service and later lived in Suffolk. His style is a continuation of that of his father.
Illustrated: C.W.D. Fife: *Square Rigger Days*, 1938.
Bibliography: *Studio*, XXVIII, 1906.

HINE, Henry George, R.I.
1811 (Brighton) - 1895 (London)
The son of a coachman, he was self taught and began by copying the vicar's Copley Fieldings (q.v.). He spent some years painting Sussex coastal scenes before being apprenticed to the engraver Henry Meyer in London. Thereafter he spent two years in Rouen and in 1841 became a wood engraver for Landells. From 1841 to 1844 he drew for *Punch* and afterwards for rival publications. He had begun to exhibit landscapes in 1830 and in 1863 was elected A.N.W.S. He became a full Member the following year and was Vice-President from 1888 to 1895. From 1840 he lived mostly in London.

His style remained based upon Fielding, and his subjects chiefly in Sussex. He was also a friend of T. Collier (q.v.), whose influence can be seen in his work.
Illustrated: A.B. Reach: *The Natural History of Bores*, 1847. H. Mayhew: *Change for a Shilling*, 1848. I.M. Beeton: *Book of Household Management*, 1861. &c.
Examples: B.M.; V.A.M.; Williamson A.G., Birkenhead; Towner Gall., Eastbourne; Fitzwilliam; Hitchin Mus.; Hove Lib.; Leeds City A.G.; Leicestershire A.G.; Maidstone Mus.; City A.G., Manchester; Beecroft A.G., Southend; Sydney A.G.
Bibliography: *I.L.N.*, 1868. *Mag of Art*, 1893. *A.J.*, 1895. *Studio*, XXVIII, 1906.

HINE, William Egerton (1852-1926)
A country cottage. *Watercolour, signed and dated Sept. 1876, 11in. x 17¾in.*

HINE, Victoria Susannah, Mrs., née Colkett 1840 (Norwich) - 1926
The daughter of S.D. Colkett (q.v.) and wife of H.T. Hine (q.v.), she painted views of Oxford and Cambridge colleges which are very much in the manner of G. Pyne (q.v.). They lived in Suffolk.
Examples: Fitzwilliam.
Bibliography: *A.J.*, 1893. J. Walpole: *Art and Artists of the Norwich School*, 1997.

HINE, William Egerton 1852 - 1926 (Haslemere)
A son of H.G. Hine, he studied in London, Nuremberg, and Paris under Gerôme. He was Art Master at Harrow from 1892 and exhibited landscapes in oil and watercolour from 1873 to 1920.

HINES, Frederick
A landscape painter in oil and watercolour who lived in London and exhibited at the R.I. and elsewhere from 1875 to 1897. He wrote and illustrated a number of religious books. He may have been working in Essex as early as 1842.

His brother **Theodore HINES** was also an artist and was active from about 1876 to 1889.

HISCOX, George Dunkerton 1830 (North Wootton, Norfolk) - 1901
A landscape painter who studied at the Bristol School of Art. He lived in Windsor, and many of his subjects were taken from the area. He exhibited from 1879, and his wife **Laura M. HISCOX,** who painted farmyards, streams and flowers, from 1880 to 1884.
Bibliography: B. Hiscox and M.A. Langdale: *In Memoriam G.D.H.*, 1901.

HITCHINGS, J
A painter of landscapes and costume subjects who was active from 1860 for at least ten years. He lived in South London and sometimes painted in Herefordshire.

HIXON, James Thompson, A.N.W.S. 1836 - 1868 (Capri)
A painter of North African and Eastern scenes who exhibited from 1856. He died of consumption shortly after his election as A.N.W.S.
Bibliography: *I.L.N.*, 1868.

HOARE, Rev. Arthur Malortie 1821 - 1894
The son of the Ven. C.J. Hoare, Archdeacon of Winchester and Surrey, he was a member of the banking family. He was educated at Cambridge and became Rector of Fawley, Hampshire. He painted Alpine and Cornish subjects which are weakly Lear-like, exhibiting one such at the R.A. in 1872.

HOARE, Prince 1755 (Bath) - 1834 (Brighton)
The son and pupil of William Hoare, R.A. (1707 nr. Eye - 1792 Bath), he was educated at Bath Grammar School. He entered the R.A.

HINES, Frederick
Primrose gatherers. *Watercolour, signed and indistinctly dated, 22in. x 15in.*

Schools in 1772, visited Rome in 1776 and was for a time a pupil of Mengs. He exhibited portraits and historical subjects at the R.A. in 1781 and 1782 and became Hon. Foreign Secretary to the Academy. He was also a dramatic author. His compositions and figures can be reminiscent of those of Fuseli (q.v.), but his colours tend to be rather messy.
Examples: B.M.; V.A.M.

HOARE, Sir Richard Colt, 2nd Bt., F.R.S., F.S.A.
1758 (Barn Elms, Surrey) - 1838 (Stourhead)
A patron of the arts and an amateur watercolourist, he was educated at schools run by Devis at Wandsworth, and Dr. Samuel Glasse at Greenford. He worked briefly in the family bank. On the death of his wife in 1785 he began a tour of France, Italy, Switzerland and Spain, returning in July 1787, in which year he succeeded to the baronetcy. From 1788 to 1791 he travelled in Holland, Germany, Bohemia, Austria, Italy and the islands, and in

the Tyrol. Later he toured Wales and Monmouth, and Ireland in 1807.

His later years were primarily taken up with antiquarian and archaeological pursuits, and he published numerous books and pamphlets. In the course of his tours he made large numbers of pen and sepia wash drawings.

His younger half-brother, **Peter Richard HOARE (1772-1849),** produced a number of drawings of the West Country, which are much in the manner of J.B. Knight (q.v.) although with less detailed outlining. Their sister was H.A. Fortescue (q.v.).
Examples: B.M.; Brighton A.G.; Nat. Mus., Wales; Nat. Lib., Wales.

HOARE, Sarah 1777 - 1856
The daughter of Samuel Hoare and Sarah Gurney. She was a flower painter of merit and probably studied under W. Henry Hunt (q.v.). She did not marry.
Published: *The Pleasures of Botanical Pursuits,* 1823. *Poems on Conchology and Botany,* 1831.

HOBDAY, William Armfield
1771 (Birmingham) - 1831 (London)
A portrait painter in watercolour and miniature who was apprenticed to an engraver and studied at the R.A. Schools. He exhibited at the R.A. from 1794 and lived in Bristol from 1804 to 1817 when he returned to London. In 1829 he became bankrupt through a gallery speculation.
Examples: B.M.; Leicester A.G.

HOBDEN, Frank **- c.1930**
A genre painter who lived in Islington from 1882 to 1892, Chiswick until 1906, and South Benfleet, Essex, until 1915. He was a member of the R.B.A.

HOBSON, Alice Mary, R.I.
1860 **- 1954**
A peripatetic landscape painter who lived at various times in Leicester, Bedford, London, Doncaster, Midhurst, Chichester and Marazion. She was elected R.I. in 1888 and resigned in 1931.

HOBSON, Cecil James, R.I.
1874 **- 1915**
A landscape painter and illustrator who was elected R.I. in 1901. He lived in London.

HOBSON, Henry Edrington
1820 (London) - 1870
The son of **Henry HOBSON**, a Bath engraver, watercolourist and musician, and an artist mother, he married the daughter of J. Hardy (q.v.). He studied at the R.A. Schools from 1843 and exhibited genre and rustic subjects from 1857 to 1866.
Examples: V.A.M.; Wakefield A.G.

HODGE, Ann
A figure and landscape painter who was working in the 1840s.

HODGE, Thomas
1827 (Truro) - 1907 (London)
A golfing painter, schoolmaster and expert on fortification, he spent most of his life at St. Andrews. There he ran a school, played golf and painted the course and its denizens. He retired south in disgust when the game became popular in about 1898. His work is much esteemed by golfers. He used a wet technique, slightly reminiscent of that of N.E. Green (q.v.). A collection of his work was sold at Sotheby's in July, 1985.

HODGES, Walter Parry
1760 (Dorset) - 1845
A sporting artist working in the 1830s. He signed with initials. His original name was Parry, and he also adopted the manner of H.T. Alken (q.v.).

HODGES, William, R.A.
1744 (London) 1797 - (Brixham, Devonshire)
He picked up the rudiments of drawing while employed as an errand boy at Shipley's. He became a pupil of Richard Wilson and later worked in London and Derby, partly as a scene painter. He exhibited at the S.A. from 1766. In 1772 he was appointed draughtsman to Captain Cook's second voyage to the South Seas, returning in 1775, when he superintended the engraving of his drawings for the official account. In 1778 he left for India, where he remained until 1783, travelling extensively and even visiting Nepal. In 1784 he settled in London, and was elected A.R.A. in 1786 and R.A. in 1789. In about 1790 he travelled widely on the Continent, visiting St. Petersburg. His landscapes in the Wilson manner and large, allegorical pictures had little appeal, and in 1795 he retired to Dartmouth where, again unsuccessfully, he tried to run a bank.
Published: *Select Views in India,* 1786-8.
Examples: B.M.; V.A.M.; Admiralty; India Office Lib.; R.G.S; Soane Mus.
Bibliography: Sir W. Foster: *W.H. in India,* 1925. G,. Tillotson: *The Artificial Empire: the Indian Landscapes of W.H.,* 2000. *Geographical Mag.* XIX, 1947. *Burlington,* CXV, Oct. 1973.

HODGSON, Charles
c.1770 **- 1856 (Liverpool)**
An architectural painter in oil and watercolour. He taught English at North Walsham Grammar School and in 1802 he was running a school in Norwich and teaching mathematics. Drawing and painting were at first his hobby, but they gradually took precedence. He visited North Wales in 1805. He became maths master at the Norwich Free School, but also had a reputation as a private drawing master and helped to found the Norwich Society in 1803. He was President in 1813 and in 1825 was appointed Architectural Draughtsman to the Duke of Sussex. He appears to have given up exhibiting in the same year. Later he retired to London and then Liverpool.
His views are generally in Norwich, but he also exhibited copies of Swiss landscapes.
Examples: Castle Mus., Norwich.
Bibliography: W.F. Dickes: *The Norwich School,* 1905. J. Walpole: *Art and Artists of the Norwich School,* 1997.

HODGSON, David
1798 (Norwich) - 1864 (Norwich)
A pupil of J. Crome (q.v.) and his father C. Hodgson (q.v.) whom he accompanied on sketching tours. He built up a teaching practice and became drawing master at Norwich Grammar School. He exhibited not only at Norwich from 1813 to 1833 but also at Liverpool, Manchester and Newcastle.
His subjects, both in oil and watercolour, are generally old houses and lively street scenes in Norwich and Norfolk.
Examples: Castle Mus., Norwich.
Bibliography: W.F. Dickes: *The Norwich School,* 1905. *Burlington Mag.,* VII, 1905. J. Walpole: *Art and Artists of the Norwich School,* 1997.

HODGSON, Edward, F.S.A.
1719 (Dublin) - 1794 (London)
An Irish drawing master who practised in London and exhibited with the Free Society from 1763 to 1783 and at the R.A. in 1781, 1782 and 1788. He became Treasurer of the A.A. of Great Britain.
He painted fruit and flower pieces in watercolour and chalk, and occasionally made academic drawings.
His daughter exhibited flower pieces with the Free Society from 1770 to 1775.

HODGSON, Edward
A painter of landscapes and coastal subjects who was working in Northumbria from the 1880s.
Edward S. HODGSON was active as a landscape painter and illustrator between about 1906 and 1925. He lived at Bushey.

HODGSON, George
1847 **- 1921 (Ruddington, Nottingham)**
The son of a Nottingham braid manufacturer, he became a member of the Nottingham Society of Artists. He painted landscapes and allegories, mainly in watercolour, and was a cartoonist.
Illustrated: E.W. Robinson: *The Lay of Saint Lucundus,* 1887.
Examples: Castle Mus., Nottingham.

HODGSON, Harold 1867 **- 1953**
A doctor who practised at Alresford and painted in the southern counties and no doubt elsewhere. He exhibited at the R.A. and R.I. and also drew portraits.

HODGSON, John James
1871 (Carlisle) - 1906 (Carlisle)
A landscape and architectural painter and an illustrator. He studied under Herbert Lees, at the Windsor School of Art and the Slade. He then returned to Carlisle where he taught. He died just before establishing his name.

HODGSON, William
A landscape and portrait painter from Gateshead who studied under Boniface Muss (q.v.). He was active in the late eighteenth century. He moved to London, took further lessons from the engraver Schiavonetti and died at Castle Howard while painting a copy.

HODGSON, William J
An illustrator from Gateshead who worked in London from 1878. His style is reminiscent of that of Caldecott. He also painted in Devon, Scotland and on the Yorkshire coast. He enjoyed sporting themes, contributed to *Punch,* and illustrated a number of poems by the barrister F.E. Weatherley, for whom H.B. Potter (q.v.) also worked.
Examples: B.M.

HODSON, Edward
A Birmingham landscape and coastal painter in oil and watercolour who exhibited there from 1849 to 1881.

HOLDING, Henry James (c.1833-1872)
Haymaking. *Watercolour, signed and dated 71, 12in. x 35in.*

HODSON, Sir George Frederick, 3rd Bt.
1806 (Bray, Co. Wicklow) - 1888
The second son of Sir Robert Hodson of Hollybrook, Bray, he was in Italy in 1830 and succeeded his brother as 3rd baronet in 1831. He exhibited landscapes, still lifes and figure subjects at the R.H.A. from 1827, and in 1871 was made an Honorary Member. He was also an amateur architect.
Examples: Ulster Mus.

HODSON, Samuel John, R.W.S.
1836 (London) - 1908
A lithographer and illustrator who studied at Leigh's and the R.A. Schools from 1853 and exhibited from 1858 to 1906. He worked for the *Graphic* and was a member of the R.B.A. He was elected A.R.W.S. in 1880 and R.W.S. in 1891. He specialised in architectural subjects and romantic Continental views.
Illustrated: P. Slater: *History of the Parish of Guiseley,* 1880.
Examples: B.M.; Haworth A.G., Accrington.
Bibliography: *A.J.,* 1901. *The Year's Art,* 1909.

HOFLAND, Thomas Christopher
1777 (Worksop, Nottinghamshire) -
1843 (Leamington)
The son of a wealthy manufacturer of cotton mill machinery, he painted occasional landscapes until the family moved to London in 1790, where, being reduced to poverty, Hofland made painting his profession. He studied briefly under J. Rathbone (q.v.) and exhibited at the R.A. between 1799 and 1805. At this time the King employed him in making botanical drawings. From 1805 to 1808 he taught at Derby. He lived briefly in Doncaster and Knaresborough, where he married the writer Barbara Hoole as her second husband, before returning to London in 1811. There he continued to teach, and he exhibited at the S.B.A., of which he was a founder member, the B.I. and the R.A. The commission from the Duke of Marlborough for Mrs Hoole and himself to describe the seat of White Knights was not paid for, leaving them with all the

expenses and much out of pocket. He held a one-man exhibition in New Bond Street in 1821. In 1840 he spent nine months in Italy, making sketches which he later worked up for his patron, Lord Egremont. G. Haugh (q.v.) of York was a great friend.
His son, T.R. Hofland, is separately noticed.
Published: *The British Angler's Manual,* 1839.
Illustrated: B. Hoole: *A descriptive account...of White Knights,* 1819. E. Rhodes: *Yorkshire Scenery,* 1826.
Examples: V.A.M.; Brighton A.G.
Bibliography: Ramsay: *The Life and Literary remains of Barbara Hofland,* 1849.

HOFLAND, Thomas Richard
1816 (London) - 1876 (Durham)
The son of T.C. Hofland (q.v.), he was permanently ill and lame from youth. He was a drawing master and landscape painter, and he travelled in America and elsewhere.
Bibliography: *A.J.,* 1876.

HOLBECH
– see MORDAUNT, Lady, and Bowles Family Tree

HOLBEIN, Hans, Yr.
1497 (Augsburg) - 1543 (London)
The first major artist to use watercolour in England. In about 1515 his family moved to Berne, and he worked there, at Lucerne and perhaps in Italy, before his first visit to England in 1526/7-1528. He settled in London in 1532, revisiting the Continent in 1538-1539. His paintings and portraits need no mention here, except to note that in some of his memoranda, and in some miniatures and portrait drawings, he used watercolour.

HOLDEN, Fanny, Mrs, née Sterry
1804 - 1863
The daughter of B.W. Sterry, she married Luther Holden, F.R.C.S. in 1851. They honeymooned at Passy, visited the Riviera and lived near Ipswich. She painted interiors and exteriors, which are reminiscent of the work of

M.E. Best (q.v.), and she sometimes signed phonetically 'Van Nye'.

HOLDING, Henry James G   H
c.1833 - 1872 (Paris)
A painter of Tudor scenes and landscapes in oil and watercolour who lived and worked in Manchester.
In the V.A.M. and the Manchester City A.G. there are a Shakespearian scenes by his brother **Frederick HOLDING (1817-1874)** who also illustrated Southey's *Battle of Blenheim,* 1864.
Examples: Williamson A.G., Birkenhead.
Bibliography: *A.J.,* Oct. 1872.

HOLDSWORTH, Arthur Howe
1786 - 1860 (Torquay)
A pupil of Samuel Evans at Eton, which he entered in 1796. In later life he was Governor of Dartmouth Castle and for twenty years M.P. for the town.

HOLE, William Brassey, R.S.A., R.S.W.
1846 (Salisbury) - 1917 (Edinburgh)
An etcher, painter, sculptor and designer of stained glass windows. He was educated at the Edinburgh Academy and University, and trained to be a civil engineer. On turning to art he studied at the Trustees' School and the R.S.A. life class. He was elected A.R.S.A. and R.S.A. in 1878 and 1889, and R.S.W. in 1885. His watercolours are usually Highland landscapes or scenes around Edinburgh, and he illustrated a number of R.L. Stevenson's books, including *Kidnapped,* and works by Barrie and Burns. He contributed to *The Quiver.*
Bibliography: Hole: *Memories of W.H.,* 1920. *Portfolio,* 1881; 1892. *A.J.,* 1882; 1897; 1902. *Mag. of Art,* 1902.

HOLIDAY, Henry James
1839 (London) - 1927 (London)
An illustrator, historical genre painter, sculptor and stained glass designer. He studied at Leigh's School and the R.A. Schools and worked with Burne-Jones before starting his own glass works in 1890 in Hampstead. He

HOLLAND, James (1800-1870)
Bathing Machines at Eastbourne. *Signed with monogram, dated 9 Sept. '61 and inscribed, pencil and watercolour heightened with white, 3⅞in. x 6in.*

exhibited from 1858 and his early work shows a strong Pre-Raphaelite influence.
Published: *Reminiscences*, 1914.
Illustrated: L. Carroll: *The Hunting of the Snark,* 1876. H.C. Andersen: *The Mermaid* (n.d.).
Examples: B.M.
Bibliography: *A.J.,* 1859; 1884; 1890; 1901; 1904; 1906; 1906. *Studio,* XXXIV, 1905; XLVI, 1909; Year Book, 1909; LXX, 1917. *Walker's Quarterly,* 1930.

HOLL, Francis Montague, 'Frank', R.A., A.R.W.S. 1845 (London) - 1888 (London)
The son of Francis Holl, A.R.A., the engraver, he was mainly a portrait painter in oil, but also made chalk drawings and occasional watercolours. He entered the R.A. Schools in 1861 and gained two silver medals for drawings and a gold medal for a historical painting. He exhibited at the R.A. from 1864 until his death. In 1866 he visited Betws-y-coed where he met and later married **Annie Laura HO LL**, daughter of C. Davidson (q.v.). She was a flower painter in watercolours. He worked for the *Graphic* from 1874 to 1876, and was elected A.R.A. in 1878, after which time he became inundated with commissions for portraits. He was elected A.R.W.S. and R.A. in 1883.
Illustrated: A. Trollope: *Phineas Redux,* 1874.
Examples: B.M.; N.G., Scotland.
Bibliography: A.M. Reynolds; *Life and Work of F.H.,* 1912, *A.J.,* 1876, 1889. *Portfolio,* 1888.

HOLL, John
A painter of charming, rather naïve, views of Kentish ports seen from the sea, he was active from about 1760 to 1785. His water is very

horizontal, his figures are stilted, and there is often a lettered key, as for a print.

HOLLAND, James, O.W.S.
1800 (Burslem, Staffordshire) -
1870 (London)
His family were designers and painters of pottery, and his own earliest drawings were flower pieces. He came to London in 1819 and gave drawing lessons while teaching himself mastery of landscape and architecture. In 1831 he paid his first visit to France, and came under the influence of Bonington (q.v.) who had died only two years previously. This influence is very strong in his works during the next decade. In 1835 he was elected A.O.W.S. for the first time and he made his first visit to Venice. In 1837 he went to Portugal, in 1841 he visited Paris, in 1844 Verona, 1845 Holland, 1850 Normandy and North Wales, 1851 Genoa, and in 1857, Innsbruck. In 1842 he resigned from the O.W.S. in order to attempt to enter the R.A. as an oil painter. The failure of his ambitions led him back to the O.W.S. in 1856 and he became a full Member in 1857.
Early flower pieces attributed to him should be approached with some caution, as many of these comparatively crude or, perhaps more precisely, stylised drawings are in fact by an elder brother, **Thomas HOLLAND (c.1795-c.1865).**
To modern tastes his best work was produced before 1845, when the influence of Bonington was still comparatively strong, and before he became over-elaborate in his colour. At the time there were two opinions about him; Ruskin refers to his irrevocable fall from

a peak of perfection in about 1837. Roget, on the other hand, praises his 'poetry of the palette in the late Venetian drawings'. Amongst the most attractive of his works are the sketches which were never meant for general circulation. Many of them, taken at various places on the Kent coast, are mere memoranda for his future use, but their freedom and verve are extremely appealing. His remaining works were sold at Christie's, 26 May 1870.
Illustrated: W.H. Harrison: *The Tourist in Portugal,* 1830.
Examples: B.M.; V.A.M.; Ashmolean; Blackburn A.G.; Ferens A.G., Hull; Greenwich; Newport A.G.; City A.G., Manchester; Reading A.G.; Ulster Mus.
Bibliography: *A.J.,* April, 1870. *Portfolio,* 1892. *Connoisseur,* 1913; 1914. *Studio,* Special No., 1915; Winter No., 1922-23. *Walker's Quarterly,* XXIII, 1927. O.W.S. Club, VII, 1930; XLII, 1967.
See Colour Plate

HOLLAND, John
1799 - 1879 (Nottingham)
A Nottingham landscape and coastal painter who exhibited at the B.I. and Suffolk Street between 1831 and 1879. He sometimes worked in charcoal like G. Sheffield (q.v.).
His son, **John HOLLAND Yr. (1830-1886)** painted landscapes in watercolour and, towards the end of his life, portraits in oil. He signed 'jnr'.
Samuel HOLLAND (c.1807 Nottingham - 1887), a Nottingham picture dealer and painter of landscapes and seascapes, was probably a brother of the elder John Holland.
His son, **Samuel HOLLAND Yr. (c.1835 Nottingham -c.1895)** exhibited at the R.A. and Suffolk Street from 1877 to 1890.

HOLLAND, Sir Nathaniel DANCE, Bt. R.A. 1735 (London) -
1811 (Cranborough House, nr. Winchester)
The third son of George Dance, the elder, and elder brother of G. Dance, Yr. (q.v.). He attended Merchant Taylor's School, and studied art under Francis Hayman and in Rome, where he lived from 1754 to 1765. During the '60s he worked there with Batoni. In 1761 he was elected to the Incorporated Society, and he was a Foundation Member of the R.A., exhibiting portraits and historical and classical subjects in oil until 1776. In 1790 he retired from painting as a profession, and, taking the name Holland, entered Parliament as the member for East Grinstead, which seat he held for many years. He was created baronet in 1800, but died without issue.
Like his brother's, his work in watercolour and wash consists primarily of spirited caricatures and grotesques.
Examples: B.M.; Towneley Hall, Burnley; Fitzwilliam; N.G., Scotland.

HOLLAND, Peter 1757 - 1812
A landscape and miniature painter who entered

Drawings, 1979. *Country Life,* 25 April 1928; 26 Sept. 1963. Manchester City A.G.: Exhibition Cat., 1963. Institution Neerlandais, Paris: Exhibition Cat., 1979. Staatliche Mus., Berlin: Exhibition Cat., 1984. *Burlington,* CVI, Feb., 1964.

HOLLINS, John, A.R.A.
1798 (Birmingham) - 1855 (London)
One of the sixteen children of William Hollins (1763-1843), a Birmingham painter, sculptor and architect, he showed early enthusiasm for art. He sent portraits to the R.A. in 1819 and 1821. In 1822 he came to London and was in Italy from 1825 to 1827. He returned to London and exhibited at the R.A., being elected Associate in 1842, and at the B.I. As well as portraits he painted historical subjects, and, later, landscapes and figure subjects.

Among his brothers were **Peter HOLLINS (1800-1886)** and **William HOLLINS (1788-1831),** both sculptors.
Examples: V.A.M.; Fitzwilliam.
Bibliography: *A. J.,* 1855.

HOLLIS, Vice Admiral Aiskew Pafford
- 1844 (Southampton)
A landscape painter who entered the Navy in 1774. He saw action in 1778 and again in 1791 on the Glorious First of June. In 1797 he was at the Cape, in 1801 off Gibraltar and Egypt, and from 1804 to 1807 in the West Indies. He then served in the Baltic in 1809 and the Mediterranean and Adriatic in 1811. Thereafter he commanded guard ships at Portsmouth from 1816 to 1821.

HOLLIS, George
1793 (Oxford) - 1842 (Walworth)
An etcher who was a pupil of George Cooke. He also produced watercolour studies of monuments, portraits and views of colleges.
Published: with T. Hollis (q.v.): *The Monumental Effigies of Great Britain,* 1840.
Examples: B.M.; Ashmolean.

HOLLIS, Thomas
1818 - 1843 (Walworth)
The son and collaborator of G. Hollis (q.v.), he studied with Henry William Pickersgill and at the R.A. Schools from 1836. His landscapes, often around Dulwich, are a little Constable-like and full of greens and blues.
Examples: B.M.

HOLLOWAY, Charles Edward, R.I.
1838 (Christchurch, Hampshire) - 1897 (London)
A fellow pupil at Leigh's School with F. Walker, Sir J.D. Linton and C. Green (qq.v), Holloway worked with William Morris (q.v.), producing stained glass, until 1866. After that date he began to exhibit marine subjects and drawings of the Fens and the Thames Valley at the R.A. and elsewhere. He was elected A.N.W.S. in 1875 and a Member in 1879. He visited Venice in 1875 and 1895. His

HOLLIS, George (1793-1842)
'Cross in Headington Church Yard, Oxfordshire, looking S.E.'

the R.A. Schools in 1779, winning a silver medal in 1781. He exhibited from that year to 1793. C. Rosenberg (q.v.) aquatinted a set of Lake District views after his drawings in 1792. Latterly he lived in Liverpool.

HOLLAR, Wenceslaus
1607 (Prague) - 1677 (London)
He came to London from Cologne and Antwerp in 1637 with the Earl of Arundel, for whom he acted as draughtsman. In 1639 or 1640 he was appointed Teacher of Drawing to the Prince of Wales, later Charles II. With the exception of the years 1644 to 1652, when he fled to Holland as a Royalist, and a mission to Tangier in 1669 with Lord Henry Howard, he remained in England for the rest of his life. Many of his most important English engravings, however, were produced during the exile in Amsterdam.

He is one of the most important artists to have worked in England at this period, and he gives us the best idea of the scenery and buildings of the time. He was one of the first people to use watercolour in this country, and although in his drawing he is very much the print-colourer, the use of tinted washes adds a new dimension to the development of the art. He sometimes worked from sketches by native artists such as D. King (q.v.) and T. Johnson (q.v.) and his influence was spread by his friend and (despite himself) disciple, F. Place (q.v.).

His son who, Aubrey says, was 'an ingeniose youth' and 'drew delicately', died of the plague.
Examples: B.M.: J. Rylands Lib., Manchester; N.G., Scotland.
Bibliography: G. Vertue: *A Description of the Works of W.H.,* 1745. F. Sprinzels: *H. Handzeichnungen,* 1938. J. Urzidel: *H.,* 1942. F.G. Springell: *Connoisseur and Diplomat,* 1963. V. Denkstein: *H.*

watercolours, especially the sea pieces, are generally impressionistic and show the influence of Whistler in their colouring.

An exhibition of his work was held at the Goupil Gallery, London, in 1897.

Examples: V.A.M.; Cartwright Hall, Bradford; Leeds City A.G.

Bibliography: *A.J.*, 1896; 1897. *Studio*, 1906; Special No., 1919.

HOLMES, Sir Charles John, A.R.W.S., F.S.A. 1868 (Preston) - 1936 (London)
Nephew of Sir R.R. Holmes (q.v.) and a landscape painter in watercolour and oil. He was educated at Eton and Brasenose College, Oxford. From 1903 to 1909 he edited the *Burlington Magazine* and from 1904 to 1910 he was Slade Professor of Fine Art at Oxford. In 1916 he was appointed Director of the National Gallery. He signed his work, either with his full names, or with initials and date.

Published: *Constable*, 1902. *Notes on the Science of Picture Making*, 1909. *The National Gallery*, 1923, 1925.

Examples: B.M.; V.A.M.; Aberdeen A.G.; Blackburn A.G.; Dundee City A.G.; Fitzwilliam; Leeds City A.G.; Leicestershire A.G.; Maidstone Mus.; City A.G., Manchester; Stalybridge A.G.; Ulster Mus.; Wakefield A.G.

Bibliography: C.H. Collins Baker: *Sir C.H.*, 1924. *Studio*, 1921. *Burlington Mag.*, LXXVII, Aug. 1940.

HOLMES, George
An Irish illustrator and landscape draughtsman who studied at the R.D.S. Schools, winning a medal for a landscape in 1789. He worked on the *Sentimental and Masonic Magazine* and the *Copper Plate Magazine* and drew for Ledwich's *Antiquities of Ireland* and Brewer's *Beauties of Ireland*, 1825-1826. In 1797 he toured South West Ireland with J. Harden (q.v.). He moved to London in 1799, where he exhibited at the R.A. until 1802. Although said to have died in 1804, he was active at least until 1809, when he signed a drawing of Bristol.

There was also a **George HOLMES** of Plymouth who exhibited English and Irish views at the R.H.A. in 1841 and 1843. The two may be related or even identical.

Published: *Sketches of some of the Southern Counties of Ireland collected during a Tour in the autumn*, 1797, in a series of *Letters*, 1801.

Examples: B.M.; Ashmolean. City A.G., Bristol.

HOLMES, James 1777 (Burslem) - 1860 (London)
A figure and portrait painter who was apprenticed to Meadows the engraver, and studied at the R.A. Schools as an engraver from 1796, but who turned to watercolour painting as soon as his articles were out. He was a member of the A.A. from 1809 to 1812 and the Oil and Watercolour Society from 1812 to 1821. In 1824 he was a founder of the S.B.A. G.B. Brummell (q.v.) was an early

friend and patron, and Byron wrote that one of his portraits by Holmes was 'the very best of me'. His figure and genre subjects have titles like 'The Doubtful Shilling' and 'Hot Porridge'. He painted three portraits of George IV, of whom he was a favourite, so much so that he was dubbed 'the King's hobby' in Court circles. After 1821 he devoted himself chiefly to oil painting, and his later years were spent in Shropshire. A number of his drawings were engraved for the Annuals.

His son, **James HOLMES, Yr.** painted portraits and figure subjects in oil and watercolour, exhibiting between 1836 and 1859.

Bibliography: *See* A. Gilchrist: *Life of William Blake*, 1863. A.T. Storey: *J.H. and John Varley*, 1894. *Connoisseur*, XXX, 1911.

HOLMES, Sir Richard Rivington, F.S.A. 1835 - 1911
The son of an assistant keeper of manuscripts at the B.M., he was educated at Highgate, and succeeded his father in 1854. In 1860 he worked with Henry le Strange and T.G. Parry (q.v.) in decorating Ely Cathedral, and he produced stained glass designs. In 1868 he went with the Abyssinian expedition as archaeologist. In 1870 he was appointed Librarian at Windsor.

He worked in a number of media including full watercolour. His Abyssinian landscapes are in brown wash.

Examples: B.M.

HOLMES, R Sheriton 1829 (S. Shields) - 1900
A civil and railway engineer who was an amateur antiquary and landscape painter. He was educated in Wharfedale and articled to a Newcastle engineer. He then worked in the North-East and London for a while before returning to Tyneside. He wrote and illustrated a number of books including *The Walls of Newcastle*, 1895. He also painted ships.

Examples: Newcastle Univ. Lib.; Laing A.G., Newcastle.

HOLMS, Alexander Campbell, R.S.W. 1862 - 1898
An illustrator and painter of flowers, figures and religious subjects in oil and watercolour, he lived at Paisley. He studied in Glasgow and Paris and was elected R.S.W. in 1893. He illustrated the poems of Spencer, Rossetti and Tennyson.

HOLROYD, Sir Charles 1861 (Leeds) - 1917
An etcher and painter who was educated at Leeds Grammar School and the Yorkshire College of Science. He studied at the Slade, winning a two year travelling scholarship to Italy, and later becoming Legros' assistant. He exhibited at the R.A. from 1883 and was Director of the N.G. from 1906 to 1916. His

wife, Fannie Fetherstonehaugh Macpherson, was the daughter of a Prime Minister of Victoria, Australia, and she also painted.

Examples: B.M.; V.A.M.; Haworth A.G., Accrington.

Bibliography: *Studio*, XXIII, 1898; XXX, 1904; XLVIII, 1910; LXXII, *1918.Connoisseur*, Jan. 1919.

HOLST, Theodore Matthias, Von 1810 (London) - 1844 (London)
A genre painter who was the son of a music teacher and of Livonian descent. He studied at the B.M. and at the R.A. Schools under Fuseli (q.v.), in whose manner he worked. His drawings are generally rather more colourful, and many subjects come from romantic literature. As with many fairy painters, opium played its part in his art. His death certificate gives him the middle names of Richard Edward. Elsewhere he has a middle initial M, which is generally stated to have been Matthias, but he signed at least one letter (to George Richmond) 'Theodore Maria'. He was a great-uncle of the composer, Gustav Holst.

Examples: B.M.; V.A.M.

Bibliography: *Burlington*, CV, 1963. Cheltenham A.G., Exhibition Cat., 1994.

HOLWORTHY, James, O.W.S. 1781 (Bosworth, Leicestershire) - 1841 (London)
A pupil of J. Glover (q.v.) in the 1790s, and a close friend of J.M.W. Turner (q.v.), Holworthy exhibited three Welsh views at the R.A. in 1803 and 1804. He was at this time living in Mount Street, and he was a founder member of the O.W.S. He retired in 1814 but continued to practise in London until after his marriage to a niece of J. Wright of Derby (q.v.) in 1821. Thereafter he bought a property in Derbyshire where he lived until his death. His subjects are picturesque views in England and Wales, with a bias towards ruined castles, and his style is closely modelled on that of his master.

Examples: V.A.M.

Bibliography: O.W.S. Club, LVIII, 1983.

HOME, Robert 1752 (Hull) - 1834 (Cawnpore)
A portrait painter and brother of Sir Everard Home, the anatomist. At an early age he voyaged to Newfoundland on board a whaler. He helped his brother-in-law, Dr. John Hunter, with anatomical diagrams and had lessons from A. Kauffmann (q.v.). He entered the R.A. Schools in 1769, exhibiting at the R.A. in 1770 and 1771 and was in Rome from 1773 to 1778. He returned to London, and the following year went to Dublin, where for ten years he had a successful practice. He returned to London in 1789 and in 1790 left for India. His sketches of the Mysore war were published as engravings in 1794. In 1795 he went to Calcutta, and in 1802 was appointed Secretary to the Asiatic Society, whose rooms he decorated with

portraits. In 1814 he became Court Painter to the King of Oudh. He is said to have made a fortune, chiefly out of military and ceremonial subjects. In 1825 he retired to Cawnpore.

Published: *Select Views in Mysore*, 1794.

Examples: V.A.M.; Asiatic Soc., Calcutta; N.G., Ireland; N.P.G.; N.G., Scotland.

Bibliography: Sir H.E.A. Cotton: *R.H.*, 1928.

HONE, Nathaniel, Yr., R.H.A.
1831 (Armagh) - 1917 (Dublin)

The great-nephew of Nathaniel Hone, I (1718-1784), he was primarily an oil painter. However, he is a strangely neglected member of the Barbizon School, and was also a fine and prolific landscape painter in watercolour. He did not sell or exhibit these, leaving them all to the N.G.I. He was trained as an engineer, but turned to painting in Paris. From about 1856 to 1870 he lived at Barbizon and Fontainebleau, visiting Italy before returning to Ireland in 1872. In 1861 he was in London for the census when he gave his place of birth as above. He also travelled to Holland, Greece, Turkey and Egypt, as well as to other parts of France and England. He was much influenced by Corot.

Examples: N.G.I.

Bibliography: T.Bodkin: *Four Irish landscape Painters*, 1920. *A.J.*, 1909. *Studio*, LXIV, 1908.

HOOD, Hon. Albert   1841 -   1921

The second son of the 3rd Viscount Hood, he was a talented landscape painter. Before his marriage to the daughter of a former Governor of Madras in 1868, he had served as a lieutenant in the Rifle Brigade. He painted in India, Italy, Norway, Britain and doubtless elsewhere.

HOOD, George Percy JACOMB-
1857 (Redhill, Surrey) - 1929 (Alassio, Italy)

Illustrator, etcher and portrait painter, he studied at the Slade and under J.P. Laurens in Paris. He exhibited at the R.A. from 1878 and, for most of his career, kept a Chelsea studio. For a time he worked for the *Graphic* , which sent him to Greece in 1896, and he was on the King's staff during the Delhi Durbar. In his early days he was influenced by the Pre-Raphaelites. He was also a friend of H.S. Tuke (q.v.) and visited the nascent Newlyn School in Cornwall in the 1890s. A memorial exhibition was held by the Walker A.G., Liverpool, in 1934.

Published: *With Brush and Pencil*, 1925.

Illustrated: L. Morris: *Odatis, An Old Love Tale*, 1888. H. Rider Haggard: *Lysbeth, A Tale of the Dutch*, 1900.

Examples: Hove Lib.

HOOD, John

A Limehouse shipwright who exhibited stiff and crude Indian ink drawings of shipping from 1762 to 1771.

Examples: B.M.; Greenwich.

HOLWORTHY, James, O.W.S. (1781-1841)
Conway Castle by Moonlight. *Ink and watercolour, inscribed in the sky, 10in. x 14½in.*

HOOD, Thomas
1799 (London) - 1845 (London)

The poet and humorist. Between 1815 and 1818 he lived in Dundee for the sake of his health. There he sketched and wrote for local newspapers. On his return to London he was apprenticed to his uncle, an engraver, and to Le Keux, before turning to full time writing as a career.

In the B.M. are several small and colourful landscapes by Hood, in which the drawing is poor, also a Blake-like figure in a landscape.

His son **Thomas HOOD, Yr.** was also a humorist and a caricaturist.

Examples: B.M.

Bibliography: D. Jerrold: T.*H., His Life and Times,* 1907. J.C. Reid: *T.H.*, 1963.

HOOK, James Clarke, R.A.
1819 (Clerkenwell) - 1907 (Churt, Surrey)

A pupil of J. Jackson (q.v.), he entered the R.A. Schools in 1836. Between 1845 and 1848 he travelled in France and Italy on a scholarship. From 1864 to 1867 much of his work was done in Cornwall and the Scilly Islands. He was elected A.R.A. and R.A. in 1850 and 1860, retiring a few months before his death.

Until about 1859 he specialised in genre and historical subjects, thereafter turning to landscapes and coastal scenes. He was noted for his vivid colouring.

Bibliography: A.H. Palmer: *J.C.H.*, 1888. F.C. Stephens: *J.C.H., His Life and Work*, 1890. A.J. Hook: *Life of J.C.H.*, 1929. *A.J.*, 1856; 1888; 1907; 1908. *Portfolio*, 1871.

HOOKER, Sir William Jackson, F.R.S.
1785 (Norwich) - 1865 (Kew)

A botanist, author and artist, and a son-in-law of D. Turner (q.v.) with whom he botanised in Scotland in 1806. He visited Iceland in 1809 and France, Switzerland and North Italy in 1814. After his marriage the following year he lived in Suffolk, and in 1820 took the post of Professor of Botany at Glasgow University. In 1841 he was appointed Director of Kew Gardens. He was elected to the Linnaean Society in 1806 and the Royal Society in 1812.

Until 1835 he himself drew the majority of the illustrations for his books; after this date they were executed by W. Fitch (q.v.).

His son, **Sir Joseph Dalton HOOKER, O.M., P.R.S. (1817 Halesworth - 1911)** followed his careers with quite as much distinction, and was also a surgeon. He accompanied Ross to Antarctica, 1839-1843, travelled widely, and succeeded his father at Kew. He published four botanical books.

Published: *Musci Exotici*, 1818-1820. *Flora Scotica*, 1821. *Exotic Flora*, 1823-1827. *Catalogue of the Plants in the Glasgow Botanical Garden*, 1825. *British Flora*, 1830-1831. *The Journal of Botany*, 1834-1842. *Companion to the Botanical Magazine*, 1835-1836. *Guide to Kew Gardens*, 1847-1865.

Examples: R.H.S.

HOPKINS, Arthur, R.W.S.
1848 (Stratford, Essex) - 1930 (London)

A brother of Gerard Manley Hopkins the poet – himself a fine draughtsman – and of **Edward HOPKINS,** an occasional black and white artist who married **Frances Anne HOPKINS,** a grand-daughter of Sir W. Beechey. He was educated at Lancing College, studied at the R.A. Schools from 1872, and for twenty-five years worked for the *Graphic* and *Punch*. He also painted country genre scenes in the manner of H. Allingham (q.v.) and strong landscapes and coastal views which are very effective in their clear colours and discipline of detail. He was elected A.R.W.S. and R.W.S. in 1877 and 1896.

Published: *Sketches and Skits*, 1900.

Examples: B.M.; Ashmolean; Exeter Mus.

Bibliography: A.J., 1899. *Studio*, LXXXIII, 1922.

HOPKINS, Everard
1860 (London) - 1928
Another of the seven siblings of G.M. Hopkins, like A. Hopkins (q.v.) he also painted watercolours, but was primarily a graphic artist. In this line he was the most distinguished of the family. He studied at the Slade, and became assistant editor of *The Pilot*.

Illustrated: M.Gray: *A Costly Freak*, 1894. &c.

HOPKINSON, Anne E
A flower painter who was awarded a gold medal by the Society of Female Artists in 1879. She exhibited at Suffolk Street and the R.A. from 1877 to 1887, and lived at Forest Hill.

HOPLEY, Edward William John
1816 (Whitstable) - 1869 (London)
A painter of literary and genre subjects who lived at Lewes before moving to Islington. He studied medicine initially, but then turned to genre, historical and fairy painting, as well as portraits. He was an unsuccessful candidate for the N.W.S. in 1844 and exhibited at Suffolk Street from that year until 1851, which was also the year that he first showed at the R.A. He invented a trigonometrical system of facial measurement for the use of artists.

Bibliography: A.J., 1853; 1869.

HOPPNER, John, R.A.
1758 (London) - 1810 (London)
The portrait painter. Like his friend Dr. Monro (q.v.) he produced a number of Gainsborough-like chalk drawings, usually on bluish paper. He also made similar drawings in brown wash. He was elected A.R.A. and R.A. in 1793 and 1795.

Examples: B.M.; V.A.M.

Bibliography: H.P.K. Skipton: *J.H.*, 1905. F. Rutter (ed.): *Essays of Art by J.H.*, 1908.

HOPWOOD, Henry Silkstone, R.W.S.
1860 (Markfield, Leicestershire) - 1914 (Edinburgh)
A genre and landscape painter in oil and watercolour who was a Manchester and Belfast businessman before studying in Manchester, Antwerp and Paris. He visited North Africa, and Australia and Japan between

1888 and 1890. He exhibited from 1884 and was elected A.R.W.S. and R.W.S. in 1896 and 1908. Many of his landscapes are of the area around Montreuil.

Examples: V.A.M.; Leicestershire A.G.

Bibliography: *Studio*, XXVII, 1903; XL, 1907; XLI, 1907; LIV, 1912; LXIII, 1915. *A.J.*, 1906; 1907; 1909. *Connoisseur*, XL, 1914.

HORNBROOK, Captain A
A Plymouth marine painter who visited Spain in 1837. He was presumably related to T.L. Hornbrook (1780-1850), also of Plymouth, who was Marine Painter to the Duchess of Kent and Queen Victoria.

HORNBROOK, Major Richards Lyde
c. 1783 - 1856 (Plymouth)
A marine officer who was stationed in Canada from about 1826 to 1830. His view of Montreal was lithographed by T.M. Baynes (q.v.) in 1828. He worked in pen and washes.

He was presumably a brother of the marine painter Thomas Lyde Hornbrook (1780-1850), who was well established in Plymouth. At the same period a Thomas Beckford Hornbrook was serving as a captain in the marines; if he was a relative, he too may have painted.

HORNE, Herbert Percy
1864 (London) - 1916
An architect, designer, connoisseur and landscape painter who visited Italy with F.J. Shields (q.v.) in 1889. He settled in Florence three years later, where he wrote a number of biographies of Italian painters. He was a collector of the works of A. Cozens (q.v.), as well as of Italian paintings and sculptures which he left to the state with his palazzo.

Examples: B.M.; Birmingham City A.G.

Bibliography: C. Gamba: *Il Museo Horne a Firenze*, 1961.

HORNER, Thomas   1785 (Hull) - 1844
A topographer who was working between 1800 and 1844 and was in South Wales from 1816 to 1820. He also painted rather Grimm-like Swiss views, perhaps copied from prints. He was the proprietor of the Regents Park Colosseum where he employed E.T. Parris and G. Chambers (qq.v.) on a huge Panorama from the top of St. Pauls. This enterprise broke him.

Examples: B.M.; Cardiff Co. Record Office; Swansea Lib.; Nat. Lib., Wales; Nat. Mus., Wales.

HORNSEY, J
A topographer and cattle painter who worked in Yorkshire for the *Copper Plate Magazine* between 1795 and 1800. His cows, in slightly tinted grey wash, are unusually lifelike.

Examples: B.M.

HORTON, George Edward
1859 (North Shields) - 1950 (London)
A self-taught artist who specialised in Dutch townscapes. He was particularly fond of

sketching in Rotterdam and Dordrecht. He exhibited in France and Holland as well as at the R.A. He moved to London in 1918.

Examples: Shipley A.G., Gateshead; Laing A.G., Newcastle.

HORTON, Wartley
An animal and rustic painter who was active at the end of the nineteenth century. In mood he is akin to M.B. Foster (q.v.) and H. Allingham (q.v.) although in subject matter he is closer to E. Alexander (q.v.). His Christian name may be a catalogue mistake for Westley. There was a landscape painter of this name working in Birmingham in 1874 and 1875.

HOTHAM, Hon. Amelia, Mrs. Woodcock
- 1804
The daughter of the 2nd Lord Hotham, she married John Woodcock in 1798. She painted landscapes. The 1793 example in the B.M. is distinctly Payne-like.

Examples: B.M.

HOTHAM, Sir Charles
1806 (Dennington, Suffolk) - 1855 (Melbourne, Australia)
A naval commander, colonial governor and a pupil of T.S. Cooper (q.v.). He entered the Navy in 1818 and was promoted lieutenant, commander and captain in 1825, 1828 and 1833. In 1845 he took part in the Para expedition and was the hero of the first Battle of the River Plate. He was knighted the following year. He was appointed Lieutenant-Governor of Victoria in 1854 and Governor in 1855.

By her previous and subsequent marriages, his wife, Hon. Jane Sarah Hood (d.1907) was connected to the family of Oldfield Bowles (q.v.).

See Bowles Family Tree

HOUGH, William B
1819 - 1897 (Wolverhampton)
An imitator of W. Henry Hunt (q.v.) painting meticulous still lifes of fruit, flowers and birds. He exhibited at the N.W.S. and elsewhere from 1857 to 1894, and also painted competent and attractive landscapes. He lived in Coventry and London.

Examples: V.A.M.; Glasgow A.G.; Newport A.G.

HOUGHTON, Arthur Boyd, A.O.W.S.
1836 (Kotagiri, Madras) - 1875 (London)
He was a pupil at Leigh's Art School. Early in his career he concentrated on providing illustrations for periodicals, such as the *Graphic*, for which he visited India and America, and books such as Dalziel's edition of the *Arabian Nights*, 1865. After attempting oil painting and wood engraving – in which he was hampered by the loss of an eye – he turned to watercolours and was elected A.O.W.S. in 1871, exhibiting with them in 1871, 1872 and 1874. However, he became an alcoholic, which killed him.

HOUGHTON, Arthur Boyd (1836-1875)
The Transformation of King Beder. *Watercolour, 19½in. x 23½in.*

He is best known as an illustrator of the Walker/Pinwell group. His colours are rich and powerful, and his black and white effects striking. Many of his subjects are Oriental in inspiration.

His remaining works were sold at Christie's, 17 March 1876.
Examples: B.M.; V.A.M.; Cecil Higgins A.G., Bedford.
Bibliography: L. Housman: *A.B.H.: Selection of Work*, 1896. P. Hogarth: *A.B.H.*, 1981. *A.J.*, 1876. *Burlington Mag.*, XL, 1922. *Studio*, Special Nos., 1922; 19234. *Print Collectors' Quarterly*, X, i, ii, 1923.

HOUGHTON, Elizabeth Ellen
1853   - 1922
An illustrator of children's books who lived in Lancashire and worked in the manner of R. Caldecott (q.v.). She signed with initials.
Examples: V.A.M.

HOUGHTON, Georgiana
- 1884 (Kensington)
An exhibition of her 'Spirit Drawings in Watercolour' was held at the New British Gallery, London, on 22 May 1871. These were done under the guidance of her sister Zilla (d.1851) who had been 'an accomplished artist while upon earth'; her brother Cecil Angelo Houghton; Henry Lenny who had been a deaf and dumb artist; and other spirits including those of H.R.H. the late Prince Albert (q.v.), W. Blake (q.v.) and W. Shakespeare.
Published: *Evenings at Home in Spiritual Seance*, 1881. *Chronicles of the Photographs of Spiritual Beings*, 1882.

HOUSTON, George, R.S.A., R.I., R.S.W.
1869 (Dalry, Ayrshire) - 1947 (Dalry)
A painter of Ayrshire and Argyllshire landscapes. He lived in Glasgow and was elected R.S.W. in 1908, A.R.S.A. in 1909, R.I. in 1920 and R.S.A. in 1924.
Examples: Glasgow A.G.
Bibliography: *Studio*, XXXVIII, 1906; LXIII, 1915; Special Winter No., 1917; LXXII, 1918. *A.J.*, 1908.

HOUSTON, John Adam Plimmer, R.S.A., R.I.
1802 (Gwydyr Castle, Wales) - 1884 (London)
A landscape painter who studied in Edinburgh, at the R.A. Schools, in Paris and Germany, and settled in London in 1858. He exhibited at the R.S.A. from 1833 and was elected A.R.S.A. and R.S.A. in 1842 and 1845. After an unsuccessful attempt in 1868 he was elected A.N.W.S. and N.W.S. in 1874 and 1879. As well as landscapes he painted Cattermole-like Civil War and genre subjects.
Examples: Ashmolean; Maidstone Mus.; N.G., Scotland.
Bibliography: *A.J.*, 1869. *The Year's Art*, 1885. *Portfolio*, 1887.

HOUSTON, John Rennie McKenzie, R.S.W.
1856 (Glasgow) - 1932
A painter of figures and interiors in oil and watercolour, he was trained in Glasgow and lived at Rutherglen until he retired to Edinburgh in about 1930. He was elected R.S.W. in 1889, and his watercolours are inspired by the Dutch school.

His brother **Charles HOUSTON (d.?1936)** was a painter of landscapes and flower studies, occasionally in watercolour. He too lived in Glasgow and latterly at Rutherglen.
Examples: Kirkaldy A.G.

HOUSTON, John Adam Plimmer (1802-1884)
Loch Lomond. *17in. x 27in.*

HOWITT, Samuel (1756-1822)
A country inn, with coaches. *Watercolour, 5in. x 8in.*

HOWARD, Edward Stirling
1809   - 1878
A Sheffield artist who exhibited landscapes and rustic subjects on infrequent occasions from 1834 to 1870. He was an unsuccessful candidate for the N.W.S. in 1867 and 1868, in which latter year he sketched in North Wales.
Examples: V.A.M.; Mappin A.G., Sheffield.

HOWARD, Hon. Frances
1746   - 1818 (Ashstead)
The youngest daughter of Mary, **Viscountess ANDOVER (1716-1803)** who was a daughter of the 2nd Earl of Aylesford. Both mother and daughter were artists in pen and grey wash. Frances married Richard Bagot (q.v.), fourth son of Sir W.W. Bagot, Bt., in 1783, and he took her maiden name. She was the heiress of her nephew, the 13th Earl of Suffolk and 6th Earl of Berkshire. **Thomas HOWARD, 14th Earl of Suffolk AND 7th Earl of Berkshire (1721-1783)** was also a draughtsman. In style the family owed much to their double cousin, the 4th Earl of Aylesford (q.v.) and to his connection with J.B. Malchair (q.v.).
Examples: B.M.; Ashmolean.
Bibliography: *W &D*, 1987, iv.
See Aylesford Family Tree

HOWARD, George James
see CARLISLE, George James Earl of

HOWARD, Henry, R.A.
1769 (London) - 1847 (Oxford)
A classical and history painter who became

Professor of Painting at the R.A. in 1833. He himself was a pupil (and son-in-law) of Reinagle (q.v.), and had studied at the R.A. Schools, receiving a gold medal in 1790. He travelled to Rome in 1791, where his friend Flaxman influenced his figure drawing, returning in 1794 by way of Vienna and Dresden. Although largely thought of as a monumental oil painter, he did many book illustrations which can be charming, in a 'Keepsake' manner.
Examples: V.A.M.; Soane Mus.

HOWARD, Vernon 1840   - 1902
A drawing master who worked at Boston and Sutton, Lincolnshire, at Kidderminster and Grantham. He exhibited at the R.I. and elsewhere from 1864 to 1899.
Examples: V.A.M.; Castle Mus., Nottingham.

HOWITT, Samuel
1756   - 1822 (London)
A country gentleman from Chigwell in Essex, Howitt became a professional artist only because of his financial troubles. He first exhibited in 1783 and his subjects are always drawn from country and sporting life. His style is very clearly influenced by Rowlandson (q.v.), whose sister he married. His drawing, which is fairly crude at the beginning of his career, improves until it is very skilful indeed. One hallmark of his style is a fretted outline for foliage. His animal sketches, often done from life at such places as the Menagerie at the Tower of London, are very lifelike indeed. Although he illustrated a book of Oriental sports, he never went East himself.

Illustrated: T. Williamson: *Oriental Field Sports*, 1807. &c.
Examples: B.M.; V.A.M.; Brighton A.G.; Fitzwilliam; City A.G., Manchester; Newport A.G.
Bibliography: Hewitt Family: *The Pedigree of Hewitt or Howitt of London*, 1959. *The Field*, April, 1927. *British Racehorse*, 1960.

HOWLETT, Bartholomew
1767 (Louth, Lincolnshire) -
1827 (Newington)
An engraver and draughtsman who was apprenticed to James Heath. His work was mainly antiquarian and topographical. In 1817 he made several drawings for a projected *History of Clapham*. He also drew about a thousand seals of English religious houses for John Caley.
Published: *A Selection of views in the County of Lincoln*, 1801.

HOWLEY, Harriet Elizabeth, Mrs. Wright
c.1812   - 1860
The youngest daughter of William Howley (1766-1848), Archbishop of Canterbury, she married J.A. Wright, Rector of Merstham, Surrey, in 1832. She may have been a pupil of Cox (q.v.) and produced pencil and brown wash drawings of North Wales. Her elder sister, Mary Anne Howley (c.1807-1834) married the great-nephew and heir of Sir G.H. Beaumont (q.v.).

HOWMAN, Rev. George Ernest
c.1795   - 1874
The vicar of Sonning, Berkshire, from 1822, he rose in Trollopean fashion to become rural

dean of Barnsley, Gloucestershire, Master of St. Nicholas Hospital, Sarum, and a canon of Bristol. To judge by a view of the Orwell dated 1848, he was capable of good, easy effects in pencil and watercolour heightened with white.

HOWSE, George, N.W.S.   - 1860
A painter of landscape, architecture, town and coastal scenes who lived in London. He exhibited from 1830 and was elected N.W.S. in 1834. He painted in France, Holland and Wales and on the South Coast.
Examples: V.A.M.; N.G., Ireland.

HUBBACK, Catherine Anne, Mrs.
1818 (Portsdown Lodge, nr. Portsmouth) -
A niece of Jane Austen and of J. Austen (q.v.), she too became a novelist as well as an amateur painter. In 1842 she married a barrister whose family came from Northumberland, and later because of his ill health they travelled about the spas of England and Wales.

Her landscapes and drawings of family life are generally crude but always charming.
Bibliography: *Country Life*, 30 Mar. 1978.

HUDSON, William, N.W.S.
1782   - 1847
A portrait and architectural painter who lived in Croydon and London and exhibited from 1803. He was elected N.W.S. in 1834. Early in his career he also painted flower subjects.

HUEFFER, Catherine, Mrs. née Madox Brown   1850   - 1927 (London)

The younger daughter and pupil of F.M. Brown (q.v.) she was a follower of the Pre-Raphaelites and exhibited from 1869 to 1872. She married Francis Hueffer.

HUGGINS, William   1820 (Liverpool) -
1884 (Christleton, nr. Chester)
An animal painter who studied at the Mechanics' Institute, the Liverpool Academy and from the life in the zoo. In 1861 he moved to Chester and in 1876 and 1877 lived in Betws-y-coed. He exhibited at the R.A. from 1846. As well as his best known animal subjects in oil and watercolour or chalk, he painted portraits, landscapes and themes from Milton and the Bible. His drawing is good and his colour brilliant. Few artists have better painted the eye of a lion. His tombstone proclaims him a 'just and compassionate man, who would neither tread on a worm nor cringe to an emperor'.
Examples: Williamson A.G., Birkenhead; Warrington A.G.
Bibliography: *A.J.*, 1904. *Connoisseur*, 1913. *British Racehorse*, 1967.

HUGGINS, William John
1781   - 1845 (London)
A marine painter whose early life was spent as a sailor on East Indiamen, visiting China and the Far East. He exhibited at the R.A. from 1817, having settled in Leadenhall Street. He retained links with the East India Company and was regularly employed to paint pictures of their ships. He was marine painter to

George IV and William IV. There are many aquatints after his works.

Although primarily an oil painter he made occasional watercolours. His drawing is good and accurate, but his colour and composition are weak.

His daughter **Bertha HUGGINS** produced grey wash drawings and married E. Duncan (q.v.). There is an example of her work at Greenwich.

It is likely that **James Miller HUGGINS,** who lived nearby in Leadenhall Street and was active as a marine painter in oil and watercolour from about 1830 until at least 1849, was William's son and pupil.
Examples: Greenwich.

HUGHES, Arthur
1832 (London) - 1915 (Kew)
The Pre-Raphaelite illustrator, genre and historical painter. He entered the R.A. Schools in 1847 and first exhibited two years later. In 1858 he moved out of London to Kew and the quality of his work in oil and watercolour declined. His remaining works were sold at Christie's, 21 November 1921.
Illustrated: T. Hughes: *Tom Brown's Schooldays,* 1869. &c.
Examples: B.M.; Ashmolean; City A.G., Manchester.
Bibliography: *Portfolio*, 1870. *L'Art*, LIX, 1894. *A.J.*, 1904. *Studio*, LXVII, 1916; LXXII, 1918. *Burlington Mag.*, XXVIII, 1915-16. *Apollo*, Mar. 1964. Nat Gall Wales, Exhibition Cat., 1971. L. Roberts: *A.H., His Life and Works*, 1997.

HUGGINS, William (1820-1884)
Lions. *Watercolour, signed and dated 1869.*

HULK, Abraham (1813 -1897)
Shipping in a choppy sea. *Watercolour, signed, 5¾in. x 9in.*

HUGHES, Arthur Foord
1856   - 1934
A landscape and genre painter who lived in Surrey, London and the Isle of Wight. Windmills were a favourite subject.
Illustrated: G.M. Fowell: *Windmills in Sussex*, 1930.
Examples: Haworth A.G., Accrington; Hove Lib.; Maidstone Mus.

HUGHES, Edward
1827   - 1905 (S. London)
An antiquary and topographer who prepared two volumes of *Kent Sketches and Annotation* which were presented to the Maidstone Mus. in 1905. As well as original drawings these contain copies of works by his cousin W. Alexander (q.v.).
    The illustrator **Edward HUGHES** II (1832-1908) lived and worked in London, producing literary and historical subjects. He was the son of the painter George Hughes and exhibited at the R.A. from the age of fourteen. He is now best remembered for royal and society portraits.
Examples: Maidstone Mus.
Bibliography: *A.J.*, 1859.

HUGHES, Edward Robert, R.W.S.
1851 (London) - 1914 (St. Albans)
A painter of romantic genre subjects who studied at the R.A. Schools and with his uncle A. Hughes (q.v.) and Holman Hunt (q.v.). He exhibited from 1870 and was elected A.R.W.S. and R.W.S. in 1891 and 1895.

Examples: Ashmolean; Maidstone Mus.; Melbourne A.G.; Sydney A.G.
Bibliography: *W&D, 1990, iv.*

HUGHES, John
1790 (Uffington) - 1857 (London)
An author, he was educated at Westminster and Oriel. He lived at Uffington, where his father was vicar, from about 1820 to 1833 when he moved to Donnington Priory, Berkshire. He was an etcher and sculptor as well as an accomplished draughtsman. His sketches were worked up by P. de Wint (q.v.) and engraved by William Bernard Cooke for *Views in the South of France*, 1825.
Published: *An Itinerary of Provence and the Rhone &c.*, 1822.

HUGHES, John Joseph
1820   - 1909 (W. Bromwich)
A Birmingham landscape painter who worked extensively in Wales and the Lake District. He exhibited in London from 1838 to 1867 and in Birmingham from 1862 to 1908. He also painted coastal and town subjects, churches and still lifes, and he worked in oil and watercolour.

HUGHES, William 1842-1901
– see under **STANTON, Sir H.E.P. Hughes-**

HUGHES, William W., Yr.
A landscape painter who lived at Welbatch near Shrewsbury and in London. He exhibited

between 1830 and 1853, and painted in Wales and on the Thames as well as in Shropshire. He also showed at least one watercolour portrait, which may have been a miniature.

HULK, Abraham
1813 (Amsterdam) - 1897 (London)
A marine and landscape painter, primarily in oil. He studied under the portraitist J.W. Daiwaille and at the Amsterdam Academy from 1828 to 1834. He then visited America and worked in Holland·before settling in London in 1870. He specialised in Dutch barges.
    The son, **Abraham HULK, Yr.,** painted landscape and coastal watercolours, in a manner even less distinguished than the father, between 1876 and 1898. He lived in Dorking.
    William Frederick HULK, who exhibited animal subjects at the N.W.S. and elsewhere from 1875, may have been another son.

HULL, Clementina M   , Mrs
A sketcher of flower and figure subjects who lived in Kensington and was active from 1866 to 1904. She also painted genre subjects in oil.

HULL, Edward
A lithographer and topographical draughtsman working between 1820 and 1834. He may be the 'Dealer in Curiosities' in London whose stock was sold up in 1845 and 1846. He painted in France and was an acquaintance of T.S. Boys (q.v.).
Examples: B.M.

HULL, Edward, II
1823 (Keysoe, Beds.) - 1905 (Sharnbrook)
The son of a farmer, rather than of his name-
sake, he painted genre subjects, landscapes
and illustrations and exhibited from 1860 to
1877. His brother W. Hull (q.v.) who had
encouraged his early efforts, used his
Stockwell address in 1867.
Illustrated: A.J. Buckland: *The Little Warringtons*,
1861. Sir S. Lee: *Stratford on Avon*, 1885. A.J.
Church: *The Laureate's Country*, 1891.
Examples: Coventry A.G.
Bibliography: S. Houfe (publ.): *The William Cowper
Album by E.H.*, 1981.

HULL, George
A Leicester artist who exhibited at the R.I.
from 1875 to 1900. He was probably related to
Samuel Hull, active as a sculptor in Leicester
from 1818 to 1850.

HULL, William
1820 (Grafham, Huntingdonshire) -
1880 (Rydal)
The son of a farmer, Hull was intended for a
minister of the Moravian Church at Ockbrook,
Derbyshire, where he trained for three years, at
the same time taking drawing lessons from the
Germans Petersen and Hassé. He spent a year
as assistant at the settlement at Wellhouse,
Yorkshire, and two or three years from 1838 at
Grace Hill, Ballymena. He gave up his
appointment in 1840 and worked as a printer's
clerk in Manchester, where he also studied at
the school of design. He travelled on the
Continent as a tutor from 1841 to 1844,
thereafter returning to Manchester, where he
lived until 1870 when he he moved to Rydal.
He was left lame and deaf by a stroke in 1850.
His best known works are fruit and flower
pieces closely modelled on those of W. Henry
Hunt (q.v.), but he also produced landscapes in
wash, and book illustrations. In his earlier
works his colour is weak, as Ruskin told him,
but it improves.
An earlier **William HULL** was at the
Portsmouth Naval Academy at the beginning
of the 19th century. The watercolours with
which he illustrated his navigation exercises
are excellent examples of the military amateur.
They may have been influenced by the
Cleveleys (qq.,).
Examples: V.A.M.; Abbot Hall A.G., Kendal.
Bibliography: Manchester Literary Club: *In
memoriam W.H.*, 1880. *Portfolio*, 1886; 1887.

HULLMANDEL, Charles Joseph
1789 (London) - 1850 (London)
One of the foremost lithographers of his time.
He travelled on the Continent, studying and
sketching, before turning to printmaking in
1818. His first publication, produced in that
year, was *Twenty-Four Views of Italy* from his
own drawings. He later reproduced the
drawings of artists such as C. Stanfield, D.
Roberts, L. Haghe and G. Cattermole (qq.v).

Published: *The Art of Drawing on Stone*, 1824.
Ancient Castellated Mansions in Scotland, 1833.

HULME, Frederick William
1816 (Swinton, Yorkshire) - 1884 (London)
The son of an artist, he produced figure studies
before turning to landscape. He first exhibited
at Birmingham in 1841, and later at the B.I.,
the Manchester Institution and the R.A. He
moved to London in 1844 and worked for the
A.J. and other publications. He taught drawing
and painting.
His watercolours, which are often views of
Betws-y-coed, are very much in the manner of
T. Creswick (q.v.).
Published: *A graduated Series of Drawing copies on
Landscape subjects for use in Schools*, 1850.
Bibliography: *A.J.*, April 1858. *Studio*, Spring No.,
1915.

HUME, Rev. John, Dean of Derry
c.1743 (Oxford) - 1818
A competent topographer and antiquarian
draughtsman who lived at Glenalla House,
near Rathmullen, Co. Donegal. He was Dean
of Derry from 1783.

HUMPHREYS, Captain Henry
1773/4 (America) -
He entered the Navy as a midshipman in 1792
and two years later was master of the *Chatham*
on Vancouver's circumnavigation. Two plates
were taken from his drawings for the official
account: *Voyage round the World*, 1798.

HUNN, Thomas Henry
1856 (Hackney) - 1928 (Tonbridge)
A landscape and Thames painter who lived in
Hackney and Surrey and exhibited at the R.A.
and Suffolk Street from 1878 to 1910.
Sometimes his work can be Allingham-like
and is brightly coloured.

HUNSLEY, William
A topographer and military artist who also
worked as a draughtsman for the East India
Company in Madras. He was active between
1837 and 1843.
Examples: India Office Lib.

HUNT, Alfred William, R.W.S.
1830 (Liverpool) - 1896 (London)
The son of A. Hunt (q.v.), he was educated at
Corpus Christi, Oxford, of which he became a
Fellow in 1853. Although he first exhibited at
the age of twelve, he was destined for an
academic career. It was only on his marriage to
the novelist Margaret Raine in 1861, which
meant automatic resignation of his Fellowship,
that he turned to art full-time. He had already
become a member of the Liverpool Academy
in 1856, and was exhibiting Pre-Raphaelite
works at the R.A. He had visited Scotland,
Cumberland, Devonshire and Wales in his
youth, the Rhine in 1850, and Wales again in
1854. In 1862 he moved to London and was

elected A.O.W.S. He became a full Member in
1864 and Vice-President in 1888. He and his
wife were at the centre of an artistic and
literary circle.
Hunt's main sketching grounds were
Scotland, the Lakes, the Thames Valley and
Whitby, but his first love was always North
Wales. He also visited Mont St. Michel and
Oberwesel, the Rhine and Moselle, and in
1869-70 made a nine month tour of Italy,
Sicily and Greece. At some point he visited
America. Although influenced by Turner's
middle period, he always works with a Pre-
Raphaelite minuteness of detail. Having
achieved this he sometimes works backwards
again so as to reduce the finish and secure
atmospheric effect. Some of his Welsh
sketches are reminiscent of Linnell.
A memorial exhibition was held at the
Burlington Fine Arts Club in 1897.
Examples: B.M.; V.A.M.; Ashmolean; Leeds City
A.G.
Bibliography: *Portfolio*, 1876. *A.J.*, 1896; 1897;
1903. *Studio*, Winter No., 1917-18. O.W.S. Club, II,
1925.

HUNT, Andrew
1790 (Erdington, nr. Birmingham) -
1861 (Liverpool)
A pupil of S. Lines (q.v.) and a lifelong friend
of D. Cox (q.v.), he moved to Liverpool quite
early in life, becoming a leading member of
the Academy there. He was a landscape
painter and a drawing master. One of his
children was A.W. Hunt (q.v.).

HUNT, Arthur Ackland
A landscape painter who lived in London until
at least 1902 and exhibited from 1863. He
painted in Cornwall and also produced still
lifes and literary subjects. In the 1890s he was
Instructor of Freehand Drawing at Greenwich.

HUNT, Cecil Arthur, R.W.S.
1873 (Torquay) - 1965 (Burnham)
A landscape painter in watercolour, oil and
tempera. He was educated at Winchester and
Trinity College, Cambridge. He was elected
A.R.W.S. and R.W.S. in 1918 and 1925, and
was a member of the R.B.A. from 1914 to
1921. He lived in London and South Devon.
Examples: B.M.; V.A.M.; Blackburn A.G.;
Cartwright Hall, Bradford; Exeter Mus.;
Fitzwilliam; Glasgow A.G.; India Office Lib.; Leeds
City A.G.; City A.G., Manchester; Newport A.G.
Bibliography: *Athenaeum*, II, 1919. *Burlington
Mag.*, XLIV. *Studio*, LXVI, 1916; LXXXV, 1923.
O.W.S. Club XXXVIII, 1963.

HUNT, Captain George Henry
c.1820 - ?1858
A draughtsman who joined the 57th Foot in
1838 and transferred to the 78th on promotion
to captain ten years later. He served in India at
least between 1849 and 1851, and he appears
to have died, or at least retired, in 1858.

HUNT, William Henry (1790-1864)
Still life with apples and holly. *Watercolour, signed, 6in. x 8¼in.*

HUNT, Thomas, A.R.S.A., R.S.W.
1854 (Skipton) - 1929 (Glasgow)
A painter of Scottish landscapes and characters in watercolour and oil. He studied at the Glasgow School of Art and in Paris and lived in Glasgow. He served as Vice-President of the R.S.W. and was elected A.R.S.A. in 1914. He was known as the 'Highland cattle man'.
Examples: Glasgow A.G.: Leeds City A.G.; Wakefield A.G.
Bibliography: *A.J.*, 1898. *Studio*, LXIII, 1915; LXIX, 1917; LXXXIV, 1922.

HUNT, William Henry, O.W.S.
1790 (London) - 1864 (London)
The son of a Covent Garden tinman. Since he had deformed legs, he was thought incapable of anything better than art. He was apprenticed to J. Varley (q.v.) in about 1804 and one of his fellow pupils was J. Linnell (q.v.). The two aspiring artists seem to have had a good influence on each other's work, and they made a number of sketching tours together, including a visit to Hastings in 1809. In 1808 he entered the R.A. Schools, but probably he did not stay there very long. He was, however, one of the group of students who were selected to help redecorate Drury Lane Theatre after the fire of 1809. His earliest important private patrons were the Duke of Devonshire and the Earl of Essex, who commissioned drawings of the staterooms at Chatsworth and Cassiobury.

At the latter place he met Dr. Monro (q.v.) who also employed him. By 1815 he had set up on his own as an architectural and rustic painter. He exhibited with the Oil and Watercolour Society, but failed to gain election to the O.W.S. in 1823. He was elected associate, however, in the following year, and became a full member in 1826. By this time he was turning from pure landscapes and buildings to studies of rustics and to still lifes.

Throughout his life Hunt visited Hastings and the South Coast, and he rarely seems to have left the Southern Counties. His work can be divided into two periods; in the first, up to about 1825, he was in some ways a traditional topographical draughtsman, working carefully with the pen and using thin washes of pale colour. In the second period his work is marked by a massing and building up of colour by a technique of hatching with a number of different tints to obtain a lifelike texture. His colours in this period are generally laid over a ground of white bodycolour to give them luminosity. He had a keen sense of humour, not without its malicious edge, and enjoyed poking fun at the foibles of his rustics. Unfortunately the popularity of these works and of the still lifes which earned him the nickname of 'Bird's nest Hunt' caused him to neglect his great talent for landscape.

His remaining works were sold at Christie's, May 16-17, 1864. His few pupils included

A.M. Fitzjames (q.v.) and J. Sherrin (q.v.).
Examples: B.M.; V.A.M.; Aberdeen A.G.; Haworth A.G., Accrington; Ashmolean; Williamson A.G., Birkenhead; Blackburn A.G.; Blackpool A.G.; Grundy A.G., Blackpool; Cartwright Hall, Bradford; Brighton A.G.; Derby A.G.; Dudley A.G.; Glasgow A.G.; Leeds City A.G.; Leicestershire A.G.; Newport A.G.; Reading A.G.; N.G., Scotland; Ulster Mus.
Bibliography: J. Ruskin: *Notes on S. Prout and W.H.H.*, 1879; J. Witt: *W.H.H.*, 1982; *A.J.*, April, 1864; 1895. *Fraser's Mag.*, Oct. 1865; *Portfolio*, 1888; 1891. *Mag. of Art*, XXII, 1898. *Studio*, XXXVII, 1906; Special No., 1919; 1922-23. Connoisseur, XXXXIX, 1914. O.W.S. Club XII, 1936; *Country Life*, 27 April 1972.
See Colour Plate

HUNT, William Holman, A.R.S.A., R.S.W., Hon. R.W.S.1827 (London) - 1910 (London)
The Pre-Raphaelite Brother. He worked for an estate agent before studying with H. Rogers, the portrait painter, and at the B.M., N.G. and the R.A. Schools from 1844. He exhibited from 1846. 1848-9 was the great year of the Brotherhood, and in 1849 Hunt visited the Continent with Rossetti. He first visited Egypt and Syria in 1854. He was in Italy from 1865 to 1867 and the Holy Land from 1869 to 1871. He was again in Palestine from 1875 to 1878 and in 1892. He was elected A.O.W.S. and O.W.S. in 1869 and 1887, but retired in 1893.

His watercolours, often studies for, or derived from, his oil paintings, show the meticulous handling that one would expect. They can be very fine indeed.
Examples: B.M.; V.A.M.; Ashmolean; Coventry A.G.; City A.G., Manchester.
Bibliography: *A Memoir of W.H.H.'s Life*, 1860; F.W. Farrar: *W.H.H.*, 1893; H.W. Shrewsbury: *Brothers in Art*, 1920; A.C. Gissing: *W.H.H.*, 1936; D. Holman Hunt: *My Grandmothers and I*, 1960. D. Holman Hunt: *My Grandfather, His Wives and Loves*, 1969. A.C. Amor: *W.H.H., The True Pre-Raphaelite*, 1989. J.Maas: *H.H. and The Light of the World*, 1984. *A.J.*, 1910; *O.W.S. Club* XIII, 1935-6; Walker A.G., Liverpool, Exhibition Cat., 1969; *Country Life*, 3 April 1969.

HUNT, William Howes
1806   -1879
A painter of beaches and fishing boats who lived at Great Yarmouth. His work is good enough to make one wish that it were better.
Examples: B.M.; Castle Mus., Norwich; Gt. Yarmouth Lib.

HUNTER, Colin, A.R.A., R.I., R.S.W.
1841 (Glasgow) - 1904 (London)
Best known for his seascapes in oil, for which he was elected A.R.A. in 1884, he also painted marine watercolours and was elected R.I. in 1882. In his youth he lived in the Western Highlands, and the pictures he painted there best show his particular skill at rendering the changing effects of water.
His remaining works were sold at Christie's, 8 April 1905.
Bibliography: *A.J.*, 1884; 1885. *Portfolio*, 1887. *The Scots Pictorial*, 1898. *Studio*, Special No., 1919.

HUNTER, Lieutenant James - 1792 (India)
An artilleryman who served under Cornwallis against Tippoo Sultan.
Illustrated: Blagdon: *A Brief History of Ancient and Modern India. Pictorial Scenery in the Kingdom of Mysore*, 1804-5.

HUNTER, Mason, A.R.S.A., R.S.W.
1854 (Broxburn) - 1921 (Edinburgh)
A landscape and marine painter in oil and watercolour. He studied in Edinburgh and Paris, exhibited from 1881, and was elected R.S.W. in 1896 and A.R.S.A. in 1913.
Bibliography: *Studio*, XXVII, 1903; XLII, 1908; LXIV, 1915; LXVII, 1916; LXVIII, 1916. LXXIII, 1918.

HUNTINGDON, Francis H
A landscape painter in oil and watercolour who lived at Ipswich and exhibited from 1849 to 1894. He painted in the West Country Wales and Scotland as well as in East Anglia.

HUNTINGFIELD, Louisa, Lady
- 1898
The daughter of Andrew Arcedeckne, she married the future 3rd Lord Huntingfield in 1839. He succeeded to the title in 1844. She painted landscapes in the manner of her teacher, H. Bright (q.v.).

HUNTLY, Maria Antoinetta, Marchioness of   c.1822   - 1893
The daughter of the Rev. P.W. Pegus and the Countess Dowager of Lindsey who was a daughter of the Dean of Bristol and a niece of the archaeologist Sir H.A. Layard. In 1844 she married as his second wife Lord Aboyne, M.P. for East Grinstead and afterwards Huntingdonshire. In 1853 he succeeded to the marquisate. She gave him seven sons and after his death in 1863 presumably had more time for painting. She travelled widely, visiting among other countries Turkey, Japan, New Zealand, Australia and Canada. She was a good landscape painter, although her mannerism of drawing foliage with a downward zigzag may be more effective for tremulous birches than for other trees.

HURDIS, James Henry
1800 (Southampton) - 1857 (Southampton)
After an education at Southampton and in France he was articled to C. Heath (q.v.), who taught him drawing and engraving. He was never a professional artist, but drew and etched many caricatures in the style of G. Cruikshank (q.v.). He lived mostly at Newick, Sussex, but returned to Southampton towards the end of his life. He also dabbled in architecture.

HURLSTONE, Frederick Yeates
1800 (London) - 1869 (London)
Great-nephew of Richard Hurlstone, the portraitist and friend of Wright of Derby, he was a pupil of Beechey and Lawrence, and possibly Haydon. He entered the R.A. Schools in 1820 and first exhibited at the R.A. in the following year. In 1831 he was elected to the S.B.A. and became President in 1835. He paid a number of visits to Italy, Spain and Morocco between 1835 and 1854.
He was a portrait and historical painter and, in his later years, produced many rather weak studies of Continental and Arab peasants.
His wife **Jane HURLSTONE, née CORAL (d.1858)** exhibited watercolours and portraits at the R.A. and S.B.A. from 1846 to 1850.
Examples: B.M.
Bibliography: *A.J.*, 1869; 1870.

HUSON, Thomas, R.I.
1844 (Liverpool) - 1920 (Bala)
A landscape painter in oil and watercolour and an etcher, he worked as a chemist before taking up painting as a profession. He was elected R.I. in 1883, and he lived in Liverpool until about 1907 when he moved to Bala.
His wife was also an artist.
Published: *Round about Snowdon*, 1894; *Round about Helvellyn*, 1895.
Bibliography: *Studio*, Summer No., 1902; XXVIII,

1903; XXXIX, 1907. *A.J.*, 1904; 1905; 1907; 1909. *The Year's Art*, 1921.

HUSSEY, Henrietta, Mrs., née Grove
1819 (Salisbury) - 1899
An amateur landscape painter in watercolour and oil, she was a pupil of D.C. Read (q.v.) in Salisbury, where she lived after her marriage in 1839. She visited the Continent and North Wales as well as making sketches on the South Coast. Her watercolours show a freedom possibly influenced by Whistler (q.v.), but they can be oversplashy.

HUTCHESON, Walter   - 1910
A landscape, rustic genre and figure painter in oil and watercolour who lived in Glasgow, where he was active from around 1869. His favourite subjects were found on the West Coast, especially on Arran. He may have had a painting namesake in Glasgow during the 1880s.

HUTCHINSON, Robert Gemmell, R.S.A., R.W.S.   1860 (Edinburgh) -
1936 (Coldingham, Berwickshire)
A genre, portrait and landscape painter who was much influenced by Josef Israels both in style and subject. He studied at the Board of Manufacturers' School of Art, Edinburgh, and lived in Edinburgh and Musselburgh. He exhibited from 1878 and was elected R.S.W. in 1895 and A.R.S.A. and R.S.A. in 1901 and 1911.
His son **George Jackson HUTCHISON (1896-1918)** painted pastoral scenes in oil and watercolour, which he had begun to exhibit before being killed in the First World War.
Illustrated: T.R. Barnett: *Reminiscences of Old Scots Folk*, 1913.
Bibliography: *A.J.*, 1900. *Studio*, 1913; 1915.

HUTCHINSON, Samuel
A marine painter who lived in London and exhibited at the R.A. and elsewhere from 1770 to 1802. His work can be like that of S. Atkins (q.v.).

HUTH, Frederick, Yr.   - 1906
A painter of landscapes, town scenes, interiors and portraits who lived in Edinburgh and exhibited at the R.A. and R.S.A. from 1881. He was also an etcher and engraver, often after such old masters as Rembrandt and Gainsborough.

HUTTULA, Richard Carl
c.1839   - 1893 (Edmonton)
A genre painter who exhibited at Suffolk Street and in Brighton from 1866 to 1887. He lived in London.
Published: *The Young Dragoon*, 1874.
Illustrated: W.H.G. Kingston: *Hurricane Harry*, 1874.

HYDE, Henry James
A London painter of genre subjects who exhibited at the R.I. from 1883.

I'ANSON, Charles 1848 - 1907 (London)
Perhaps a younger son or nephew of the architect and surveyor Edward I'Anson, yr. (1812-1888). He painted landscapes, coastal and river scenes. He entered the R.A. Schools in 1874, and he lived in London.

Frederick I'ANSON (b.1813/4), presumably a younger son of the elder Edward I'Anson (1775-1853), was admitted to the Schools as a painter in 1830. He exhibited portraits (with or without pets) between 1833 and 1837.

IBBETSON, Sir John Thomas Selwin, 6th Bt 1789 - 1869
An amateur landscape painter who lived at Down Hall, Essex, and Denton Park, Otley, Yorkshire. In 1825, he assumed the additional surname of Selwin on receiving an inheritance from his mother's family, and he sometimes used this name alone as a signature. He exhibited drawings at the R.A. in 1811 and 1812 as well as in his friend Walter Fawkes' exhibition of 1817. In that year he toured Italy and Sicily, and he also sketched in Devon and Cornwall. His son was created Lord Rookwood.

Denzil O. IBBETSON (1775-1857) who fought in the Peninsula and sketched Napoleon and his companions on St. Helena, seems to have been a member of the same family.

IBBETSON, Julius Caesar
1759 (Farnley Moor, Leeds) - 1817 (Masham)
The 'English Berghem' was apprenticed to a ship painter in Hull in 1772. He remained there for five years, also painting scenery for Tate Wilkinson, before leaving for London. There he worked for a picture restorer until 1784, studying techniques and gradually making himself a name, and he exhibited at the R.A. for the first time in 1785. In 1787 and 1788 he sailed as draughtsman to the Chinese Embassy of the Hon. Charles Cathcart, visiting Madeira, the Cape, and Java, where the Ambassador died. On Ibbetson's return he painted in South Wales, staying at Cardiff Castle with Lord Bute, in 1789, and on the Isle of Wight in 1791. Naval subjects, smugglers and sailors ashore were popular during the French wars. He also moved out of London to Kilburn and later to Paddington. In 1792, he made an extensive tour of North Wales with the Hon. R.F. Greville (q.v.). From the death of his first wife in 1794 he went through a period of great personal and professional difficulty culminating in a disastrous contract to work for the dealer Vernon in Liverpool in 1798. In 1800 he was in Edinburgh and Roslin during the summer and he won the friendship and

IBBETSON, Julius Caesar (1759-1817)
View on the Serpentine River looking towards Hyde Park Corner. *Pen and black ink and watercolour, signed. 8¾in. x 12in.*

patronage of Lady Crawford. He then settled at Ambleside and remarried in 1801. He moved to Troutbeck in 1803 and, following commissions at Swinton and crippling rheumatism brought on by the climate of the Lake District, to Masham in the North Riding.

His work, both in oil and watercolour, is based on the Dutch landscape tradition, but he has an elegance and wit which are entirely his own. His figures have a superficial resemblance to those of Wheatley or La Cave, but he is by far the greater artist, for his are not pretty stereotypes, but real people. His comparatively rare portraits are fine studies in character.

His daughter by his first marriage was adopted and brought up by Sir G. Beaumont (q.v.), and his eldest son, **Julius Caesar IBBETSON, Yr. (1783-1825)**, followed him to Liverpool and the Lake District. In 1805 he set up as a drawing master at Richmond in place of G. Cuitt (q.v.), and he died there, a respected councilman as well as artist and landlord of the Fleece Inn.

Published: *An Accidence or Gamut of Painters in Oil and Watercolours*, 1803. *Process of Tinted Drawing*, 1805.
Illustrated: J. Trusler: *Modern Times*, 1785. J. Hassell: *A Picturesque Guide to Bath*, 1793. *Church: Cabinet of Quadrupeds*, 1796.
Examples: B.M.; V.A.M.; Aberdeen A.G.; City Mus., Bristol; Darlington A.G.; Fitzwilliam; Greenwich; Leeds City A.G.; Leicestershire A.G.; N.G., Ireland; Newport A.G.; Nat. Lib. Wales.
Bibliography: ?Bella Ibbetson: *A Memoir of the Author's Life* (in the second edition of Ibbetson's *An Accidence of Painting in Oil)*, 1828. B.L.K.

Henderson: *Morland and Ibbetson*, 1923. R.M. Clay: *J.C.I.*, 1948. J. Mitchell: *J.C.I, the Berchem of England*, 1999. *Gentleman's Mag.*, 1817, p.637. J. Mitchell & Son, London, Exhibition Cat., 1999.
See Colour Plate

IKEN, Jonathan Alfred
An artist who visited Brazil and the Cape Verde Islands in 1858-9. He painted panoramic view of the towns in which he stayed; they are poorly drawn but well coloured.

IMAGE, Rev. Selwyn
1849 (Bodiam) - 1930
The clergyman, academic, stained glass designer, watercolour painter, illustrator and poet, he was educated at Marlborough and New College, Oxford, and he studied at the Slade School, Oxford, with Ruskin (q.v.). He was ordained in 1872, serving as a curate in London. He was President of the Art Workers' Guild in 1900 and Professor of Fine Art at Oxford from 1910 to 1916. He designed stained glass windows for the 1900 Paris Exhibition and for churches in London and Devon, and designed *ex libris* as well as illustrating books.
Illustrated: L. Binyon: *Lyric Poems*, 1894. &c.

INCE, Joseph Murray
1806 (Presteigne, Radnor) - 1859 (London)
A pupil of Cox (q.v.) at Hereford from 1823 to 1826, when he came to London and began to exhibit at the R.A. and the S.B.A. By 1832 he had moved to Cambridge, where he worked as

INCHBOLD – INNES

an architectural draughtsman, and he returned to Presteigne about three years later, remaining there for the rest of his life. However, although his memorial is in the church there, he actually died in London and is buried in Kensal Green.

He was best known for his small landscapes and coastal subjects and was particularly adept at handling the texture of brick and stone.

Published: *Views illustrating the County of Radnor*, 1832.

Examples: B.M.; V.A.M.; Haworth A.G., Accrington; Coventry A.G.; Fitzwilliam; Maidstone Mus.; Newport A.G.; Ulster Mus.

Bibliography: *Studio*, 1902.

INCHBOLD, John William
1830 (Leeds) 1888 - (Headingley)
A landscape painter who was the son of the owner and editor of the *Leeds Intelligencer*. He began his career as a draughtsman for Day and Haghe, taking lessons from L. Haghe (q.v.). He entered the R.A. Schools in 1847 and exhibited from 1849. He travelled widely in Germany, Austria and Switzerland and visited Algeria a year or two before his death.

He enjoyed little popular or Academic success although he had many literary admirers and supporters. His style is hard and overfaithful with rather lurid effects that are reminiscent of MacWhirter (q.v.). He also used thick splashes of bodycolour on occasion. His poetry is perhaps more attractive than his painting.

Published: *Annus Amoris*, 1877.

Examples: V.A.M.; Ashmolean; Leeds City A.G.

Bibliography: *A.J.*, 1871. *Portfolio*, 1874; 1876; 1879. *Athenaeum*, 4 Feb. 1888. Leeds City A.G., Exhibition Cat., 1993.

INCHBOLD, Stanley 1856 -
An artist who studied under Herkomer, lived in Bushey and later at Brading on the Isle of Wight, and who exhibited North African scenes at the R.I. and elsewhere from 1884.

Illustrated: A.C. Inchbold: *Under the Syrian Sun*, 1906; A.C. Inchbold: *Lisbon and Cintra*, 1907; A. Beckett: *The Spirit of the Downs*, 1909; G.N. Whittingham: *The Home of Fadeless Splendour* (Palestine), 1921.

INGALL, John Spence
1850 - 1936
A painter who was living in Barnsley when he exhibited a marine subject at the N.W.S. in 1892. By 1901 he was painting Arabs.

INGLEBY, John 1749 - 1808
A topographer who was active from about 1770. He was in Wales around 1795.

Examples: Nat. Lib., Wales.

INGLEFIELD, Admiral Sir Edward Augustus, F.R.S.
1820 (Cheltenham) - 1894 (London)
The son of a rear-admiral, his own distinguished naval career included the Arctic Expedition of 1853 in search of Franklin, and a period as C. in C., North American Station.

He was Chairman of the Arts Section of the Chelsea Naval Exhibition of 1891, at which he also exhibited. He showed both oil and watercolour paintings at the R.A. He was best known as a practical and scientific man, and the inventor of the 'Inglefield Anchor'. His watercolours are extremely professional, somewhat in the manner of Edward Duncan (q.v.).

Examples: Greenwich.

INGLIS, Jane - 1916
A fruit and flower painter in oil and watercolour who exhibited at the R.A., the N.W.S. and elsewhere from 1859 to 1905.

She should not be confused with **Jean Winifred INGLIS (1884 London - 1959)**, an art mistress and painter in various media.

INGRAM, Hon. Mrs Emily Charlotte MEYNELL, née Wood
1840 - 1904
The eldest daughter of the 1st Viscount Halifax, in 1863 she married H.C. Meynell Ingram, M.P. of Temple Newsam, Leeds (d.1871). They had no children and eventually she left the house to her nephew the 3rd Viscount and 1st Earl. She painted landscapes and copied portraits, before, during and after her marriage. She visited the Scottish islands and many parts of the Continent, and in 1890 she voyaged up the Nile.

On that occasion she was accompanied by her niece, the **Hon. Mary Agnes Emily WOOD (b.1877)**, who was also an accomplished watercolourist and in 1903 married G.R. Lane-Fox, M.P. of Bramham Park.

INGRAM, William Ayerst, R.I.
1855 (Glasgow) - 1913 (Falmouth)
Primarily an oil painter, he also made a number of watercolours of coastal and marine subjects, and was a pupil of J. Steeple (q.v.). He exhibited at the R.A. from 1880 and was elected R.I. in 1907. He travelled widely, becoming President of the Royal British Colonial Society of Artists in 1888. From the 1880s he spent much of his time in St. Ives and Falmouth, and he opened a gallery there in about 1894 with H.S. Tuke (q.v.).

In 1877 his brother, **R.S. INGRAM**, exhibited a watercolour in Glasgow.

Examples: V.A.M.; Greenwich; Sydney A.G.

INNES, James Archibald
A figure and genre painter who lived in Brixton and exhibited at Suffolk Street between 1866 and 1870.

His sister, wife or daughter, **Alice INNES**, exhibited watercolours of flowers in 1869 and 1870. It is possible that they were related to A.I. Withers (q.v.).

INNES, James Dickson
1887 (Llanelly) - 1914 (Swanley, Kent)
A figure and landscape painter in oil and watercolour, who studied at the Slade and was influenced by Augustus John. He painted in Wales, France and Spain, and from 1908 he spent some time in North Africa and Teneriffe because of poor health.

A memorial exhibition was held at the Chenil Gallery, London, in 1923.

Examples: B.M.; V.A.M.; Cartwright Hall, Bradford; Cecil Higgins A.G., Bedford; Fitzwilliam; Leeds City A.G.; Newport A.G.

Bibliography: J. Fothergill and L. Browse: *J.D.I.*, 1946.

IBBETSON, Julius Caesar (1759-1817)
A Long-Fin Albacore. *Signed and inscribed 'An Albacore caught Jan.ᵗ 28. 1788. By Skinner a Mulatto seaman in Lat 2.N. about 18 inches in length – on opening him a number of small fish were found together with a white substance Resembling a Heart from whence he probably takes his name, Julius Ibbetson del ad Nat. Vestal.' Blue and grey washes, 9in. x 14½in.*

INSKIPP, James 1790 - 1868 (Godalming)
An official in the army commissariat who turned professional artist in 1820. He exhibited portraits and figure subjects in oil and watercolour at the R.A. and elsewhere from 1816 to 1864. In the 1830s he made illustrations for an edition of *The Compleat Angler* which was only published in 1875.
Published: *Studies of Heads from Nature*, 1838.

IRELAND, Samuel   - 1800 (London)
Primarily an author, collector and engraver, he made some slightly amateurish architectural and landscape drawings in watercolour. He lived for the most part in London and became deeply involved in the unravelling of the Shakespeare forgeries of his son William

Henry. This affair cast a blight over the latter part of his career.
His daughter, Jane, exhibited miniatures at the R.A. in 1792 and 1793.
Published: *A Picturesque Tour through France, Holland &c, made in the Autumn of 1789, 1790. &c.*
Examples: B.M.

IRELAND, Thomas Tayler
A painter who lived in North London and was particularly fond of pools and rippling streams. He was active from about 1880 to 1927.
In much the same period **James IRELAND** of Liverpool was producing genre subjects in watercolour.

**IRTON, Lieutenant-Colonel Richard
                    - 1847**
An amateur landscape painter who was commissioned in the Rifle Brigade in 1815. He was promoted captain in 1826 and lieutenant colonel in 1841.
Illustrated: G.N. Wright: *The Rhine, Italy and Greece*, 1840. G.N. Wright: *The Shores and Islands of the Mediterranean*, 1840.

IRWIN, Clara   c.1870   -
Probably a daughter of Lt.-Col. De la C.T. Irwin of Carnagh House, A.D.C. to two Governors-General of Canada. She was a painter of Armagh street scenes who was working between 1891 and 1916 and lived in Dublin and Carnagh, Ireland.

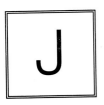

**JACKSON, Rev. Frederick Christian
                1825   - 1898 (Great Stanmore)**
A marine, coastal and landscape painter who was educated at St. John's College, Cambridge and ordained in 1849. For thirty years he was rector of Ruan Minor in Cornwall, and not unnaturally many of his subjects are wrecks on the Cornish coast. He exhibited them at Suffolk Street from 1868 to 1873 and at the R.A. from 1878 to 1884. In 1883 he moved to the less tempestuous rectory of Great Stanmore in Middlesex.

**JACKSON, Frederick Hamilton
                1848   - 1923**
An illustrator and designer who trained at the R.A. Schools, was Master of the Antique School at the Slade, and, in 1880, co-founder of the Chiswick School of Art. He was a member of the R.B.A. and the Langham Sketching Club.
Published: *Sicily*, 1904; *The Shores of the Adriatic*, 1906. &c.

**JACKSON, Frederick William
                1859 (Oldham) - 1918**
Marine and landscape painter in oil and watercolour, and a ceramic designer, he studied at the Oldham School of Art, the Manchester Academy and in Paris. He visited Italy and Morocco and mostly lived at Hinderwell, Yorkshire. He exhibited from 1880 and is particularly noted for his broad and atmospheric sketches.
Examples: Brighton A.G.

Bibliography: *Studio*, XXX, 1904; XLIV, 1908; XLVII, 1907; L, 1910.

JACKSON, George Bryant
A landscape painter who was an unsuccessful candidate for the N.W.S. in 1836. Doubtless he was a relative or godson of G.B. Campion (q.v.) who proposed him, and he may have been the G. Jackson who exhibited a picture of dead game at the R.A. in 1844.

JACKSON, James Eyre
A landscape painter who exhibited between 1876 and 1886. He lived in Sussex, Lancashire and at Torquay, and also painted in Brittany and Berkshire.

**JACKSON, John, R.A.
                1778 (Lastingham, Yorkshire) -
                1831 (London)**
A portrait painter, he was the son of a tailor who discouraged his artistic tendencies. However, he won the patronage of Lord Mulgrave at Whitby, who in turn introduced him to the Earl of Carlisle and Sir G.H. Beaumont (q.v.). The latter sent him to the R.A. Schools in 1804, where he became a close friend of Wilkie and Haydon (qq.v.). He also copied at the B.M. He was elected A.R.A. in 1815 and in 1816 toured the Netherlands with General Phipps, Lord Mulgrave's brother (*see* under Phipps, A.). In 1817 he was elected R.A. and two years later travelled through Switzerland to Rome with Sir F. Chantrey (q.v.).

Although he exhibited regularly, and had an extensive practice, producing very sensitive likenesses, he never achieved the popularity of Lawrence.
Examples: B.M.; V.A.M.; Greenwich; N.P.G.; Newport A.G.
Bibliography: *A.J.*, 1899.

**JACKSON, Mason
                1819 (Ovingham) - 1903 (London)**
Art Editor, and from 1875 Editor, of the *I.L.N.*, he was a wood engraver, illustrator, and landscape painter in oil and watercolour. He painted in his native Northumbria and elsewhere in Britain.
His elder brother **John JACKSON, II (1801-1848)** was his teacher as a wood engraver and also painted genre subjects.
Published: *The Pictorial Press*, 1885.
Illustrated: I. Walton: *Compleat Angler*.

**JACKSON, Samuel, A.O.W.S.
                1794 (Bristol) - 1869 (Clifton)**
The son of a merchant for whom he worked until 1820, when the end of the business and sketching holidays in Scotland and Ireland turned him to art. He was strongly influenced by F. Danby (q.v.) but, unlike his mentor, he remained in Bristol and became the father figure and mainstay of the Bristol School. He built up a successful practice as a drawing master and developed a complex and highly sophisticated technique of painting, with much sponging, stopping, scratching and glazing with thin bodycolour. The majority of his

JACKSON, Samuel Phillips (1830-1904)
Sty Head Tarn, Cumberland, early morning. *Watercolour, signed and dated 1858 and inscribed on an old label to reverse, 22½in. x 36in.*

subjects are British landscapes, particularly from Wales and Devon, but he seems to have visited the West Indies, perhaps for his health, in 1827, and he toured Switzerland in 1854 and 1858. He was elected A.O.W.S. in 1823 and retired in 1848.
Examples: B.M.; V.A.M.; Preston Manor, Brighton; City A.G., Bristol; Fitzwilliam; Glasgow A.G.; Newport A.G.
Bibliography: F. Greenacre and S. Stoddard: *The Bristol Landscape*, 1986. *A.J.*, Feb. 1870.
See Colour Plate

JACKSON, Samuel Phillips, R.W.S.
      1830 (Clifton) - 1904 (Bristol)
The son and pupil of S. Jackson (q.v.), he began by exhibiting oil paintings in London from about 1850. However, after his election as A.O.W.S. in 1853, he turned almost entirely to watercolour painting. He became a full member of the Society in 1876. He moved from Clifton to Streatley-on-Thames in 1870 and in 1876 to Henley. Later, however, he returned to Clifton.

His earlier coastal subjects were mostly found in Cornwall and Devon, with a few in the Channel Islands and Wales. He also made a single Continental tour, to Switzerland with his father in 1858. After 1870 his subjects are largely taken from the Thames Valley. He uses sober colours, greys, greens and browns which, with his clean handling, were praised by Copley Fielding (q.v.). He has a talent for conveying moist and hazy atmosphere. Sometimes he over-uses bodycolour. He was a

dog lover.
Examples: B.M.; V.A.M.; City A.G., Bristol.
Bibliography: *A.J.*, 1904. *Western Daily Press*, 2 Feb., 1904. *Studio*, Spring No., 1905.

JACKSON, Sir Thomas Graham, Bt., R.A., F.S.A.   **1835 (Hampstead) - 1924**
An architect who was educated at Brighton College, and Wadham, Oxford, where he later became a Fellow. While in Oxford he took lessons from W. Turner (q.v.), and he then became a pupil of Gilbert Scott. His buildings, such as the Examination Schools, 'contributed greatly towards changing the appearance of Oxford'. He was elected A.R.A. and R.A. in 1892 and 1896, and was created a baronet in 1913. He lived in Surrey. In the Fitzwilliam there are a number of pretty wash drawings of Cambridge by him, and the Ashmolean holds a number of book plates.
Bibliography: B.H. Jackson (ed.): *Recollections of T.G.J.*, 1950. *A.J.*, 1892. *The Times*, 9 Jan. 1925.

JACKSON, William, of Exeter
    1730 (Exeter) - 1803 (Exeter)
Composer, *littérateur* and occasional painter and draughtsman in the manner of his friend T. Gainsborough (q.v.). He had Liverpool connections, exhibiting there on three occasions. His music has been described as displaying 'refinement and grace, but little character'. One might expect his drawing to have been of a similar quality. He published a number of works on music.

JACOB, Alice
    1862 (?New Zealand) - 1921 (Dublin)
The daughter of Irish Quakers who had emigrated to New Zealand but returned to Dublin. She won a scholarship at the Dublin Metropolitan School of Art in 1882 and a prize from the R.D.S. in 1890. She designed and decorated a set of Belleek porcelain, designed lace and exhibited widely on the Continent. In 1898 she was appointed teacher of design at her old art school. In 1908 she followed L. Shackleton (q.v.) at the Botanic Gardens, Glasnevin. By 1919 she had produced about 150 portraits of orchids. Her vivid watercolours, sometimes on coloured papers, are often inscribed in Celtic script. She was also an illustrator.
Examples: National Botanic Gardens, Dublin.
Bibliography: P.Butler: *Irish Botanical Illustrators*, 2000.

JAMES, Charles Stanfield
A landscape painter who lived in London and exhibited views in Wales, Yorkshire and southern England between 1854 and 1862.

JAMES, Edith Augusta
    1847 (Eton) - 1898 (Tunbridge Wells)
Painter of flowers, portraits and St. Paul's Cathedral. She studied in Paris and exhibited in London from 1884. Her St. Paul's interiors date from the last three years of her life.

Other painting James ladies include **Charlotte J. JAMES,** who exhibited flower

pieces in the 1860s and 1870s, and **Sarah JAMES** who was living in Essex in 1900.
Examples: V.A.M.

JAMES, Francis Edward, R.W.S.
1849 (Willingdon, Sussex) -
1920 (Gt. Torrington, Devon)
A painter of landscapes, flowers and church interiors, he was the son of the Vicar of Willingdon and was a friend of H.B. Brabazon (q.v.). He was a member of the N.E.A.C. and was elected A.R.W.S. and R.W.S. in 1908 and 1916.
Examples: B.M.; V.A.M.; Aberdeen A.G.; Leeds City A.G.; Leicestershire A.G.
Bibliography: *Studio,* XII, 1898; XXXVII, 1906. *A.J.,* 1901. *Connoisseur,* LVIII; LX.

JAMES, Harry E
A painter of boats and landscapes who lived in London and Cornwall, and who was active between at least 1888 and 1902.

JAMES, Marianne Jane, Mrs, née Reeves
The fourth daughter of Frederick Reeves of East Sheen and Mangalore, she married the **Rev. John Thomas JAMES (1786-1828)** in 1823. He was son of a headmaster of Rugby, and after Christ Church, Oxford, he had travelled to Moscow, 1813-14, and in 1816 to Italy where he studied painting. As vicar of Flitton-cum-Silsoe, Bedfordshire, he also wrote on art and published illustrations. In 1827 he was appointed Bishop of Calcutta, and they sailed out to India by way of Madeira and Cape Town. They were in Calcutta only for the first eight months of 1828, when his illness demanded a sea voyage. He died after two weeks, and she came home via Penang, Singapore and St Helena. She produced ink and watercolour or wash views which are more than competent, and also kept a diary of her voyages.

JAMES, William
Canaletto's assistant during his London visit, James exhibited rather Bellotto-like views of London from 1761 to 1771 and became a member of the Society of Artists in 1766.
Examples: V.A.M.

JAMESON, T   (Ambleside) -
A landscape painter who was living at Ambleside in the early nineteenth century. He became a protégé of J. Harden (q.v.), who introduced him to Farington and Constable (qq.v.) and brought him to London, where he was probably the 'T. Jamison' who was an unsuccessful candidate for the O.W.S. in 1806. He probably knew W. Havell (q.v.) while living in the Lake District, as the influence of the latter is shown strongly in his work.
Examples: B.M.

JARDINE, Sir William, 7th Bt., H.R.S.A.
1800 (Edinburgh) - 1874 (Sandown, IoW)
The naturalist, geologist and botanist, he was

also a painter of still lifes and an illustrator. He was educated at York and Edinburgh University, and succeeded to the title in 1820. In the same year he married the daughter of Daniel Lizars, the engraver. He wrote many books on natural history, the first with P.J. Selby (q.v.), as well as memoirs of naturalists. Again with Selby, in 1837 he founded *The Magazine of Zoology and Botany,* later renamed the *Annals and Magazine of Natural History,* and he was joint editor of the *Edinburgh Philosophical Journal.* He also formed a museum containing 6,000 species at Jardine Hall, and was a fine shot and fisherman. He was elected H.R.S.A. in 1827.
Published: with P.J. Selby: *Illustrations of Ornithology,* 1830. *The Naturalist's Library* (ed.), 1833-45. *The Ichnology of Annandale,* 1853. *British Salmonidae,* 1861. &c.
Bibliography: *Nature,* 26 Nov. 1874. *Proceedings* of the Royal Soc., Edinburgh, ix, 207.

JAY, J   Isabella Lee
A painter of fruit and flowers who lived in London and exhibited from 1873 to 1896. She also produced Turner copies, perhaps under the influence of Ruskin.
Bibliography: *Connoisseur,* XLVII.

JEAKES, Joseph 1778   - c.1829
An engraver who made prints after D. Serres (q.v.), and an occasional draughtsman. He exhibited at the R.A. between 1796 and 1809, but only entered the Schools in 1807. There was a 'small rather formal monochrome landscape' in I.A. Williams' collection which is now in the B.M.

JEE, David – *see* **GEE, David**

JEFFERSON, Charles George
1831 (South Shields) - 1902 (South Shields)
An accomplished amateur painter of river and marine subjects. He exhibited at the R.S.A. and in Glasgow as well as locally and worked in oil and watercolour.

JEFFERSON, John
A topographer who provided illustrations for J. Britton (q.v.). His style is rather woolly. He also painted portraits in oil and was active in Newcastle, North Shields and Sunderland between 1811 and at least 1825.
Examples: B.M.

JEFFERY, Emmanuel 1806   - 1874
An Exeter artist who painted views of the city and local landscapes from about 1821. His perspective is not perfect and his colour can be rough, but generally his drawing is good. He preferred views with streams in them.
Examples: Exeter Mus.

JEFFREY, J
A drawing master at Portsmouth Naval Academy from 1774 to 1794.

JEFFERYS, James
1751   - 1784
A painter who studied at the R.A.Schools from 1772, winning a gold medal two years later. He was in Florence and Rome in 1777. His ink and wash drawings vary in style, but many are in the Mortimer-Fuseli-Barry or Romney manners. Some identify him with the hand otherwise known as 'The Master of the Giants'.
Examples: Maidstone A.G.
Bibliography: *Burlington Mag.,* CXVIII, 1976; CXIX, 1977.

JEKYLL, Gertrude
1843 (London) - 1932 (Godalming)
The great garden designer has rightly been described as a polymath, and one of her many talents was as a watercolourist. Her early ambition was to be an artist, and in 1861 she studied at South Kensington, exhibiting at the R.A. four years later and thereafter with the Society of Female Artists. She had many artist friends, both amateur and professional, including Mme. Bodichon (q.v.) and H.B. Brabazon (q.v.), for whom she carried out interior decorations. She travelled widely in Europe with family and friends, and for a couple of months in 1868 she studied at Gigi's in Rome. At Wargrave, whither her family moved from Surrey in that year, she painted inn signs as well as landscapes, portraits and flowers. In about 1872, probably because of weak sight, she gave up painting along with many of her other interests, and concentrated on gardening and later writing for the young *Country Life.*

An exhibition of her drawings, with some oil sketches, was held at the Museum of Garden History, Lambeth, in 1993.

JELLEY, James Valentine
1856 (Lincoln) - 1943
A painter of landscapes, coastal scenes and flowers who exhibited from 1885 and lived in Aston, Birmingham, where he was an 'Art teacher' in the 1881 census, and at Hampton in Arden, Worcestershire. His flowers can be very impressive. He was descended from a family of grocers and corn millers with no known artistic interests.

His wife, **Edith M. JELLEY** showed her work in Warwickshire exhibitions.

JENKINS, John
c.1798   - 1844 (London)
A student at the R.A. Schools from 1821, winning a silver medal in 1823, he was in Italy in 1824 and exhibited views and drawings of temples at the R.A. from 1825 to 1832. His brother **William Wesley JENKINS, Yr. (d.1864),** travelled in Greece in 1820 and exhibited Greek views from 1822 to 1827. They may have been practising architects, as they were the sons of the Rev. William Jenkins (c.1763-1844), a Wesleyan minister and

JENKINS, Joseph John (1811-1885)
View across a pond to a village. *Watercolour, signed and dated 1868, 8¼in. x 18½in.*

architect, of Red Lion Square. W.W. Jenkins exhibited views of the Acropolis at the R.A. in 1822, 1823 and 1827. He is probably the 'Mr Wily Wesleyan' whose sharp conduct is censured in a letter to the *Builder,* 21 July 1855.
Published: with W. Hosking: *A Selection of Ornament drawn from museums in Italy,* 1827.

JENKINS, Joseph John, O.W.S., F.S.A.
1811 (London) - 1885 (London)
The son of an engraver, he began drawing and engraving early and seems to have exhibited when only fourteen. In his younger days he travelled much about the Continent and the British Isles, visiting Belgium, which he disliked, and Brittany in 1846. He was a member of the N.W.S. but seceded in 1847 and became an Associate and Member of the O.W.S. in 1849 and 1850. From this time until his death he was engaged in the research for a history of watercolour painting, his notes and papers forming the basis for Roget's *History of the O.W.S.* He was a very active Secretary of the Society from 1854-64 and was well known for his benefactions to and encouragement of his fellow artists. He was a figure draughtsman of the genre school, but latterly turned more to pure landscape. There are many engravings after his works. His own collection and remaining works were sold at Christie's, 1 March 1886.
Examples: V.A.M.; Blackburn A.G.; Reading A.G.

JENKINSON, Lady Catherine Julia
– *see* **HARCOURT, Lady C.J. VERNON-**

JENKINSON, Lady Louisa Harriet, Lady Louisa Cotes
1811 - 1887 (Atcham, Shropshire)
The third daughter of the 3rd Earl of Liverpool, and the niece of the Premier 2nd Earl, her mother died in giving birth to her. She was brought up at her father's seats, Buxted Park, Sussex, where the young Princess Victoria stayed with them, and Pitchford Hall in Shropshire. In 1839 she married John Cotes of Woodcote Hall, Shropshire. She was a very competent water-colourist, and on the evidence of drawings in the Royal collection she visited the Rhine, Switzerland and the Italian Lakes in 1831, and perhaps Normandy in 1834, but the latter supposition is partly based on a copy of a French drawing by 'Mr Henderson', perhaps Charles Cooper Henderson, in that year. She also probably visited Brazil after her marriage.

JENKINSON, Lady Selina Charlotte, Lady Milton 1812 - 1883 (London)
The second daughter of the 3rd Earl of Liverpool. There is a drawing of the Rhine dated 1829 in the royal collection, together with English coastal subjects dated 1831 and 1832. She married Viscount Milton (d.1835) in 1833, and George Foljambe in 1845. Her elder sister was Harcourt, Lady C. Vernon- (q.v.).

JENKYNS, Caroline, Mrs Gaisford
The sister of R. Jenkyns (q.v.) and also a pupil of Turner of Oxford. Her copies of his drawings in pencil and wash are almost indistinguishable from the originals. She married the Rev. Thomas Gaisford (1779-1855), Dean of Christ Church, as his second wife.

JENKYNS, Rev. Richard
1782 (Evercreech, Somerset) - 1854
Master of Balliol College and Dean of Wells. He went up to Balliol in 1800 and was elected Master in 1819, serving as Vice-Chancellor from 1824 to 1828 and holding the Deanery of Wells from 1845. He was a reformer in College affairs and a strong antitractarian. He was a pupil of Turner of Oxford (q.v.), but may only have done pencil drawings.

JENNINGS, Edward
A landscape painter who was active at least from 1865 to 1888. He painted in North Wales, the Lake District, Sussex, Cornwall and Arran, and he lived in London.

JENNINGS, William George
1797 - 1843
A draughtsman and landscape painter who seems to have been active as early as 1811, and who exhibited an Italian view in 1830.

JERSEY, Julia, Countess of, 'Tooti'
1821 - 1893
The eldest daughter of Sir Robert Peel, she was a pupil of H. Bright (q.v.). She travelled and painted on the Continent with her parents, accompanying them on the dramatic return from Rome to assume the premiership in 1834, and in France in 1837. In 1841 she married Lord Villiers, who was briefly 6th Earl of Jersey in 1859. In 1865 she married Charles Brandling of Middleton, Yorks.

JERVIS, Hon. Mary Anne
c.1813 - 1893
The daughter of the 2nd Viscount St. Vincent, she was a pupil of H. Bright (q.v.). In 1840 she married the romantic and eccentric D.O. Dyce-Sombre, who inherited the private possessions of H.H. the Begum of Sombre Sirdanah. However, they separated when he was declared lunatic. He died in 1851, and in 1862, in Geneva, she married the 3rd Lord Forester (d.1886). Her sisters-in-law were G. Anson and Lady Chesterfield (qq.v).

JOBLING, Robert (1841-1923)
A harbour scene. *Signed, watercolour with scratching out, 10½in. x 17½in.*

JEWITT, Arthur   1772 (Sheffield) - 1852 (Headington, nr. Oxford)
A schoolmaster and topographical writer who painted landscapes in watercolour, he served an apprenticeship under his father, a cutler, after which he opened a private school. Among the towns in which he later taught were Chesterfield, and Kimberworth from 1814 to 1818, in which year he retired. He moved to Duffield, near Derby. In 1838 he joined some of his family at Headington. He contributed to various periodicals and in 1817 started up *The Northern Star, or Yorkshire Magazine,* which only appeared for three volumes. The following year he brought out *The Sylph, or Lady's Magazine for Yorkshire, Derbyshire and the adjoining Counties.*
Published: *The History of Lincolnshire,* 1810. *The History of Buxton,* 1811. *Matlock Companion,* 1835. *Handbook of Practical Perspective,* 1840. *Handbook of Geometry,* 1842.

JEWITT, Thomas Orlando Shelton
1799 (Derbyshire) - 1869 (London)
The second son of A. Jewitt (q.v.), he became a wood engraver and an architectural and archaeological draughtsman. He assisted his father on the *Northern Star* before working in Oxford and London. He was an enthusiastic naturalist and botanist.
He often collaborated with his youngest brother **Llewellyn Frederick William JEWITT, F.S.A. (1816 Kimberworth, Yorks. - 1886 Duffield),** an antiquary and newspaperman.
Illustrated: Bloxham: *Gothic Architecture,* 1829. Bohn: *Glossary of Ecclesiastical Ornament,* 1846.

J.H. Parker: *Glossary of Architecture,* 1849. G.E. Street: *Brick and Marble Architecture of Italy,* 1855. &c.

JOBBINS, William H
After teaching at the Nottingham School of Art, he went to Venice in about 1880, and later to India on Government service. He painted landscapes both in oil and watercolour, and he exhibited at the R.A. and Suffolk Street from 1872 to 1886.
Examples: Castle Mus., Nottingham.

JOBLING, Robert
1841 (Newcastle-upon-Tyne) - 1923 (Whitley Bay)
Until he was sixteen Jobling worked as a glassmaker, but spent his free time sketching and attending Cosens-Way's (q.v.) evening classes. Thereafter he was a foreman painter in a shipyard, only devoting himself entirely to art in 1899. His subjects are mostly river and coastal scenes. He occasionally exhibited at the R.A. and, in 1910, was elected President of the Bewick Club.
His wife Isa, née Thompson (1850-1926), was also a painter, as was their son, Joseph Jobling (1870-1930).
Illustrated: Wilson: *Tales of the Borders.*
Examples: Laing A.G., Newcastle.
Bibliography: *A.J.,* 1904.

JOCELYN, Frances Elizabeth, Lady
1820   - 1880
Daughter of the 5th Earl Cowper. she married Viscount Jocelyn in 1841. She was a

trainbearer at Queen Victoria's wedding, and a Lady of the Bedchamber from 1841 to 1867. She painted J.D. Harding-inspired views when accompanying the Queen in England, Scotland and the Channel Islands.

JOEL, H   B
A landscape and marine painter in oil and watercolour who worked in a rather Dutch manner. He is sometimes miscatalogued as A.J. Boel because of the complexities of his signature. He was working between 1880 and 1905.

JOHNSON, Alfred George
c.1820   -
An Irishman who was trained at the R.D.S. Schools. He exhibited oil and watercolour paintings at the R.H.A. between 1846 and 1850, and later worked as a draughtsman at the Ordnance Survey.
His elder brother **Blucher JOHNSON (1816-1872)** was a sculptor and draughtsman. He studied at the R.D.S. and later worked as a designer and modeller for Dublin silversmiths.

JOHNSON, Charles Edward, R.I.
1832 (Stockport) - 1913 (Richmond)
A landscape, marine and historical painter who studied at the R.A. Schools and began his career in Edinburgh. He moved south in 1864 and opened an art school in Richmond, Surrey. He exhibited Scottish and West of England subjects from 1855 and was elected R.I. in 1882.
Bibliography: *A.J.,* 1896; 1897; 1900. *Studio,* LVIII, 1913; 1914.

JOHNSON, Charles William, 'Purple'
1870 (Winchcombe) -
1937 (Washington, Sussex)
He succeeded Struan Robertson (q.v.) as the drawing master at Charterhouse in 1902, retiring in the summer of 1937, just a week before his death. Among the hundreds of Carthusians who must have 'looked back with pleasure and gratitude to the time spent in his studio or at his sketching classes in the open air as among the most enjoyable and fruitful hours of their life here', was Sir Osbert Lancaster, the cartoonist. His own work varied from the Turneresque, where he earned his nickname, to the careful black and white of the illustrator.
Bibliography: Sir O. Lancaster: *With an Eye to the Future*, 1986, pp.513. *The Carthusian*, XVII, No. 13, Nov. 1937.

JOHNSON, Cyrus, R.I.
1848 (Cambridge) - 1925 (London)
A genre and landscape painter who studied at the Perse School, Cambridge, and worked in London. He exhibited from 1871 and was elected R.I. in 1887. Later in life he also painted portraits.

JOHNSON, Edward Killingworth, R.W.S.
1825 (Stratford-le-Bow) - 1896 (Halstead)
A self-taught painter of contemporary genre scenes, he attended a few classes at the Langham Life School and only took up painting full time in 1863, although he had exhibited from 1846. He was elected A.O.W.S. and O.W.S. in 1866 and 1876 and in 1871 moved from Wembley to a family property near Halstead in Essex.
His work is often intensely detailed and highly finished, but somehow lacks true depth of feeling.
Bibliography: *I.L.N.*, 1868. *A.J.*, 1876. *The Year's Art*, 1897.
See Colour Plate

JOHNSON, Harry (Henry) John, R.I.
1826 (Birmingham) - 1884 (London)
A pupil of Müller, whom he accompanied on Sir Charles Fellows' expedition to Lycia in 1843. On his return he took lessons from S.R. Lines (q.v.) and settled in London in 1844. He was a founder member of the Clipstone Street Academy. He accompanied Cox (q.v.) on his first visit to Betws-y-coed in 1844 and on other sketching tours in North Wales. He was unanimously elected an Associate of the R.I. in 1868 and a member in 1870.
In style he remained a disciple of Müller (q.v.) and, to a lesser extent, of Cox, using fluent washes and careful draughtsmanship. This care is especially noticeable in his studies of boats. He seems to have called himself 'Harry' to avoid confusion with the **Henry JOHNSON** who exhibited figure subjects from the 1820s to the 1840s.
Examples: B.M.; V.A.M.; Fitzwilliam; Abbot Hall A.G., Kendal.

JOHNSON, Isaac
1754 (Woodbridge) - 1835 (Woodbridge)
An antiquary and surveyor who worked in the Woodbridge area of Suffolk. He painted landscapes and tree studies.
Examples: Ipswich Lib.

JOHNSON, James
1803 (Bristol) - 1834
The son of a Bristol innkeeper, he was probably a pupil of H. O'Neill (q.v.) and of F. Danby (q.v.) who certainly influenced him greatly. His earliest dated drawing is of 1819, and he was one of the organisers of the first Bristol exhibition. He moved to London soon afterwards, returning in 1826. The following year he was teaching in Bath, and by 1829 he suffered a first bout of mental illness. He planned a visit to Jamaica for his health, but it is unlikely that he actually went there.
He painted poetic landscapes in oil that are very close to those of Danby in inspiration and execution. As a watercolourist his forte was for very detailed architectural work, especially church interiors. These, and his more extensive topographical works, are among the most impressive products of the Bristol School.
Published: *Bristol Scenery*, 1862.
Examples: City A.G., Bristol.

JOHNSON, Lieutenant-Colonel John
c.1769   - 1846
A surveyor in the Bombay Engineers from 1785. He worked in many parts of India, and in 1817 he returned to England by way of Persia, Russia and Georgia. He retired in 1819. His landscapes and topographical subjects are in a traditional, rather stilted style and his figures are weak.
Published: *A Journey from India to England*, 1818.
Examples: B.M. ; India Office Lib.

JOHNSON, Robert
1770 (Shotley, Northumberland) -
1796 (Kenmore, Perthshire)
In 1788 he was apprenticed to T. Bewick (q.v.) and W. Beilby (q.v.) in Newcastle, at the same time making sketches from nature in watercolour. He turned from copperplate engraving to painting, and at the time of his death was copying the portraits at Taymouth Castle. These copies were later reproduced in Pinkerton's *Iconographia Scotica*. The engraving from his drawing of St. Nicholas' Church, Newcastle, by his friend C. Nesbit, was claimed to be 'the largest engraving on wood ever attempted in the present mode'. His drawings are delicate and detailed.
Illustrated: T. Bewick: *Fables*. Goldsmith and Parnell: *Poems*, 1795. J. Pinkerton: *Iconographia Scotica*, 1797.
Examples: Laing A.G., Newcastle.

JOHNSON, Thomas
A topographer who made drawings of

Canterbury and Bath churches in about 1675. He worked in the style of W. Hollar (q.v.).
Examples: B.M.

JOHNSON, Sir William, Bt.
1715 (Smith Town, Co. Meath) -
1774 (Johnson, N.Y.)
A soldier, draughtsman and negotiator with Indian tribes, he went to America with his uncle (and adoptive father) Sir Peter Warren, and served there against the French. The Mohawks made him a Sachem with the name '"Warrahiaghy" – he who has charge of affairs'. He was also created baronet as Johnson of New York in 1755. His only legitimate son was equally distinguished in North American affairs.
Bibliography: W.L. Stone: *Life of Sir W.J.*, 1885.

JOHNSTON, Rev. George Liddell
1817 (Sunderland) - 1902 (London)
He was educated at University College, Durham, and began his clerical career near Exeter becoming, in 1856, Chaplain to the British Embassy in Vienna. Although he retired in 1885, he returned to Austria regularly thereafter. He left sketchbooks of grotesque studies which, *en masse*, have the impact of a *danse macabre*. He may well have met Freud and seems to have been influenced by his writings. The drawings are, in fact, a splendid example of the decadence of the later Habsburg Empire. They are mostly done in pen with light washes.
Examples: Shipley A.G., Gateshead.

JOHNSTON, Henry, N.W.S.
- ?1858 (?Derby)
A landscape, figure and genre painter who exhibited from 1834 to 1858. He was elected to the N.W.S. in 1838, but was thrown out again in 1842. He painted Brazilian and Neapolitan as well as more homely subjects.
A **Miss M.H. JOHNSTON**, who lived in the Strand, was an unsuccessful candidate for the N.W.S. between 1843 and 1847. She exhibited at the S.B.A., where she is spelled without a 'T', from 1842 to 1852.

JOHNSTON, Sir Harry Hamilton, Bt.
1858 Kennington) - 1927 (Sussex)
As an explorer and consul his career began in Tunis, continued in Central and West Africa and proceeded to Uganda and Central Africa before completing the circle as Consul general at Tunis. He had been educated at King's College, London, and he had studied at the R.A. Schools from 1876 and at South Kensington. He wrote about Africa, and painted watercolours in a sharp and impressive manner. He was knighted in 1901 and later created baronet.
Published: *The Story of my Life*, 1923.

JOHNSTONE, George Whitton, R.S.A., R.W.S. **1849 (Glamis) - 1901 (Edinburgh)**
A landscape painter who began as a cabinet

JOHNSTONE, Henry James (1835-1907)
'Awaiting His Return.' Signed, *watercolour, 10¼in. x 7in.*

maker in Edinburgh and then studied at the R.S.A. Life School. As a painter he started with portraits and genre subjects, later specialising in Scottish glens, rivers and coasts. He also painted at Fontainebleau. He exhibited at the R.S.A. from 1872 and was elected A.R.S.A. and R.S.A. in 1883 and 1895. In 1892 he moved to Largs. As his work developed it became more mannered under the influence of Corot.
Bibliography: A.J., 1899.

JOHNSTONE, Henry James
1835 (Birmingham) - 1907
A painter of figure and genre subjects who was active in England from about 1881. He lived in Great Marlow and Wadhurst, and also painted at St. Ives. Previously he had worked for twenty years from 1853 in Australia as a photographer, and then in America.

JOHNSTONE, Rev. James Barbour
1815 (Nr. Annan) - 1885 (Dumfries)
A minister who painted Dumfriesshire scenes. In 1862 he moved to Warrington. He exhibited twice at the R.S.A.

JOHNSTONE, William Borthwick, R.S.A.
1804 (Edinburgh) - 1868 (Edinburgh)
He abandoned a career as a lawyer and began to exhibit at the R.S.A. in 1836. From 1840 to 1842 he attended Sir William Allen's evening classes at the Trustees' Academy. He was elected A.R.S.A. and R.S.A. in 1840 and 1848. In 1850 he was appointed Treasurer, and he exhibited at the Academy until his death. In 1842, with C. Vacher (q.v.), he visited Venice and Rome, returning to Scotland in 1844. He was well known as a collector and connoisseur and in 1858 was appointed first Principal

Curator of the newly formed N.G., Scotland. He compiled a catalogue of the Gallery.
He had studied miniature painting under Robert Thorburn, and he painted figure subjects.
Examples: V.A.M.; Abbot Hall A.G., Kendal.
Bibliography: A.J., Aug. 1868.

JOLLY, Fanny C
A painter of landscapes and still lifes who was working from about 1856 to 1875. She exhibited in London, Scotland and Brighton and lived in Bath.

JONES, Captain Adrian
1845 (Ludlow) - 1938
An army vet who became a sculptor and watercolourist on retirement. He was a pupil of C.B. Birch, A.R.A. and exhibited from 1884, horses naturally being a favourite subject. He was responsible for some of the best known war memorials in London.
Published: *Memoirs of a Soldier Artist*, 1933.
Bibliography: *Country Life*, Sept. 1984.

JONES, Anna M
A landscape and portrait painter who lived in Guernsey and exhibited in London from 1868. As well as local scenes, she painted on the Thames.

JONES, Rev. Calvert Richard
1804 (Swansea) - 1877 (Bath)
The son of a Swansea dignitary, whose estate he inherited in 1847. After Oriel College, Oxford, he was ordained and in 1829 was appointed rector of Loughor, near Swansea. He is wrongly said to have worked in the studio of G. Chambers (q.v.), but he was an admirer, and for the most part he painted shipping subjects. He travelled extensively in Europe and lived in Colchester and Bath. He was also an able mathematician and musician. In photography he was a pupil of Fox-Talbot.

JONES, Charles, A.R.S.A.
1836 (Barnham) - 1892
An animal painter in oil and watercolour who exhibited in London from 1860. He worked in Scotland and the South of England.
Bibliography: See Cat. N.G., Sydney. A.J., 1892. *The Year's Art*, 1893.

JONES, Sir Edward Coley Burne, BURNE-, Bt., A.R.A., R.W.S.
1833 (Birmingham) - 1898 (Fulham)
He was educated at King Edward's School, Birmingham and Exeter College, Oxford, where he and W. Morris (q.v.) formed the nucleus of the romantic 'Brotherhood'. Encouraged by Rossetti (q.v.) and the Pre-Raphaelites they became artists and designers. He was elected A.O.W.S. in 1863, but until 1877 his work was virtually submerged in that of Morris & Co. After that date his independent reputation grew apace, cul-

JONES, George (1786-1869)
A ruined abbey, with figures. *Pencil and blue wash. 7in. x 11in.*

minating in his creation as a baronet in 1894. He was elected R.W.S. in 1886 and A.R.A. in 1885. Many of his drawings are designs and cartoons rather than finished works, and pure watercolours are rare. Sales of his work took place at Christie's in July 1898 and June 1919. Note also Mrs. Mackail's sale in December 1954.
Examples: B.M.; V.A.M.; Ashmolean; Cecil Higgins A.G., Bedford; Fitzwilliam; City A.G., Manchester.
Bibliography: M. Bell: *Sir E.B.J.*, 1898. A.L. Baldry: *B.J.*, 1909. D. Cecil: *Visionary and Dreamer*, 1969. M. Harrison & B. Waters: *B.J.*, 1973. P. Fitzgerald: *B.J.*, 1975. J. Christian: *Letters to Katie from E.B.J.*, 1988. *A.J.*, 1898. O.W.S. Club, IX, 1932. *Burlington*, CXV, Feb. 1973. *Apollo*, Nov. 1975. Arts Council, Exhibition Cat., 1975. *Antique Collector*, March 1989.

JONES, Eliza
A painter of portraits and miniatures who lived in London and exhibited at the O.W.S. and elsewhere between 1807 and 1852.

JONES, Frederick Wood
A naturalist whose late 19th and early 20th century drawings of reptiles are attractive and impressive.
Published: *Life and Living*, 1939.

JONES, George, R.A.
1786 (London) - 1869 (London)
The son of an engraver, he entered the R.A. Schools in 1801 and exhibited portraits, landscapes and genre from 1803 to 1811. He then joined the Army and served in the

Peninsula and in Paris after the Occupation. Thereafter he painted military subjects. In 1822 he was elected A.R.A., and R.A. in 1824. He was Librarian from 1834 to 1840, Keeper from 1840 to 1850, and acting President from 1845 to 1850. He was a 'genial, well-bred man, strongly resembling the Duke of Wellington', indeed he was the 'Mr Jones, I believe', who prompted the famous putdown 'If you believe that, you'll believe anything'. His watercolours are usually in blue, grey or brown wash and he painted landscapes in France, Belgium, Germany and Ireland as well as in many parts of Britain.
Published: *Waterloo*, 1817; 1852. *Sir Francis Chantrey*, 1849.
Examples: B.M.; Fitzwilliam; Newport A.G.
Bibliography: *A.J.*, 1869; 1903.

JONES, George KINGSTON-
1865   - 1948
A painter of the East Anglian coast who lived in London in the 1890s. He was a *Graphic* illustrator.

JONES, Harry E
A competent painter of rustic genre subjects who was active between about 1882, when he was living at Brentford, and 1916. He painted in the South-East.

JONES, Inigo
1573 (London) - 1652 (London)
In his youth Inigo Jones was sent to Italy by Lord Pembroke to study architecture. He returned by way of Denmark in 1604, and he visited Italy again in 1613-14. Although his

greatest importance is as an architect, for a major part of his career, between 1605 and 1640, he produced designs for the scenery and costumes for a series of court masques. His splendidly baroque costume designs are usually in pen and ink with a brown or grey wash. However, nine coloured drawings survive. His imaginative landscape designs for stage settings are also in pen and ink, with grey wash, and in them can be seen the influence of the great Italians as well as that of Rubens. There is also an affinity with Claude's broadest drawings.
Examples: B.M.; Chatsworth; R.I.B.A.
Bibliography: J.P. Collier: *I.J., remarks on his sketches for masques, &c.* 1848. S.C. Ramsay: *I.J.*, 1924. J.A. Gotch: *I.J.*, 1928. *Festival Designs by I.J.*, 1967. S. Orgel and R. Strong: *I.J., The Theatre of the Stuart Court*, 1973. J. Orrell: *The Theatres of I.J. and John Webb*, 1985. J. Harris and G. Higgott: *I.J.: Complete Architectural Drawings* (with comprehensive bibliog.), 1989. J. Peacock: *The Stage Designs of I.J.*, 1995. Walpole Society, XII, 1924. *Apollo*, LXXXVI, Aug. 1967. *Burlington*, CXV, June 1973. Fraser and Harris: Cat. of Drawings by I.J. (typescript in V.A.M.). *W&D*, 1990, i.

JONES, John Rock, Yr.
c.1836 (Isle of Man) - c.1898 (nr. Newcastle)
The son of a portrait painter who settled on Tyneside, he first copied Cox, Fielding, Richardson and others, and then became a landscape painter in his own right and a teacher. He exhibited locally from 1866.

JONES, Thomas (1742-1803)
View of Larici from the Via Appia leading towards Gensano.
Watercolour over pencil, inscribed in pencil, 11in. x 16½in.

JONES, Josiah Clinton
1848 (Wednesbury, Staffordshire) - 1936
A landscape and marine painter in watercolour and oil who exhibited North Welsh subjects from 1885 and lived at Conway.
Examples: Blackburn A.G.

JONES, Owen Carter
1809 (London) - 1874 (London)
A designer and architect who was a pupil of Louis Vulliamy for six years before entering the R.A. Schools in 1830. He then travelled in France, Italy, Egypt and Spain, returning in 1836. He was a member of the circle about Henry Cole (q.v.) which aimed at higher standards in 'art manufactures', and whose ideas later influenced William Morris (q.v.). He produced designs and illustrations for Cole's *Journal of Design and Manufactures,* founded in 1849. In 1851 he supervised the decoration of the building for the Great Exhibition and again in the following year on its re-erection as the Crystal Palace. He exhibited at the R.A. from 1831 to 1861.

Apart from his designs for wallpapers, textiles and the like, Jones also produced topographical drawings, most notably a series of Cairene views which were lithographed.
Published: *The Grammar of Ornament,* 1856. &c.
Examples: B.M.
Bibliography: See N. Pevsner: *Pioneers of Modern Design,* (Penguin, 1960). *A.J.,* 1874.

JONES, Sir Philip BURNE-, 2nd Bt.
1861 - 1926
The son of Sir E. Burne-Jones (q.v.), he was educated at Marlborough and University College, Oxford. He painted genre and decorative subjects in oil and watercolour, and exhibited from 1886. Towards the end of his life he gave up painting to concentrate on drawing and caricaturing.
Published: *Dollars and Democracy,* 1904. *With Amy in Brittany,* 1904.
Examples: B.M.
Bibliography: *Studio,* Special No., 1898. *The Graphic,* 28 May 1910.

JONES, Reginald T
1857 (Old Charlton, Kent) - 1904
A landscape painter in oil ·and watercolour who exhibited at the R.A. and the R.I. from 1880. He visited Italy, Switzerland, Corsica and France, particularly Brittany and Pont Aven, and had an especial love of the Essex countryside. In England he also sketched on the Dorset and Devon coasts.
Examples: Wakefield A.G.
Bibliography: *Studio,* XXX, 1904; LXVII, 1916.

JONES, Richard - ?1812
A painter of portraits, landscapes and architectural subjects in the manner of J. Bourne (q.v.). He was an Honorary exhibitor at the R.A. from 1780 to 1812.
Examples: V.A.M.

JONES, Samuel John Egbert
- ?1849 (Clapton)
A landscape, genre and sporting painter who was active between 1820 and 1849. He lived in London.
Examples: B.M.; V.A.M.

JONES, Theodore
A landscape painter who lived in London and exhibited for ten years from 1879. His favourite subjects were Hampstead Heath, Harrow and the East Anglian coast.

JONES, Thomas
1742 (Aberedw, Radnorshire) - 1803 (Aberedw, Radnorshire)
In 1759 he went to Oxford and in 1762 came to London where he studied under Richard Wilson (q.v.) from 1763 to 1765. He first exhibited at the Society of Artists in 1765, later becoming a member. He spent the winter of 1773-4 with O. Bowles (q.v.) at North Aston. From 1776 to 1783 he lived in Rome and Naples, and after his return exhibited Italian scenes at the R.A. On his brother's death he inherited the family estate at Pencerrig and became High Sheriff of Radnorshire.

He painted Welsh scenery in the manner of Wilson. Occasionally J.H. Mortimer (q.v.) would add figures to his landscapes. His small works in oil are often painted on paper.

His diaries were published by the Walpole Society in 1951. Exhibitions of his work were held at Marble Hill, Twickenham, and Nat. Mus., Wales, in 1970.
Examples: B.M.; Fitzwilliam; Nat. Mus., Wales.
Bibliography: Walpole Soc., XXXII. *Country Life,* 16 and 23 Nov. 1945; 9 July 1970. *Connoisseur,* CLXVIII, 1968; CLXXIV, 1970.

JONES, Sir Thomas Alfred, P.R.H.A.
1823 (Dublin) - 1893 (Dublin)
He studied at the R.D.S. from 1833, before

going up to Trinity. He exhibited at the R.H.A. from 1841, and between 1846 and 1849 he travelled on the Continent. He was elected P.R.H.A. in 1869, and was the first President to be knighted. Although he is best known for his portraits in oil, he began by painting literary and genre subjects as well as small portraits in watercolour and pastel. His use of watercolour can be Pre-Raphaelite, with brilliant colours and small brush strokes.

JONES, Thomas Howell
An artist working between 1836 and 1848. In the former year he produced a crude series of London characters. Their poses are awkwardly forced into profile like an Egyptian frieze.
Examples: B.M.

JOPLING, Joseph Middleton, A.N.W.S.
1831 (London) - 1884 (London)
The son of a clerk at the Horse Guards, and perhaps related to Joseph Jopling (1789-1867), an architect, author and draughtsman, he worked for a few years as a clerk in the War Office, meanwhile teaching himself to paint. In 1859 he was elected Associate of the N.W.S. He joined the 3rd Middlesex Volunteers and was officially commissioned to make drawings of the Queen inspecting the Troops. He was a member of the Arts Club, Hanover Square, and he exhibited still lifes and historical and genre subjects at the R.A. and elsewhere from 1848. His studio sale was held by Christie's, 12 February 1885.
In 1874 he married **Louise GOODE (1843 Manchester - 1933)**, formerly Mrs. Frank Romer, herself an artist. Her third husband was a lawyer, G.W. Rowe. She published *Hints to Amateurs,* 1891, and *Twenty Years of My Life,* 1925.
Examples: B.M.; V.A.M.; Williamson A.G., Birkenhead.

JOY, Arthur, R.H.A.
c.1808 (Dublin) - 1838 (London)
An historical, landscape and subject painter in oil and watercolour who studied under Robert Lucius West, R.H.A., a portraitist, in Dublin, and afterwards in Paris and Holland. He was elected A.R.H.A. and R.H.A. in 1836 and 1837, in which year he moved to London. He exhibited at the B.I. in 1838, the year of his death.

JOY, William
1803 (Great Yarmouth) - 1867
JOY, John Cantiloe
1806 (Great Yarmouth) - 1866 (London)
Marine painters who generally collaborated. They were educated at Wright's Academy, Yarmouth, of which they made sketches which were engraved. They were given the use of a room in the Royal Hospital, from which they taught themselves to paint the sea. In about 1832 they moved to Portsmouth, where they worked as government draughtsmen. They later lived in London, Chichester, Putney, and London again,

JOY, William (1803-1867) and John Cantiloe (1806-1866)
A Transport preparing to disembark Troops. *Pen and brown ink and watercolour, 11in. x 15¾in.*

where John died in 1866. William moved to the country, where he died the next year.
Their work shows careful observation in the detail of ships and rigging. However, John's figure drawing tends to be weak and William over-uses a lurid green in his seas.
Examples: B.M.; V.A.M.; Greenwich; Gt. Yarmouth.
Bibliography: J. Walpole: *Art and Artists of the Norwich School,* 1997.

JUDKIN, Rev. Thomas James
1788   - 1871
A pupil of H. Bright (q.v.), he was Private Chaplain of Somers College, Somers Town, from 1828 to 1868. He exhibited landscapes at the R.A. and elsewhere from 1823 to 1849. His watercolour work is full of techniques such as scraping and white heightening. He was a friend of Constable (q.v.), whose funeral service he conducted in 1837. He published several religious works.

JUKES, Francis
1745 (Martley, Worcestershire) -
1812 (London)
An engraver who coloured his works by hand. He made topographical views and shipping scenes, and most of his later printed work is done in aquatint. His watercolours are muddy and traditional and lack the discipline of line necessary to a print.

JULIAN, Lieutenant Humphrey John
- 1850
He entered the Navy in 1824, and was promoted lieutenant in 1840 and sent to Africa,

where he was involved in the destruction of a slave factory at Corisco. In 1841 he sailed to the East Indies, from which he visited China. Later he was in the Mediterranean. He painted shipping subjects.
Examples: Greenwich.
Bibliography: *Gentleman's Mag.,* Nov. 1850.

JUSTYNE, Percy William
1812 (Rochester) - 1883 (London)
A landscape painter and book illustrator who worked for, among others, the *I.L.N.,* the *Graphic* and the *Floral World.* He exhibited landscapes at the R.A. and Suffolk Street. From 1841 to 1848 he was in Grenada.
Illustrated: Dr. Smith: *History of Greece.* Dr. Smith: *Biblical Dictionary.* Fergusson: *Handbook of Architecture.* C. Kingsley: *Christmas in the Tropics.* &c.
Examples: Castle Mus., Nottingham.

JUTSUM, Henry
1816 (London) - 1869 (London)
After an education in Devonshire, where he drew landscapes, he returned to London, and drew frequently in Kensington Gardens. He exhibited at the R.A. and elsewhere from 1836. In 1839 he became a pupil of J. Stark (q.v.) and in 1843 was elected A.N.W.S. He resigned in 1847, after which date he painted chiefly in oil.
His remaining works and collection were sold at Christie's, 17 April 1882.
Examples: Blackburn A.G.; Cartwright Hall, Bradford; Coventry A.G.; Leeds City A.G.; Maidstone Mus.; Newport A.G.
Bibliography: J. Walpole: *Art and Artists of the Norwich School,* 1997. *A.J.,* 1859; 1863; 1869.

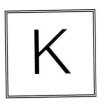

KARR, Captain Heywood Walter SETON-
1853 (?St Boswells) - 1938
A game hunter and watercolourist, he was younger brother of Sir Henry Seton-Karr, M.P. of Kippilaw, St. Boswells, Roxburghshire. He was educated at Eton, Oriel College, Oxford and the University of Florence. He then spent about four years in the army, serving with distinction in Egypt. Later he discovered prehistoric flint mines in Somaliland and amethysts in Egypt, and explored and shot in Africa, India and the Arctic regions of Europe. He was a landscape painter and was a war artist in Palestine from at least 1917 to 1919. He also painted in Cyprus in 1921 and 1922, using an effective bright and splashy style. Other interests included golf and cycling.
Published: *Shores and Alps of Alaska. Ten Years' Wild Sports in Foreign Lands. Bear Hunting in the White Mountains.*
Examples: Cyprus Archeological Museum; Imp. War Mus.

KAUFFMANN, Maria Anna Angelica Catharina, R.A.
1741 (Chur, Switzerland) - 1807 (Rome)
The daughter of Johann Josef Kauffmann (1707-1772), a minor Austrian painter who encouraged her early artistic leanings. The family happened to be in Switzerland at the time of her birth, and later travelled widely in Italy. Angelica studied art and music in Milan, Florence and Rome. They came to London in 1766. She received commissions for portraits from the Royal Family and nobility, including the Princess of Brunswick, Queen Charlotte, and Christian III of Denmark. Her effect on literary and artistic circles was dramatic, both Reynolds and Nathaniel Dance falling for her. She was a Foundation Member of the R.A., exhibiting there between 1769 and 1797. She visited Ireland in 1771. In 1781 she married A. Zucchi (q.v.). They immediately left for Italy where Angelica lived, mainly in Rome, for the rest of her life. Among her circle of admirers in Rome was Goethe, whose portrait she painted.
She painted mainly in oil, but some of her portraits are in pastel. She also painted fans and allegorical compositions in watercolour. Her works are in the neo-classical tradition. She was employed by the Adam brothers, and greatly contributed to the concept of the 'Adam style'. Her figure drawing, though, is weak and her colour can be overdone.
Examples: B.M.; V.A.M.; Fitzwilliam; N.G., Scotland.
Bibliography: G.G. de Rossi: *A.K.,* 1810. Lady V. Manners: *A.K.,* 1924. A. Hartcup: *Angelica: portrait of an 18th century artist,* 1954. D.M. Mayer: *A.K.,* 1972. Kenwood: Exhibition Cat., 1955. Brighton A.G.: Exhibition Cat., 1992.

KAY, Alexander
A series of aquatints of Edinburgh were made from his drawings in about 1814. He was active until about 1863 and he also painted landscapes and coastal subjects in a style derived from that of 'Grecian' Williams (q.v.).
Examples: V.A.M.

KAY, Archibald, R.S.A., R.S.W.
1860 (Glasgow) - 1935 (Glasgow)
A landscape painter in oil and watercolour who lived in Glasgow. He studied in France in about 1886 and exhibited at the R.A. from 1890 to 1921. He also lived in Edinburgh and worked in Belgium, France, Italy, Holland and Denmark as well as Scotland.
Examples: Glasgow A.G.
Bibliography: *Studio,* XXVII, 1903; XXIX, 1903; LXVIII, 1916; LXXXVII, 1924. *A.J.,* 1909.

KAY, James, R.S.A., R.S.W.
1858 (Lamlash, Isle of Arran) -
1942 (Whistlefield, Dumbartonshire)
A painter of landscapes, street scenes, marine and Continental subjects who threw up a career in insurance for art. He studied at the Glasgow School of Art and was elected R.S.W. in 1896 and A.R.S.A. and R.S.A. in 1893 and 1938. He lived in Dumbartonshire. His subjects were found above all on the Clyde, and on Dutch rivers and the French coast. He specialised in the less romantic aspects of ships and shipping, and his style can be a little monotonous and overworked.
Bibliography: *Studio,* XXVII, 1903; XXVIII, 1903; XXXIX, 1907.

KAY, John
1742 (Dalkeith) - 1826 (Edinburgh)
A caricaturist and miniature painter, he was apprenticed to a barber – often synonymous with printseller. A grateful customer gave him a pension in 1782 and he set up as an artist, publishing his first caricatures two years later. He was sued several times.
His drawing is a little crude, but his likenesses were thought good. The satire seems good humoured to a modern eye and it covers a wider social spectrum than was usual, from senators to sweeps. His son was W. Kay (q.v.).
Published: *Kay's Edinburgh Portraits,* 1784-1813.
Bibliography: H. & M. Evans: *J.K. of Edinburgh,* 1973.

KAY, Joseph   1775 - 1847 (London)
A distinguished architect who had been a pupil of S.P. Cockerell, he was also a painter working between 1793 and 1813. He visited Italy, probably in 1802. His style is a mixture of precision and sketchiness. He uses clear colour washes and much blue and brown. He was a son-in-law of the architect William Porden, and he was secretary to the London Architects' Club and a founder of the R.I.B.A.
Examples: V.A.M.; R.I.B.A.

KAY, Robert
1740 (Cairnton, nr.Penicuik) -
1818 (Edinburgh)
A distant relative of J. Kay (q.v.) who drew a caricature of him, he began in a small way as a carpenter, but became a builder and drawing master and an architect. He designed Hebridean and Orcadian lighthouses as well as buildings in Edinburgh.
Bibliography: J. Kay: *Original Portraits,* ii, 1838. *Book of the Old Edinburgh Club,* XXIV, p.167.

KAY, William
A portrait and miniature painter, who worked in both oil and watercolour, and a printmaker, he was the son of John Kay (q.v.). He worked very much in his father's manner and was active in Edinburgh from 1795 to 1830.

KEANE, Harriet Edith   - 1920
KEANE, Frances Annie   - 1917
The daughters of Sir John Keane, 3rd Bt., of Glensheelin, near Cappoquin, they were among the six founders of the Irish Amateur Drawing Society at Lismore in 1870. After a number of name changes, this evolved into the Water Colour Society of Ireland in 1888, and from 1891 the exhibitions have been held in Dublin.

KEARNAN, Thomas, N.W.S.
A landscape painter who was working for W.H. Pyne (q.v.) in London from 1821. He was also a pupil of the elder Pugin, for whom he worked on *Paris and its Environs,* 1828 and 1831. He was elected N.W.S. in 1837 and resigned in 1851, when he seems to have given up painting.

KEARNEY, William Henry, N.W.S.
1800   - 1858 (London)
A landscape and genre painter who joined the N.W.S. in 1833 and later became Vice-President. He exhibited at the R.A. from 1823, the year in which he entered the Schools. He painted in London and in Wales and his work can be rather charming and old-fashioned in the manner of P. Sandby. Despite a studio sale at Christie's on 30 March 1859, his widow was left in poverty.
Published: *Illustrations of the Surrey Zoological Gardens,* 1832.
Examples: B.M.; V.A.M.; Guildford Mus.; N.G., Ireland.
Bibliography: *A.J.,* 1858.

KEARSLEY, Harriet
1802 - **1881 (London)**
A copyist of old masters in watercolour and a figure painter in oil and watercolour. She lived in London and exhibited from 1824 to 1858.
Examples: V.A.M.

KEATE, George, F.R.S., F.S.A.
1729 (Trowbridge, Wiltshire) -
1797 (London)
An antiquary, naturalist and poet as well as a prolific amateur artist. After an apprenticeship as clerk to the steward to the Duke of Bedford, he entered the Inner Temple in 1751. He was called to the bar in 1753, but never practised. He lived abroad for some years, in Geneva, where he became a friend of Voltaire, and in Rome in 1755. He then returned to England and exhibited at the R.A. in an honorary capacity between 1766 and 1789.

He generally painted views of English and Continental towns, and the major part of his work is in bodycolour. He was the father of G.J. Henderson (q.v.).
Published: *Sketches from Nature in a Journey to Margate*, 1779. *An Account of the Pelew Islands*, 1788. &c.
Examples: B.M.; V.A.M.
Bibliography: C.E. Engel: *G.K. et la Suisse*, 1948.

KEATS, C   J
An artist who sketched in France, Holland and on the Rhine in 1885. He also worked in the Lake District, on the Severn and the Italian lakes.

KEELEY, John
1849 - **1930 (Birmingham)**
A Birmingham landscape painter. He exhibited from 1872 and became a member of the Royal Birmingham Society in 1902.
Bibliography: *A.J.*, 1905.

KEELING, William Knight, R.I.
1807 (Manchester) -
1886 (Barton-upon-Irwell)
After an early apprenticeship to a Manchester wood-engraver, he moved to London to work under W. Bradley (q.v.). Returning to Manchester in about 1835, he set himself up as a painter of portraits and genre, as well as giving drawing lessons. He exhibited at the Royal Manchester Institution, once each at the B.I. and the R.A., and was a member of the original Manchester Academy. He helped found the Manchester Academy of Fine Arts, of which he was President from 1864 to 1877, and exhibited with them until 1883. He was elected Associate and Member of the N.W.S. in 1840 and 1841.

The style of many of his earlier works, in particular his illustrations to Sir Walter Scott and other authors, owed much to his friend H. Liverseege (q.v.).
Examples: V.A.M.
Bibliography: *Art Union*, 1842.

KEENE, Charles Samuel (1823-1891)
Mr Caudle having come home a little late declares he will henceforth have a key.
Watercolour.

KEENE, Alfred John, 'Jack'
1864 (Derby) - 1930 (Derby)
Son of a Derby art dealer and photographer, his family had been known as Midlands artists for nearly a century. He was a co-founder of the Derby Sketching Club and at the time of his death was President.

He specialised in landscapes and old Derbyshire buildings, the latter done with extreme accuracy, often in pale colours and vignette form. His later work became more atmospheric and colourful. His figure drawing is good.

His wife, Mrs. A. Keene, née Brailsford, was also an artist.

A brother **William Caxton KEENE (1855-1910)** studied under Sir E.J. Poynter (q.v.) and became an illustrator, working for, amongst others, the *Magazine of Art* and *Picturesque London*. Examples of his watercolour landscapes are in the Derby A.G.
Examples: Derby A.G.

KEENE, Charles Samuel
1823 (Hornsey, North London) -
1891 (Hammersmith)
Keene's family moved from London to Ipswich during his childhood, but returned after the death of his father, a solicitor, in 1838. He was briefly articled to a solicitor and then to an architect, but as soon as his apprenticeship was over he was re-articled to Charles Wymper and then set up as a professional artist. The first book with his illustrations appeared in 1842 and thereafter he worked on many books and periodicals, including *I.L.N.* His drawings for *Punch*, which made his name, began in 1851. From about 1848 he was a regular attender at the Clipstone Street Academy, where he not only sketched, but also produced a number of very striking etchings. Early in his career he made short trips to Brittany and the Rhine but on the whole he preferred the scenery of the Suffolk coast and Scotland.

Whistler described him as the 'greatest English artist since Hogarth', and he is certainly the best pen and ink draughtsman that this country has produced. His drawings are generally social rather than political, and it is through his eyes that we see the late Victorian era. In his economy of line he comes close to Impressionism. His watercolours are rare, mostly dating from early in his career, and are very competent wash drawings, with a preference for light greys, browns and pinks. Generally, his pure watercolours, as distinct from his coloured pen drawings, do not have the clarity of line which one would expect. He did occasional landscape sketches as well as

KELLY, Robert George Talbot (1861-1934)
A sunset scene with an Arab in the foreground mounted on a camel.
Signed and dated 1893, watercolour, 14¾in. x 9¼in.

figures.
Examples: B.M.; Ashmolean; Fitzwilliam; N.G., Scotland; Tate Gall.
Bibliography: G.S. Layard: *The Life and Letters of C.S.K.*, 1892. G.S. Layard: *The Work of C.K.*, 1897. J. Pennell: *The Work of C.K.*, 1897. Sir L. Lindsay: *C.K.*, 1934. F.L. Emmanuel: *C.K.*, 1935. D. Hudson: *C.K.*, 1947. M. Piper: *C.K.*, 1952. S. Houfe: *The Works of C.K.*, 1995. *The Spectator*, 21 Sept. 1861. *A.J.*, 1891. *Studio*, 1902-22. *Pall Mall Mag.*, Oct. 1908. Arts Council: Exhibition Cat., 1952. Christie's: Exhibition Cat., 1991.

KELLY, Robert George Talbot, R.I.
1861 (Birkenhead) - 1934
The son of Robert George Kelly (1822 Dublin - 1910 Chester) a portrait, figure and landscape painter, he was a painter of Eastern scenes, especially in Egypt, which he visited on several occasions, and Burma. He also painted in Iceland. He was a member of the

R.B.A. and was elected R.I. in 1907. He lived in Liverpool and London, and he also painted genre subjects.
An exhibition of his Egyptian views was held at the Fine Art Society, London, in 1902.
His son **Richard Barrett Talbot KELLY, R.I. (1896-1971)** painted birds and historical subjects, and was elected R.I. in 1925. On occasions he painted mildly Vorticist landscapes, but he could not bring himself to Vorticise any ducks that might appear in them. He taught at Rugby School for many years.
Published: *Egypt*, 1902. *Burma*, 1905.
Illustrated: Sir R.C. Slatin: *Fire and Sword in the Sudan*, 1896. &c.
Bibliography: *Connoisseur*, LXIX.

KELSEY, Frank
A painter of ships, coasts and flowers. He lived in Hampstead and was active from the 1880s to the 1920s.

KEMP, George Meikle
1795 (Hillrigs, Biggar) -
1844 (Edinburgh Canal)
The son of a Pentland shepherd whom he assisted before an apprenticeship with a carpenter and working as a millwright. He twice met Walter Scott, whose memorial is his only architectural work, but on the first occasion he did not recognise him, and on the second he was too shy to speak. He sketched in the Borders and studied Gothic architecture before going to London and Paris in 1824 and 1825. On his return to Edinburgh he studied perspective, made models and projected a Scottish equivalent of Britton's *Antiquities*. In 1838 he won the competition for the Scott Memorial, but before it was completed he fell into the canal one foggy night. He married a sister of W. Bonnar, R.S.A. His watercolours can be similar in style to those of T. Hamilton (q.v.).
Examples: N.G.S.; R.I.A.S.
Bibliography: J. Colston: *History of the Scott Monument*, 1881. T. Bonnar: *Biog. Sketch of G.M.K*, 1892. *Country Life*, 5 Aug. 1971.

KEMP, John   **1833 (?Cork) - 1923**
A portrait and landscape painter, and a drawing master. He studied at the Cork School of Art, 1852-3, and the R.A. Schools, and taught at the Gloucester School of Art. He is said to have emigrated to Australia around 1877. While he could produce Prout-like French town scenes, he also painted Irish landscapes. His pupils included P. Wilson Steer (q.v.) and the caricaturist George Belcher.
Examples: V.A.M.

KEMPE, Mary Harriet, Mrs. Marks
1847/6   **-**
A painter of fruity still lifes and humorous genre subjects. She studied at Heatherley's and at the R.A. Schools, which she entered in 1870. She exhibited under her maiden name from 1867 until about 1893 when she married H.S. Marks (q.v.). She exhibited for the last time in 1900. She lived in London for the most part and also exhibited in Birmingham and Brighton.

KEMPSON, M   Freeman
A landscape painter who was in India from around 1856 to 1861. Later she lived in Croydon and exhibited at Suffolk Street, with the Female Artists and elsewhere from 1870 to 1884. Her subjects were often from the West of Scotland and North Wales, but she also painted in the Lake District and at Lynmouth.

KENDRICK, Emma Eleonora
1788   - 1871
The daughter of a sculptor, she was a miniaturist and occasional subject painter. She exhibited at the R.A., O.W.S., N.W.S. and S.B.A. from 1811 to 1840 and was appointed Miniature Painter to William IV in 1830.

KENDRICK, Matthew, R.H.A.
c.1797 (Dublin) - 1874 (London)
A marine painter, occasionally in watercolour, who began as a sailor and entered the R.D.S. Schools in 1825. He exhibited at the R.H.A. between 1827 and 1872 and was elected A.R.H.A. and R.H.A. in 1832 and 1850, and served as Keeper from 1850 to 1866. He lived in London from 1840 until 1848, exhibiting at the R.A., and the S.B.A. He then went back to Dublin where he practised until 1872 when, his right hand having become paralysed, he retired to London.

KENNEDY, Charles Napier, A.R.H.A.
1852 (London) - 1898 (St. Ives, Cornwall)
A portrait and figure painter in oil and watercolour who studied at the Slade and in Paris. He exhibited at the R.A. from 1872 to 1894, the S.B.A., and the R.H.A. from 1886, and was elected A.R.H.A. in 1896.

His wife **Lucy KENNEDY, née Marwood,** painted genre subjects in watercolour.
Bibliography: *A.J.,* 1890.

KENNEDY, Edward Sherard
A London genre painter in oil and watercolour who was working between 1863 and 1890.

His wife **Florence KENNEDY, née Laing,** was also a painter.

KENNEDY, John
A Scottish landscape painter who was working about 1855. He was Master of the Dundee School of Art for a time.
Published: *The first grade Freehand Drawing Book,* 1863. *The first grade Practical Geometry,* 1863.
Examples: V.A.M.; N.G., Scotland.

KENNEDY, Joseph
A genre painter who lived in Chelsea and at Barnstaple. In 1867 he was at the Government School of Design at Kidderminster, and in about 1873 at the Aberdeen School of Art. He exhibited from 1861 to 1888.

KENNEDY, William
1859 (Glasgow) - 1918 (Tangiers)
A landscape, military and genre painter in various media including watercolour. He studied at the Paisley and Glasgow Schools of Art and in Paris and Grez-sur-Loing. From 1885 to 1898 he worked in Stirling and was associated with the Glasgow School, being the first President of the Glasgow Boys' society. From around 1900 he spent much time in Berkshire, and in 1911 he emigrated to Tangiers for his health. He developed from detail to breadth, and could be very effective, but he was a very uneven painter, signing his name to 'many mediocre and some downright bad paintings'.

His wife Lena Kennedy, née Scott, painted landscapes in oil.

KENNEDY, William Denholm
1813 (Dumfries) - 1865 (London)
After being educated in Edinburgh, he came to London, and in 1833 entered the R.A. Schools. He exhibited at the R.A. almost every year from 1833 until his death. In 1835 he won a gold medal for a historical painting, and from 1840 to 1842 he was sketching and studying in Rome. He frequently made designs for stained glass for Thomas Willemont.

He painted a variety of subjects, including portraits. His style was marked by his friendship with W. Etty (q.v.); and, after his stay in Rome, Italian influence is felt in his work.
Examples: B.M.
Bibliography: *A.J.,* 1865.

KENNEDY, Admiral Sir William Robert
1838 - 1916
The artist of a folio of watercolours and plans relating to the China War of 1857 to 1860. He served in the Crimean War, off Newfoundland and in the Pacific. He was promoted lieutenant in 1857, captain in 1874, rear-admiral in 1889, vice-admiral in 1896 and admiral in 1901, when he retired to Sussex. He was made a K.C.B. in 1897.
Examples: Greenwich.

KENNION, Edward, F.S.A.
1744 (Liverpool) - 1809 (London)
Educated in Liverpool and London, he sailed for Jamaica in 1762 and accompanied the Cuban expedition. He returned to England after the capture of Havana but was in Jamaica again from 1765 to 1769 as manager of a cousin's estates and aide-de-camp to the Commander-in-Chief. From 1769 to 1782 he was in trade in London. He lived near Malvern for the next few years but was back in London as a drawing master during the winters of 1787 and 1788 and permanently from the following year. He became a member of the S.A. and exhibited at the R.A. from 1790 to 1807. From about 1782 he was working on a book on landscape painting, which he never finished. He made frequent visits to Liverpool and the Lakes and sometimes with G. Barret (q.v.).

His earlier drawings are in ink or pencil, later tints are added and finally full colour. His drawing is accurate and he manages to differentiate between different types of foliage.

His son **Charles John KENNION (1789-1853)** exhibited at the R.A. and Suffolk Street from 1804 to 1853 when he died in London. His work is similar to that of his father.
Published: *Elements of Landscape and Picturesque Beauty,* 1790. *An Essay on Trees in Landscapes,* 1815.

KEPPIE, Jessie
1868 (Glasgow) - 1951 (Prestwick)
A painter of flowers, architecture and topographical subjects, she was the sister of the architect, draughtsman and etcher **John KEPPIE, R.S.A. (1860-1945).** She studied under Fra Newbery (q.v.) and James Dunlop at the Glasgow School of Art, and she was a friend of the Macdonald sisters and Kate Cameron (q.v.). Although she was engaged to C.R. Macintosh for a while, she never married. She was a designer as well as an illustrator, and was a member of the Glasgow Lady Artists' Club.

KER, Sophia, Mrs. Mahon
1780/1 -
The eldest daughter of David Ker of London, who bought several properties in Co. Down, and his wife Madalena Guardi, making her a grand-daughter of Francesco Guardi. She became an amateur watercolour painter and was active in the early 19th century. In 1813 she married George Mahon of Mount Pleasant, Co. Mayo.

KERR, Fred – see ALTHAUS, Fritz B.

KERR, Frederick James
1853 (Neath, Glamorgan) -
A landscape painter who began by working in oil but turned to watercolour. He studied at the Swansea School of Art and at South Kensington. He lived at Barry, South Wales, and was for a time Chairman of the South Wales Art Society. He should not be confused with 'Fred Kerr'.

KERR, Commander George Cochrane
c.1825 - c.1907
A naval officer who retired in about 1864 to become a marine painter in oil and watercolour. He had been promoted lieutenant in 1845. He lived in Kensington and near Gillingham on the Medway and exhibited from 1873 to 1897. Many of his subjects are on the Channel and Norfolk coasts. In 1898 he had a show at the Fine Art Society.

KERR, Henry Wright, R.S.A., R.S.W.
1857 (Edinburgh) - 1936 (Edinburgh)
A genre, portrait and landscape painter who studied in Dundee and at the R.S.A. Schools. He visited Connemara in 1888 and exhibited in London from 1890. He was elected A.R.S.A. and R.S.A. in 1893 and 1909. He was influenced by his Dutch contemporaries as well as the Glasgow School.
Illustrated: E.B. *Ramsay: Scottish Life and Character,* 1909. J. Galt: *Annals of the Parish,* 1910. G.A. Birmingham: *The Lighter Side of Irish Life,* 1911. J. Galt: *The Last of the Lairds,* 1926.
Examples: Dundee City A.G.; N.G., Scotland.
Bibliography: *Scotsman,* 18 Dec. 1936.

KERR, Johnson – see CARR, Johnson

KERR, Vice-Admiral Lord Mark
1776 - 1840
A naval officer, topographer, caricaturist and

KILBURNE, George Goodwin (1839-1924)
'The Portfolio.' *Watercolour, signed and dated 1877, 13½in. x 17½in.*

painter of weird grotesques, he was a younger son of the 5th Marquess of Lothian. In 1799 he married Charlotte, younger daughter of the Marquess of Antrim, who became Countess of Antrim in her own right in 1834, but died the next year. He had learned to draw in the navy, where he illustrated his logs, notably that of the voyage to China with Earl Macartney's embassy, 1792-94. His wash grotesques, as Crookshank and Glin point out, anticipate Lear's nonsense drawings.

KETTLE, Sir Rupert Alfred
1817 (Birmingham) - 1894 (Wolverhampton)
Barrister, industrial arbitrator and amateur artist, he practised at Oxford and in 1859 was appointed judge of the Worcestershire County Courts. He established a system of arbitration in Wolverhampton which was followed in other towns. In 1880 he was knighted, and in 1882 elected a bencher of the Middle Temple.
Several of his pictures were exhibited.
Examples: V.A.M.

KEYS, Frances M
A landscape painter who lived at Mitcham and Croydon and exhibited at Suffolk Street from 1857 to 1877. Her favourite sketching grounds were Surrey, Dartmoor and North Wales. She liked to emphasise trees and flowers.

KEYS, George Scott
A landscape painter who lived in London and exhibited from 1856 to 1875. The majority of

his subjects were found in North Wales, and he also painted in Surrey.
A **G.F. KEYS** exhibited Dartmoor and Sussex views at Suffolk Street in the 1890s.

KEYS, John   1798 (Derby) - 1825 (Derby)
Son of Samuel Keys, a decorator at the Derby Porcelain works. He painted on china and, on being discharged in 1821, taught flower painting in Derby. His watercolours are very neat.
Published: *Sketches of Old Derby,* 1895.

KIDD, J
A topographer who visited Orkney in 1805.
Examples: N.G., Scotland.

KIDD, Joseph Bartholomew
1808 (Edinburgh) - 1889 (Greenwich)
A pupil of Thomson of Duddington (q.v.), Kidd was one of the original A.R.S.A.s, becoming R.S.A. in 1829. In 1836 he moved from Edinburgh to London and resigned from the Academy two years later. He became a drawing master at Greenwich.
His subjects are generally Highland or Lake District views. He also painted portraits.
Illustrated: Sir T.D. Lauder: *The Miscellany of Natural History,* 1833.

KILBURN, William
1745   - 1818
An immensely talented Irish textile designer, who may have studied at the R.D.S. Schools and was trained under Jonathan Sisson at

Lucan before moving to England in about 1766. At first he sold designs to calico printers and shops, but then, under the influence of the botanist William Curtis, he turned to botanical illustration. In both areas his work is of very high quality. His textile designs are in bodycolour and based on natural forms.
Examples: V.A.M.; R.Botanical Gdns., Kew.
Bibliography: Irish Georgian Soc., XXIV, i and iii, 1981. *W&D,* 1989, ii.

KILBURNE, George Goodwin, R.I.
1839 (Norfolk) - 1924 (London)
A genre painter who worked for the Dalziels for five years and exhibited at the R.A. from 1863. He was elected N.W.S. in 1866. Many prints were made from his work, which is almost entirely set in the eighteenth century.
It is likely that the **Miss S.E. KILBURNE** who exhibited a watercolour in 1871 was his sister.
His son, **George KILBURNE, Yr. (1863-1938)** painted very similarly to himself.
Examples: Haworth A.G., Accrington.
Bibliography: *Connoisseur,* LXX, 1924.

KINDON, Mary Evelina
1849   - 1919 (Watford)
A Herkomer student who became a portrait, genre and landscape painter in oil and watercolour. She exhibited from 1874 to 1919 at the R.A., the R.I. and elsewhere, and lived in Chelsea, Croydon, Chalk Hill, Bushey and Watford.

KING, Daniel
c.1622 (Chester) - c.1664 (London)
An engraver who was apprenticed to Randle Holme, the elder, for ten years from 1630. He moved from Chester to London where he produced drawings and engravings in the manner of Hollar (q.v.). He was said to be a 'most ignorant, silly fellow', and he made a bad marriage.
Published: *The Vale Royall of England,* 1656. *The Cathedrall and Conventuall Churches of England and Wales,* 1656. *Universal Way of Dyaling by G. de Desargues* (trans.), 1659. *An Orthographical Design of Severall Views upon ye Road in England and Wales,* c.1660.
Examples: B.M.

KING, Mrs. E.B. –
see **BROWNLOW, Emma**

KING, Haynes
1831 (Barbados) - 1904 (London)
A landscape and genre painter who came to England in 1854 and studied at Leigh's Academy. He exhibited from 1855 and became a member of the S.B.A. in 1864. For a time he shared a house with his namesake H.J.Y. King (q.v.), and he was killed by a train. He specialised in cottage interiors.
Examples: V.A.M.; Derby A.G.
Bibliography: *A.J.,* 1904. *The Times,* 21 May 1904.

KING, Jessie Marion, Mrs. Taylor (1875-1949)
'None with her save a Little Maid, a Novice.' *Pen and ink wash, 7¾in. x 6in.*

and he was present at the occupation of Paris in 1815. He was promoted captain in 1830, in which year he retired. He was made a Military Knight of Windsor in 1852.

He often exhibited his views of Spain, Portugal, Killarney, Boulogne, and elsewhere at the R.A. and B.I.
Bibliography: *A.J.*, 1863.

KING, Thomas Richard
A landscape painter who lived in Islington and exhibited from 1839 to 1846. He worked in Kent and also painted French and German subjects. His wife, or widow, exhibited in 1848.

KINNAIRD, Henry J   - c.1920
A landscape and cattle painter of small talent, who exhibited in London from 1880 to 1908. He lived in London until 1886 and thereafter at Chingford, Arundel and Lewes. His name is sometimes spelled 'Kinniard' in catalogues.

KINNAIRD, Wiggs
**   c. 1870   - 1930**
If the work of H.J. Kinnaird (q.v.) lacks inspiration, that of Wiggs Kinnaird is worse in its rustic way. His name too has been variously spelled.

KINNARD, William
**   c.1788   - 1839**
An architect who studied at the R.A. Schools from 1805, winning a gold medal that year. He was District Surveyor of St Giles and St George, Bloomsbury, until dismissed after a quarrel with Soane. This will have made it easier for him to travel with C. Barry (q.v.) and C. Eastlake (q.v.) in Italy, Greece and Turkey from 1817 to 1819 He was a good

KING, Henry John Yeend, R.I.
**   1855 (London) - 1924 (London)**
A landscape painter who began his career in a glassworks. He became a pupil of William Bromley, a historical painter, and studied in Paris, and he exhibited in London from 1874. He was elected R.I. in 1887 and became Vice-President in 1901. His work is very typical of his period with bright colours and a slight crudeness of handling, and he sometimes shows the influence of Brabazon.
Examples: Reading A.G.; Walker A.G., Liverpool.
Bibliography: *A.J.*, 1897; 1898.

KING, Jessie Marion, Mrs. Taylor
**   1875 (Bearsden, nr. Glasgow) -**
**   1949 (Kirkudbright)**
An illustrator who exhibited from 1901 to 1940. She lived in Glasgow from 1901 to 1908, Manchester from 1909 to 1910 and in 1912, Paris in 1911 and from 1913 to 1915, and thereafter at Kirkcudbright. She married E.A. Taylor, an artist. She illustrated many authors including Kipling and Milton and produced many lightly coloured pen and ink drawings of fairytale princesses in a style that is very much her own, if influenced by the great late nineteenth century illustrators.
Published: *The Grey City of the North*, 1910. *The City of the West*, 1911. &c.
Bibliography: *Studio*, 1902; 1906. Scottish Arts Council: Exhibition Cat. (n.d.).

KING, Captain John Duncan
**   1789 (Ireland) - 1863 (Windsor Castle)**
King entered the Army in 1806, served in the Walcheren expedition and the Peninsular War

KINNAIRD, Henry J (c.1920-)
Near Bury, Sussex. *Watercolour heightened with bodycolour, signed and inscribed, 10in. x 14½in.*

watercolourist, and he exhibited views from his travels, as well as designs, at the R.A. However, according to Barry's friend J.L.Wolfe, he 'went mad from time to time'.
Edited: Supplementary volume to *The Antiquities of Athens*, 1830.

KINNEAR, James Scott
A landscape painter in oil and watercolour, he lived in Edinburgh and exhibited detailed scenes at the R.S.A., the R.S.W., the R.I. and elsewhere from 1870 to 1917. He enjoyed winter subjects.
Bibliography: *A.J.*, 1894.

KINSLEY, Albert, R.I.
1852 (Hull) - 1945
A painter of woods, moors and rivers in oil and watercolour who was brought up in Leeds and moved to London in 1879. He was a drawing master and exhibited from 1881, being elected R.I. in 1896.
Bibliography: *A.J.*, 1896; 1900.

KIPLING, John Lockwood
1837 (Pickering) - 1911 (Tisbury)
An architect, sculptor and illustrator who was educated at Woodhouse Grove and studied at South Kensington, taught at the Bombay School of Art and was Principal of the Mayo School of Art, Lahore, from 1865 to 1875. He was then Curator of the Central Museum at Lahore until his retirement in 1893 when he settled in Tisbury, Wiltshire. In 1898 he went to South Africa via Madeira with his son Rudyard, and the following year they went to Sutherland.

He provided illustrations in a number of media for Rudyard's Indian books and also produced wash drawings of Indians. He edited the *Indian Art Journal*.

His wife was sister-in-law of Sir E.J. Poynter and Sir E.C.B. Burne-Jones (qq.v.), and aunt of Stanley Baldwin.
Published: *Beast and Man in India*, 1891.
Examples: India Office Lib.

KIRBY, John Joshua, F.R.S., F.S.A.
1716 (Wickham Market) - 1774 (Kew)
A friend of Gainsborough who began his career in Ipswich as a coach and house painter. In 1745 Gainsborough came to live in the town and encouraged Kirby to try landscape painting. He began with a series of drawings of the monuments of Suffolk and later worked for Boydell and others. He gave three lectures on perspective at the St. Martin's Lane Academy in 1764 and taught George III architectural drawing. The King appointed him Clerk of the Works at Kew Palace. He was briefly President of the Incorporated Society of Artists in 1768. His grave at Kew is close to that of Gainsborough.

He is a neat and pleasant, if unadventurous, artist, working in the topographical tradition which continued down to the Bucklers.

His son **William KIRBY**, who died at Kew

in 1771, was a member of the Incorporated Society from 1766.
Published: *Monasteries, Castles, Ancient Churches and Monuments in the County of Suffolk*, 1748. *Dr. Brook Taylor's Method of Perspective made Easy*, 1754.
Examples: B.M.
Bibliography: Walpole Soc., XXVII. Gainsborough Ho. Mus., Sudbury, Exhibition Cat., 1980.

KIRCHHOFFER, Henry, R.H.A.
1781 (Dublin) - 1860 (London)
The son of Francis Kirchhoffer, a cabinet-maker working in Dublin, he entered the R.D.S. Schools in 1797, after which he practised as a miniature painter in Cork. He returned to Dublin in 1816, where he was a frequent exhibitor, and he became one of the original A.R.H.As., being elected R.H.A. in 1826. He exhibited there from 1826 to 1834, and acted as Secretary for a period up to 1830. He moved to London in 1835 and exhibited at the R.A. and elsewhere between 1837 and 1843. He lived for some years in Brighton.

He painted landscapes, portraits and figure subjects in watercolour and occasionally in oil.
Examples: N.G., Ireland.

KIRK, Thomas   1765 - 1797 (London)
A pupil of R. Cosway (q.v.), he was a miniaturist, historical painter and engraver. He studied at the R.A. Schools from 1784 and exhibited at the R.A. from 1765 to 1796. Drawings of his were used for 'Cooke's series of Poets', and he worked on Boydell's Shakespeare. He died of consumption, and should not be confused with his Irish name-sake (1777-1845), a sculptor. His drawings manage to be both theatrical and insipid.

KIRKPATRICK, Joseph
1872 (Liverpool) - 1936
A painter of landscapes and rustic scenes rather in the manner of M.B. Foster (q.v.) or W.S. Coleman (q.v.). He trained at the Liverpool School of Art and Julian's in Paris, worked in the Liverpool area and may have visited Jamaica in about 1903. He also lived at Curdridge, Hampshire for a time.
Examples: Haworth A.G., Accrington; Newport A.G.
Bibliography: *Connoisseur*, XLV.

KIRKUP, Seymour Stocker
1788 (London) - 1880 (London)
The son of a London diamond merchant, he entered the R.A. Schools in 1809. He became a friend of Blake and Haydon. In 1816 he paid his first visit to Italy and subsequently settled in Rome and Florence. In 1840 he was one of the discoverers of Giotto's missing portrait of Dante, for which he was later made a Cavaliere di SS Maurizio e Lazzaro. Owing to a misunderstanding he referred to himself as 'Baron' thereafter. In 1872 he moved to Leghorn and in 1875 married a twenty-two year old Italian.

He was a dilettante in his approach to painting and is best known for his chalk and watercolour portraits in the manner of Lawrence.
Examples: Ashmolean.

KIRWAN, William Bourke
c.1814 (Dublin) - p.1852
A miniaturist, landscape and genre painter in the Morland (q.v.) tradition who exhibited in Dublin and London from 1836 to 1846. His work can be weak. In 1852 he was tried for the murder of his wife and sentenced to transportation for life. He is said to have died in America.
Examples: B.M.

KITCHEN, Thomas Samuel
- 1853 (London)
A landscape painter who lived in Peckham and exhibited from 1833 to 1852. He produced excellent studies of trees in pen and wash which are reminiscent of those of D.S. McColl (q.v.).

A **Miss E.M. KITCHEN** of Windsor was an unsuccessful candidate for the N.W.S. in 1856 and 1857. She exhibited fruit and flower subjects at the S.B.A. from 1850 to 1852. In Scotland **James KITCHEN** exhibited watercolour portraits and figure subjects infrequently between 1855 and 1885. He lived in Leith and Dumbarton.

KITTON, Frederick George
1856 (Norwich) - 1903 (St. Albans)
A writer on art and painter of London views who exhibited with the Norwich Art Circle in 1886 and 1887. He was a prolific illustrator of, and commentator on, the works of Dickens, and he also illustrated books on St. Albans and Herefordshire houses.
Published: *Phiz. – A Memoir*, 1882. *John Leech, Artist and Humourist*, 1883. *Dickensiana*, 1886. &c.
Bibliography: Anon. *F.K., a Memoir*, 1895.

KNEEN, William
1862 (Isle of Man) - 1921 (London)
A pupil of Professor Fred Brown, he lived at Richmond, Surrey and painted landscapes, beach scenes and genre subjects.
Examples: V.A.M.

KNELL, William Adolphus
1802 - 1875 (London)
The best known and best of a family of marine painters. He lived in London and perhaps Bristol, and exhibited in London from 1825 to 1866. He painted in oil and watercolour on the southern coasts of England and off France, Belgium and Holland. He used a distinctive dark green and rubbing for his seas.

William Callcott KNELL who worked between 1848 and 1871 and **Adolphus KNELL** were probably his sons, and **J.H. KNELL**, working in 1833 and 1834, perhaps a brother.
Examples: Greenwich; N.G., Scotland.
Bibliography: *Art Union*, 1847. *A.J.*, 1857; 1860.

KNEWSTUB, Walter John
1831/2   - 1906

A caricaturist and genre painter who was D.G. Rossetti's (q.v.) assistant in the 1860s and F.M. Brown's (q.v.) at Manchester Town Hall from 1878 to 1893. His caricatures belong to the early part of his career, and he entered the R.A. Schools in 1862 and exhibited from 1865 to 1881. His daughter married Sir William Rothenstein.

Bibliography: W.M. Rossetti: *Some Reminiscences,* III, 1906. *Studio,* XXXVIII, 1906. *Artwork,* IV, 1930.

KNIGHT, Adam   - 1931

A landscape painter who lived at West Bridgford, Nottinghamshire. He exhibited from 1892, both in London and Liverpool.

KNIGHT, Ellis Cordelia
1757 (? London) - 1837 (Paris)

Authoress, landscape painter and Royal companion, she was the daughter of Rear-Admiral Sir Joseph Knight. She was educated in London by a Swiss pastor, and the family were intimate with Reynolds and Dr. Johnson's circle. On the death of her father in 1775 she went to Italy with her mother and became a friend of the Hamiltons. The mother died in 1799, and Miss Knight returned to England with the Hamiltons and Nelson. She was appointed a companion to Queen Charlotte in 1805, but transferred to Princess Charlotte in 1813. In the following year she was sacked by the Prince Regent, together with the Princess's other attendants, and two years later she returned to the Continent, where she lived thereafter, although she made frequent visits to England.

Her watercolours are those of a distinguished amateur, and make one feel that she knew 'Grecian' Williams (q.v.) in Rome, or at least knew his work. In a private letter dated 1790 J.T. Serres noted that 'she draws *very well.*' She was also an etcher.

Published: *Autobiography* (edited), 1861; *A Description of Latium or La Campagna,* 1805. &c.
Bibliography: B. Luttrell: *The Prim Romantic,* 1965.

KNIGHT, Henry Gally
1786   - 1846 (London)

An architectural writer, playwright and polemicist, educated at Eton and Trinity College, Cambridge. In 1810 and 1811 he travelled in Spain, Sicily, Greece, Egypt and Palestine, producing publications in verse to illustrate these journeys. He studied architecture in Normandy in 1831 and Sicily in 1836. In England he managed his estate, Langold Hall, Yorkshire, and served in Parliament intermittently between 1824 and 1837, and from 1837 until his death as member for North Nottinghamshire. He was a friend of J.M.W. Turner (q.v.).

The drawings he made to illustrate his travels are in pencil with light washes.

Published: *An Architectural Tour of Normandy,*

KNIGHT, John Baverstock (1788-1859)
Totnes. *Inscribed and dated, watercolour.*

1836. *The Normans in Sicily,* 1838. *Saracenic and Norman Remains to illustrate the 'Normans in Sicily',* 1840. *The Ecclesiastical Architecture of Italy from... Constantine to the 15th Century,* 1842-4.

KNIGHT, John Baverstock
1788 (Langton, nr. Blandford, Dorset) - 1859 (Piddle Hinton, Dorset)

The son of a land agent and connoisseur who encouraged his many talents. He was educated at home and at Child Okeford. Later he assisted his father and toured Britain, Ireland and the Continent painting in oil and watercolour and sketching in chalk and pen and ink. He also made etchings and miniatures. He is said to have painted between five and six in the morning leaving the rest of the day for agriculture, sport and his other love, poetry.

His style is rather stilted and old-fashioned and his drawings have some affinity with the Towne (q.v.) school. An exhibition of his work was held at the Goupil Gallery, London, in 1908.

Examples: B.M.; V.A.M.; Victoria A.G., Bath; Williamson A.G., Birkenhead; Blackburn A.G.; Brighton A.G.; Wiltshire Mus., Devizes; Co. Mus., Dorchester; Exeter Mus.; Fitzwilliam; Glasgow A.G.; Leeds City A.G.; Leicestershire A.G.
Bibliography: Rev. F. Knight: *J.B.K.,* 1908; D.S. MacColl: *Burlington Mag.,* May 1919; *Dorset Year Book,* XXI, 1925.

KNIGHT, John Prescott, R.A.
1803 (Stafford) - 1881 (London)

A genre and portrait painter in oil and watercolour, he was the son of a comedian and came to London as a boy. He worked as a

junior clerk to a West India merchant before studying at Sass's, with G. Clint (q.v.) and at the R.A. Schools from 1823. As a portraitist he was largely unsuccessful so he turned to rustic genre, exhibited from 1824 and was elected A.R.A. and R.A. in 1836 and 1844. He was Professor of Perspective in 1839 and Secretary in 1848.

His studio sale was at Christie's, 2 July 1881.
Examples: B.M.; V.A.M.
Bibliography: *A.J.,* 1849; 1881. Stafford Historical and Civic Society, *J.P.K.: A Catalogue,* 1971.

KNIGHT, John William Buxton
1843 (Sevenoaks) - 1908 (Dover)

Although the son of a landscape painter, he was self taught to begin with. He worked for a while at Knole Park with J. Holland (q.v.) and was advised to enter the R.A. Schools by Landseer (q.v.), which he did in 1860. He exhibited from 1863 and won a gold medal at Paris in 1889. His subjects are often views of Kent and are a fusion of the English and French traditions of landscape. He painted in oil and watercolour and was an etcher and engraver.

An exhibition of his work was held at the Goupil Gallery in 1897, and a memorial exhibition was held at the British Galleries, Bradford, in 1908.

Examples: B.M.; V.A.M.; Williamson A.G., Birkenhead; Cartwright Hall, Bradford; Derby A.G.; Fitzwilliam; Leeds City A.G.
Bibliography: *A.J.,* 1907; 1908. *Studio,* XLII, 1908. *Morning Post,* 17 Feb. 1908. *The Year's Art,* 1909. *Burlington Mag.,* XXXI, 1917. *Connoisseur,* LVIII, 1924.

KNOWLES, George Sheridan (1863-1931)
Garden tea party. *Signed, 49½in. x 29½in.*

KNIGHT, Joseph, R.I.
1837 (London) - 1909 (Bryn Glas, Conway)
A landscape painter in oil and watercolour. Despite having lost his left arm at the age of seven, he taught himself to paint while working for a photographer. He then attended the Manchester Academy and exhibited in London from 1861. He moved to London in 1871 and to North Wales in 1875. He was elected R.I. in 1882. Sometimes his Welsh landscapes are in the Birket Foster (q.v.) manner. He also etched.
Examples: V.A.M.; Tate Gall.
Bibliography: Manchester Brazenose Club: Exhibition Cat., 1878. *A.J.,* 1909.

KNIGHT, Joseph, of Bury
1870 (Bolton) - 1950
A landscape painter and etcher who studied in Paris and became Headmaster of Bury Art School.
Published: with H.B. Carpenter: *Introduction to the History of Architecture,* 1929.

KNIGHT, Richard Payne
1750 - 1824 (London)
A collector and amateur artist, Knight was the son of the Rev. Thomas and a member of the Shropshire ironworks family. He spent several years in Italy from 1767 and returned there in 1777, visiting Sicily with Philipp Hackert and C. Gore (q.v.). He was a prolific writer, usually on artistic subjects, and his collections of bronzes, statues, pictures and coins in London and at Downton, Herefordshire, were justly famous. He was M.P. for Leominster from

1780 and Ludlow from 1784 to 1806. He was Townley trustee of the B.M. from 1814.
Examples: Townley Hall, Burnley.

KNIGHT, William - 1845 (Kidderminster)
An architect who exhibited landscapes as well as architectural subjects at the R.A. and Suffolk Street from 1807 to 1846, from addresses in London, Chelmsford and Sevenoaks. However, his practice was in Kidderminster, where in 1822 he was clerk of the works to F. Goodwin (q.v.), and later he worked with T. Rickman (q.v.).
W.S. KNIGHT and **Mary KNIGHT,** who exhibited views of Knole in the 1860s and 1870s, were presumably his children.
Bibliography: *Berrow's Worcester Journal,* 25 May 1837.

KNIVETON, William
A Dublin landscape painter who exhibited at Parliament House in 1802 and Dame Street in 1804. Two aquatints after his drawings were published by del Vecchio in Dublin.

KNOWLES, George Sheridan, R.I.
1863 (Manchester) - 1931
A medieval and Imperial genre painter who lived in London. He was the son of the journalist Richard Brinsley Knowles, and a nephew of the Irish painter Nicholas Joseph Crowley (1819-1857). He entered the R.A. Schools in 1883, exhibited from 1885, and was elected R.I. in 1892, later serving as Treasurer. He was also a member of the R.B.A.
Bibliography: *A.J.,* 1901.

KNOWLES, William Pitcairn
A landscape painter who lived at Burton, near Christchurch, Hants., and exhibited local subjects between 1882 and 1892.

KNOX, Archibald 1864 - 1933
A landscape painter who sketched and taught in many parts of the country. He was the founder of the Knox Guild of Design and Crafts and lived in Douglas, Isle of Man, from 1895.
Examples: Manx Mus.

KNOX, Commander George James
1810 - 1897
The painter who signs G.J. Knox is perhaps to be identified with the grandson of the 1st Earl of Ranfurly. His watercolours, which are fairly common, show a decided penchant for sunsets and snow-covered landscapes, usually in combination. He also painted beach scenes. He exhibited at the R.A. and Suffolk Street from 1839 to 1859.
Examples: Cape Town A.G.

KOEHLER, Brigadier-General George Frederic - 1800 (Jaffa)
A pupil of Sandby at Woolwich, he made reconnaissances in Corsica with Sir John Moore in 1794. His drawings of enemy positions, which Moore praised highly, were included in his official report. He was of German origin and was commissioned 2nd lieutenant in the Royal Artillery during the siege of Gibraltar in 1780. He distinguished himself and became a favourite aide-de-camp of Lord Heathfield, with whom he later travelled and who recommended him to the Belgian rebels against the Austrians in 1790. Thereafter he served in Gibraltar, Toulon in 1793, Corsica and Newcastle-upon-Tyne, and he headed a mission to Constantinople in 1799 and visited Cyprus in 1800. He died while visiting the Syrian front. The cannon in the background of the famous portrait of Heathfield was designed by Koehler.
Examples: Greenwich.

'KYD' 1856/7 - 1937 (Hampstead)
The *nom d'artiste* of Joseph Clayton Clarke who made a series of spirited watercolour sketches of Dickens' characters. They were published in 1889.
Examples: Portsmouth City Mus.

KYD, James 1813 -
A genre painter who lived in Worcester, London and Edinburgh. He studied at the Government School of Design in Worcester and entered the R.A. Schools in 1850. He exhibited from 1855 to 1875, and he enjoyed Highland themes.

L

LA CAVE, Peter

A painter of rustic figures and landscapes in the Bergham tradition, who was probably a member of a family of French artists working in Holland. He was in England from at least 1789 to 1816 and painted in Worcestershire, Berkshire, Devonshire and Wilton, where he was in prison in 1811 on a charge of felony, which was thrown out by the Grand Jury. He was a friend of Ibbetson (q.v.) and probably an assistant to Morland (q.v.). On reading the report of his imprisonment (in which the name is given as 'le Cave'), Blake noted that he considered La Cave to be a much better artist than Morland: 'It confirms the suspition I entertained concerning those two I Engraved From for J.R. Smith – That Morland could not have Painted them, as they were the works of a Correct Mind & no Blurer'.

His finished watercolours are pretty, conventional and rather weak. His pencil drawings are much stronger and were admired by Cotman. He had a number of pupils, some of whom seem to have added their signatures to his work. Among them were J.R. Morris (q.v.) and John Thomas Gower.

Examples: B.M.; V.A.M.; Derby A.G.; Fitzwilliam; Leeds City A.G.; London Mus.; Newport A.G.

Bibliography: *Bell's Weekly Messenger*, 29 July 1811. *The Examiner*, 4 Aug. 1811. *Walker's Quarterly*, July, 1922. *Walker's Monthly*, Aug. 1929. *Apollo*, Dec. 1947.

LA CAVE, Peter
Coming Home from Market. *Pencil, pen and black ink and watercolour, 11¼in. x 14¼in.*

LACY, George
c.1814 (London) - 1884 (Bathurst, N.S.W.)

One of the ten children of a London banker, he went to Sydney, Australia, in 1842. There he began by 'shooting, stuffing strange birds and reptiles, and preserving insects' and tried his hand at gold digging before becoming a teacher. He revisited England in about 1859. He was also something of a journalist and illustrator, contributing to *The Southern Courier* and *The Illustrated Sydney News*. He painted topographical and gold mining subjects, and what were virtually strip cartoons. His wash sketches are lively.

Examples: Nat. Lib., Australia.

LADBROOKE, Henry
1800 (Norwich) - 1870 (Norwich)

Second son of R. Ladbrooke (q.v.), he was a landscape painter and drawing master at North Walsham and King's Lynn. He exhibited at Norwich and in London from 1818 to 1865.

Bibliography: J. Walpole: *Art and Artists of the Norwich School*, 1997.

LADBROOKE, John Berney
1803 (Norwich) - 1879 (Norwich)

A pupil of his uncle, John Crome (q.v.), he was primarily an oil painter. He exhibited at Norwich from 1816 to 1833 and in London from 1822 to 1859. Although almost all of his life was spent in Norfolk, he seems to have visited the Lakes in the 1850s.

His younger brother Frederick was a portrait painter at Bury St. Edmunds.

Published: *Select Views of Norfolk and its Environs*, 1820.

Examples: Castle Mus., Norwich.

Bibliography: W.F. Dickes: *The Norwich School*, 1905. J. Walpole: *Art and Artists of the Norwich School*, 1997.

LADBROOKE, Robert
1770 (Norwich) - 1842 (Norwich)

A landscape painter in oil and watercolour who was apprenticed to an engraver and shared a boyhood studio with his friend J. Crome (q.v.). In 1793 he married Crome's sister-in-law. He set up as a teacher and picture dealer. In 1803 he helped to found the Norwich Society and was a keen supporter of the exhibitions from 1805. He seems to have visited Wales at about this time. He was Vice-President of the Society in 1808 and President for the following year. In 1816 he quarrelled with Crome and led the secession from the Society. His rival exhibition collapsed after 1818, and by 1824 he had returned to the fold. By this time he had given up teaching in order to concentrate on his Norfolk Churches.

His work is generally disappointing, especially the churches, which are very ordinary. His colour is generally muddy and his drawing indistinct. However, he could sometimes rise to higher things, and then his work is a little reminiscent of Varley.

Published: *Views of the Churches of Norfolk*, 1843.

Examples: B.M.; Castle Mus., Norwich.

Bibliography: W.F. Dickes: *The Norwich School*, 1905. Bibliography: J. Walpole: *Art and Artists of the Norwich School*, 1997.

LAING, James Garden, R.S.W.
1852 (Aberdeen) - 1915

He trained and worked as an architect in Aberdeen before he began painting watercolours. Although he produced landscapes, he was best known for his church interiors, which are influenced by Bosboom and other Dutch contemporaries whom he met on sketching tours of Holland.

His wife **Annie Rose LAING, née Low**

LADBROOKE, Robert (1770-1842)
View on the Norfolk Broads at evening. *Watercolour, 8½in. x 11in.*

(1869-1946) painted landscapes and children, occasionally in watercolour.
Examples: Glasgow A.G.; Paisley A.G.
Bibliography: *Studio,* XXVIII, 1903; XXXVII, 1906; LXI, 1914; LXVII, 1916. *Morning Post,* 18 April 1910.

LAIRD, Alicia H

A painter of Scottish genre scenes who exhibited at the Society of Female Artists and elsewhere from 1846 to 1865. She lived in London and Edinburgh.
Examples: Hove Lib.

LAIT, Edward Beecham

A painter of landscapes with figures who was living in London in the 1860s and in Brighton in 1874. His work seems to be influenced by his neighbours, the Earps (q.v.).

LAMB, S

An artist who visited Iona in 1838. His work is light and pleasing. It is possible that he should be identified with Captain Somerville Waldemar Lamb, the third son of the 1st Lamb baronet, who was a Grenadier and wounded at Waterloo.

LAMBERT, Clement
1855 - 1925 (Brighton)

A landscape, coastal and genre painter who lived in Brighton and exhibited from 1880. He was a member of the Brighton Fine Art Committee.

Examples: Hove Lib.
Bibliography: *Connoisseur,* LXXI, 1925.

LAMBERT, George
1700 (Kent) - 1765

A landscape and scene painter who studied under Warner Hassells and John Wootton. He worked for John Rich at Lincolns Inn Fields Theatre and at Covent Garden. The Beefsteak Club is sometimes said to have originated in his suppers in the painting loft. He was a friend of Hogarth and occasionally collaborated with S. Scott (q.v.). He was a member of the Society of Artists, with whom he exhibited from 1761 to 1764, and a founder and first President of the Incorporated Society. T.T. Forrest (q.v.) was a pupil.

Although his oil paintings were painted in the manner of Poussin and Rosa, his watercolours belong to the typically English group embracing Taverner and Skelton, and independent of the Sandby tradition. As opposed to Sandby's method of careful outlining with the pen, the watercolour is applied loosely with a characteristic dappled effect, especially in the foliage, over a soft pencil basis. He also produced Italian landscapes in pen and brown wash, sometimes in collaboration with Zuccarelli (q.v.). A loan exhibition of his work was held at Kenwood in 1970.

In the Brighton A.G. are two works by **George LAMBERT, Yr.,** one dated 1827.
Examples: B.M.; Brighton A.G.; N.G., Scotland.
Bibliography: Country Life, 23 July 1970.

LAMBERT, James
1725 (Jevington, Sussex) - 1788 (Lewes)

A self-taught landscape painter, Lambert began his career in Lewes producing inn signs. He exhibited at the S.A., the R.A. and elsewhere from 1761. Sir William Burrell commissioned several hundred watercolours of Sussex antiquities. Lambert was also a musician and was organist of St. Thomas-at-Cliffe. His colour is said to have been good, but his drawings have usually faded badly. They are a little primitive in style.

His son **James LAMBERT, Yr. (1742-1799)** worked in a similar manner.
Illustrated: Watson: *History of the Earls of Warren.*
Examples: B.M.; V.A.M.; Leeds City A.G.
Bibliography: W.H. Challen: *Baldy's Garden, the Painters Lambert, &c.* 1952.

LAMBERT, John
c.1640 (Calton, Yorkshire) - 1701 (York)

Son of General John Lambert, he was an amateur artist and friend of F. Place (q.v.). On the death of his father – who had painted flowers and Oliver Cromwell – in 1683 he inherited the family's Yorkshire estates, which had been held in trust since the Restoration. He was said by Thoresby to be 'a most exact limner'.

LAMBORNE, Peter Spendelowe
1722 (London) - 1774 (Cambridge)

An engraver, miniaturist and architectural draughtsman, he studied in London under Isaac Basire, but practised in Cambridge. He exhibited with the Incorporated Society from 1764 to 1774.

LAMONT, Thomas Reynolds, A.R.W.S.
1826 (Greenock) - 1898

A Scot who studied in Paris – he was 'the Laird' in du Maurier's *Trilby* – and in Spain. He painted landscapes and figures and was elected A.O.W.S. in 1866, having stood unsuccessfully for the N.W.S. in the previous year. After about 1880 he painted little. He lived in St. John's Wood and on an estate near Greenock.
Examples: V.A.M.; Glasgow A.G.
Bibliography: See L. Ormond: *George Du Maurier,* 1969.

LAMPLOUGH, Augustus Osborne, R.W.S.
1877 (Manchester) - 1930 (Abergele)

A North African and Venetian architectural painter who studied at Chester School of Art. Later he lectured at Leeds School of Art. His architectural and Venetian subjects generally occur early in his career. From about 1902 he concentrated on North Africa and, in particular, Egypt. He lived in North Wales. Various exhibitions of his work were held in London, including Egyptian views at the Fine Art Society in 1917.
Published: *Cairo and its Environs,* 1909. *Winter in Egypt. Egypt and How to see it. The Flight of the*

Turkish Invaders.
Illustrated: P. Loti: *La Mort de Philae*, 1908. P. Loti: *Egypt*, 1909.
Examples: Grosvenor Mus., Chester; Newport A.G.

LANCASTER, Percy, R.I.
1878 (Manchester) - 1950
A landscape painter in the tradition of Cox and Collier. He studied at the Manchester School of Art and lived at Southport. He was elected R.I. in 1921.
Examples: Towner Gall., Eastbourne; Leicestershire A.G.; Newport A.G.; Preston A.G.

LANCE, George   1802 (Dunmow, Essex) -
1864 (Sunnyside, near Birkenhead)
Primarily an oil painter of fruity and floral still lifes, Lance studied under B.R. Haydon (q.v.), and at the R.A. Schools. He was encouraged by Beaumont to paint still lifes, and exhibited at the B.I. from 1824 and the R.A. from 1828. He also exhibited historical and genre subjects in oil. In 1839 he had a studio in Paris. He was brother-in-law of J.W. Archer (q.v.). His watercolours are merely versions of his oil paintings. Sir J. Gilbert (q.v.) and W. Duffield (q.v.) were pupils.
Examples: B.M.
Bibliography: *A.J.*, Oct. 1857; Aug. 1864.

LANDELLS, Ebenezer
1808 (Newcastle-upon-Tyne) -
1860 (London)
A wood-engraver, illustrator and founder of *Punch*, he was apprenticed to Bewick and then worked for John Jackson and William Harvey in London. He also worked for the *I.L.N.*, the *Lady's Newspaper* and the *Queen*, and had numerous pupils and assistants including M.B. Foster (q.v.), the Dalziels and Edmund Evans (q.v.). He was artist-correspondent for the *I.L.N.* and specialised in sketching Royal tours.
His eldest son **Robert Thomas LANDELLS (1833-1877)** was also an artist and war correspondent for the *I.L.N.*, covering the Crimean, Prusso-Danish and Franco-Prussian wars. He also painted in oil.

LANDMANN, Isaac
1741   - c.1826
The professor of artillery and fortification at Woolwich from 1777 to 1815, he drew local landscapes rather weakly in the manner of his colleague P. Sandby (q.v.), as well as plans and illustrations. Previously he had taught at the Royal Military School in Paris and served as an aide-de-camp to Marshal Broglie, and he was personally invited to Woolwich by George III. He published eight works on his subjects, of which the most notable was *The Principles of Fortification*, 1806. This went through five editions in his lifetime and was revised and republished by his son in 1841.
The son, **Lieutenant-Colonel George Thomas LANDMANN, 1779 (Woolwich) -**

LAMPLOUGH, Augustus Osborne (1877-1930)
A scene on the Nile at sunset near the ruins of Luxor. *Signed and inscribed, watercolour, 12in. x 30in.*

1854 (Shacklewell) served with distinction in Canada from 1797 to 1802 and in the Peninsula from 1804 to 1812. He had been a cadet at Woolwich in 1795 and was commissioned into the Royal Engineers in the same year. Between 1813 and 1819 he served in Ireland and Yorkshire, and in retirement he wrote *Recollections of my Military Life*, 1854, and two other books of Peninsular memoirs. He was a member of the Institute of Civil Engineers. Like his father he drew landscapes as well as plans.
Bibliography: *Records of the R.M.A. Woolwich*, 1851. *Royal Military Calendar*, 1826, vol.v. *Gentleman's Mag.* 1854, i.

LANDSEER, Charles, R.A.
1799 (London) - 1878 (London)
The second son of John Landseer A.R.A., the engraver, he was a pupil of B.R. Haydon (q.v.) and entered the R.A. Schools in 1816. He went to Portugal with Lord Stuart de Rothesay's mission and on to Rio de Janeiro. The sketches and drawings which resulted were exhibited at the B.I. in 1828. In the same year he began to exhibit literary and costume pictures at the R.A. He was elected A.R.A. and R.A. in 1837 and 1845 and was Keeper from 1851 to 1873.
Illustrated: W. Scrope: *Days of Deerstalking*, 1883. W. Scrope: *Days and Nights of Salmon Fishing*, 1898.
Examples: B.M.; V.A.M.; Ashmolean.
Bibliography: *A.J.*, 1879.

LANDSEER, Sir Edwin Henry, R.A.
1802 (London) - 1873 (London)
The youngest son of John Landseer A.R.A., he was one of the most fashionable painters of the nineteenth century. He can hardly be called a watercolourist, but his drawings are very fine and he made brown wash studies and

caricatures which are very close to those of his friend Wilkie (q.v.).
Examples: B.M.; V.A.M.; Fitzwilliam; Maidstone Mus.; Nottingham Univ.; N.G., Scotland.
Bibliography: S. Maun: *The Works of Sir E.L.*, 1843. A. Chester: *The Art of Sir E.L.*, 1920. I.B. Hill: *L.*, 1973. C. Lennie: *L the Victorian Paragon*, 1976. S. Tytler: *L's Dogs and their Stories*, 1977. V.A.M. MSS, c.1820-1919; *Fraser's Mag.*, July 1856. *A.J.*, 1873. *Apollo*, XLIX, 1949. *Country Life*, 24 Feb 1972. R.A. Exhibition Cats., 1874; 1961. Mappin A.G., Sheffield: Exhibition Cat., 1972. Tate Gall.: Exhibition Cat., 1982.

LANDSEER, George
1829   - 1878 (London)
Son of T. Landseer (q.v.), he was admitted to the R.A. Schools in 1846, exhibited from 1850 to 1858, and went to India. There he painted landscapes and portraits of prominent Indians in oil and watercolour. He returned to England in about 1870 and gave up painting because of poor health. However, in 1876 he shared an exhibition at the Fine Art Society with A.W. Hunt (q.v.).
Examples: V.A.M.
Bibliography: *A.J.*, 1876.

LANDSEER, Jessica
1807 (London) - 1880 (Folkestone)
Sister and housekeeper to Sir E.H. Landseer (q.v.), she was a landscape and miniature painter and an etcher. She copied her brother's paintings in watercolour, and although she lived in his shadow, her talent was not of the same order as his, and her work does not justify the claims that have sometimes been made for it by feminists.
Her younger sister, **Emma LANDSEER, Mrs. McKENZIE,** was an occasional painter and copyist.

LANGLEY, Walter (1852-1922)
'Mending Nets.' *Watercolour, signed, 9½in. x 14in.*

LANDSEER, Thomas, A.R.A.
1795 (London) - 1880 (London)
The eldest son of John Landseer A.R.A. whose assistant he became. Like his brothers he was a pupil of Haydon (q.v.). Most of his life was spent in engraving his brother Edwin's pictures including a splendid study of Turner taking tea, which he lithographed in 1851. He also made occasional designs of his own, notably the series *Monkeyana*, 1827. He was elected A.R.A. in 1868.
Published: *The Life and Letters of W. Bewick*, 1871.
Examples: B.M.

LANE, Rev. Charlton George
1836 - 1892 (Berkhamstead)
Educated at Christ Church, Oxford, he was first curate of Great Witley, Worcestershire, from 1866 to 1868, then of Eddlesborough from 1868 to 1870. In that year he was presented with the living of Little Gaddesden and became librarian to Earl Brownlow at Ashridge, Hertfordshire. He visited Venice early in his career and most of his exhibited works are of Venetian scenes. He often worked on a small scale and his style is a mixture of that of W. Callow (q.v.) and the best of T.B. Hardy (q.v.). He was a most muscular Christian and a notable cricketer.

LANE, Theodore
1800 (Isleworth) - 1828 (London)
The son of a drawing master from Worcester, he was apprenticed to J.C. Barrow (q.v.). He exhibited watercolour portraits and miniatures at the R.A. in 1819, 1820 and 1826. He also produced a number of humorous prints including *A Trip to Ascot Races,* 1827. He took up oil painting in about 1825 with the encouragement of Alexander Fraser, R.S.A., but fell through a skylight in Grays Inn Road before his promise could be realised. He was left-handed.
Published: *The Life of an Actor,* 1825.
Illustrated: P. Egan: *Anecdotes of the Turf,* 1827.
Examples: B.M.

LANGLEY, Walter, R.I.
1852 (Birmingham) - 1922 (London)
Apprenticed to a Birmingham lithographer, he became a partner in the business after studying at South Kensington. However, in 1880 he went to Newlyn, Cornwall, for a holiday and in 1881 to Brittany. This unsettled him, and the following year he settled in Newlyn and took up painting full time. He was elected R.I. in 1883 and exhibited in London from 1880 to 1919. He was in Holland in 1905-1906. He was one of the founders of the Newlyn colony, and H.S. Tuke (q.v.) described him as: 'I should think the strongest watercolour man in England'. His work is truthful and traditional in technique and his favourite subjects Cornish and Breton fisherfolk.
Examples: Leicestershire A.G.
Bibliography: *A.J.,* 1889.

LANSDOWN, Henry Venn
1806 - 1860
A landscape painter and topographer who settled in Bath in 1830 and was a pupil of B. Barker of Bath (q.v.). He produced both watercolours and brown wash drawings. Some of the latter were used to illustrate Meehan's *Famous Houses of Bath.*
Examples: Victoria A.G., Bath.

LANSDOWNE, Louisa Emma, Marchioness of c.1789 - 1851
The fifth daughter of the 2nd Earl of Ilchester, she married the future 3rd Marquess of Lansdowne and 4th Earl of Kerry in 1808. Their seats were in Wiltshire and Kerry, and she also sketched in Waterford and Co. Down and elsewhere in Ireland and Britain.

LAPORTE, George Henry, N.W.S.
1802 (London) - 1873 (London)
The son of J. Laporte (q.v.), and probably a pupil of his father's old friend Henry Bernard Chalon, he exhibited sporting subjects at the R.A. and elsewhere from 1818. He was a member of the N.W.S. from 1834 and was Animal Painter to the Duke of Cumberland, later King of Hanover. Some of his works were engraved for the *New Sporting Magazine.* His strongest work is said to date from the 1830s.
Bibliography: *A.J.,* 1859.

LAPORTE, John Peter
1761 (?Dublin) - 1839 (London)
A pupil of J.M. Barralet in London, he became a notable drawing master himself, although he never taught at Addiscombe Military Academy as is usually stated. His many pupils included Dr. Monro (q.v.). He exhibited at the R.A. and B.I. from 1785 and was a founder of the short-lived A.A. He and W.F. Wells (q.v.) produced a series of softground etchings after Gainsborough. Laporte worked in both water and bodycolour, occasionally combining them with softground etching. He also produced a few oil paintings. Much of his topographical work is influenced by Sandby (q.v.), but occasionally there are hints of early Turner (q.v.). He frequently uses the compositional device of a strong line – of a wood or cliff – at a diagonal to the horizon. He frequently visited (or re-visited) Ireland. He also painted in Wales, the Isle of Wight and the Lake District, and he may have visited Madeira in 1807 or 1808. However, his views there, and later Swiss and Italian subjects, may have been worked up from drawings by other travellers.

His daughter **Mary Anne LAPORTE** (b.c.1795) exhibited portraits and fancy subjects at the R.A. and B.I. from 1813 to 1822. She was a member of the N.W.S. from 1835 to her retirement, because of illness, in 1846. She lived first with her father, and then with her brother.
Published: *Characters of Trees,* 1798-1801. *A Drawing Book,* 1800. *Progressive Lessons Sketched from Nature,* 1804. *The Progress of a Water-Colour Drawing,* 1812.
Examples: B.M.; V.A.M.; Aberdeen A.G.; Haworth A.G., Accrington; Leeds City A.G.; Leicestershire A.G.; Newport A.G.
Bibliography: H.L. Mallalieu: *Understanding Watercolours,* 1985. *Walker's Quarterly,* July, 1922.

LAW, David (1831-1901)
River Landscape. *Signed, watercolour, 6¼in. x 10¾in.*

LASCELLES, Edward, Viscount
1764   - 1814
The elder son of the first Earl of Harewood, with whom he was a patron of J. Varley, Turner and Girtin (qq.v.). He was a pupil of the last, for whom a painting room was kept at Harewood. Because of his likeness to the Prince Regent he was known as 'Prince' Lascelles, except to the Prince, who referred to him as 'The Pretender.' His landscapes show talent.
Examples: Harewood House.

LATHAM, Oliver Matthew
c.1828   - p.1860
An Irish soldier and amateur artist who entered the R.D.S. Schools in 1844. He enrolled as an ensign in the 48th Regiment in 1847 and was promoted captain in 1852. He exhibited at the R.H.A. in 1849 and the R.I.A. in 1859, and he retired from the Army in 1860. Apart from some drawings of the Crimean War which he worked up from sketches, he painted landscapes for the most part.

LATHAM, Captain William
A captain in the Royal Lancashire Militia who toured the Isle of Man with S.D. Swarbreck (q.v.) in 1815 – they brought the news of Napoleon's abdication to the island. He also sketched in Wales, the Lake District, Yorkshire, Lancashire, Cheshire, Buckinghamshire, Sussex, the Isle of Wight, Somerset and the Hebrides. He may have been the editor of a projected history of Cheshire in 1800.
Examples: Manx Mus.; Co. Record Office, Preston; N. Lib., Wales.

LAUDER, Charles James, R.S.W.
1841 (Glasgow) - 1920 (Glasgow)
The son of a portrait painter, he studied in Glasgow and painted landscapes. Many of his subjects were found in Venice and on the Thames.
Examples: Dundee City A.G.; Paisley A.G.
Bibliography: *Connoisseur,* LVIII, 1920.

LAUDER, Robert SCOTT, R.S.A.
1803 (Silvermills, nr. Edinburgh) -
1869 (Edinburgh)
A highly influential teacher, whose pupils dominated Scottish art in the third quarter of the 19th century, he was primarily a history and genre painter in oil. He studied at the Trustees' Academy, of which he became Master in 1852. He was in London from 1823 to 1826, and from 1838 to 1852, spending the intervening years in Italy. He was incapacitated by a stroke in 1861. His forte was colour.
He married a daughter of J. Thomson (q.v.), and their daughter **Isabella SCOTT LAUDER (1839-1918)** painted portraits, landscapes figures and interiors in oil and watercolour. She lived in Edinburgh.
Bibliography: *A.J.,* 1850; 1869; 1898.

LAUDER, Sir Thomas Dick, 7th Bt.
1784   - 1848 (E. Lothian)
An author, historian, landscape and portrait painter, he succeeded to the title in 1820. He served briefly in the 79th regiment, and then married an heiress from Moray, where they settled for a while. In 1832 he moved back to The Grange, near Edinburgh, and involved himself in Whig politics. He was Secretary to

the Board of Scottish Manufacture (incorporating the Board of White Herring Fishery), which encouraged the establishment of art and design schools, and of the Royal Institution for the Encouragement of the Fine Arts. He published and illustrated a number of works, and contributed scientific papers to the *Annals of Philosophy,* as well as a story to *Blackwood's* and papers to *Tait's Magazine.*

Lord Cockburn said that he could have made his way as 'a player, or a ballad-singer, or a street-fiddler, or a geologist, or a civil engineer, or a surveyor, and easily or eminently as an artist or a lawyer'.
Published: *Lochindhu,* 1825. *The Wolf of Badenoch,* 1827. *Account of the Great Moray Floods of 1829,* 1830. *Highland Rambles,* 1837. *Legends and Tales of the Highlands,* 1841. *A Tour round the Coast of Scotland,* 1842. *Memorial of the Royal Progress in Scotland,* 1842. &c.

LAW, David, R.S.W
1831 (Edinburgh) - 1901 (Worthing)
A landscape painter and etcher who was apprenticed to an engraver and studied at the Trustees' Academy from 1845 to 1850. Thereafter he worked for twenty years as an engraver in the Ordnance Office in Southampton before resigning to concentrate on his watercolours. He painted Scottish, Welsh and Southern landscapes and often made etchings from his own watercolours, as well as after Turner and Corot.
Illustrated: O.J. Dullea: *The Thames,* 1882.
Examples: Dundee City A.G.; Sydney A.G.
Bibliography: *Portfolio,* 1879; 1880; 1883; 1884; 1902. *A.J.,* 1902.

LAWES, Caroline, Lady (-1895)
On the Laxford. *Pencil and watercolour, 12½in. x 25¼in.*

LAW, Edward
A landscape painter who lived in London and painted in Scotland and Wales as well as England. He exhibited from 1860 to 1883.

LAWES, Caroline, Lady   - 1895
The daughter of Andrew Fountain of Narford Hall, Norfolk, she married J.B. Lawes of Rothamsted, Herts., in 1842. He was F.R.S. and was created baronet in 1882. Their son, Sir C.B. Lawes-Wittewronge, was a sculptor. She painted in Scotland, Wales, Italy (1884) and the Tyrol.

LAWLESS, Matthew James
1837 (Dublin) - 1864 (London)
Chiefly known for his book illustrations, he also drew and painted genre subjects and exhibited at the R.A. from 1858. On leaving Dublin for London he studied at the Langham School and under H. O'Neill (q.v.). His numerous illustrations for books and periodicals met with great success. He was a member of the Junior Sketching Club.
Examples: B.M.
Bibliography: *The Quarto*, 1898. *Studio*, Winter No., 1923-24; XC, 1925.

LAWRENCE, Mary, Mrs. Kearse
She exhibited flower pieces at the R.A. between 1794 and 1830, and in 1799 published a monograph on roses. In 1804, when she was living in Queen Anne Street, London, and giving lessons in botanical drawing, she attempted to use the patronage of Charles Greville (q.v.) and the influence of Farington (q.v.) to promote her pictures at the Academy. Farington declined to help. She married Mr. Kearse in 1813. Her works were said to be 'more remarkable for the beauty of their execution than for their botanical accuracy'.
Published: *The Various Kinds of Roses cultivated in England*, 1799.
Bibliography: Farington *Diary*, 9 April 1804.

LAWRENSON, Edward Louis
1868 (Dublin) -
A landscape painter who was active between 1908 and 1934 and lived in London and at Hadlow Down, Sussex.
Examples: Hove Lib.

LAWSON, Cecil Gordon
1851 (Wellington, Shropshire) -
1882 (London)
His father, William Lawson, was a Scottish painter who brought Lawson to London with him in 1861. He was self taught, making fruit studies in the meticulous manner of W.H. Hunt (q.v.). Most of his brief career was taken up with large scale oil paintings, but he also made small preliminary studies and vigorous landscapes in watercolour. His form of impressionism was well fitted to catch the atmosphere and to hint at the detail of his subjects, which were taken from many different parts of the country, including Kent, Yorkshire and Scotland. In the winter of 1881 he went to the Riviera for his health. He shares something of the inspiration of Cox and Cotman (qq.v.) in their last years, and has a kinship with A.W. Rich (q.v.), although he does not employ Rich's technical formulae.
    His wife **Constance LAWSON**, daughter of John Birnie Philip, the sculptor, exhibited watercolours of flowers at the R.A. and elsewhere. They were married in 1879.
Examples: B.M.; V.A.M.; Ashmolean; Cecil Higgins A.G., Bedford; Cartwright Hall, Bradford; Glasgow A.G.; Leeds City A.G.; N.G., Scotland.
Bibliography: Sir E.W. Gosse: *C.L. Memoir*, 1883.

Mag. of Art, 1893. *A.J.*, 1882; 1895; 1908; 1909. *Studio*, LXVI, 1916; Special No., 1919. *Connoisseur*, CXIV, 1944.

LAWSON, George Stodart
A figure and flower painter who lived at Henfield, Sussex, for some years before returning to his native Edinburgh in 1886. He was a very occasional exhibitor in Edinburgh and Glasgow.

LAWSON, John   - 1909 (Carmunnock)
An illustrator and landscape painter, who was drawing figures for popular magazines and papers from the 1860s. He was working in Sheffield in 1892-93, and was a keen painter of Welsh landscapes at the end of his life, but lived for the most part in Ayrshire.

LAWSON, Brigadier-General Robert
c.1742   - 1816 (Woolwich)
A pupil of Sandby (q.v.) at Woolwich who made good use of his talent in his military career. He entered the Academy in 1758 and was commissioned at the end of the following year. He served at the siege of Belle Isle, and at Gibraltar and in America from 1776 to 1783. He then commanded the artillery in Jamaica for three years. In 1799 he was in command at Newcastle-upon-Tyne and subsequently throughout the Egyptian campaign. He was in charge of the anti-invasion fortifications of London and Chatham from 1803. His son Lieutenant-Colonel Robert Lawson (d.1819) served in the Peninsula.
    Lawson was the author of several military memoranda which he illustrated with exquisite fully coloured drawings in the Sandby manner.

LEADBETTER, Margaret M
A painter of domestic genre and figure subjects who exhibited in Scotland from 1885 to 1891. She lived in Edinburgh.

LEAR, Edward
1812 (Highgate, London) - 1888 (San Remo)
With childhood lessons and encouragement from his sister Ann, by the age of fifteen Lear was already showing a talent – and even finding a market – for natural history drawings. He produced bird drawings for the publisher Gould, who claimed authorship of some of them, and took a number of lessons from T.H. Cromek (q.v.). In 1831 he was working at the Zoological Gardens as a draughtsman, and in the following year published his first book. He attracted the notice of Lord Derby, and spent four years at Knowsley, working on the bird illustrations for Derby's privately printed *Knowsley Menagerie*, 1856. Through Derby he built up a good practice as a drawing master, and in 1846, rather awkwardly, he gave lessons to the Queen.
    Lear's extensive travels began in 1831 or 1832 with a visit to Holland, Switzerland and Germany. He was in Ireland in the summer of

1835 and went to Rome, by way of Belgium, Germany and Switzerland, in 1837. He based himself there until 1848, making a visit to England in 1845 and his first tour of Greece, Albania and Malta in 1848. In 1849 he was in Egypt and again in Greece, and then returned to England to enter the R.A. Schools. At this point he came under the influence of Holman Hunt (q.v.), with whom he worked near Hastings. In December 1853 he went to Egypt again in 1855 and from 1855 to 1857 based himself in Corfu for the winters, visiting Greece, the Holy Land and London in the summers. The winters of 1858 and 1859 were spent in Rome, those of 1860 and 1861 in Corfu, 1864 in Nice, 1865 in Malta, 1866 in Egypt and thereafter generally at Cannes where he settled, passing many of his later summers at Monte Generoso, Switzerland. He revisited Athens in 1864, Rome in 1871, set out for India, reaching Suez, in 1872 and actually went to India in the following October, leaving Ceylon in

LEAR, Edward (1812-1888)
Valetta from Pieta, Malta, 1866. *Numbered and inscribed, pen, ink and watercolour, 7⅜in. x 21in.*

December 1874. His last visit to England was in 1880. In 1881 he made his last move from Cannes to San Remo.

At his death he left more than ten thousand cardboard sheets of sketches. They vary from the merest pen and ink jottings to elaborate and even highly coloured pieces. Almost all are well annotated with times, dates, colour hints, reference numbers and so forth. He was, in fact, a watercolour draughtsman in the school of Towne (q.v.) rather than a typical Victorian watercolour painter. Even in his finished works, in which he employs brilliant colours, it is almost always the drawing in brown ink which takes first place. The colours in both sketches and finished works are generally laid on in a very smooth and characteristic manner. He never achieved the success and popularity which he sought as a painter – he was perhaps saddened that his fame as a nonsense writer should overshadow what he considered his real achievements as an artist. He tried to achieve academic recognition by painting in oil, often on a large scale, but he rarely matched up to his skill with watercolour.

Published: *Journal of a landscape painter in Albania, S. Calabria, Corsica,* 1870. &c.
Examples: B.M.; V.A.M.; Ashmolean; Cartwright Hall, Bradford; Brighton A.G.; Glasgow A.G.; Greenwich; Harvard Lib.; India Office Lib.; Leeds City A.G.; Newport A.G.; N.G., Scotland; Southampton A.G.; Ulster Mus.
Bibliography: A. Davidson: *E.L.,* 1938. P. Hofer: *E.L. as a Landscape Draughtsman,* 1967. V. Noakes: *E.L.: the Life of a Wanderer,* 1968. S.E. Kelen: *Mr. Nonsense; A Life of E.L.,* 1973. S. Hyman: *E.L.'s Birds,* 1980. S. Hyman: *E.L. in the Levant,* 1988. R. Pitman: *E.L.'s Tennyson,* 1988. V. Noakes: *The painter E.L.,* 1991. *Country Life,* 9 Nov. 1929; 8 Oct. 1964. *Antique Collector,* Aug. 1963. *Connoisseur,* CLXIV, 1967. R.A., Exhibition Cat., 1985.
See Colour Plates

LEAR, William Henry
1860 (Darlington) - 1932 (Darlington)
An ironmonger and amateur painter of landscapes and animals.
Examples: Darlington A.G.

LEATHAM, William J
A marine painter with a penchant for storms. He lived in Lambeth and Brighton, and exhibited from 1840 to 1855. He also painted portraits of ships on the Atlantic run. His work is good in a Bentley-like way.

LEAR, Edward (1812-1888)
A rare preliminary watercolour sketch done by Lear during the preparation of his book *The Family of Psittacidae* (published 1832), inscribed in pencil. *7¼in. x 4⅝in.*

LEAVER, Noel Harry (1889-1951)
'An Eastern Gateway.' *Watercolour, signed, inscribed on reverse,*
14½in. x 10¾in.

LEAVER, Noel Harry
1889 (Austwick, Yorkshire) - 1951
A painter of North African street scenes. He studied at the Burnley Art School and at South Kensington, where he won a travelling studentship, and the R.I.B.A. For a time he taught at the Halifax Art School, before returning to live at Burnley.

His work is notable for the hot blue skies which often contrast with shadowed buildings. Early examples have A.R.C.A. after the signature.

LE CAPELAIN, John
1814 (Jersey) - 1848 (Jersey)
A marine painter who worked in London from 1832. After Queen Victoria's visit to Jersey a volume of his drawings of the island scenery was presented to her, and she commissioned him to paint the Isle of Wight, where he caught T.B. He specialised in coast scenes and a misty or foggy effect. There are lithographs after his work, and he also published his own Channel Island scenes.
Examples: B.M.; Jersey Mus.

LECKY, Susan, Mrs.
1837 - 1896
The wife of R.J. Lecky, partner of J. Beale (q.v.), the shipbuilder. They lived at Ballinskelligs Abbey, Kerry, from about 1863, and she painted landscapes and botanical studies.

LE CONTE, John 1816 - 1877
A painter of landscapes and townscapes and an engraver, he lived and worked in Edinburgh. He was a pupil of, and later assistant to, the engraver Robert Scott, and most of his drawings are of Edinburgh. He was a keen sketcher.
Examples: Edinburgh City Coll.

LEE, Lady Elizabeth, née Harcourt
1739 - 1811
Sister of the 2nd Earl Harcourt, she was trainbearer to Queen Charlotte at her marriage. In 1763 she married Sir William Lee, Bt. Like her brothers (q.v.), she was a pupil and friend of Sandby (q.v.), and she made small monochrome landscapes in his manner. She also attempted Cozens' (q.v.) blot method, which she claimed to study six hours a day.

Louis XVIII lived at the Lees' Hartwell House, Bucks., during his exile.
Examples: B.M.
Bibliography: W.H. Smyth: *Ædes Hartwellianae,* 1851.

LEE, Frederick Richard, R.A.
1794 (Barnstaple) -
1879 (Vleesch Bank, Malmsay, Sth. Africa)
After a period in the Army serving in the Netherlands, Lee entered the R.A. Schools in 1818. He exhibited at the B.I. from 1822 and the R.A. from 1824. He lived mainly in Devon but visited the coasts of France, Spain and Italy in his yacht. He was elected A.R.A. in 1834 and R.A. in 1838. He retired in 1870 and died on a visit to some of his family in South Africa. His subjects were usually coast scenes or river and woodland landscapes, but he also produced still lifes. Figures were often added to his work by T.S. Cooper, Landseer (qq.v.) and others. He was primarily an oil painter but left many sketches as well as finished watercolours.

His brother **John LEE** was an architect and occasional exhibitor of drawings.
Examples: B.M.; V.A.M.
Bibliography: *A.J.,* 1879; 1908.

LEE, Rev. Sir George, 6th Bt.
1767 - 1827
The younger son of Lady E. Lee (q.v.), he succeeded his brother in 1801, becoming the last Lee baronet of Hartwell. He was a pupil of H. Bright (q.v.), and he exhibited a view of Marseilles, perhaps in oil, at the R.A. in 1846.

LEE, John c.1869 - p.1934
A genre painter in oil and watercolour who exhibited from 1889 to 1900. He lived in London, Middleton-in-Teesdale and Darlington.
Examples: Bowes Mus., Durham.

LEE, Sir Richard
c.1513 (?Hertfordshire) - 1575
Descended from a Hertfordshire family, Lee was a page of the king's cups in 1528, and was serving in the army by 1533 at Calais. He was primarily a military engineer and surveyor, but in the course of these duties he made maps and probably panoramic views of strongpoints and ports. No doubt he built up a team to help in this work, rather like the later Drawing Room at the Tower, and he may have used draughtsmen such as Anthonis van den Wyngaerde and Vincent Volpe 'the King's Painter'. In 1540 he was

appointed surveyor of the king's works. As well as at Calais and Boulogne he served in Scotland, the North of England, especially Berwick, and around the southern coasts. His employment was continued throughout the various changes of regime between Henry VIII and Elizabeth, and in 1557 he accompanied the English troops in the Netherlands. In 1562 he went with another force to Dieppe and Le Havre. At the same time he built up considerable estates around St Albans in his native county and in Gloucestershire. His drawings (if they are his rather than by assistants) are impressive exercises in pen and wash. Most notable is the 1538 picture-map of Dover in the British Library. The prominent fox figurehead of a vessel in the foreground, however, makes one wonder whether this is not in fact by Volpe.
Examples: ?British Library.

LEE, William, N.W.S.
1810   - 1865 (London)
A member and secretary of the Langham Sketching Club, he was elected A.N.W.S. in 1845 and N.W.S. in 1848, occasionally exhibiting there as well as at the R.A. and S.B.A. He was best known for rustic subjects and French coastal scenes.
Published: *Classes of the Capital*, 1841.
Examples: V.A.M.; N.G., Ireland.
Bibliography: *A.J.*, May, 1865.

LEECH, John
1817 (London) - 1864 (London)
The son of John Leech, proprietor of the London Coffee House and an amateur artist, he was educated at Charterhouse and trained to be a surgeon. He even worked as a doctor for a while but had turned professional artist by 1835. From this time he became one of the most prolific and successful illustrators. He was a keen huntsman and many of his most successful drawings and etchings are of the hunting field. Millais taught him to paint in oil, and he held an exhibition of his oil paintings in the Egyptian Hall, Piccadilly, in 1862. This proved such a success that he was inundated with orders for copies of his pictures, which he produced with the aid of a rubber stamp, and sold for a hundred guineas each.
Examples: B.M.; Brighton A.G.; Fitzwilliam; Leicestershire A.G.; Ulster Mus.
Bibliography: F.G. Kitton: *J.L.*, 1883. W.P. Frith: *J.L.*, 1891. C.E.S. Chambers: *A List of Works containing illustrations by J.L.*, 1892. G. Tidy: *A Little about L.*, 1931. T. Bodkin: *The Noble Science*, 1948. J. Rose: *The Drawings of J.L.*, 1950. S. Houfe: *J.L. and the Victorian Scene*, 1984. *A.J.*, Dec. 1864. *Scribners*, Feb. 1879. *Strand Mag.*, March, 1903. *The Critic*, Oct. 1964; Jan. 1977. *Country Life*, 20 Jan. 1977; 5 Oct. 1989. *Antique Collector*, Aug. 1984.

LEFEVRE, Rachel Emily, SHAW
see **GORDON, Rachel Emily, Lady HAMILTON**

LEGGE, Arthur 1862   - p.1936
A landscape painter who lived at Doncaster and later in Essex when he was head of the West Ham School of Art. He was active from at least 1886 to 1921. He spent much time in Cyprus between at least 1928 and 1936, painting admirable romantic views, often with an emphasis on people and colourful costume.
His daughter, **Phyllis Mary LEGGE**, was also an art teacher, and the **G.E. LEGGE** who is represented by a local view dated 1917 in the Derby A.G. may have been a relative.

LEGGE, Lady Barbara Maria   - 1840
The fourth daughter of the 3rd Earl of Dartmouth, her drawings show the influence of her kinsman Lord Aylesford (q.v.). She married Francis Newdegate in 1820.

LEGGE, Lady Charlotte Neville
1789   - 1877 (Wells)
The second daughter of the 3rd Earl of Dartmouth, in 1816 she married the Very Rev. and Hon. George Neville Grenville, Master of Magdalen, and Dean of Windsor. She, together with her sister Barbara Maria (q.v.), was influenced by Lord Aylesford (q.v.), their first cousin. Their father **George LEGGE, Earl of Dartmouth**, was a pupil of J.B. Malchair (q.v.) and produced drawings in the same tradition.
See Aylesford Family Tree

LEGGE, Charlotte Anne, Hon. Mrs. Perceval c.1800   - 1856
The daughter of Augustus George, fifth son of William, 2nd Earl of Dartmouth, she married in 1825 the Hon. and Rev. Arthur Philip Perceval. She was perhaps the best of her family as a landscape painter, and her work has sometimes been mistaken for that of Lear (q.v.).

LEGGE, Lady Harriet   - 1855 (Warwick)
The third daughter of the 3rd Earl of Dartmouth, she was a pupil of P. de Wint (q.v.). In 1815 she married Gen. the Hon. Sir Edward Paget (1775-1849), Governor of Chelsea Hospital. His first wife, who died in 1806, had been Frances, daughter of the 1st Lord Bagot.
There were three younger unmarried sisters: **Lady Georgina Caroline LEGGE (1795-1885)**; **Lady Mary LEGGE (1796-1886)**; and **Lady Anne LEGGE (1797-1885)**. No doubt they too drew.

LEICESTER, Anne Amelia, Countess of
1803   - 1844
A landscape painter and a pupil of H. Bright (q.v.), she was the daughter of the 4th Earl of Albemarle. In 1822 she married Thomas Coke of Holkham, who was created Earl of Leicester in 1837. He died in 1842, and in the following year she married the Rt. Hon. Edward Ellice, M.P.

LEICESTER, Sir John Fleming – *see* **DE TABLEY, Lord**

LEIGH, James Mathews
1808 (London) - 1860 (London)
The founder of the Newman Street drawing school, rival to that of Sass. He studied under W. Etty (q.v.), entered the R.A. Schools in 1824, and first exhibited at the R.A. in 1830. He made two Continental visits. He painted historical and religious subjects. His remaining works were sold at Christie's, 25 June 1860.
Published: *Cromwell*, 1838. *The Rhenish Album*.
Bibliography: *A.J.*, 1860.

LEIGHTON, Frederic, Lord, P.R.A., R.W.S.1830 (Scarborough) - 1896 (London)
The son of a doctor who travelled widely, Leighton was determined to become an artist after a visit to G. Lance's (q.v.) studio in Paris in 1839. He was educated in London, Rome, Dresden, Berlin, Frankfurt and Florence. In 1848 he spent a year studying in Brussels, and he was in Paris in 1849. Thereafter he returned to Frankfurt for a three year study under Johann Eduard Steinle. He finally settled in London only in 1860, moving to Leighton House six years later. In 1868 he went up the Nile with de Lesseps. He was elected A.R.A. and R.A. in 1864 and 1868, becoming President in 1878. In 1873 he revisited Egypt. He was created a baronet in 1886 and a peer on the day before his death.
He was primarily an oil painter in the classical mould of Burne-Jones and Poynter (qq.v.). His drawings and watercolours are usually preliminary studies for oil paintings. His remaining works were sold at Christie's, 11 and 13 July 1896. The catalogue was reprinted to mark the centenary.
Examples: B.M.; V.A.M.; Ashmolean; Fitzwilliam; Reading A.G.
Bibliography: Mrs. A. Lang: *Sir F.L. Life and Works*, 1884. E. Rhys: *Sir F.L.*, 1895. G.C. Williamson: *Frederic, Lord L.*, 1902. A. Corkran: *L.*, 1904. E. Staley: *Lord L.*, 1906. Mrs. R. Barrington: *The Life, Letters and Work of F.L.*, 1906. L. & R. Ormond: *Lord L.*, 1975. C. Newall: *The Art of Lord L.*, 1990. *A.J.*, 1896. *Sunday Times* (colour suppl.), 2 Nov. 1969. R.A. Exhibition Cat., 1996.

LEIGHTON, Mary, Lady, née Parker
c.1810 (Sweeney Hall, Oswestry) - 1864
The daughter of Thomas Netherton Parker of Sweeney Hall, Oswestry. In 1830, two years before her marriage to Sir Baldwin Leighton, 7th Bt., of Loton Hall, Shropshire, she accompanied her brother, Rev. John Parker (q.v.) to Palestine, where they both sketched. Some of his work is in the National Library of Wales. Her honeymoon was also spent in the Near East and North Africa. The portrait that she painted of her husband in Egyptian costume on their return to Loton Hall in 1833 is an intriguing mixture of M.E. Best (q.v.) and the Orient.
Her second son **Stanley LEIGHTON, M.P. (1837-1901)** was the author and illustrator of *Salop Houses Past and Present*, 1902.

LEITCH, William Leighton (1804-1883)
Village scene with royal progress. *Watercolour.*

LEITCH, William Leighton (1804-1883)
The bridge at Pau. *Watercolour, signed and dated 1839, 8in. x 12in.*

LEIPER, William, R.S.A.
1839 (Glasgow) - 1916 (Helensburgh)
A successful architect who studied in Paris and London as well as serving an apprenticeship in Glasgow. From the mid-1860s he practised in Glasgow, building churches, and houses whose interiors made him a leading proponent of the Anglo-Japanese manner. His water-colours are mainly of West Coast subjects.

LEITCH, Richard Principal
c.1827 (Glasgow) - 1882
The eldest son of W.L. Leitch (q.v.), he became 'an excellent painter and a good draughtsman on wood', as well as a successful drawing master, writing several instructional books. He exhibited from 1840, and later he painted scenes for Gordon Cumming's South Africa entertainment 'The Lion Slayer at Home'. One of his scenes was reproduced in the *I.L.N.*, 5 Jan. 1856. He may have gone to China in 1857 for the *I.L.N.*, but probably only worked up the drawings of C. Wirgman (q.v.), as he certainly went to Normandy later in that year, on a commission for the Queen. He took over his father's royal pupils from 1859-1861. He painted landscapes in a formalised manner, using a characteristic grey for all shadows. He was also active as an illustrator.

Published: with J. Callow: *Easy Studies in Water-Colour Painting*, 1881, &c.
Examples: B.M.; V.A.M.; Brighton A.G.; Maidstone Mus.; Newport A.G.
Bibliography: A. MacGeorge: *Memoir of William Leitch*, 1884.

LEITCH, William Leighton, R.I.
1804 (Glasgow) - 1883 (London)
A landscape painter who was apprenticed in Glasgow to a lawyer and to a weaver, meanwhile practising drawing at night with Daniel Macnee, later P.R.S.A. He next worked under Mr. Harbut, a decorator and sign painter. In 1824 he was painting scenery at the Glasgow Theatre Royal, and, on the theatre's collapse, spent two years in Mauchline, painting snuff box lids. He then moved to London, worked for the Pavilion Theatre, and took lessons from Copley Fielding (q.v.). He exhibited at the S.B.A. in 1832. He also drew for Mr. Anderden, a stockbroker, who in 1833 gave him the money to visit Italy, where he remained until July 1837, having journeyed through Holland, Germany and Switzerland. He travelled widely in Italy and Sicily, sketching and teaching. On his return he built up a successful practice as a landscape drawing master, his pupils including Queen Victoria (q.v.), to whom he was introduced by Lady Canning (q.v.), and he exhibited at the R.A. and elsewhere. In 1862 he was elected to the N.W.S., serving as Vice-President for twenty years.

His work is pleasant and competent, but in no way original. Despite the idyllic haze in which his landscapes bask, they seldom portray any true depth of feeling. This is especially true of his late paintings, when he has found his own formula. The drawings of his earlier years, particularly those inspired by Italy, show more freedom and imagination. His colours are warm, and he is fond of a misty purple for distant hills. His recipe for landscape became the over-romanticised 'trees – lake – mountain' formula employed by many Victorian artists. His remaining works were sold at Christie's, 13-17 March and 17 April 1884, and drawings from the sale bear a studio stamp.

His elder son was R.P. Leitch (q.v.), and among his six other children were Georgiana Leitch (1826-1879), William Leitch, yr., and David Roberts Leitch (d.1868).
Examples: B.M.; V.A.M.; Williamson A.G.; Birkenhead; Cartwright Hall, Bradford; Dundee City A.G.; Glasgow A.G.; N.G., Scotland.
Bibliography: A. MacGeorge: *Memoir of W.L.*, 1884. *Portfolio*, 1883. *A.J.*, 1884.

LE JEUNE, Henry, A.R.A.
1820 (London) - 1904 (Hampstead)
Of a musical family and himself a musician and chess player, he showed an early inclination towards art, and was sent to study in the B.M. In 1834 he entered the R.A. Schools, and from 1845 to 1848 taught at the Government School of Design, leaving this post to become curator of the R.A. He first exhibited at the R.A. in 1840 and was elected A.R.A in 1863. He painted historical and rustic genre subjects and children.
Bibliography: *A.J.*, Sept. 1858; 1904.

LE LIEVRE, Peter
1812 (St Peter Port) - 1878 (St Peter Port)
A very accomplished Guernsey amateur watercolourist, he was the son of a wine and general merchant. After an education at Elizabeth College he took over the family business. He was a prominent citizen, and a member of the militia, rising to command the Royal Guernsey Artillery Regiment in 1868. He painted very occasionally in oil, but generally concentrated on watercolours of the island, its coasts and people. His skies are admirable.
Examples: Guernsey Mus.

LEMAN, Robert 1799 - 1863
A talented amateur landscape painter who was a follower of J.S. Cotman (q.v.) at Norwich. He was a member of the Norwich Amateur Club in the 1830s, exhibited at the Norwich Society and was a friend and patron of many of the later Norfolk painters. He was manager of the Norwich Union Fire Insurance Company. On 23 April 1863 there was a sale of his collection at the Exhibition Rooms, Norwich, which included an impressive accumulation of Cotmans as well as some 1,500 of his own watercolours and drawings.
Examples: B.M.; V.A.M.; Norwich Castle Mus.
Bibliography: *W&D*, 1986 iv. J. Walpole: *Art and Artists of the Norwich School*, 1997.

LE MARCHANT, Major-General John Gaspard 1766 (Amiens) - 1812 (Salamanca)
The head of an ancient Guernsey family, he was commissioned in the Inniskilling Dragoons and stationed in Dublin and Gibraltar. Having incurred heavy gambling debts, he turned to sketching and music to keep himself from further temptation. On returning to England he commanded the King's Escort from Dorchester to Weymouth, and his drawings of Gibraltar were shown to the King, winning him Royal patronage. He was promoted rapidly and fought through the Flanders Campaign of 1793. In 1802 he was the co-founder of the Military College at High Wycombe and Marlow, and was engaged in a complicated dispute with General and Mrs. Harcourt (later Countess of Harcourt, q.v.) over the appointment of the first drawing master, although both parties eventually

settled upon W. Alexander (q.v.). He fought in the Peninsula and was sketching up to the morning of his death, which occurred whilst leading a charge at the Battle of Salamanca. He was the inventor of the sword exercise.

His earlier landscapes are in the manner of Farington (q.v.) who had taught his brother-in-law P. Carey (q.v.) in 1791. Le Marchant later took lessons from W. Payne (q.v.), from whom he learnt to make watercolours rather than tinted drawings. Alexander, at Marlow, completed his artistic education, and his later drawings show a distinct professionalism.
Bibliography: Sir D. Le Marchant: *Memoirs of the late Major General Le M.*, 1841.

LE MOYNE DE MORGUES, Jacques
1533 (Dieppe) - 1588 (London)
A Huguenot who was cartographer and artist on de Laudonnière's expedition to Florida in 1564. He escaped to London after St. Bartholomew and became a friend of Sir Philip Sidney, Hakluyt and Sir Walter Raleigh, who commissioned him to make new versions of his American maps and drawings.
Published: *La clef des champs…*, 1586.
Illustrated: T. de Bry: *America*, 1591.
Examples: B.M.
Bibliography: S. Lorant: *The New World*, 1946. *B.M. Quarterly*, XXVI.

LENNOCK I   George Gustavus
A marine painter and ship portraitist who entered the navy as a captain's servant in 1789. Six years later he made lieutenant. His service was mostly in the West Indies and Americas.

LENOX, A
A painter of figures and genre subjects she exhibited with the Female Artists and at the S.B.A. in the 1870s when living in London. She may have visited Algiers and Italy.

LENS, Bernard, III
1682 (London) - 1740 (Knightsbridge)
The son and pupil of Bernard Lens, II, who had made many topographical drawings in England, he was a miniaturist and drawing master. He studied at the Academy of Painting in Great Queen Street. He became Limner to George I and George II, taught at Christ's Hospital from 1705, and his private pupils included the Duke of Cumberland, the Princesses Mary and Louisa, and Horace Walpole. His work includes grey wash topographical views of London, Herefordshire, Shropshire, Bristol and Somerset, Portsmouth and elsewhere, as well as watercolour copies of Rubens, Vandyck and others, and *trompes l'oeil*.

Unfortunately, although all officially miniaturists, any of the members of this dynasty may have made wash and watercolour landscapes which could be confused with those of Bernard III. They are his grandfather **Bernard I (1631-1708)**, his father **Bernard II (1659-1725)** and his three sons **Bernard IV,**

Peter Paul (c.1714-c.1750) and **Andrew Benjamin (c.1713-c.1780)**. Also **Edward LENS** taught at Christ's Hospital to about 1749, and **John LENS (1703-1779)** taught in Norwich from 1761 to 1763 before becoming a land steward.
Examples: B.M.

LEONARD, John Henry
1834 (Patrington) - 1904 (London)
Between 1849 and 1860, he worked as an architectural draughtsman and lithographer and was a pupil of W. Moore (q.v.). He was then in Newcastle for two years before settling in London in 1862. From this time he concentrated on landscapes, occasionally reverting to architectural subjects. He painted in France, Belgium and Holland, and from 1886 until his death he was Professor of Landscape Painting at Queen's College, London. He remains always a precise and often rather old-fashioned draughtsman, but at his best his landscapes are Mole-like, and his sheep in the manner of T.S. Cooper (qq.v.).
Examples: B.M.
Bibliography: *A.J.*, 1909.

LE PIPER, Francis - 1695 or 1698 (London)
The son of Noel Le Piper, a member of a prosperous Walloon family settled in Canterbury, he was well educated and affluent enough to spend all his time drawing, in taverns, travelling, or all three together. He made many tours on the Continent and even visited Cairo. He was a fine draughtsman and caricaturist, but does not seem to have bothered with colour, although he was an admirer of Titian as well as Rembrandt and the contemporary Italians. Thus his work is usually in charcoal and grey washes. Some of his grotesque heads have so modern a feel that people have been convinced that they are by Mervyn Peake. Little is known of his life and anecdote, and one of his few biographers places his death forty-five years too late. He made drawings for *Hudibras*.
Illustrated: Sir P. Rycaut: *History of the Turks*, 1687.
Examples: B.M.
Bibliography: Buckeridge: *An Essay Towards an English School*, 1706.

LESLIE, Charles Robert, R.A.
1794 (Clerkenwell) - 1859 (London)
A literary and historical painter in oil and watercolour, whose family emigrated to Philadelphia in 1800. There he studied with George Sully and was apprenticed to a New York bookseller before returning to England and Benjamin West (q.v.) in 1811. He entered the R.A. Schools in 1813 and first exhibited at the R.A. in the following year. He was elected A.R.A. and R.A. in 1821 and 1826. He visited Brussels and Paris in 1817, and in 1833 he went back to America as drawing master at West Point, but returned the following spring. From 1847 to 1852 he was Professor of

LE PIPER, Francis (-1695 or 1698)
Grotesque Heads. *Pen and grey ink and grey wash, each 1⅝in. diameter.*

Painting at the R.A. He was a close friend of Constable, and a perceptive critic. His drawings are often in brown wash and of humorous subjects, in the vein and manner of J.J. Chalon (q.v.).

His sons were Robert Charles Leslie the marine painter, Sir Bradford Leslie (1831-1926), a distinguished civil engineer, and G.D. Leslie (q.v.).
Published: *Life of Constable*, 1845. *Handbook for Young Painters*, 1854. *Life of Sir Joshua Reynolds. Autobiographical Recollections*, 1860.
Examples: B.M.; V.A.M.; Williamson A.G., Birkenhead; Derby A.G.; Hove Lib.; Castle Mus., Nottingham.
Bibliography: J. Dafforne: *Pictures by C.R.L.*, 1875. J. Constable: *The Letters of J.C. and C.R.L.*, 1931. *A.J.*, March-April, 1856; 1859; 1902; 1911.

LESLIE, Colonel Francis Seymour
1851   - 1925 (Woolwich)
A most competent landscape painter with a liking for water, especially the lower reaches of the Thames. He was commissioned in the R.E. in 1871, making captain in 1883, major in 1890 and lt.-col. in 1898. He served in Egypt and the Sudan, and at home he also painted on the Isle of Wight and Dartmoor. He visited Norway. He signed with initials, liked small, oblong compositions and enjoyed sunsets.

LESLIE, George Dunlop, R.A.
1835 (London) - 1921 (Lindfield, Sussex)
The younger son of C.R. Leslie (q.v.) and brother of Robert Charles Leslie, the marine painter. He studied at the R.A. Schools, exhibited from 1857 and was elected A.R.A. and R.A. in 1868 and 1875. He painted figures

in gardens or interiors as well as landscapes, usually in the Thames Valley, and occasional historical scenes. He was mainly an oil painter but produced watercolours in a similar vein. He was a member of the St. John's Wood Clique and later lived at Wallingford.
Published: *The Inner Life of the Royal Academy*, 1914.
Bibliography: *Portfolio*, 1894. *Studio*, LXXI, 1921. *Connoisseur*, LIX, 1921. *Apollo*, June 1964.

LESLIE, Sir John, 1st Bt.
1822 (London) - 1916 (London)
An amateur artist who inherited Glaslough, Co. Monaghan from a brother, and was M.P. for the county. He was educated at Christ Church, Oxford, served as a captain in the Life Guards to 1850, and was created baronet in 1876. He painted hunting subjects and portraits, and in 1856 was a pupil of K.F. Sohn in Düsseldorf, moving on to R. Buckner (q.v.) and Rome. One of his sisters married the 4th Marquess of Waterford, and he became a close friend and painting companion of Louisa Waterford (q.v.).
Examples: County Mus., Armagh.
Bibliography: *American Art News*, XIV, 1916.

LESLIE, Thomas
A painter of Devonshire views who was active in the 1820s. He exhibited with the S.B.A. in 1828.

LESSELS, John Archibald
1808   - 1883
An Edinburgh architect who painted landscapes and interiors in oil and watercolour. One of his best known pictures was a view of the Acropolis worked up from an 1861 drawing by T.W.O. McNiven (q.v.).

LESSORE, Jules, R.I.
1847 (Paris) - 1892
The son and pupil of Emile Aubert Lessore, a French painter and engraver, he worked for the most part in England from 1871 painting landscapes and genre subjects. He exhibited from 1879 and was elected R.I. in 1888.
Examples: V.A.M.; Glasgow A.G.

LESSORE, Jules (1847-1892)
A beached fishing boat. *Watercolour, signed, 7in. x 10¾in.*

**LETHABY, William Richard
1857   - 1931**
An architect and draughtsman who was admitted to the R.A. Schools in 1880 and worked under Norman Shaw before setting up on his own in 1891. He was much associated with Philip Webb and became Principal of the Central School of Arts and Crafts. In 1906 he was appointed Architect to Westminster Abbey. He lived in London and was F.R.I.B.A. He wrote copiously on architectural and artistic subjects.
Examples: B.M.; City A.G., Manchester; R.I.B.A.
Bibliography: Sir R.T. Blomfield: *W.R.L.*, 1932; Tate Gall: Exhibition Cat., 1932.

**LETHERBROW, John Henry
1836   - 1883**
A Manchester landscape painter who was the brother of T. Letherbrow (q.v.), and whose work was influenced by the Pre-Raphaelites.

LETHERBROW, Thomas 1825   -
Elder brother of J.H. Letherbrow (q.v.), he worked in a similar, if softer, style. He was also a book illustrator.

LEVEN & MELVILLE, Ronald Ruthven, 11th Earl of   1835   - 1906
The third surviving son of the 9th Earl, he succeeded his half-brother in 1859. He was a representative peer and Keeper of the Privy Seal of Scotland. In 1909 a memorial exhibition of his watercolours was held at the Fine Art Society.

LEVIN, Victoria
The daughter of the German born portrait and genre painter Phoebus Levin, she painted domestic genre subjects in watercolour. She lived in London, sometimes with her father, and was active at least between 1869 and 1887.

**LEVINGE, Sir Richard Augustus, 7th Bt.
1811   - 1884**
An amateur artist whose family seat was Knockdrin Castle, Co. Westmeath. An army career took him to Canada in the 1830s, where he served with W. Herries (q.v.), and although he retired as a captain, he later became a lt.-col. of militia. He was in North Wales in 1844 and toured France, Italy and Switzerland in the following year. His drawings are in rather old-fashioned brown wash.
His next brother **Major George Charles Rawdon LEVINGE (1812-1854)** was an accomplished draughtsman, but died at Varna on his way to the Crimea.
Published: *Echoes from the Backwoods*, 1846. *A Day with the Brookside Harriers at Brighton*, 1858. *Historical Records of the 43rd Regiment*, 1867. *Jottings for Early History of the Levinge Family*, 1873.

LEWIN, John William 1770   - 1819
The brother of W. Lewin (q.v.), he was also a naturalist, and he spent some nine years, from 1800, in Paramatta, New South Wales, drawing the aborigines, fauna and insects. He moved to Sydney in 1808, and later travelled in the interior with Governor Macquarie.
Published: *Prodromus Entomology*, 1805. *The Birds of New Holland*, 1808-22. *The Birds of New South Wales*, ?1817.
Examples: B.M.
Bibliography: P.M. Jones: *J.W.L.*, 1953.

LEWIN, William   - 1795
A naturalist who was elected a fellow of the Linnaean Society in 1791, he lived in Kent in 1792 and Hoxton in 1794. The first edition of *The Birds of Great Britain Accurately Figured* was published in seven volumes, 1789-95, and was engraved and coloured by Lewin. His sons helped with the descriptions. The second edition was published in eight volumes, 1795-1801. He also engraved the plates for *The Insects of Great Britain systematically Arranged, Accurately Engraved, and Painted from Nature*, 1795, but unfortunately delegated the colouring to assistants.
His work is lively despite the crude colouring, and sometimes the poor proportions of the birds.
His brother J.W. Lewin is separately noticed.

**LEWIS, Charles James, R.I.
1830 (London) - 1892 (London)**
He exhibited at the R.A. from the age of seventeen, and at the S.B.A. and the B.I. In 1882 he was elected R.I. He lived for many years in Chelsea. He painted small genre scenes and, later in his career, landscapes.
Examples: Newport A.G.
Bibliography: *A.J.*, 1869.

**LEWIS, Frederick Christian
1779 (London) - 1856 (Enfield)**
The elder brother of G.R. Lewis (q.v.), he was an engraver and landscape artist. He studied under J.C. Stadler and at the R.A. Schools. He met Girtin (q.v.), whose Paris etchings he aquatinted (published 1803). He worked under John Chamberlain, aquatinted pl. 43 of Turner's *Liber Studiorum,* and between 1808 and 1812 was engaged on Ottley's *Italian School of Design.* He also worked for Sir Thomas Lawrence and for members of the Royal Family. He exhibited landscapes in oil and watercolour at the R.A., the B.I. and the O.W.S. His early views are taken from Enfield, where he lived for some years, and later from Devonshire, which he visited frequently, and where his patrons included the Duke of Bedford, Lord Mount-Edgecumbe, and Sir J. Dyke Acland.
Published: *Scenery of the Devonshire Rivers*, 1821-7.
Examples: B.M.; V.A.M.; Fitzwilliam; Newport A.G.; Nat. Lib., Wales.
Bibliography: *Gentleman's Mag.*, 1857, i. *A.J.*, Feb. 1857; 1875; 1880; 1910. *Print Collectors' Quarterly,* XII, 1925; XIII, 1926. *Walker's Monthly,* May, 1929.

**LEWIS, George Lennard
1826 (London) - 1913 (London)**
A cousin of J.F. Lewis (q.v.), he exhibited landscapes from 1848 including French and Portuguese views. He was an unsuccessful candidate for the N.W.S. in 1857 and 1861 and is perhaps the least talented of the family. His wife painted views in Brittany.
Examples: B.M.; V.A.M.; Sydney A.G.

LEWIS, George Robert (1782-1871)
Ayez Pitié du pauvre Aveugle. Signed and dated 1828, watercolour, 10⅛in. x 7⅛in.

**LEWIS, George Robert
1782 (London) - 1871 (Hampstead)**
Younger brother of F.C. Lewis (q.v.), with whom he lived at Enfield. He studied at the R.A. Schools under Fuseli, exhibiting landscapes there from 1805 to 1807. He worked with his brother for John Chamberlaine and Ottley, and in August 1812 he toured North Wales with J. Linnell (q.v.), being joined by F.C. Lewis. In 1818 he was draughtsman to Dr. Dibden on his Continental tour. He exhibited at the R.A., B.I., Suffolk Street and the Oil and Watercolour Society between 1820 and 1859.
He painted landscapes, figure subjects and portraits, several of the latter being engraved.
Published: *Views of the Muscles of the Human Body,* 1820. *Banks of the Loire illustrated Tours; The Ancient Font of Little Walsingham Church,* 1843. &c.
Illustrated: Dibden: *Bibliographical and Picturesque Tour through France and Germany,* 1821.
Examples: B.M.; Leeds City A.G.

LEWIS, John Frederick (1805-1876)
Lilium Auratum.

Society and in 1830 sketched in the Highlands. At this point he was still primarily an animal painter, but his rare landscapes, with their use of Chinese white and their attention to minute detail, point the way to his later development. In 1832 he went to Spain, and returned to England in 1834. This led not only to a change in his subject matter but also to a change in style. His colour becomes more striking and his handling is looser. His work is in some ways reminiscent of that of Cotman (q.v.) at the same time. He left England again in 1837 and went to Rome by way of Paris and Florence. He remained there for two years, leaving for the East in 1840. He went first to Constantinople, passing through Albania and Athens. In November 1842 he moved on to Egypt and based himself on Cairo for ten years. Although he painted profusely whilst there, he sent nothing to London for exhibition between 1841 and 1850, and was asked to resign from the O.W.S. Consequently he sent to London a picture entitled 'Hhareem' which caused a sensation by its technical brilliance and won Ruskin's unqualified praise. He returned home in 1851, having accumulated enough material to last the rest of his career. He was elected P.O.W.S. in 1855 but in 1858 resigned both Presidency and membership to become an oil painter, both because this was more lucrative and because he wished to gain membership of the Academy. He was elected A.R.A. in 1859 and R.A. in 1865.

Although never one of the Pre-Raphaelite brethren, his style and technique in many ways anticipated theirs. He was a craftsman of brilliance, using bright, gemlike colours and showing a fascination for the effects of light in all its aspects, which won the admiration of Holman Hunt and Millais as well as of Ruskin (qq.v.). He is perhaps the most accomplished user of bodycolour in English painting. His career can be clearly divided into three phases, the early animal drawings and studies from Italy and the Highlands; the Spanish subjects; and the full maturity of his Eastern works.

On July 5 1855 he sold 140 of his sketches, including studies in Spain, Belgium, Italy, Greece and the East, at Christie's. His remaining works were also sold at Christie's, 4-7 May 1877.

Examples: B.M.; V.A.M.; R.S.A.; Aberdeen A.G.; Ashmolean; Blackburn A.G.; Cartwright Hall, Bradford; Fitzwilliam; Leeds City A.G.; Leicestershire A.G.; City A.G., Manchester; Portsmouth City A.G.; N.G., Scotland.

Bibliography: H. Stokes: *J.F.L.,* 1929. M.I. Wilson: *A Man who loved Beasts,* 1976. M. Lewis: *J.F.L.,* 1978. *A.J.,* Feb. 1858; 1876; 1908. *Portfolio,* 1892. *Connoisseur,* 56, 1920. O.W.S. Club, III, 1926. *Walker's Quarterly,* XXVII, 1929. *Burlington,* LXXX, May 1942. *Country Life,* Dec. 1976. Laing A.G., Newcastle: Exhibition Cat., 1976. Guildford House Gallery: Exhibition Cat., 1976. Sotheby's, Sale Cat., Nov. 20, 1996. *Country Life,* 12 Dec. 1996.
See Colour Plate

LEWIS, Jane Mary, Lady, née Dealy, R.I.
1857 - 1939 (Blackheath)
A genre painter and illustrator of children's books who exhibited from 1879, the year in which she entered the R.A. Schools. She was elected R.I. in 1887 and married Sir Walter Lewis, Chief Justice of British Honduras, in the same year. She lived in Blackheath and North Wales.
Examples: Sunderland A.G.; Ulster Mus.

LEWIS, John Frederick, R.A., P.O.W.S.
1805 (London) - 1876 (Walton-on-Thames)
His father F.C. Lewis (q.v.) and uncle being distinguished engravers, Lewis learnt to etch and draw almost as soon as he could read. He was a childhood friend of Edwin Landseer

(q.v.), and shared his practice of sketching the animals in the menagerie at Exeter Change. Since he was more interested in drawing than engraving, his father agreed that he could become a painter if he could sell a picture at a London Exhibition. This he did at the age of fourteen. Sir Thomas Lawrence was impressed by his talent and employed him for a year as an assistant to work on the backgrounds of his portraits. In 1822 he began to exhibit at the R.A. and in 1824 and 1825 he published six mezzotints after his own drawings of lions and tigers. George IV then employed him to paint sporting subjects at Windsor. In 1827 he was elected A.O.W.S. and made his first foreign journey to Germany, the Tyrol and Northern Italy. In 1829 he became a full member of the

LEWIS, John Frederick (1805-1876)
Sir Edwin Landseer, R.A., in the act of angling. *Watercolour, signed, 19¼in. x 25½in.*

LEWIS, John Frederick (1805-1876)
Highland Hospitality. *Watercolour heightened with white, 21⅝in. x 29½in.*

LEWIS, John Hardwicke
1842 (Hyderabad) -
1927 (Veylaux, Switzerland)
The nephew of J.F. Lewis (q.v.), he painted portraits, genre subjects and landscapes in oil and watercolour. He was a pupil of his father Frederick Christian 'Indian' Lewis, Yr. and of Couture in Paris. From 1875 to 1885 he was in California drawing for newspapers, and thereafter he settled in Switzerland, where he illustrated a number of books. His work is thin and accurate.
Examples: V.A.M.; Worcester City A.G.

LEWIS, Shelton
A landscape painter who lived in Wiltshire, Henley and London and exhibited a North Welsh view at Glasgow in 1878. He also exhibited at the S.B.A. in 1877 and 1880.

LEWIS, William
An uncle of J.F. Lewis (q.v.), he was an amateur landscape painter in oil and watercolour, exhibiting at the R.A., the N.W.S. and elsewhere from 1804 to 1838. His work can look a little like that of W.F. Varley (q.v.).
Examples: V.A.M.; Newport A.G.; Nat. Lib., Wales.

LEYDE, Otto Theodore, R.S.A., R.S.W.
1835 (Wehlau, Prussia) - 1897 (Edinburgh)
A lithographer and genre painter in oil and watercolour who settled in Edinburgh in 1854. He was elected A.R.S.A. and R.S.A. in 1870 and 1880 and served as Librarian. At the end of his career he turned to etching.
Examples: Williamson A.G., Birkenhead.
Bibliography: *A.J.*, 1897.

LEYMAN, Alfred
1856 (Exeter) -   1933
A landscape painter of very modest talents who painted almost exclusively in Devon, with occasional excursions to Dorset. He was the son of a merchant seaman, and he moved from Exeter to Honiton in 1888. Thereafter he was art master at Allhallows School until his death.

LIDDELL, Thomas Hodgson
1860 (Edinburgh) - 1925 (London)
A writer and topographer who was educated at the Royal High School, Edinburgh, and travelled in China. He later worked at Worcester and became a member of the R.B.A.
A **W.F. LIDDELL** painted London views from about 1900 to 1927.
Published: *China: its Marvel and Mystery*, 1909.

LIDDELL, Hon. Thomas
1800 (Ravensworth Castle) - 1856
The second son of the 1st Lord Ravensworth and brother of the 1st Earl, he was a marine and landscape painter in oil and watercolour. He appears to have visited North America. He superintended his father's rebuilding of Ravensworth Castle and performed similar services for his brother-in-law Lord Barrington at Beckett Park, Berkshire. His consequent familiarity with Gothic won him a place on the committee to select the design for the new Houses of Parliament.
His brother **Henry Thomas, Earl of RAVENSWORTH (1797-1878)**, sister-in-law **Isabella Horatia, Countess of RAVENSWORTH (1801-1856)**, youngest sister Lady Bloomfield (q.v.), and nephew **Captain the Hon. Hedworth LIDDELL (1825-1863)** were all amateurs, for the most part in oil.

LINDSAY, Thomas (1793-1861)
At Brighton. *Signed, inscribed and dated 1837, pencil and watercolour, 8¾in. x 13in.*

LIDDERDALE, Charles Sillem
1830 - 1895
A rustic figure and landscape painter who was admitted to the R.A. Schools in 1849, exhibited from 1851, and lived in London. He generally painted on a small scale in both oil and watercolour and occasionally produced metropolitan genre subjects. He was a member of the R.B.A.
Bibliography: *A.J.*, 1859; 1868.

LIGHT, Colonel William
1784 - 1838 (Adelaide)
The son of Captain Francis Light and a daughter of the Sultan of Kedah in Malaya, whose dowry was the island of Penang (Prince of Wales Island). He joined the Army in 1807, serving with the 4th Dragoons, the 3rd Buffs and the 13th Fusiliers. In the Peninsula his talents as a draughtsman led him to intelligence duties. He provided de Wint with the sketches which were worked up for his *Sicilian Scenes* in 1823, and in that year he took part in the abortive Spanish revolution, and was wounded. Thereafter he served in the Egyptian Navy of Mehemet Ali. In 1836 he went to South Australia as Surveyor-General of the new colony, and he settled on the site of Adelaide. In a private capacity he surveyed the port. In his coffin is a statement that he was the founder of the city.
Published: *Sicilian Scenery*, 1823; *Views of Pompeii*, 1828; *A Trigonometrical Survey of Adelaide; Views*
of Adelaide; A Plan of Adelaide.
Bibliography: A.F. Stewart: *A Short Sketch of the Lives of Francis and W.L.*, 1901.

LIGHTBODY, Robert
A painter of Wilson-Steer-like views who was on the Riviera in 1882, in Venice in 1887, and exhibited at the R.I. in 1891. He also showed at Birmingham, Liverpool and Manchester in the 1880s, but lived in Brighton.

LIGHTON, Sir Christopher Robert, 7th Bt.
1848 - 1929
An occasional marine painter who was educated at Trinity College, Cambridge, and called to the bar in 1874, the year before he succeeded his father in the Irish baronetcy. He was a deputy lieutenant for Herefordshire, and High Sheriff in 1885. He also lived in Kent, and he exhibited at the R.I. in 1891, when spending the summer at Brighton.

LILLIE, Denis Gascoigne
An amateur caricaturist who served as Marine Biologist aboard H.M.S. *Terra Nova* on Scott's last expedition, 1910-1913. He produced caricatures while living in Cambridge in 1908 and 1909, and may have done others while at Westward Ho! and Birmingham University. In 1919 he suffered a breakdown from which he never fully recovered, and although he survived for several years after, it put an end to his drawing. An example of his work in pencil
and watercolour is illustrated in a letter to *Country Life*, 12 September 1968.
Examples: Scott Institute for Polar Research, Cambridge.

LINDNER, Moffatt Peter, R.W.S.
1852 (Birmingham) - 1949
A landscape and marine painter in oil and watercolour who studied at the Slade and Heatherley's. He was a member of the N.E.A.C. and of the R.I. from 1906 to 1916, transferring to the R.W.S. in the following year. He worked in London and St. Ives and was noted for Venetian views, some of which were exhibited, together with views of Holland, at the Fine Art Society in 1913.
Bibliography: *Studio*, Special No., 1900; XXXII, 1904; XLIV, 1908; XLVII, 1909; LIX, 1913; LX, 1914; LXVIII, 1916; Special No., 1919; LXXXXIX, 1925. *Athenaeum*, 1920.

LINDSAY, Sir Coutts, Bt., R.I.
1824 (Balcarres) - 1913 (London)
A soldier and playwright who painted portraits and genre subjects in watercolour, exhibiting from 1862. He founded the Grosvenor Gallery in 1878 with his wife, **Caroline Blanche FITZROY (1844-1912),** a still-life painter. Until their separation and its closure in 1890, the Gallery provided a centre for the aesthetic movement. Lindsay was elected R.I. in 1879.
Bibliography: V. Surtees: *Sir C.L.*, 1993.

LINES, Henry Harris (1800-1889)
Vale of Cliveden. *Watercolour, signed and inscribed, 10½in. x 13½in.*

LINDSAY, Hon. Robert 1754 - 1836
The second son of the 5th Earl of Balcarres, he was a rather weak topographer working in the 1780s.
Examples: B.M.

LINDSAY, Thomas, N.W.S.
1793 (London) - 1861 (Hay-on-Wye)
A landscape painter who was elected to the N.W.S. in 1833. He lived in London and Greenwich drawing Thames views, and later retired to Hay-on-Wye and Welsh scenery. His drawing and colouring are generally weak.
Examples: B.M.; V.A.M.; Nat. Lib., Wales.
Bibliography: A.J., 1859; 1861.

LINDSAY, Thomas M
A painter of coastal and genre subjects and landscapes. He lived at Rugby and exhibited with the Birmingham Society from 1881 to 1898 and at the R.I. in 1893.

LINES, Henry Harris
1800 (Birmingham) - 1889 (Worcester)
The elder brother of S.R. Lines (q.v.), he painted landscapes in Warwickshire and on the Welsh borders. He exhibited in London from 1818 to 1846 and may have stayed there for a while towards the end of his life. In about 1830 he settled in Worcester as a drawing master and a sale of his remaining works was held there in 1889.
Examples: V.A.M.; City A.G., Birmingham;

Grosvenor Mus., Chester; Maidstone Mus.; Worcester City A.G.
Bibliography: G. Potter: *A Provincial from Birmingham...Life and Times of H.H.L....*, 1969.

LINES, Samuel Restell
1804 (Birmingham) - 1833 (Birmingham)
A son of **Samuel LINES (1778-1863),** a Birmingham drawing master who was a co-founder of a life academy in Peck Lane, New Street, and of the Birmingham School of Art and later treasurer of the Birmingham Society of Artists. Samuel Restell was taught by his father, showed a talent for sketching trees, and was employed in making drawings for lithographs in exercise books. He exhibited at the N.W.S. and elsewhere in 1832 and 1833. He also specialised in views of picturesque buildings, such as Haddon Hall.
Two other brothers, **William R. LINES (1801-1846),** and **Edward LINES,** were sculptors.
Examples: V.A.M.; City A.G., Birmingham; Maidstone Mus.

LINNELL, John
1792 (Bloomsbury) - 1882 (Redhill)
A landscape painter in oil and watercolour, he was the son of a wood-carver and picture dealer and was copying pictures and drawings by the age of ten. He entered the R.A. Schools in 1805 and was a pupil of B. West and J. Varley (qq.v.). At Varley's house he met W. Henry Hunt (q.v.) and W. Mulready (q.v.), with whom he sketched and shared rooms. He was also a member of the Monro circle. He sketched on the Thames between 1805 and 1809 and in the latter year visited Hastings with Hunt. From 1811 to 1815 he made many sketches in the London Parks as well as at Windsor, in Wales and the Isle of Wight, and he was employed by A. Pugin (q.v.). He was a

LINNELL, John (1792-1882)
Woodland landscape near Windsor. *Watercolour over pencil and black and white chalk on grey paper, 4¾in. x 6¾in.*

LINNELL, John (1792-1882)
Mowers in the Field in Porchester Terrace, Bayswater. *Signed with initials, inscribed and dated June 9th 1830 and also signed in full, pencil and watercolour, 5¾in. x 7⅞in.*

member of the Oil and Watercolour Society from 1813 to 1820 and was Treasurer in 1817. He painted portraits at this time and built up a teaching practice. In 1818 he met Blake (q.v.) and he introduced him to Varley. He toured Wales with G.R. and F.C. Lewis (qq.v) in 1812 and visited Derbyshire in 1814. He moved to Hampstead in 1824, and to Bayswater in 1829. In 1852 he built himself a house at Redhill. He abandoned portrait painting in 1847, having amassed a considerable fortune, and concentrated on landscape. His watercolours are really adjuncts to his oil paintings, but he was a brilliant sketcher and he is seen to great advantage in the scraps and memoranda which he made in the sandpits at Hampstead or Paddington. His finished watercolours tend to be rather laboured.

He was the father-in-law of S. Palmer (q.v.), whose art he is traditionally, and unjustly, held to have ruined. His sons all became painters, for the most part in oil. They were: **John LINNELL Yr. (1821-1906)**, who was also a naturalist; **James Thomas LINNELL (1823-1905)**; and **William LINNELL (1826-1906)**, who studied in Italy and lived in Surrey. All three were admitted to the R.A. Schools on the same day in 1840. **Mary Anne LINNELL (1828-1903)**, who lived with her brother William from 1869, was an excellent painter of landscapes and flowers.
Examples: B.M.; V.A.M.; Aberdeen A.G.;

Ashmolean; Cartwright Hall, Bradford; Fitzwilliam; Leeds City A.G.; Newport A.G.; Ulster Mus.; Walsall A.G.
Bibliography: A.T. Story: *Life of J.L.*, 1892. D.

Linnell: *Blake, Palmer, L. & Co.*, 1994. *A.J.*, 1850; 1851; 1859; 1862; 1865; 1872; 1882; 1883; 1892; 1893. *Portfolio*, 1872; 1882. Colnaghi, London, Exhibition Cat., 1973. *Burlington Mag.*, CXXIV, March, 1982. Fitzwilliam Mus., Exhibition Cat., 1982. Martyn Gregory Gall, London, Exhibition Cat., 1982.
See Colour Plate

LINTON, Sir James Dromgole, P.R.I.
1840 (London) - 1916 (London)
A historical, figure and portrait painter who studied at Leigh's School and began his career as a black and white illustrator for the *Graphic*. He exhibited from 1863 and was elected A.N.W.S. and N.W.S. in 1867 and 1870, twice serving as President, from 1884 to 1898 and from 1909 until his death. He was knighted in 1885. His work is in the medieval and Stuart tradition of G. and C. Cattermole (q.v.), but lacks their conviction.
Examples: V.A.M.; Ashmolean; Cartwright Hall, Bradford; Dundee City A.G.
Bibliography: *Portfolio*, 1885.; 1893. *A.J.*, 1891; 1904; 1905. *Studio*, Special No, 1898; XXXVIII, 1906; LX, 1914; LXIX, 1917. *Connoisseur*, XXXVI, 1913; XXXIX, 1914; XLII, 1915.

LINTON, William
1791 (Liverpool) - 1876 (London)
At about sixteen he was apprenticed to a Liverpool merchant, meanwhile taking any opportunity to escape to North Wales and the Lakes to sketch. He also copied the Richard Wilsons at Ince Blundell Hall, Lancashire. He came to London, and first exhibited at the R.A. and B.I. in 1817. He helped found the S.B.A. He left for Italy in 1828, where he remained

LINTON, James Dromgole (1840-1916)
The Petition. *Watercolour, 18in. x 26in.*

for fifteen months. In 1840 he travelled through Italy, Sicily, Calabria and Greece. The drawings from this tour were exhibited at the N.W.S. In 1842 he resigned his membership of the S.B.A., but continued to exhibit with them until 1871, and in 1869 he was made an honorary member.

He painted landscapes, classical and religious compositions and worked up his Italian and Greek sketches for many years after his visits. His remaining works were sold at Christie's, 15 February 1877.
Published: *Ancient and Modern Colours...*, 1852. *The Scenery of Greece and its Islands*, 1856. *Colossal Vestiges of the Older Nations*, 1862.
Examples: B.M.; V.A.M.
Bibliography: *A.J.*, 1850, Jan. 1858; 1876. *Connoisseur*, LXVIII, 1924.

LINTON, William James
1812 (London) - 1898 (New Haven, Conn.)
An engraver, poet and political reformer. He was apprenticed to the wood engraver George Wilmot Bonner and later did much important work, particularly for the *I.L.N.* He also ran a succession of libertarian and republican papers. He lived for a time in Northumberland and at Brantwood, later Ruskin's Lake District home, returning to London in 1855 and emigrating to the U.S.A. in 1866. There he had a profound influence on wood engraving and illustration.
Published: *The Masters of Wood Engraving*, 1890. *Memoirs*, 1895. &c.
Bibliography: F.B. Smith: *Radical Artisan*, 1973.

LINTOTT, Edward Barnard
1875 (London) - 1951 (Chelsea)
A landscape and portrait painter in oil and watercolour, he studied in Paris with brilliant academic success. In 1915 he was acting Librarian at the R.A. He was also art editor of the woman's supplement of *The Times* in 1918 and 1919 and art adviser to *The Times* in the following year. Thereafter he worked as an examiner for the Board of Education. He visited America and Russia during the Revolution.
Published: *The Art of Watercolour Painting*, 1926.
Illustrated: W.G. King: *The Philharmonic-Symphony Orchestra of New York*, 1940.
Examples: V.A.M.

LISTER, Harriet –
see GREEN, Harriet, Mrs.

LITTLE, Robert W   R.W.S., R.S.W.
1854 (Greenock, Glasgow) -
1944 (Tunbridge Wells)
The son of a ship-owner, he sailed to France, Spain and the Mediterranean as a youth. After studying at the R.S.A. Schools from 1876 to 1881 he went to Rome, where he worked at the British Academy, and to Paris, where he studied under Dagan-Bouveret. In 1886 he was elected R.S.W. and in 1892 A.R.W.S.,

becoming a full Member in 1899. He was Vice-President of the R.W.S. from 1913 to 1916. He painted not only landscapes, often Italian views, but also domestic genre subjects. His work is perhaps too soft in technique and in sentiment.

An exhibition of his Italian landscapes was held at the Fine Art Society in 1907.
Examples: Derby A.G.; Dundee City A.G.; Greenock A.G.
Bibliography: *Studio*, Summer No., 1900; XXIII, 1901; XLI, 1907; LV, 1912; Winter No., 1917-18.

LITTLETON, Lucy Ann
A painter who lived in Greenlaw, Glasgow and Bridport, Dorset, she exhibited a Lake District view in Glasgow in 1878.

LIVERSEEGE, Henry
1803 (Manchester) - 1832 (Manchester)
In 1827 he moved to London to study at the B.M., and to copy the old masters at the B.I. However, he failed to gain admission to the R.A. Schools and returned to Manchester in the following year. He revisited London in 1829, returning once more to Manchester after a year. He made only one further visit to London.

He painted historical and romantic compositions and portraits. He was the brother-in-law of A.G. Vickers (q.v.).
Examples: B.M.; V.A.M.
Bibliography: C. Swaine: *Memoirs and engravings from the works of H.L.*, 1835. G. Richardson: *The works of H.L.*, 1875.

LIVESAY, Richard
1753   - 1826 (Portsmouth)
A pupil and assistant to Benjamin West P.R.A. (q.v.), he entered the R.A. Schools as a designer in 1774, and began to exhibit at the R.A. in 1776. In the 1790s he lived at Windsor, working as a portrait painter, and giving drawing lessons to the Royal children. In about 1797 he was appointed drawing master to the Portsmouth Naval Academy and described himself as a 'portrait, landscape and marine painter'. At some point in his career he lived in Bath.

John LIVESAY, who was a writing master at Portsmouth Dockyard from about 1799 to 1832, painted watercolours of ships. There is an example of his work at Greenwich. A later **F. LIVESAY** of Portsmouth and the Isle of Wight exhibited watercolours of local Swiss and Scottish scenes at the R.S.A and S.B.A. from 1869 to 1877. He was an architect, and a pupil of J. Adams (q.v.).
Examples: Greenwich.
Bibliography: *Bath Chronicle*, Dec. 6, 1826.

LLANOVER, Augusta Hall, Lady, née Waddington
1802 (Llanover)   - 1896
The daughter of Benjamin Waddington of Llanover, nr. Abergavenny, she married

Benjamin Hall, M.P., in 1823. He was made a baronet in 1835 and created Lord Llanover in 1859, dying in 1867. He was the Commissioner of Works for whom 'Big Ben' was named. She was an able political wife as well as a student of Welsh costumes, traditions, folklore, agriculture, music, literature, husbandry, cookery and housekeeping. Her watercolours of the costumes of South Wales, like her recipes, are often the only surviving records.
Published: (ed.): *Autobiography of Mrs. Delany*, 1861; *Good Cookery*, 1867. &c.
Bibliography: B. Freeman: *First Catch your Peacock*, 1980.

LLOYD, Edward
An animal painter from Ellesmere in Shropshire. He painted in oil and watercolour and was active from about 1846. His work is signed, dated and inscribed 'Ellesmere'.

LLOYD, John Hugh 1803   - 1866
A landscape painter who was active from about 1830 to the end of his life. He lived in London and Llanwrst and painted in Wales, England, Normandy and on the Bosphorus. He used white heightening.

LLOYD, Robert Malcolm
A marine, coastal and landscape painter who was working in London, Kent, Sussex and Northern France between 1879 and 1900. He lived at Catford Bridge, Kent, and in Central London.

LLOYD, Robert Malcolm
Fishing boats leaving Penzance. *Watercolour, signed, 12in. x 9in.*

LLOYD, Thomas James (1849-1910)
'The Soft West Wind.' *Watercolour, signed, dated 1896 and inscribed on back, 15½in. x 31in.*

LLOYD, Thomas James, R.W.S.
1849   - 1910
A landscape, genre and marine painter who exhibited from 1870 and was elected A.R.W.S. and R.W.S. in 1878 and 1886. He lived in London and then at Walmer Beach and Yapton, Sussex. He was generally known as 'Tom Lloyd'.
Examples: Cardiff A.G.; Shipley A.G., Gateshead; Glasgow A.G.
Bibliography: *A.J.,* Aug. 1877.

LLOYD, Walter Stuart   - 1926
A painter of landscape and marine watercolours which are at worst ghastly and at best sub-T.B. Hardy (q.v.). He lived in Brighton, worked between 1875 and 1913 and was a member of the R.B.A.

LOAT, Samuel
1802 (London) - 1876 (Kingston, Ontario)
An architect who entered the R.A. Schools in 1823 and gained the Gold Medal in 1827. In

1828 he was awarded a Travelling Studentship and went to Italy. He exhibited an architectural view at the R.A. in 1832. Later he emigrated to Canada.

LOBLEY, James
1829 (Hull) - 1888 (Bradford)
He studied at the Leeds School of Art and taught at the Mechanics Institute, Bradford, before resigning to devote himself to painting. He lived in Bradford and Brighouse and exhibited at the R.A. from 1865 to 1887. He painted church interiors in the manner of Webster, and portraits. He was to a certain extent influenced by the Pre-Raphaelites, particularly by Holman Hunt (q.v.).
Examples: Cartwright Hall, Bradford.
Bibliography: Bradford A.G., Exhibition Cat., 1983.

LOCK, William, of Norbury, né Wood
1732 (London) - 1810 (Norbury)
The illegitimate son of William Lock, M.P.

(d.1761), from whom he inherited a considerable fortune. He travelled in Italy with Richard Wilson in 1749, and became a patron, collector and amateur artist. He purchased the estate of Norbury, near Mickleham, Surrey, in 1774. G. Barret (q.v.) painted murals, with help from S. Gilpin (q.v.) and G.B. Cipriani (q.v.). Lock's circle included Sir T. Lawrence, Fanny Burney, Mme. de Staël and the French refugees. His work is Italianate, in pen and wash. John Julius Angerstein, founder of the National Gallery, was one of his grandsons.
Examples: Wakefield A.G.
Bibliography: Duchess of Sermoneta: *The Locks of Norbury,* 1940.

LOCK(E), William, of Norbury, Yr.
1767   - 1847 (Paris)
A friend and pupil of Fuseli (q.v.) who drew landscape in various media as well as figure compositions and caricatures in Fuseli's manner. These can be very free in a rather

LLOYD, Walter Stuart (-1926)
Sunset on the Avon. *Watercolour, signed and dated 1903, 15¾in. x 39in.*

modern way with light blue and brown washes. He added an 'e' to his name on the death of his father, and sold Norbury in 1819. Thereafter he lived in Rome and Paris.

His son **William LOCKE III (1804-1832)** was a captain in the Life Guards and also an amateur artist. He was drowned in Lake Como in 1832.

Examples: B.M.; V.A.M.; Ashmolean; Leicestershire A.G.

Bibliography: Duchess of Sermoneta: *The Locks of Norbury*, 1940.

LOCKER, Edward Hawke, F.R.S.
1777 (East Malling, Kent) - 1849 (Iver)
A competent topographical watercolourist, he was educated at Eton and in 1795 entered the Navy Pay Office. In 1804 he became Civil Secretary to Lord Exmouth, serving with him in the East Indies from 1804 to 1809, the North Sea in 1810 and the Mediterranean from 1811 to 1814. He lived at Windsor from 1815 to 1819, when he became secretary of Greenwich Hospital. He was civil commissioner there from 1824 to 1844. He was co-editor of the magazine *The Plain Englishman*, 1820-23. In 1823 he contributed works from his collection to the first loan exhibition at the O.W.S. and organised the establishment of the gallery of naval pictures at Greenwich. He was the father of F. Locker Lampson.

His watercolours are generally charming if a little unsure in handling.

Published: *Views in Spain*, 1824. *Memoirs of Celebrated Naval Commanders…*, 1832.

Examples: B.M.; V.A.M.; Greenwich; Victoria A.G., Bath.

LOCKHART, William Ewart, R.S.A., A.R.W.S., R.S.W.
1846 (Annan, Dumfriesshire) - 1900 (London)
A painter best known for his large oil paintings of Victorian ceremonies and Spanish landscapes. He was elected R.S.A. and A.R.W.S. in 1878. In 1863 he went to Australia for health reasons and in 1867 made the first of several visits to Spain. His watercolours, both landscapes and figures, are quieter and less studied and sometimes show a kinship with Bough's informality.

Examples: Dundee City A.G.; Glasgow A.G.; Paisley A.G.; N.G., Scotland.

Bibliography: *Portfolio*, 1878; 1883; 1887.

LODDER, Commander Charles Arthur
c.1826 - 1885 (Edinburgh)
A sailor who served on the Syrian coast at the bombardment of Acre, elsewhere in the Mediterranean, and off Portugal. He was promoted lieutenant in 1846 and commander in 1858. In retirement he lived in Edinburgh, becoming a friend of S. Bough (q.v.), and exhibiting coastal, marine and Scottish subjects in London between 1874 and 1882. He sometimes used white heightening and also

LOCKER, Edward Hawke (1777-1849)
God's House Gate, Southampton, Hants. *Pencil and watercolour, 6in. x 8¾in.*

exhibited at the R.S.A. and the R.H.A.

His son **Charles LODDER, Yr.,** painted similar subjects and was active in Edinburgh between at least 1876 and 1902.

LODGE, William 1649 - 1689
One of the 'York Virtuosi' with F. Place (q.v.). He visited Italy and was an amateur draughtsman of no great skill.

LOFTHOUSE, Mary, Mrs –
see **FORSTER, Mary**

LOMAX, J O'BRYEN
A landscape and coastal painter who lived at Bognor, Chichester and Brighton and exhibited from 1853 to 1881. He painted in Ireland, on the Severn, in Sussex, the Lake District and elsewhere.

LOCKHART, William Ewart (1846-1900)
Aberdeen. *Watercolour, signed, inscribed and dated 1898, 14½in. x 20in.*

LOUND, Thomas (1802-1861)
Bridge over a stream, with figures. *Watercolour, 7½in. x 10in.*

LONDONDERRY, Elizabeth Frances Charlotte, Marchioness of
1814 - 1884 (London)
A landscape painter and pupil of H. Bright (q.v.), she was the daughter of the 3rd Earl of Roden. In 1836 she married the 6th Viscount Powerscourt, who died in 1844, and in 1846 Lord Castlereagh who became 4th Marquess of Londonderry in 1854. He died in 1872.

LONG, Hon. Eleanor Julian, née Stanley
1821 - 1903
The elder daughter of Edward Stanley and Lady Mary Maitland, she married Lt.-Col. Samuel Long as his second wife in 1866. She was a pupil of J.D. Harding (q.v.), and of Chopin. She was a maid of honour to the Queen from 1841, and she gave her lessons in chalk drawing. Her watercolours are a credit to her own master. She was stepmother to M.E. Long (q.v.).

LONG, John O., R.S.W. - 1882
A Scot who lived in London from about 1860 and painted coastal subjects in oil and watercolour. He exhibited from 1868 to 1882 and found subjects in Scotland and the West Country. He was a founder member of the R.S.W. in 1878.

LONG, John St. John
1789 (Newcastle, Co. Limerick) -1834 (London)
A painter, drawing master and engraver who

studied at the R.D.S. Schools. In 1822 he came to London and studied under J. Martin (q.v.). He worked briefly as an engraver under W.J. Ottley (q.v.), afterwards taking up painting full-time and exhibiting at the S.B.A. and B.I. In 1827 he turned to medicine, advocating a cure for rheumatism, but one of his patients died under his treatment and he was charged with manslaughter. He was later acquitted, and continued to live in Harley Street. Bonington was brought to him from Paris, but got no benefit from the experience, dying within days.

LONG, Mary Euphemia, Hon. Mrs Hugh Elliott 1856 - 1934
Not, as stated in previous editions, a Gurney, but the daughter of Lt.-Col. Samuel Long of Bromley Hill, and thus a niece of Lord Farnborough (q.v.). Her mother was Emily Herbert of Muckross, Killarney. In 1879 she married a son of the Earl of Minto, and they lived at Newton Stewart. She was a very able painter of small and pretty landscapes in the manner of Birket Foster (q.v.).

LONGBOTTOM, Sheldon
A landscape painter who lived and worked at Barnard Castle in the late nineteenth century. He occasionally exhibited with the Bewick Society in Newcastle and at Carlisle.
Examples: Bowes Mus., Barnard Cas.

LONGCROFT, Thomas 1811 -
A topographer working in London and then India from 1784. He painted landscapes in watercolour and monochrome wash. He was a friend, and perhaps pupil, of Zoffany at Lucknow, but soon gave up hope of a professional career, married an Indian and turned indigo planter. There is a touch of the Daniells in his work, but he conveys the heat of India far better.
Bibliography: *Connoisseur*, Feb., 1980.

LONGMIRE, William Taylor
1841 (Troutbeck) - 1914 (Ambleside)
An artist who lived at West Bromwich and painted Lake District views in the 1870s and 1880s. He was the son of a butcher and was left deaf by a childhood accident. His work is varied in quality because it was often produced on a conveyor-belt system to pay bills.

LONSDALE, James
1777 (Lancaster) - 1839 (London)
A portrait painter in oil who studied under Romney and at the R.A. Schools. He had an extensive and fashionable practice and produced occasional watercolours. His son, Richard Threlfall Lonsdale (b.1813), was also an artist, and presumably precocious since he exhibited from 1826 to 1849.
Examples: B.M.

LORIMER, John Henry, R.S.A., R.W.S., R.S.W.
1856 (Edinburgh) - 1936 (Edinburgh)
He was primarily a portrait and subject painter in oil. In 1882 he was elected A.R.S.A. and for two years went to study in Paris. In 1900 he was elected R.S.A. as a result of his paintings of Scottish country life. He became an Associate and Member of the R.W.S. in 1908 and 1932. His watercolours are generally in a low key and show a feeling for the effects of light.
Bibliography: *A.J.*, 1893; 1895; 1906. *Portfolio*, 1893. *The Artist*, 1899. *Studio*, XXXIV, 1905; LXVIII, 1916.

LOTT, Frederick Tully
A painter of views and fruit in oil and watercolour who exhibited from 1852 to 1879. He moved to London from Jersey in 1855 but continued to produce Channel Island subjects. He also painted in France, Belgium and Germany, and in Sussex and the Lake District.

LOUISE, Caroline Alberta, H.R.H. Princess, Duchess of Argyll 1848 (Windsor Castle) - 1939 (Kensington Palace)
The fourth daughter of Queen Victoria (q.v.) and Prince Albert (q.v.), she married the future 9th Duke of Argyll (1845-1914) in 1871. She painted views in Canada and elsewhere.
As **John Douglas Sutherland, Marquess of LORNE,** her husband illustrated his own books, such as *Canadian Pictures,* and even contributed to the *Graphic* in 1883.

LOW, Charles
Barge people with horses and a dog by a lock. *Watercolour, signed, 9in. x 15in.*

Examples: B.M.; Dundee City A.G.; Maidstone Mus.
Bibliography: D. Duff: *The Life Story of H.R.H. Princess L.*, 1940. J. Roberts: *Royal Artists*, 1987.

LOUND, Thomas 1802 - 1861 (Norwich)
A brewer and amateur landscape painter, he was a pupil of J.S. Cotman (q.v.), whose work he began by copying, as well as that of J. Crome, J. Stannard and Cox (qq.v.). He joined the Norwich Society in 1820 and exhibited with them until 1833. He entertained and sketched with all the leading Norwich artists and collected their work. He exhibited in London from 1845 to 1857, and in 1856 he was an unsuccessful candidate for the N.W.S.

His subjects are almost all in Norfolk, although he exhibited a view of Windermere in 1825 and one of Richmond, Yorkshire, in 1854. He also visited Wales. He had a strong colour sense and a dashing sketchy style. Sometimes the detail is a little clumsy, but generally his watercolours are rich and impressive. A sale of his artistic effects was held on 6 March 1861 at the Bazaar Room, Norwich.
Examples: B.M.; V.A.M.; Leeds City A.G.; Castle Mus., Norwich; Gt. Yarmouth Lib.
Bibliography: W.F. Dickes: *The Norwich School*, 1905. J. Walpole: *Art and Artists of the Norwich School*, 1997.

LOVE, Horace Beever
1780 (Norwich) - 1838
A portraitist who exhibited at the R.A. from 1833 to 1836. He was working in Norwich earlier than this and in 1830 he drew a portrait of Cotman (q.v.) which is typical of the formal, lithographic style of the time. In the same year he joined Cotman in founding the Norwich Artists' Conversaziones.
Examples: B.M.; V.A.M.
Bibliography: J. Walpole: *Art and Artists of the Norwich School*, 1997.

LOVER, Samuel, R.H.A.
1797 (Dublin) - 1868 (Jersey)
A miniaturist, painter, illustrator, songwriter and novelist, he was intended for his father's profession of stockbroking. In 1814 he was sent to work in London, and after his return he left home to become an artist. He gave drawing lessons from the age of seventeen, teaching himself marine and landscape painting at the same time, and he also studied at the R.D.S. Schools and with the miniaturist John Comerford. Among his own pupils was F.W. Burton (q.v.). He exhibited with the R.D.S. in 1817 and 1819, and from 1826 exhibited landscapes and miniatures at the R.H.A. He was elected A.R.H.A. and R.H.A. in 1828 and 1829. In 1831 he illustrated *The Parson's Horn-Book*, which caricatured the established Church. These illustrations were badly received, losing him many of his customers, and they may partly account for his move to London in 1835. Before moving, he helped to start up the *Dublin University Magazine* in 1833, which he illustrated. In London he had a successful practice as a miniaturist, and in 1836 started to write novels and plays. This was as well, since his sight deteriorated, and from 1844 he ceased to paint miniatures. From 1846 to 1848 he toured America and Canada with his one-man entertainment of songs and stories. He returned to London, and exhibited landscapes at the R.A. between 1851 and 1862, as well as at the R.H.A. He retired to Jersey for the last four years of his life. His body was brought back to Kensal Green.
Published: *Legends and Stories of Ireland*, 1831. *Rory O'More, a National Romance*, 1837. *Handy Andy*, 1842. &c.
Examples: B.M.; Ulster Mus.
Bibliography: B. Bernard: *The Life of S.L., R.H.A., with Selections from his Papers*, 1874; A.J. Symington: *Sketch of the Life of S.L.*, 1880. P. Caffrey: *S.L.: His Life and Work*, 1985. *Irish Arts Review*, III, i, 1986.

LOVERING, Ida Rose
1854 (Greenwich) -
The niece of A. and H. Tidey (q.v.), she painted domestic scenes and landscapes in oil and watercolour. She entered the R.A. Schools in 1878 and exhibited from 1881 to 1914.
Illustrated: A.A. Procter: *Legends and Lyrics*, 1895. E. McMahon: *A Modern Man*, 1895. D. Wyllarde: *A Lovely Little Lady*, 1897.
Examples: Brighton A.G.

LOW, Charles
A landscape painter who occasionally essayed flowers and lived in Islington, Hungerford and Witley. He worked in Wales, Derbyshire and the Lake District as well as the Southern counties, and he exhibited from 1870. He was a member of the S.B.A.

LOWRY, Matilda, Mrs. Heming
1787/8   - 1861 (London)
A daughter of Wilson Lowry (1762-1824), the engraver, and half-sister of Joseph Wilson Lowry (1803-1879), and of Delvalle Elizabeth Rebecca Lowry (1800-1860), the second Mrs John Varley, she won a gold medal from the Society of Arts in 1804 and exhibited landscapes, miniatures and portraits from 1808 to 1855. She may have been an engraver herself, and she visited the West Country. Her watercolour style is pretty and close to that of J. Cristall (q.v.) or J.S. Hayward (q.v.).
Examples: B.M.; V.A.M.; N.P.G.

LOWTHER, Lady Mary   - 1863
A daughter of the 1st Earl of Lonsdale, she married Major-General Lord W.F. Cavendish-Bentinck in 1820, but he died eight years later. She was a pupil of C. Metz, J. Farington and P. de Wint (qq.v.).

LUARD, Lieutenant-Colonel John
1790   - 1875
He was commissioned in the 4th Regiment of Dragoons in 1809 as second lieutenant, and promoted lieutenant in 1811, captain in the 30th Regiment of Foot in 1821, and major in 1834. In 1838 he became a lieutenant-colonel in the 21st Fusiliers, and he was retired on half-pay in 1845. He was commissioned by Mrs., later Lady, Parkes, wife of Sir Harry Parkes, to make sixty watercolour sketches of India. These were exhibited, under the title 'A Grand Moving Diorama of Hindustan' in the Asiatic Gallery, Portman Square, in 1851, and were later taken to America.
Published: *History of the Dress of the British Soldier*, 1852.
Examples: B.M.

LUARD, John Dalbiac 1830 (Blyborough) -
1860 (Winterslow, nr. Salisbury)
Son of J. Luard (q.v.). He served in the Army from 1848 to 1853. Thereafter he studied with J. Phillip (q.v.), and visited the Crimea. At one point he shared lodgings with his friend J.E. Millais (q.v.). He exhibited military subjects at the R.A. from 1855.
Lowes Dalbiac LUARD (1872-1944), a notable horse painter and illustrator, continued the family tradition.
Bibliography: *see* J.G. Millais: *Life and letters of Sir J.E. Millais*, 1899.

LUCAN, Margaret, Countess of
1814   -
A miniaturist and illustrator. She was the daughter of James Smith, M.P., of Devon and Somerset, and married the 1st Earl of Lucan in 1760. Walpole was very flattering about her talents. Between the ages of fifty and sixty-five she filled five folio volumes with illustrations to the historical plays of Shakespeare.
Examples: Althorp.

LUCAS, Anne Florence, Lady
see under DE GREY, Amabel, Countess

LUCAS, John Seymour, R.A., R.I.
1849 (London) - 1923 (Southwold)
Figure, historical and portrait painter in oil and watercolour, he was the nephew of John Lucas, a portraitist. He studied at St. Martin's School of Art and the R.A. Schools and exhibited from 1872. He was elected A.N.W.S. and N.W.S. in 1876 and 1877 and A.R.A. and R.A. in 1886 and 1898.
His wife **Marie Elizabeth Seymour LUCAS, née CORNELISSEN (1855 Paris - 1921)** also painted portraits and illustrated children's books. Before her marriage she had studied in France and Germany as well as at the R.A. Schools.
Illustrated: S.R.Crockett: *The Grey Man*, 1896.
Examples: B.M.
Bibliography: M.E.S.L., *Connoisseur*, LXVI, 1923.

LUCAS, Ralph W 1796   - 1874
A landscape, portrait and genre painter who lived in Greenwich and Blackheath and exhibited at the N.W.S. and elsewhere from 1821 to 1852. His wife was also a painter.

LUCAS, Samuel
**1805 (Hitchin, Hertfordshire) -
1870 (Hitchin)**
Educated at a Quaker school in Bristol, he was apprenticed to a ship-owner at Shoreham. His religion only allowed him to paint as an amateur and he very rarely exhibited his works. After his marriage in 1838 he returned to Hitchin. He was paralysed in 1865. He painted landscapes around Hitchin, portraits, birds, animals and flowers, some of the latter being engraved in *The Florist*.
Many members of his family painted, including his son **Samuel LUCAS, Yr. (1840-1919)**, his wife **Matilda LUCAS, née HOLMES,** and his daughters and granddaughters, **Alice Mary LUCAS (1844-1939), Florence LUCAS, Matilda LUCAS (1849-1943), Rosa LUCAS, Ann Rachel LUCAS (d.1971)** and **Constance LUCAS.**
Examples: B.M.; Hitchin Mus.; Glynn Vivian A.G., Swansea.
Bibliography: *Walker's Quarterly*, XXVII.

LUCAS, William
1840 (London) - 1895 (London)
The brother of J.S. Lucas (q.v.), he exhibited portraits and W.H Hunt-like figure subjects from 1856 to 1880. In 1858 he was admitted to the R.A. Schools to study both painting and engraving. He was A.N.W.S. from 1864 to 1882 but then his health broke down and he gave up painting for lithography. He lived in St. John's Wood.

LUDBY, Max, R.I.
1858 (London) - 1943
A landscape painter who lived and worked at Cookham. He exhibited from 1886, was elected R.I. in 1891 and was a member of the R.B.A.
Examples: Melbourne A.G.

LUDOVICI, Albert 1820   - 1894
A genre painter in oil and watercolour who worked in Paris and London, where he exhibited at the R.A. and the R.I. from 1854 to 1889. He was elected to the S.B.A. in 1867.

LUDOVICI, Albert, Yr.
1852 (Prague) - 1932 (London)
Son of A. Ludovici (q.v.), he too painted genre subjects and lived much in Paris. He exhibited there, in Geneva and in London where he was a member of the R.B.A. He was influenced by Whistler (q.v.).
Published: *An Artist's Life in London and Paris*, 1926.
Examples: Brighton A.G.

LUKER – *see* MARGETTS

LUND, Neils Moeller, R.A.
1863 (Faaborg, Denmark) - 1916 (London)
A landscape and portrait painter who studied at the R.A. Schools and at Julian's in Paris. His parents had moved to Newcastle when he was four, and he had also studied at the Art School there. He was chiefly noted for his large oil paintings but also worked in watercolour, often in Scotland and Northumbria.

LUNDGREN, Egron Sellif, O.W.S.
1815 (Stockholm) - 1875 (Stockholm)
He studied in Paris for four years, and went to Italy in 1841, where he remained for eight years. He served under Garibaldi at the siege of Rome in 1849. After this he left for Spain, where he lived for ten years. He met F.W. Topham (q.v.) and J. Phillip (q.v.) in Seville in about 1852, and they encouraged him to come to London in 1853. He seems to have worked in London for some time as an illustrator before going to India, where he was on Lord Clyde's staff during the campaigns of 1857. He made a large number of drawings in 1857 and 1858, including Indian landscapes and portraits. A collection of 271 of these was sold at Christie's on 16 April 1875 for 3,050 guineas. He visited England again on his return, and undertook several commissions for the Queen. He then revisited Scandinavia and by 1861 had gone to Cairo. In 1862 he visited Spain once more and by 1865, Italy. His last years were divided between London and

Stockholm. In 1864 he was elected A.O.W.S. and in the following year a full Member.

The majority of his subjects are taken from Spain, Italy and Egypt. Although he often produced single figure studies of peasants, he is happiest with small group subjects such as fiesta or bullfighting scenes. His colours are generally pale and fairly limited, laid on in thin washes, but with a dashing style of execution which can be most attractive. His portrait drawings, although rather conventional in the manner of A.E. Chalon (q.v.), can also be very pretty. A retrospective was held at the Nationalmuseum, Stockholm in 1879, and a further exhibition was mounted there in 1995.
Published: *Letters from Spain, 1873-4. Old Swedish Fairy Tales,* 1875. *Letters from India,* 1875. *Leisure Hours Abroad,* 1879.
Illustrated: G.O. Hyltén-Cavallius: *Old Norse fairy tales,* 1882.
Examples: B.M.; V.A.M.; Fitzwilliam; Maidstone Mus.; Nationalmuseum, Stockholm; Göteborg Kunstmuseum;
Bibliography: K. Asplund: *E.L.,* 1974. 1975. S.Nilsson and N.Gupta: *The Painter's Eye,* 1992. *A.J.,* 1876.

LUNY, Thomas
1759 (London) - 1837 (Teignmouth)
A marine artist who served in the Navy and was a pupil of Francis Holman. He exhibited at the S.A. in 1777 and 1778 and at the R.A. from 1780. He probably spent most of his time at sea until 1810 when he was paralysed and settled at Teignmouth, where he managed to paint. One hundred and thirty of his pictures were exhibited in Bond Street three months before his death.
Examples: Exeter Mus.; Greenwich; Portsmouth City Mus.
Bibliography: C.J. Baker, *T.L.,* 1982.

LUSCOMBE, Henry Andrews
1820 (Plymouth) -
Perhaps a son of Lt. Edward Luscombe, R.N. (d.1851), he was a marine and town painter and lived in Plymouth. He worked in oil and watercolour until at least 1865, specialising in pictures of the modern Navy and Rayner-like street scenes.
Examples: Exeter Mus., Greenwich.

LUSHINGTON, Maria
1800 (London) - 1855 (London)
The eldest daughter of Sir Henry Lushington, Bt., British Consul-General in Naples from 1815 to 1832. Her reconstructions of Pompeii are probably based on the original sketches for Sir W. Gell (q.v.), *Pompeiana,* 1832, to which they show a striking similarity. The fact that she knew Gell may be deduced from his inclusion in one of her drawings. Her landscapes and interiors are accomplished although the overall effect is rendered rather charmingly naïve by her fanciful colours and uncertain drawing of fixtures and fittings. She signed 'Maria' *tout court.*

Her sister Louisa married Sir C. Burrard (q.v.). At least one of their cousins was a pupil of T.S. Cooper (q.v.).

LUTTRELL, Rev. Alexander Fownes
1793 - 1888
A pupil of W. Callow (q.v.). He was the fourth son of J.F. Luttrell of Dunster Castle and was educated at Eton and Exeter College, Oxford. He was Rector of East Quantoxhead from 1819 until his death.

LUTTRELL, Captain the Hon. James
1751/2 (Four Oaks, Warwickshire) - 1788
The fourth and youngest legitimate son of the 1st Lord Carhampton (1713-1787), he was promoted lieutenant in the Navy in 1770 and captain in 1781. In the following year, commanding the *Mediator,* he captured two American vessels and disabled two more. From 1783 he was surveyor-general of the ordnance. He was M.P., first for Stockbridge and then for Dover. His sister married Henry Frederick, Duke of Cumberland, and he painted Sandbyish views in Windsor Great Park, of which the Duke was Ranger and T. Sandby (q.v.) his Deputy Ranger. He died of consumption.
Bibliography: *Gentleman's Mag.,* 1788, ii.

LUXMOORE, Arthur Coryndon Hansler
1842 - 1881
A sculptor and a landscape and genre painter who entered the R.A. Schools in 1861, and was living in London in the 1860s and 1870s. He was a descendant of the Luxmoores of Oakhampton, Devon, and his maternal grandfather was Sir R.J. Hansler, P.R.S. He painted in Northern France as well as England. He also lived at St. Lawrence, Thanet, and records have sometimes confused him with his father, Coryndon Henry Luxmoore, F.S.A. (1812-1894), who was elected F.S.A. in 1854. His own son, Sir Fairfax Luxmoore, was a distinguished judge.

LUXMORE, Myra Elizabeth
1851 - 1919
A historical and portrait painter who exhibited from 1887. She lived in Somerford, near Newton Abbot, Devon, and in London. She was kin to the above, but the Luxmores (and moores) went in for a confusion of similar names in the same generation.

LYNDON, Herbert
1855 (London) - c.1922
A landscape painter in oil and watercolour who entered the R.A. Schools in 1880, exhibiting from the previous year until 1898 when he went to India. He also lived in London and continued to exhibit until 1922.
Examples: India Office Lib.

LYNN, William Henry
1829 - 1915
Probably a Belfast architect, he painted views in Ireland and Wales.
Examples: Ulster Mus.

LYON, Captain George Francis
1795 (Chichester) - 1832 (at sea)
A traveller who joined the Navy in 1808, serving in the Mediterranean. In 1818 he joined Ritchie's expedition to Tripoli and the Fezzan. After Ritchie's death, he struggled back, reaching London in 1820. In the following year he was sent to the Arctic with Parry, returning in 1823. A second voyage in the following year was unsuccessful. In 1825 he married a daughter of Lord Edward Fitzgerald, and soon after he toured Mexico studying mines. Later he went to South America on the same business, but died on the return voyage from Buenos Aires.

His North African drawings are in the Turkish manner of T. Allom (q.v.).
Published: *A Narrative of Travels in North Africa,* 1821; *The Private Journal of Captain G.F.L.,* 1824; *A Brief Narrative of the Unsuccessful Attempt to reach Repulse Bay,* 1825; *Journal of a Residence and Tour in the Republic of Mexico,* 1828.

LYUS, T
A topographer who drew Suffolk churches in the 1780s. A large group of these watercolours was in an album of ecclesiastical antiquities apparently begun by John Ives (1751-1776), Suffolk Herald Extraordinary. They are neat and competent, and Lyus was not afraid to push a spire through a borderline if necessary.

Antique Collectors' Club

THE ANTIQUE COLLECTORS' CLUB was formed in 1966 and quickly grew to a five figure membership spread throughout the world. It publishes the only independently run monthly antiques magazine, *Antique Collecting*, which caters for those collectors who are interested in widening their knowledge of antiques, both by greater awareness of quality and by discussion of the factors which influence the price that is likely to be asked. The Antique Collectors' Club pioneered the provision of information on prices for collectors and the magazine still leads in the provision of detailed articles on a variety of subjects.

It was in response to the enormous demand for information on 'what to pay' that the price guide series was introduced in 1968 with the first edition of *The Price Guide to Antique Furniture* (completely revised 1978 and 1989), a book which broke new ground by illustrating the more common types of antique furniture, the sort that collectors could buy in shops and at auctions rather than the rare museum pieces which had previously been used (and still to a large extent are used) to make up the limited amount of illustrations in books published by commercial publishers. Many other price guides have followed, all copiously illustrated, and greatly appreciated by collectors for the valuable information they contain, quite apart from prices. The Price Guide Series heralded the publication of many standard works of reference on art and antiques. *The Dictionary of British Art* (now in six volumes), *The Pictorial Dictionary of British 19th Century Furniture Design*, *Oak Furniture* and *Early English Clocks* were followed by many deeply researched reference works such as *The Directory of Gold and Silversmiths*, providing new information. Many of these books are now accepted as the standard work of reference on their subject.

The Antique Collectors' Club has widened its list to include books on gardens, garden design, garden history and architecture. All the Club's publications are available through bookshops world wide and a full catalogue of all these titles is available free of charge from the addresses below.

Club membership, open to all collectors, costs little. Members receive free of charge *Antique Collecting*, the Club's magazine (published ten times a year), which contains well-illustrated articles dealing with the practical aspects of collecting not normally dealt with by magazines. Prices, features of value, investment potential, fakes and forgeries are all given prominence in the magazine.

Among other facilities available to members are private buying and selling facilities and the opportunity to meet other collectors at their local antique collectors' club. There are over eighty in Britain and more than a dozen overseas. Members may also buy the Club's publications at special pre-publication prices.

As its motto implies, the Club is an organisation designed to help collectors get the most out of their hobby: it is informal and friendly and gives enormous enjoyment to all concerned.

For Collectors — By Collectors — About Collecting
ANTIQUE COLLECTORS' CLUB
Sandy Lane, Old Martlesham, Woodbridge, Suffolk, IP12 4SD, UK
Tel: 01394 385501 Fax: 01394 384434
e-mail: sales@antique-acc.com website: www.antique-acc.com
or
Market Street Industrial Park, Wappingers' Falls, NY 12590, USA
Tel: (845) 297 0003 Fax: (845) 297 0068 Orders: (800) 252 5231
e-mail: info@antiquecc.com website: www.antiquecc.com